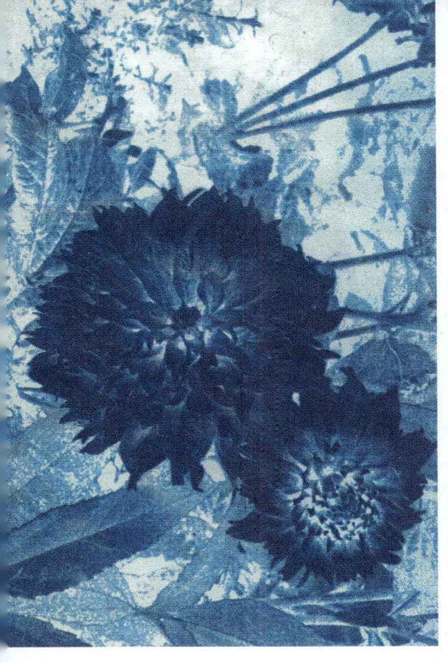

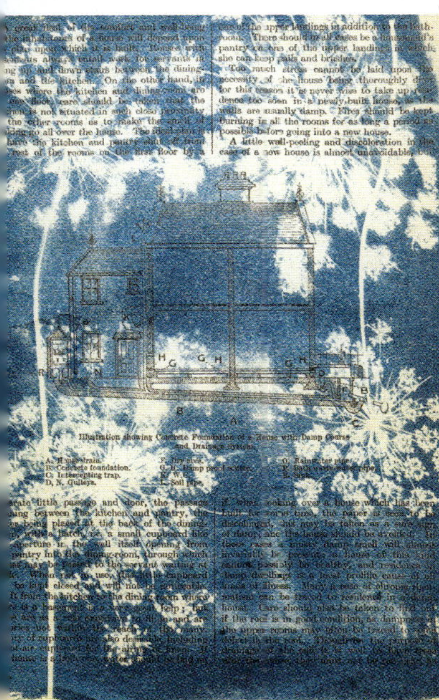

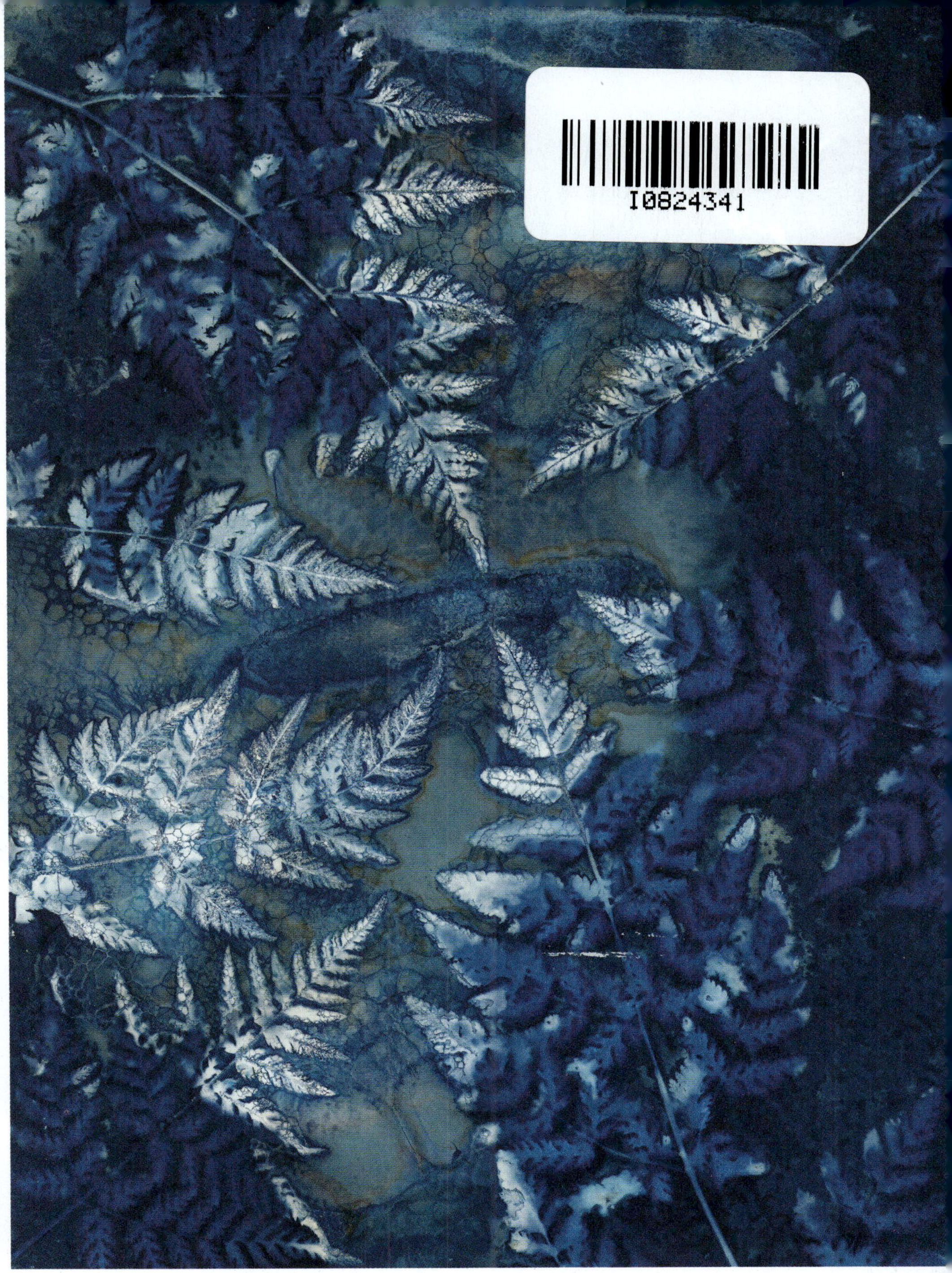

pantry on one of the upper landings in which
she can keep pails and brushes.
Too much stress cannot be laid upon the
necessity of the house being thoroughly dry;
for this reason it is never wise to take up resi-
dence too soon in a newly built house, as the
walls are usually damp. Fires should be kept
burning in all the rooms for as long a period as
possible before going into a new house.
A little wall-peeling and discoloration in the
case of a new house is almost unavoidable,




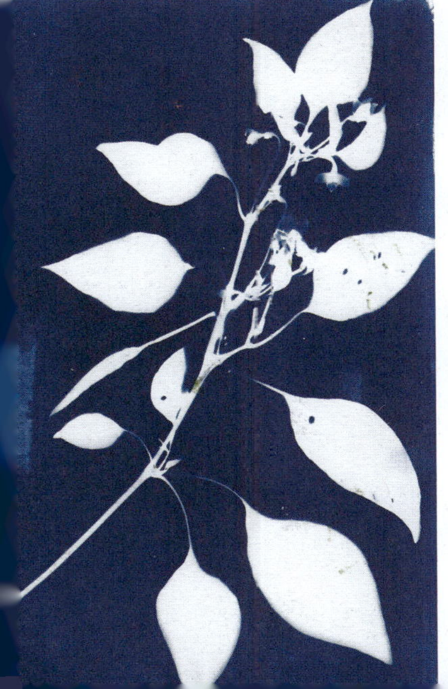

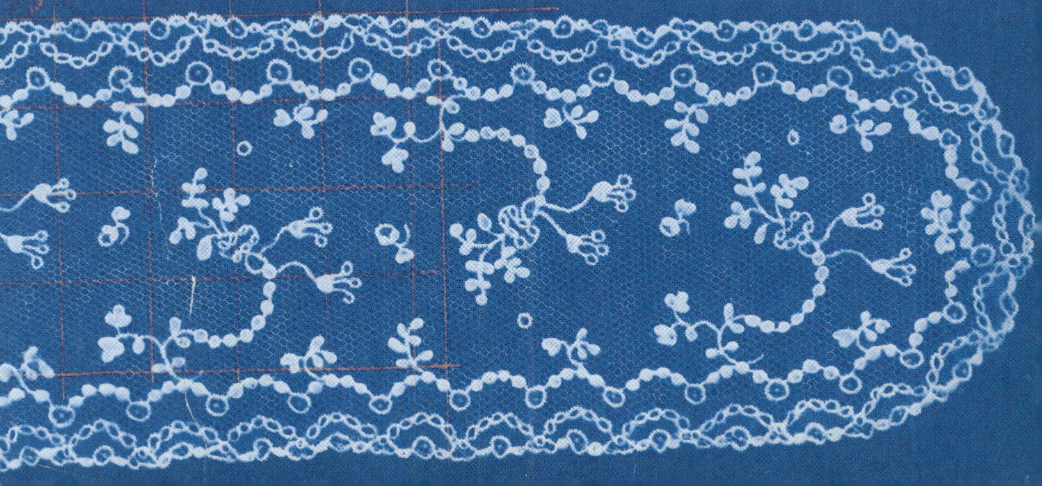

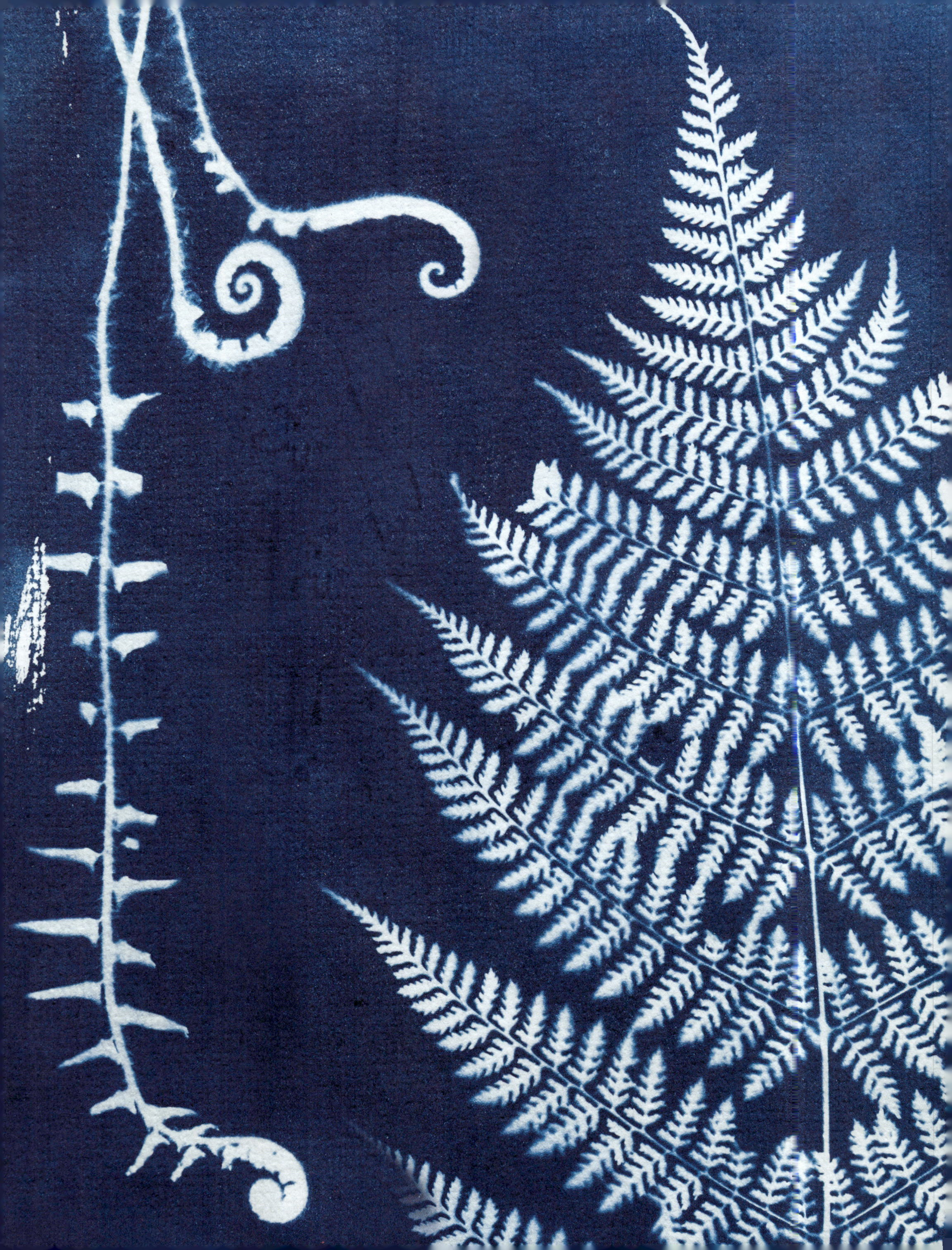

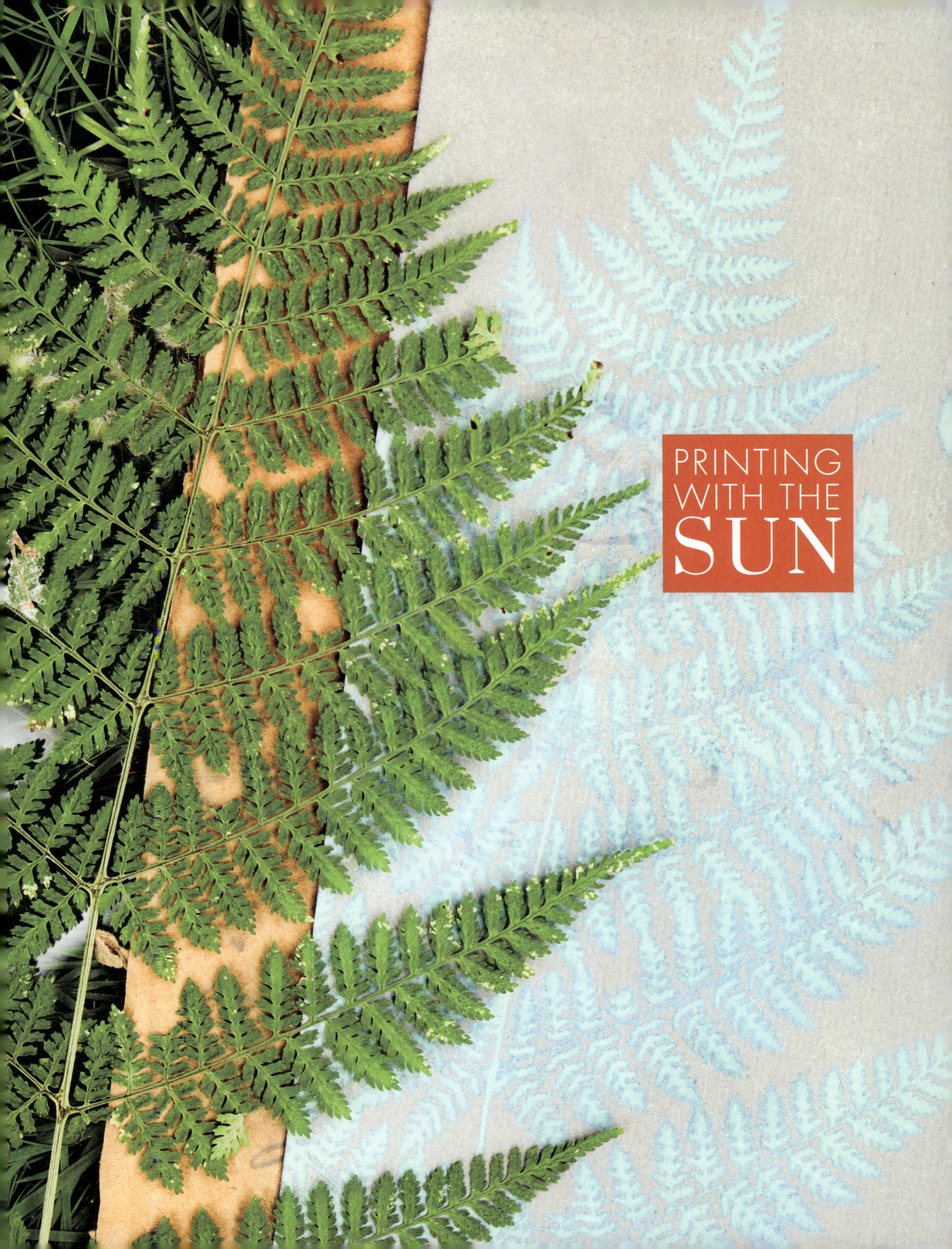
PRINTING
WITH THE
SUN

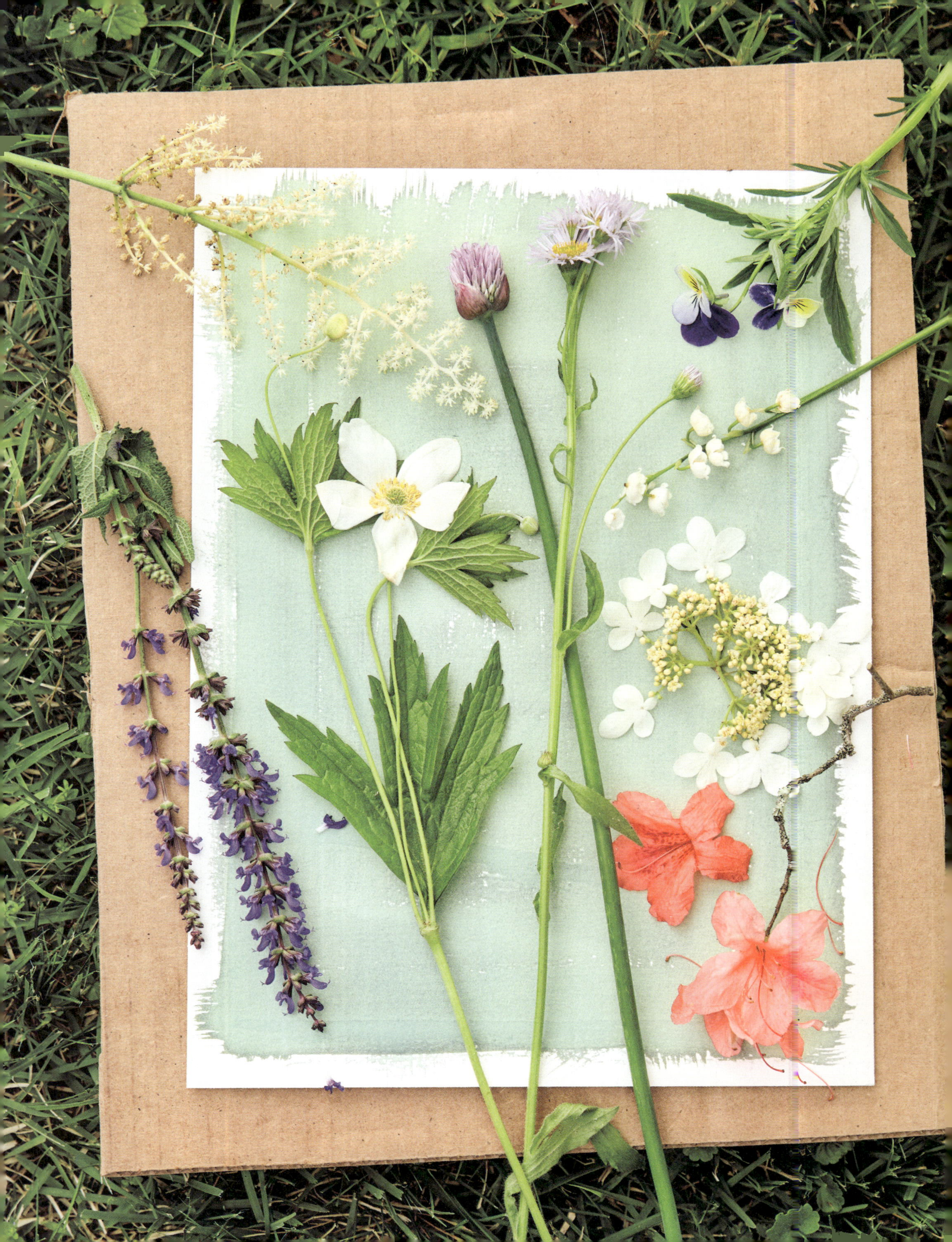

# PRINTING WITH THE SUN

## Capturing the Beauty of Nature with Cyanotypes

MADGE EVERS

Storey Publishing

**The mission of Storey Publishing is to serve our customers by publishing practical information that encourages personal independence in harmony with the environment.**

**EDITED BY** Carleen Madigan and Gwen Hawkes
**ART DIRECTION AND BOOK DESIGN BY** Carolyn Eckert
**TEXT PRODUCTION BY** Jennifer Jepson Smith

**COVER PHOTOGRAPHY BY** © Kristin Teig, back; Mars Vilaubi © Storey Publishing, artwork by Melinda Brazell, front; Mars Vilaubi © Storey Publishing, spine

**INTERIOR PHOTOGRAPHY BY** © Kristin Teig, 1–2, 5 b., 6, 8, 22, 23, 30–32, 35 b., 50–52, 54, 56, 59, 60, 61 t.l. & t.r., 64–65, 70–81, 86–87, 135, 145, 151–153, 155 t., 162–164, 166 b., 168, 172–181, 184–190, 192–198, 199 t.r. & b.r., 218, endsheet B; Mars Vilaubi © Storey Publishing, IFC b.r., endsheet A m.l., facing half title, 3, 5 t., 6 b.l. & r.m., 24–25, 26 b., 28–29, 33–34, 35 t. & m., 36–41, 42 t., 43, 46–49, 53, 55, 58, 61 (b.l., m.r, b.r.), 62–63, 66, 68–69, 82–84, 88–91, 94–101, 103, 105–111, 114–117, 120–126, 128–133, 136, 138–144, 146–150, 154, 155 b., 156, 158, 159 (t.l., m., b.), 165, 169–171, 224, facing BC (b. all), IBC t.r. & b.r.

**PHOTO STYLING BY** Ann Lewis (Kristin Teig's photographs)

**ADDITIONAL INTERIOR PHOTOGRAPHY BY** © Angelea H. R., 183, 204 b.; © Asa Culver, *Staying Afloat*, cyanotype on cotton, 2025, 18 r.; Atkins, Anna, 1799–1871/public domain /Wikimedia Commons, IFC t.r.; Beverly Wilgus, Homage to Sir John Herschel, 16 t.; © Brooke Sauer, 10 t., 45, 209 t.; Carnegie Museum of Art/public domain/Wikimedia Commons, IFC t.c.; Chiara Chiarel/CC BY-SA 4.0/Wikimedia Commons, IFC b.l.; © Claudia Hollister, 113, 157, 205 t.; Uploaded by Cormaggio/CC BY-SA 1.0/Wikimedia Commons, 18 l.; © Dora Somosi, 10 b.l. & b.r., 112, 209 b.; Eli Alex Gresham, 42 b., 203 b.; Courtesy of Elizabeth Ellenwood, 20, 93, 201; Artwork and photo by © Elizabeth Zeschin, 12, 210 b.; Emily Crisman, 160, 200 b.; Courtesy of Erika Frank, 167, 203 t.; F. Holland Day/public domain/Wikimedia Commons, 17 t.; Fluffigkatt/CC BY-SA 4.0/Wikimedia Commons, facing IBC t.r., 23 title background, 81 title background; Courtesy of Fritz Horstman, 19, 205 b.; Hallwyl Museum/public domain/Wikimedia Commons, 21; © Heather Palecek, 57, 102, 207 b.; Hillary Waters Fayle, 44, 202 t.; Hippolyte Bayard/public domain/Wikimedia Commons, IFC t.l.; Hutschi/CC0/Wikimedia Commons, endsheet A b.l.; James Hoggard, artwork by Elizabeth Booth, 67, 127, 137 t., 200 t.; © Jeannie Hutchins, 134, 206 t.; Joy Oil Co Ltd/public domain/Wikimedia Commons, 17 b.l.; Krista McCurdy, 119, 207 t.; artwork and photo by Lesley Riley, 166 t., 208 b.; © Liliana Guzmán, 104, 137 b., 204 t.; © Linda Clark Johnson, 161, 206 b.; © Linda Ruel Flynn, 202 b.; © 2025 Madge Evers, endsheet A t.r., 9, 11, 13, 14, 85 t., 118, 159 t.r., 191, 199 l., 217, facing BC t.l.; © Marita Wai, 182, 210 t.; National Gallery of Art/Creative Commons CC0 1.0/Wikimedia Commons, 17 b.r.; Period Scrapbook/public domain/Wikimedia Commons, IFC c., facing BC r.m.; Rijksmuseum/CC0/Wikimedia Commons, IBC t.l & b.l., IFC l.m., endsheet A b.r.; © Sandra Costello, artwork by and photo courtesy of Linda Ruel Flynn, 85 b.; © Sarah Bourne Rafferty, 26 t., 208 t.; Sommerlüftchen/CC BY-SA 4.0 /Wikimedia Commons, IFC m.l.; Spencer Collection, The New York Public Library. "Cystoseira granulate" New York Public Library Digital Collections. Accessed October 22, 2025. https://digitalcollections.nypl.org/items/2d207360-c612-012f-2616-58d385a7bc34, 16 b.; Courtesy of Taylor Drouhard, 27; Thierry R/CC BY-SA 3.0/Wikimedia Commons, 92; "Zwei Blumen" by hutschinetto/licensed under CC BY-SA 2.0, recently new license for 4.0, CC BY-SA 2.0/https://creativecommons.org/licenses/by-sa/2.0/Wikimedia Commons, endsheet A t.l.

**ARTWORK BY** © Madge Evers, unless otherwise noted here or on the page



Be sure to read all the instructions thoroughly before undertaking any of the projects in this book and follow all of the safety guidelines summarized on page 29.



**Storey Publishing**
210 MASS MoCA Way
North Adams, MA 01247
storey.com

Storey Publishing is an imprint of Workman Publishing, a division of Hachette Book Group, Inc., 1290 Avenue of the Americas, New York, NY 10104. The Storey Publishing name and logo are registered trademarks of Hachette Book Group, Inc.

ISBNs: 978-1-63586-918-7 (paper over board);
978-1-63586-919-4 (ebook)

Printed in China by Toppan Leefung Printing Ltd. on paper from responsible sources
10 9 8 7 6 5 4 3 2 1

TLF

Library of Congress Cataloging-in-Publication Data on file

# Contents



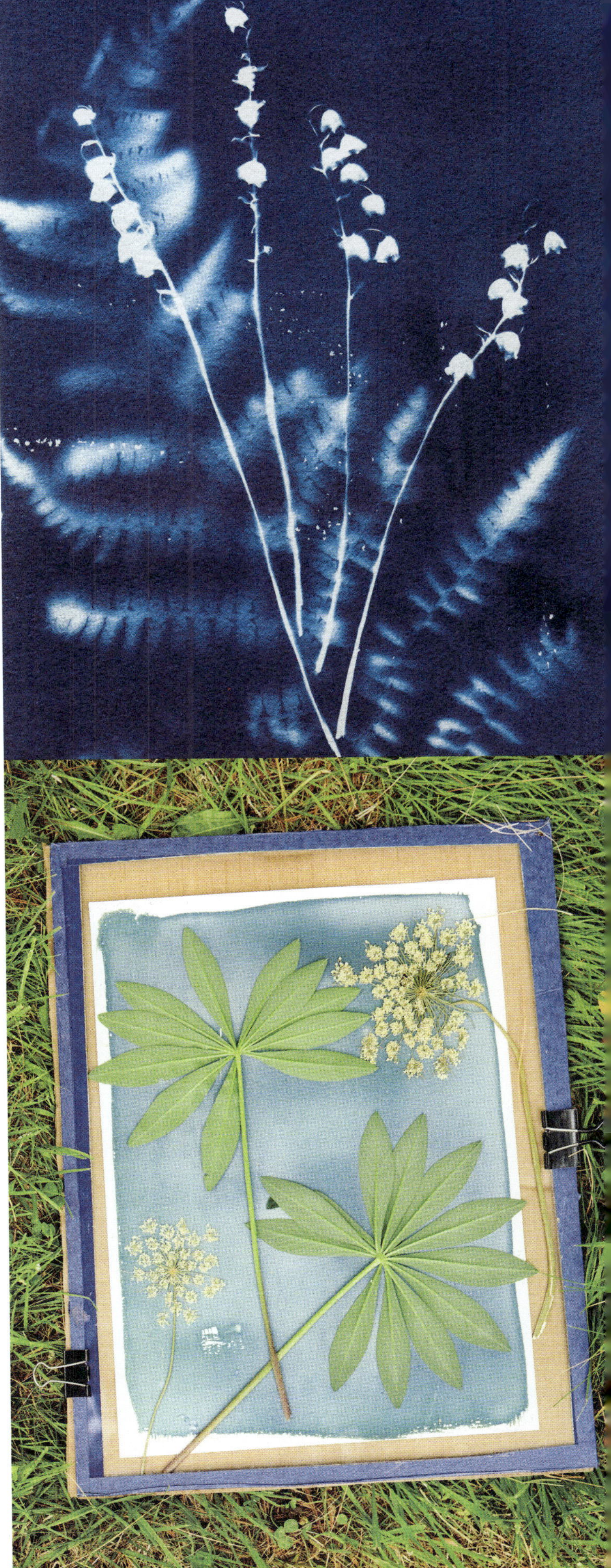

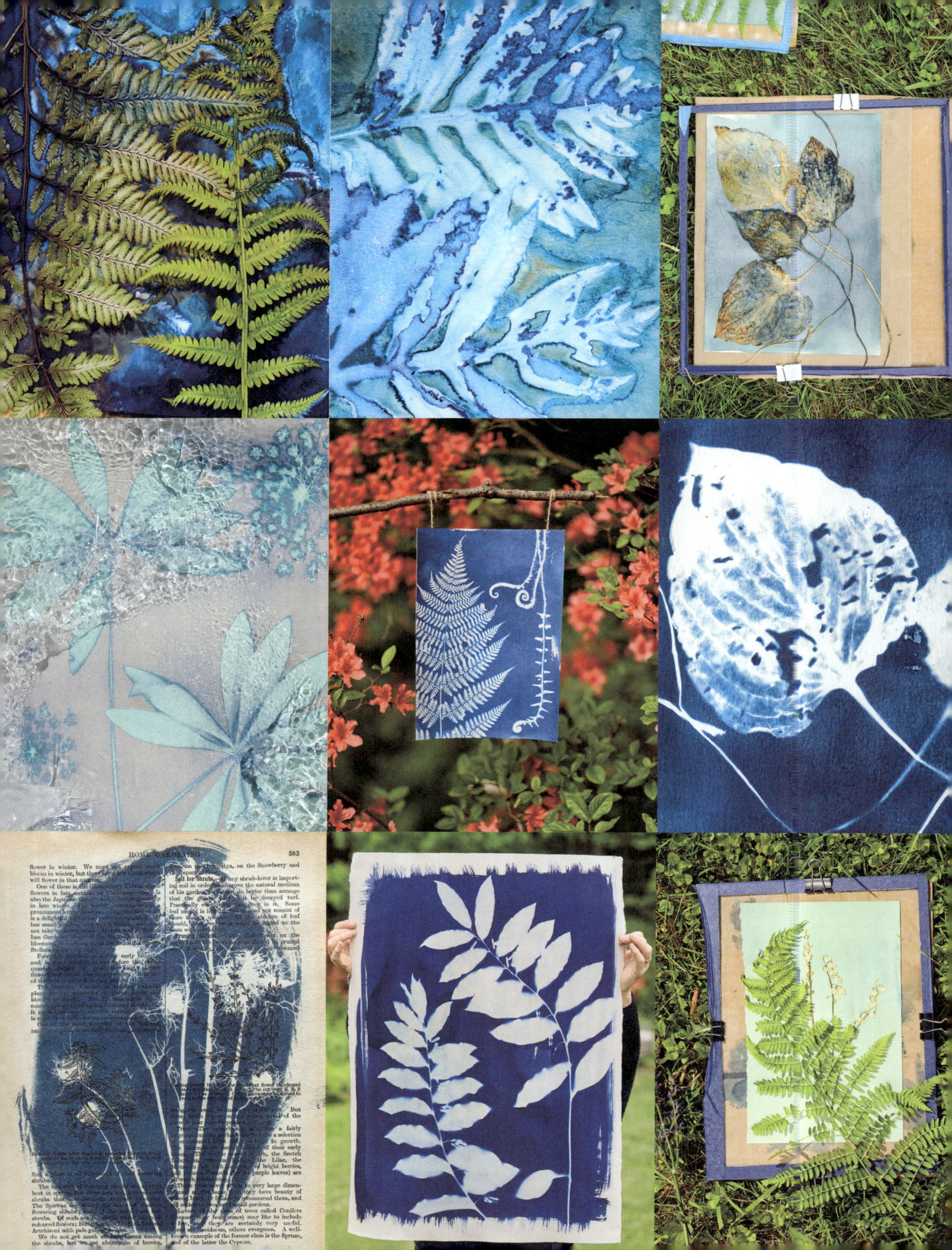

## PART 2 STEP-BY-STEP PROJECTS

# INTRODUCTION

## The Magical Art of Cyanotypes

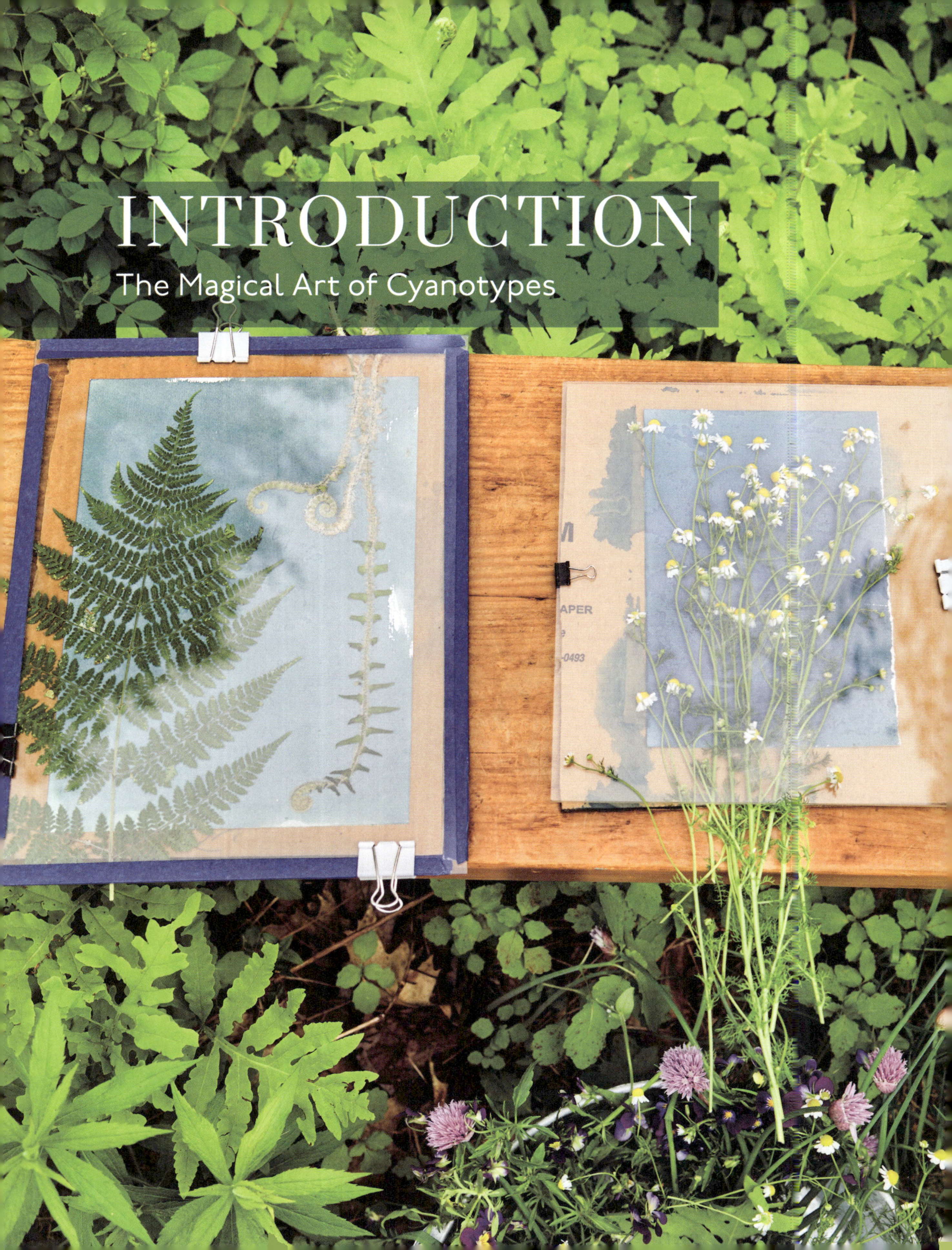

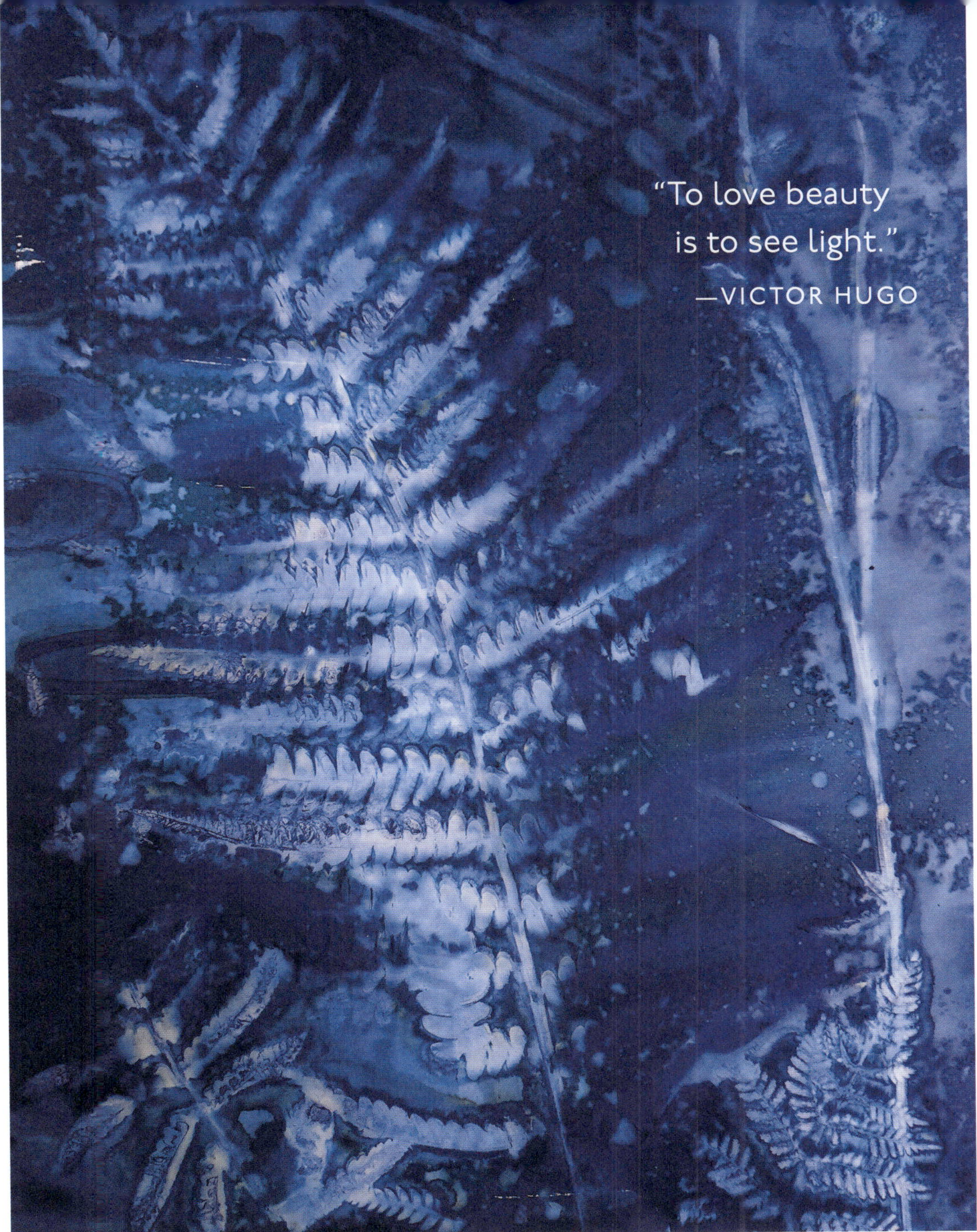


# Light as Art

Cyanotypes are born from the sun. When the sun's rays touch a surface coated with a simple mixture of two chemicals, a reaction unfolds that transforms a seemingly blank sheet of paper into a rich, vivid blue. The reaction itself may be simple, but the results feel like visual alchemy, a delightful magic that anyone can conjure.

Madge Evers, *Crowd Pleaser*

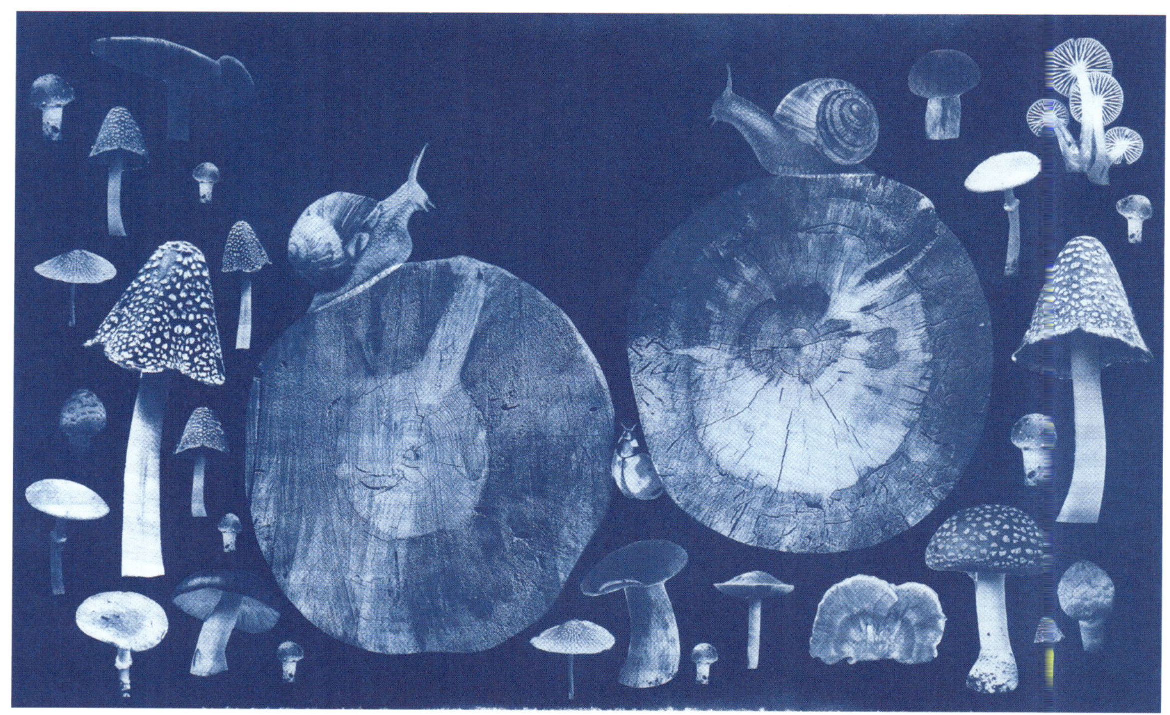

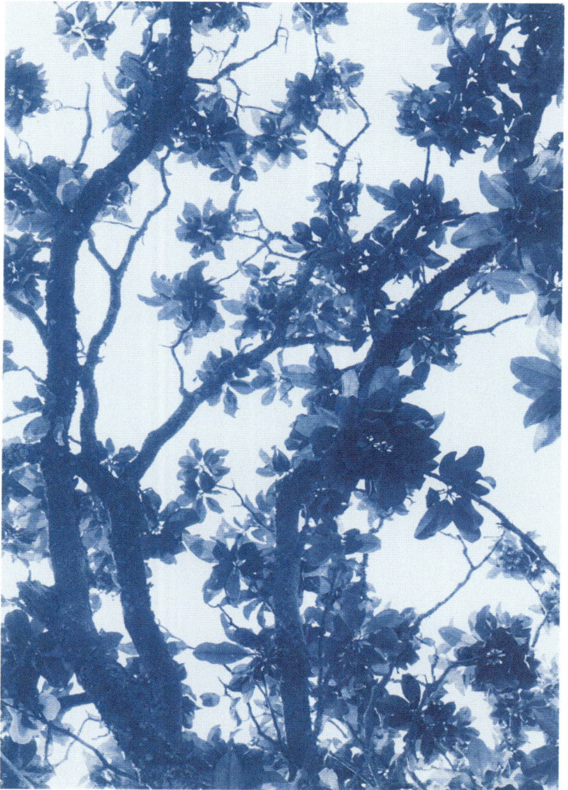

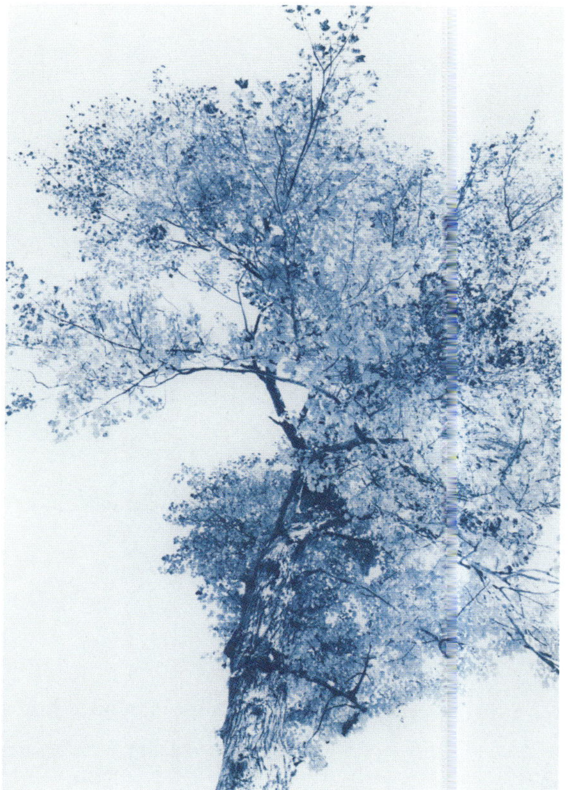

The work of artists Brooke Sauer and Dora Somosi shows the dynamic range of the cyanotype art form, whether capturing the details of various mushroom species as Sauer has done in *Travelogue* or the towering beauty of a tree as depicted in pieces from Somosi's *By Her Side* series.

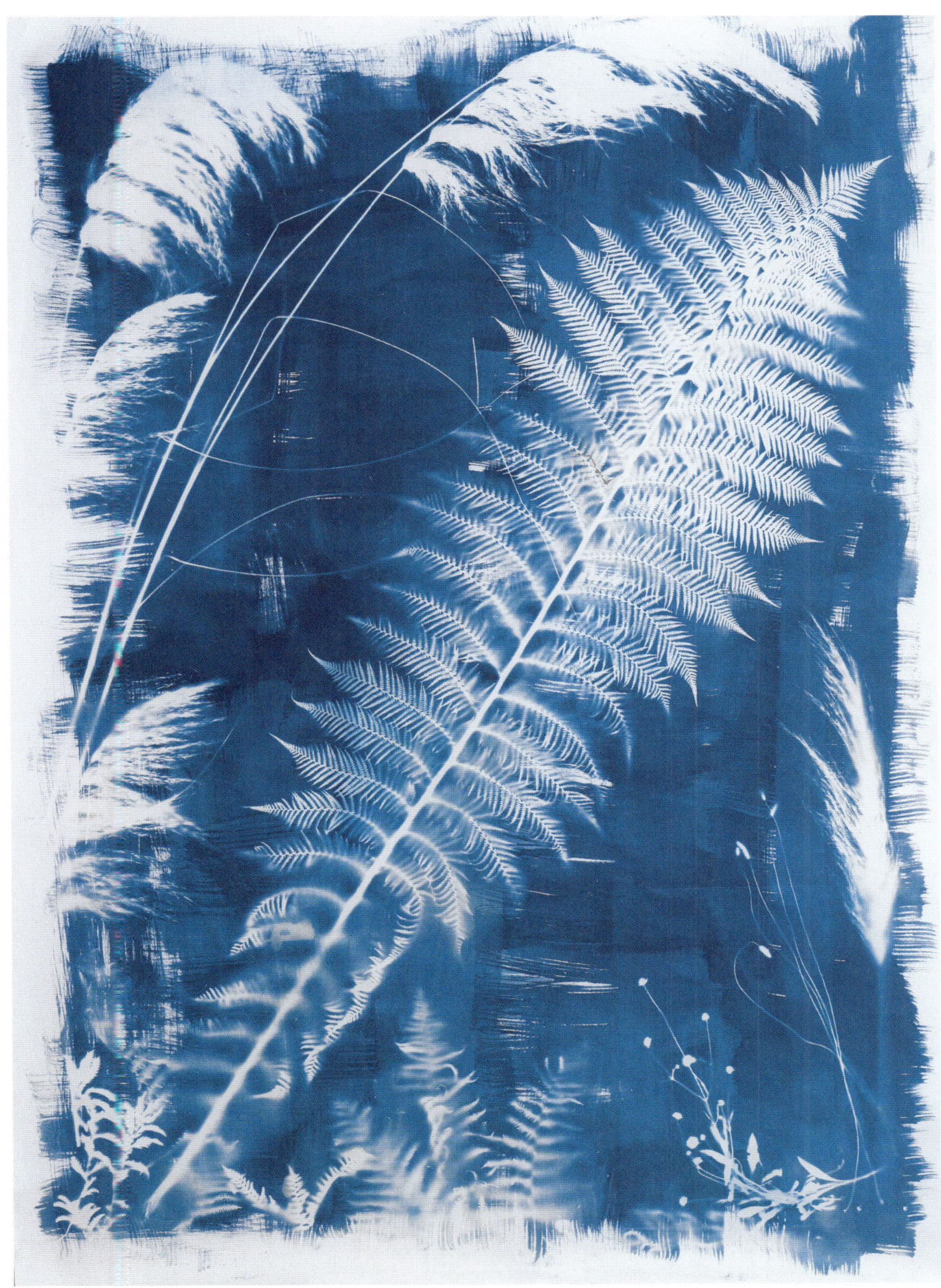

Paper of any size can be used to make a cyanotype. This large sheet depicts a 7-foot tree fern branch and the plumes of giant toetoe grasses. Madge Evers, *Tree Fern*

Cyanotypes are striking and evocative. The deep blue background and ethereal white outlines call to mind the hues of the natural world: the sky threaded with clouds, the sea frothed with whitecaps, moonflower white spilling across forget-me-not blue. Despite the simplicity of the process and the color palette, cyanotypes are wildly adaptive, capturing the minute intricacies of a fern or mushroom, even the ephemeral movement of the waves.

## *What Is a Cyanotype?*

Developed almost 200 years ago, cyanotypes were among the earliest photographic processes. Making a cyanotype is straightforward—it involves combining two iron salt chemicals in liquid form, applying that liquid to a surface, then exposing the surface to light. The sun's ultraviolet rays, or those of a UV lamp, transform the chemicals to create a striking blue. Any objects set on the chemically treated surface protect it from the light, preventing the chemical reaction from occurring. The result is a white image on a vivid blue background. This elementary form of photography does not require a camera, a darkroom, or special equipment; its simplicity allows creativity to shine.

My first encounter with the compelling blue of a cyanotype was with an image made by commercial photographer Elizabeth Zeschin, known for her striking portraits, elegant architectural interiors, and detailed still-life photos. In the 1980s I was an aspiring photographer and managed Elizabeth's studio in New York City. Elizabeth's portfolio contained a gorgeous blue-toned photo she had created with the cyanotype process. I'd never seen anything like it. The impression was lasting; Prussian blue gave the image a sense of timelessness and planted the seed of an idea I hoped one day to pursue.

As a gardener, I love the idea of dormancy, of plants saving their energy in order to emerge when the time is right. Ideas and seeds, it turns out, have

Elizabeth Zeschin's beautifully captured cyanotypes served as my introduction to the art form.

**LEFT:** Elizabeth Zeschin, *Papaver Somniferum*
**RIGHT:** Elizabeth Zeschin, *Anemone Hupehensis*

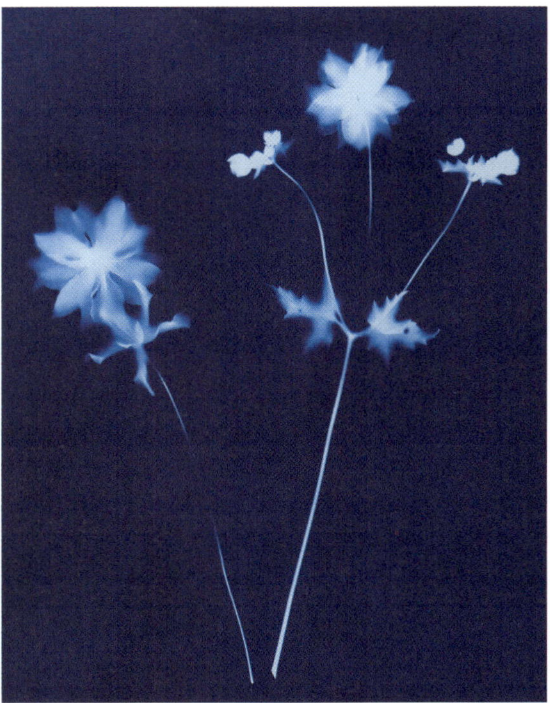

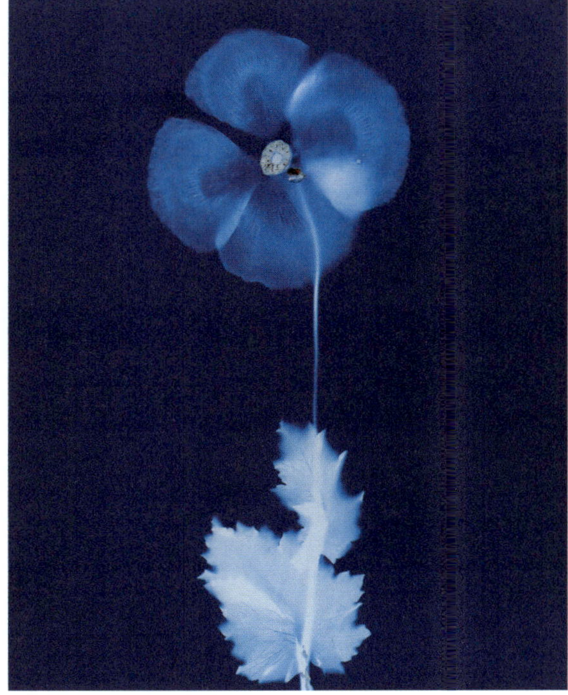

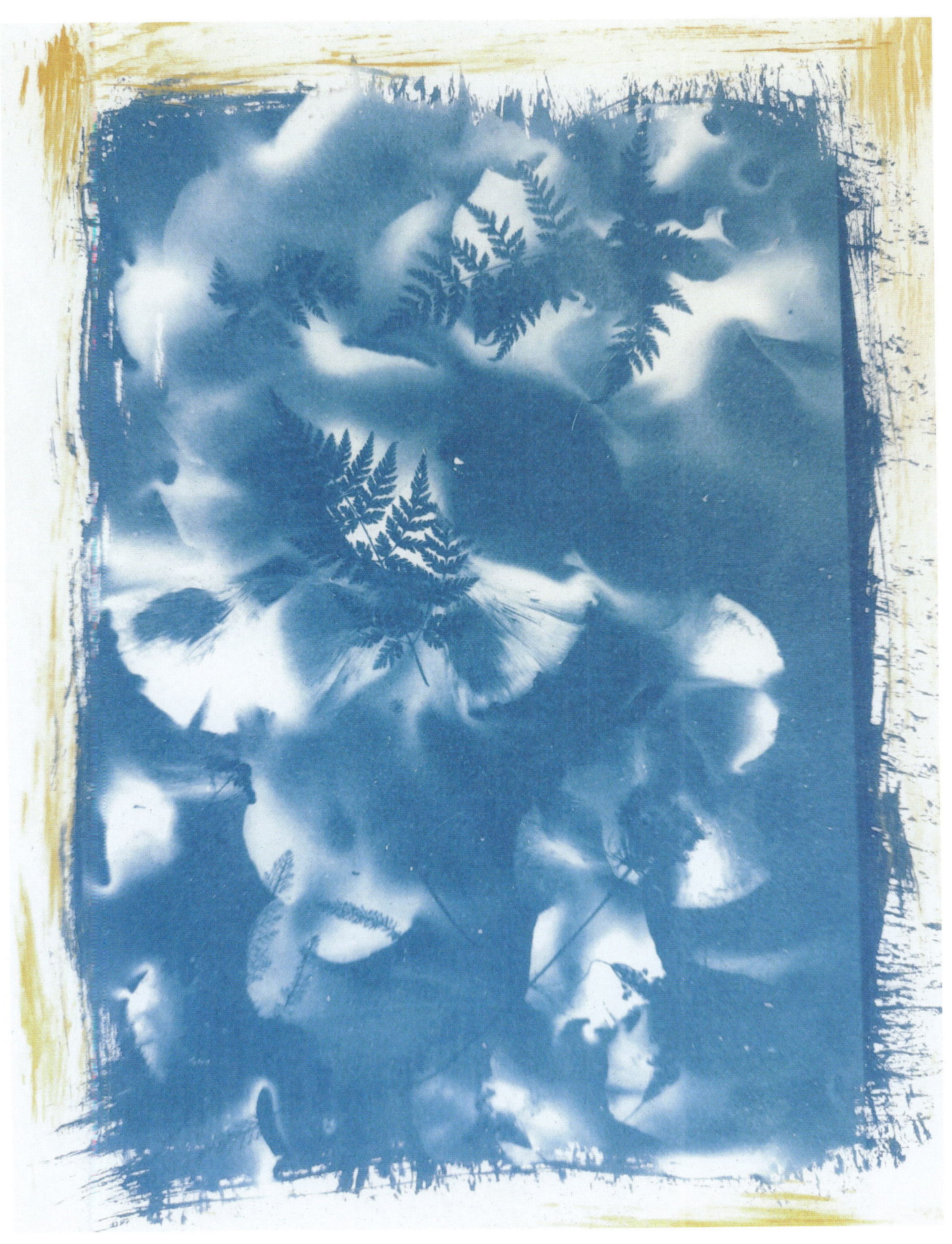

*Luminous Blue* was made by creating a digital negative of *Luminous Herbarium* (on page 14), then using the negative to make a cyanotype contact print (see page 105 for more).

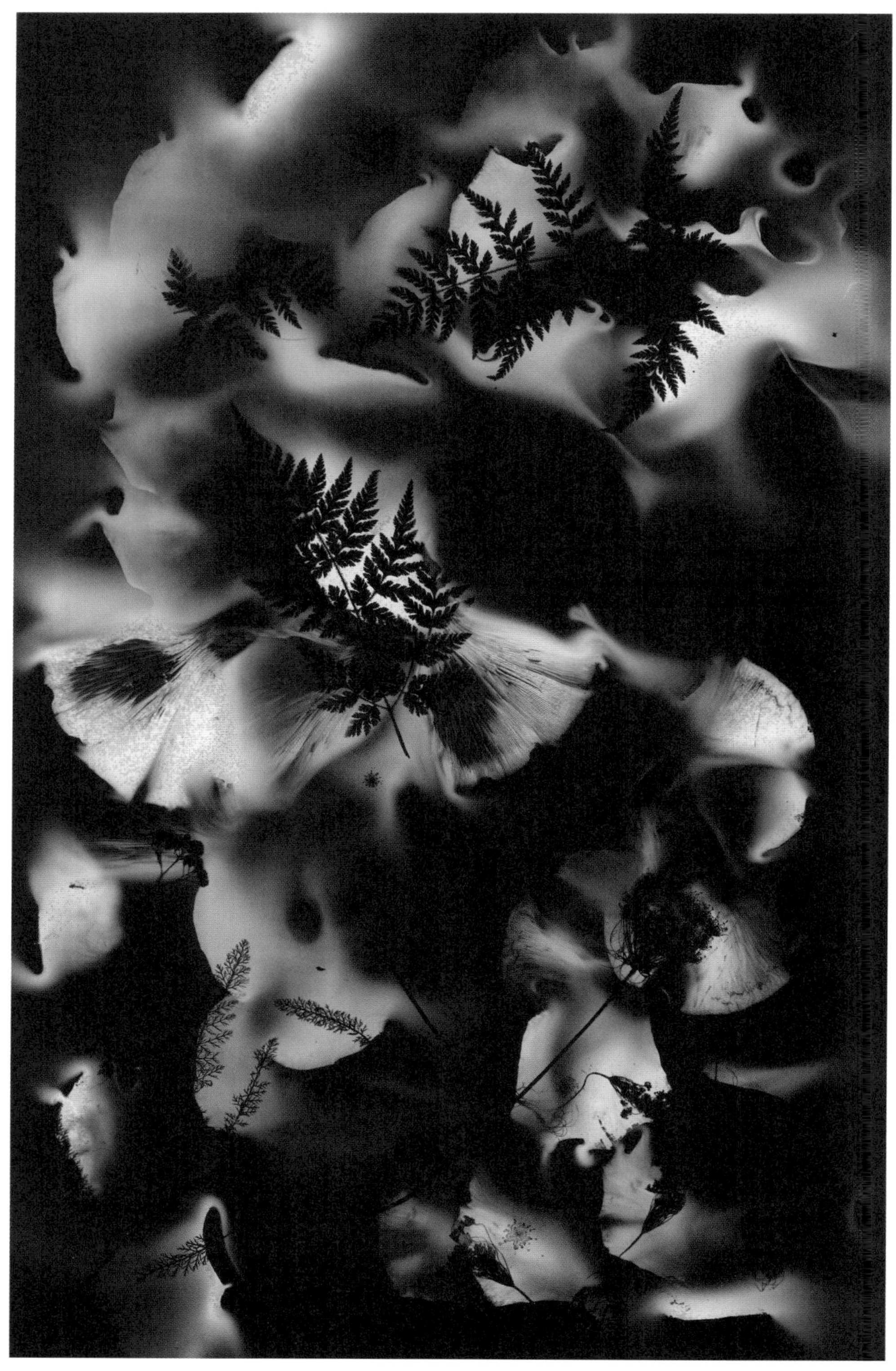

*Luminous Herbarium* depicts chervil, yarrow, and Queen Anne's lace. It's part of *The New Herbarium* series in which I use mushroom spores to reimagine the centuries-old process of collecting and preserving plants for science and art.

a great deal in common, both waiting for the right time to blossom. The ideas planted by the cyanotype I first saw in the 1980s broke dormancy in 2019 when I gathered a collection of pressed flora for a mushroom spore print series called *The New Herbarium*. The Prussian blue of the cyanotype returned to me. An internet search provided enough information to glean that, with just a few materials, I could in fact return to cultivate ideas from the past.

The ground proved to be fertile. My engagement with the cyanotype process quickly changed the way I saw the plants in my garden and in the woods near my home. In truth, it changed the way I saw everything. My attention began to linger on the texture and shape of leaves, the translucency of a flower's petal, the tiny seed sprays left once a blossom had faded. I have loved plants for a long time—their exuberant growth cycles, their culinary and medicinal uses, and the lessons they teach of decay. The cyanotype process gave me fresh eyes and new reasons to love the natural world around me.

## Why Explore the Cyanotype?

As you begin to create cyanotypes, you'll find countless reasons to love the art form, but these are some of my favorite aspects of creating cyanotypes.

**ACCESSIBILITY.** The essential components of the cyanotype process are potassium ferricyanide, ferric ammonium citrate, water, and sunlight. The two chemicals are easily obtained from art supply stores and online; water and sunlight are, for now, free. You'll also need some basic tools, but they are inexpensive or can be fashioned from materials you already have.

**IT'S MAGIC! IT'S SCIENCE!** Whenever I teach a cyanotype workshop, I'm always energized by students' enthusiasm and wonder at all stages of the process. Chemicals react with sunlight, then water, undergoing striking transformations that captivate our attention. Everyone's first cyanotype experience is punctuated by oohs and aahs.

**IT'S NOT DIGITAL.** Sometimes I find relief in analogue activities. Digital tools can be used when making a cyanotype, but today's process remains quite similar to the process used some 200 years ago. I'm no Luddite, but stepping away from a screen can be a breath of fresh air.

**IT'S FORGIVING.** There are many happy accidents in this process. It's always a bit experimental and surprising in the best way. If a cyanotype doesn't work the way I planned, I can employ techniques such as bleaching and recoating that allow me to alter the image and to add new layers.

**THAT BLUE!** Literature abounds on the positive psychological impact of the color blue, with any number of possible attributes. For me, it evokes an elemental connection with both water and sky.

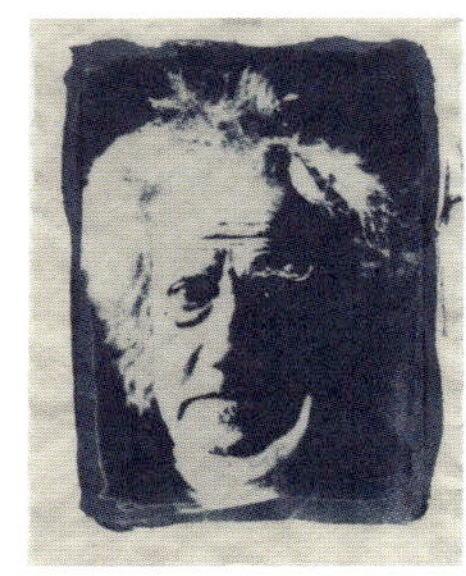

# A Visual History of Cyanotypes

## 1842

Sir John Herschel discovered the cyanotype process.

## 1843

English botanist Anna Atkins used Herschel's innovative process to create a groundbreaking book titled *Photographs of British Algae: Cyanotype Impressions*—the first book illustrated entirely with photographic images. Struggling with the difficulty of creating accurate drawings, Atkins transformed her collection of British algae into mysterious photographic images containing various shades of blue.

### SCIENTIFIC ORIGINS

Despite its seemingly magical qualities, the cyanotype process originates in science. In 1842, Sir John Herschel discovered that a chemical solution, when applied to paper and exposed to ultraviolet light, created a distinctive Prussian blue print.

Initially Herschel used the process to replicate his notes. He would coat a sheet of paper with the chemical solution, then write his notes on a sheet of transparent paper, place it on top of the coated paper, and expose the materials to sunlight, creating a perfect copy. Herschel was a photocopy pioneer—117 years before Xerox!

Herschel, a science-meets-art hero, is also credited with coining the term *photograph*, literally meaning "to draw with light."

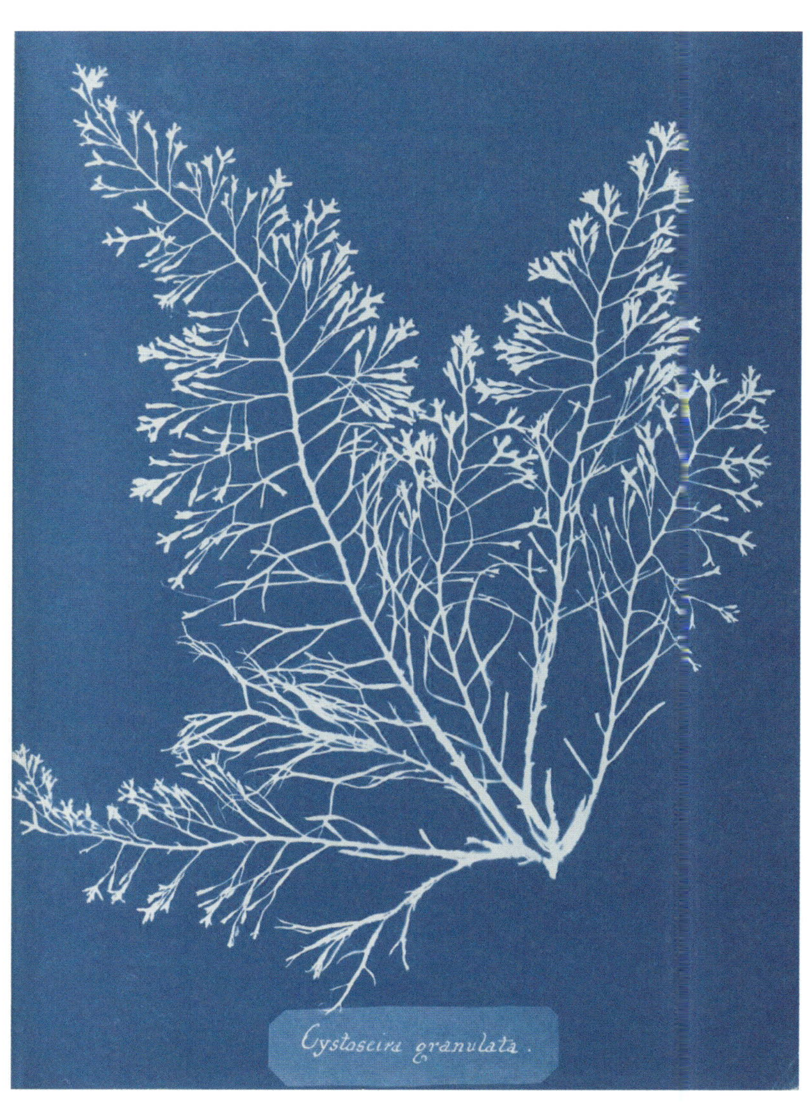

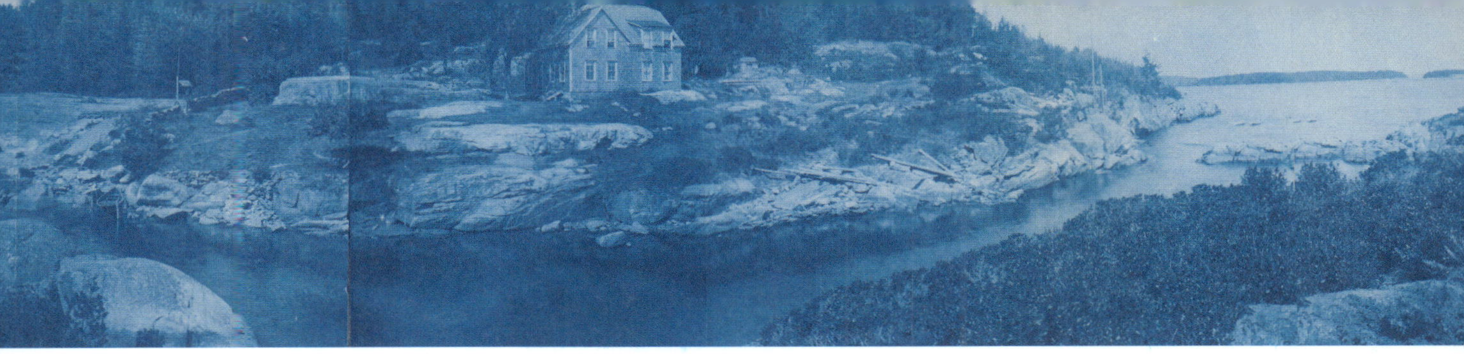

## 1870–1880

Cyanotypes became widely used in the construction industry to re-create architectural plans, giving rise to the term *blueprint* for the ubiquitous cyan schematics.

## 1900

The simplicity of the cyanotype process made it popular among amateur photographers, and cyanotypes were featured in travelogues and on postcards and birthday invitations.

## 1900–1920

During the late Victorian Arts and Crafts Movement, artists like self-taught printmaker and photographer Bertha Jaques created cyanotype photograms that demonstrated an engagement with the natural world and emphasized its elemental beauty.

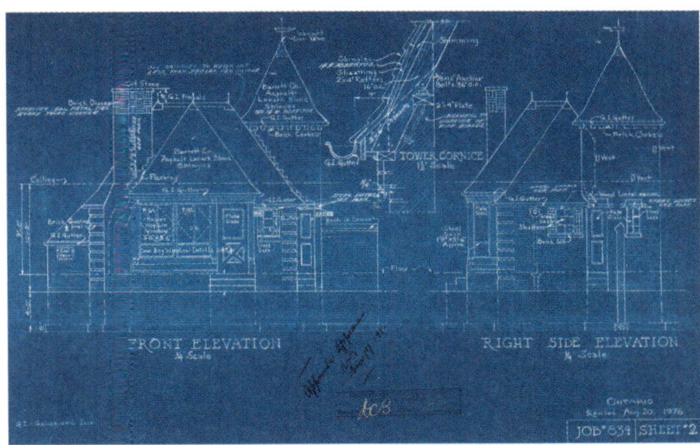


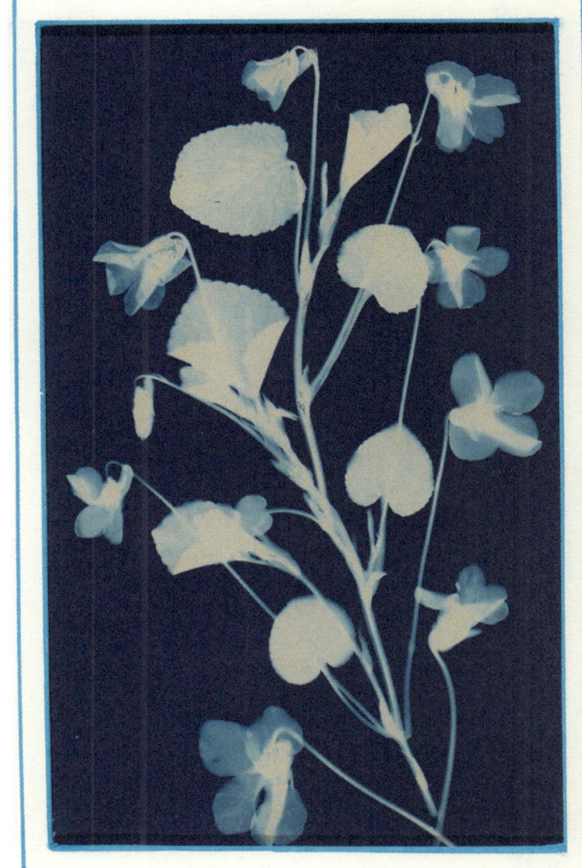

### NATURE AND THE CYANOTYPE

Cyanotypes have often been used to capture objects from the natural world. Whether it highlights the intricate fronds of seaweed or a flower in bloom, the art form is uniquely connected to the environment. The process of making a cyanotype is always slightly unpredictable and open-ended—just like the beauty of nature itself.

# A Visual History of Cyanotypes

## 1920s

The cyanotype process was used to make photograms.

## 1950

After learning how to create cyanotypes as a child, Susan Weil and her husband, Robert Rauschenberg, collaborated together on cyanotypes, using blueprint paper and processing the images in their bathtub.

## 1950–52

Rauschenberg collaborated with Jasper Johns under the name Matson Jones to create a cyanotype series for department store windows called *Blue Ceiling*.

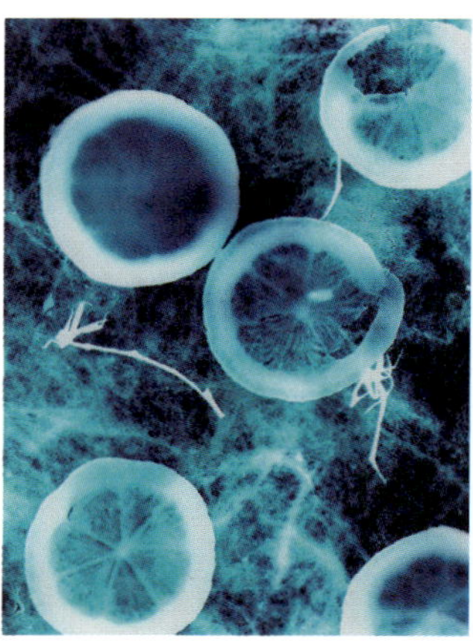

**PHOTOGRAM:**
A photographic image made without a camera by placing an object directly on the surface of light-sensitive paper, then exposing the paper to light. Photograms were popularized in the United States by the artist Man Ray, who created photograms he called "rayographs" in the 1920s.

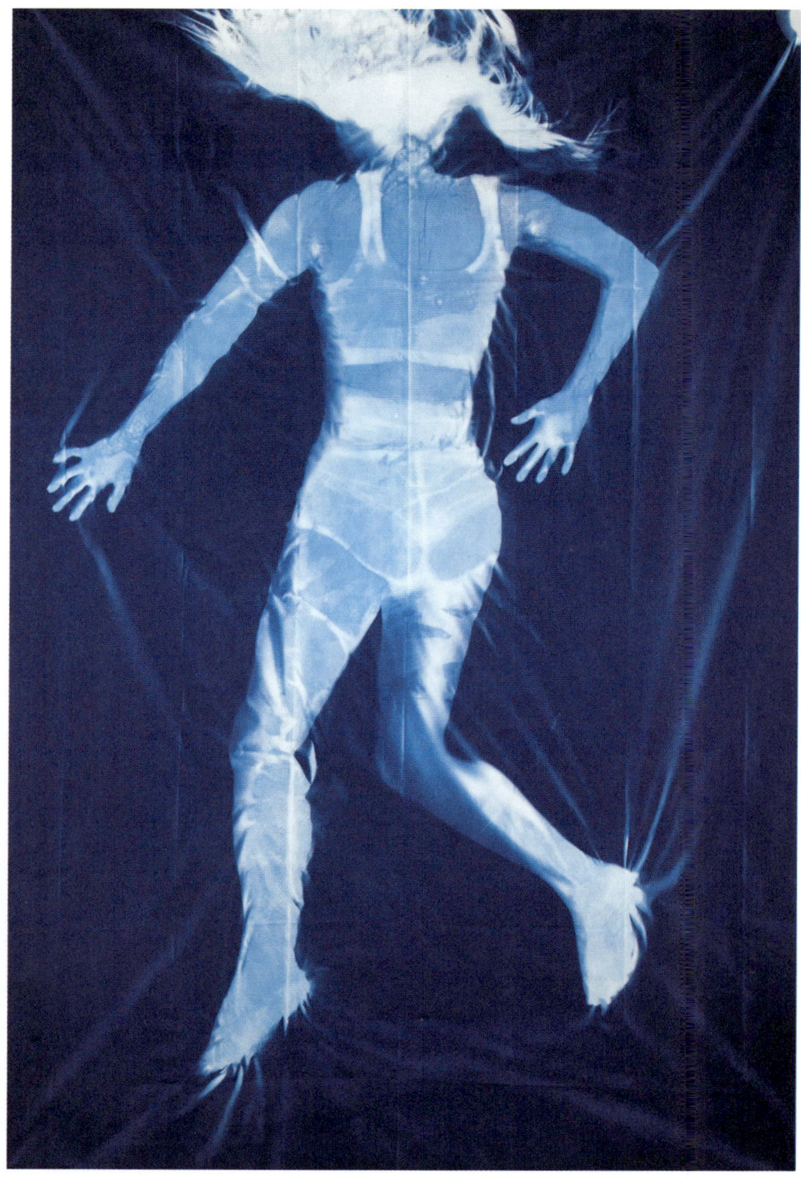

Rauschenberg and Weil pioneered the use of "full body" cyanotypes, a technique artist Asa Culver also uses in her work, creating strikingly detailed cyanotype self-portraits.

## 1974–75

Artist Barbara Kasten experimented with a camera-less photographic technique that used cyanotype-style coated paper to create her surreal and ephemeral *Photogenic Painting* series.

## 1995–2005

Nancy Wilson-Pajic's experiments with various alternative photographic processes led to the creation of several large-scale narrative cyanotype photogram series, including *Les Divas,* which depicts the biomorphic forms of theater costumes.

## 2016

The first major museum exhibition of cyanotypes, *Cyanotypes: Photography's Blue Period,* took place at the Worcester Art Museum in 2016. Curator Nancy Kathryn Burns observed that the cyanotype's availability to amateurs and use "as a primitive copier" led critics to regard it as an "imposter" within the realm of photography.

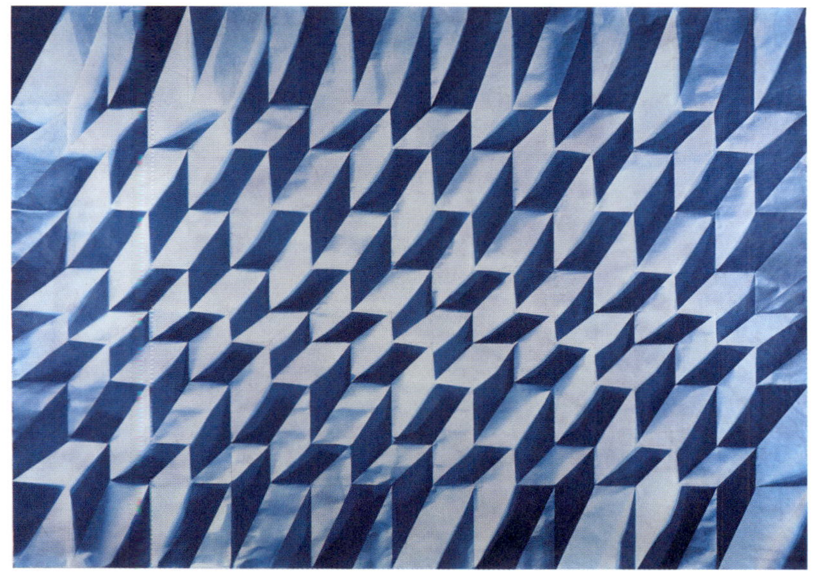

## 2019–present

Innovative cyanotype artists continue to evolve the art form, from West Coast–based artist Meghann Ripenhoff, who exposes her pieces to the elements to create a unique record of nature's impermanence, to Fritz Horstman, whose use of intricately folded cyanotype paper creates richly geometric prints.

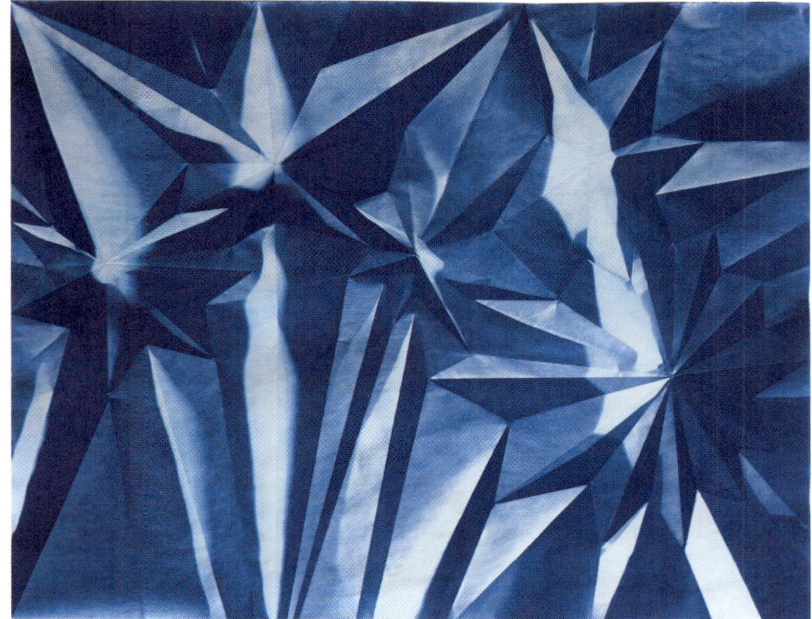

Artist, curator, and educator Fritz Horstman creates blue-and-white images of varying shades and geometric shapes in his *Folded Cyanotypes* series, exploring both high and low contrast. His innovation lies in his use of materials: folded paper, cyanotype chemicals, and sunlight.

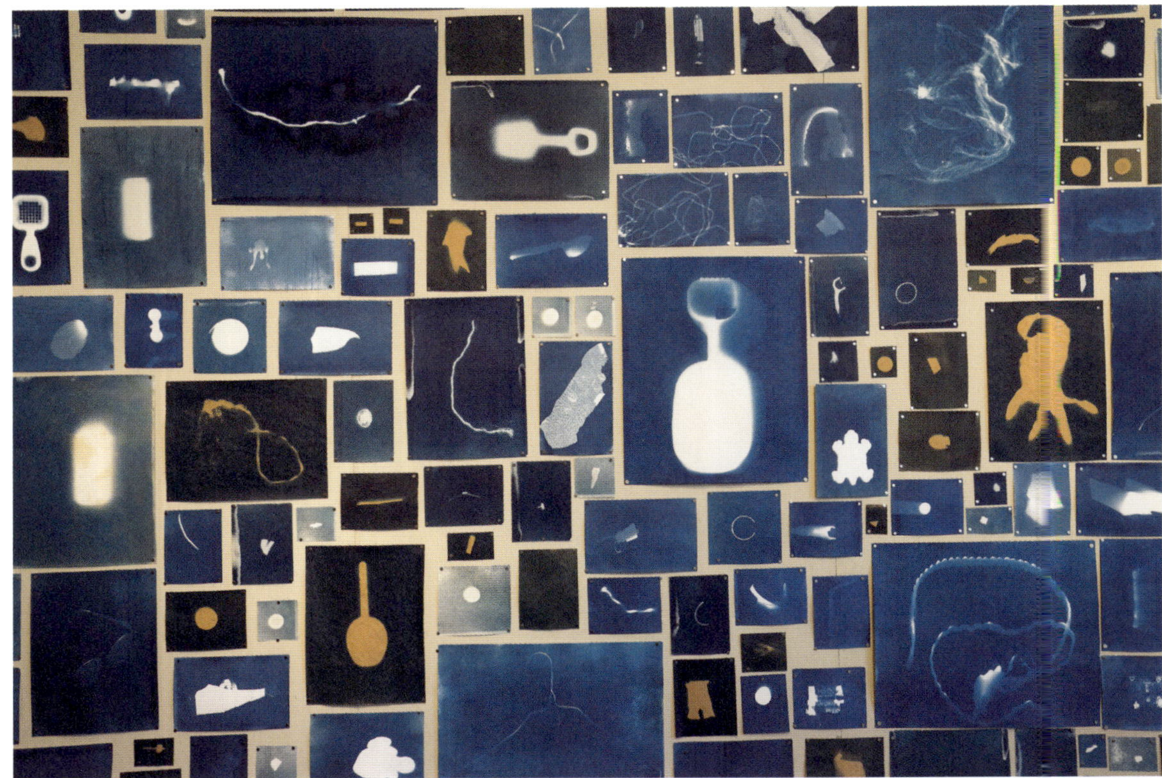

# Making It Your Own

Whether it's a blueprint or a large-scale piece of art, the cyanotype process is infinitely adaptable. One of the best parts about cyanotypes is their accessibility. You don't need to master oil paints or even learn to sketch in order to create a beautiful and unique work of art. Instead, cyanotypes are an invitation to capture the beauty of the world around you—a perfect leaf, a scrap of lace, the rippled reflection of a crystal vase—in a stunning and creative way.

In the following pages, you'll encounter other artists who are also engaged in cyanotype work today. You're about to join a vibrant community! I'm thrilled to be your guide on a journey exploring this magical process and an array of projects using it.

Elizabeth Ellerwood's cyanotype installation, *Among the Tides*, combines art and activism to document and illuminate the issue of ocean pollution.

### A BEGINNER'S BLUEPRINT:

# MAKING A CYANOTYPE

I jumped, feet-first, into the blue pool of the cyanotype process with a bare minimum of supplies and know-how, and you can do the same. We'll begin simply, with a basic overview of each step of the process.

1 **MIX UP** a light-sensitive chemical solution.

2 **APPLY THE LIGHT-SENSITIVE SOLUTION** to a sheet of paper, coating it completely. Let the paper dry.

3 **ARRANGE MATERIALS** (plants, stencils, or other objects) on top of the paper.

4 **EXPOSE THE PAPER** to ultraviolet light, whether artificial or sunlight.

5 **MONITOR THE DEVELOPMENT,** watching the light-sensitive coating on the paper turn bronze or silvery gray, until the exposure has developed to your liking.

6 **REMOVE THE OBJECTS** from the paper. Rinse the paper under running water for 5 to 15 minutes to wash off the light-sensitive chemicals.

7 **HANG THE PAPER** or lay it flat to dry.

There are many variations on this basic process, from using fabric and varying exposure time to adding unexpected materials.

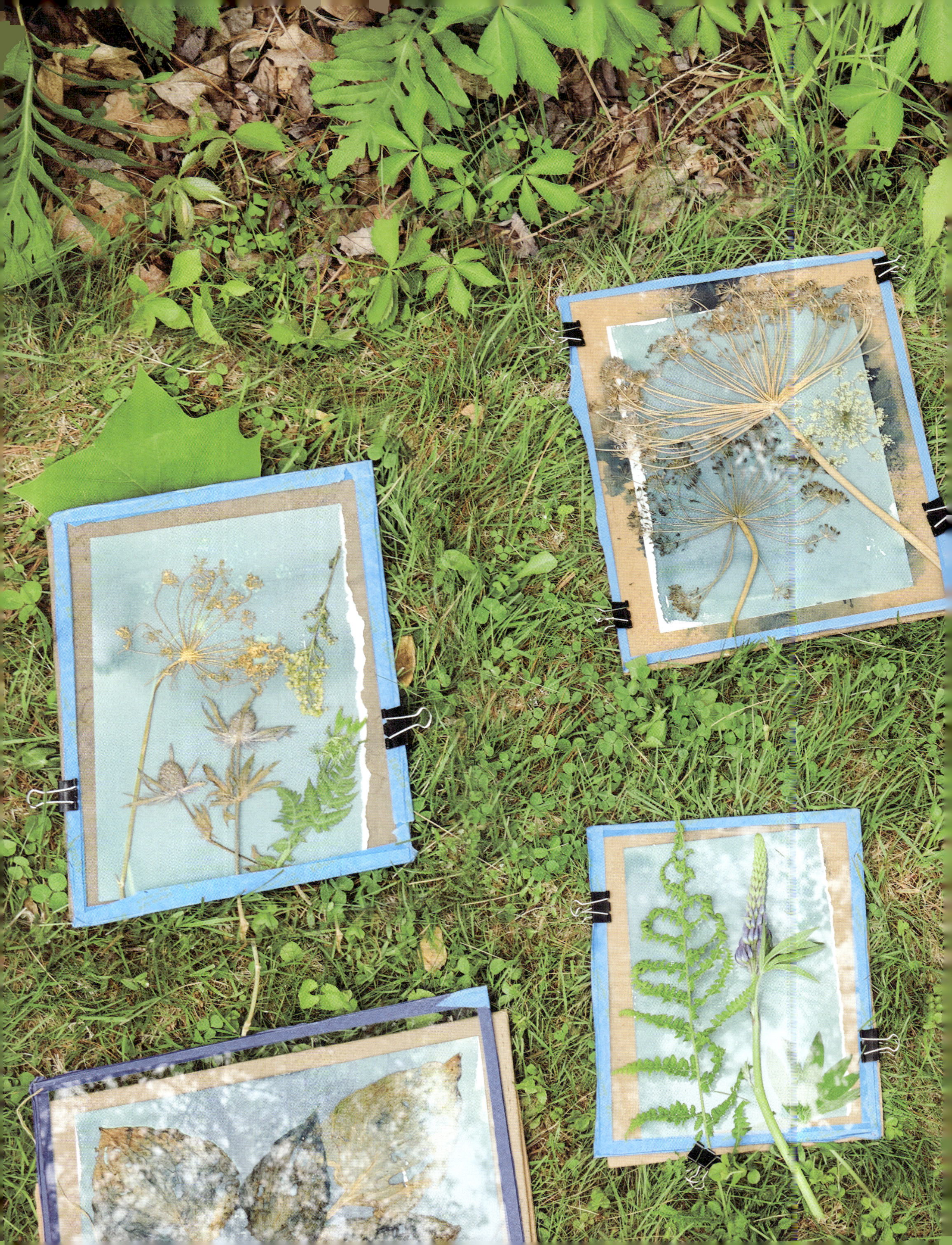

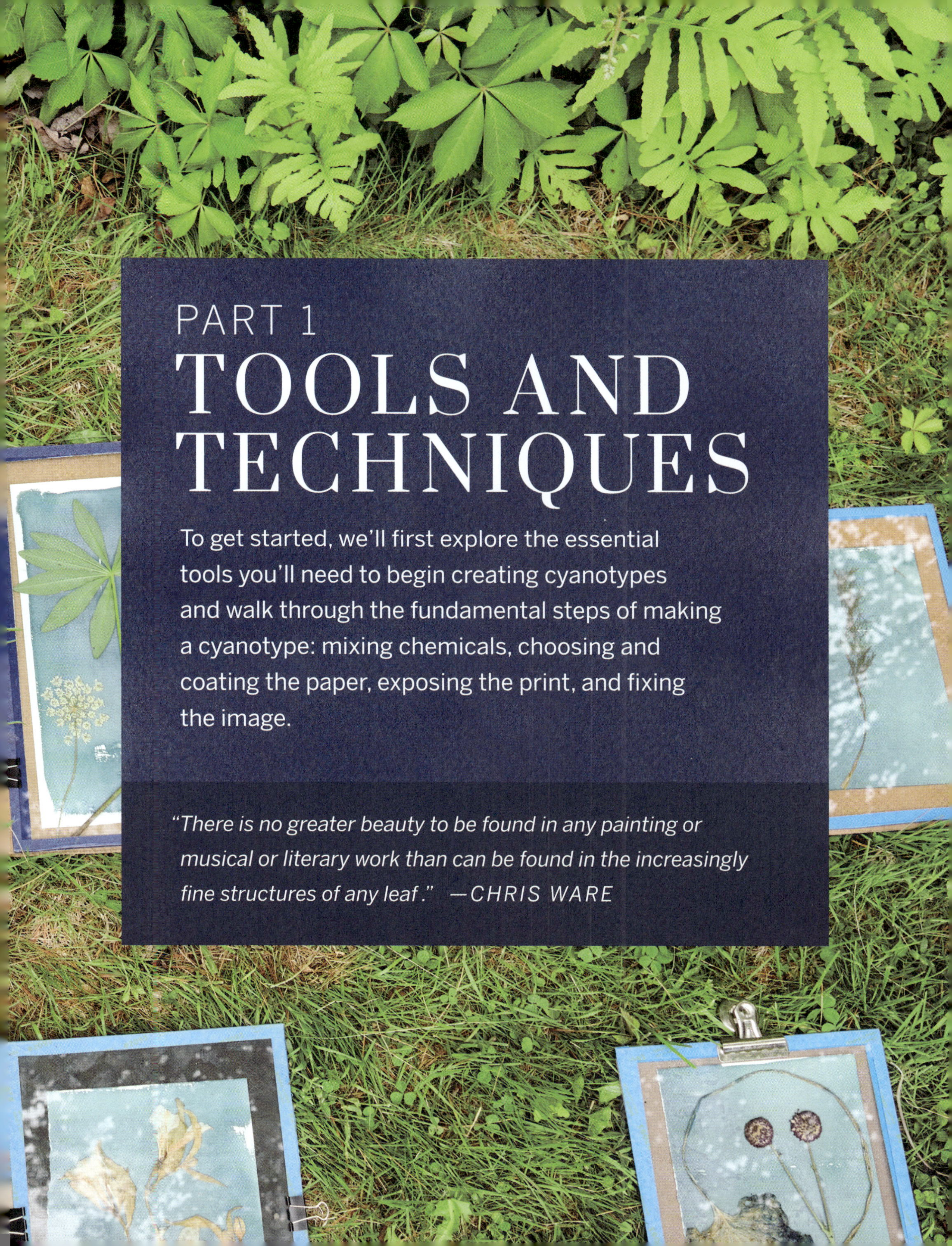

PART 1

# TOOLS AND TECHNIQUES

To get started, we'll first explore the essential tools you'll need to begin creating cyanotypes and walk through the fundamental steps of making a cyanotype: mixing chemicals, choosing and coating the paper, exposing the print, and fixing the image.

*"There is no greater beauty to be found in any painting or musical or literary work than can be found in the increasingly fine structures of any leaf."* —CHRIS WARE

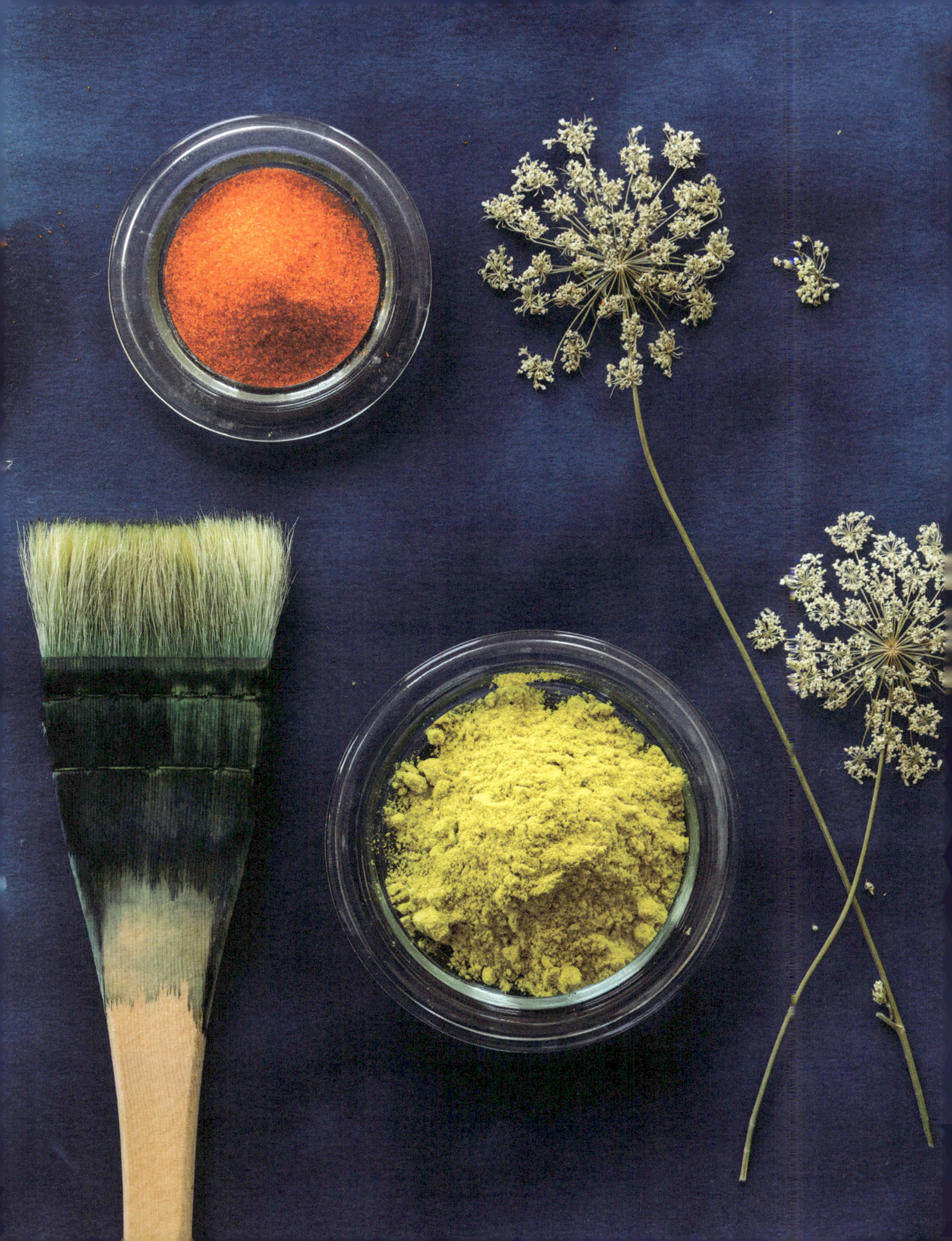

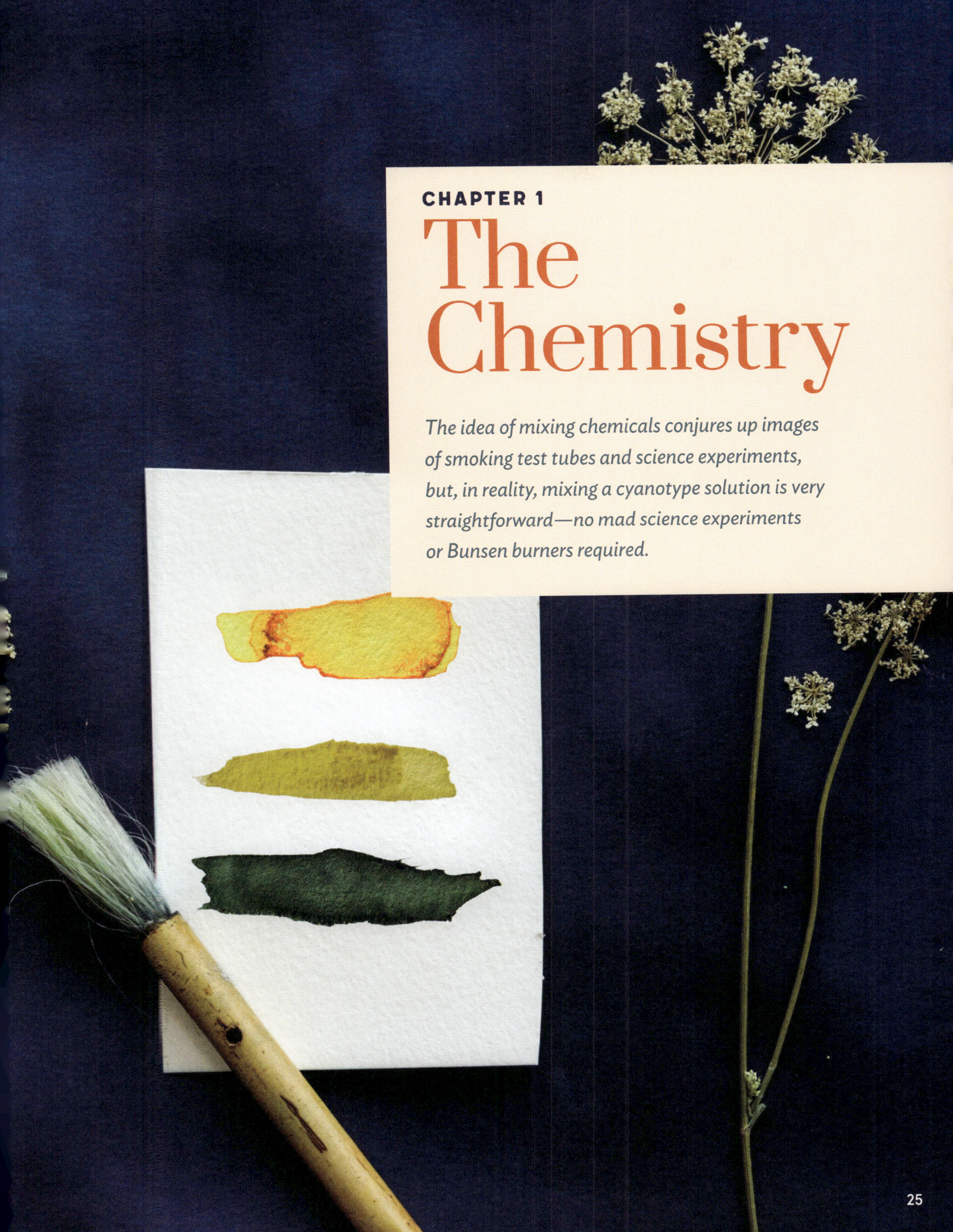

CHAPTER 1

# The Chemistry

*The idea of mixing chemicals conjures up images of smoking test tubes and science experiments, but, in reality, mixing a cyanotype solution is very straightforward—no mad science experiments or Bunsen burners required.*

# Cyanotype Chemicals

The heart of the cyanotype process lies in two iron salt chemicals: ferric ammonium citrate and potassium ferricyanide. To make a cyanotype, you mix each chemical with water to create two stock solutions. The two stock solutions are then combined to make a working solution. The working solution is sensitive to UV light; when brushed onto paper (or another surface), it creates a light-sensitive coating or emulsion that will transform into a distinctive bright blue when exposed to the sun.

Potassium ferricyanide and ferric ammonium citrate can be purchased in cyanotype kits from art supply stores and online; they can also be purchased in bulk online. (See the Resources section for more information.) They are packaged in lightproof plastic or glass containers to minimize their exposure to ultraviolet light. Neither chemical is highly sensitive to light, but prolonged exposure to UV light may cause each chemical to degrade and reduce its activity over time.

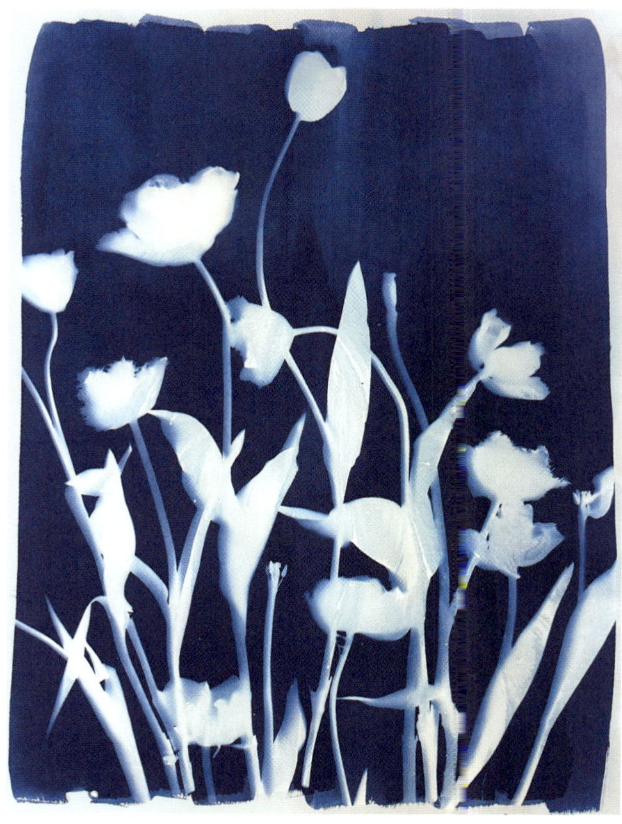

Artist Sarah Bourne Rafferty's *Field Dance* illustrates the archetypal blue for which cyanotypes are known.

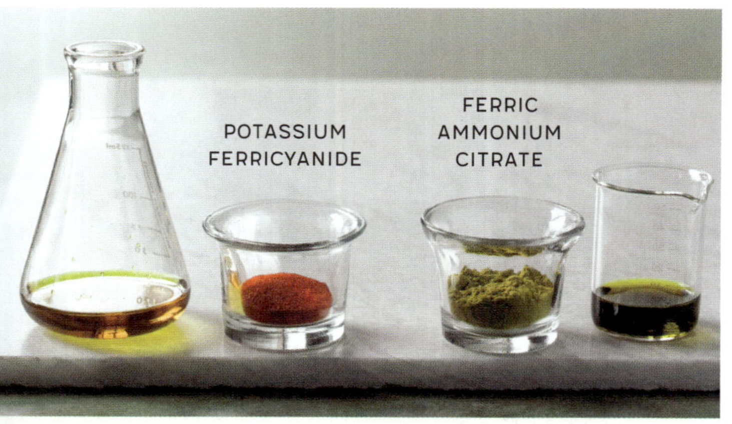


**POTASSIUM FERRICYANIDE.** A bright red salt compound that reacts with the iron compounds in ferric ammonium citrate and, when exposed to ultraviolet light, results in a cyanotype's Prussian blue color. When dissolved in water, it turns the liquid a bright green-yellow.

**FERRIC AMMONIUM CITRATE.** A water-soluble iron compound; in dry form, it is a fine brown-green powder. When dissolved in water, it turns the liquid dark green. It has several industrial uses, including as a food additive.

## AVOIDING METAL

Do not use any metal tools or containers when working with cyanotype chemicals. Contact between these iron salts and metal can cause galvanic corrosion, an electrochemical reaction that happens when two different types of metals meet, which can change the emulsion's chemical composition. Instead, use only plastic or glass tools and containers.

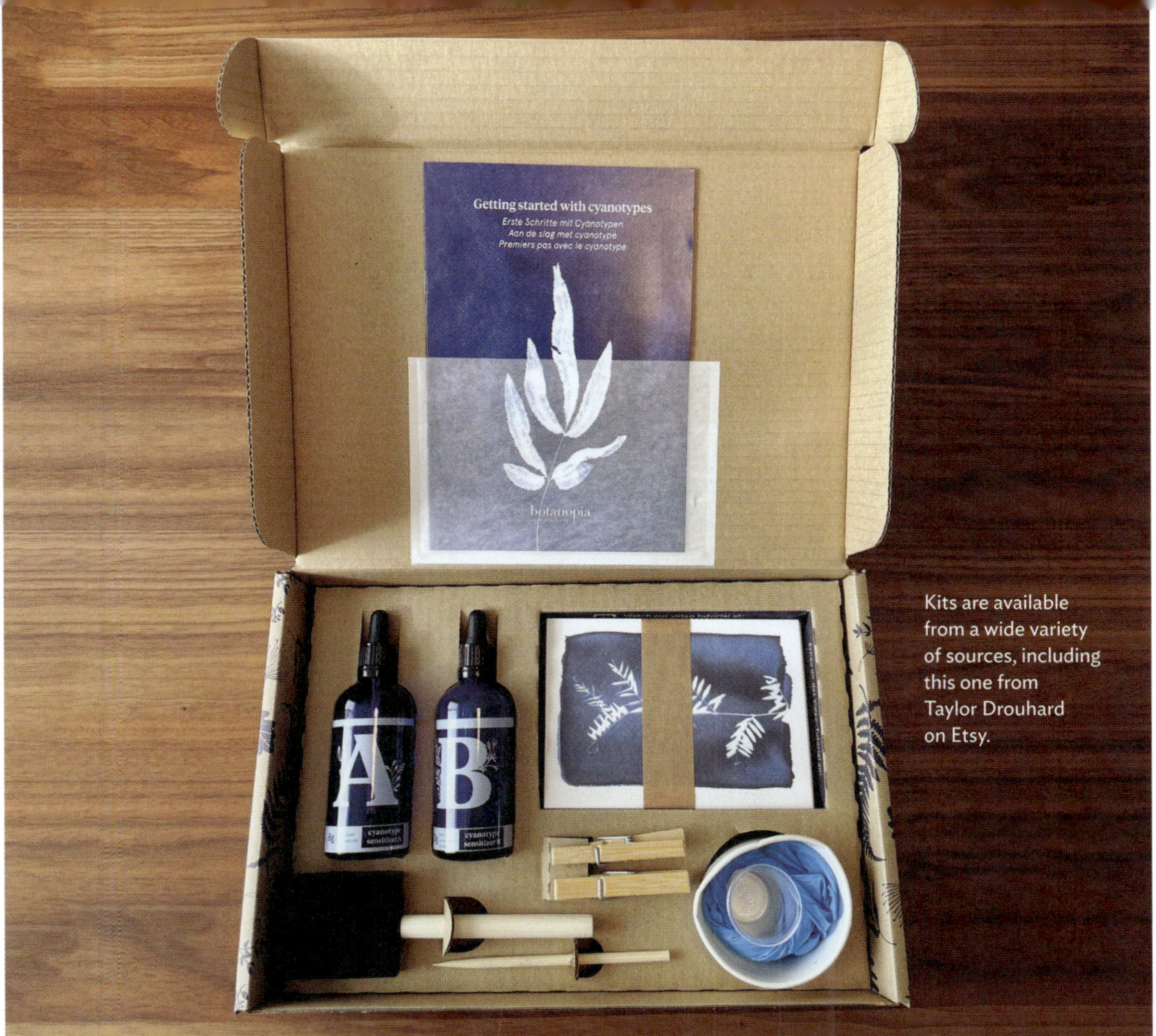


Kits are available from a wide variety of sources, including this one from Taylor Drouhard on Etsy.

## Kit Options

A kit can be a great way to try cyanotypes for the first time. If you purchase a cyanotype kit, the chemicals will be packaged in either liquid or dry form.

**LIQUID KIT.** The chemicals are prepared in liquid form and provided in two lightproof bottles, one containing a stock solution of ferric ammonium citrate and the other a stock solution of potassium ferricyanide. The kit provides instructions on mixing together the two stock solutions to prepare a working solution (you can also follow the directions included on page 35).

**DRY KIT.** The dry chemicals are premeasured and provided in two lightproof bottles. The kit provides detailed instructions for adding distilled water to each bottle to create the two stock solutions as well as how to mix them together to prepare the working solution. Or refer to page 34 for step-by-step directions.

**PRECOATED PAPER.** A third option is to purchase paper that has already been coated with a working solution and is ready to use. Throughout this book, I assume that you're mixing and applying your own chemicals. For me, coating the paper is part of the creative process. It's also the most cost-effective approach, and it gives you the most control over the finished piece. However, precoated paper or fabric is readily available and can be a great way to explore the technique for the first time. If you want to go this route, precoated paper would work well with the botanical print project on page 88, or try precoated fabric for the stencil project on page 168.

# *Bulk Chemicals*

When purchased in bulk, ferric ammonium citrate and potassium ferricyanide come in dry form. Working with these dry chemicals requires caution. Always wear a mask and gloves when handling, weighing, and mixing them. To prevent dispersal of the powder into the air, where you might breathe it in, add dry chemicals to the stock bottle before adding water. If chemical contact with your skin occurs, immediately rinse the area with cold running water.

Classic cyanotype stock solutions are typically labeled A (potassium ferricyanide) and B (ferric ammonium citrate). Stock solution A is 10 percent potassium ferricyanide (PFC), and stock solution B is 25 percent ferric ammonium citrate (FAC).

## CYANOTYPE FORMULAS

The solutions are typically mixed according to the following formulas.

- **STOCK SOLUTION A**
  10 grams or 2 teaspoons potassium ferricyanide per 100 mL distilled water
- **STOCK SOLUTION B**
  25 grams or 2 tablespoons ferric ammonium citrate per 100 mL distilled water
- **WORKING SOLUTION**
  1 part stock solution A +
  1 part stock solution B

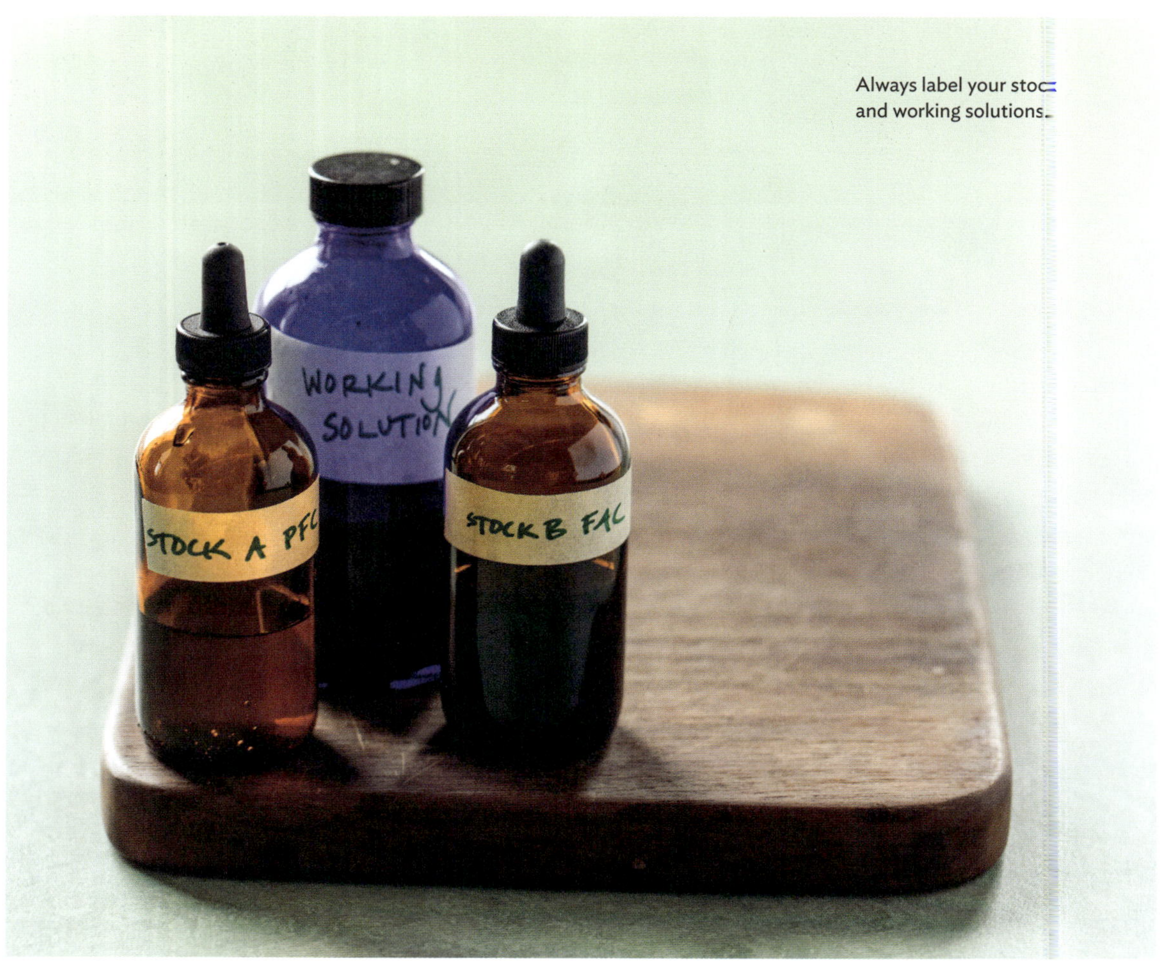


Always label your stock and working solutions.

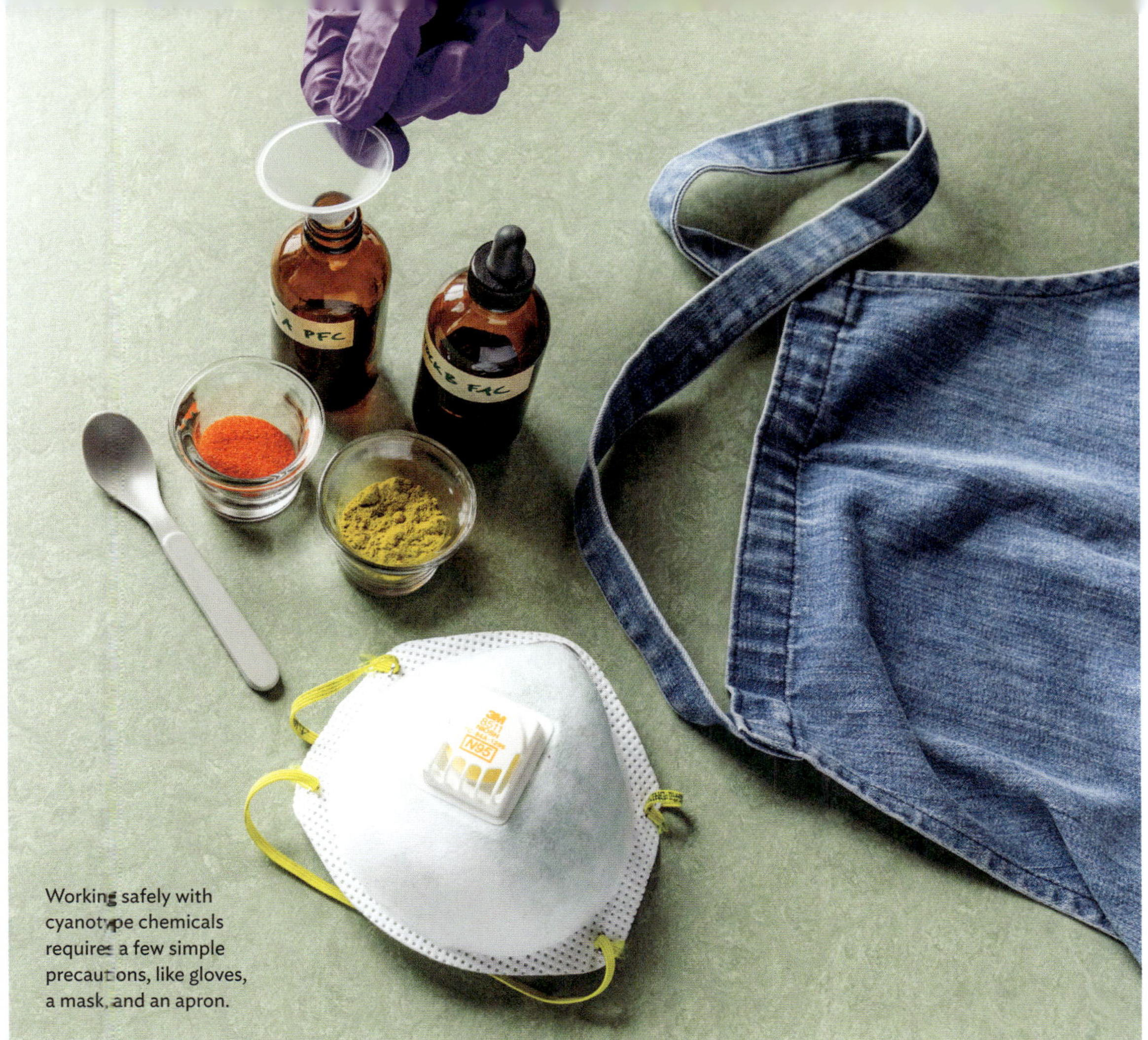


Working safely with cyanotype chemicals requires a few simple precautions, like gloves, a mask, and an apron.

## WORKING SAFELY WITH CYANOTYPE CHEMICALS

- Label all chemicals, whether in liquid or in powder form.
- Store chemicals in a childproof, pet-proof location.
- Wear a mask and gloves when handling, weighing, and mixing chemicals.
- Clean up spills with a mild dish soap; avoid using acid-based cleaners and ones with ammonia or bleach.
- When mixing dry chemicals with water, always add the dry chemicals to the bottle first to avoid dispersing powder into the air.
- If the dry chemicals come in contact with your skin, wash the area thoroughly with cold running water.
- In general, the working and stock solutions won't harm your skin. However, if your skin is sensitive, you may wish to wear gloves to avoid direct contact.
- To dispose of liquid chemicals, both stock and working solutions, mix them with clay kitty litter and throw away. See page 31 for more information.
- When working with chemical solutions, wear old clothes or an apron, as the solutions can stain.

# Creating a Prep Station

Before you begin mixing chemicals, it's ideal to set up a prep station with all your tools at hand. This is where you'll mix chemicals, coat paper, and allow the light-sensitive paper to dry (more on that in the following chapters). You can achieve low-light conditions by working at night with a low-level lightbulb (see page 43 for more information) or in a room with shades or no windows. This is also the best place to arrange your composition before exposure. The ideal prep station should have:

**CHEMICALS.** Either a cyanotype kit or dry ferric ammonium citrate and potassium ferricyanide.

**PROTECTIVE GLOVES.** Use reusable rubber gloves or disposable nitrile gloves when mixing chemicals or applying liquid emulsion to paper. If you have sensitive skin, you'll also want to wear gloves while washing exposed prints.

**FACE MASK.** I wear an N-95 mask when preparing stock solutions to avoid inhaling chemicals. Follow safety practices to prevent dispersing powder into the air.

**APRON.** Cyanotype chemicals can stain. Wear something you don't mind getting stained, like an old shirt or a denim apron. This includes shoes.

**DRY WEIGHT SCALE.** A scale is useful when working with bulk chemicals. Scales sold for use in the kitchen work well.

**DISTILLED WATER.** Use distilled water for consistent stock solutions. You can find it in grocery or first aid aisles. Municipal and well water

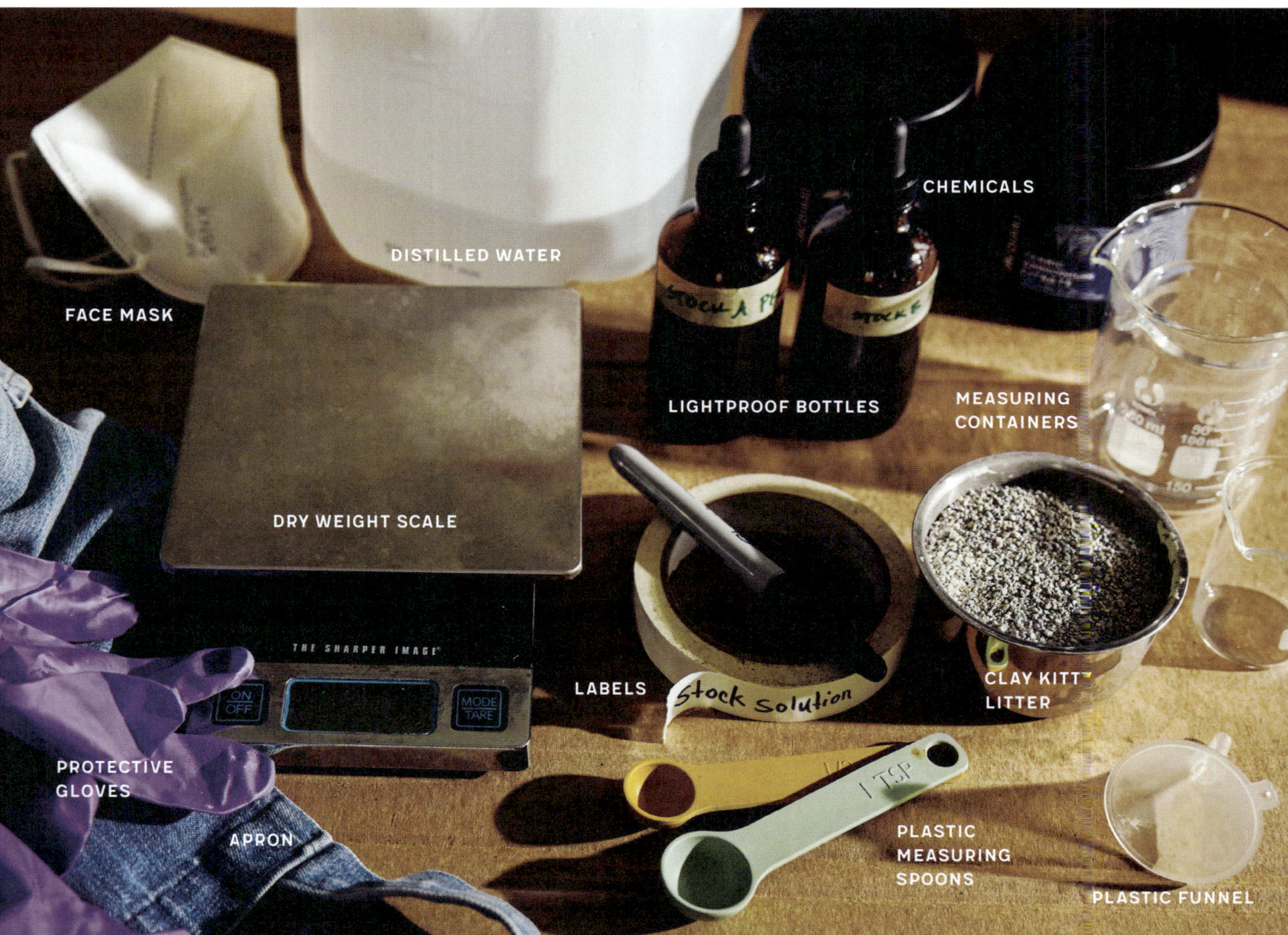

may contain components that interact unpredictably with the cyanotype chemicals. In a pinch, I have used tap water successfully, but my preference is to use distilled water to ensure consistent results.

**AMBER OR OTHER LIGHTPROOF BOTTLES.** Store solutions in lightproof plastic or glass bottles to minimize exposure to ultraviolet light. I reuse lightproof bottles from cyanotype kits, vitamins, or supplements.

**LABELS.** Label all containers, including spray bottles and jars holding liquids. I often make simple labels with blue painter's tape and a Sharpie.

**PLASTIC FUNNEL.** Use a funnel to pour liquid and dry chemicals into bottles. Always add dry chemicals before adding the water to prevent powder from dispersing.

**MEASURING CONTAINERS.** Use glass or plastic cups/beakers for mixing solutions and rinsing brushes. Designate specific containers for cyanotype use.

**PLASTIC MEASURING SPOONS.** Use separate spoons to measure chemicals and designate them only for cyanotype use.

**CLAY KITTY LITTER.** To safely dispose of any unused working solution, mix the extra working solution with enough kitty litter to fully absorb the liquid, seal the mixture securely in a plastic bag, and then dispose of it. I recommend you purchase the cheapest and most eco-friendly version of litter. Better yet, only make enough working solution for a paper-coating session.

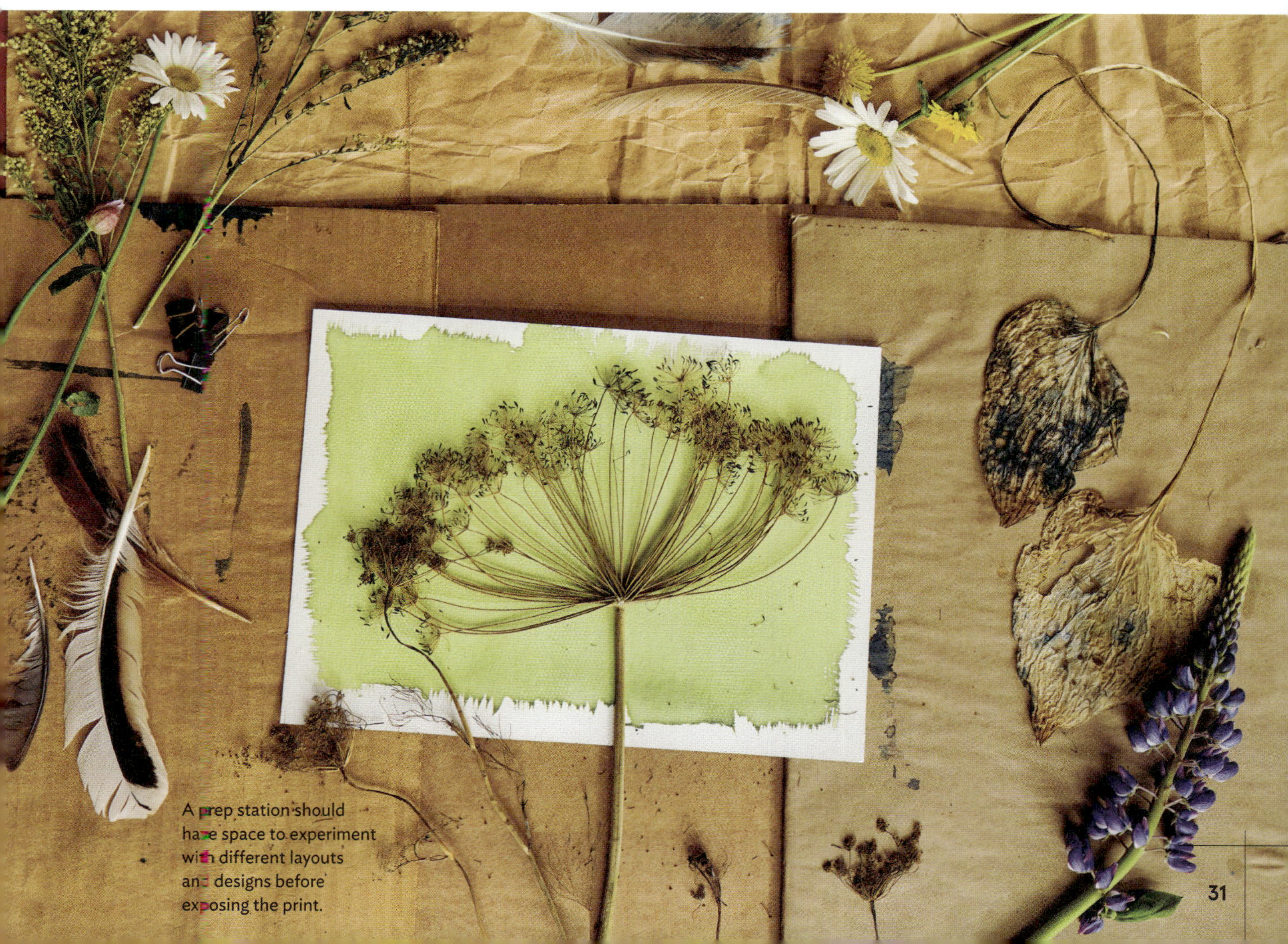

A prep station should have space to experiment with different layouts and designs before exposing the print.

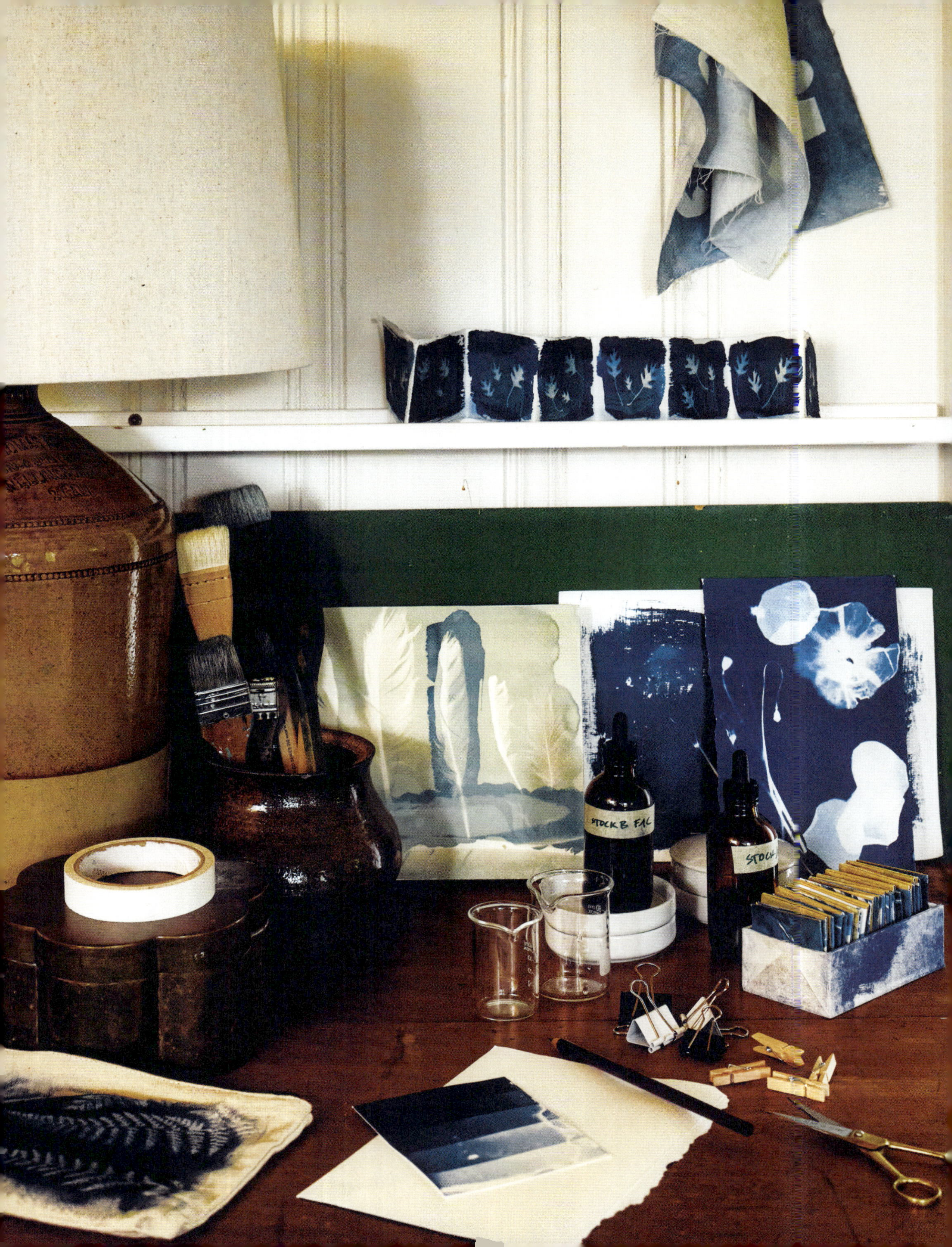
STOCK B FAC
STOCK

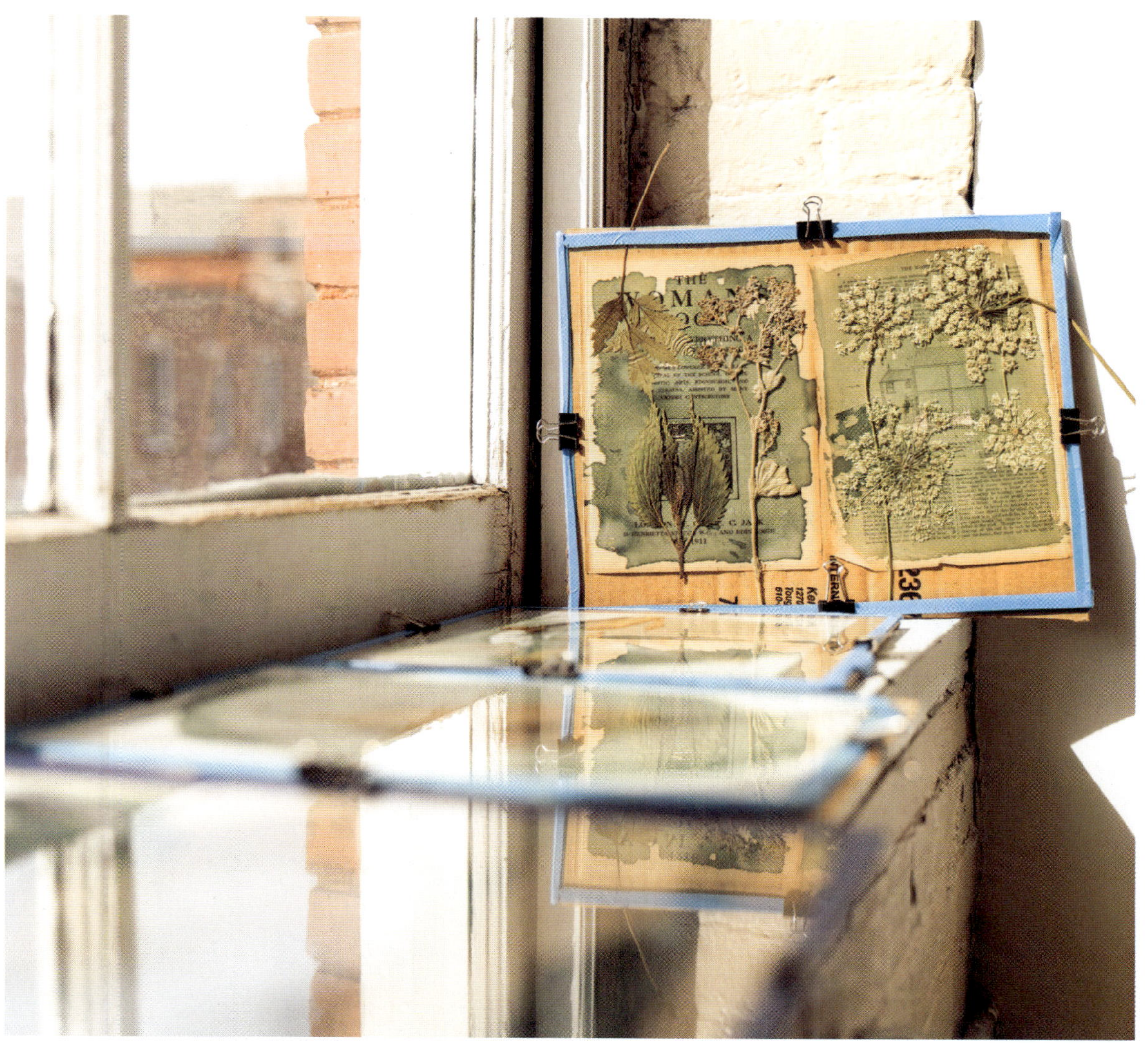

## FINDING A WORKSPACE

Creating a workspace free from distractions can be a challenge, especially when space is limited. Whether your area serves multiple purposes or is dedicated solely to project work, defining a workspace is important for your creative process. My studio is a converted room in my home, but many of my projects inevitably spill into shared living spaces, despite my efforts to contain them.

You'll need a low-light workspace for working with light-sensitive materials. You do not need a darkroom, however—just a room where you can handle the light-sensitive chemicals and coated paper away from direct sunlight. You will also need a wash station, with access to running water, and a spot where your prints can dry out of direct light. We'll discuss those spaces in more detail on pages 56 and 72.

# Mixing Solutions

The first step to creating a cyanotype is to mix your stock solutions and working solution. Distilled water is always best. Remember to wear a mask and gloves while working with chemicals!

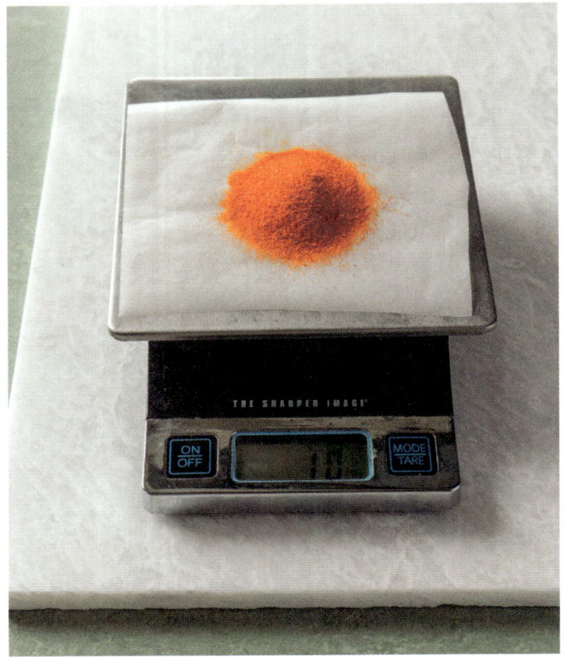


### PREPARE A STOCK SOLUTION

1. Using a scale, weigh out the appropriate amount of dry chemical: 10 grams of potassium ferricyanide or 25 grams of ferric ammonium citrate. I generally weigh out chemicals on a sheet of wax paper or parchment, making them easier to transfer. Measuring by weight is most accurate, but if you don't have a scale you can use volume measurements. Use 2 teaspoons of potassium ferricyanide or 2 tablespoons of ferric ammonium citrate.
2. Transfer the measured amount of dry chemical into a lightproof glass or plastic bottle.
3. Add 100 mL of distilled water.
4. Put the cap on the bottle and shake to mix the solution thoroughly.
5. Label the bottle, then allow the solution to rest for 24 hours before using it.

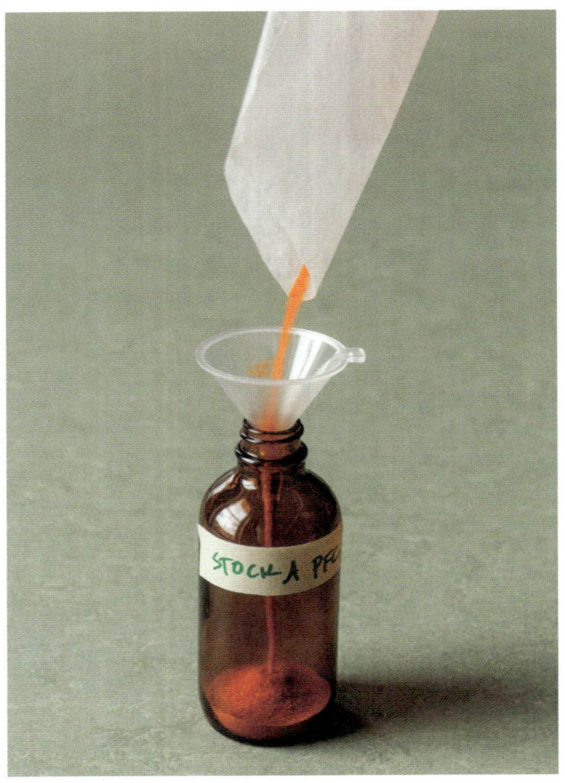


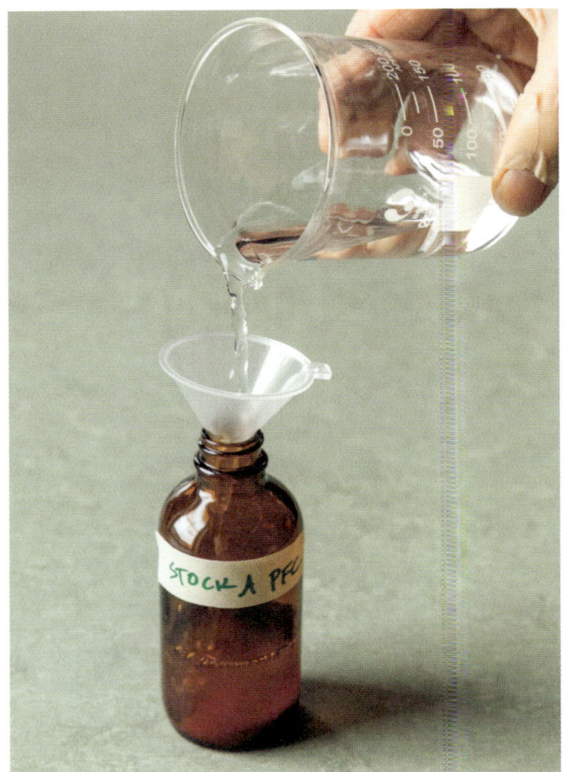

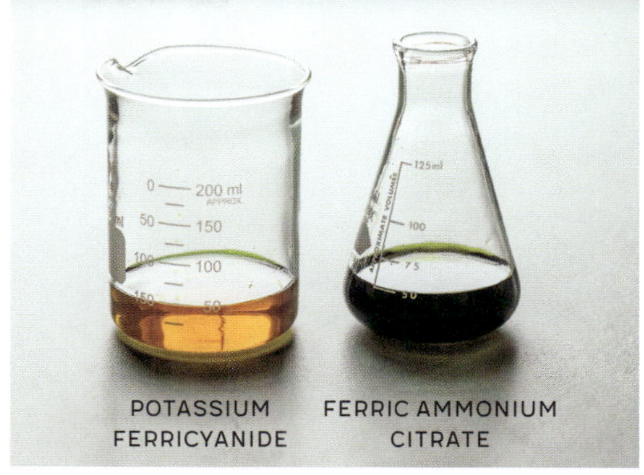


## PREPARE A WORKING SOLUTION

1. Working in a low-light space, combine equal amounts of stock solution A (potassium ferricyanide) and stock solution B (ferric ammonium citrate) in a glass or plastic container.
2. Stir to mix the solution thoroughly, using a glass or plastic utensil. If the solution will not be used right away, transfer it to a lightproof container.
3. Use the working solution within 24 hours for optimal results (though some people report positive results with older working solution).
4. Safely dispose of old working solution by pouring it into a plastic bag filled with clay kitty litter, then sealing the bag securely and putting it in the trash.

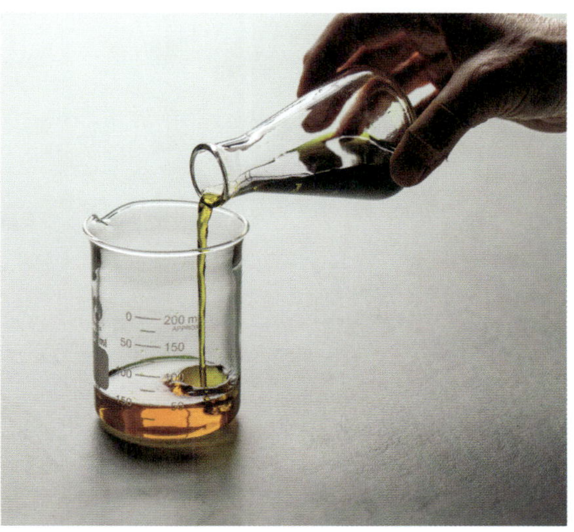

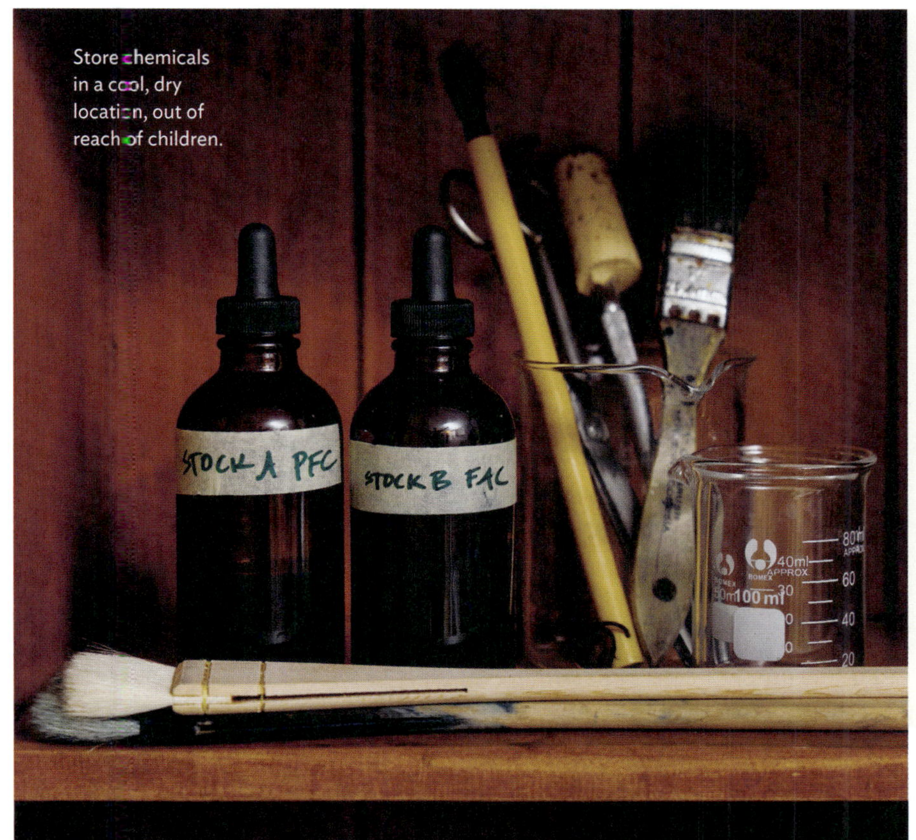


Store chemicals in a cool, dry location, out of reach of children.

## STORAGE AND SHELF LIFE.

Store all your cyanotype chemicals, dry or liquid, in a cool, dry location. Dry chemicals have a shelf life of many years; liquid stock solutions will keep for approximately 1 year. I store stock solution B in the refrigerator to minimize the harmless mold that can form in the solution. If mold develops, remove with a toothpick. Working solution should be used within 24 hours.

varieties, and can be had in all shades from palest lavender to deepest indigo.

**Evening Primroses.**—These are characterised by great profusion of bloom, and are bright border plants. The principal drawback is a tendency to straggle, but this is not so marked in one or two of the modern varieties. The most compact Evening Primroses are the species Fruticosa and its variety Youngi, both yellow flowered. The latter is perhaps the most useful that we can have, as in addition to its closeness of growth it has the merit of producing a great mass of brilliant flowers.

**Pansies.**—Considering that [illegible] a lowly plant, incapable of yielding those bo[illegible]sses of colour, which the modern flower gard[illegible]ves so much, the pansy remains a decided [illegible] especially in Scotland where the humi[illegible] seems to suit its growth. But it wi[illegible] very little coaxing in moist, cla[illegible] even [illegible] the extreme south of England.

The work of the cultivator is easier if [illegible] fairly early, say by the end of March. At that period the nights, if [illegible] cool; moreover, heavy s[illegible] may be [illegible]. A liberal rainfall and cool nights between them are a great help in [illegible] Pansies [illegible] established. If planting is not done until May or June far more attention is needed to get the plants into free growth. Pansies bloom for a long time and in[illegible] rapidly. The hardy kinds will take n[illegible] by being left out of doors all winte[illegible]

**Phloxes.**—[illegible] valuable class of garden flowers. They bear their flowers in bunches at [illegible] of [illegible] stems [illegible] with narrow [illegible]-shaped leaves. The colours are very [illegible] refined. [illegible] flower ea[illegible]

**Primr[illegible]**—[illegible] herbace[illegible] plants [illegible] ordinary acceptation of the [illegible] because they are not leafless through-out the winter. On the contrary, they grow in mild [illegible], and [illegible] in spring, when the majority of [illegible] just awakening from their [illegible] sleep. Primroses and Polyanthuses may be introduced into herbaceous borders with great advantage, as well as into ordinary flower beds; they can be shifted into beds and borders in autumn, when the herbaceous and annual plants are fading, and moved out again in the spring, when other plants are coming on.

**Pyrethrum**[illegible]ese are valuable [illegible] more ways than one. They are among the earliest of the border [illegible] bloom, and they bloom very prof[illegible] distinctly handsome, and the [illegible] varied. They are easi[illegible] very hardy.

**Gladioli.**—One of the most beautiful of late summer flowers. A neat, somewhat close flower stems closely studded with funnel-shaped flowers.

**Irises.**—These stand forth as among the most valuable of border plants. The Flag section are particularly vigorous in growth, and have large brilliant flowers. They will grow almost anywhere. Others require a very moist situation.

**Michaelmas Daisies.**—Very useful in borders, as they bloom when other flowers are beginning to fade. They have vigour of growth, free blooming and bright, varied colours.

**Ox-eye Daisies.**—A species of Chrysanthemums. There is not much variety about these flowers, but they are useful in borders. They flower well and are easily grown.

**Paeonies.**—These are among the finest of our hardy plants. The number of varieties has grown rapidly within the last few years, and they can now be had in many shades of pink and red as well as white. They require abundance of room to look well.

**Violas.**—Sometimes called the tufted pansy, [illegible] the name is not inapt, inasmuch as the growth is tufty and the plants are at least as much Pansies as Violas.

The plants are distinguished by dense, compact growth, relatively large flowers, rich and diversified colours, and great profusion and persistency in flowering. Violas are admirably adapted for forming a groundwork for other plants. They can be utilised for this purpose in herbaceous borders and in rose-beds. If [illegible] autumn along with bulbs, many charming effects can be made. They can also be used for forming edgings to beds and borders.

It is desirable to avoid planting in straight lines. When Violas are employed for an edging to wide borders, an irregular line on the inside should be followed, so that the occupants of the border may extend forward amongst the Violas at different points. If one will have a ribbon border of Violas, let nothing else be associated with them, and let the varieties be most carefully selected for the purpose.

To get the best out of Violas, plants should be bought in spring and planted in deeply-dug, well-manured soil. The earlier this is done the better, because when planted early they have a good chance of getting well established before the hot weather comes. The plants enjoy depth, coolness, moisture, and fertility. They may be planted about nine inches apart.

Constant cuttings should be practised throughout the summer [illegible] flowers will be found useful in the house, and, apart from that, the regular picking will prevent seed pods forming, and so keep the plants growing.

## ROSES

There is a charm about a beautiful Rose garden

CHAPTER 2

# The Paper

*Though you can work with other materials, such as fabric, most cyanotypes are produced on paper. You can use just about any kind of paper, but some papers are better suited to the demands of the process than others. My preferences often change, but as a general rule, I consider a paper's weight and strength, as my process involves multiple washes and the reapplication of chemicals as I add and subtract layers. Your paper preferences will reveal themselves as you develop your cyanotype practice.*

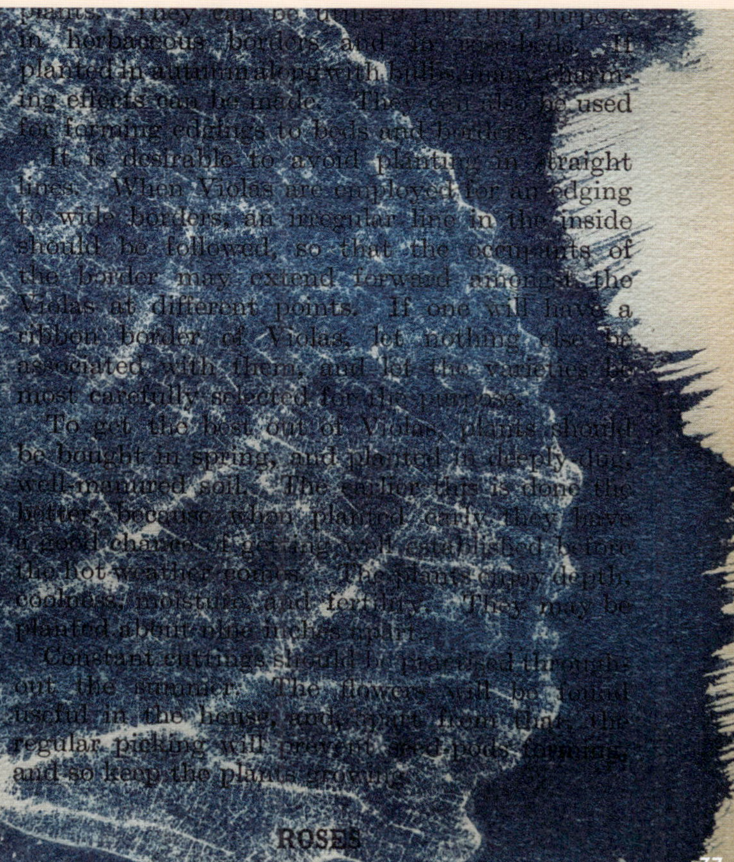

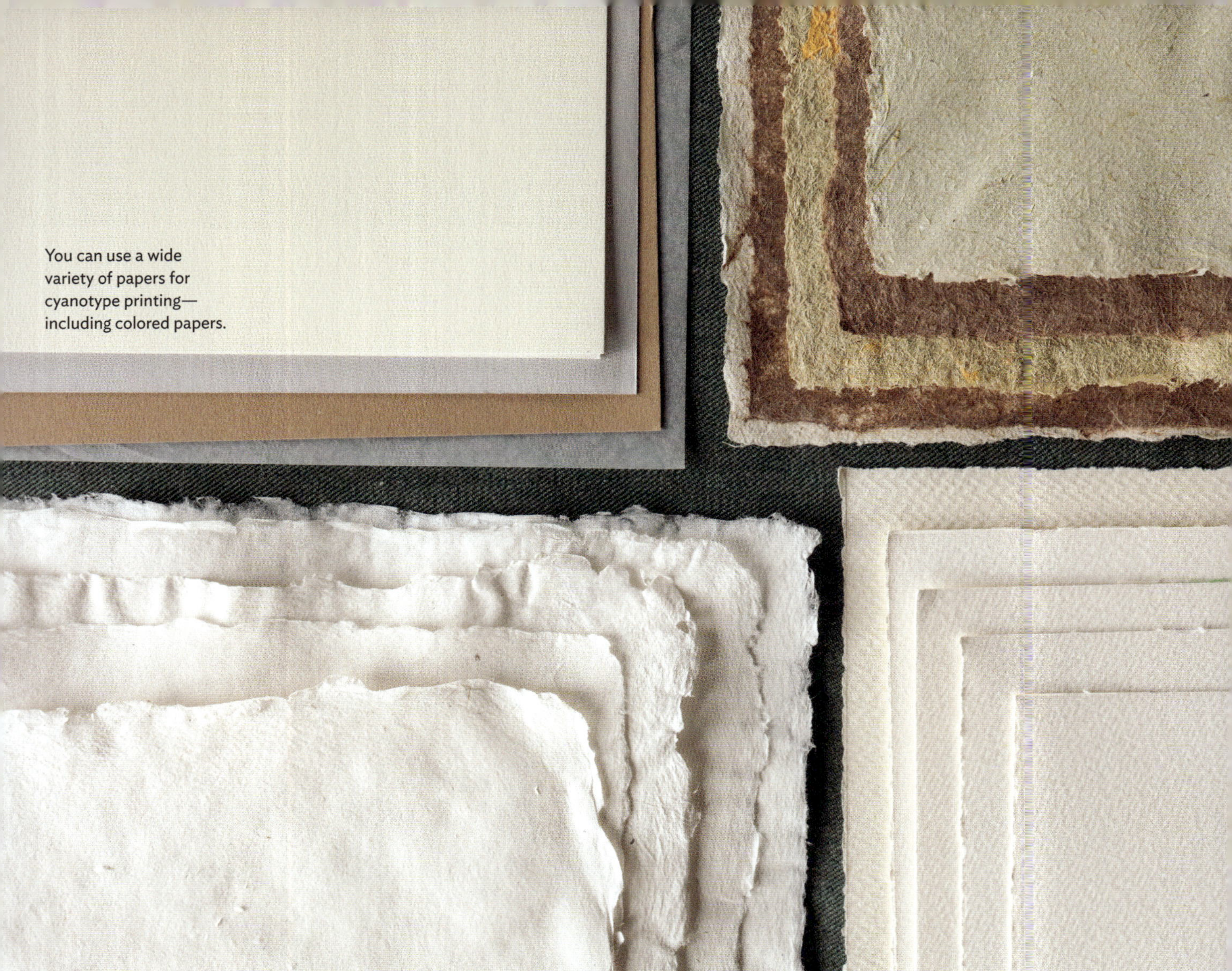
You can use a wide variety of papers for cyanotype printing—including colored papers.

# Choosing Paper

Paper is usually made from plant fibers such as cotton, bark, or wood pulp. The fibers are cooked, beaten, and then formed into sheets by hand or by a machine. It sounds simple, and it can be, but if you are interested in exploring the diversity of paper options and qualities, you'll soon find that it ranges widely and deeply. The paper section at my local art supply store offers a dizzying selection.

## *Paper Basics*

You'll find papers classified according to the following qualities.

**GSM / #.** These are units to measure a paper's weight. Gsm stands for grams per square meter, indicating the weight of a single sheet of paper that is one square meter in size. You'll also see papers categorized by their weight in pounds (indicated by the weight followed by a #, as in 140#), which refers to the weight of 500 sheets of a specific paper at its uncut size. Because the uncut sizes of various paper types can differ, gsm is often a simpler way to gauge the thickness of a paper—a higher gsm indicates a thicker paper.

**pH / ACIDITY.** Paper with higher acidity tends to deteriorate and yellow over time, reducing its longevity. You'll commonly see two terms relating to acidity on commercial papers: acid-free and pH-neutral. Acid-free paper is produced from alkaline pulp (pH of 7.0 or higher). Paper labeled pH-neutral has a pH of 7.0 (neutral). Confusingly, neither label means that the paper is completely acid-free. In general, select acid-free and/or pH-neutral paper for making cyanotypes.

**ALKALINE BUFFER.** A substance, usually calcium carbonate (chalk), added during papermaking to neutralize acids that could degrade the paper over time. Cyanotypes are sensitive to alkaline substances such as calcium carbonate, which can cause yellowing and bleaching. To avoid these problems, it's best to use unbuffered paper for creating, storing, and displaying cyanotypes.

**HOT PRESS.** Paper with a smooth surface. During papermaking, the paper is compressed onto heated rolls that smooth out the paper, like an iron.

**COLD PRESS.** Paper with a slightly textured surface. During papermaking, the paper fibers are not subjected to heated rolls and compression; this makes the surface slightly bumpy.

**ARCHIVAL.** This term is used to denote durable, acid-free paper made from pure cotton fibers or pure alpha-cellulose fibers that are made from wood; these papers have a lifespan of 100-plus years.

**DECKLED EDGE.** A standard sheet of paper has a straight-cut edge. In contrast, a deckled edge is untrimmed, leaving the edge with a rough, feathered appearance. The term comes from the wooden frame used to form sheets of paper, which is called a deckle. You most often see deckled edges on handmade papers, but some machine-made papers have artificial deckled edges.

**SIZING.** This refers to a substance, like gelatin or arrowroot, that is added to paper to decrease its absorbency and increase its strength.

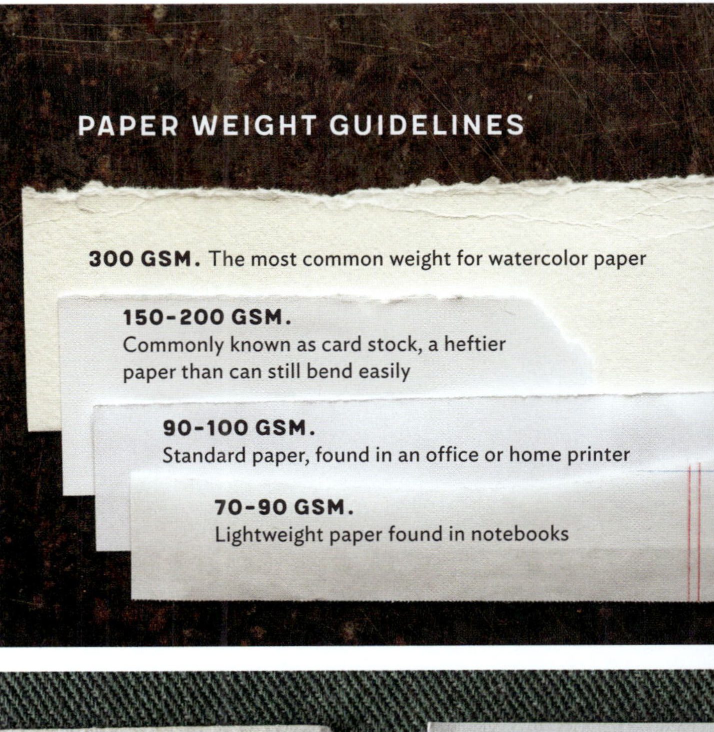


COLD PRESS

Cold-press paper is slightly textured in comparison to hot-press paper, which has a smoother finish.

HOT PRESS

## PAPER SELECTION FOR BEGINNERS

For your first foray into cyanotype making, select an acid-free watercolor paper with a weight of 300 gsm/140#. Paper with this heft provides a durable foundation for the application of cyanotype solution, for rinsing, and for some of the experimental projects you will be trying later on in this book.

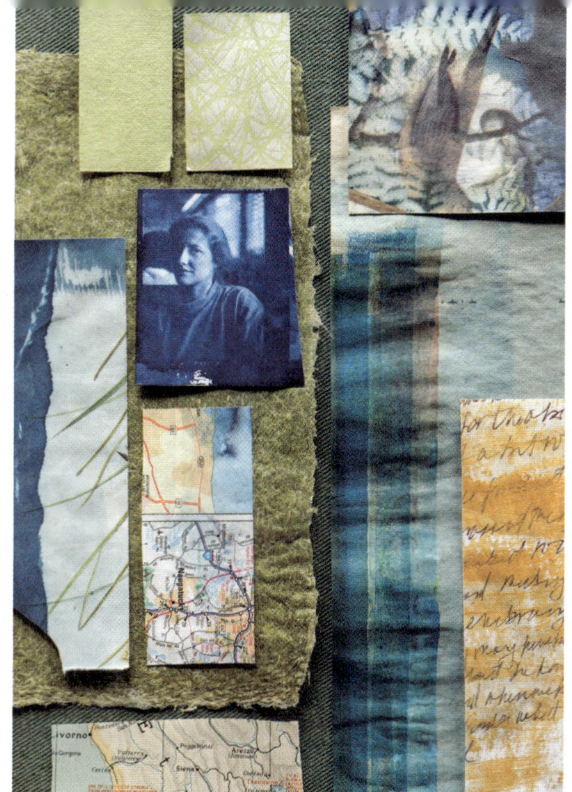


## *Handmade Papers*

Handmade papers can be a lovely option for the cyanotype process. Making paper by hand is itself an art form. My own experiences in making paper, with guidance and equipment provided by wonderful teachers, gives me appreciation for the many steps involved in creating a single sheet of paper.

If you have a sheet (or stack) of paper you have made by hand or purchased from another paper artist, use a gelatin or arrowroot sizing before applying cyanotype chemicals to the paper's surface. This will make the paper sturdier and allow the chemicals to create an emulsion on the surface.

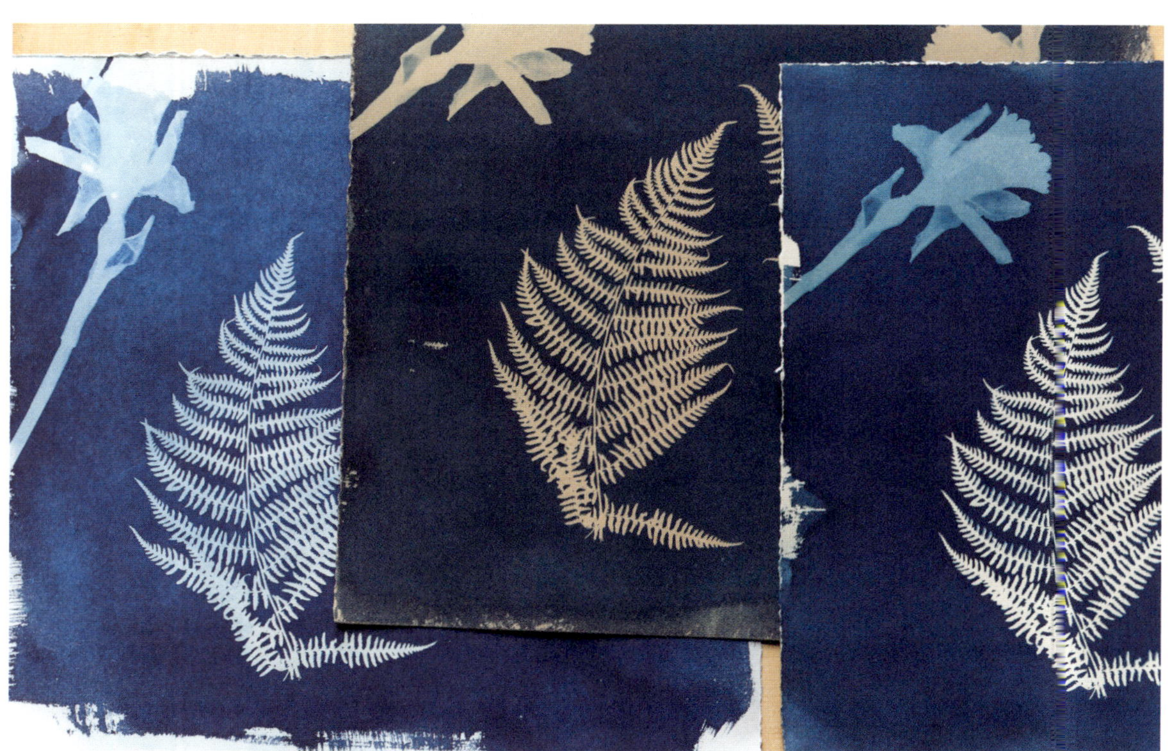

### BEYOND BLUE AND WHITE

I love the blue and white, I do. But there are moments when something different is needed. You can achieve that by altering the cyanotype itself (as we'll learn on page 128) or simply by using a colored paper. One hundred percent cotton Stonehenge paper comes in several tones; here I use a white, fawn, and steel gray.

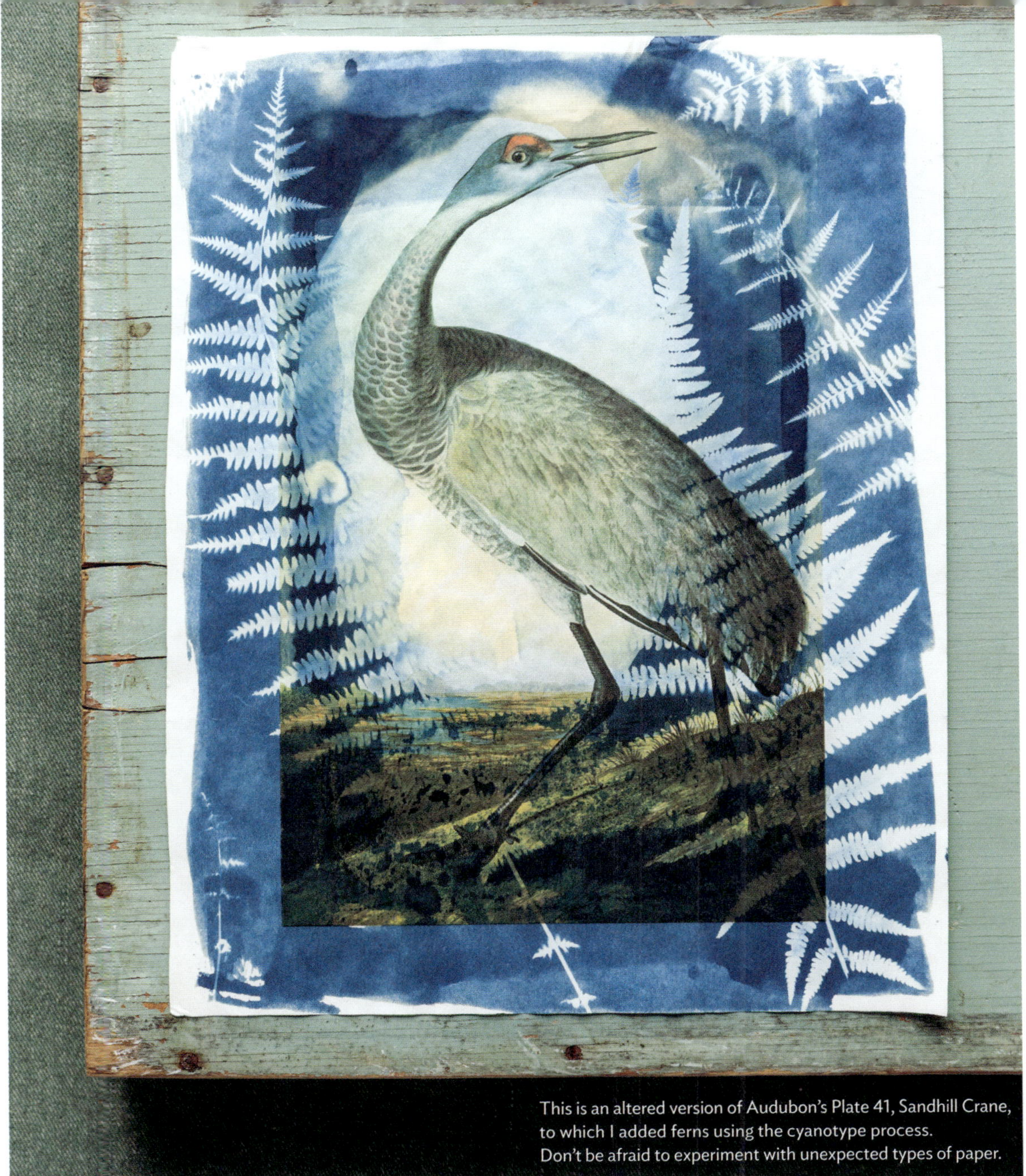

This is an altered version of Audubon's Plate 41, Sandhill Crane, to which I added ferns using the cyanotype process. Don't be afraid to experiment with unexpected types of paper.

## Paper Ephemera

If I never bought another sheet of paper, I'd still be able to make cyanotypes using paper from old books, maps, and family memorabilia for the rest of my life. A few years ago, I started pulling pages from an old copy of *Birds of America* that I've schlepped around for more than 30 years. I tore pages from the book, applied cyanotype chemicals to them, and started making something totally new. Consider using old documents, greeting cards, or handwritten letters. Coated paper such as you might find on old photographs, brochures, or some maps can be harder to work with, as it inhibits the absorption of the cyanotype chemicals.

Using paper ephemera is always unpredictable, but that's part of the fun. Keep in mind that whatever you create may not be archival, depending on the paper source.

The cyanotype solution can easily soak through thin paper. Put a second layer of absorbent watercolor paper underneath to soak it up.

## Working with Thin Paper

Washi is a type of strong but thin Japanese paper made with fiber from mulberry bark or the gampi shrub. It's generally 35 to 80 gsm. Washi paper will absorb the cyanotype liquid emulsion completely, soaking all the way through. When coating any thin, absorbent paper, place the paper on top of a sheet of watercolor paper, which will catch any solution that soaks through. Another option is to place the paper on a large sheet of sturdy glass or another wipeable surface for coating and, afterward, wiping or squeegeeing any liquid solution back into a container.

## Papers to Avoid

Although I encourage experimentation with different kinds of paper, I suggest avoiding 56 to 72 gsm notebook and copier paper for cyanotype printing. It may be similar in thickness to washi, but it lacks the structure and strength needed to survive a 10-minute wash in water and may simply dissolve. Additionally, I avoid coated or shiny papers; the finish on the paper's surface may inhibit the paper from absorbing the cyanotype solution.

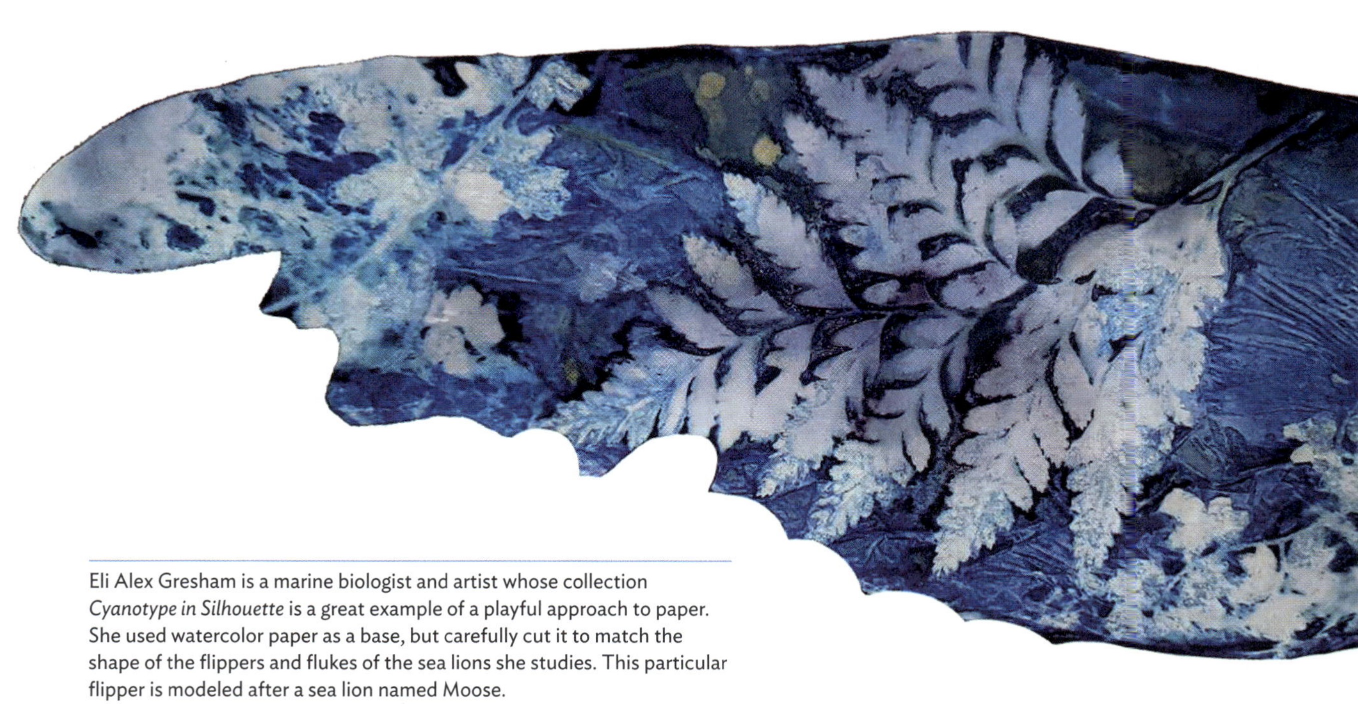

Eli Alex Gresham is a marine biologist and artist whose collection *Cyanotype in Silhouette* is a great example of a playful approach to paper. She used watercolor paper as a base, but carefully cut it to match the shape of the flippers and flukes of the sea lions she studies. This particular flipper is modeled after a sea lion named Moose.

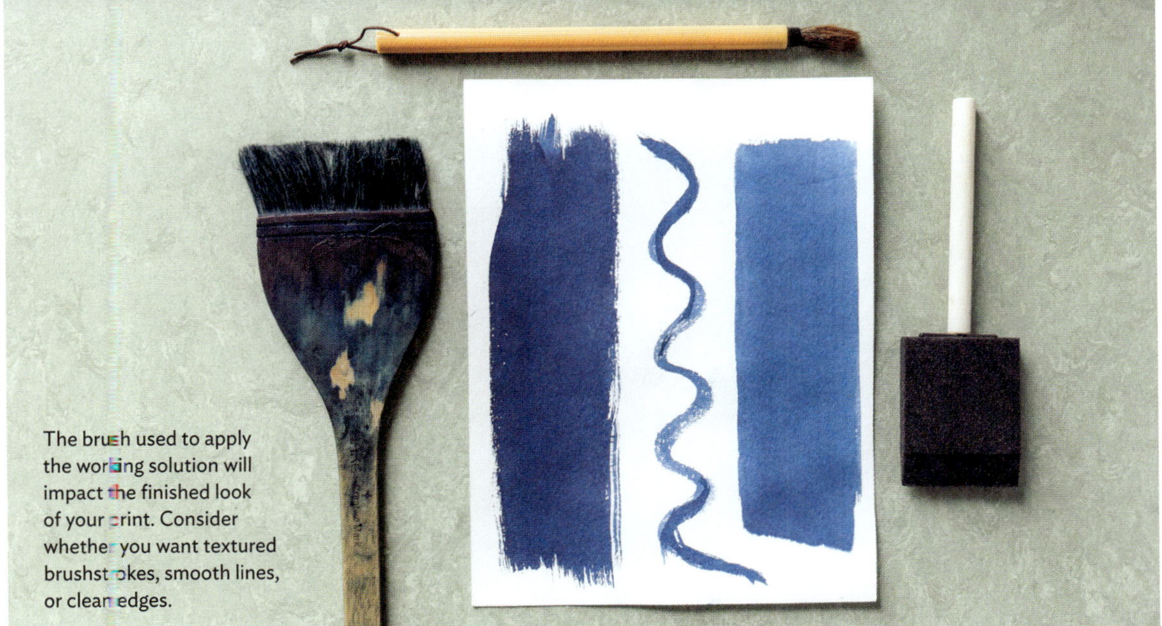

The brush used to apply the working solution will impact the finished look of your print. Consider whether you want textured brushstrokes, smooth lines, or clean edges.

# Preparing the Paper

Chemicals mixed: check. Paper selected: check. Now it's time to apply the chemicals to the paper's surface to create a light-sensitive emulsion. When exposed to ultraviolet light, the chemicals in the emulsion will interact and change, so special care must be taken to limit UV exposure during preparation and storage.

## *Light Requirements*

You'll need to work in a dim, but not completely dark, room when coating paper with the light-sensitive cyanotype chemicals. I usually coat paper in the evening, when natural light is already low. Conventional household tungsten fluorescent bulbs of 3100K and below are helpful; they will not cause the cyanotype chemicals to fog or become exposed. The same is true for standard LED home lights; they produce a minimal amount of UV light and will not interfere with the process of working with cyanotype chemicals.

## *Protective Wear*

When mixing and applying cyanotype chemicals, wear clothes and shoes that can handle a little blue spatter, as well as rubber or nitrile gloves to protect your hands. Lay cardboard, a vinyl tablecloth, or some other protective covering over your work surface.

## *Choosing a Brush*

You'll apply the working solution to the paper with a brush. The type of brush you use lends its own characteristics to the cyanotype.

**FOAM SPONGE BRUSHES.** Utilitarian 2-inch foam sponge brushes create a smooth, even emulsion without brush marks. They are an economical choice and widely available. If thoroughly rinsed after use, foam sponge brushes can last for several months and numerous applications.

**HAKE BRUSHES.** Traditional hake brushes have a wide, flat arrangement of natural goat-hair bristles on a long wooden handle, secured with glue or twine rather than metal (which avoids the possibility of galvanic corrosion). A hake brush is a beautiful tool and enjoyable to use, and it allows you to create visible brushstrokes in the emulsion on your paper.

**SUMI INK PAINTING BRUSHES.** With their fine tapered points, these brushes allow you to selectively "paint" cyanotype working solution onto paper. Be sure to look for metal-free versions.

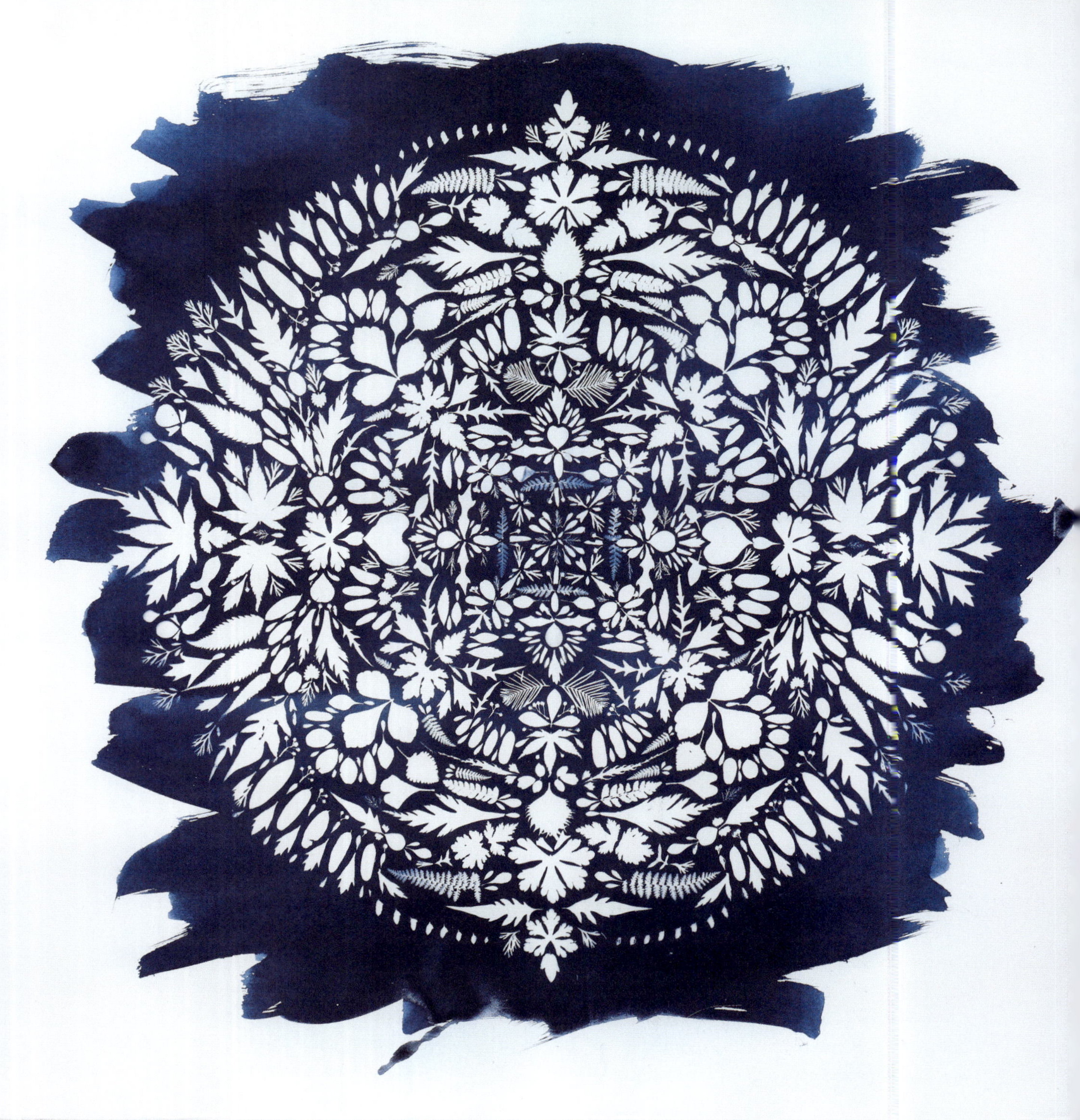

Showing brushstrokes can be a deliberate choice. Artist Hillary Waters Fayle interacts closely with the landscape, collecting as many plant specimens as possible, which she transforms into large, intricate cyanotypes. The visible brushstrokes in Waters Fayle's work *Hortus* allow her to convey a sense of movement.

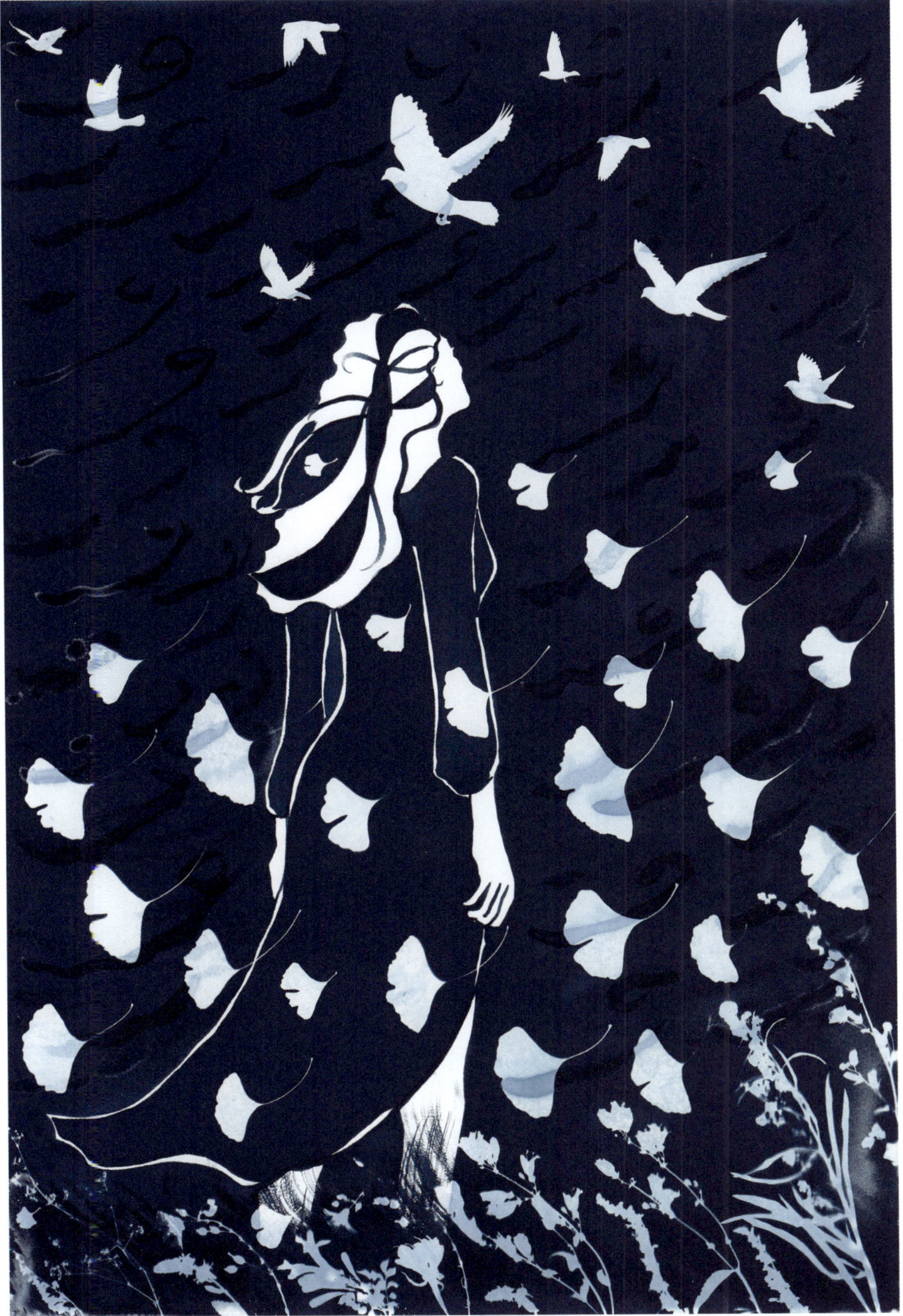

Artist Brooke Sauer's unique approach to making cyanotypes is informed by a background in painting. In *The Invitation*, Sauer combines expressive brushstrokes and wild pressed plants to create narrative works based on her emotional connection to a place.

# Applying the Working Solution

Be sure to use only glass or plastic tools and containers, and have plenty of clean rags or paper towels on hand for wiping up spills.

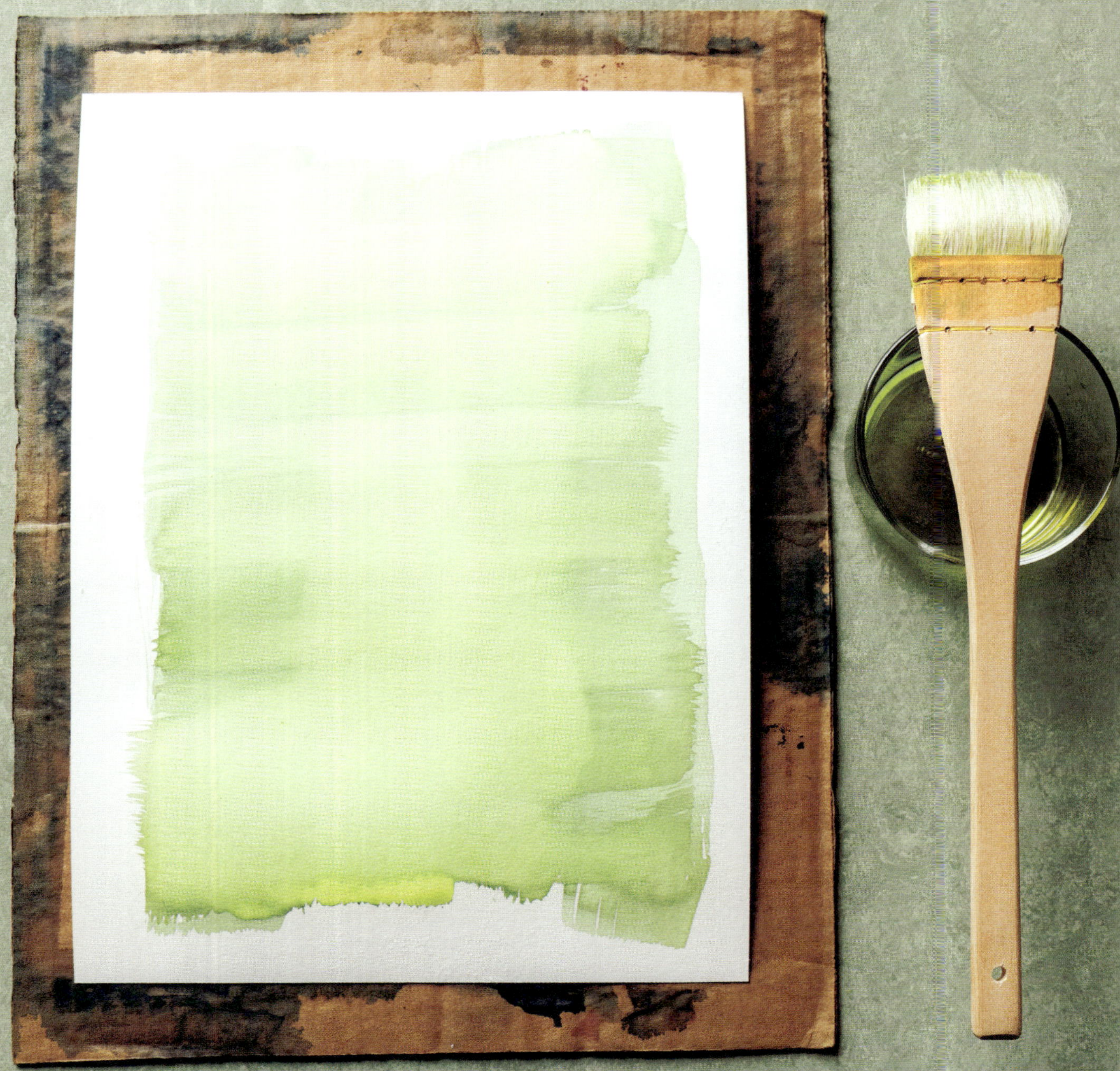

## MEASURING STOCK SOLUTION

A mixture of ½ teaspoon or 2.5 mL each of stock solution A and stock solution B is sufficient for coating an 8 × 10-inch sheet of paper. Adjust the quantities proportionally if you are coating more paper, maintaining a 1:1 ratio of solutions A and B. Try to mix only what you will use in one session to avoid waste and the need to dispose of leftover working solution.

## Materials

- Rubber or nitrile gloves
- Stock solutions A and B (see page 34)
- Paper of your choice
- Tape (optional)
- Metal-free brush
- Water

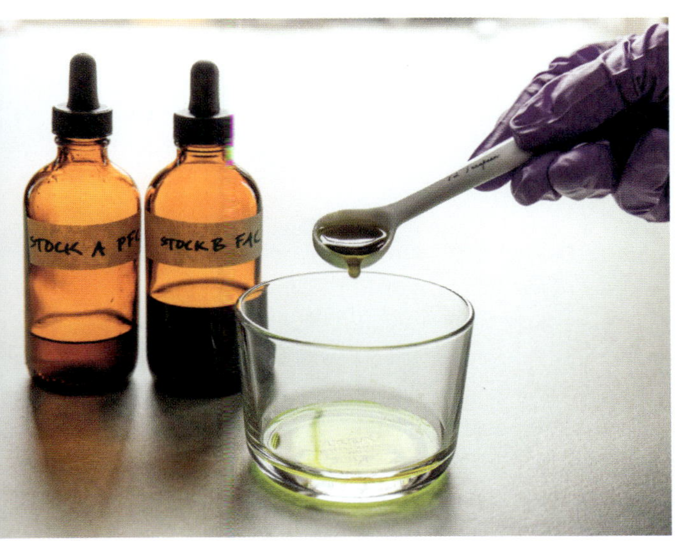


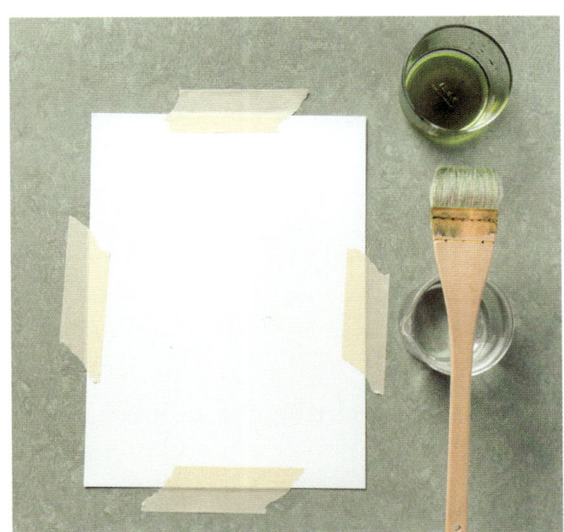

1. **MIX UP THE WORKING SOLUTION.** Wearing gloves, measure a portion of stock solution A and pour it into a glass or plastic bowl. Measure out the same volume of stock solution B and add it to the bowl.

2. **PREPARE THE PAPER.** Place your paper flat on a protected surface. Tape it down, if you like, or plan to hold it in place with your fingers as you start brushing on the solution.

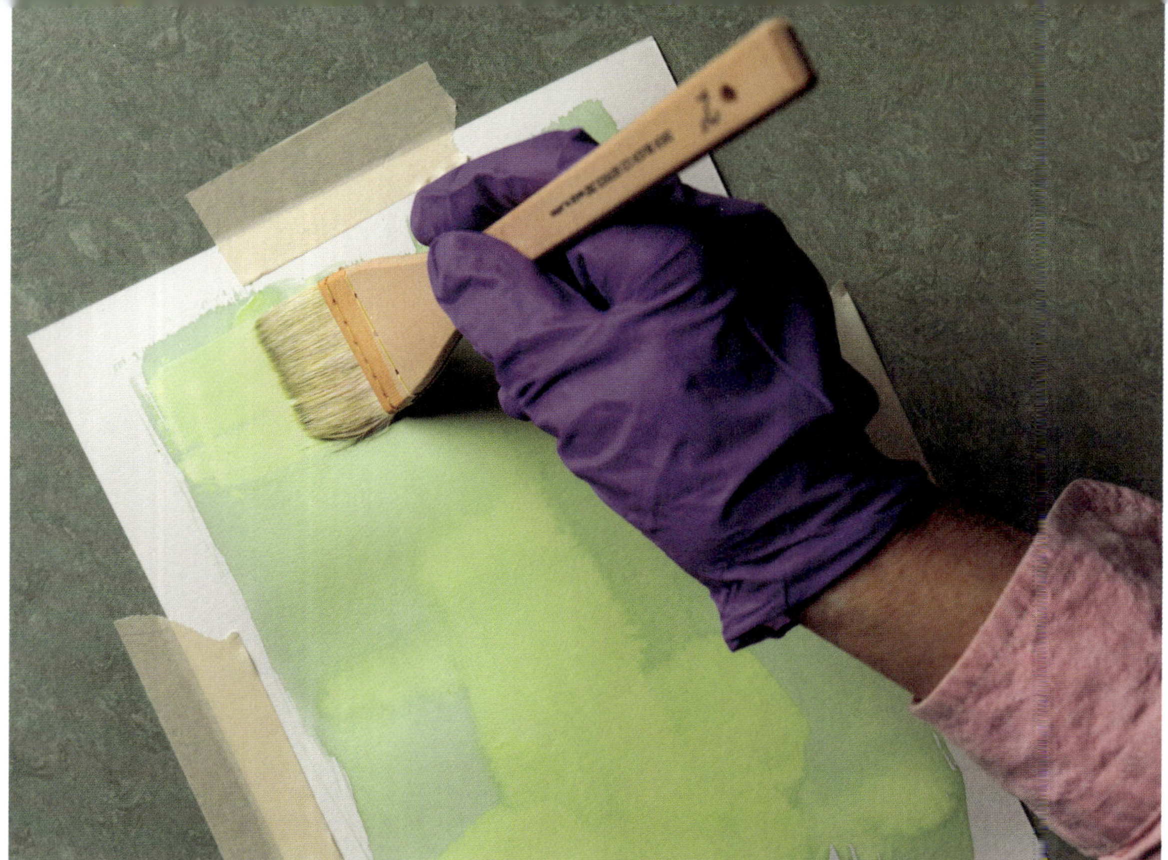

**3 PRIME YOUR BRUSH.** Dip your brush into a bowl of water, then squeeze out the excess water. Priming the brush will inhibit the bristles from absorbing the chemicals.

**4 APPLY THE SOLUTION.** Dip your brush into the yellowish-green working solution, then wipe off the excess against the side of the bowl. Brush the solution onto the paper, moving both horizontally and vertically to ensure a complete and even coating. Smooth out any puddles to achieve an even emulsion. As the solution dries, it will create a light-green emulsion on the paper.

**5 DRY THE COATED PAPER.** Dry the paper on a flat surface or hang it on a line with clothespins. Depending on the ambient temperature and humidity, the paper will dry in 30 to 60 minutes.

**NOTE** An uneven coat of working solution can cause pooling, and if the paper is hung to dry, the solution may drip. For that reason, I dry paper flat on large sheets of cardboard. If you hang your cyanotypes, note that the chemicals will stain wooden clothespins.

**6 USE OR STORE.** You can use the paper as soon as it has dried completely. If you're not going to use it right away, store the coated paper in a lightproof box or envelope in a cool, dark place. Oxidation may cause the emulsion to darken over time, so I recommend using your coated paper within 2 weeks.

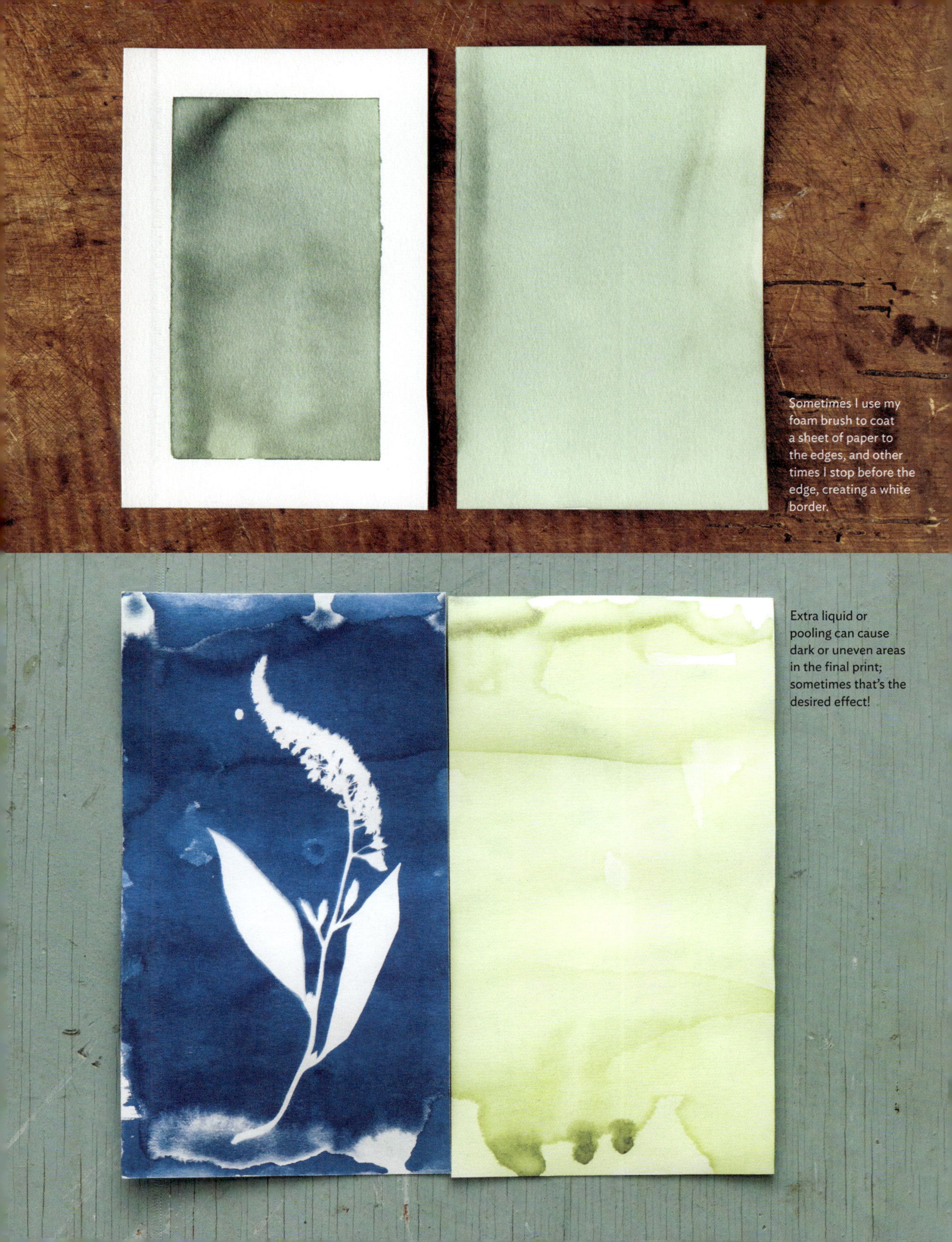

Sometimes I use my foam brush to coat a sheet of paper to the edges, and other times I stop before the edge, creating a white border.

Extra liquid or pooling can cause dark or uneven areas in the final print; sometimes that's the desired effect!

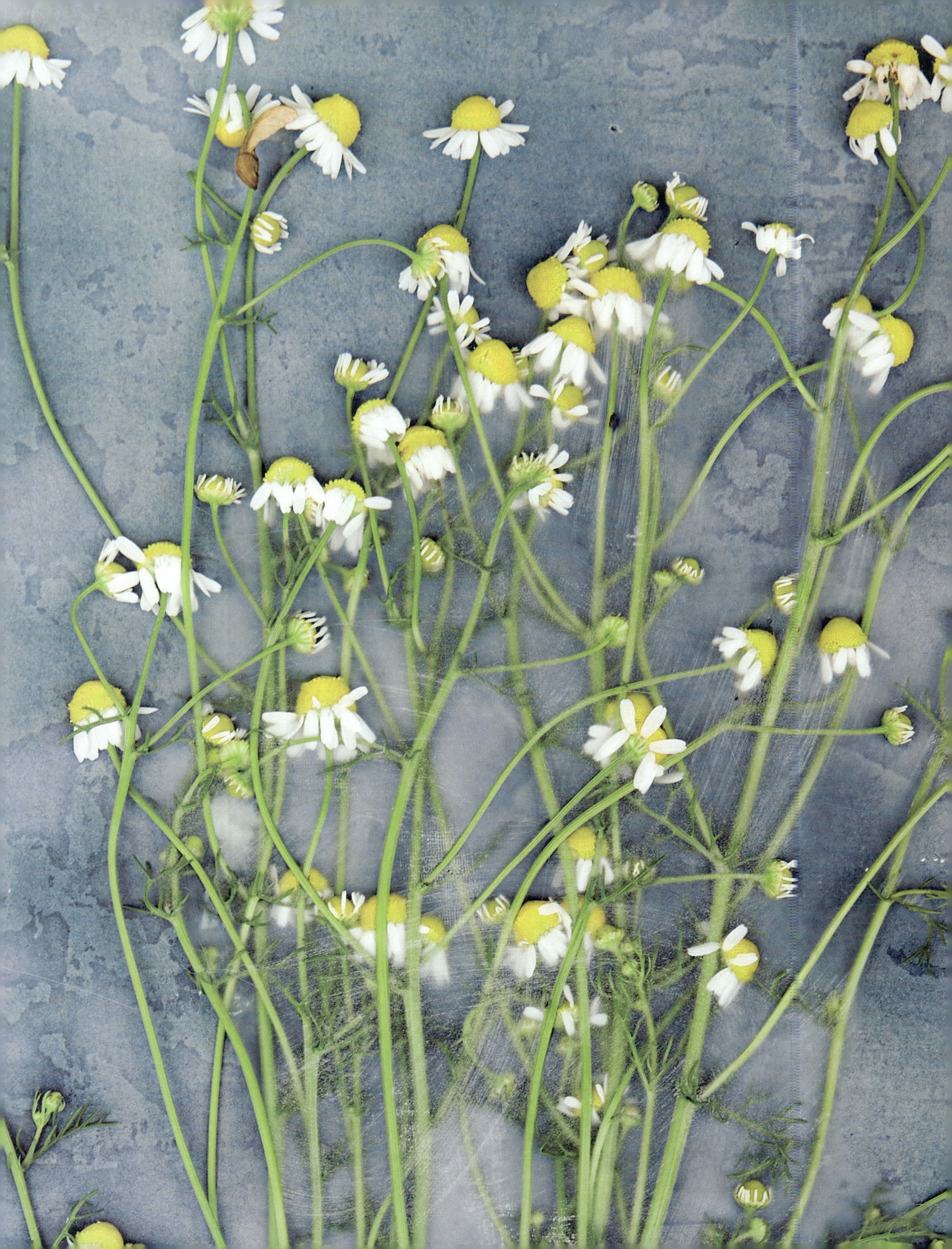

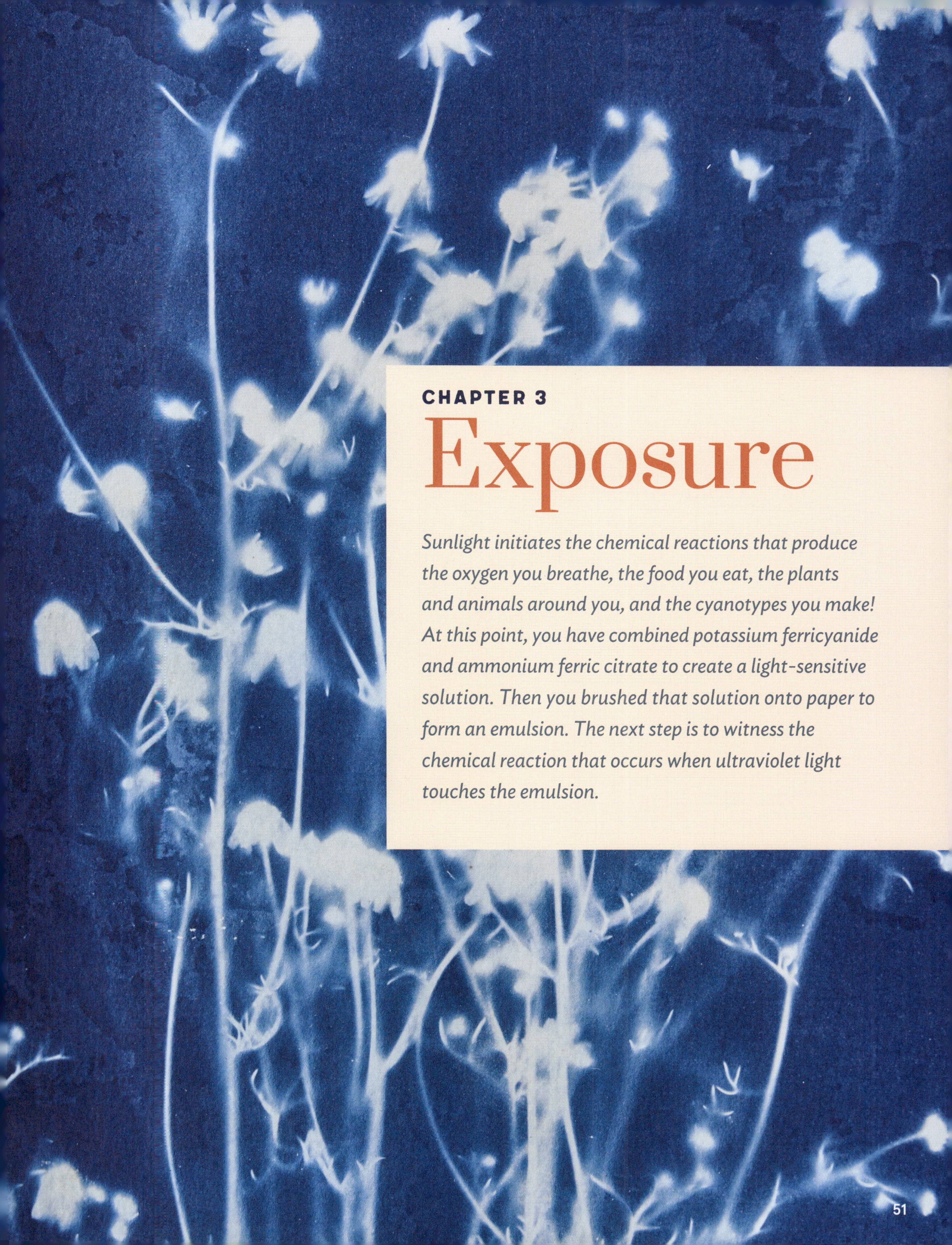

CHAPTER 3

# Exposure

*Sunlight initiates the chemical reactions that produce the oxygen you breathe, the food you eat, the plants and animals around you, and the cyanotypes you make! At this point, you have combined potassium ferricyanide and ammonium ferric citrate to create a light-sensitive solution. Then you brushed that solution onto paper to form an emulsion. The next step is to witness the chemical reaction that occurs when ultraviolet light touches the emulsion.*

# Light Sources

There are two options for a UV light source: the sun or a UV lamp set up in an exposure unit. Both options have benefits and drawbacks, but you can choose the light source that works best for your particular situation.

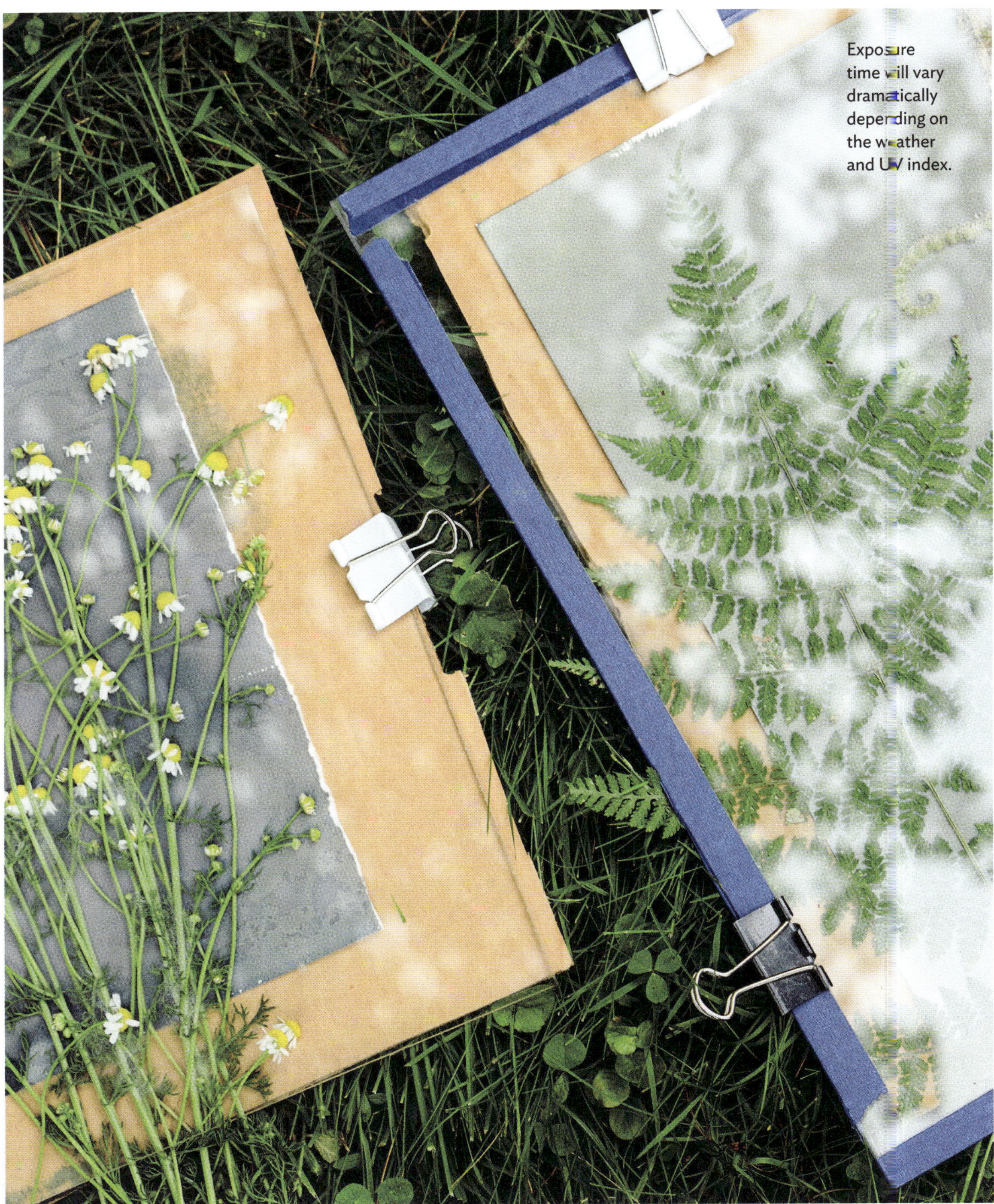

Exposure time will vary dramatically depending on the weather and UV index.

I'm partial to using the sun as a UV light source, if only because I love working outdoors. The projects in this book are based on using sunlight for exposure. That said, I do sometimes use a UV exposure unit, which you can make yourself or purchase (see Resources, page 211). Choose the exposure method that works best for your specific needs and environment.

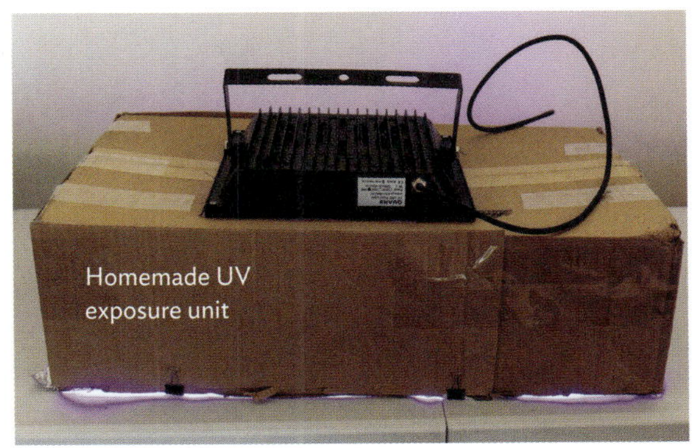

Homemade UV exposure unit

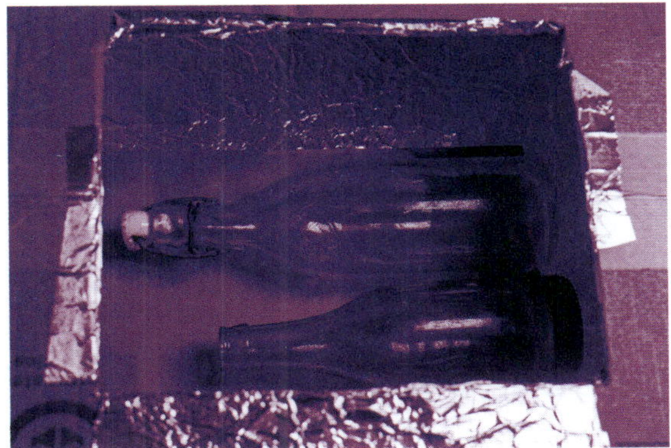

## Understanding the UV Index

If you choose to expose your cyanotypes outdoors, pay attention to the UV index, which is generally reported by various weather apps or on the news and changes based on the time of day, weather, location, and season. Higher UV numbers yield faster exposures. A UV index of 3 to 5 will require exposure times of 15 to 30 minutes. A UV index of 6 to 8 is considered high; exposure times can range from 5 to 15 minutes. A very high UV index of 9 to 11 requires short exposure times of 2 to 5 minutes and special attention to avoid overexposure. Where I live in Massachusetts, sunny summer days produce high UV indexes, ideal for exposing cyanotypes.

### SUNLIGHT

**PROS**

- It's free! No emissions!
- No limit to print size. In fact, print size is limited only by the size of your paper.
- Readily available (during daylight hours).

**CONS**

- Exposure times vary depending on weather, time of day, and season.
- Dependent on the weather.

### UV LAMP

**PROS**

- Provides a consistent UV light with repeatable exposure times.
- Available at any time, day or night.
- Allows for precision work.

**CONS**

- It's not free.
- Provides smaller coverage area; print size is limited.
- Requires access to electricity.

# Preparing to Print

Once you've decided on a light source, the next step is selecting an object or objects to print with. This is where your creativity begins to really shine—you can make a print with just about anything!

## *Choosing an Object*

While many cyanotype projects focus on pressed botanicals, other objects can also create fascinating prints. When choosing an object to print with, consider the object's relationship with light. For example, a shapely rock might form interesting lines, but its solid mass will block light from touching the paper's emulsion, leaving a large unexposed white area. A slice of transparent agate, which allows some light through, or an intricate network of twigs and branches might offer a more interesting alternative. Similarly, a snail shell would also block all the light, losing the delicate beauty of the whorled shape. A shell that's been broken open by the waves, revealing the internal structure and allowing the light to shine through, might make a better print.

The shadow an object casts gives insight into how it will print. If you're uncertain how an object will print, hold it in front of a bright light source and make note of its shadow. You can also use this technique to explore how to best position three-dimensional objects for printing, trying different angles to see how the shadows change. Objects such as lace or feathers, which let some light pass through, produce intricate, copylike images. The same applies to string, jewelry, fine metal mesh, or fruit and vegetable netting, all of which leave a unique pattern. Translucent or very thin materials, such as fabrics or paper, can also create intriguing effects.

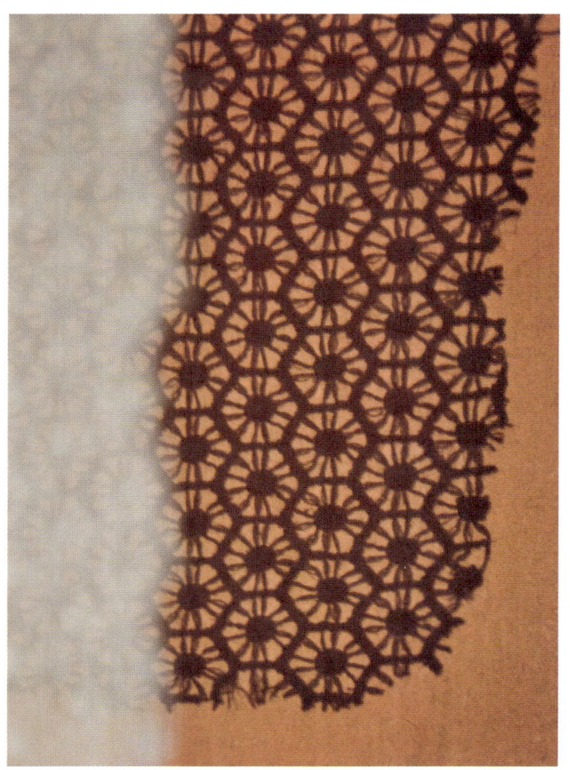

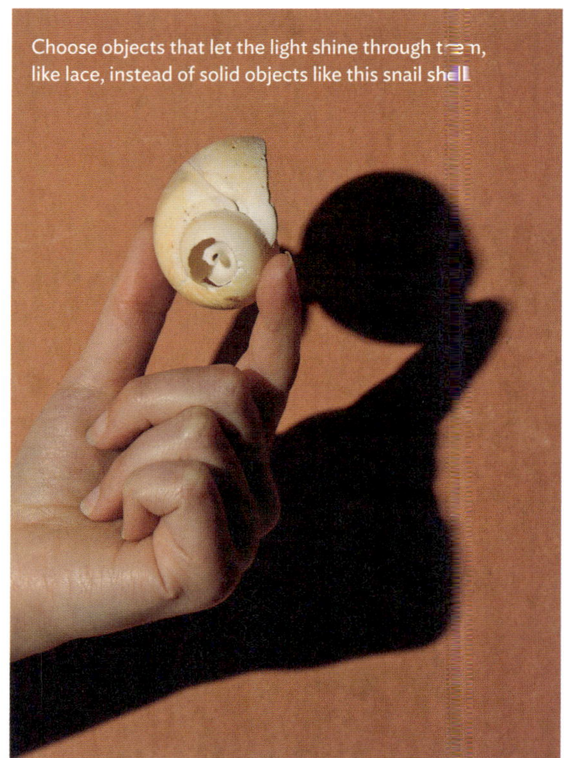

Choose objects that let the light shine through them, like lace, instead of solid objects like this snail shell.

## CYANOTYPE PRINT IDEAS

Here's a list of objects that could make excellent cyanotype prints to spark your creativity. Take a look around your home and try unexpected items—from dried pasta noodles to zipper pulls, you can make a print with just about anything.

- Glass objects or crystals
- Droplets of water
- Broken glass shards (handle with care)
- Feathers
- Stones or shells
- Seeds and dried pods
- Lace, netting, or tulle
- Fabric with interesting weaves
- Burlap or cheesecloth
- Articles of jewelry such as chains and earrings
- Metal tools such as scissors, paper clips, or safety pins
- Everyday objects such as combs, bobby pins, or utensils
- Vintage items such as antique keys or watch gears
- Bottles or jars
- Hair or fur
- Thread, string, or yarn
- Plastic or bubble wrap
- Objects related to hobbies or other interests, such as fishing lures, bike chains, or paintbrushes

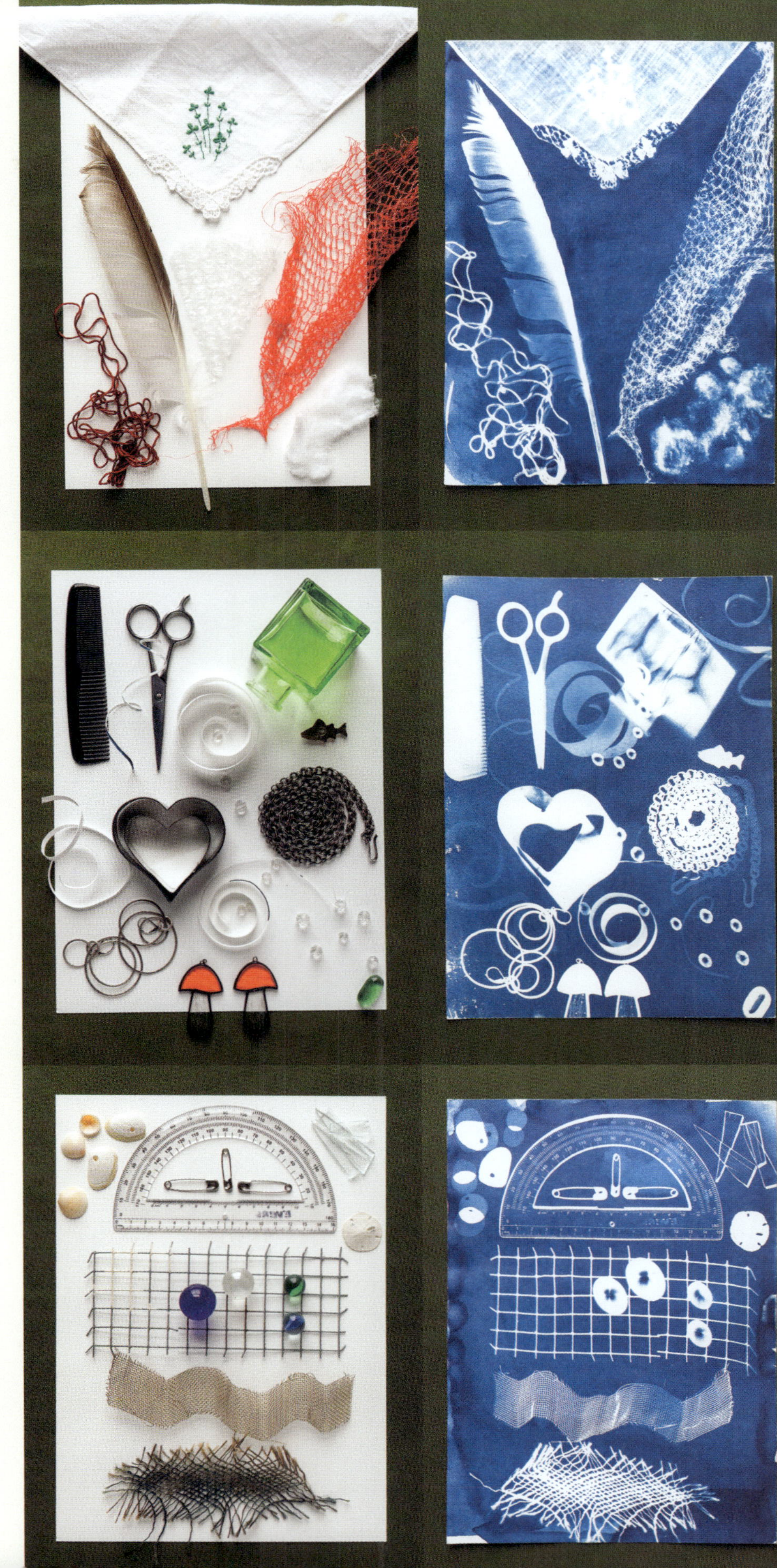

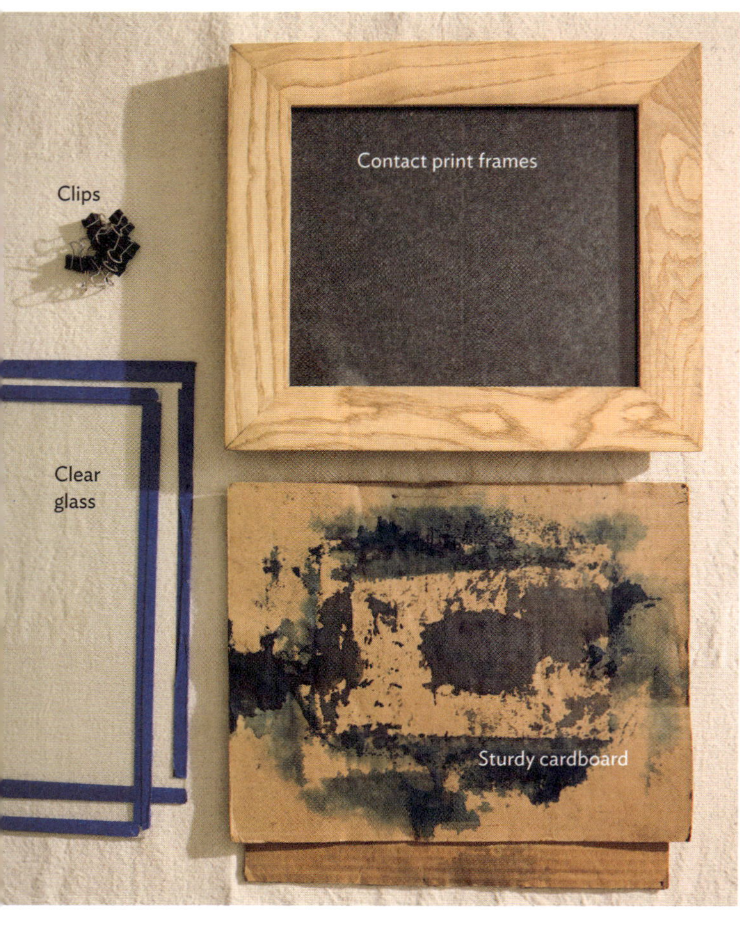


## Setting Up Your Workspace

Before you expose a print, set up a station with all your materials readily at hand, including:

**CLEAR GLASS OR AN ACRYLIC SHEET.** This should be at least 1 inch larger than the paper you are exposing and free from UV coating. Tape glass edges in case of breakage. Ensure the acrylic is thick enough to hold objects securely, about 0.06 inch.

**STURDY CARDBOARD.** This will provide a portable worksurface. It should have the same dimensions as the glass/acrylic.

**CLIPS.** Use clips to hold the glass/acrylic and cardboard without covering your composition. I use 2-inch binder clips.

**CONTACT PRINT FRAMES.** These useful tools are made with a sturdy piece of glass that fits securely into a padded frame. They hold the cyanotype paper tightly against flat materials. They can be purchased from photo supply stores and are available in sizes from 8 × 10 inches to 20 × 24 inches. They help create detailed prints, particularly when working with digital negatives.

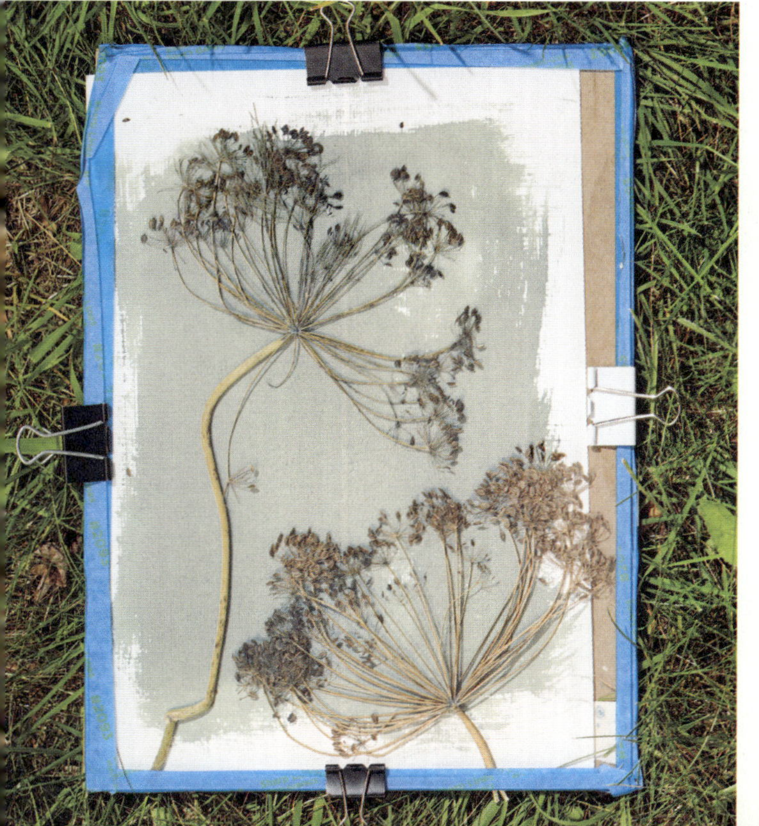

### EXPOSURE TIMES FOR PRINTING ON PAPER

- **ON A DAY WITH A HIGH UV INDEX:** 2 to 15 minutes
- **ON A DAY WITH A LOW UV INDEX:** up to 1 hour
- **WITH A UV LIGHT:** 5 to 30 minutes, depending on your particular lamp.

Look for the print to turn bronze or silver gray.

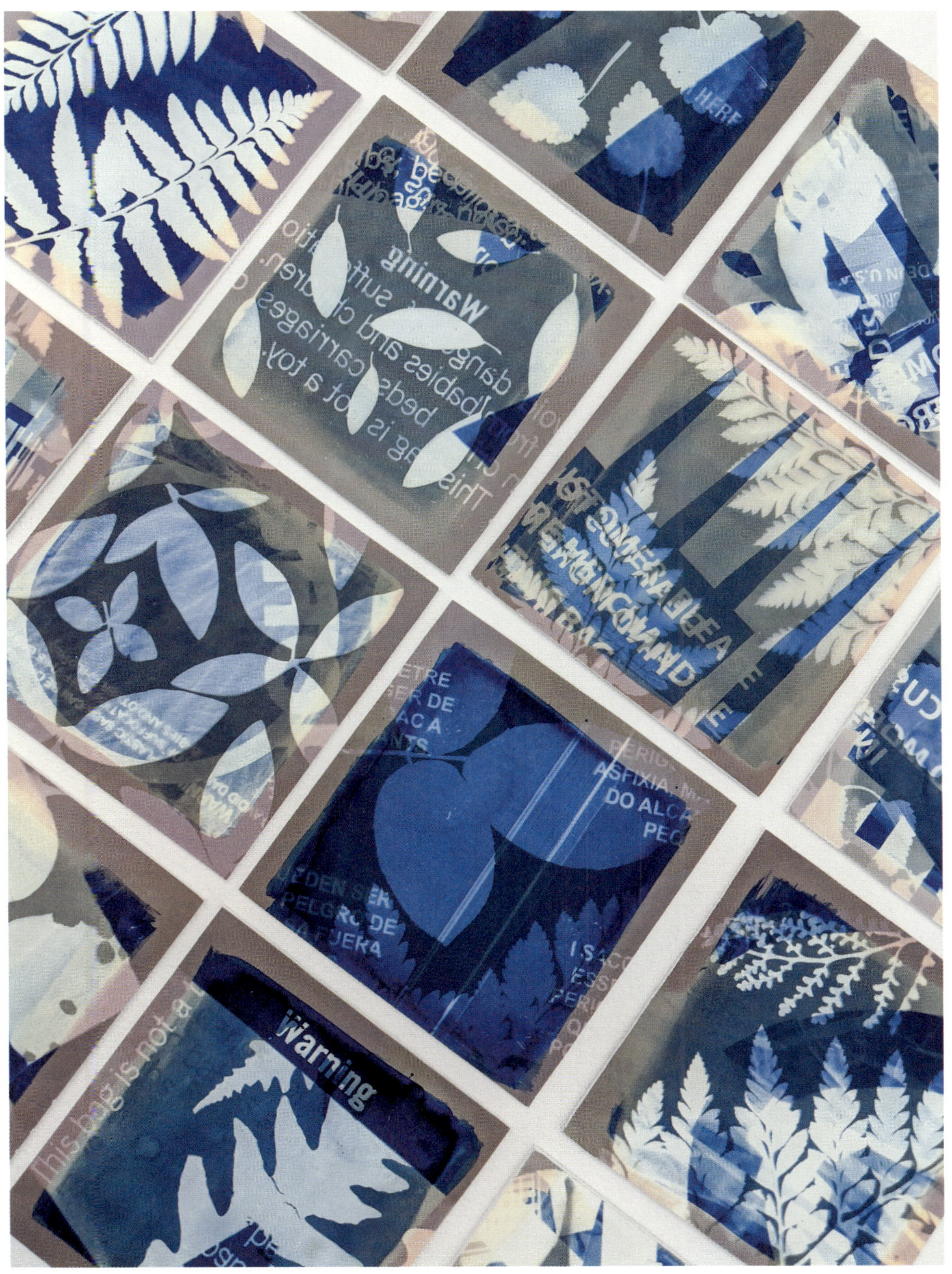


Heather Palecek's *This Bag Is Not a Toy* series uses the printed text on plastic bags to comment on the environmental impact of single-use plastics, demonstrating how nonbotanical materials can make a powerful statement in cyanotype art.

# Making an Exposure

These instructions assume that you are working with relatively flat printing material, such as a pressed plant, that can be pressed between your paper and a piece of glass or acrylic. You can adapt the instructions as needed if you're making a print using different materials by simply forgoing the glass or acrylic sheet.

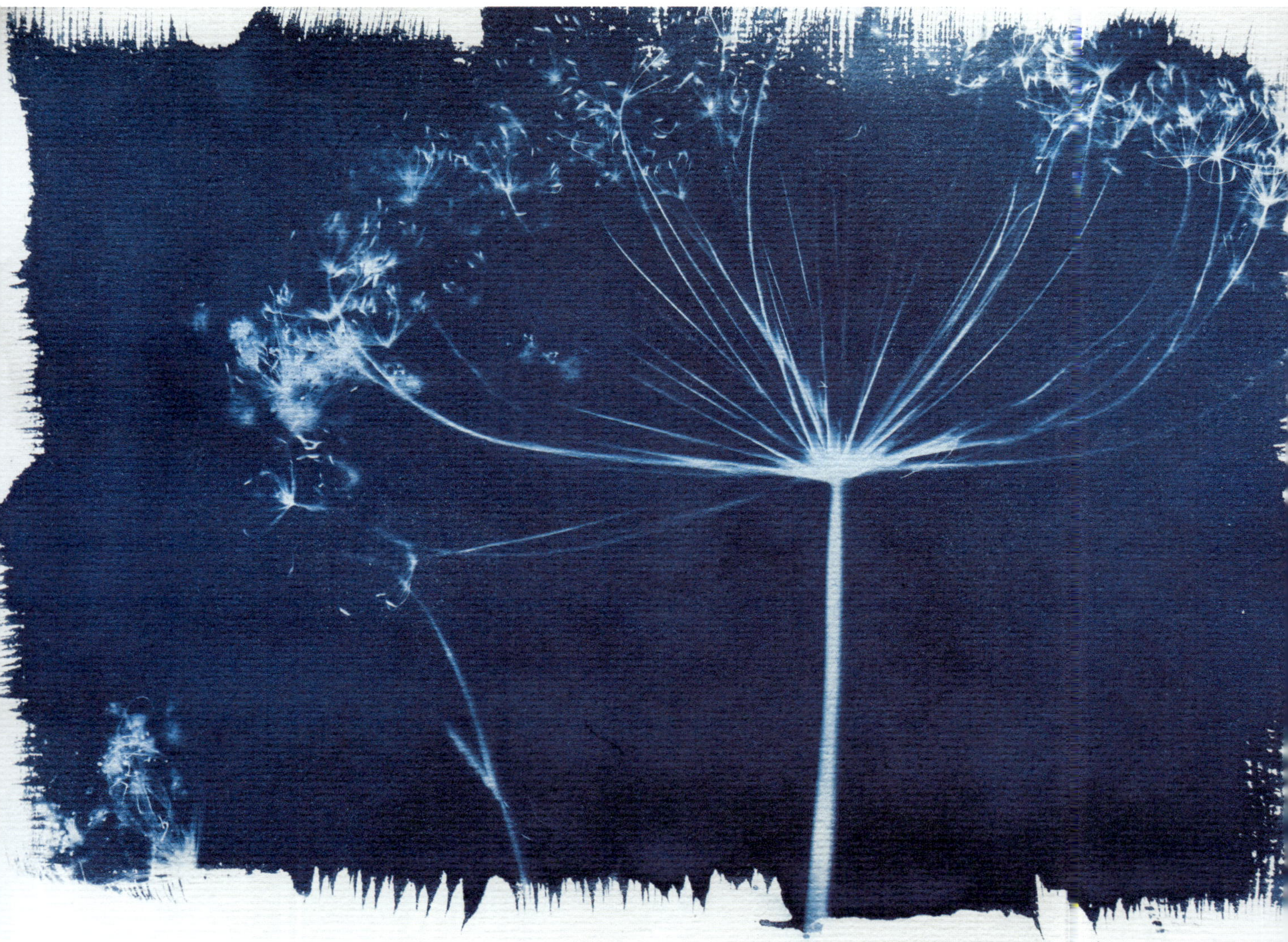

## Materials

- Sheet of cardboard (or any stiff material) the same size as the glass or acrylic
- Sheet of prepared paper (coated with cyanotype working solution and dried)
- Printing material or object of your choice
- Sheet of glass or acrylic larger than the paper
- Binder clips or similar fasteners

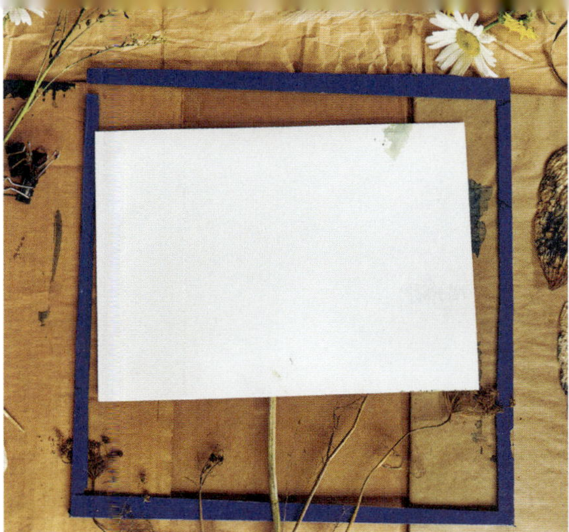

1 **SET UP.** Gather your materials in a low-light workspace.

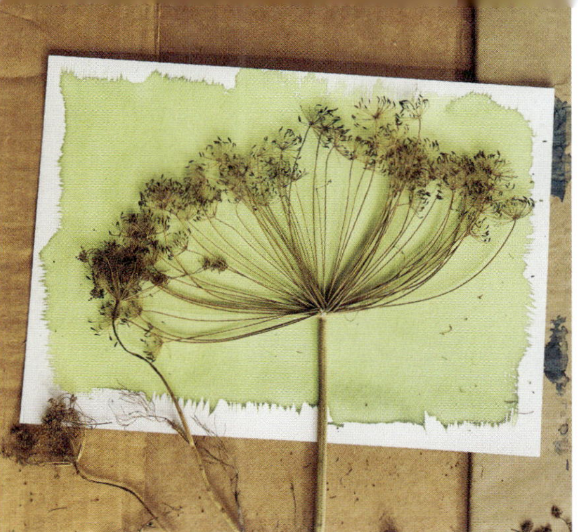

2 **ARRANGE THE COMPOSITION.** Lay the cardboard on your work surface, and place the paper, with the light-green emulsion side facing up, on top of it. Arrange the printing material on the paper.

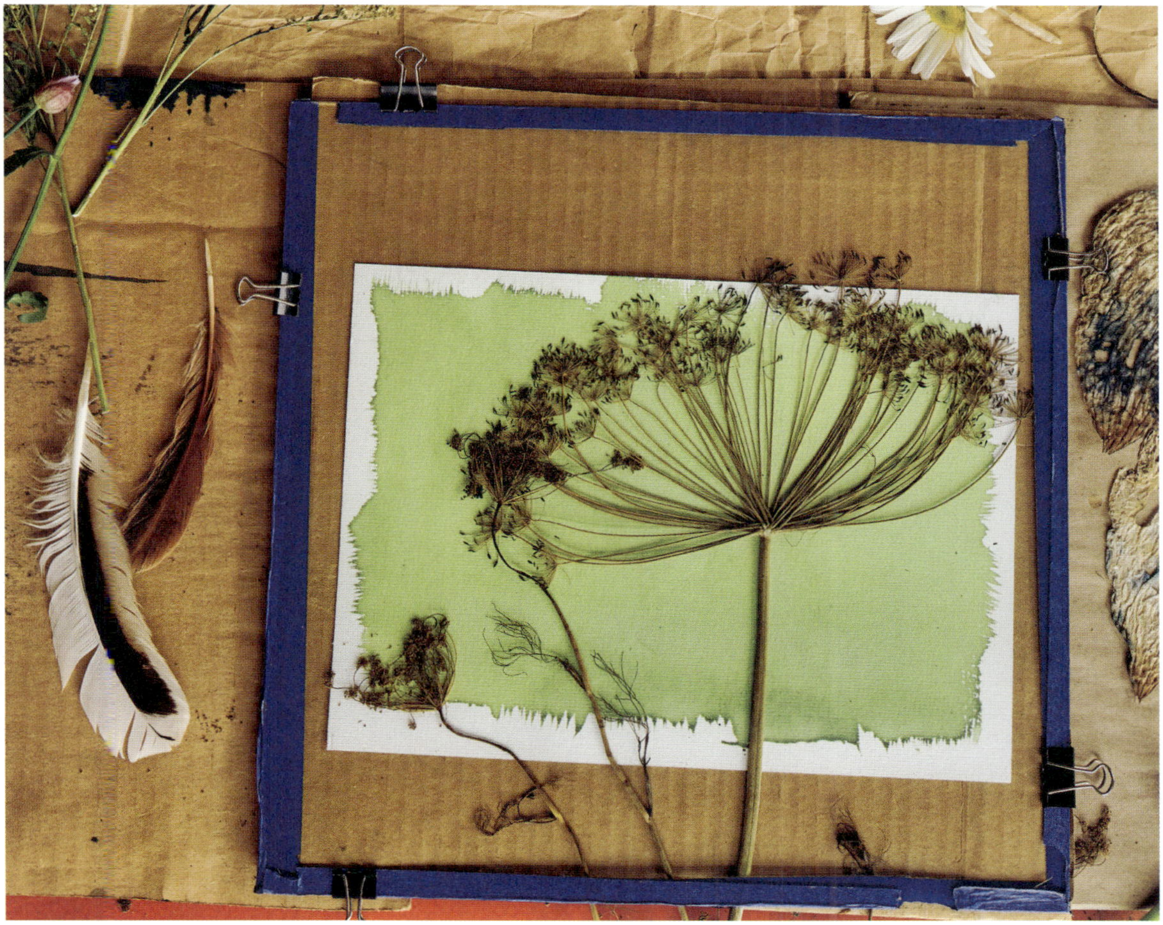

3 **SECURE THE MATERIALS.** Lay the glass or acrylic on top of the paper and printing material. Secure the glass or acrylic to the cardboard backing with binder clips. Make sure the clips don't cover any part of the paper; anything covering the emulsion on the paper will leave a mark upon exposure.

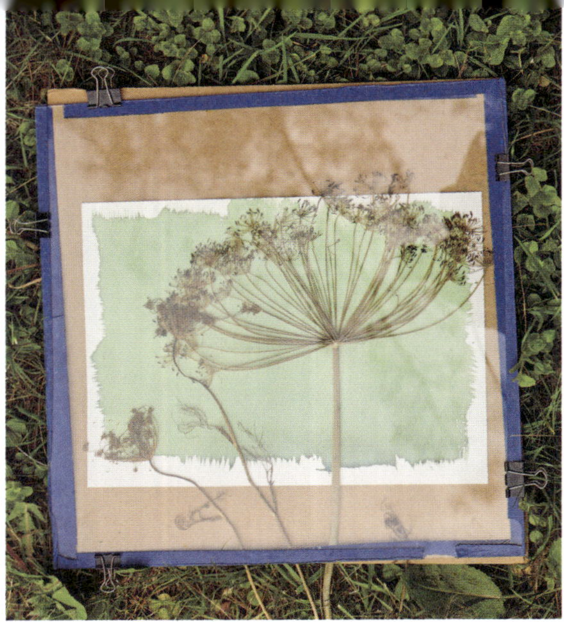

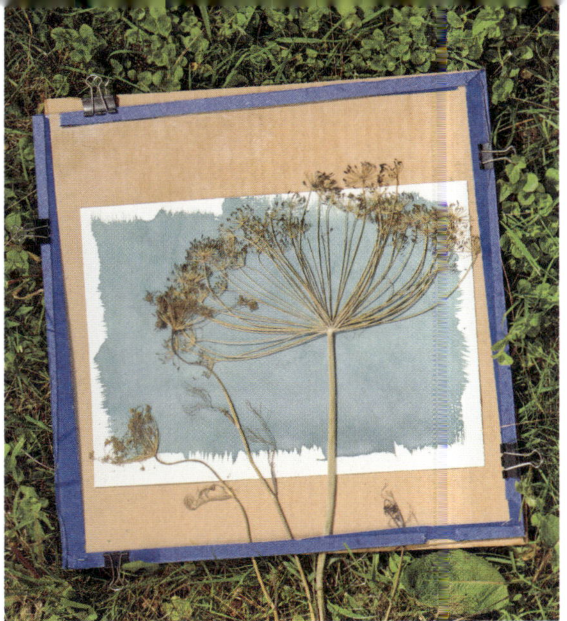

**4 EXPOSE TO SUNLIGHT.** Transfer the arrangement to a location in direct sunlight, setting it down with the emulsion side up. Don't stand where you may cast a shadow onto the setup.

**5 MONITOR THE DEVELOPMENT.** The exposure time will vary, but in general, on a bright summer day with a high UV index, a print might take 5 to 15 minutes to develop. Days with a low UV index can take an hour or more. Watch as the print develops. The light-green emulsion will immediately interact with the UV rays of the sun, turning blue-green and then continuing to change.

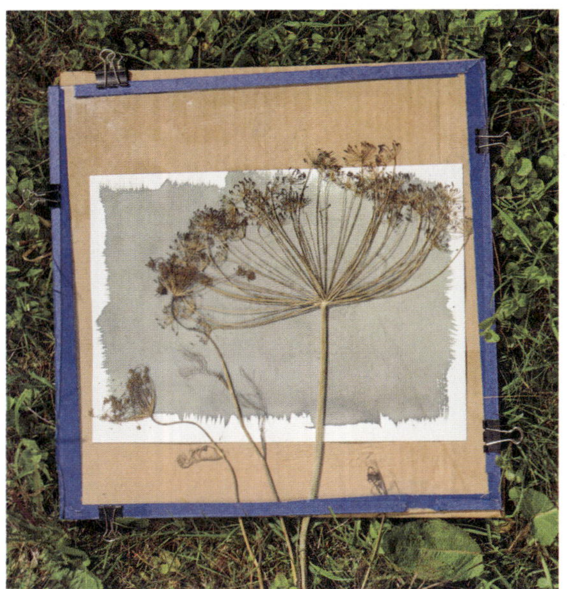

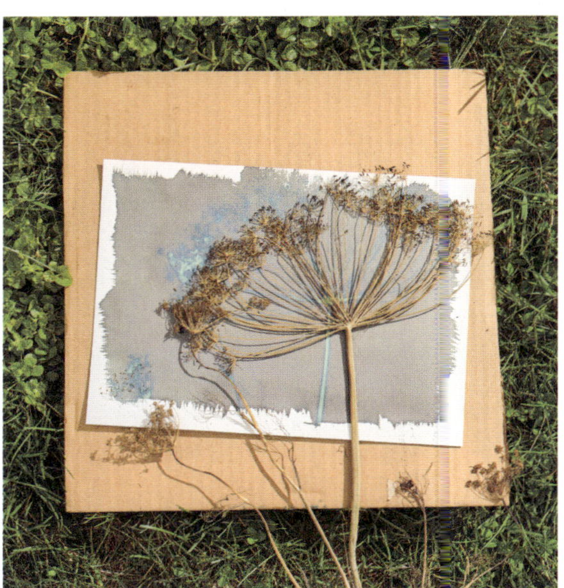

**6 STOP THE EXPOSURE.** When the emulsion turns bronze or silvery gray, the exposure is complete. (Longer exposures result in darker blues, while shorter exposures produce lighter blues; see page 64.) To stop the exposure, move the cyanotype setup out of direct sunlight.

**7 DISMANTLE.** Away from direct light, remove the clips, glass or acrylic, and printing material. Peel the exposed paper off the cardboard.

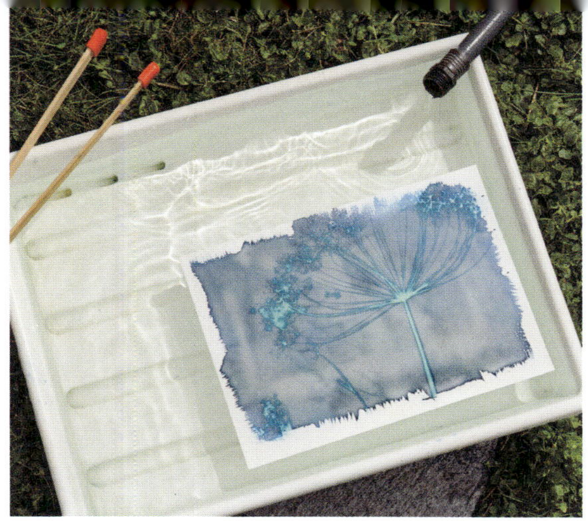

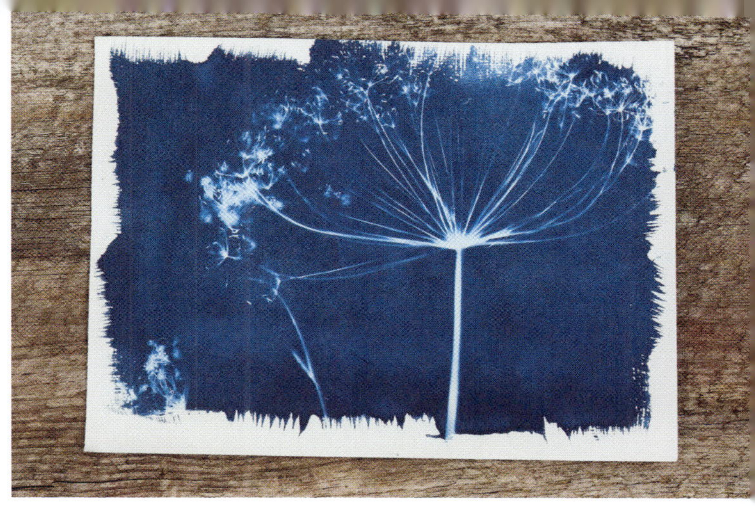

**8 WASH AND DRY THE PRINT.** Follow instructions in Chapter 4 to fix, wash, and dry the cyanotype.

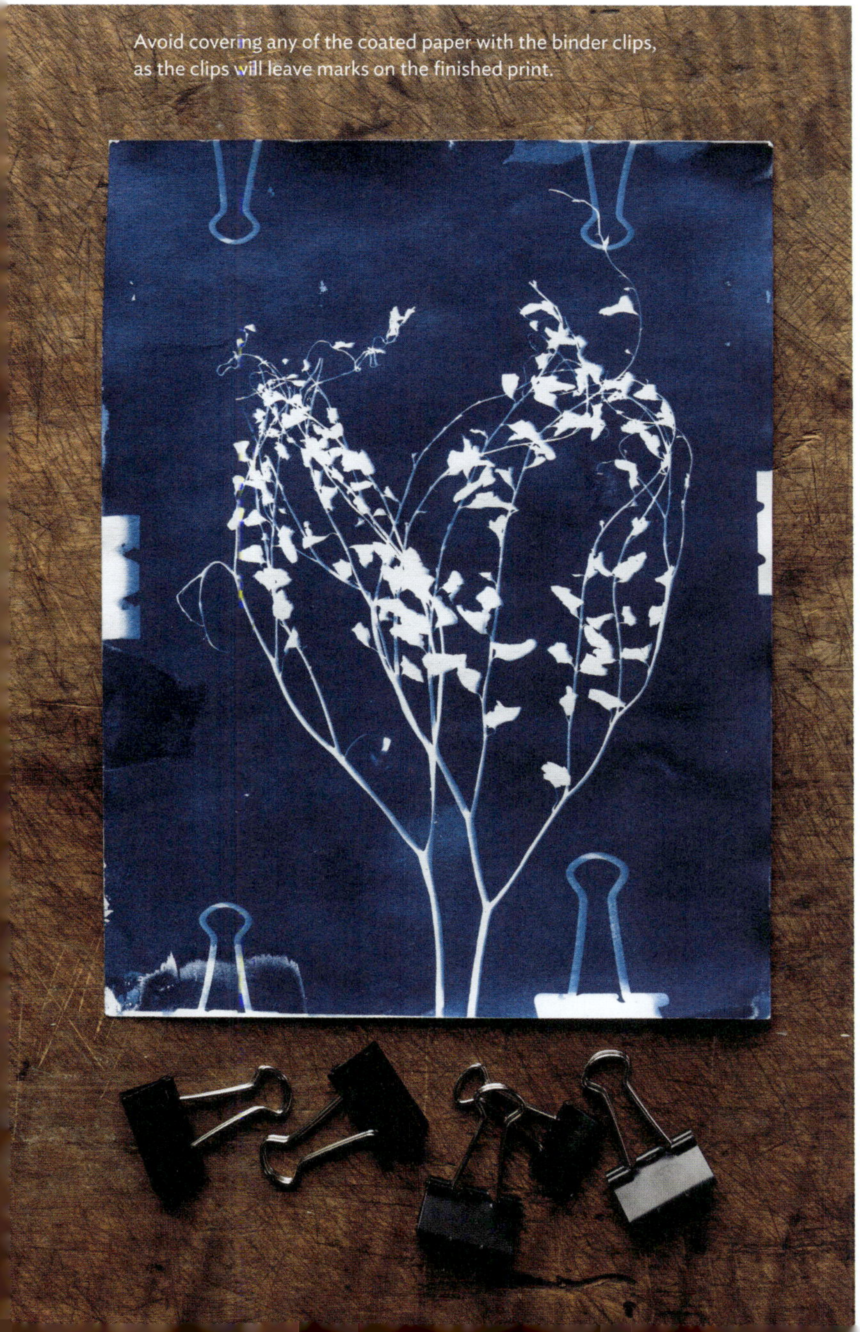

Avoid covering any of the coated paper with the binder clips, as the clips will leave marks on the finished print.

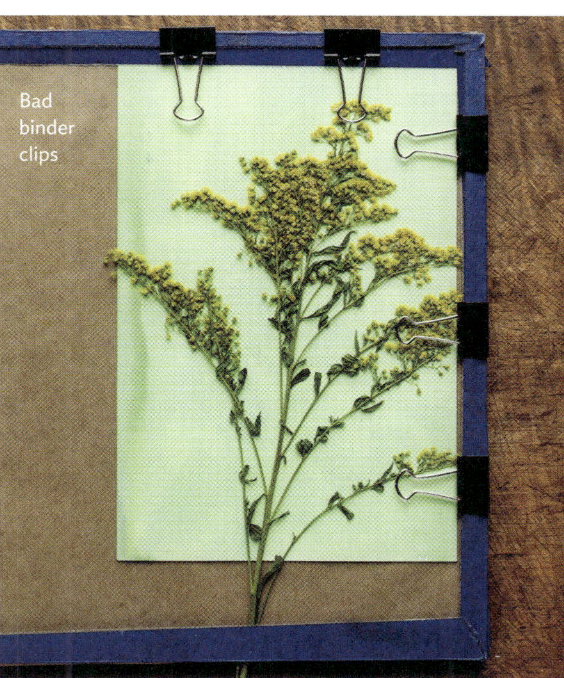


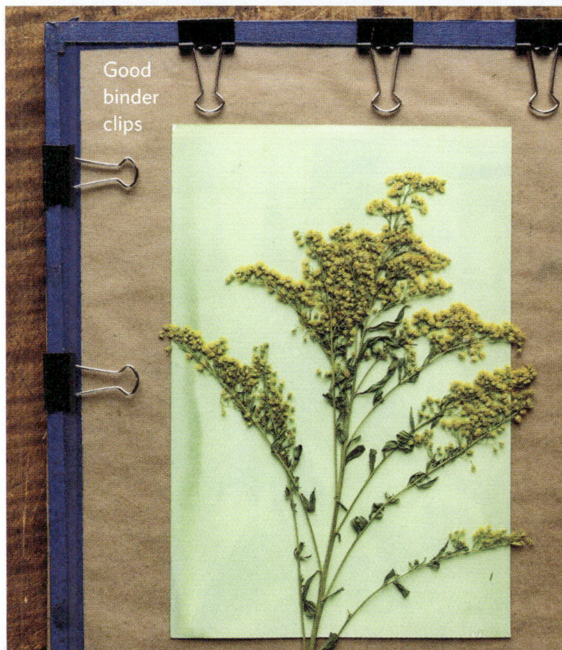

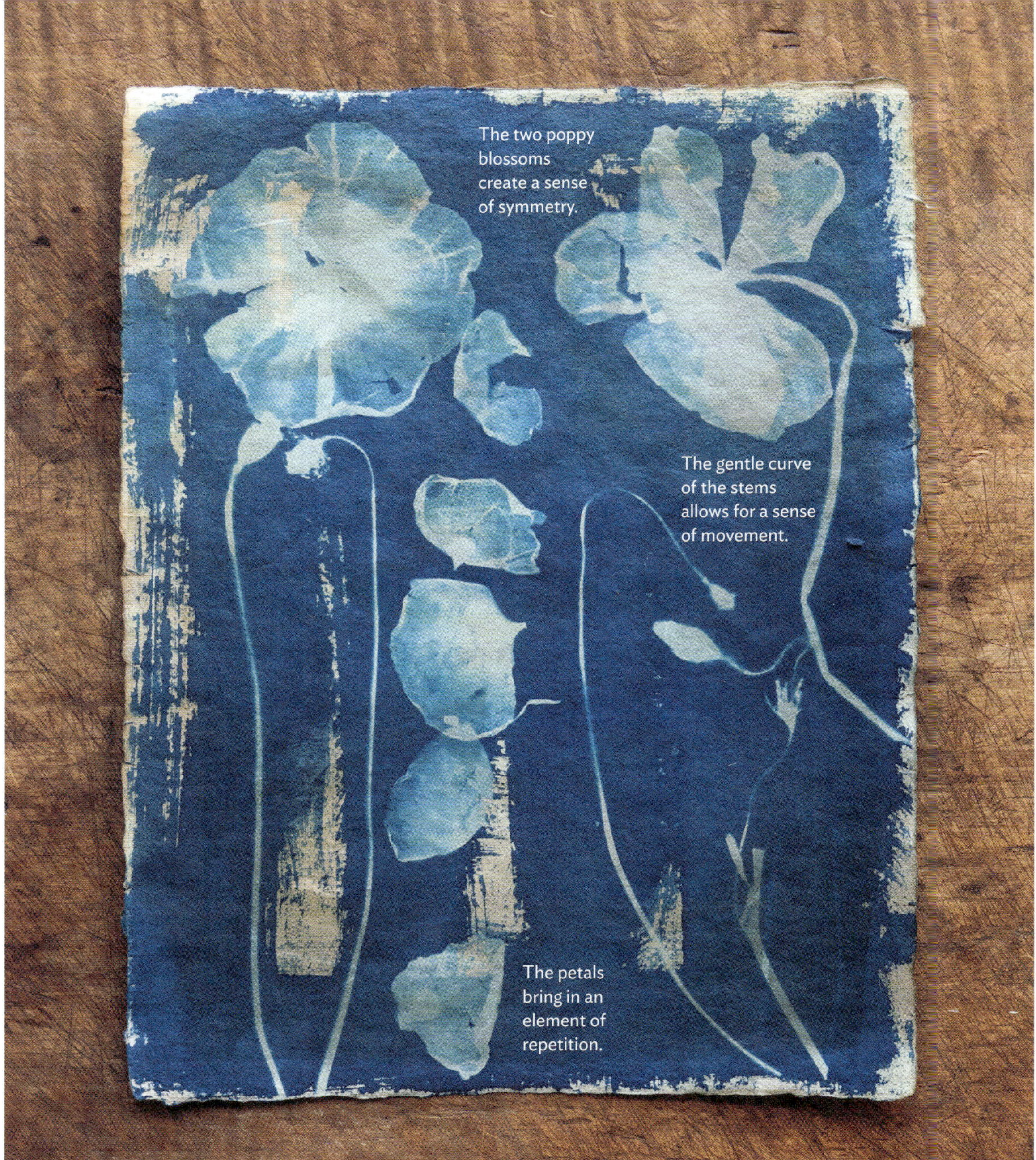


## CREATING A COMPOSITION

Composition is the way an artist arranges elements to communicate a feeling or an idea. For those new to art making, here are some questions to consider to help you compose a cohesive image.

### Compositional Elements to Consider

- Are the elements unified? Do they all seem to belong?
- Is there a sense of balance, either symmetrically or asymmetrically?
- Do the elements create movement that leads the eye around the composition?
- What is the focal point?
- Is there repetition? Are there patterns?
- Does everything fit together proportionally?

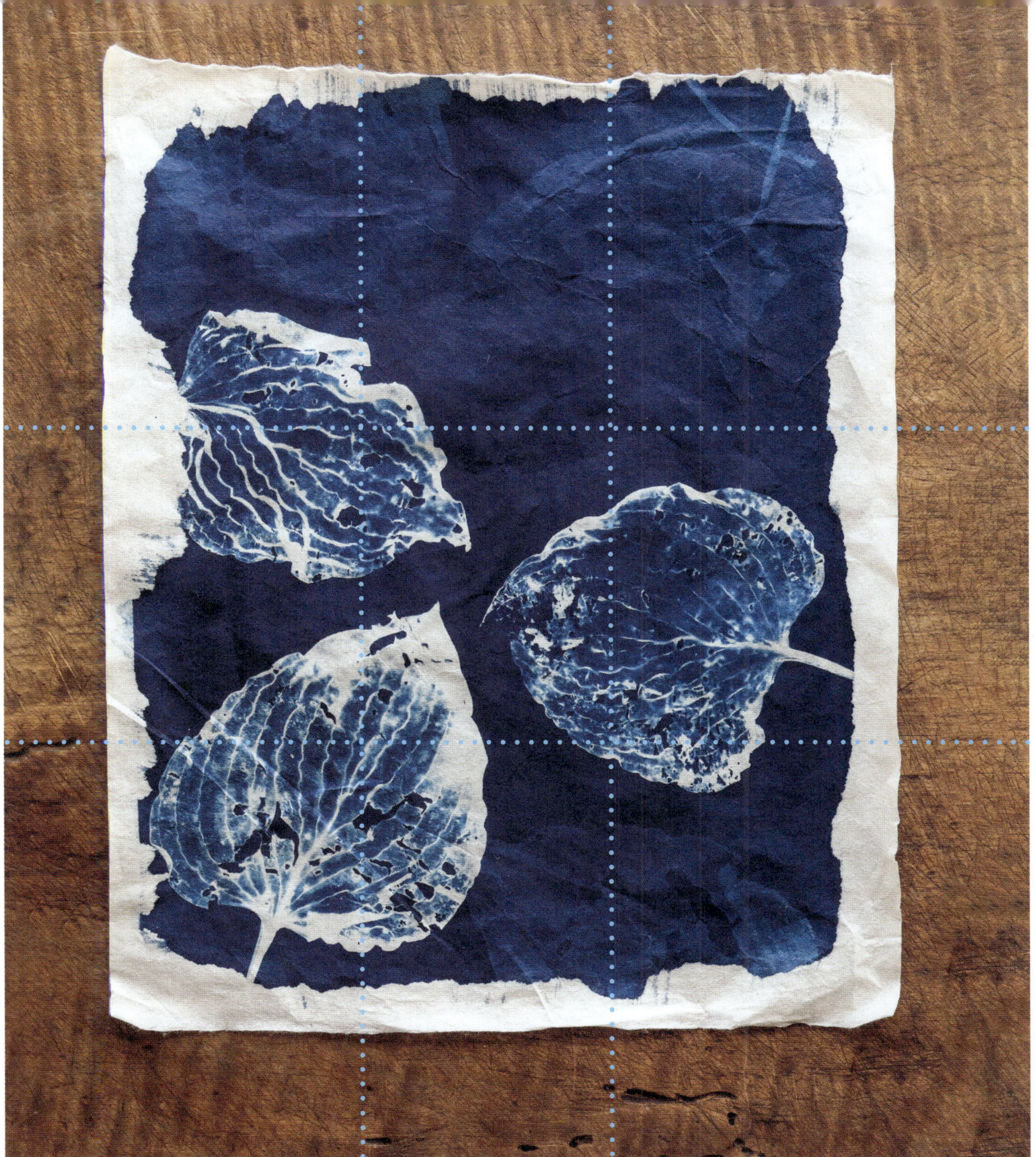

## Rule of Thirds

The rule-of-thirds approach emphasizes decentering the subject. First, we create a grid of nine equal squares with two horizontal lines and two vertical lines. Then, we place the subject of our composition on the lines or at the corners of the middle square rather than in the middle of the frame. Decentering allows the eye to move naturally across the scene.

# Playing with Exposure and Dimension

You can control exposure time to achieve lighter or darker blues in your cyanotype prints. At first, when working with sunlight, exposure times may feel unpredictable. Use the guidelines on page 56 along with your own observations to determine when a cyanotype has been exposed to your liking. It can be helpful to keep notes on your exposure setup for each print, recording how long a print was exposed and under what conditions (time of day and year, UV index, outside or in a bright window, etc.). As you gain more experience, you'll develop a feel for how much exposure is necessary.

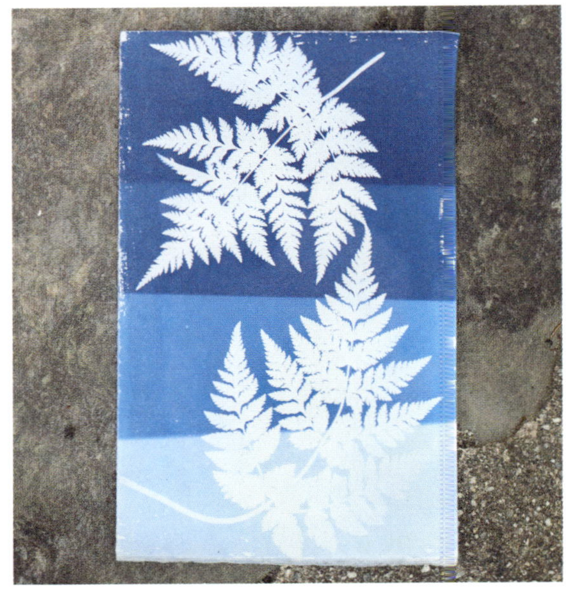

## Exposed, Rinsed, and Dried

Underexposed final prints will be a lighter blue, while over-exposed final prints will be darker. Exposure is also a creative choice. A print isn't over- or underexposed if you've achieved the color you were hoping for in your finished piece of work.

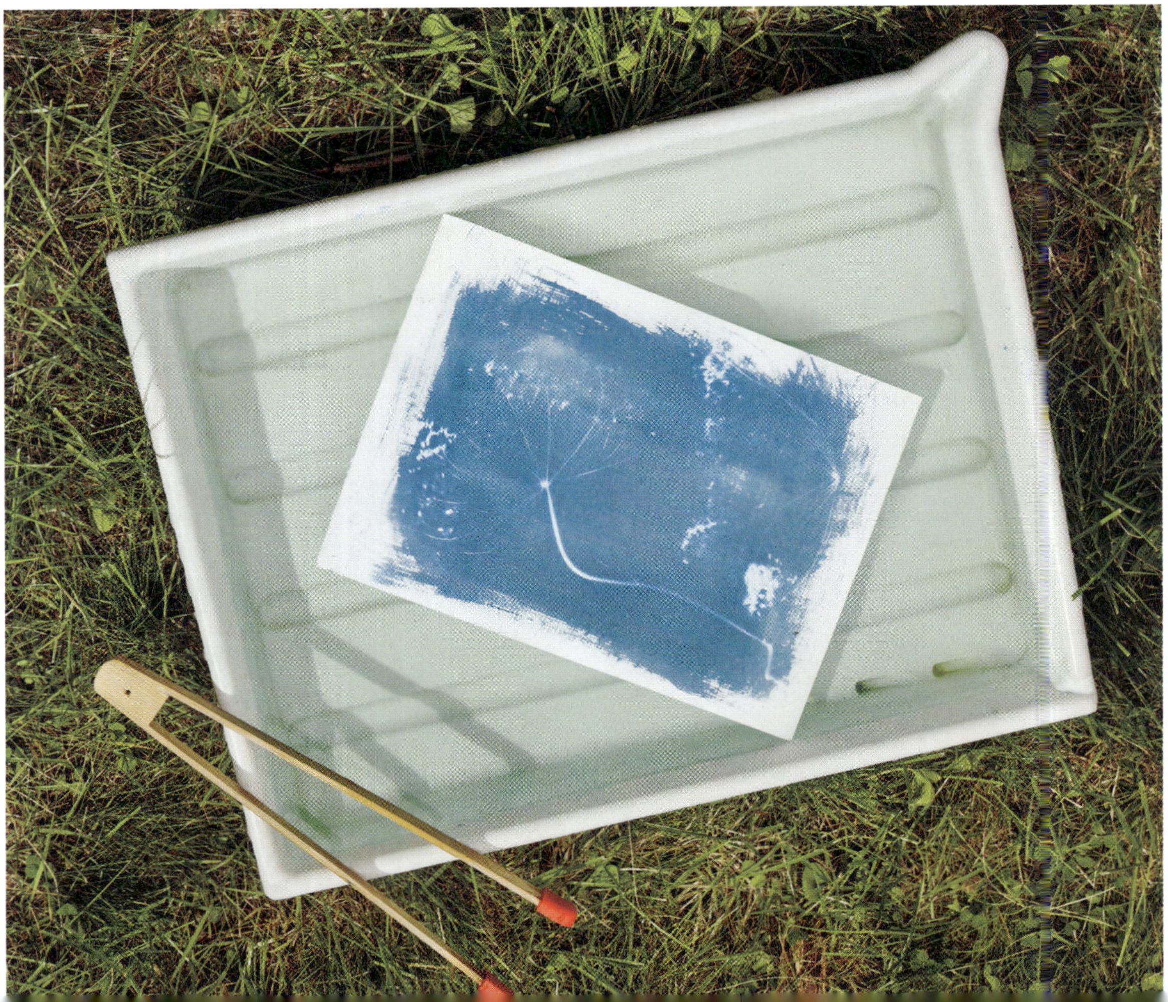

## During Exposure

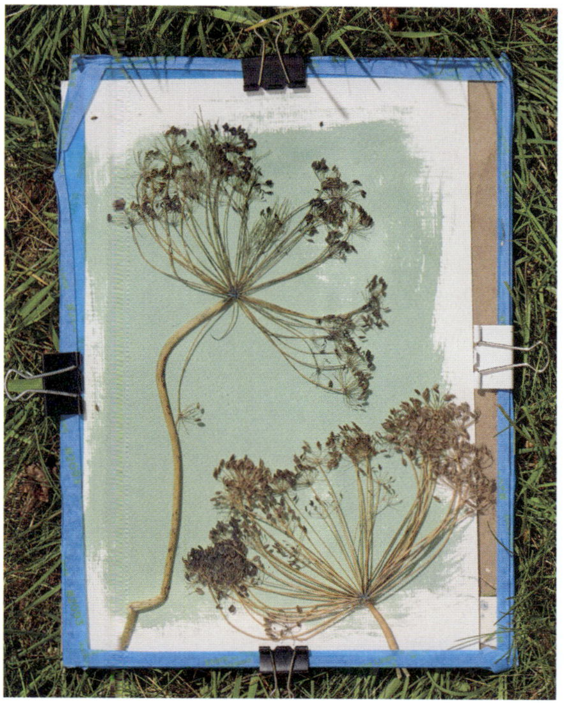

Not sufficiently exposed: Needs more time! Bring it back outside.

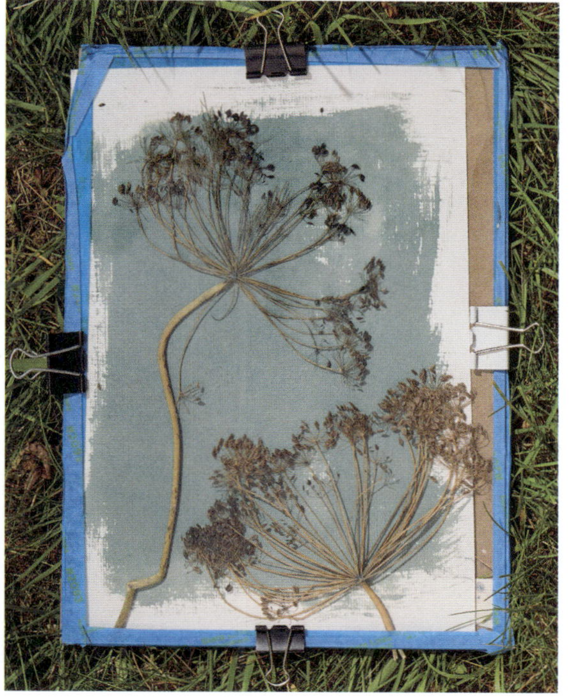

The exposure is almost finished.

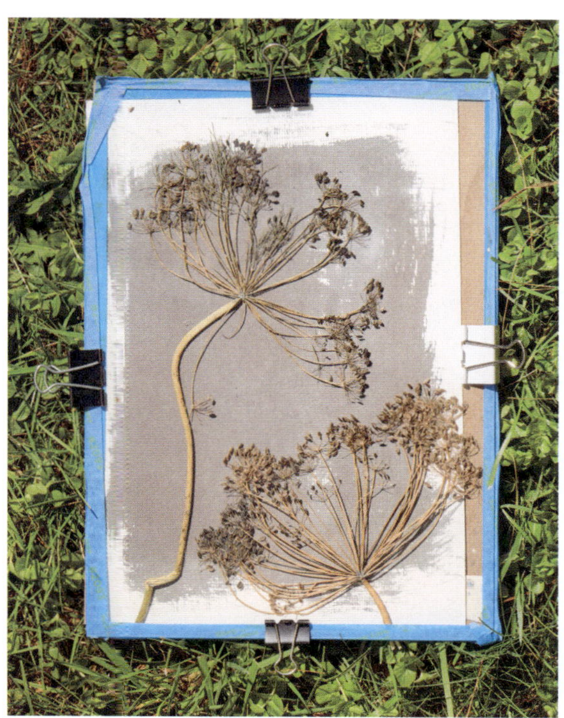

Sufficiently exposed: Looks good.

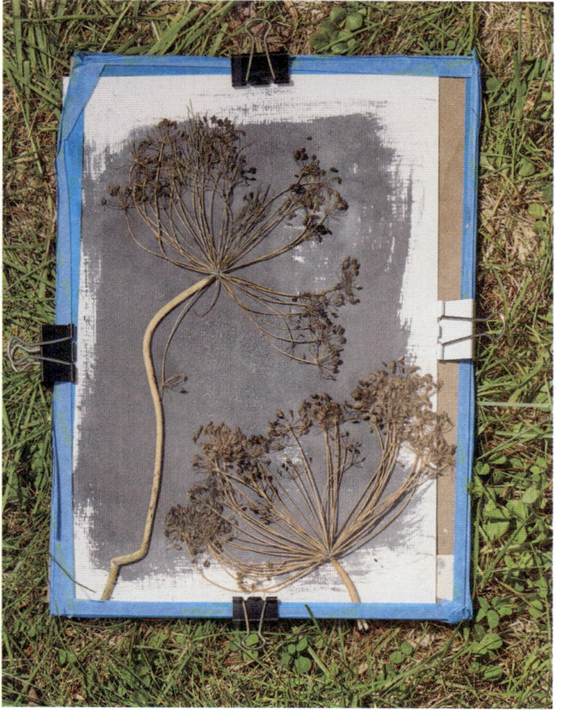

Overexposed: Too long! For tips on using a very dark print, see page 130.

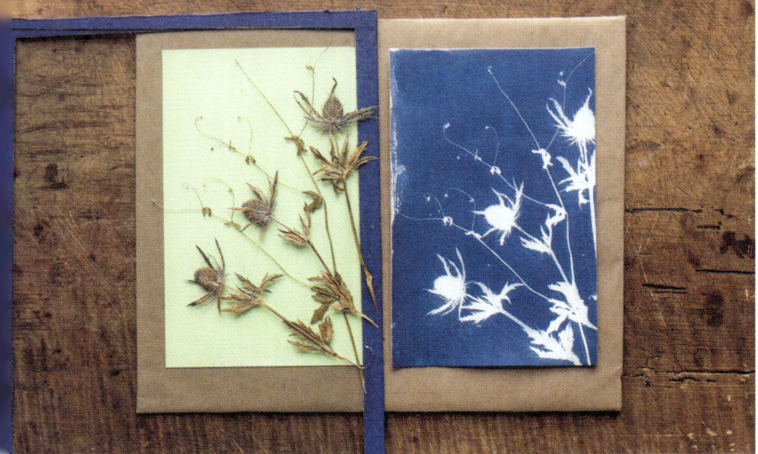

Layering directly on glass

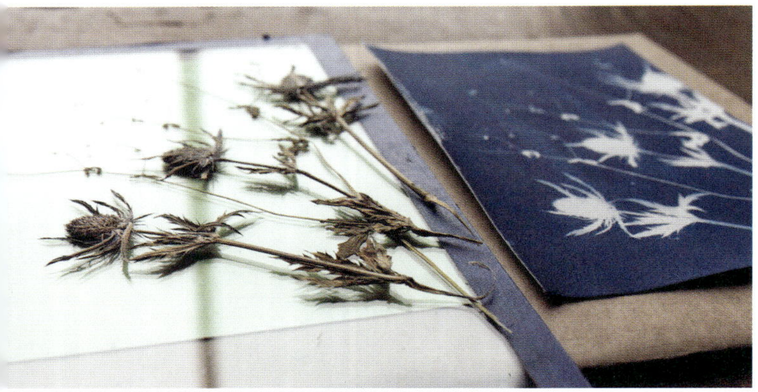

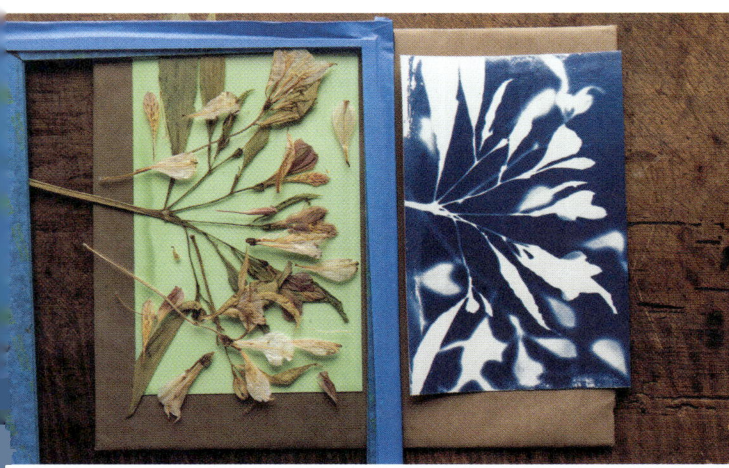

Sandwiching with additional glass

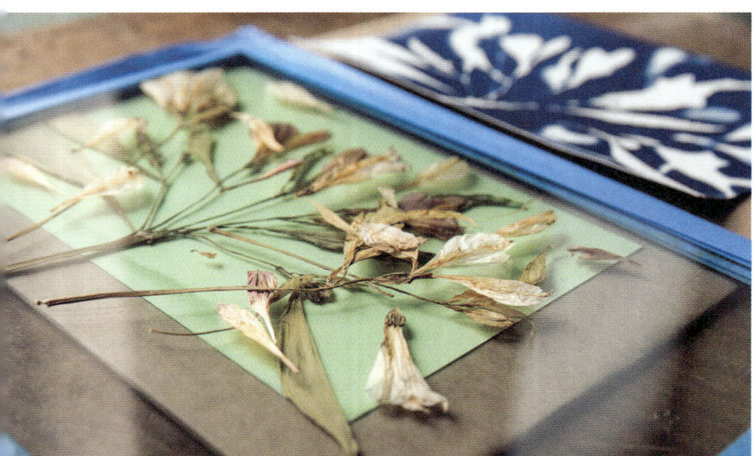

## Adding Depth to Your Cyanotypes

A traditional cyanotype exposure will result in two colors: a bright white and a deep blue. By playing with the method and time of exposure, you can add different shades of blue to your work, creating more dimension. To add depth to your cyanotypes, try layering the printing material in different ways.

**LAYERING DIRECTLY ON THE GLASS.** Place printing material directly on top of the glass instead of directly on the paper. Fresh plants with thicker silhouettes create softer edges. Layer flat objects or press plants beneath the glass to provide contrast.

**SANDWICHING WITH ADDITIONAL GLASS.** Place plant material on top of the glass and secure another sheet of glass over it. The added distance between plant and paper will result in softer, more diffused silhouettes.

Be aware that adding extra layers of glass may increase exposure times, and always use caution when stacking multiple sheets of glass to avoid breakage.

## Making Multiple Exposures

Another way to add interest and complexity to a cyanotype is by exposing it more than once. There are two ways to do this. The simplest is to pause the exposure by moving the print out of the light and adding or removing objects. Objects that you add for the second exposure will print a soft blue instead of a pure white, since the area they are covering already had some sun exposure. Similarly, if you remove an object partway through, that area will begin to expose and gain color, but will remain lighter than the surrounding space.

The results from adding and removing objects partway through the process can be quite subtle. If you're looking for more dramatic results, you can also apply a second layer of working solution and expose the whole print for a second time, varying the composition however you prefer.

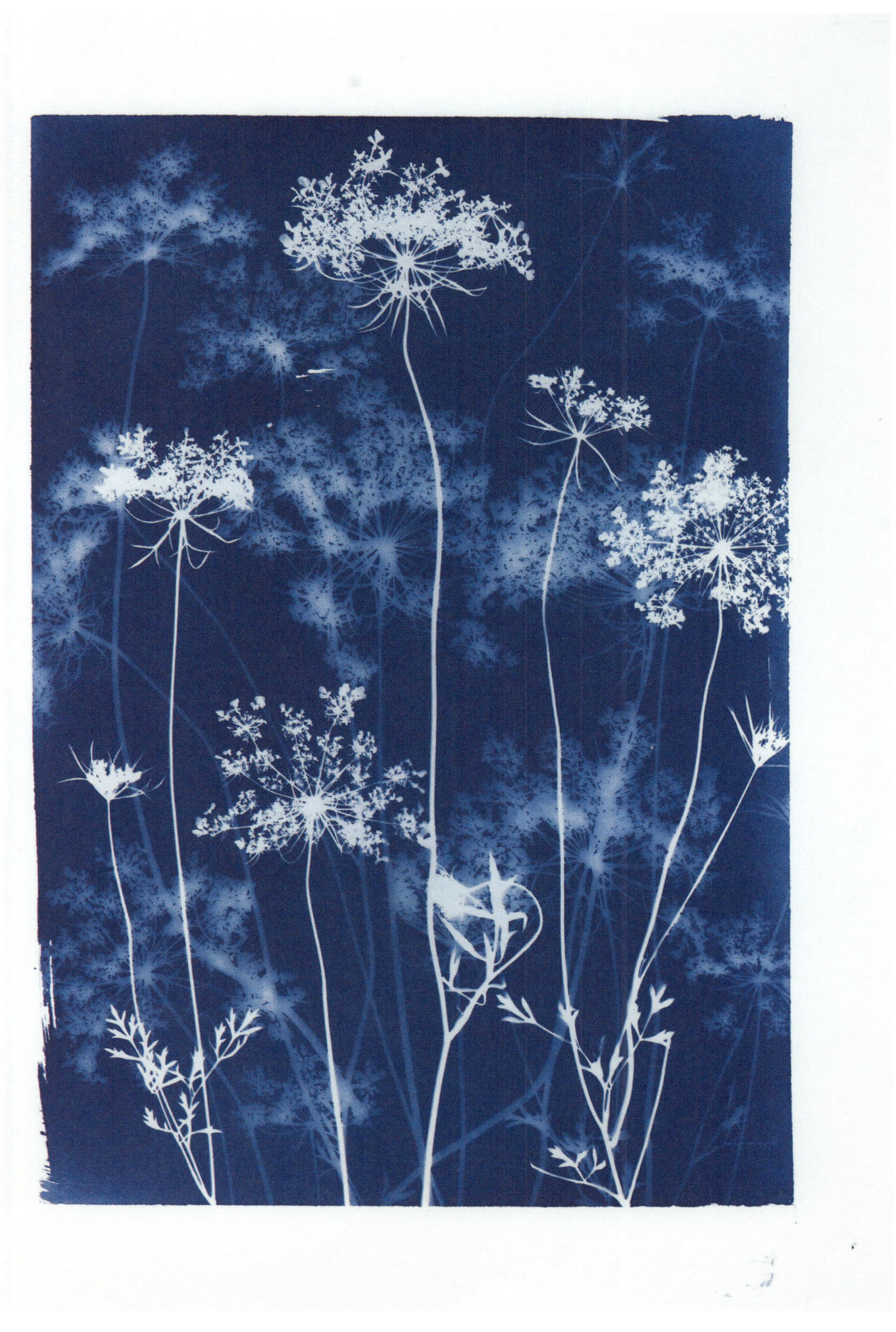

Elizabeth Booth created layers of crisp and soft silhouettes in *Queen Anne's Lace*.

# Double Exposing a Cyanotype

You can add depth and interest to a cyanotype by making a double exposure. For this process you'll begin by creating a basic cyanotype. You'll then bleach the cyanotype to soften the color, apply a second coat of cyanotype solution, and re-expose it. You can also use an underexposed, light print and forgo the bleaching. The final print will have a variety of colors from both the first exposure and the final exposure.

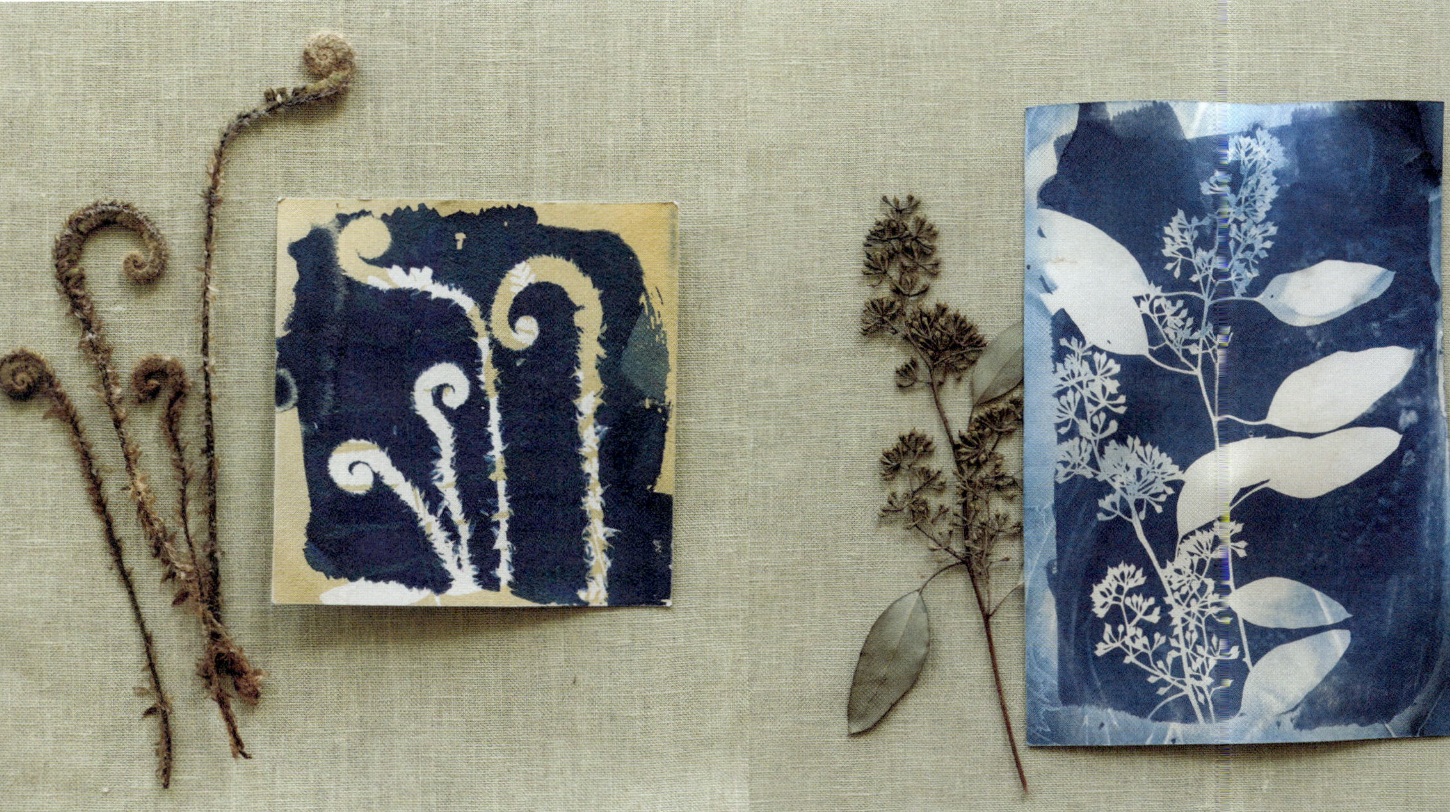

## Materials

- A finished cyanotype print
- Additional working solution (enough to coat your paper)
- Brush
- Printing material or object of your choice
- Sheet of cardboard (or any stiff material) the same size as the glass or acrylic
- Sheet of glass or acrylic larger than the paper
- Binder clips or similar fasteners

1 **BLEACH THE PRINT (OPTIONAL).** Double exposure works best with prints that are light and underexposed or with prints that are bleached. If your print is darker, follow the directions on page 130 to bleach and wash the print using washing soda. You can bleach the print all the way to a yellow color or just to a soft blue, depending on the results you want to achieve. The bleached color will be visible under the objects you choose for the second printing. If you bleach to a yellow or purple color, your finished cyanotype will have dark blue (from the second exposure) and yellow or purple (from the first, bleached exposure).

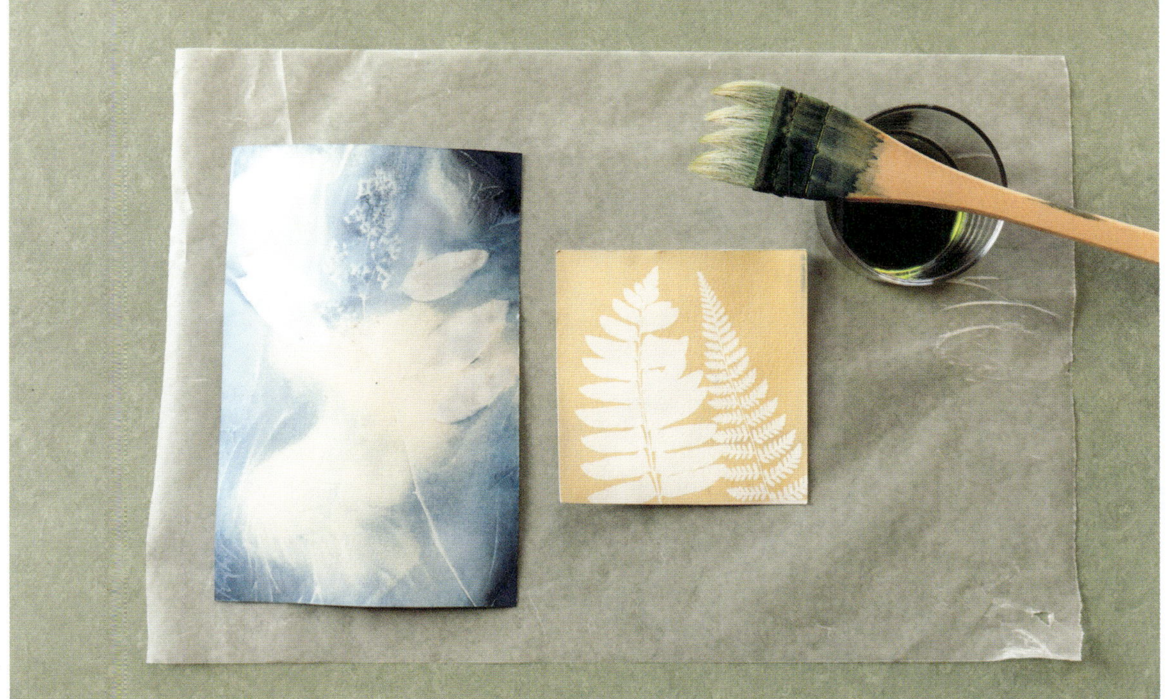

2 **APPLY A SECOND COAT OF CYANOTYPE SOLUTION.** Apply a new coat of working solution to the dry print. You can cover the whole print or only apply the working solution to selected areas. Allow the cyanotype solution to dry in a dimly lit place before proceeding.

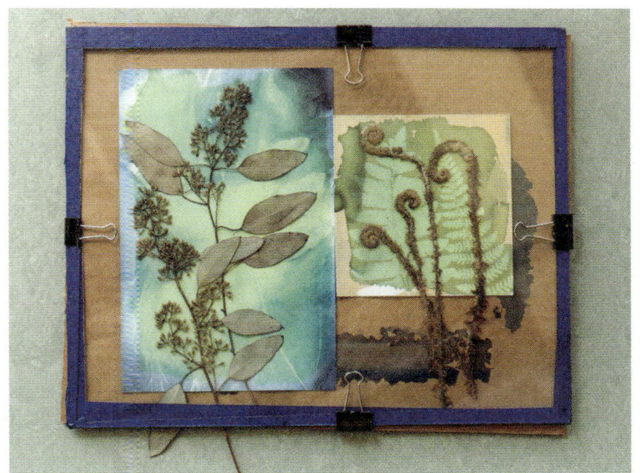

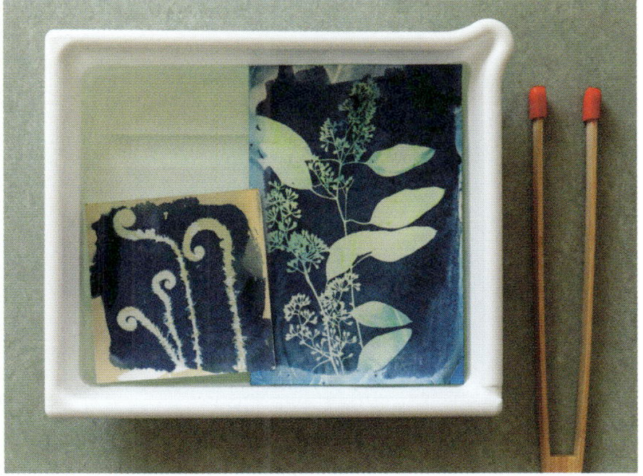

3 **ARRANGE YOUR SECOND COMPOSITION.** Place the coated paper on a sheet of cardboard and arrange your printing objects however you would like. You can use the same objects from the first exposure or choose something new. Secure the composition with a sheet of glass or acrylic and binder clips.

4 **MAKE THE SECOND EXPOSURE.** Place your printing setup in direct UV light and allow it to expose until it reaches a silvery gray color.

5 **WASH AND DRY THE PRINT.** Follow instructions in Chapter 4 to fix, wash, and dry the multiple-exposure cyanotype.

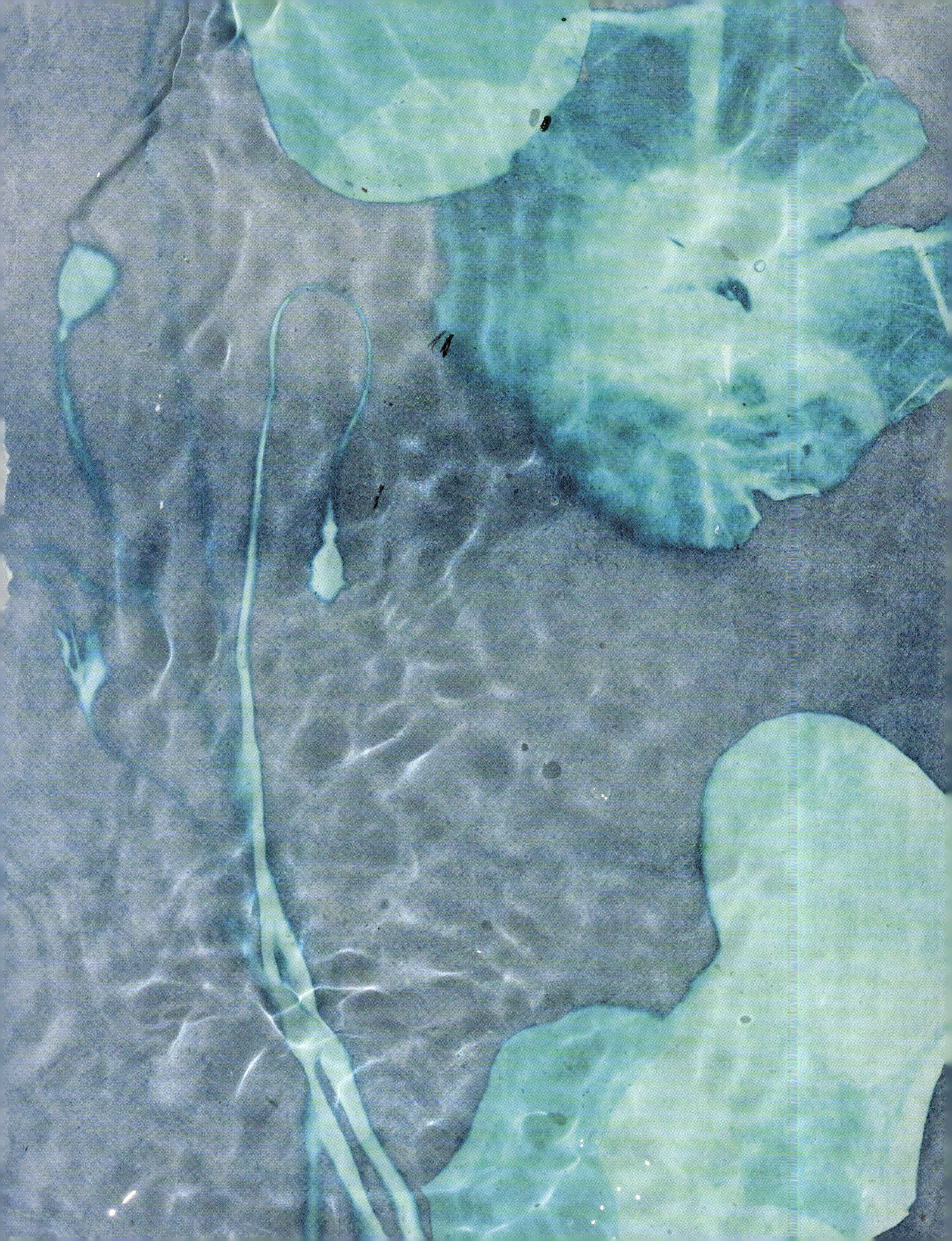

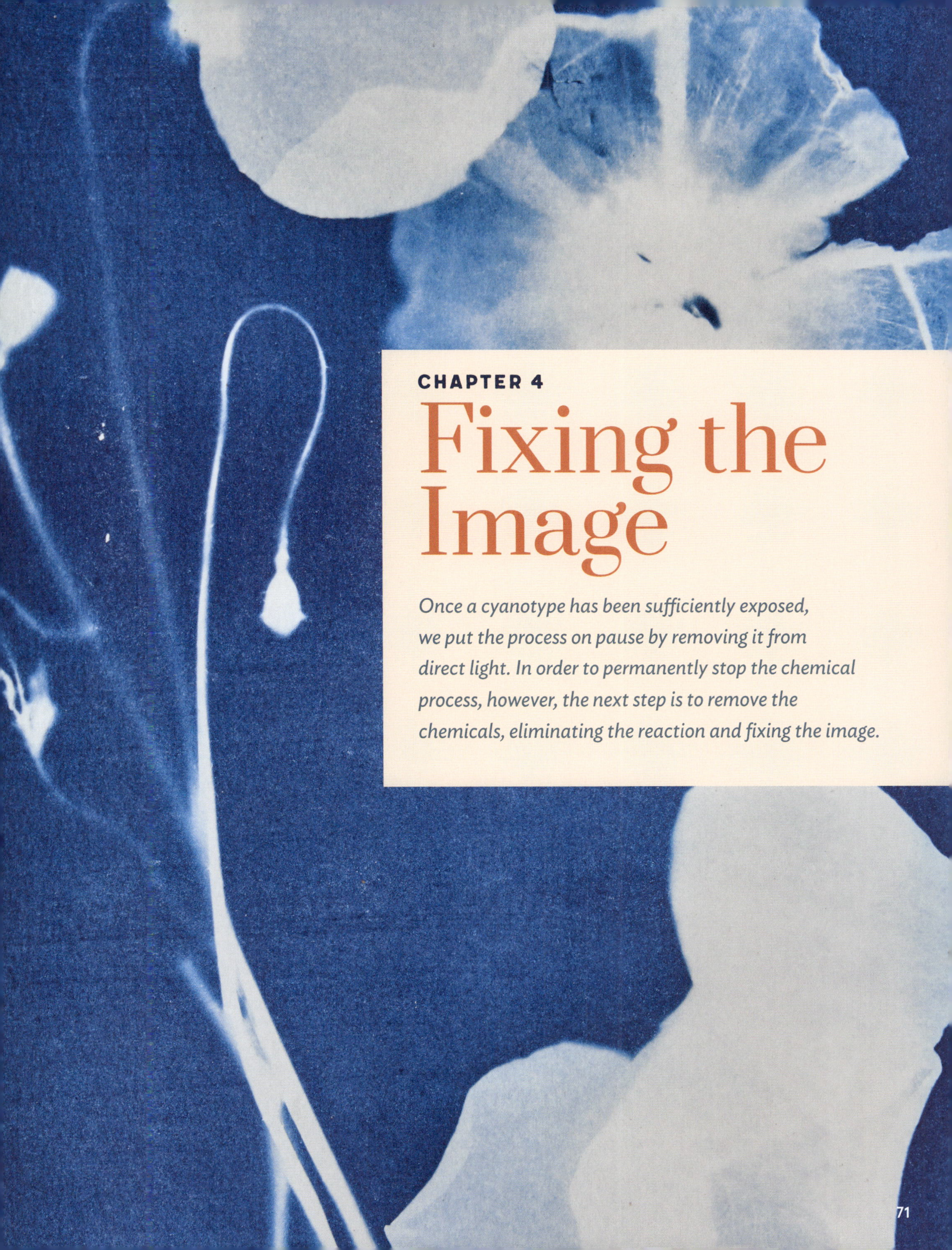

CHAPTER 4

# Fixing the Image

*Once a cyanotype has been sufficiently exposed, we put the process on pause by removing it from direct light. In order to permanently stop the chemical process, however, the next step is to remove the chemicals, eliminating the reaction and fixing the image.*

# Fixing a Cyanotype

Fixing a cyanotype image on paper (or fabric) is a fun part of the process. The goal is to rinse off the excess emulsion so that the paper is no longer light-sensitive and to increase the cyanotype's archival qualities. Rinse times are important. Too little rinsing and chemicals in the emulsion can remain on the print, making highlight areas appear yellow and eventually turn gray. If the print remains in water for too long, the Prussian blue emulsion will fade. I once left a print in the water for several hours and the image disappeared.

While there are steps to follow and tricks to employ, a tray of water is all you really need to get started. The tray should be larger than your paper and capable of holding a couple of inches of water; a plastic photo developing tray works well. You may wish to wear protective gloves or to use tongs to minimize chemical exposure. Most importantly, you will need access to running water, ideally in a spot that is not in direct light. Tap water is fine for washing prints, unlike when making stock solution.

## *Setting Up a Wash Station*

If possible, your wash station will be located out of direct sunlight. Every situation is different, but the ideal wash station includes:

**SINK OR OUTDOOR SPIGOT.** Washing prints outdoors is often the best option for less mess and cleanup.

**TRAYS.** Use photo developing trays, available in a range of sizes. Or use plastic containers designated for cyanotype use.

**DRY STATION.** Any location out of direct sunlight where wet prints can hang or dry flat; this can be in- or outdoors.

**CLOTHING LINE.** When hanging a rinsed print to dry, be mindful of where unrinsed chemicals may drip.

**CLOTHESPINS.** For hanging prints.

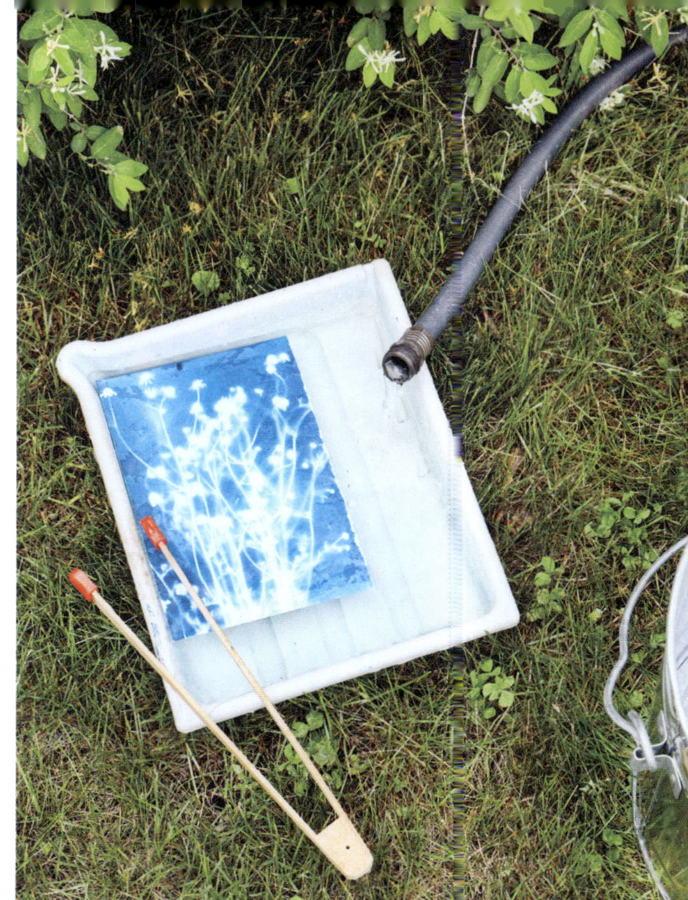

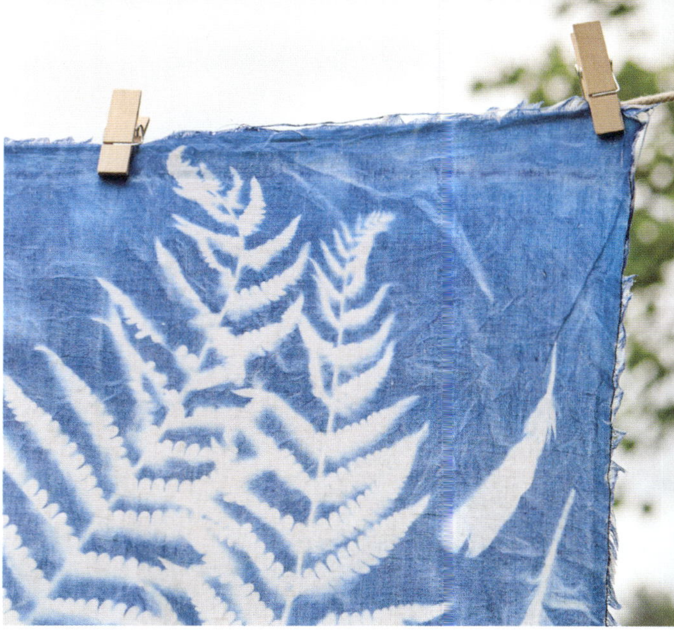

**LARGE SHEETS OF CARDBOARD.** If drying flat, use clean cardboard or lay a sheet of kraft paper down on top of a used piece of cardboard to avoid transferring dirt or chemicals onto your drying prints.

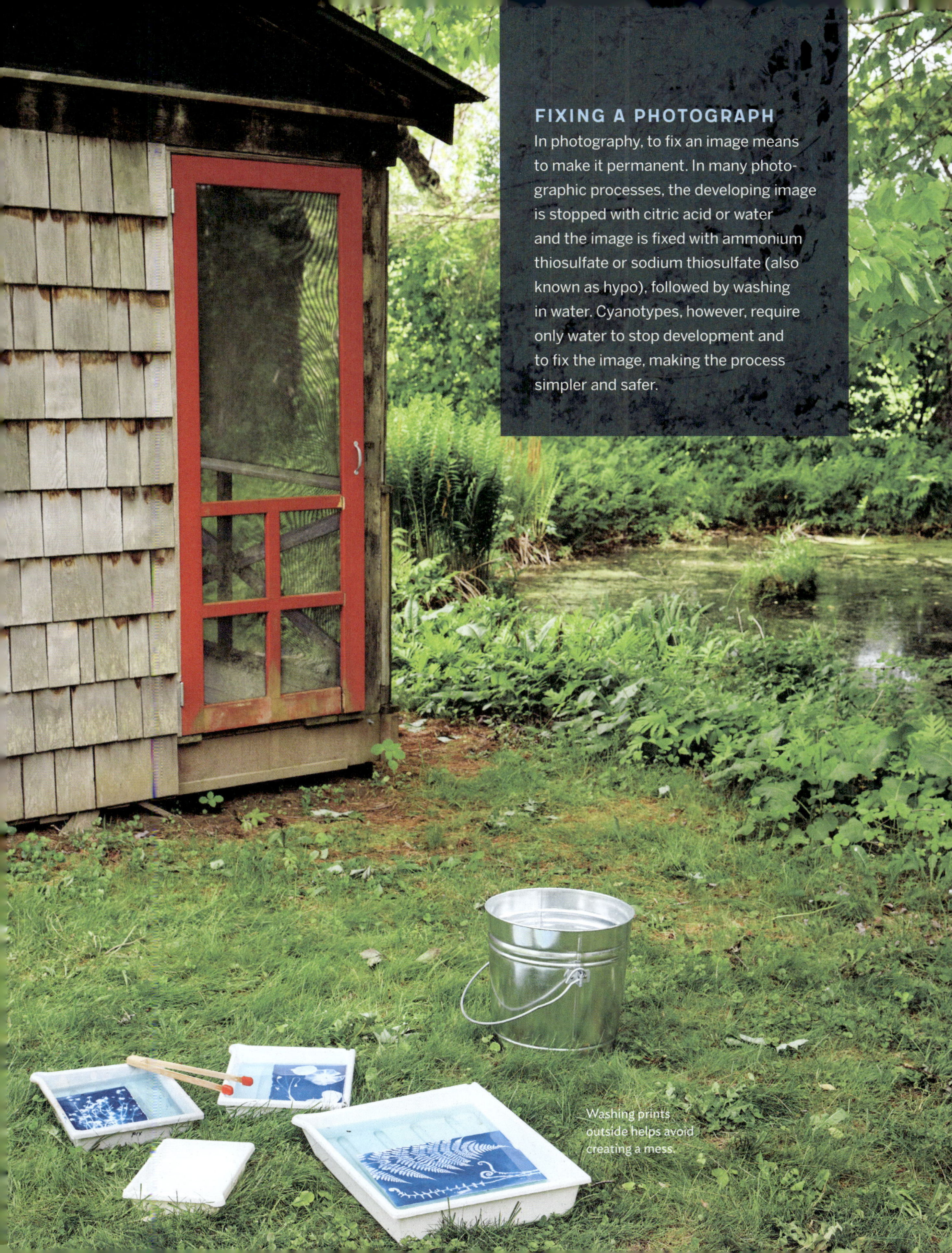

## FIXING A PHOTOGRAPH

In photography, to fix an image means to make it permanent. In many photographic processes, the developing image is stopped with citric acid or water and the image is fixed with ammonium thiosulfate or sodium thiosulfate (also known as hypo), followed by washing in water. Cyanotypes, however, require only water to stop development and to fix the image, making the process simpler and safer.

Washing prints outside helps avoid creating a mess.

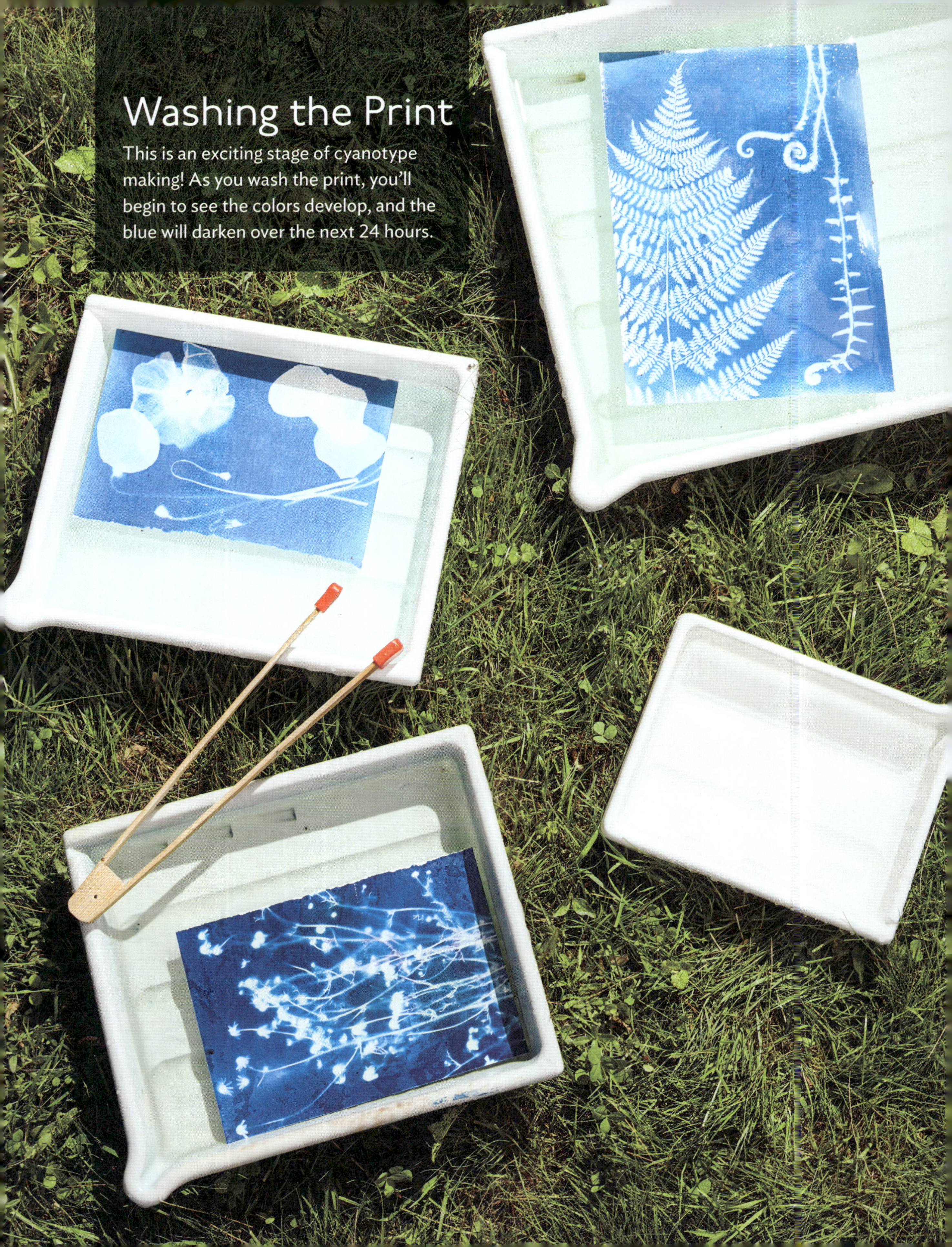

## Washing the Print

This is an exciting stage of cyanotype making! As you wash the print, you'll begin to see the colors develop, and the blue will darken over the next 24 hours.

## Materials

- Plastic washing tray, larger than the cyanotype
- Source of running water
- Gloves or tongs (optional)
- Exposed cyanotype

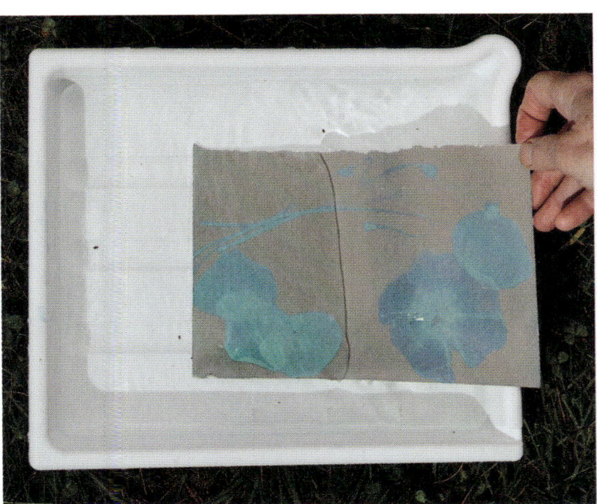

1 **SET UP.** Place the washing tray near your water source, ideally away from direct light, and fill the tray with water. Tap water can be used for washing.

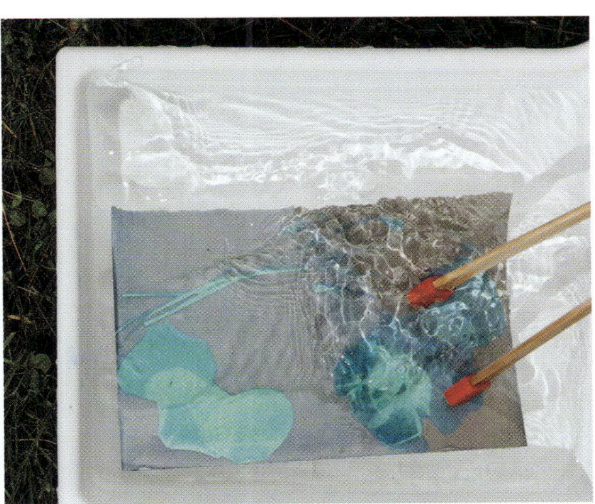

2 **SUBMERGE THE PRINT.** Wearing gloves or using tongs, slide the exposed sheet of paper into the tray of water.

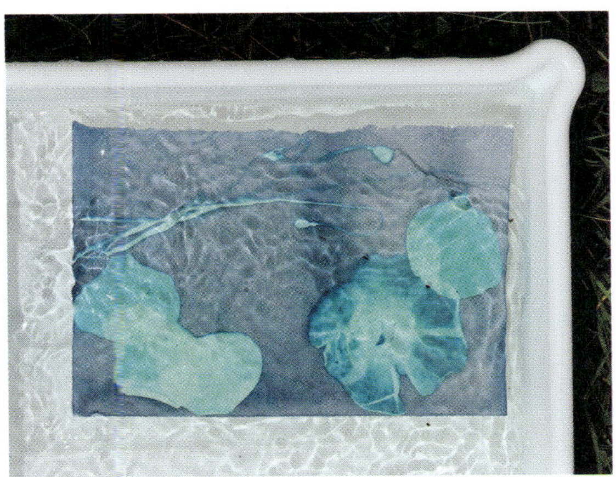

3 **WASH IN COOL RUNNING WATER.** Wash the print for 5 to 15 minutes by setting it in gently running water or by filling and dumping the tray several times, until the light-green emulsion is removed; the rinse water should be clear and there should be no yellow in the highlight or white areas of the print. If washed for too long, a print may fade as the emulsion is washed away. Proper washing ensures the print's longevity.

### SAFELY DISPOSING OF WASH WATER

I recommend consulting with your local department of environmental protection (DEP) about disposing of the water you use to rinse your cyanotype. My local DEP official said that it is generally acceptable to dispose of washed-off cyanotype chemicals in a municipal water system because they will be highly diluted. However, in the case of a septic system, the cyanotype chemicals could possibly alter the delicate pH balance within a septic tank. I have a septic system and, heeding this advice, pour my cyanotype washing water onto my lawn rather than down my drain. After five years, the grass shows no ill effects.

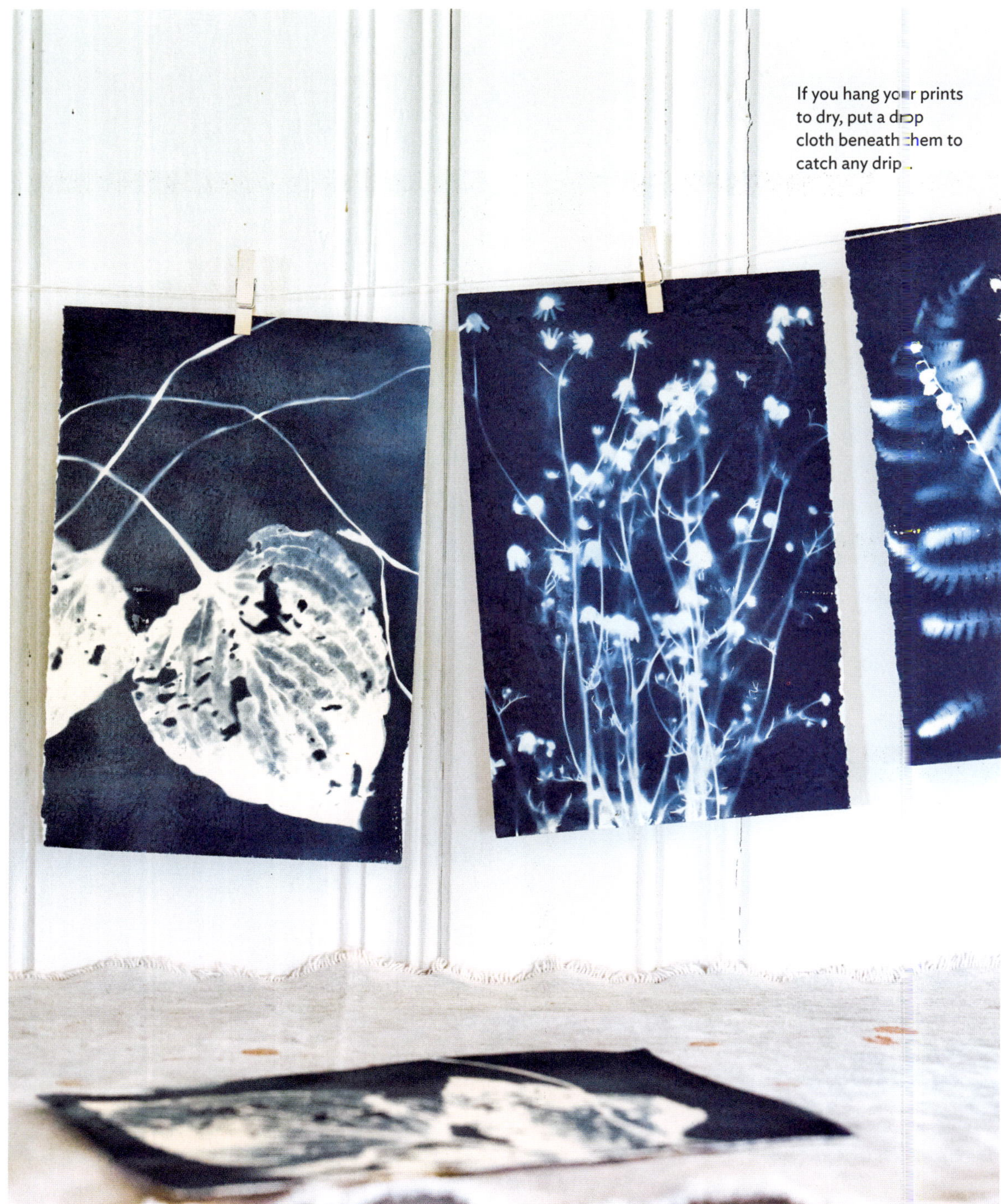

If you hang your prints to dry, put a drop cloth beneath them to catch any drips.

**4 DRY THE PRINT.** Remove the print from the wash tray. Dry the print by laying it on a flat work surface, hanging it from a line using clothespins, or placing it on a print rack. Keep the print out of direct sunlight while drying to prevent fading. If the print appears wrinkly after being dried, place it between two sheets of clean paper and cover it with books or other weights to flatten. Over the next 24 hours, the Prussian blue in the print will darken.

## Optional Explorations

**ACIDIFICATION.** In her book *Creative Cyanotype: Techniques and Inspiration*, Angela Chalmers suggests acidifying the wash water by preparing it as a 5 percent solution of white vinegar (50 mL vinegar in 1,000 mL water) to protect against any possible alkaline buffer added during the papermaking process or if you're using water with a high alkaline content. Wash the print for 5 minutes as indicated in step 3, then use the vinegar solution for a final 10-minute wash.

**SPEEDING UP THE RESULTS.** Create a solution of 3 percent hydrogen peroxide (30 mL hydrogen peroxide in 1,000 mL of water) and wash the print for 1 minute. Then follow with a 10-minute wash under running water. This will speed up the oxidation process and darken the print dramatically. This practice is wonderful to use when working with children, who will be especially eager to see the results of their efforts, but it is not required. Your cyanotype print will oxidize after 24 hours without this step.

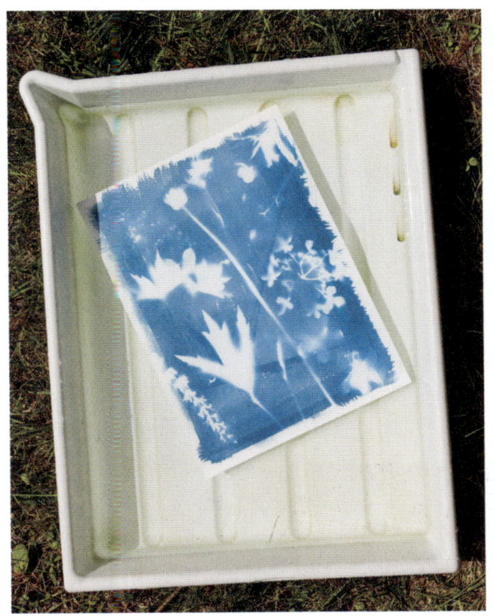

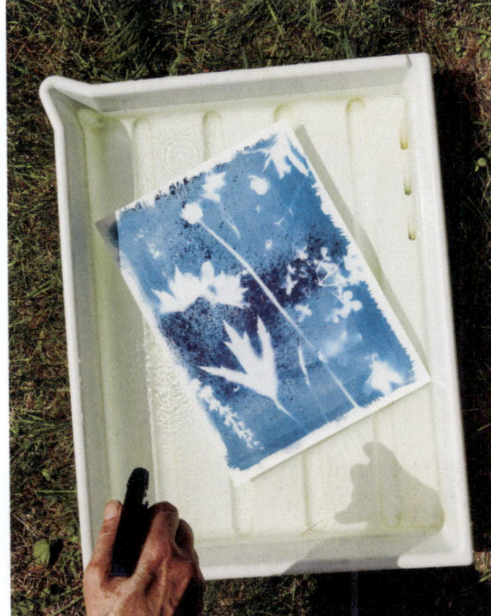

Applying a solution of 3 percent hydrogren peroxide while washing a print will darken it quickly, creating a dramatic result. However, the color will soften as it dries.

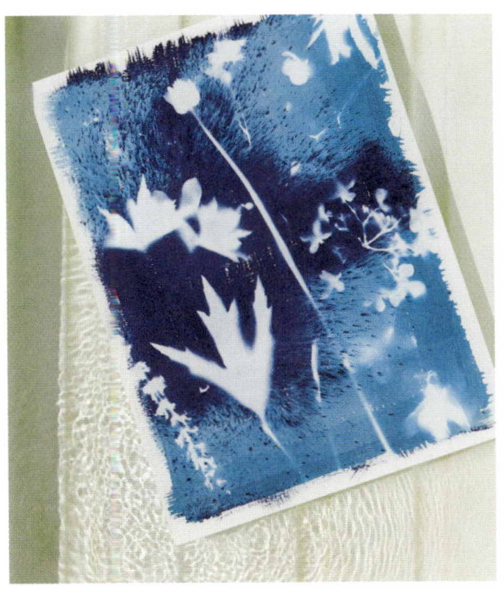

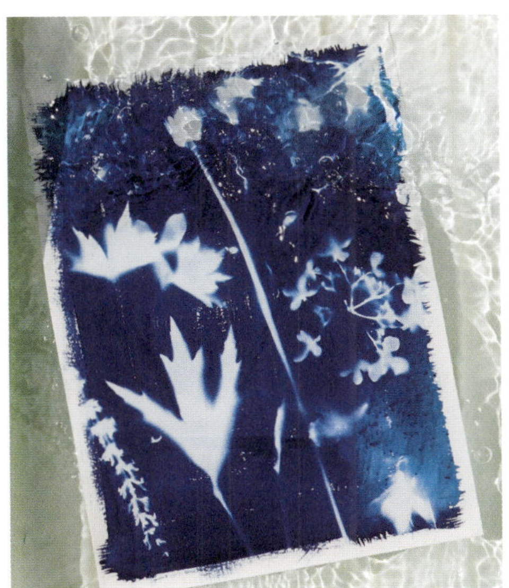

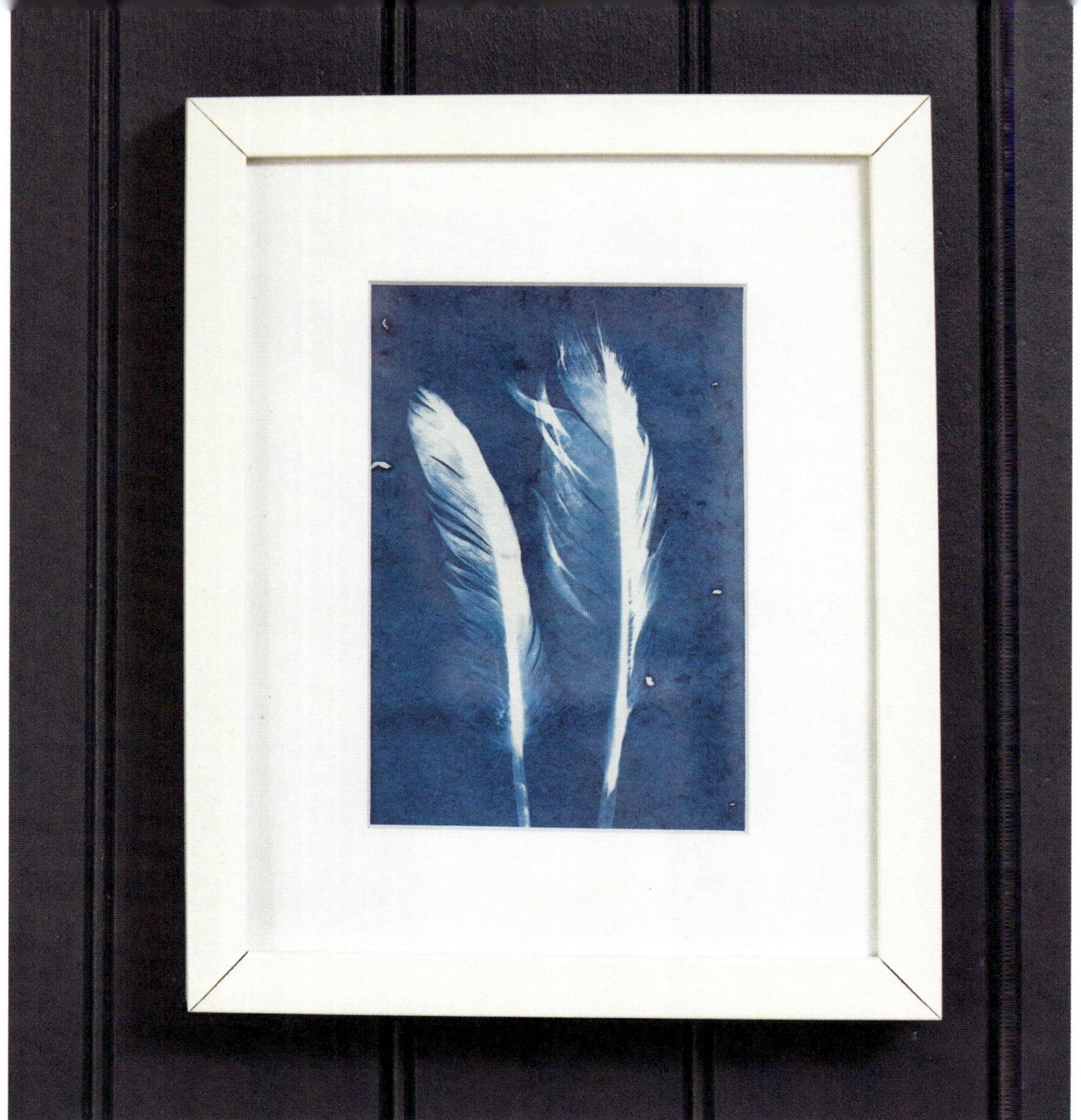

# Displaying and Storing Cyanotypes

Once you've completed the washing process, it's important to protect your cyanotype from UV light, which can cause it to fade. Do not hang a cyanotype in direct sunlight unless it is protected with 100 percent UV glazing, whether glass or acrylic. If the blues in your cyanotype fade to white due to direct sunlight exposure, place the cyanotype in darkness to regenerate the blue tones; oxygen in the air will convert the white back to blue.

One way to protect a cyanotype is with a UV-resistant coating, such as an acrylic spray with a gloss or matte finish. You can also mount your cyanotype or give it a wax finish (see instructions on pages 145 and 148).

More simply, you can showcase your favorite cyanotype by placing it in a mat and framing it with glass or acrylic. Do it yourself or take it to a professional framer. Choose unbuffered mats and archival materials to ensure the longevity of your cyanotype.

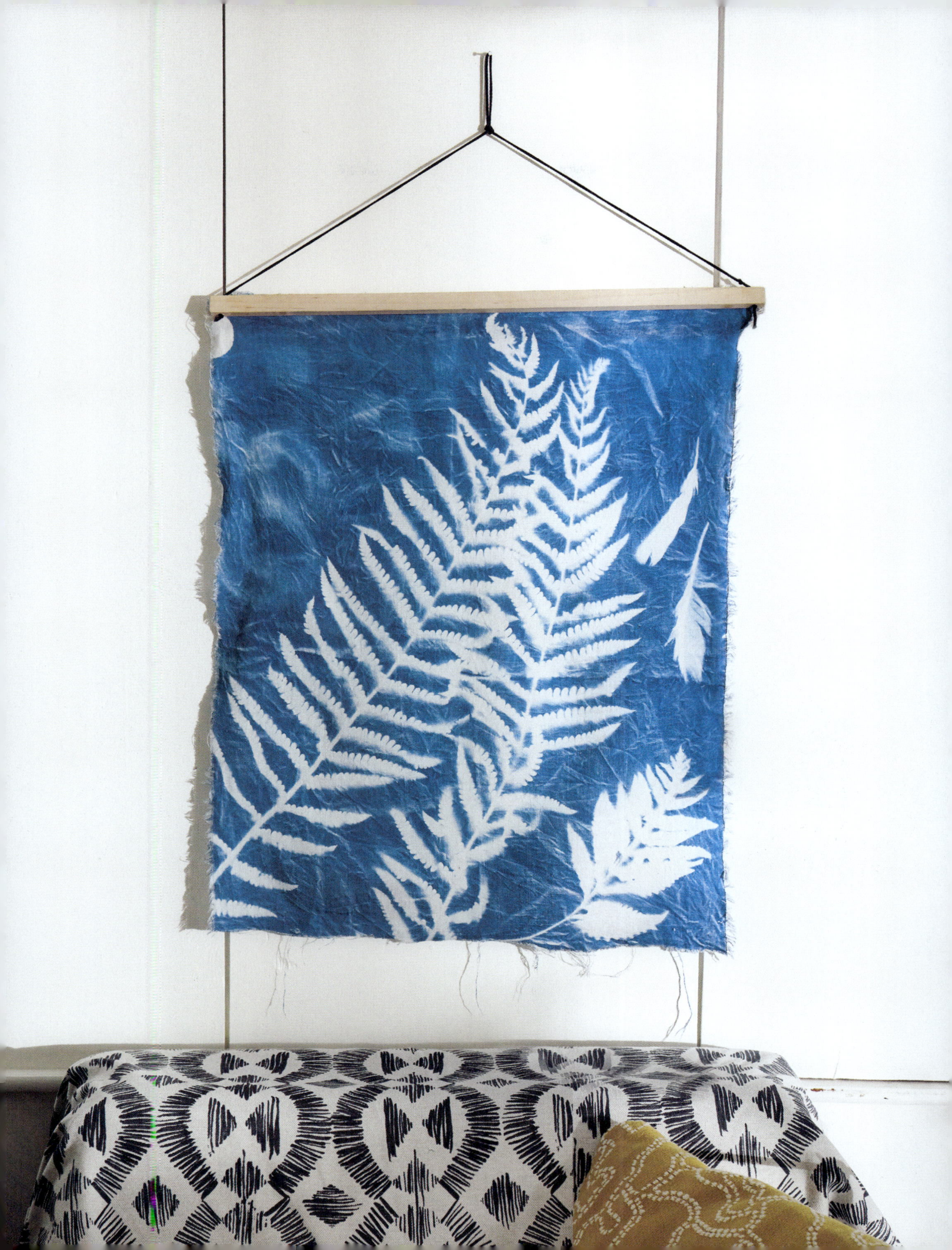

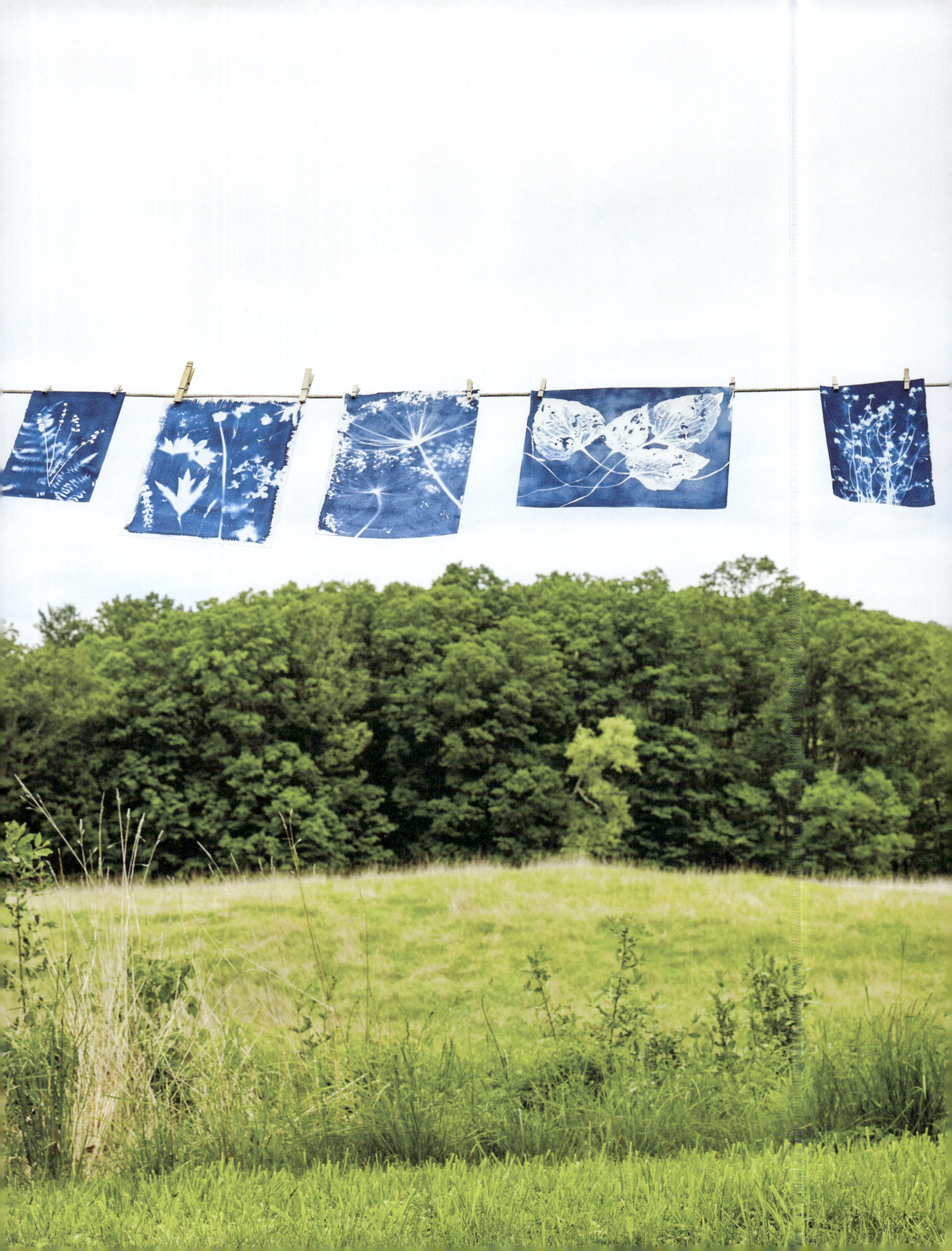

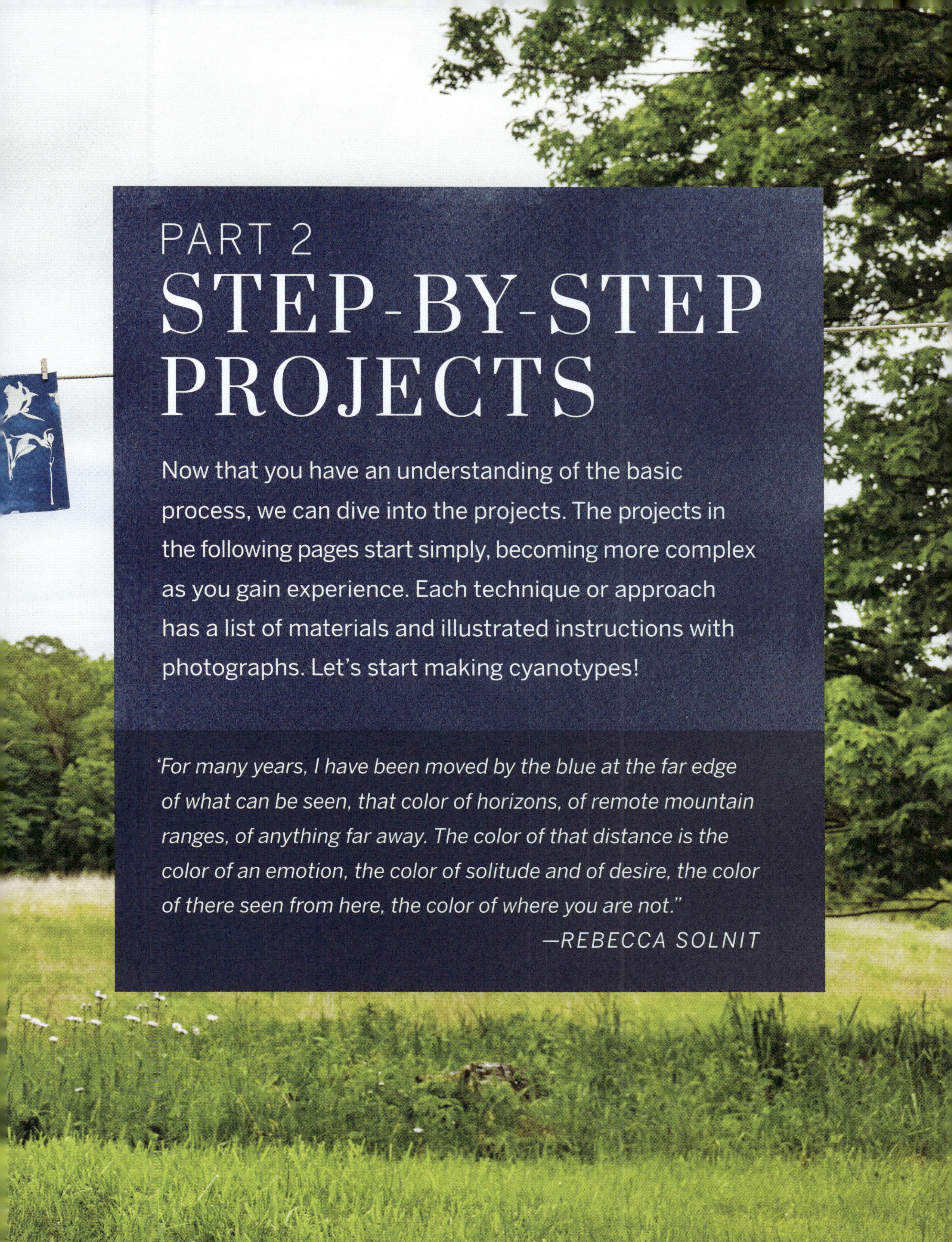

PART 2
# STEP-BY-STEP PROJECTS

Now that you have an understanding of the basic process, we can dive into the projects. The projects in the following pages start simply, becoming more complex as you gain experience. Each technique or approach has a list of materials and illustrated instructions with photographs. Let's start making cyanotypes!

*'For many years, I have been moved by the blue at the far edge of what can be seen, that color of horizons, of remote mountain ranges, of anything far away. The color of that distance is the color of an emotion, the color of solitude and of desire, the color of there seen from here, the color of where you are not."*

*—REBECCA SOLNIT*

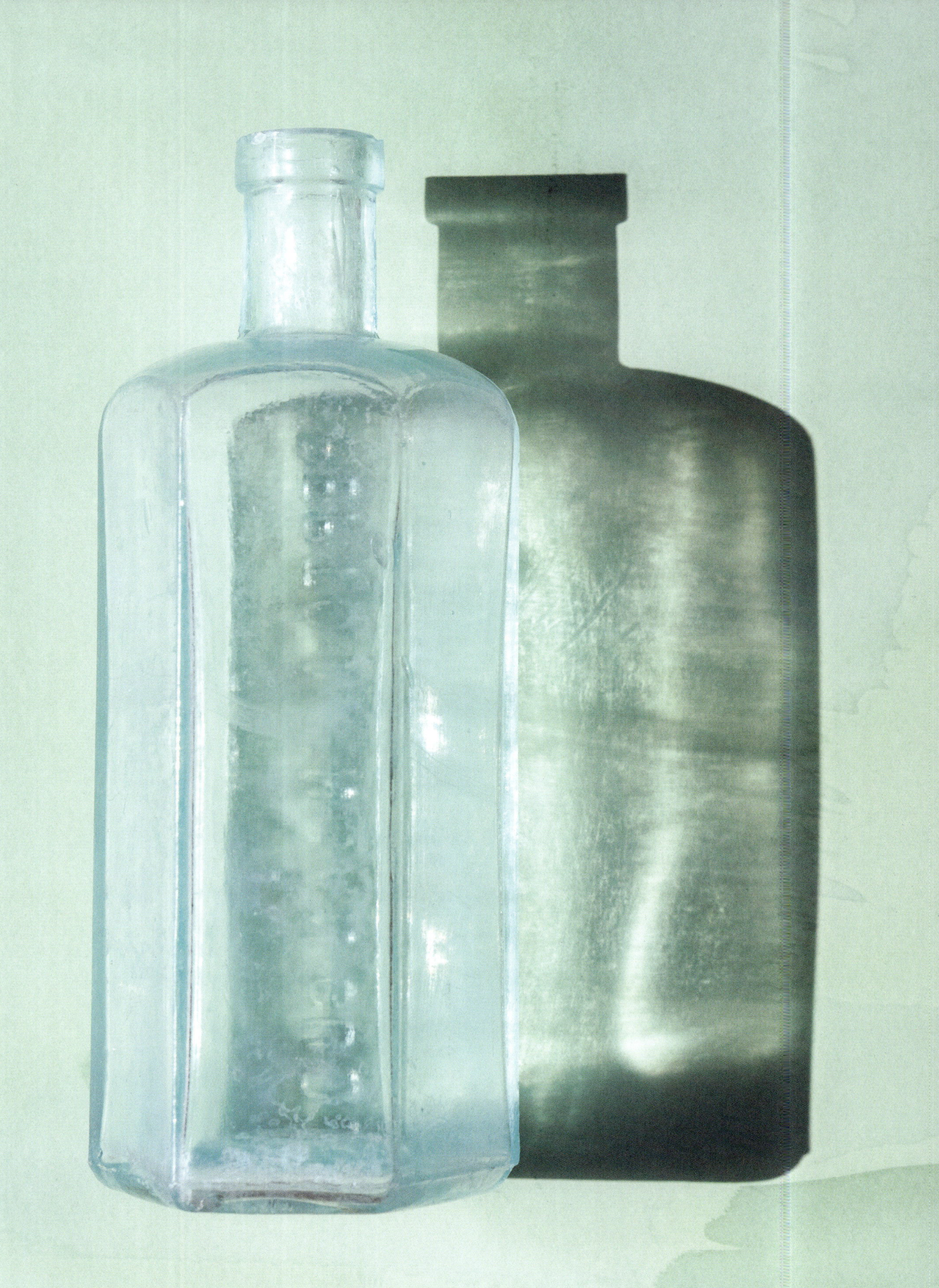

CHAPTER 5

# Simple Cyanotypes

*The projects in this chapter are a great way to start exploring the world of cyanotypes. As you begin, don't be afraid to experiment and make each piece your own. Remember, this is a forgiving and flexible process. Mistakes can often be transformed or used for other projects.*

# Working with Botanicals

Botanicals are one of the most common printing materials used when making cyanotypes. You can use both fresh and dried, pressed botanicals in your work, depending on the look you hope to achieve.

## *Dried Plants*

Botanical material such as leaves or plants that have been pressed work best for cyanotypes. They will lie flat on your paper, allowing a tighter seal between the glass or acrylic and the paper, which results in a crisper outline of the plant material.

Choose the method of plant pressing that works best for you. You might consider creating a pressed plant collection, which allows you to reuse the same specimens repeatedly.

I love the imagined history and the surprise of a pressed flower floating silently from a just-opened book. The simple act of placing a plant between the pages of a book is a technique I've used deliberately for years. Only recently have I graduated to a sturdy press with a frame, blotting paper to absorb moisture, and cardboard ventilators to promote airflow. It works nicely (see the Resources section on page 211). Even if you prefer to press flowers in a book, adding blotting paper is an inexpensive way to improve the results.

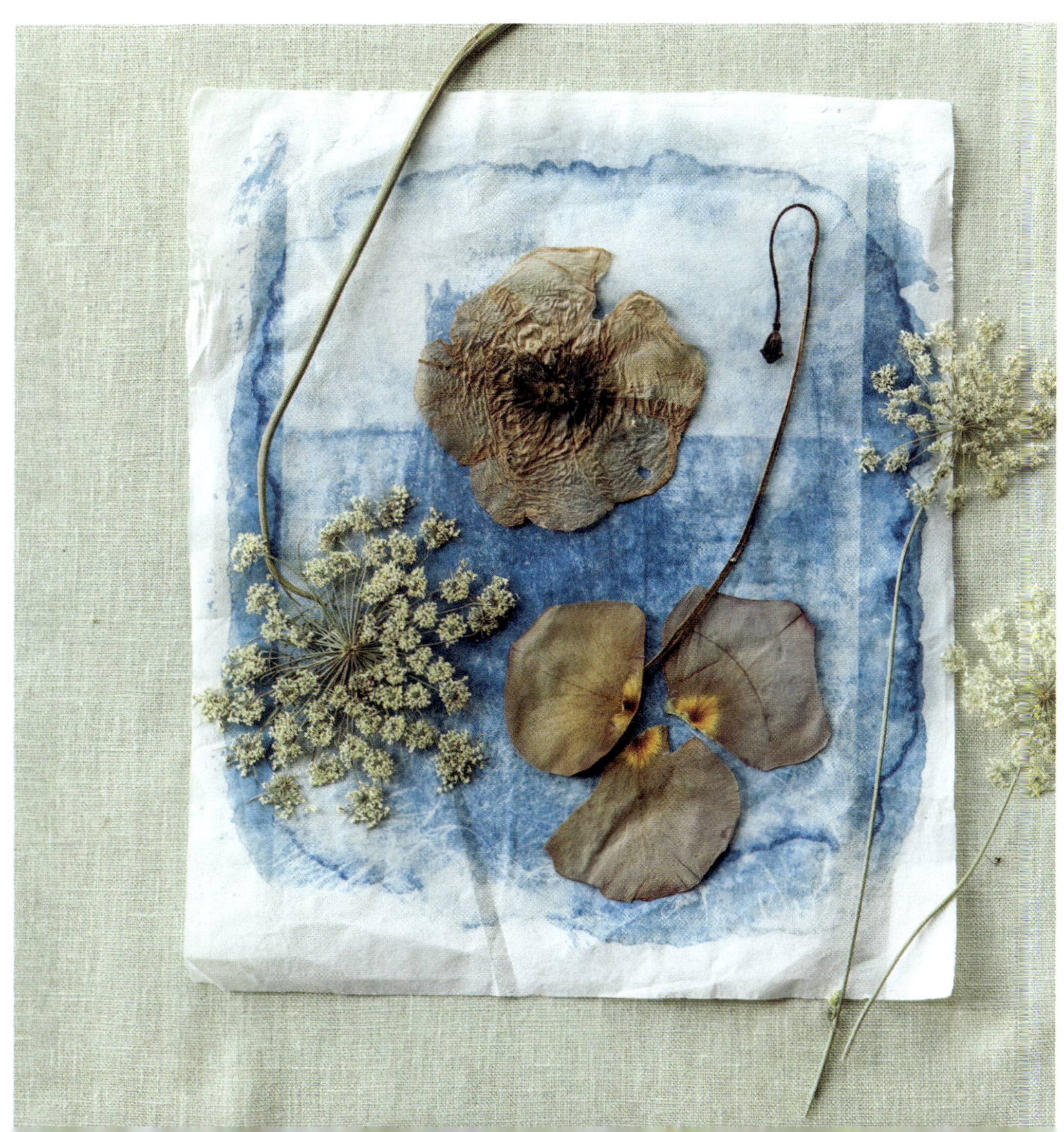

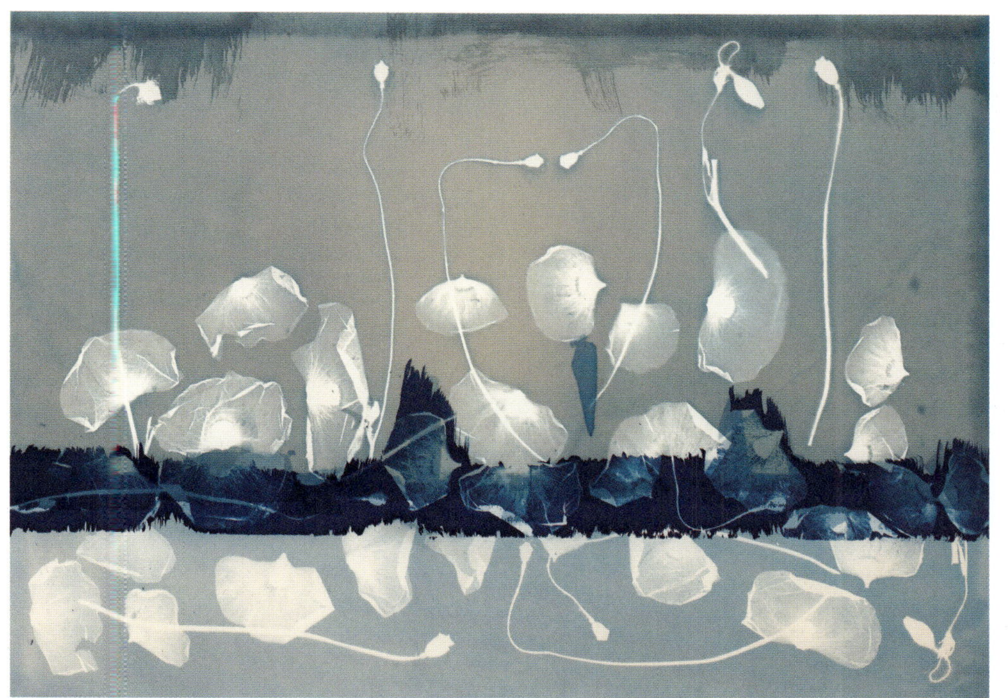

One of my favorite flowers to press and use in botanical cyanotypes is the poppy (*Papaver rhoeas*); I love the intricate details of its delicate petals.

Flower pressing is an art of its own, and flower preservationist and artist Linda Ruel Flynn has taken it to another level. Some of these pressed flowers are almost translucent, which can create a delicate and lovely effect for printing.

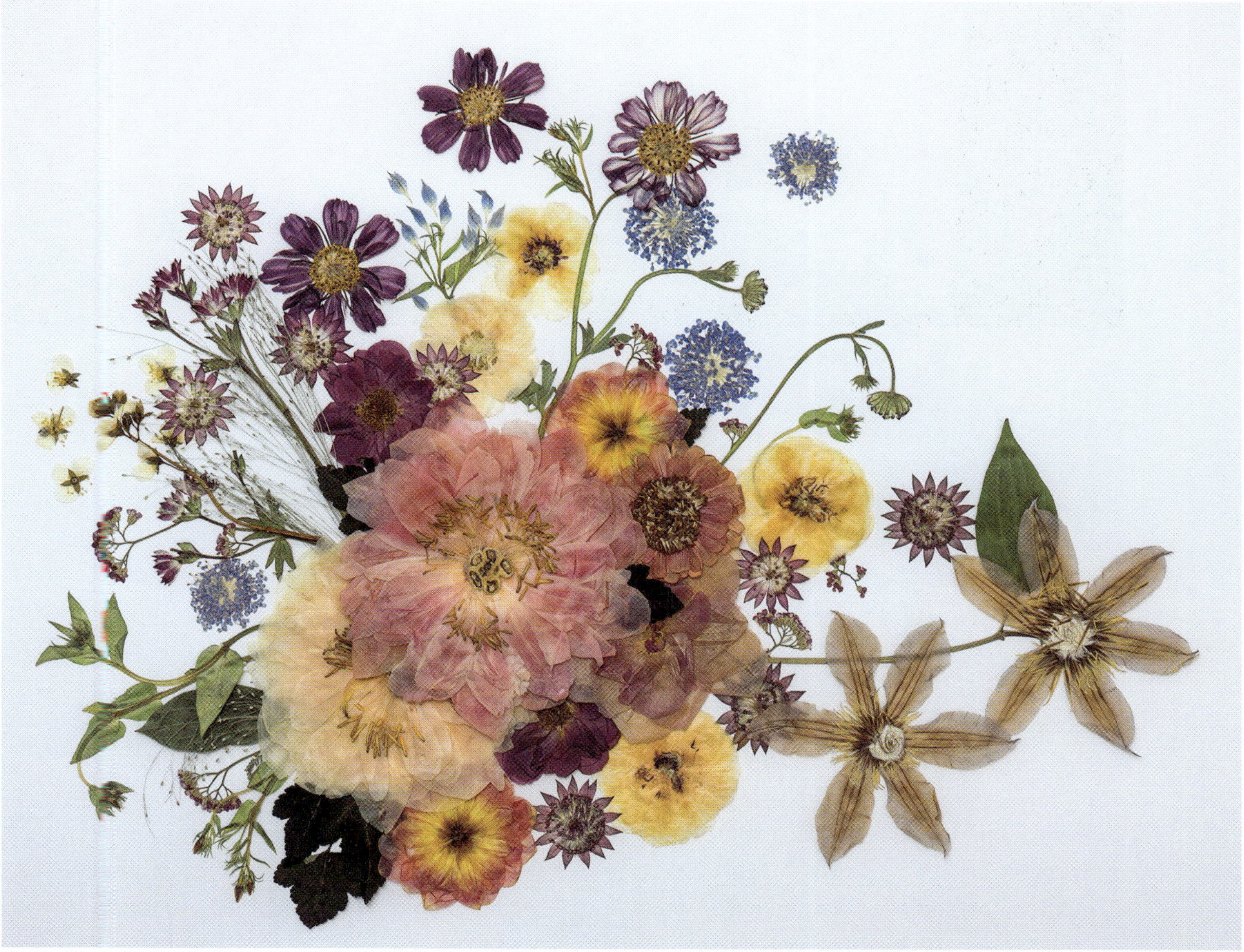

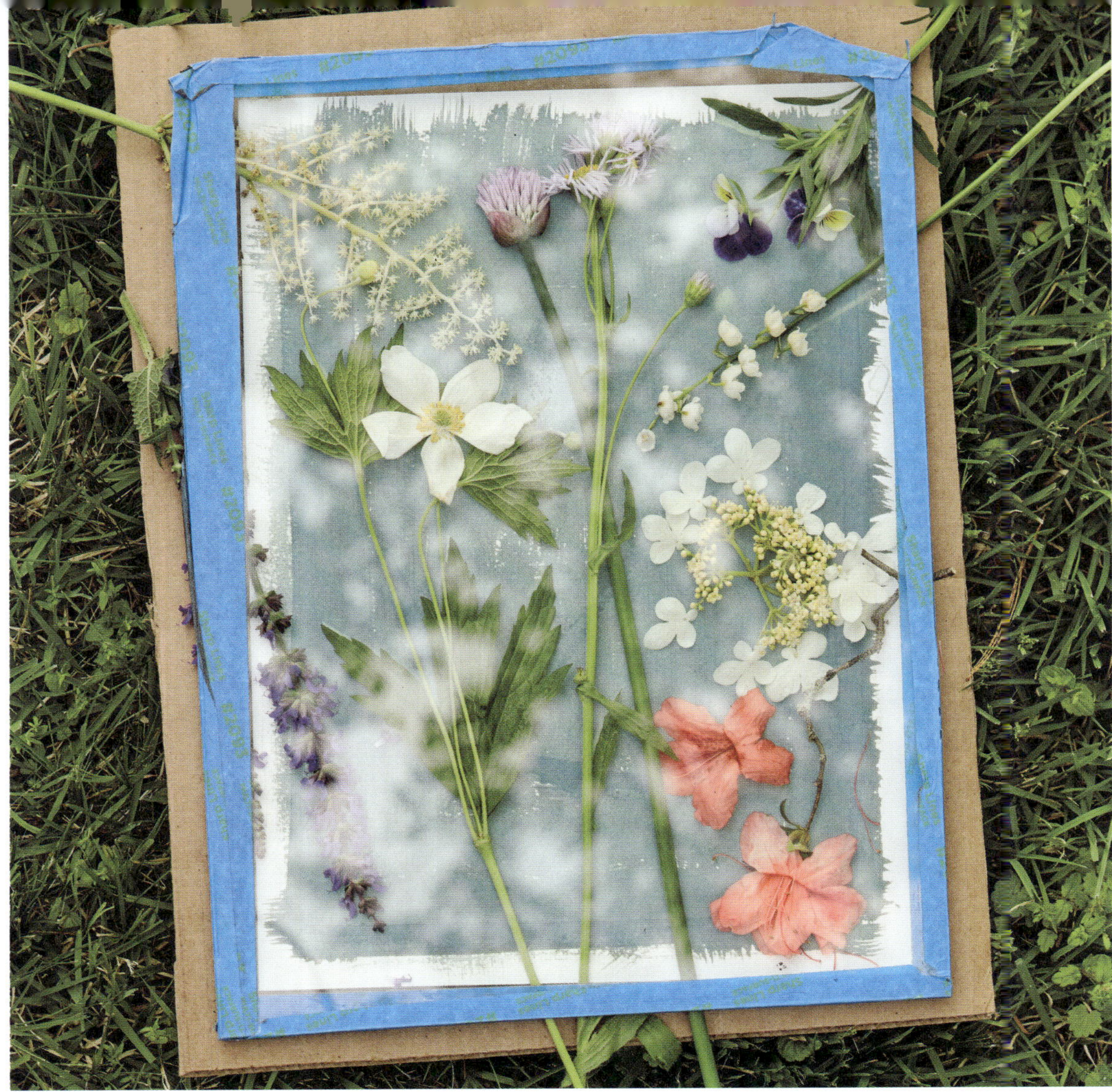

Flowers with a single arrangement of petals, like violets, press quickly, as do many ferns, but pressing thicker plants can take up to three weeks. A microwave plant press is a popular method for drying plants more quickly (see the Resources section on page 211).

## Fresh Plants

Fresh plants are usually thicker, and when sandwiched between glass and paper, they may not allow for a tight seal, leading to a softer outline of the plant in the final print. In some cases, that softness might be what you're hoping to create! To achieve this soft effect intentionally, you can also place plants on top of the glass. Keep in mind, however, that any wind during the exposure period may shift the plant material. On a windless day or when working indoors, you can skip the glass entirely by placing plants directly on the light-sensitive paper and exposing the setup to UV light. Fresh plants that are naturally flat—leaves or even flower petals—will print as crisply as dried material if they are laid beneath the glass before printing.

## Foraging for Botanicals

Plant life is all around us, but we often fail to notice it. As you begin to make cyanotypes, you'll soon find that you're on the lookout for interesting plants and flowers. Pay attention to what's growing and blooming around you. Tracking the seasons through your artwork—from the hardy Christmas ferns and skeletal leaves of the winter season to the abundant blooms of summer—is a beautiful way to engage with nature.

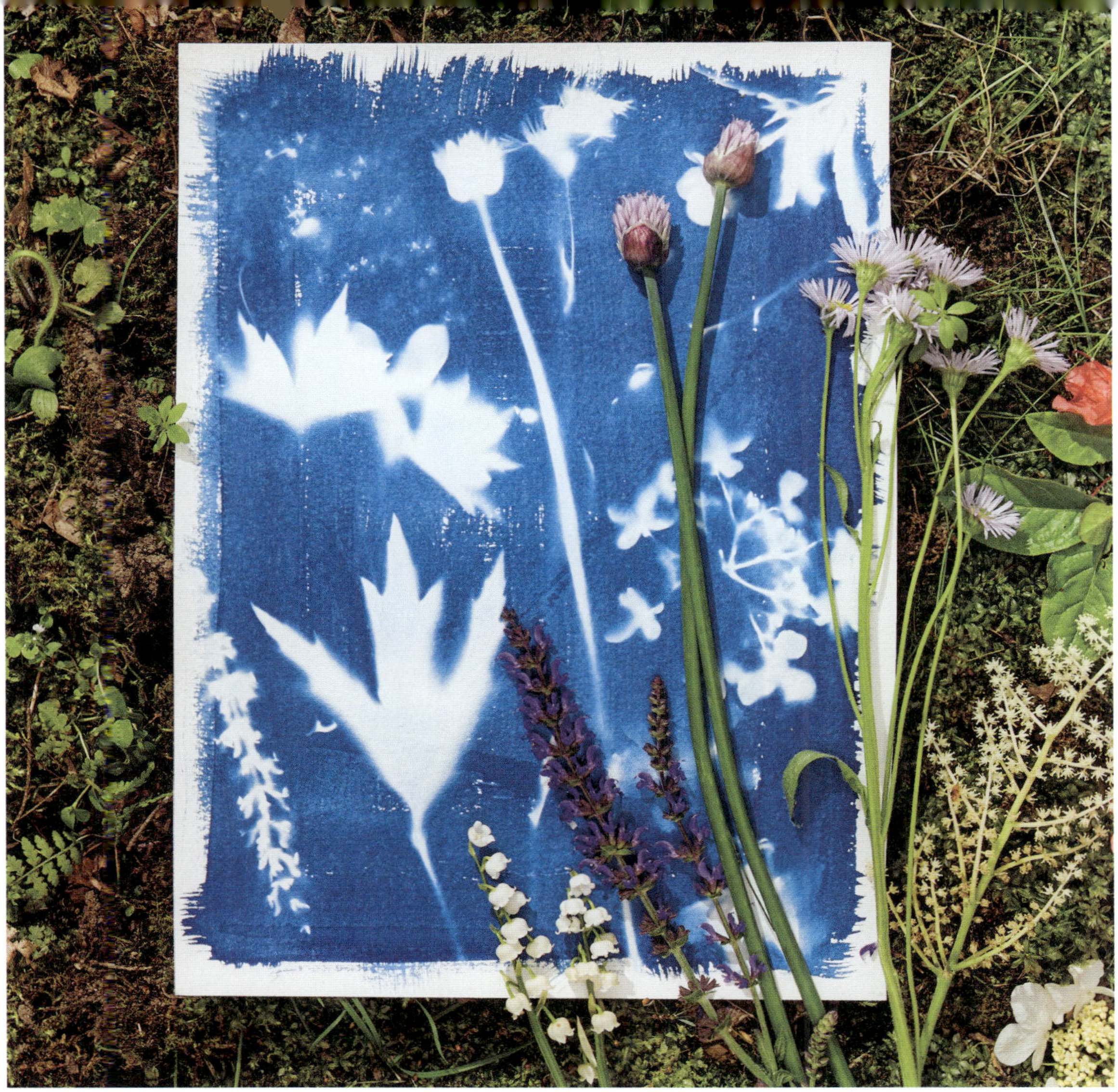

When the spring equinox rolls around and I'm eager to start making cyanotypes outside, I search fields and gardens for the previous year's worn-out plants. Overwintered plants offer an interesting perspective and craggy beauty to my cyanotype making. Desiccated hosta leaves, when I can find them, are one of my early-spring favorites. When the first daffodils arrive, I refrain from picking them until they appear in bunches. About the same time, fiddleheads unfurl, and I know that by late spring the shady edges will be a riot of ferns.

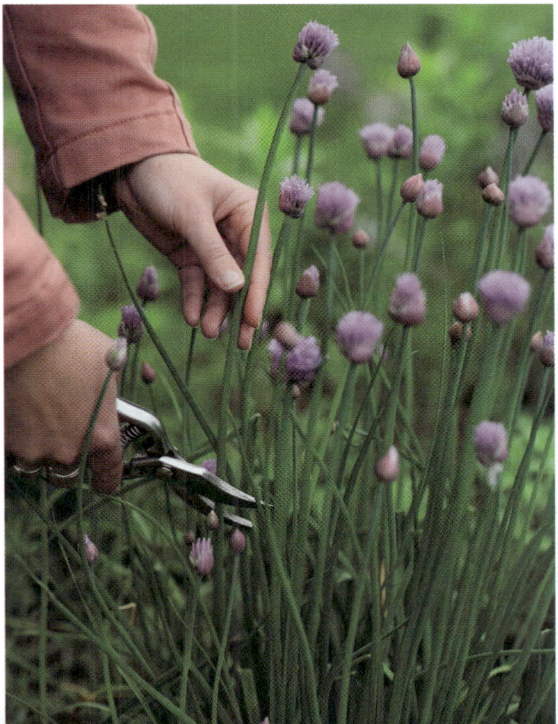

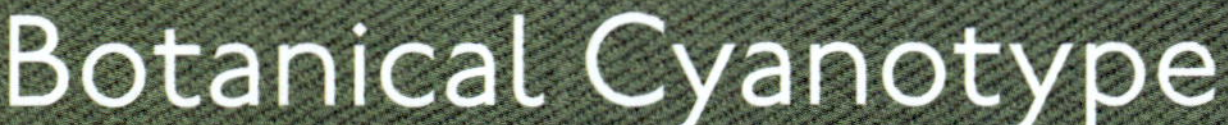

# Botanical Cyanotype

Anna Atkins's iconic work used the cyanotype process to beautifully represent flora, making botanical cyanotypes a classic form of art. Here we'll do the same.

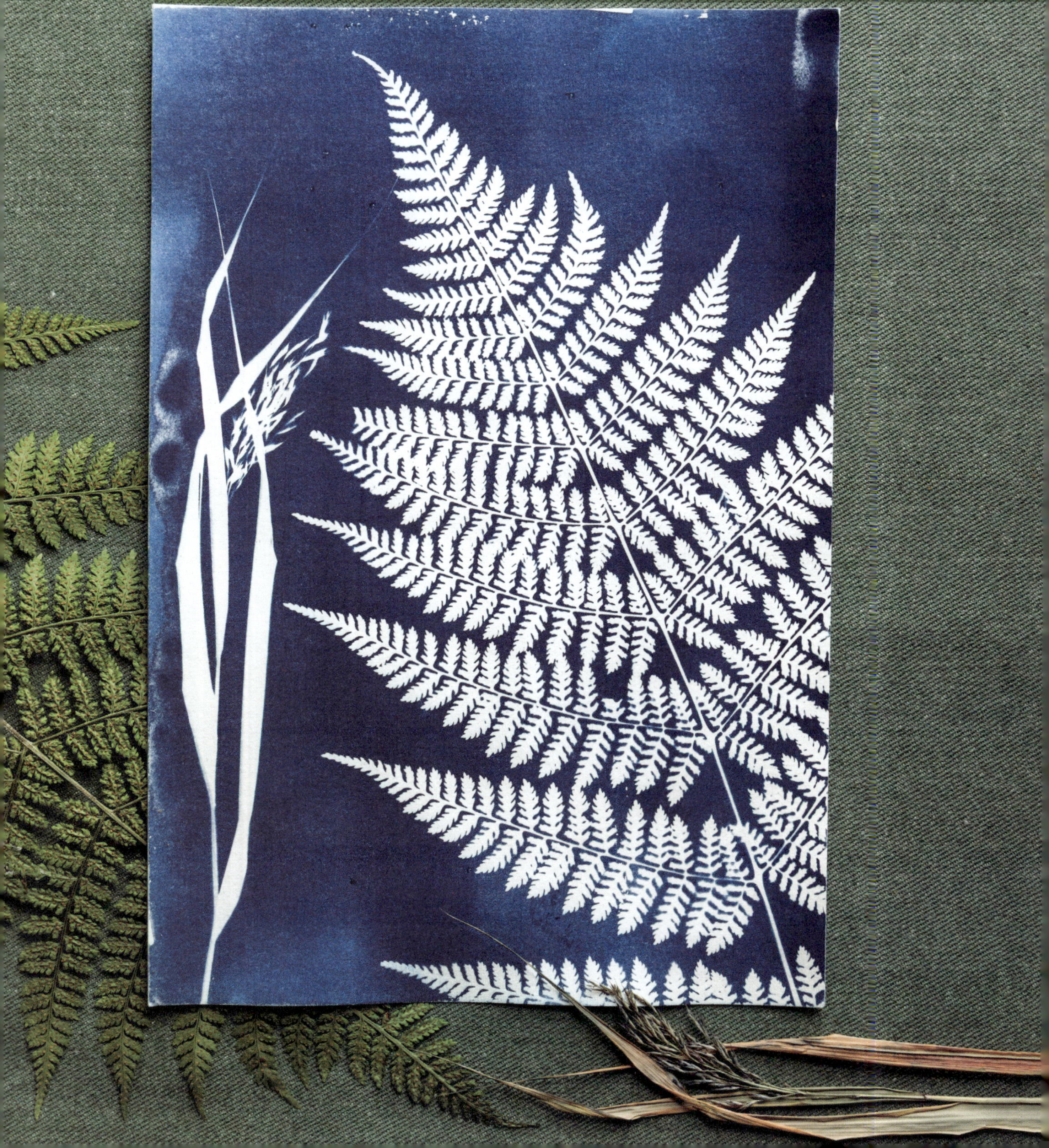

## Materials

- Plastic washing tray larger than the cyanotype
- Clothesline and clothespins or sheets of clean cardboard
- Plant material, pressed and dried or fresh
- Sheet of prepared paper (coated with cyanotype working solution, allowed to dry, and stored in a light-safe container)
- Sheet of cardboard (or any stiff material) the same size as the glass or acrylic
- Sheet of glass or acrylic larger than the paper
- Binder clips or similar fasteners
- Gloves or tongs, for handling the print while rinsing (optional)

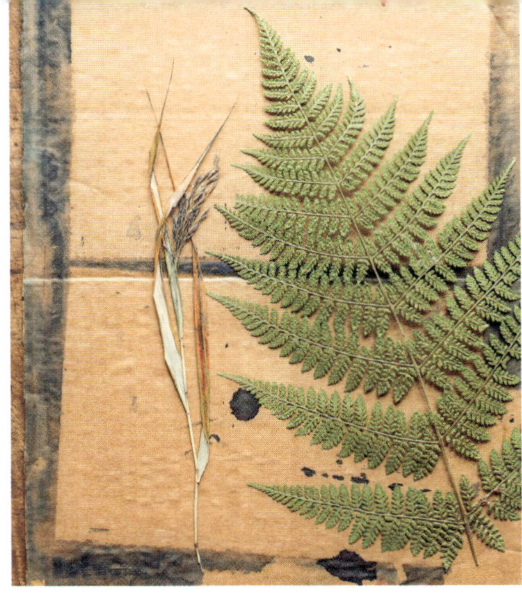

1 **SET UP.** Gather your materials in a dimly lit prep space. Place the rinsing tray in your wash area and fill it with water. Set up a clothesline or sheets of clean cardboard as a drying station, somewhere away from direct light.

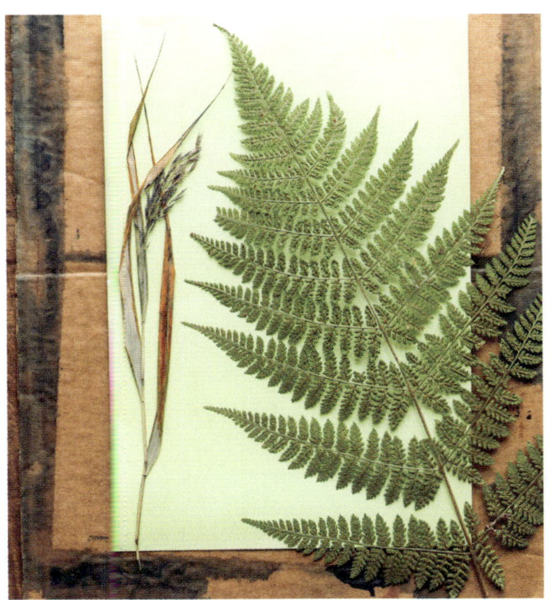

2 **ARRANGE THE COMPOSITION.** Before removing the paper from its light-safe container, play with your plant materials to create a composition (see page 62 for some guidelines). Once you are satisfied with your arrangement, remove the sheet of paper from its light-safe container and place it on the cardboard backing with the light-green emulsion side facing up. Re-create your composition by placing the plant materials on the paper. Be sure to work in low light to minimize the paper's exposure to UV light.

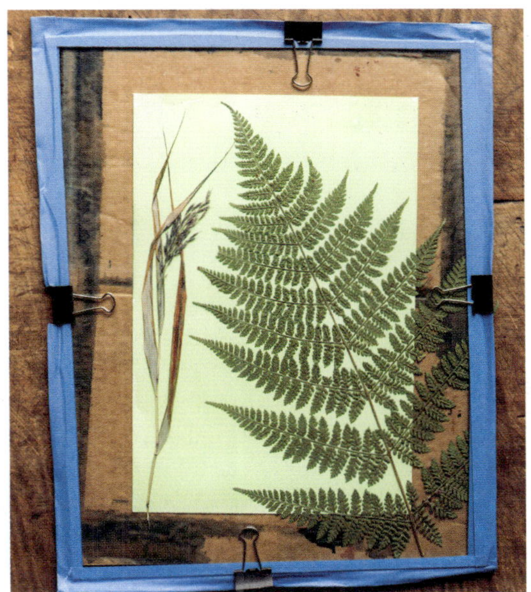

3 **SECURE THE MATERIALS.** Cover the paper and plants with a sheet of glass or acrylic. Check the arrangement of your composition; if any of the botanical materials were disrupted, adjust as needed. Secure the glass or acrylic to the cardboard backing with binder clips.

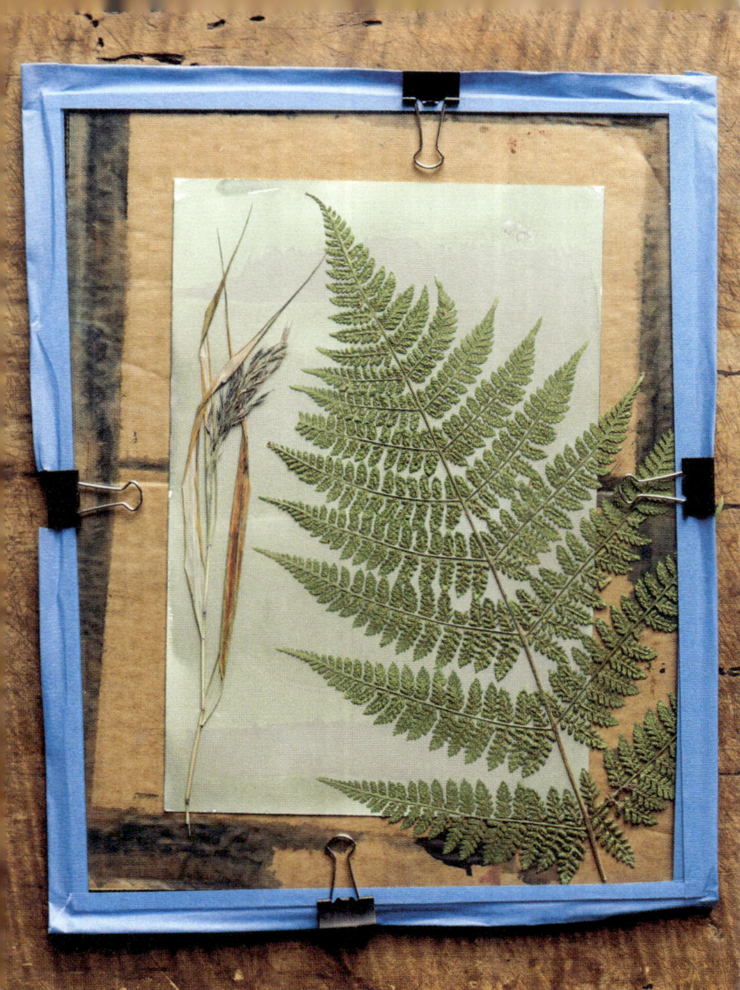

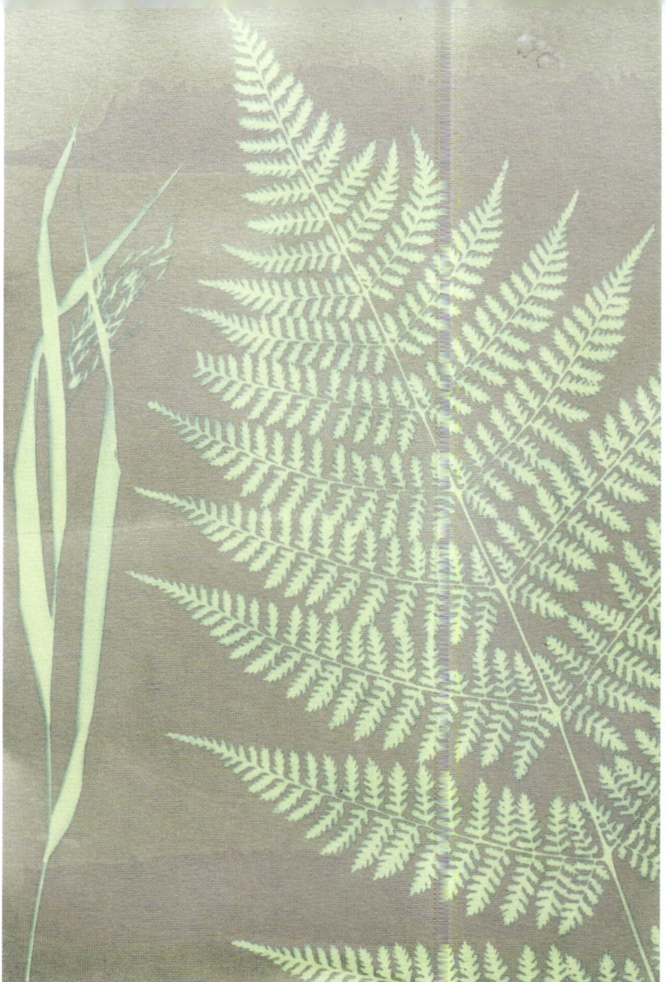

**4** **EXPOSE TO SUNLIGHT.** Place your paper and secured plant material setup in direct sunlight with the emulsion side up. Don't stand where you may cast a shadow onto the print. Exposure time varies depending on sunlight strength and time of year, as discussed on page 56. As the print develops, the light-green emulsion will interact with the UV rays of the sun, turning a blue-green color, and then continuing to change.

**5** **MONITOR THE DEVELOPMENT.** When the emulsion turns bronze or silvery gray, the print is ready. To stop the exposure, move your setup out of direct sunlight. Longer exposure results in darker blues, while shorter exposures produce lighter blues.

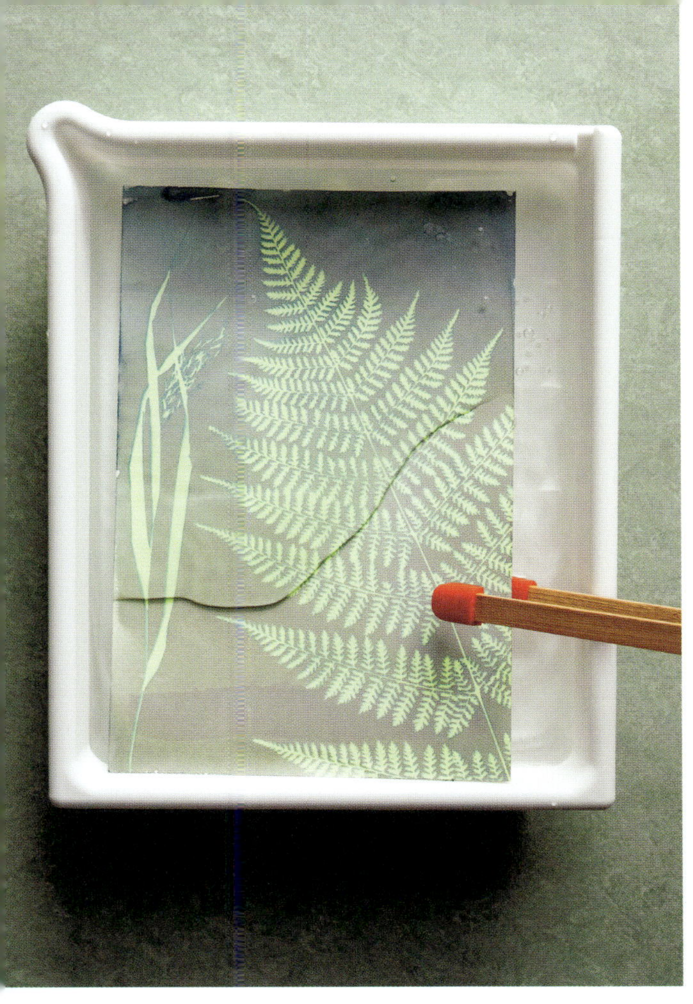

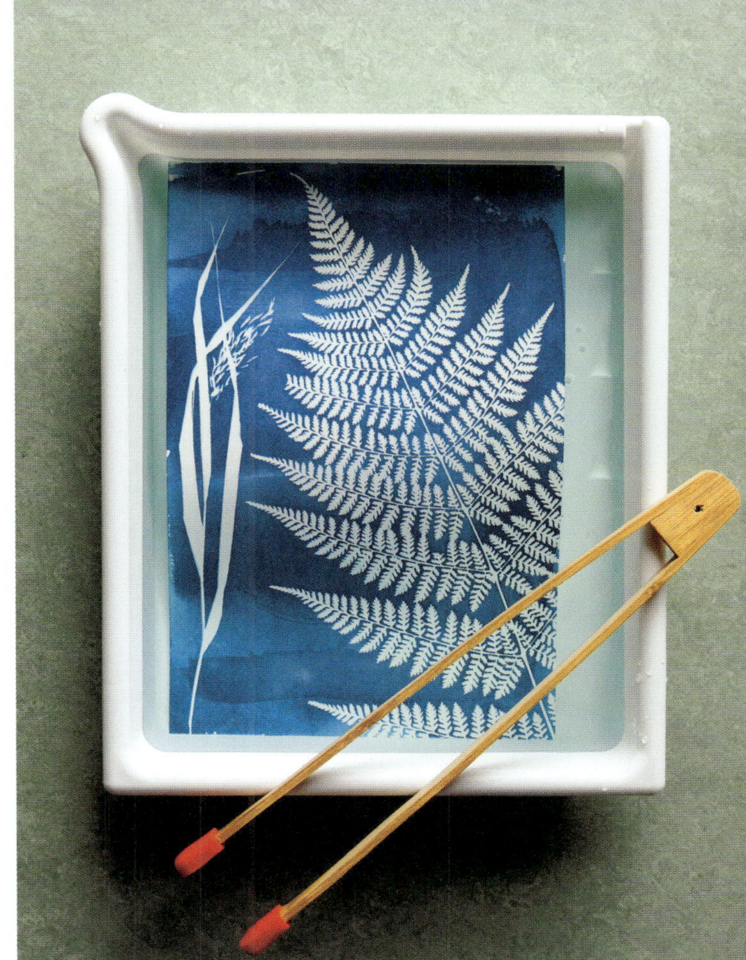

6 **DISMANTLE AND WASH.** Working out of direct light, remove the clips, glass or acrylic, and plants. Place the exposed paper in the tray of water; wear gloves or use tongs, if you like, to reduce skin contact with chemicals. Wash in slowly running water or fill and dump the tray three to five times. Wash until the light-green chemicals are removed and the water is clear, 5 to 15 minutes.

7 **DRY THE PRINT.** Lay the print on a flat work surface or hang it from a line using clothespins to dry. Keep the print away from direct sunlight during the drying period to prevent fading. After drying, if the print appears wrinkly, place it between two sheets of clean paper and cover it with books or other weights to flatten.

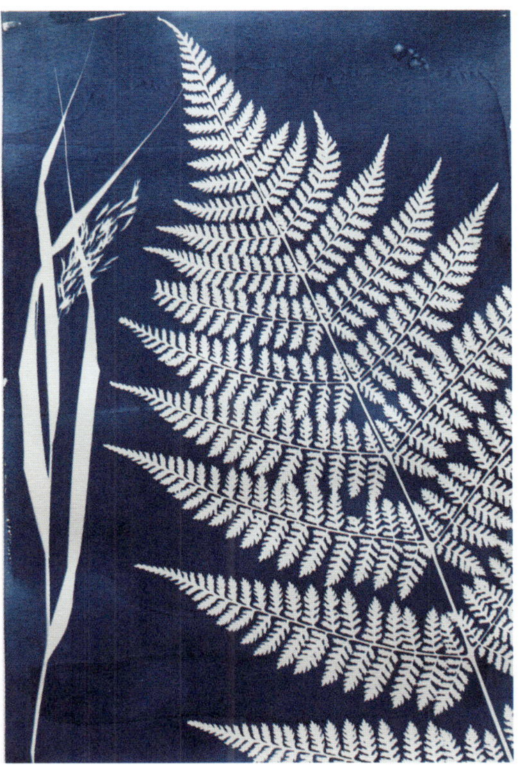

# Cyanotype Photograms

As noted in the introduction, a photogram is a photographic image made by placing an object directly on the surface of light-sensitive paper (like paper coated with cyanotype chemicals!) and then exposing the paper to light. It has a wonderful simplicity. Unlike traditional photographs, which often allow for multiple copies, each photogram is unique. Bauhaus teacher László Moholy-Nagy, who coined the term *photogram* circa 1922, made hundreds of them, using everyday objects to create both abstract and representational images.

Photograms can change the way we see everyday objects. For example, artist Elizabeth Ellenwood transforms the plastic debris she collects along the wrack lines of Rhode Island beaches for her *Among the Tides* series. The resulting abstract, beautiful, and unsettling images document the complex history of ocean trash and its effects on ecosystems.

While the following projects offer two ways to make a photogram, there are many more. The first uses glass objects and their intriguing reflections. The second explores paper textures—wrinkled, thin, thick, or folded—to create landscapelike forms.

Unexpected objects, in this case a cassette tape, can create playful prints. Look for objects that are semi-opaque.

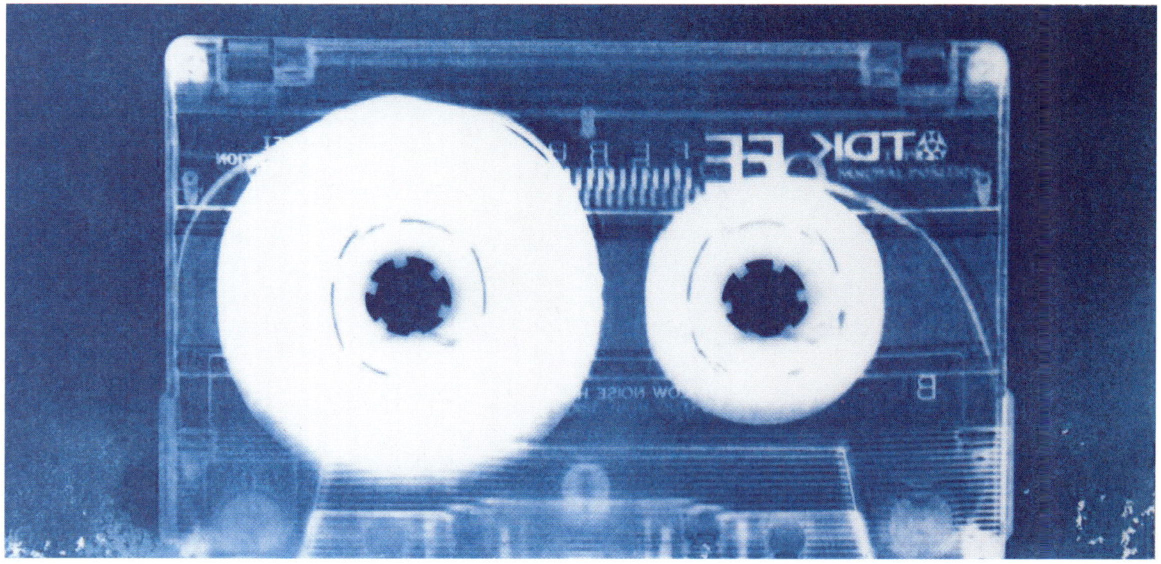

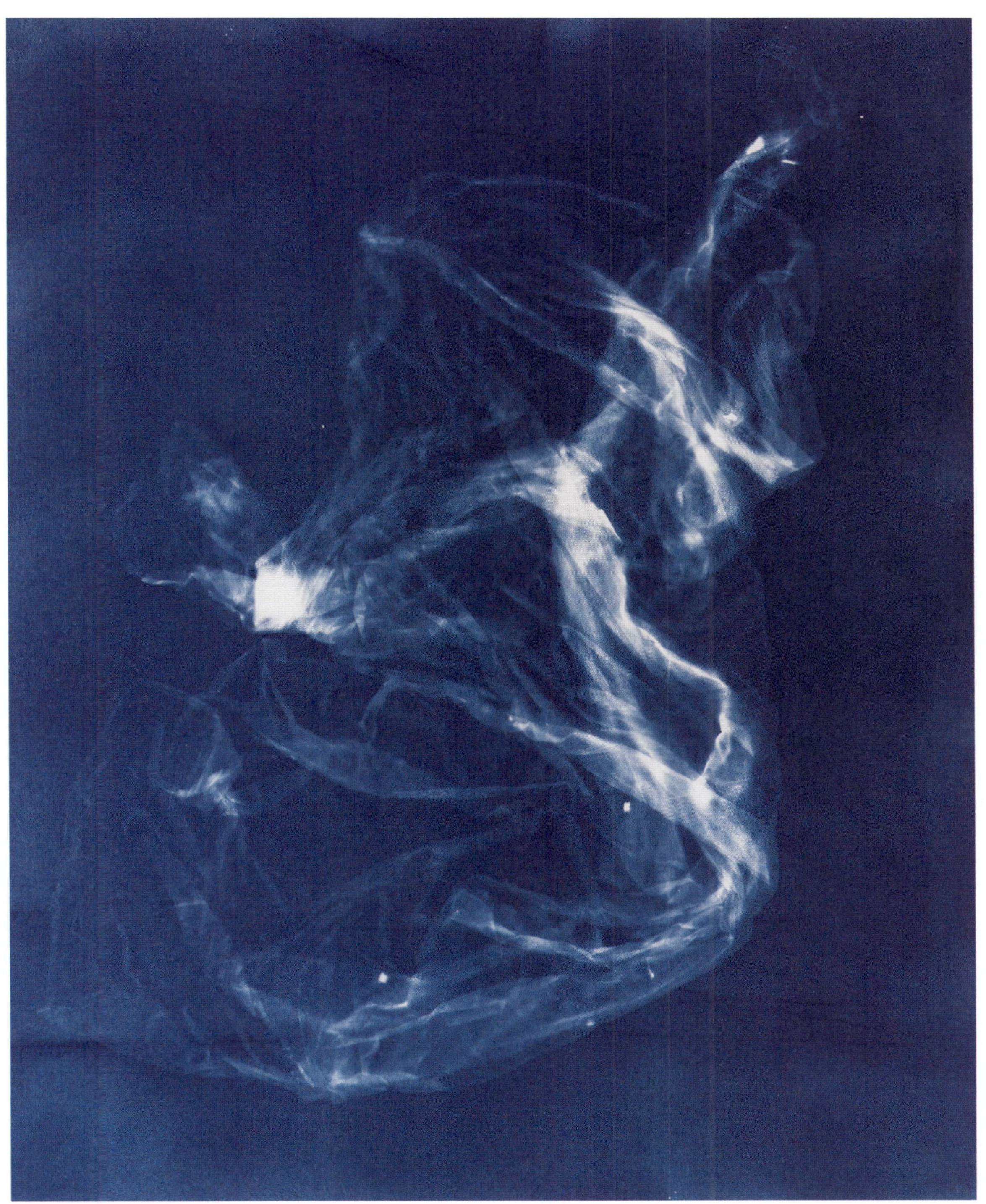

Elizabeth Ellenwood's work is a striking demonstration of how disregarded objects can create powerful art.

# Photogram with Glass Objects

This project will allow you to play with light in a unique way. By using glass objects, you can impact the way light is refracted, taking advantage of the shadows in your print. Cut crystal and glass work particularly well for this project. Be aware that as the sun moves throughout the day, it will impact how the shadows move in your composition.

## Materials

- Plastic washing tray larger than the cyanotype paper
- Clothesline and clothespins or sheets of clean cardboard
- Glass objects: bottles, vases, heavy-bottomed drinking glasses, or any cut-glass object
- Sheet of blank paper the same size as cyanotype paper
- Sheet of prepared paper (coated with cyanotype working solution, allowed to dry, and stored in a light-safe container)
- Plant material, pressed and dried or fresh, or other flat objects (optional)
- Sheet of cardboard (or any stiff material) the same size as the glass or acrylic
- Sheet of glass or acrylic larger than the cyanotype paper
- Binder clips or similar fasteners
- Gloves or tongs, for handling the print while rinsing (optional)

1 **SET UP.** Gather your materials in a dimly lit prep space. Place the rinsing tray in your wash area and fill it with water. Set up a clothesline or sheets of clean cardboard as a drying station, somewhere away from direct light.

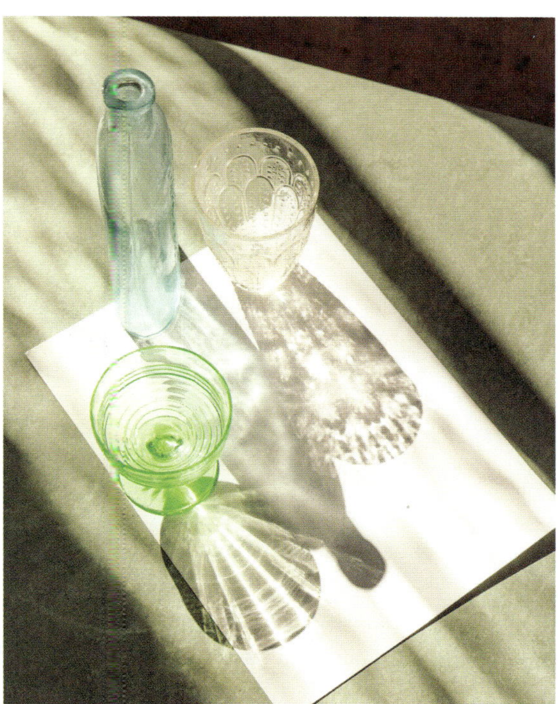

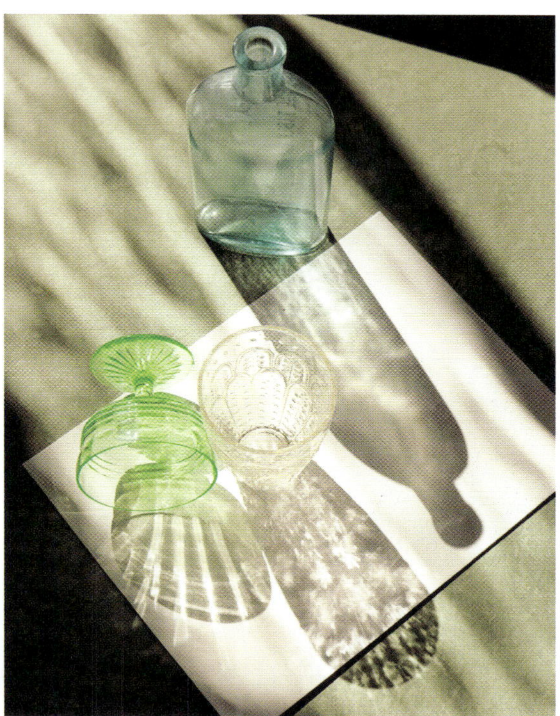

2 **ARRANGE THE COMPOSITION.** You'll begin by observing the shadows and reflections your selected objects cast in sunlight. For these observations, use a sheet of blank paper, the same size as your prepared cyanotype paper, and place it in direct sunlight. Arrange your objects on top of the paper and note how the light interacts with them—how it falls, reflects, and creates shadows. These sections of light and dark will all impact the print. If you're using pressed plants or other flat objects, include them in your arrangements. The time of day will influence the angles of these shadows. When satisfied, leave your composition in place and retrieve your cyanotype paper.

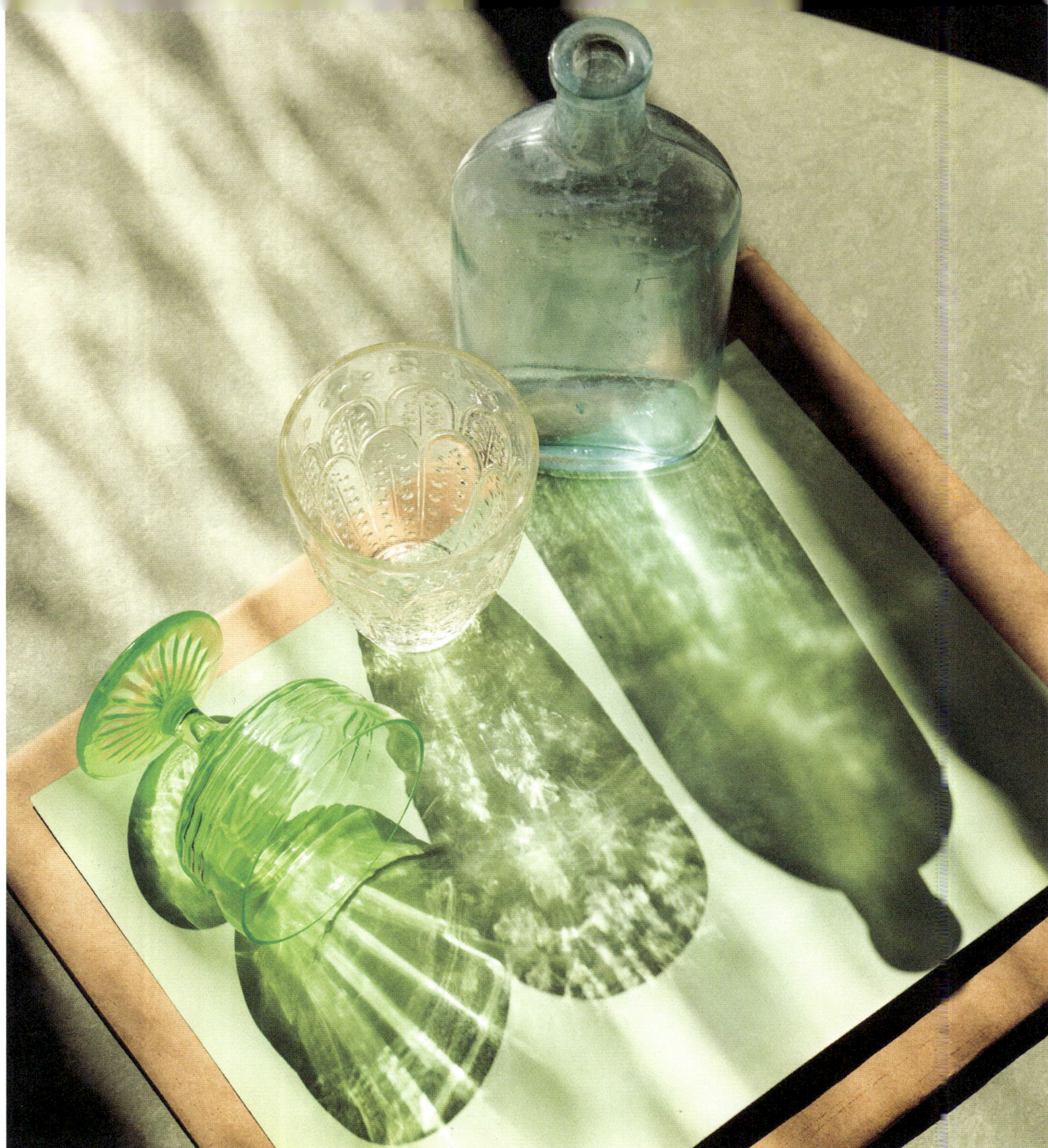

3 **PLACE THE CYANOTYPE PAPER.** Working in a low-light area, remove the cyanotype paper from its light-safe container, and place it on the cardboard backing with the light-green emulsion side facing up.

4 **SECURE THE MATERIALS (OPTIONAL).** Cover your paper with a sheet of glass or acrylic to secure it in a windy location or if you like the reflections and shadows that happen when a glass object is placed on top of a sheet of glass or acrylic. If using, secure the sheet of glass or acrylic to the cardboard backing with binder clips.

5 **EXPOSE TO SUNLIGHT.** Bring your paper and cardboard backing (along with the glass and clips, if using) to the arrangement created in step 2. Immediately position the glass objects along with any flat materials on top of the cyanotype paper to re-create the arrangement. Exposure time will vary depending on the strength of the sunlight and the time of year, as detailed on page 56. As the cyanotype develops, the light-green emulsion will react to the sun's UV rays, first turning a blue-green color, and then continuing to change.

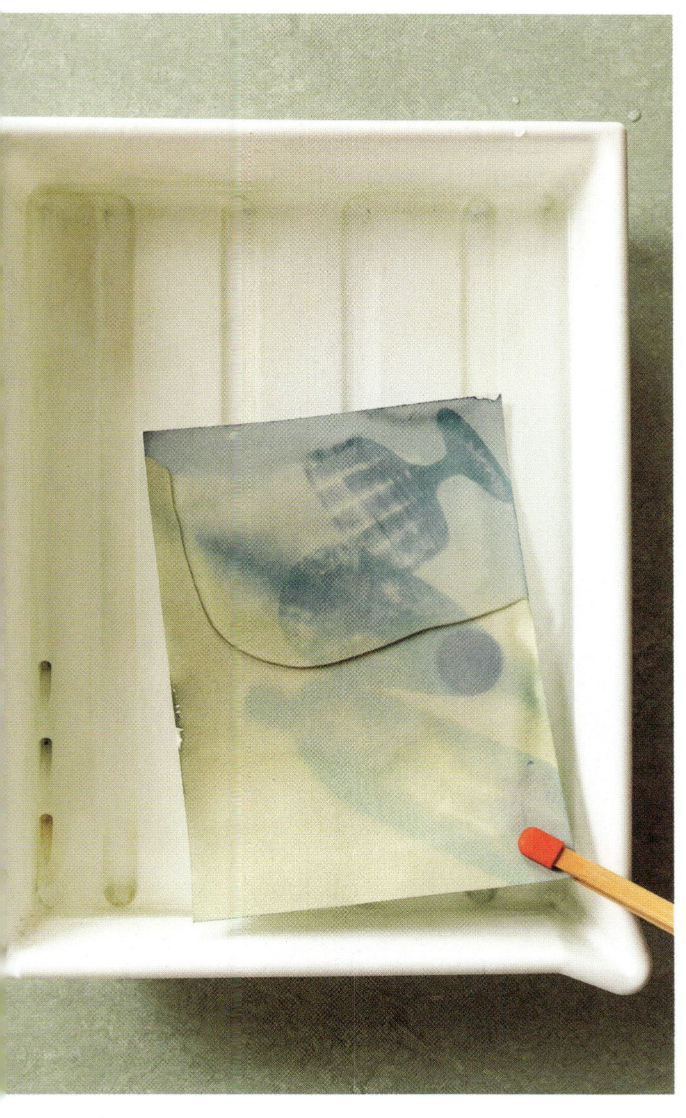

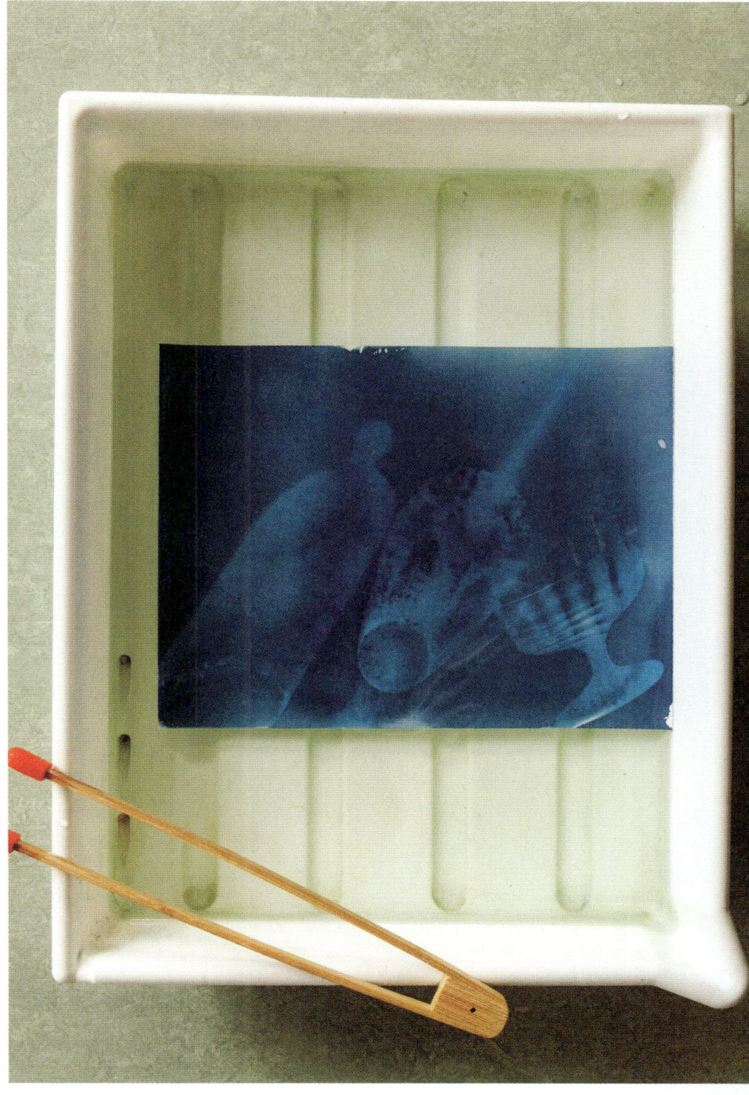

6 **MONITOR DEVELOPMENT.** When the emulsion turns bronze or silvery gray, the print is ready. To stop the exposure, move your setup out of direct sunlight.

7 **DISMANTLE AND WASH.** Carefully take the setup apart, removing the objects, clips, and the glass or acrylic. Place the exposed cyanotype paper in the tray of water; wear gloves or use tongs, if you like, to minimize skin contact with the chemicals. Wash the print under running water for 5 to 15 minutes, until the light-green chemicals are fully rinsed away and the water runs clear.

8 **DRY THE PRINT.** Lay the print on a flat work surface or hang it from a line using clothespins to dry. Keep the print away from direct sunlight during the drying period to prevent fading. After drying, if the print appears wrinkly, place it between two sheets of clean paper and cover it with books or other weights to flatten.

# Photogram Landscape with Torn Paper

This project invites a creative exploration of the abundance of paper in our everyday lives. Junk mail, notebooks, craft paper, and paper from packaging materials block more light than wax paper or typing paper. Card stock from greeting cards and manilla folders block even more light; cardboard blocks it entirely. By layering papers with different opacities in your composition, you can create depth and movement.

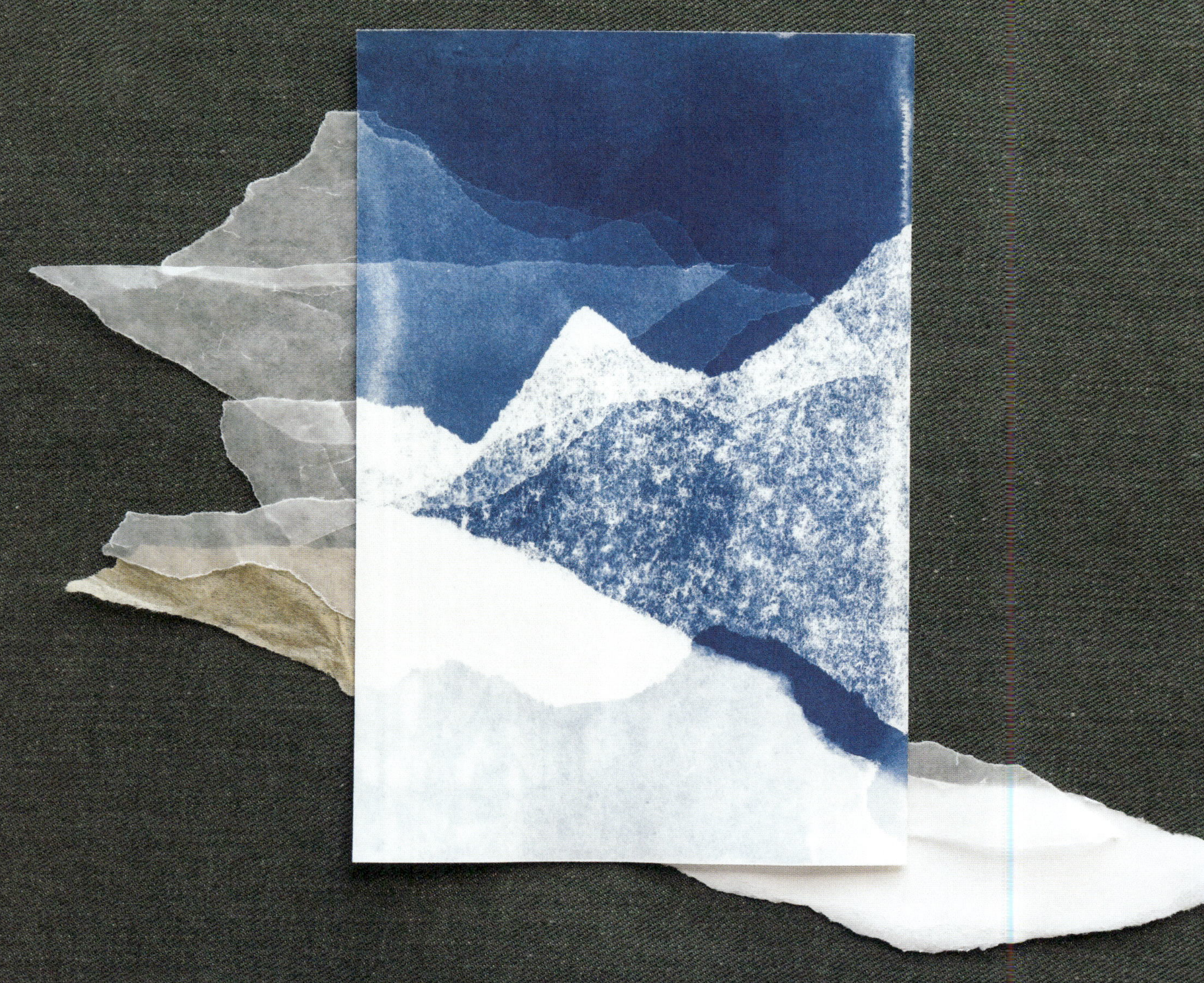

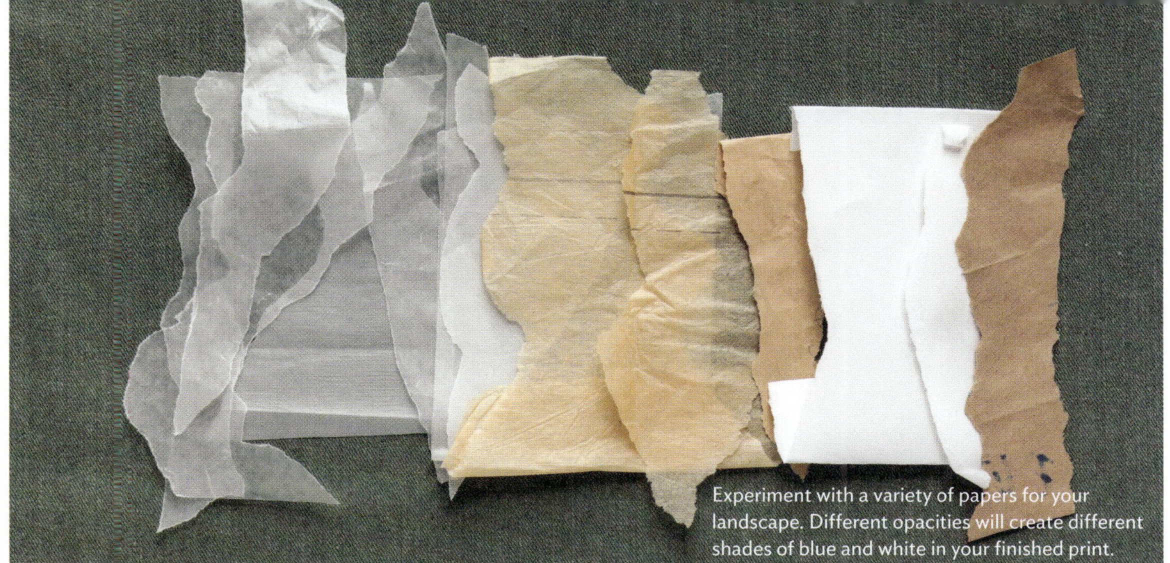

Experiment with a variety of papers for your landscape. Different opacities will create different shades of blue and white in your finished print.

## Materials

- Plastic washing tray larger than the cyanotype paper
- Clothesline and clothespins or sheets of clean cardboard
- Various types of paper (try it with wax, copy, handmade, and so on)
- Sheet of prepared paper (coated with cyanotype working solution, allowed to dry, and stored in a light-safe container)
- Sheet of cardboard (or any stiff material) the same size as the glass or acrylic
- Sheet of glass or acrylic larger than the cyanotype paper
- Binder clips or similar fasteners
- Gloves or tongs, for handling the print while rinsing (optional)

1 **SET UP.** Gather your materials in a dimly lit prep space. Place the rinsing tray in your wash area and fill it with water. Set up a clothesline or sheets of clean cardboard as a drying station, somewhere away from direct light.

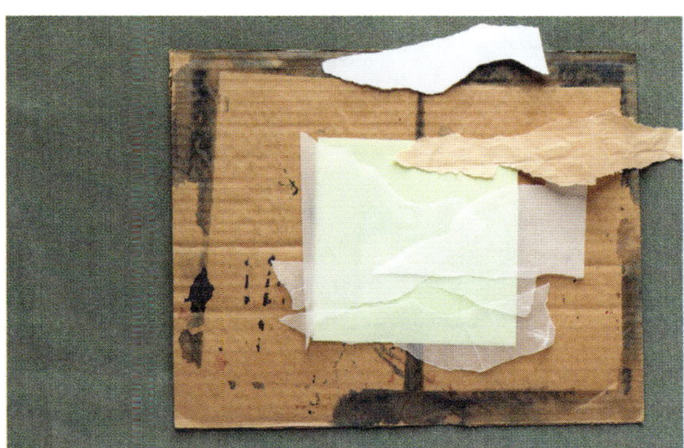

2 **ARRANGE THE COMPOSITION.** Tear your papers into various shapes. Wrinkle, crumple, and fold pieces to create interesting textures. Working in a low-light area, remove a sheet of prepared cyanotype paper from its light-safe container and place it, emulsion side up, on the cardboard backing. Arrange pieces of torn paper directly on the cyanotype paper to create a composition.

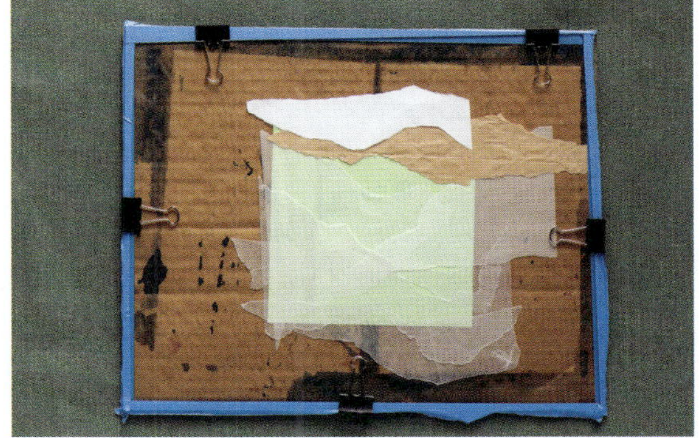

3 **SECURE THE MATERIALS.** Cover the composition with a sheet of glass or acrylic. Check the placement of your elements and make any necessary adjustments if they've shifted. Secure the glass or acrylic to the cardboard backing with binder clips.

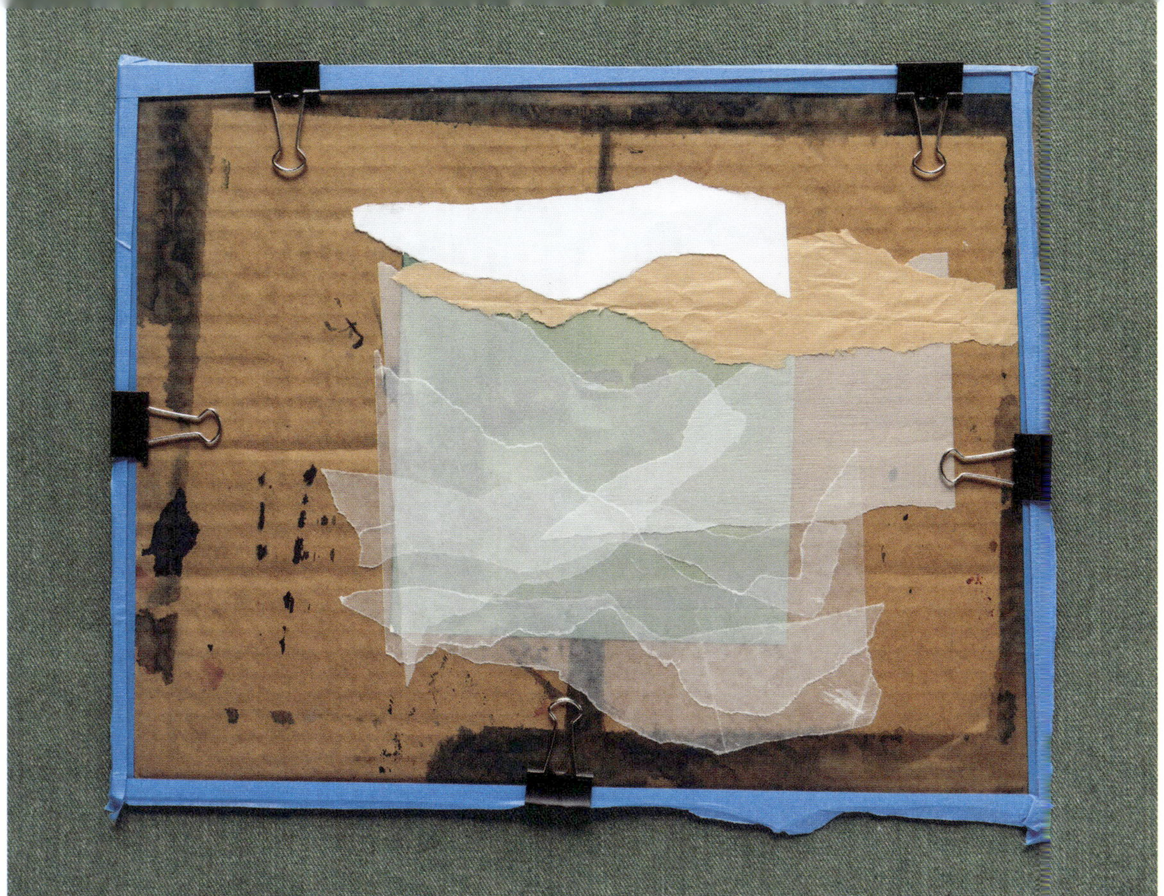

4 **EXPOSE TO SUNLIGHT.** Place your secured paper and glass setup in direct sunlight. The exposure time will vary depending on the strength of the sunlight and the time of year, as detailed on page 56. As the cyanotype develops, that light-green emulsion will react to the sun's UV rays, first turning a blue-green color, and then continuing to change.

5 **MONITOR DEVELOPMENT.** When the emulsion turns bronze or silvery gray, the print is ready. To stop the exposure, move your setup out of direct sunlight.

6 **DISMANTLE AND WASH.** Carefully take the setup apart. Place the exposed cyanotype paper in the tray of water; wear gloves or use tongs, if you like, to minimize skin contact with the chemicals. Wash the print under running water for 5 to 15 minutes, until the light-green chemicals are fully rinsed away and the water runs clear.

7 **DRY THE PRINT.** Lay the print on a flat work surface or hang it from a line using clothespins to dry. Keep the print away from direct sunlight during the drying period to prevent fading. After drying, if the print appears wrinkly, place it between two sheets of clean paper and cover it with books or other weights to flatten.

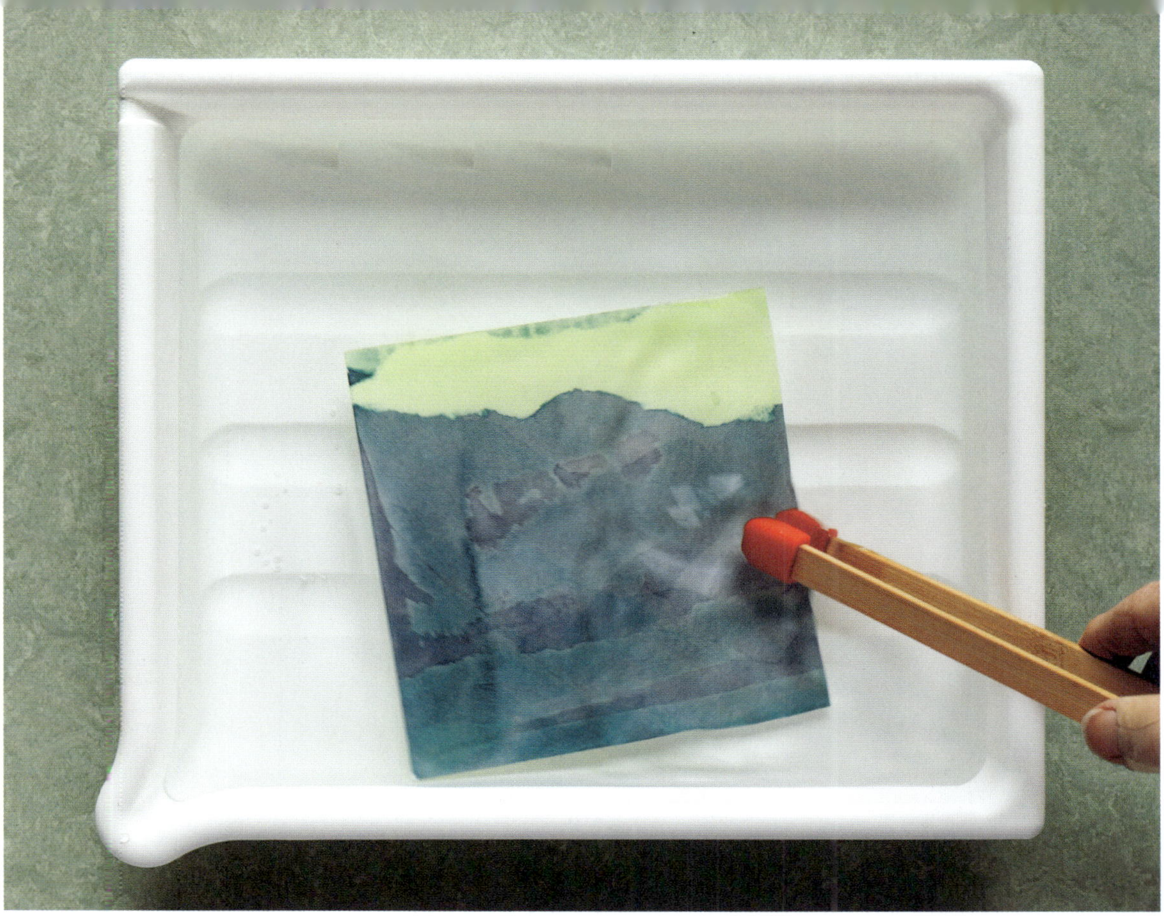

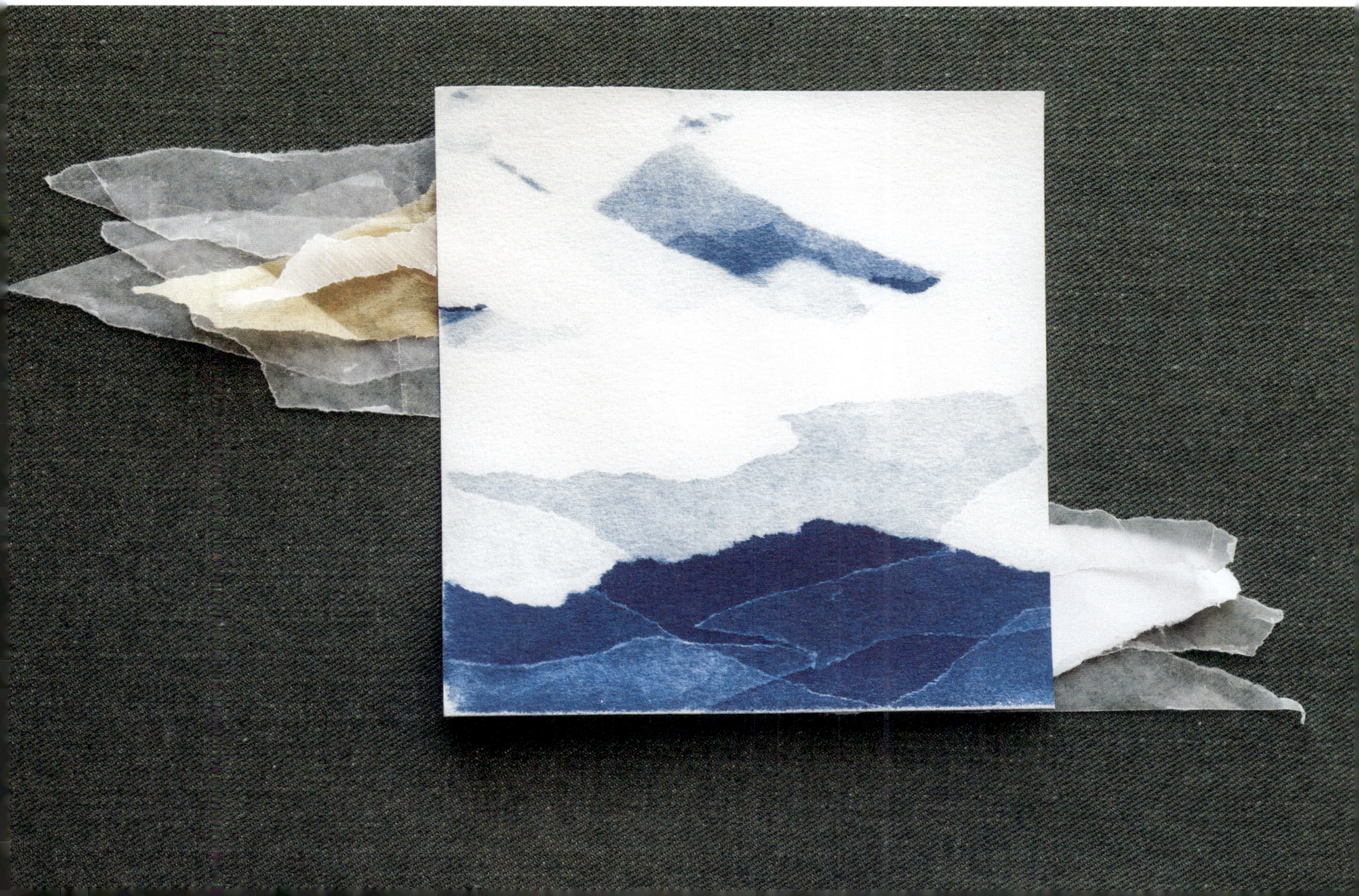

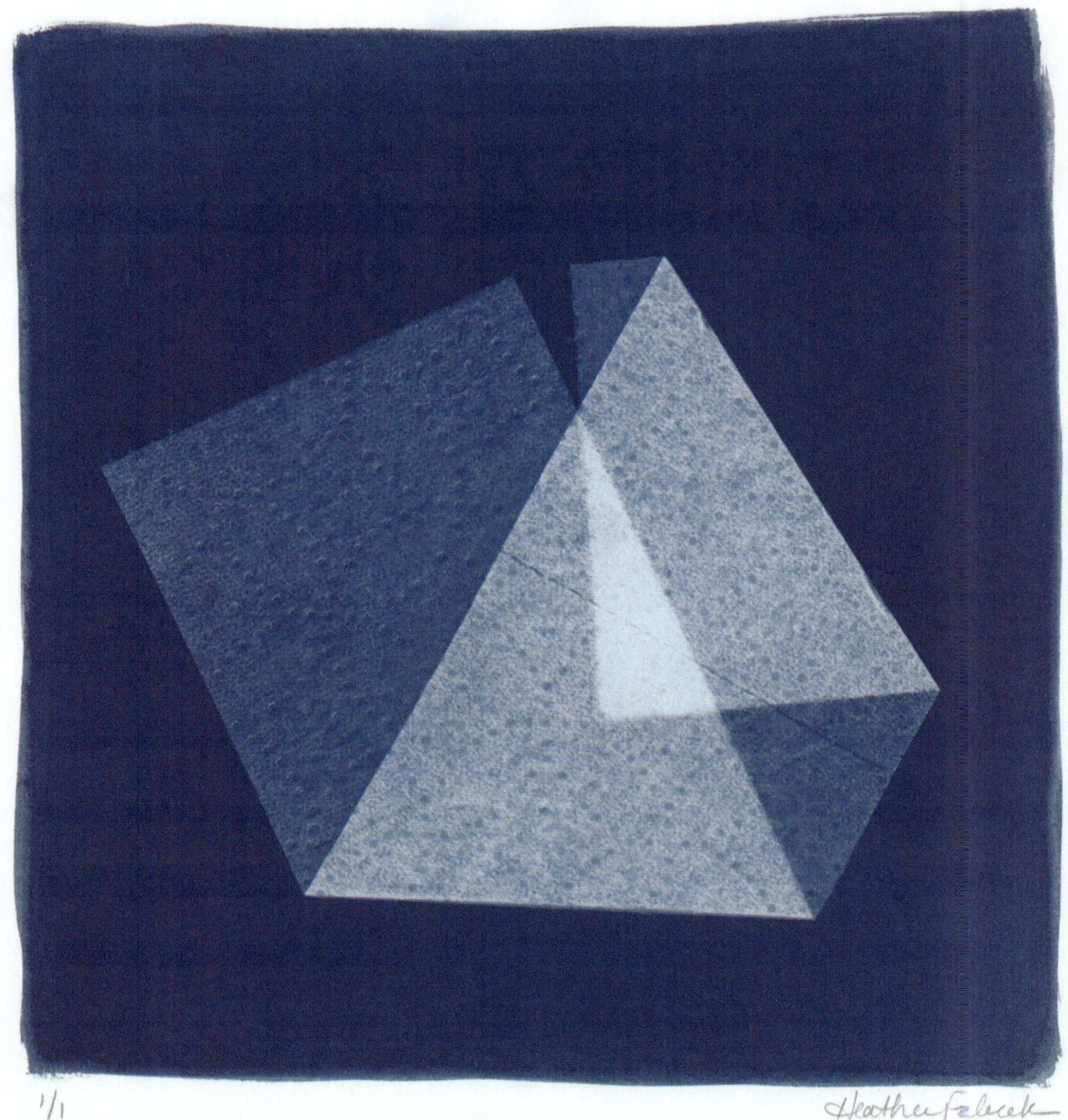


Heather Palecek's cyanotype photogram series, *Toilet Paper Art*, features meticulously folded sheets of toilet paper created in March 2020. Heather playfully observes that humans have always made "art about the things most important to us."

## RECOVERING A "FAILED" PRINT

Sometimes a print doesn't come out as expected. It might be too dark or the printed object isn't clearly visible the way you'd hoped. Before you give it up for a lost cause, there are a few different ways to redeem it. Lightening the print with bleaching (see page 130) can sometimes reveal the printed object more clearly. Or try creating a secondary exposure (see page 68) to transform your "failed" project into something stunning.

# Printing from Negatives

Even though they have little in common with what we consider to be modern cameras, cyanotypes are an early photographic method. By using digital or film negatives, you can combine modern photographic techniques with the handcrafted nature of the cyanotype. Negatives reverse the values of an image, showing the light parts of the image as dark and the darker parts as light. When placed over paper coated with a cyanotype emulsion, the darker, opaque parts of the negative shield those sections of the paper from light, creating a true representation of the image.

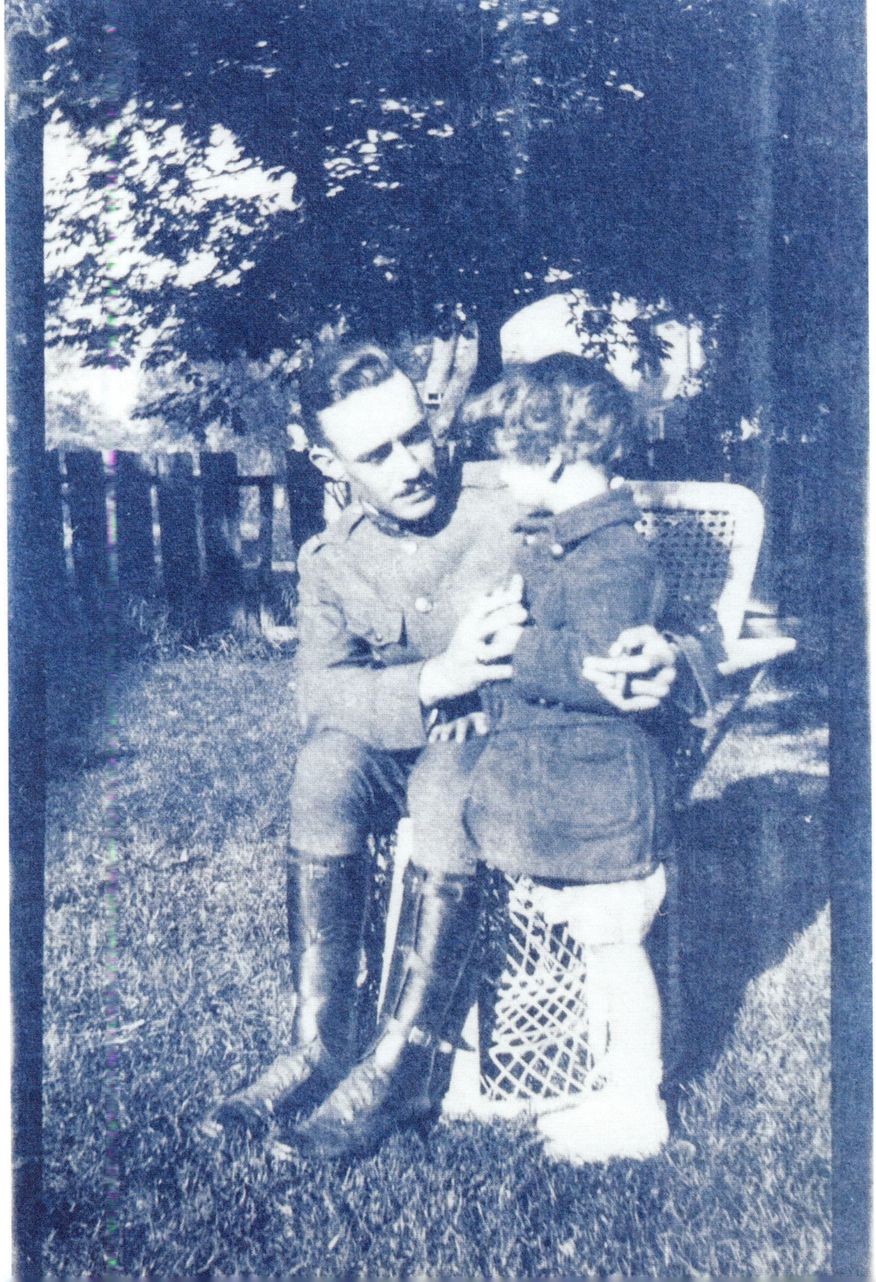

In 2020, while going through my mother's papers, I discovered a cache of black-and-white negatives. I was able to create a photograph from the negative using prepared cyanotype paper. The result is a photograph of my mother, Sheila Megargee Evers, and grandfather, J. Wilfred Megargee, in Beach Haven, New Jersey, circa 1932. The tenderness with which my grandfather holds his daughter, my mother, brought back my own memories of Tata, as I called him, who was a kind and loving man.

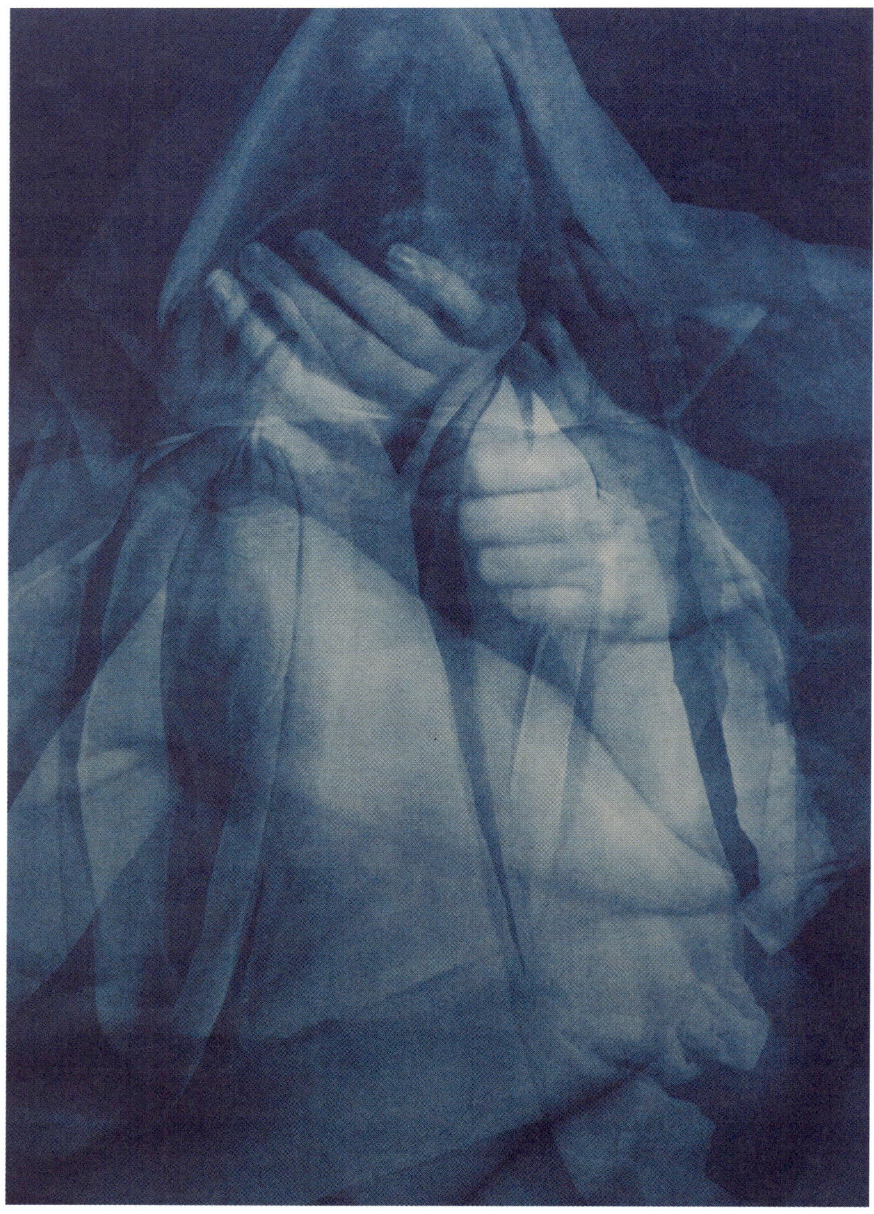

Liliana Guzmán's *Waiting* is a beautiful example of visual storytelling; the piece was created with a digital negative.

## *Working with Digital Negatives*

Another method for working with negatives is creating them digitally using tools like Gimp or Photoshop, or with Jacquard's online digital negative creator, and printing them on plastic transparencies. While this book doesn't cover the technical process of making digital negatives, the steps for creating a contact print with a digital negative are the same as with film negatives. Check out the Resources section on page 211 for guidance on creating a digital negative. You can also purchase cyanotype stencils online, which are negatives printed on a transparency, if you wish to add intricate elements to your work without creating a digital negative yourself. A key advantage of digital negatives is that you can customize them to any size you need.

# Contact Print with a Film Negative

To make a contact print, a negative is placed directly onto a sheet of photographic paper, in this case paper coated with cyanotype chemicals, secured with a piece of glass, exposed to light, and then fixed.

The exposure time will vary depending on the light, the negative, the paper, and other factors. I recommend running an exposure test to assess the quality of the print before making your finished piece of art. This is particularly important if you want to use the negative as a part of a large composition and thus can't easily redo it if the finished print isn't to your liking. An exposure test is a great use for any odd bits of coated paper you may have on hand.

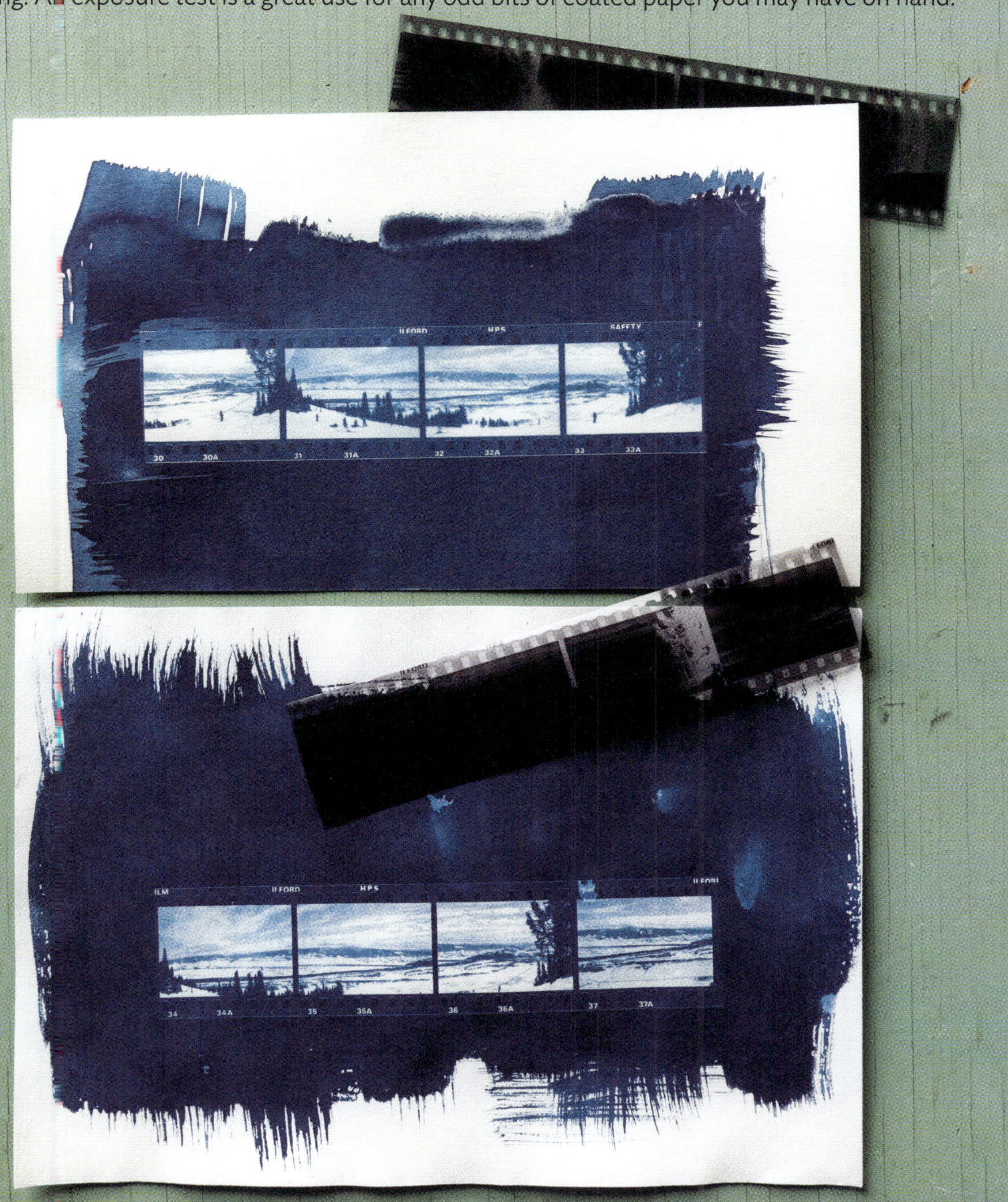

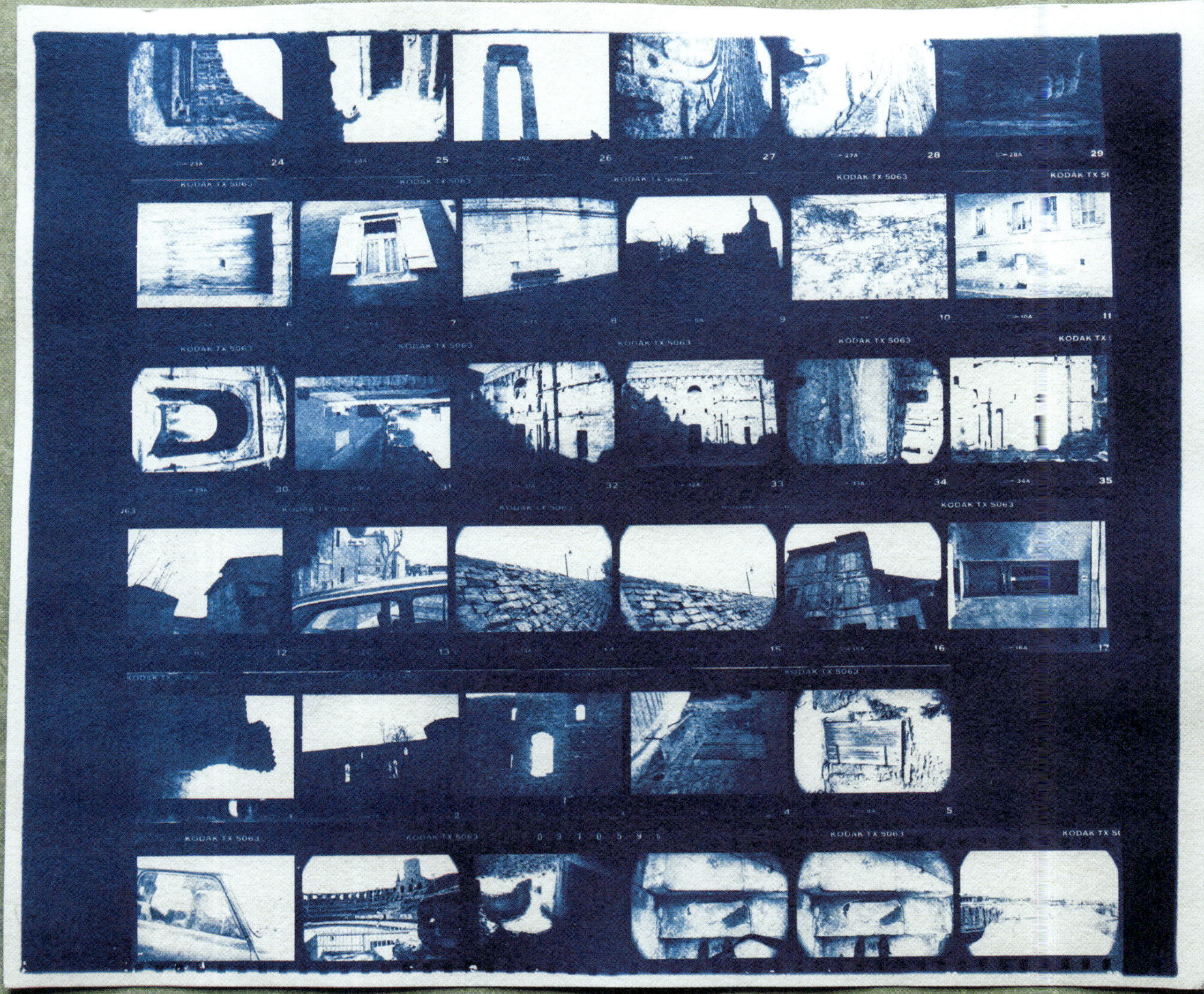


Contact printing these 35 mm negatives allowed me to resurrect a formative trip to Barcelona where I focused my camera on doorways and windows. So many portals!

## A NOTE ON FILM SIZE

When you make a cyanotype photograph from a black-and-white negative, the size of your photograph will match the size of your negative, which corresponds to the camera used to capture it. Film cameras are designed to hold specific film, ranging in size from 35 mm to 8 × 10 inches. If you have old negatives, they are likely to be 35 mm, and while the resulting image will be small, there's something special about creating a miniature photograph from the past.

Your negatives may be stored in a clear plastic sleeve that holds an entire roll of 35 mm negatives. If so, you can make an 8 × 10-inch contact sheet, called a proof sheet, by placing the entire sleeve, without removing the negatives, directly onto a sheet of cyanotype paper. An advantage to this method is that it minimizes direct contact between the negatives and the oils present on your skin. If made in this manner, the proof sheet, like the one above, will contain 24 to 36 small images.

## Materials

- Scrap piece of prepared paper
- Black-and-white negative
- Piece of prepared paper (coated with cyanotype working solution, allowed to dry, and stored in a light-safe container)
- Sheet of cardboard (or any stiff material) the same size as the glass or acrylic
- Sheet of glass or acrylic larger than the paper
- Binder clips or similar fasteners
- Plastic washing tray larger than the cyanotype
- Gloves or tongs, for handling the print while rinsing (optional)
- Clothesline and clothespins or sheets of clean cardboard

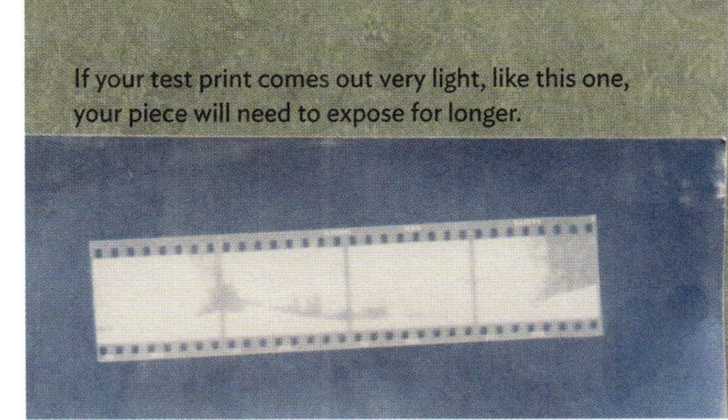

If your test print comes out very light, like this one, your piece will need to expose for longer.

**1 MAKE A TEST PRINT.** Use a scrap piece of coated paper to create a test print, following steps 2 to 5 in order to evaluate for highlights (light or white areas), shadows (dark areas), and tone (areas of color). The duration of exposure will vary depending on your negative's density and age. On a bright day, I recommend starting with an exposure time of 15 minutes. Once you've washed the print, evaluate it and increase or decrease the exposure time as needed before making your final print.

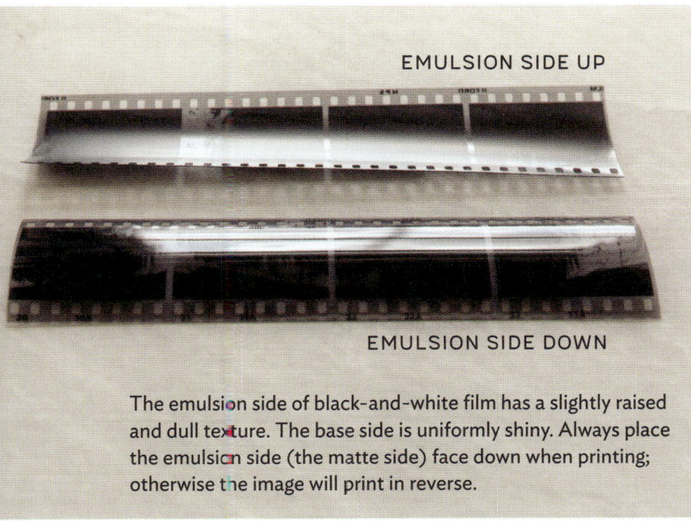


The emulsion side of black-and-white film has a slightly raised and dull texture. The base side is uniformly shiny. Always place the emulsion side (the matte side) face down when printing; otherwise the image will print in reverse.

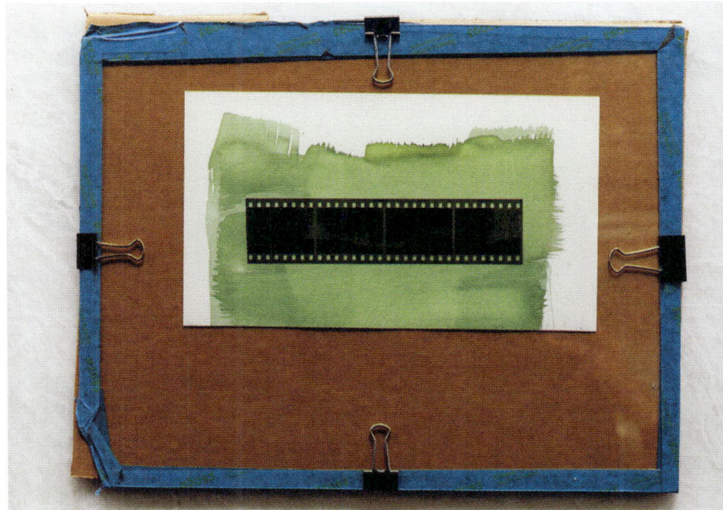

**2 ARRANGE THE PAPER AND NEGATIVE.** In low light, remove a sheet of prepared cyanotype paper from its light-safe container. Place the paper on a cardboard backing with the light-green emulsion side facing up. Position the negative, emulsion side (the matte side) down, on top of the paper. If the paper is coated only in a specific area, ensure that the negative is placed on the coated section.

**3 SECURE WITH GLASS OR ACRYLIC.** Cover the paper and negative with a sheet of glass or acrylic and secure the arrangement to the cardboard backing with binder clips.

**4 EXPOSE TO SUNLIGHT.** Place your setup in direct sunlight. Start a timer to run for the length of time you determined based on your exposure test.

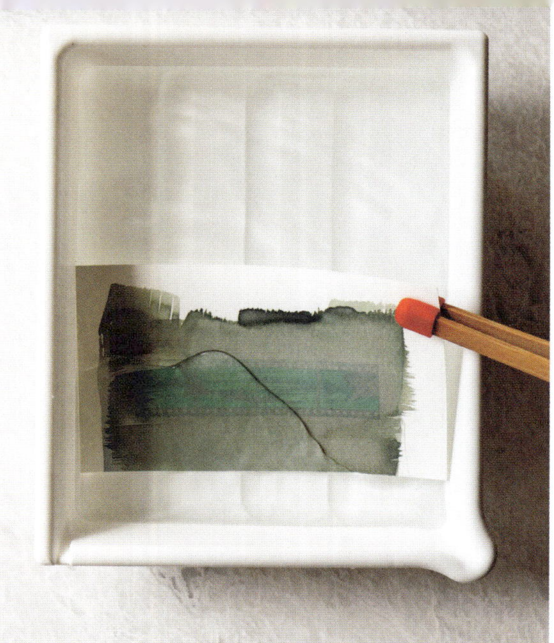

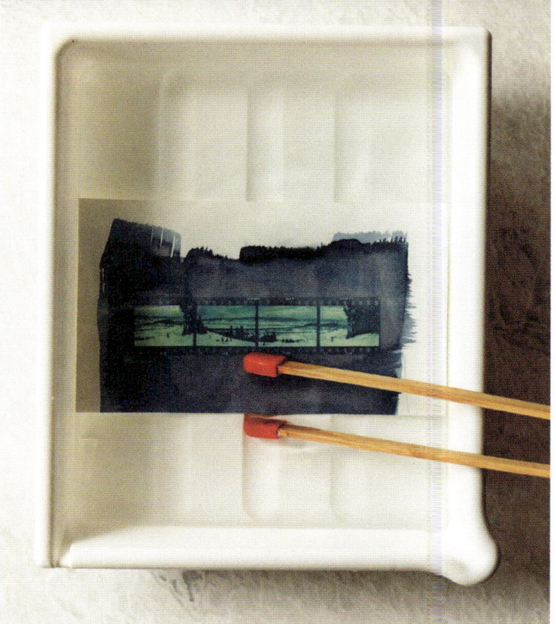

**5** **STOP THE EXPOSURE.** When the time is up, remove the setup from the UV light.

**6** **DISMANTLE AND WASH.** Remove the clips, glass or acrylic, and negative. Place the exposed paper in the tray of water; wear gloves or use tongs, if you like, to reduce skin contact with chemicals. Rinse the print in slowly running water or by filling and dumping the tray until the light-green chemicals are removed and the water is clear, 5 to 10 minutes.

**7** **DRY THE PRINT.** Set up a clothesline or sheets of clean cardboard as a drying station somewhere away from direct light. Hang or lay out the print and let it dry completely.

**NOTES** This process will not work with color negatives, which are calibrated for color photographic paper.

Always place the negative emulsion side (matte side) down; otherwise the image will print in reverse.

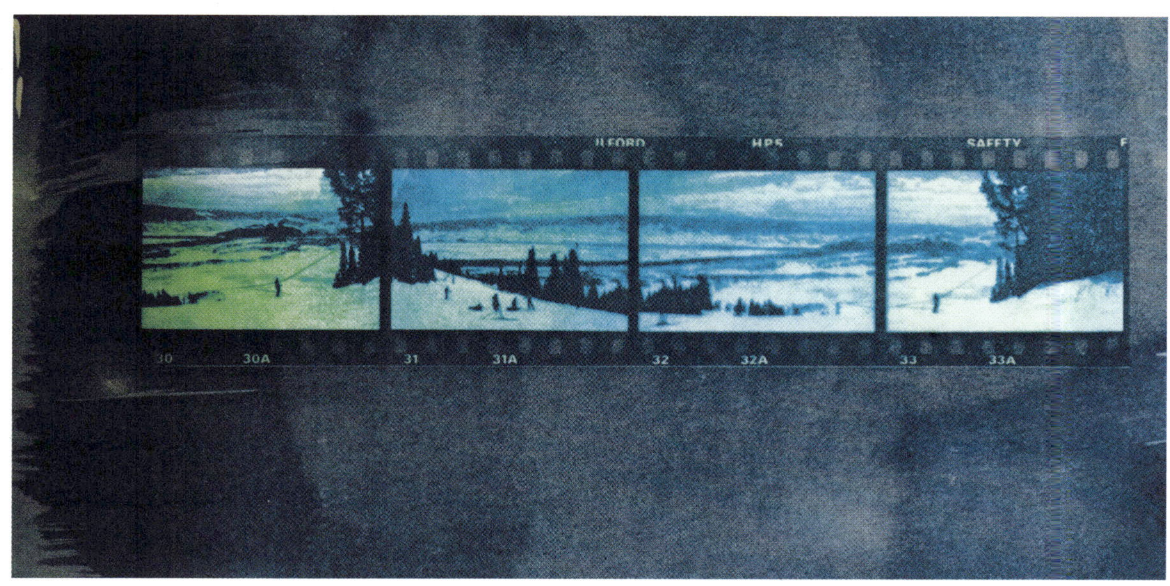

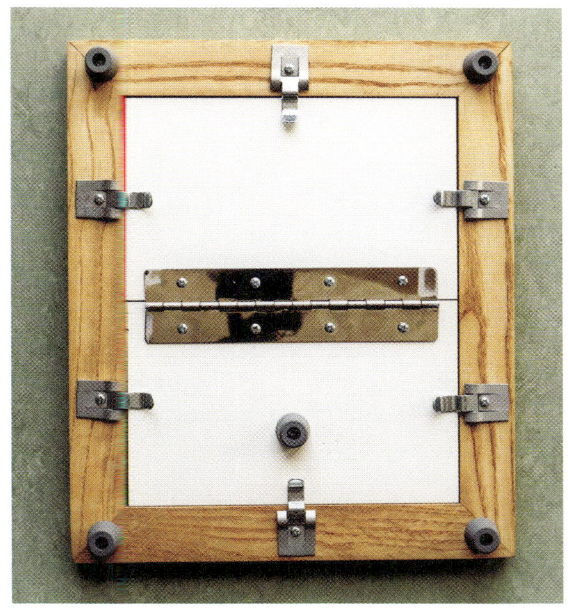

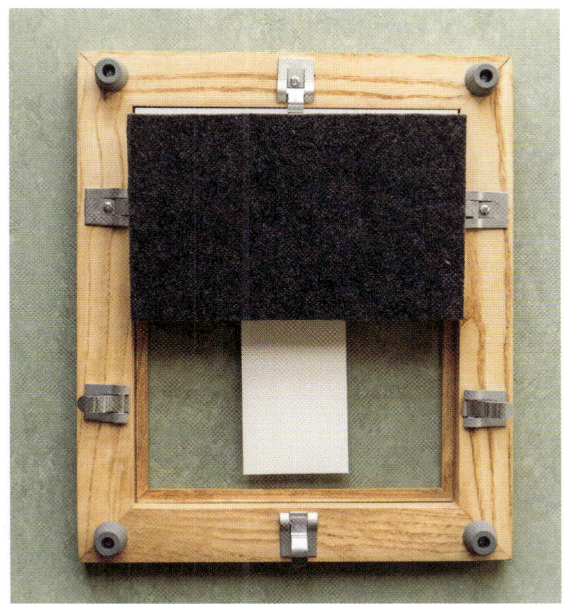

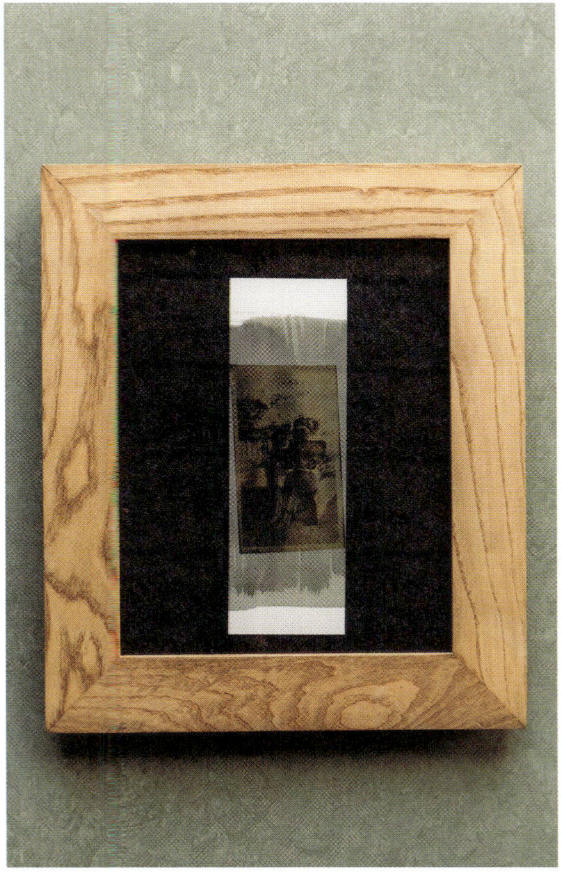

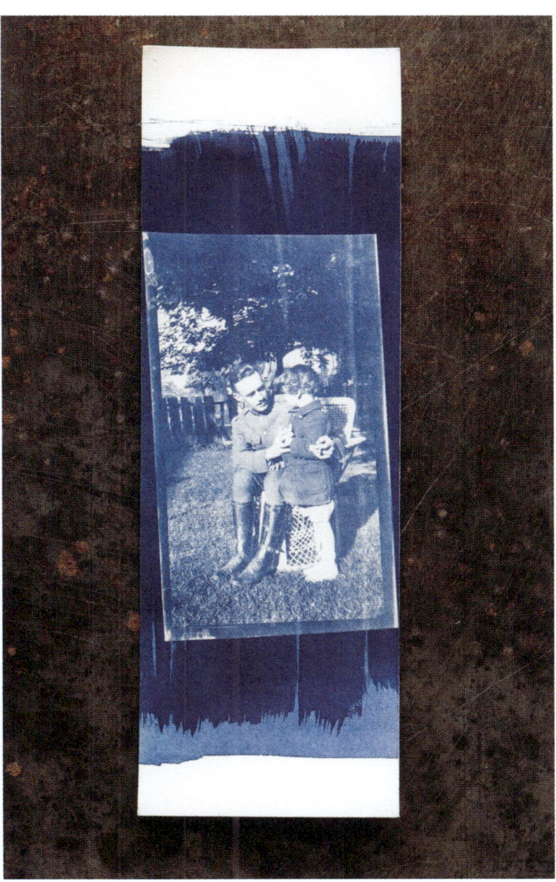

A contact print frame is a convenient and effective device for making contact prints and photograms; it can be purchased through photo supply stores (see the Resources section on page 211). Made with a hardwood frame, a piece of glass, and a felt-lined plywood back, the contact frame provides a tight fit between paper and negative or other flat objects.

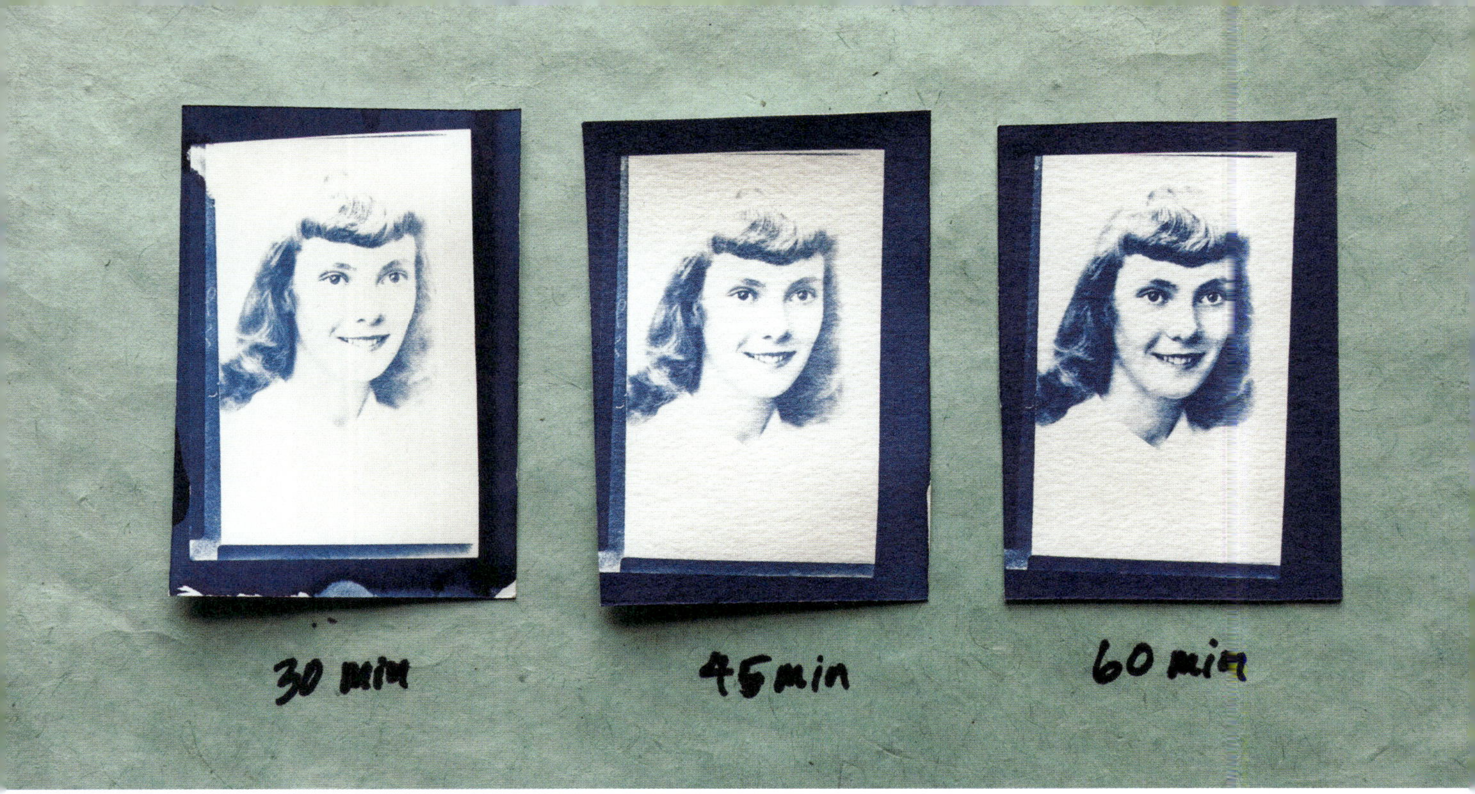

30 min

45 min

60 min

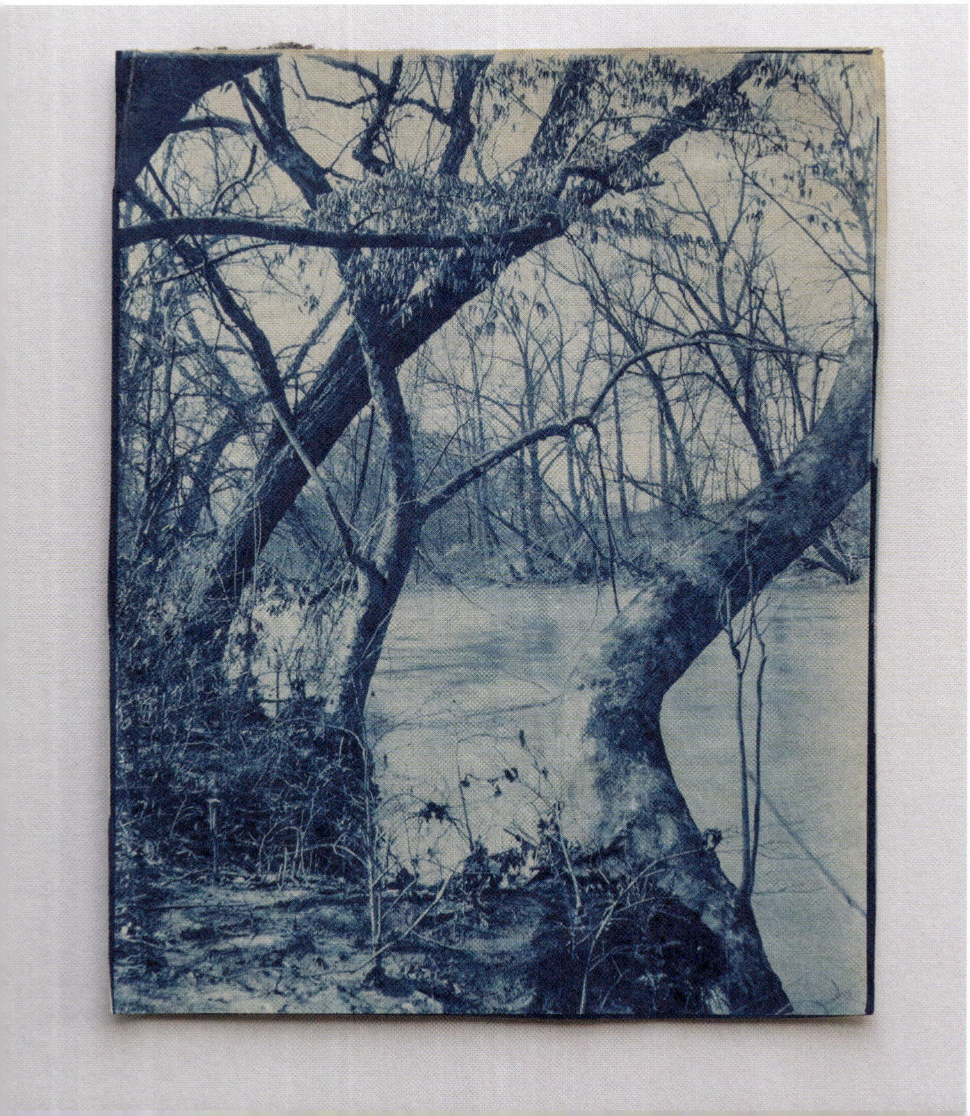

**ABOVE:** The printing time required for a negative can be highly variable, which is why creating a test print is helpful. This series was printed on a day with a low UV index. It took an hour to create a dark, high-contrast print using the negative from my mother's high school yearbook picture, circa 1947.

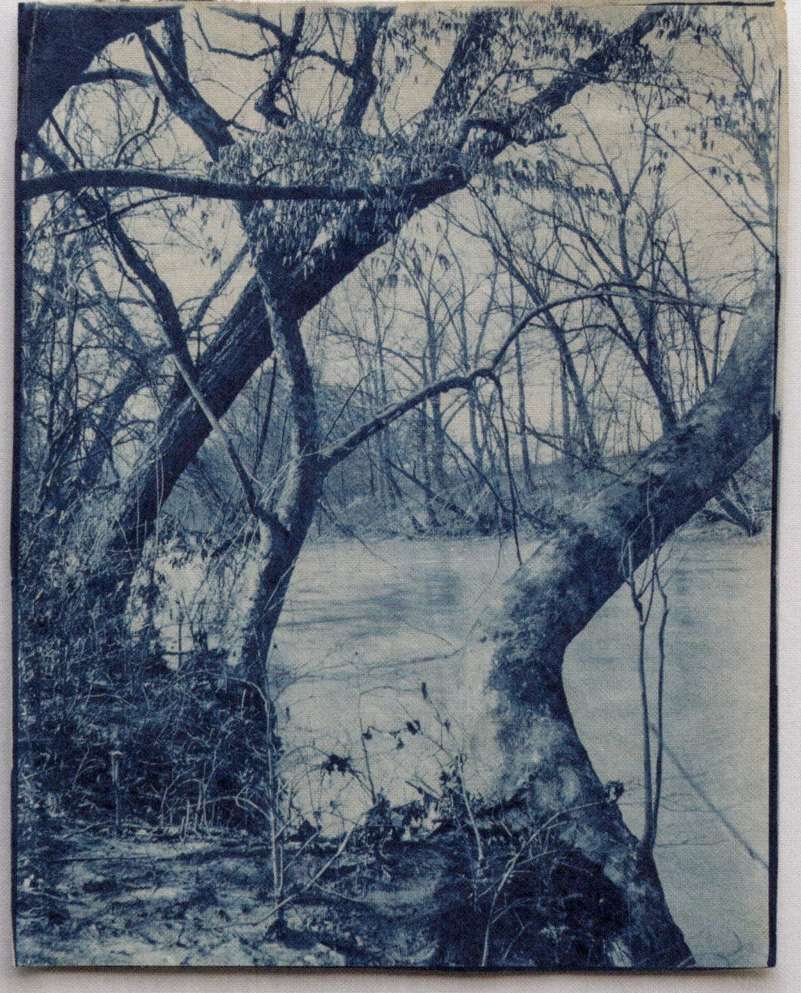

**LEFT:** I purchased this cyanotype landscape from a dealer of vintage photography and ephemera. It's a beautiful example of printing from a negative.

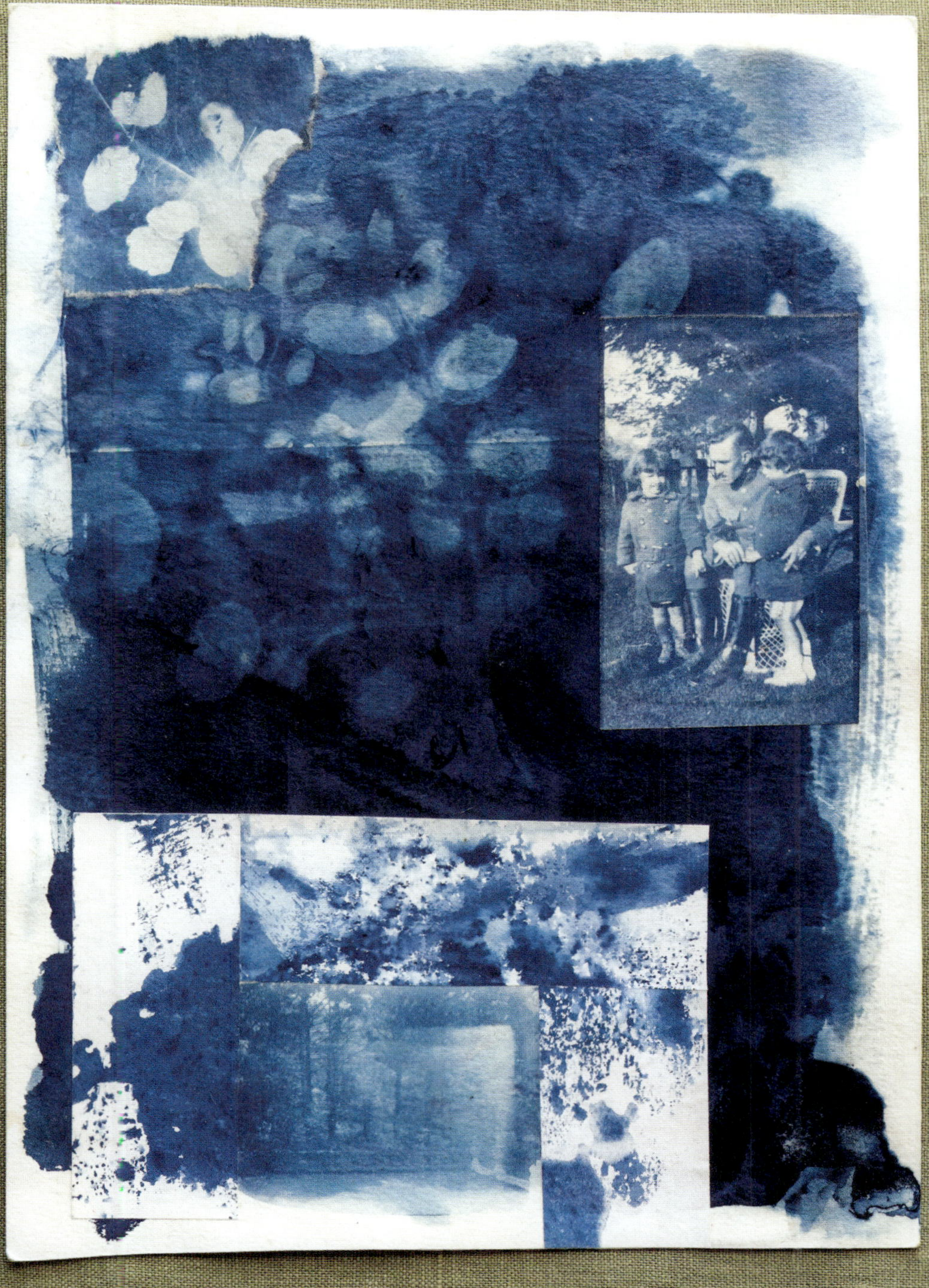

This collage was created by adhering contact prints made from vintage negatives and small cyanotype print "discards" to a larger botanical photogram. The finished piece was given more texture with cold wax medium.

## USING A 35 MM CONTACT PRINT

A 35 mm contact print on a large sheet of paper holds many possibilities for mixed-media work. Although very small, the image can be a compositional element for a larger piece. You could, for example, coat a small area on large sheet of paper with cyanotype chemicals and use the 35 mm negative to make a contact print, and then, afterward, apply cyanotype emulsion to other areas of the paper to create a photogram with botanical or other forms. You can also use it as a collage element, as I did above, or simply frame it with a large mat to create a tiny treasured piece of art.

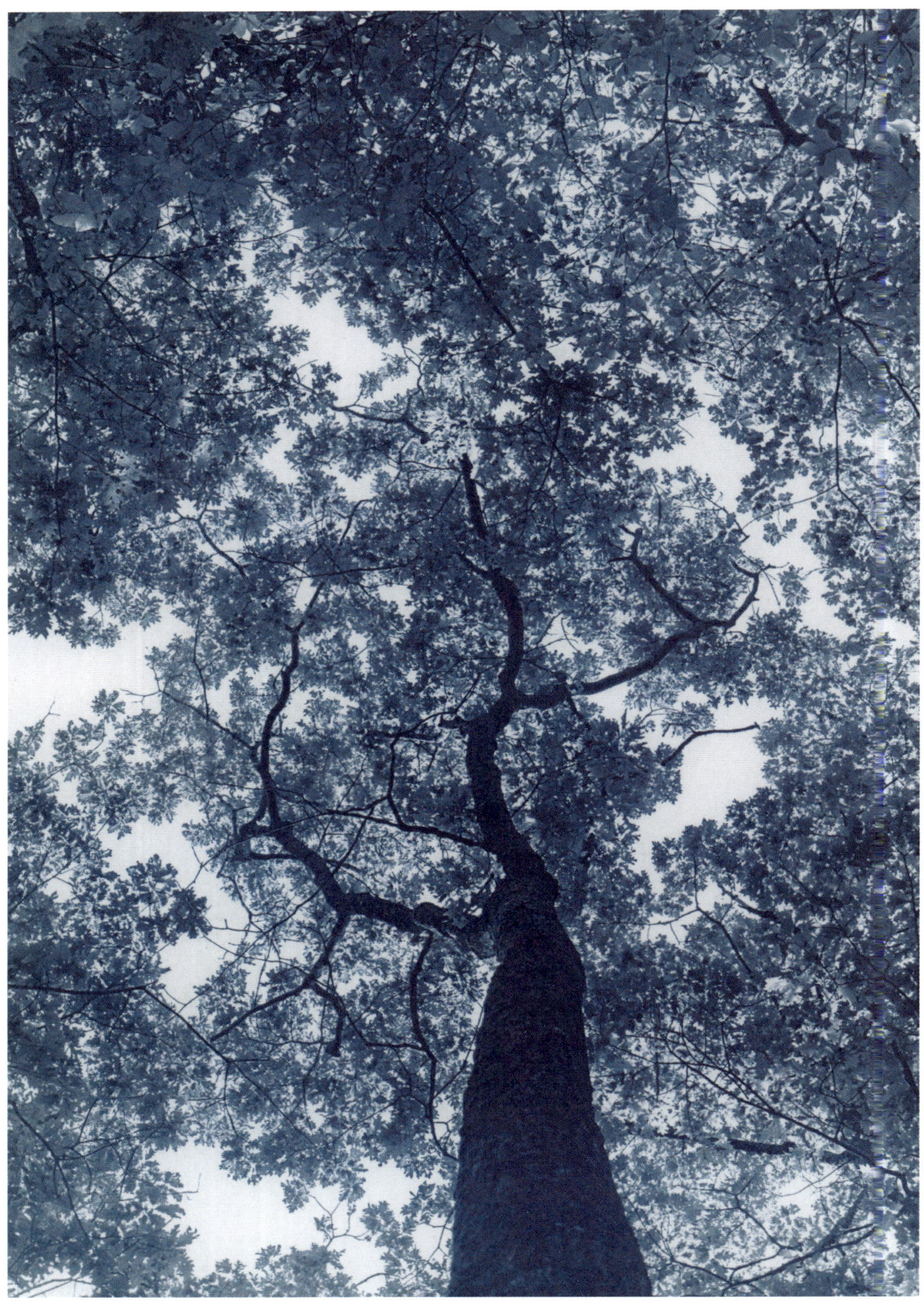

In the *By Her Side* series, Dora Somosi captures images of trees found at the homes and studios of women whose ideas have shaped history. Using oversize negatives, she creates strikingly immersive contact prints that bring these monuments to life. This piece, titled *Edna St. Vincent Millay*, *Steepletop, Austerlitz, NY*, honors the famous author.

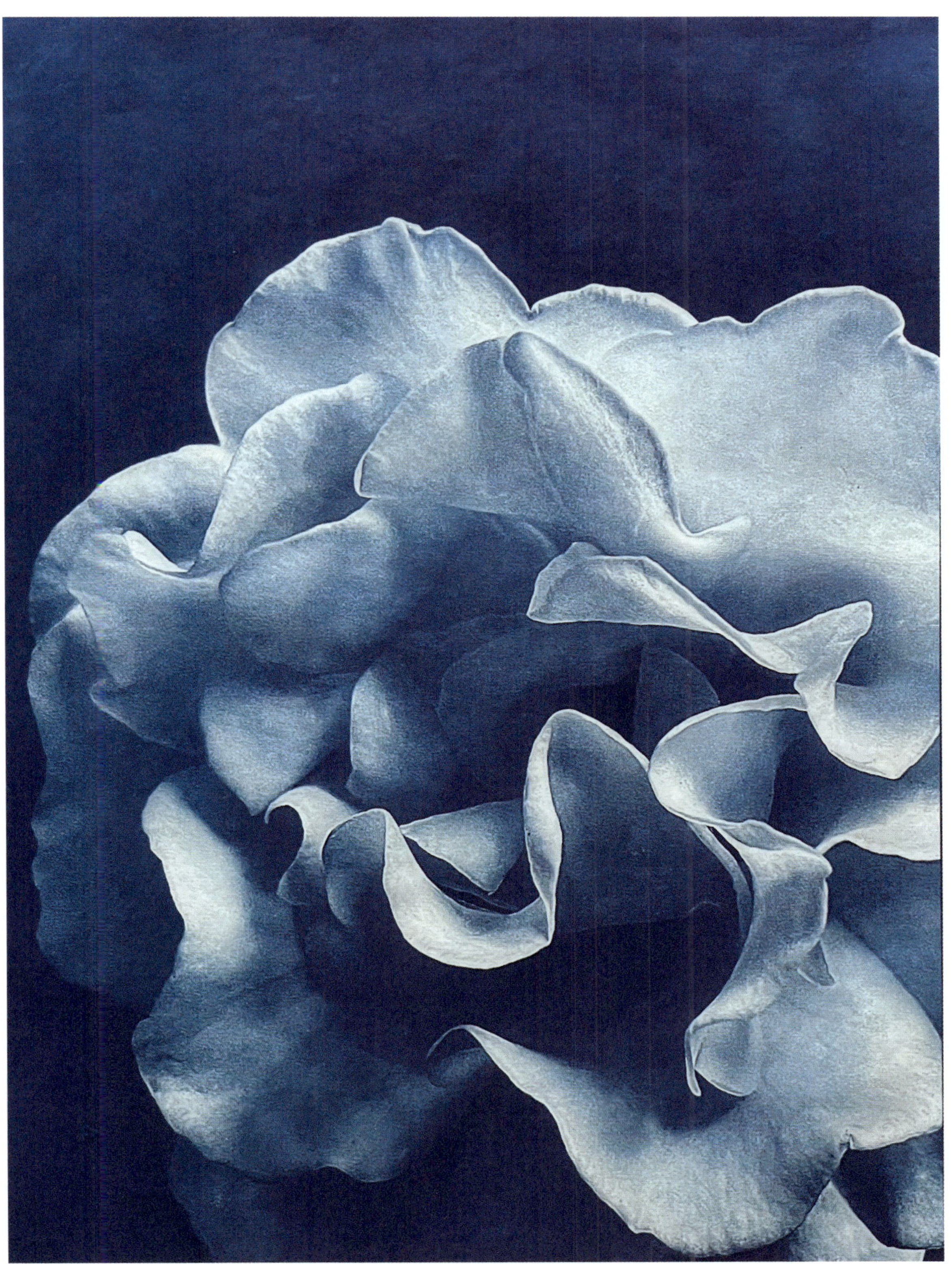

In *Luscious Waves*, Claudia Hollister uses a negative to create a contact print rich with evocative details.

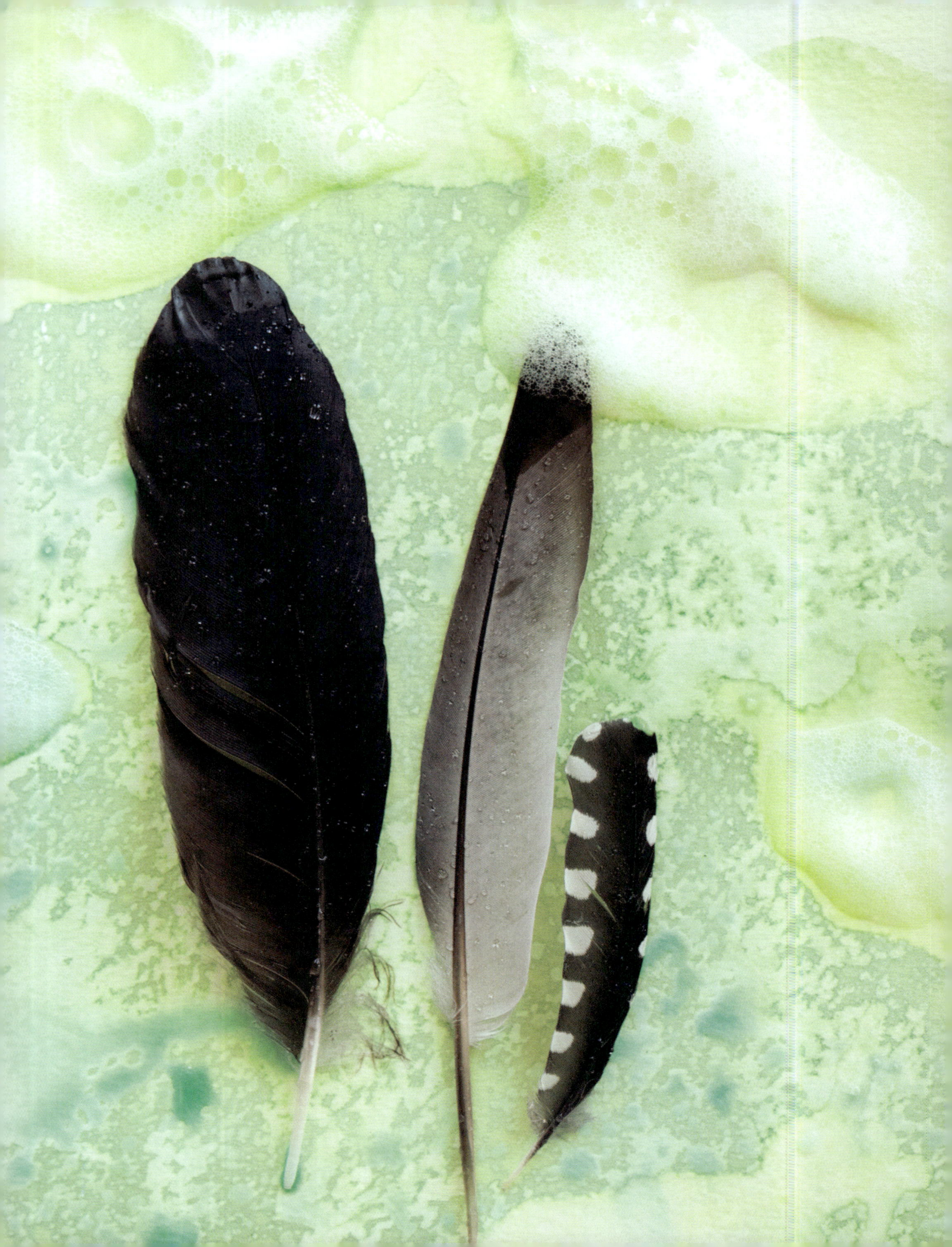

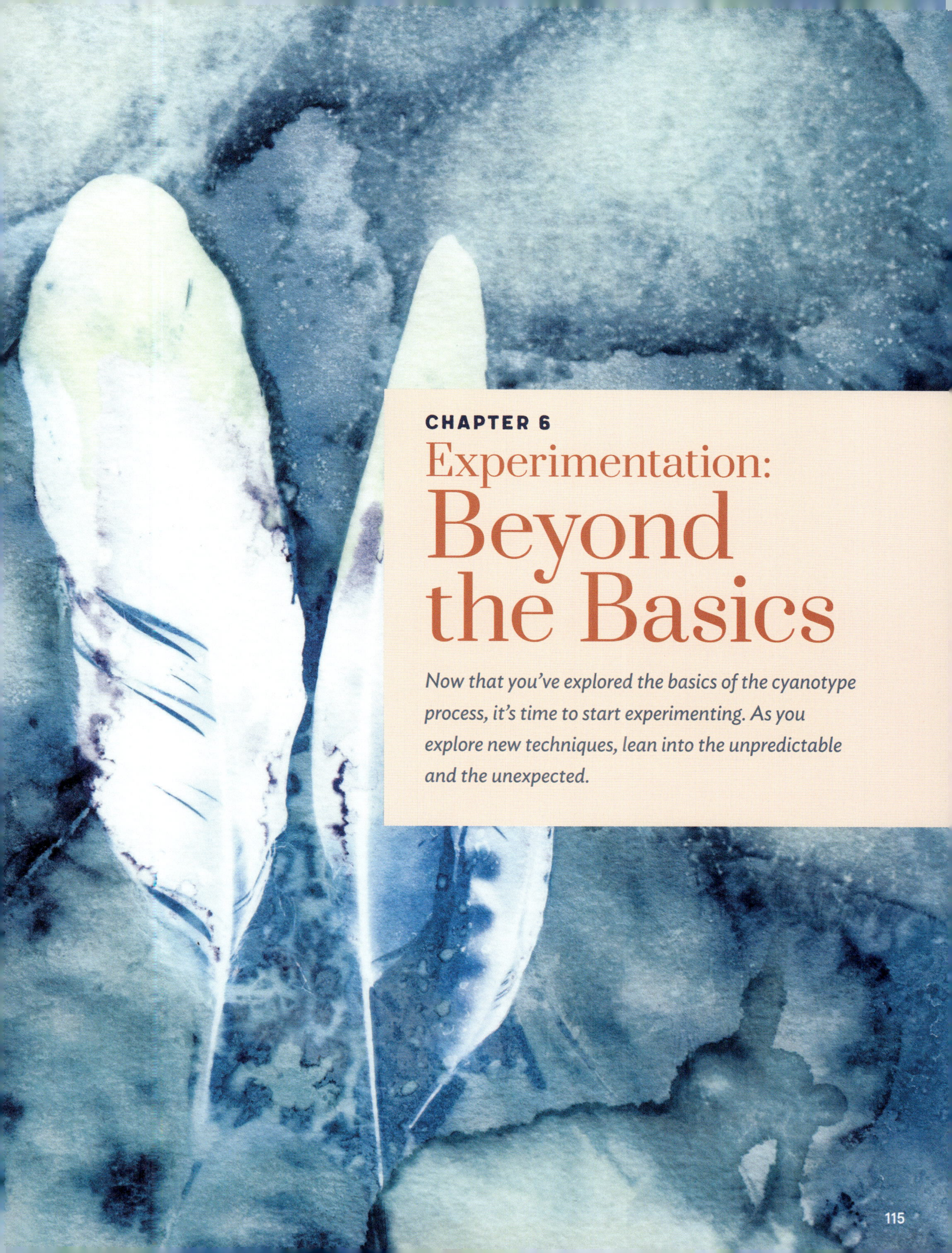

CHAPTER 6

# Experimentation: Beyond the Basics

*Now that you've explored the basics of the cyanotype process, it's time to start experimenting. As you explore new techniques, lean into the unpredictable and the unexpected.*

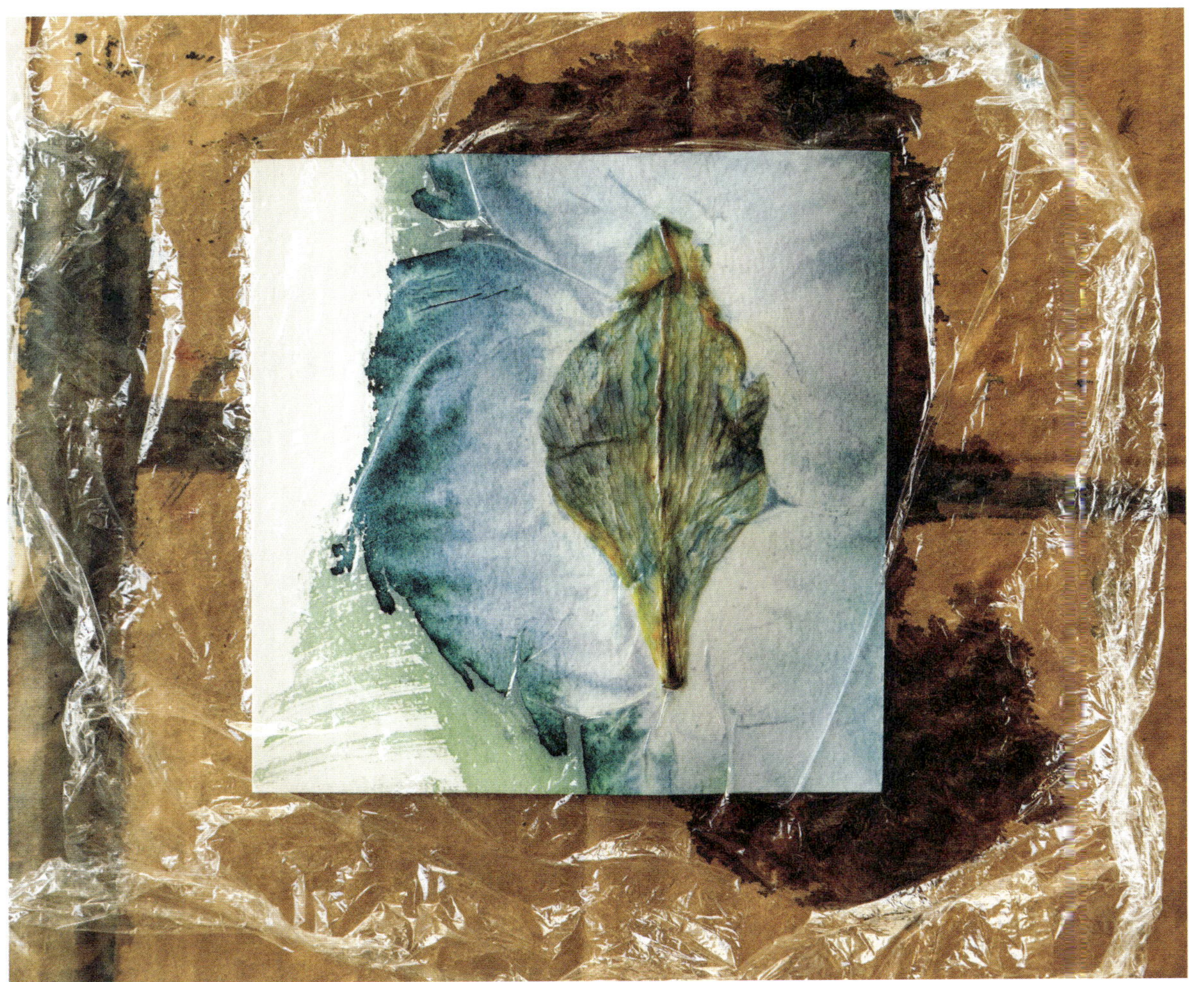

# Playing with pH

It's time to start exploring variations on the cyanotype process! While the basic equation of a cyanotype always remains the same—ferric ammonium citrate + potassium ferricyanide + light—there are numerous ways to tweak the process to create different colors and textures, as well as ways to alter your cyanotypes after you've created them.

The first method we'll explore is wet cyanotypes. By using vinegar, which contains acetic acid, you can lower the pH of the cyanotype chemicals. This enhances contrast, reduces fading during washing, and helps to create unexpected, multicolor cyanotypes. You can take the process even further by incorporating surprising elements like spice and soap bubbles.

The wet process was popularized by a video tutorial shared by artist Krista McCurdy in 2017. Embracing experimentation, McCurdy demonstrated how adding water to cyanotype-coated paper before exposure, combined with extended exposure times, could result in prints with wonderful variations in green, blue, and beige tones.

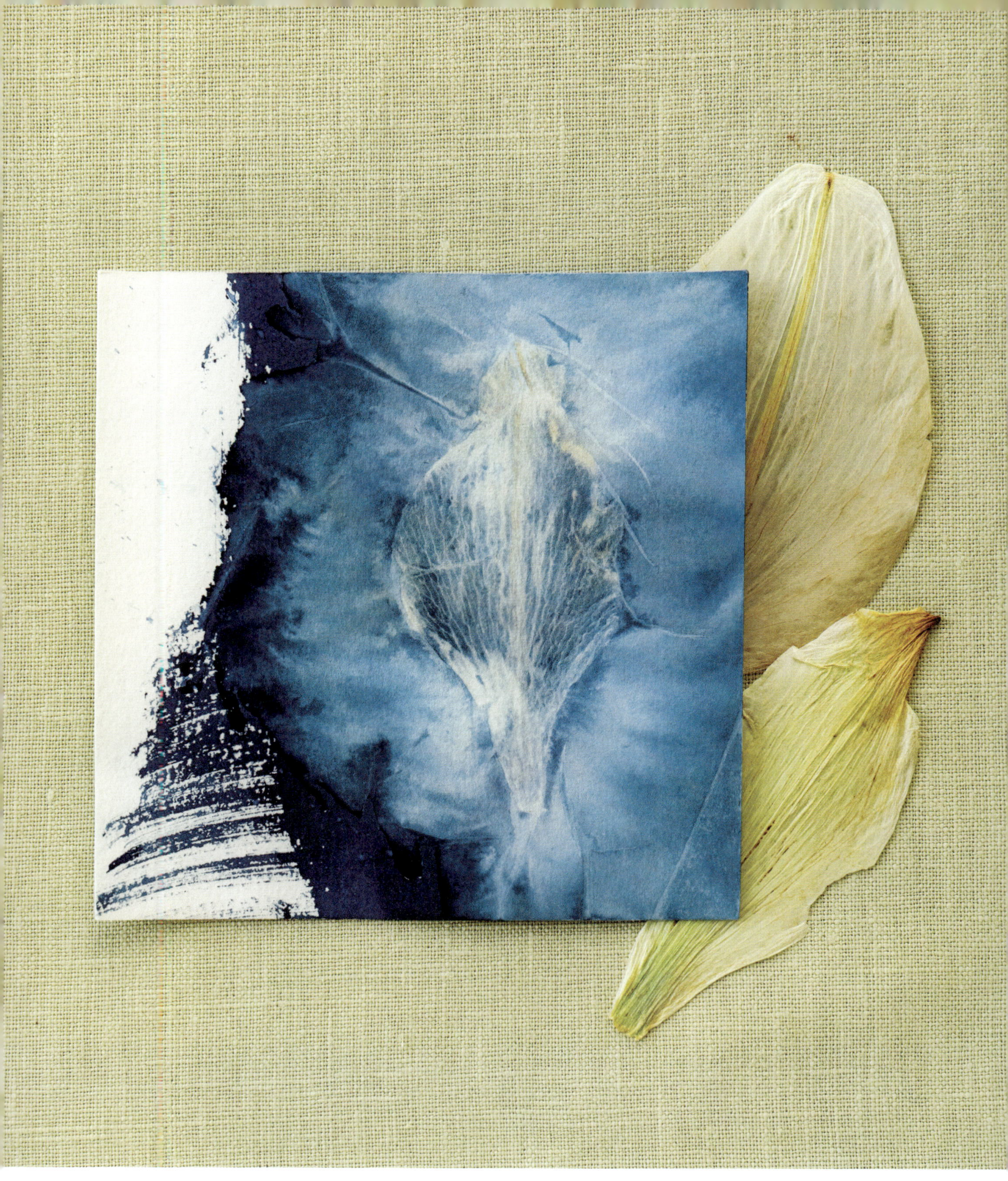

The wet cyanotype process creates beautiful results, but it's highly unpredictable. The print will continue to change as it exposes, during washing, and as it dries, so don't get too attached to the look of your piece while it's in process.

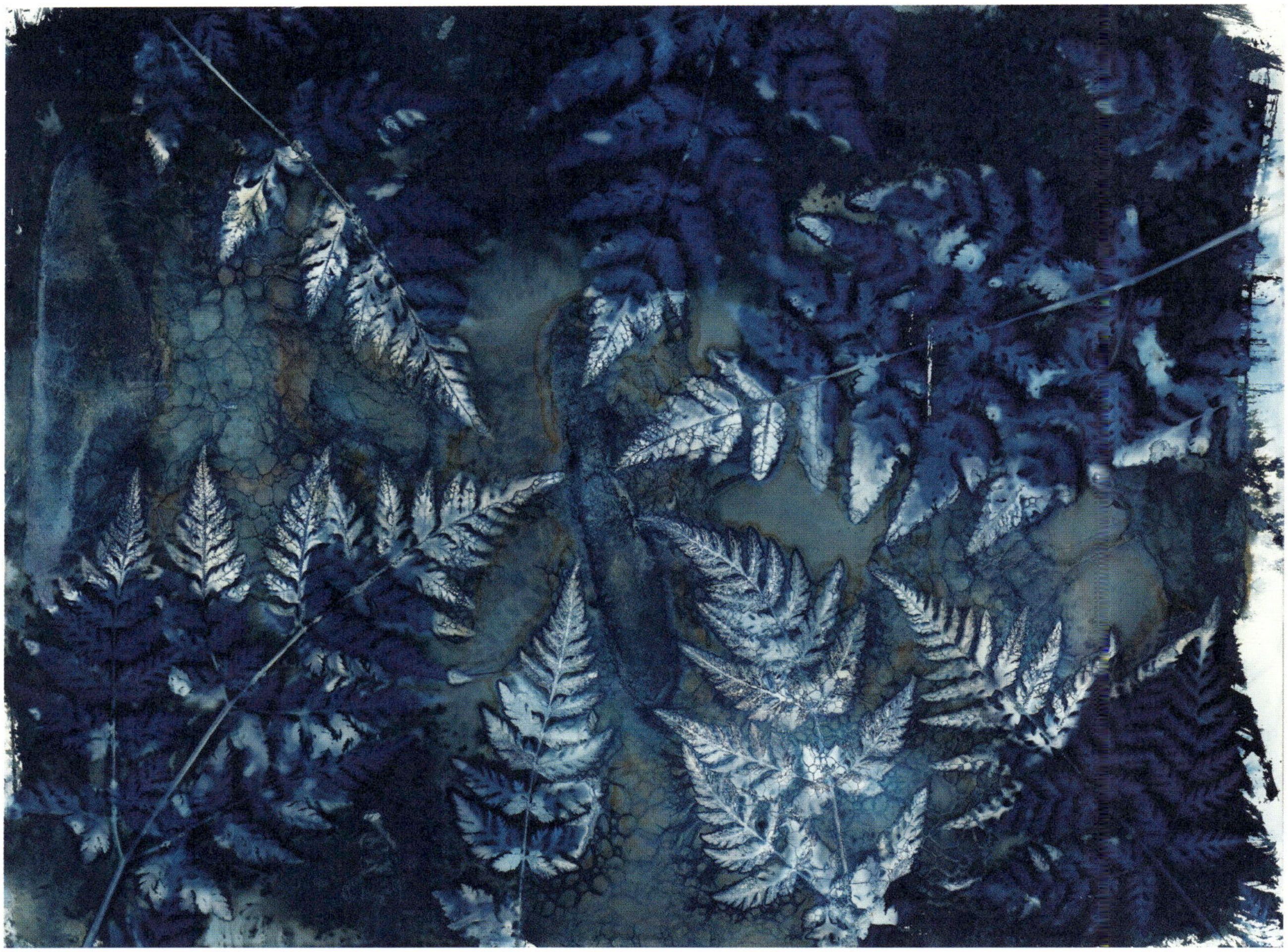

Madge Evers, *Six Beauty Tips*

## THE EPHEMERAL ART OF CYANOTYPE MAKING

Cyanotype making always involves unexpected results, but that is even more true when working with wet cyanotypes. Your image will continue to change and evolve until it has been fully washed and dried. Oftentimes, the colors will appear more vibrant during exposure than they do once the image has been washed, so keep this in mind. Making cyanotypes is a beautiful way to celebrate the ephemeral, but if you find that you're deeply attached to how your piece looks during the exposure process, you can also take a picture to capture that stage.

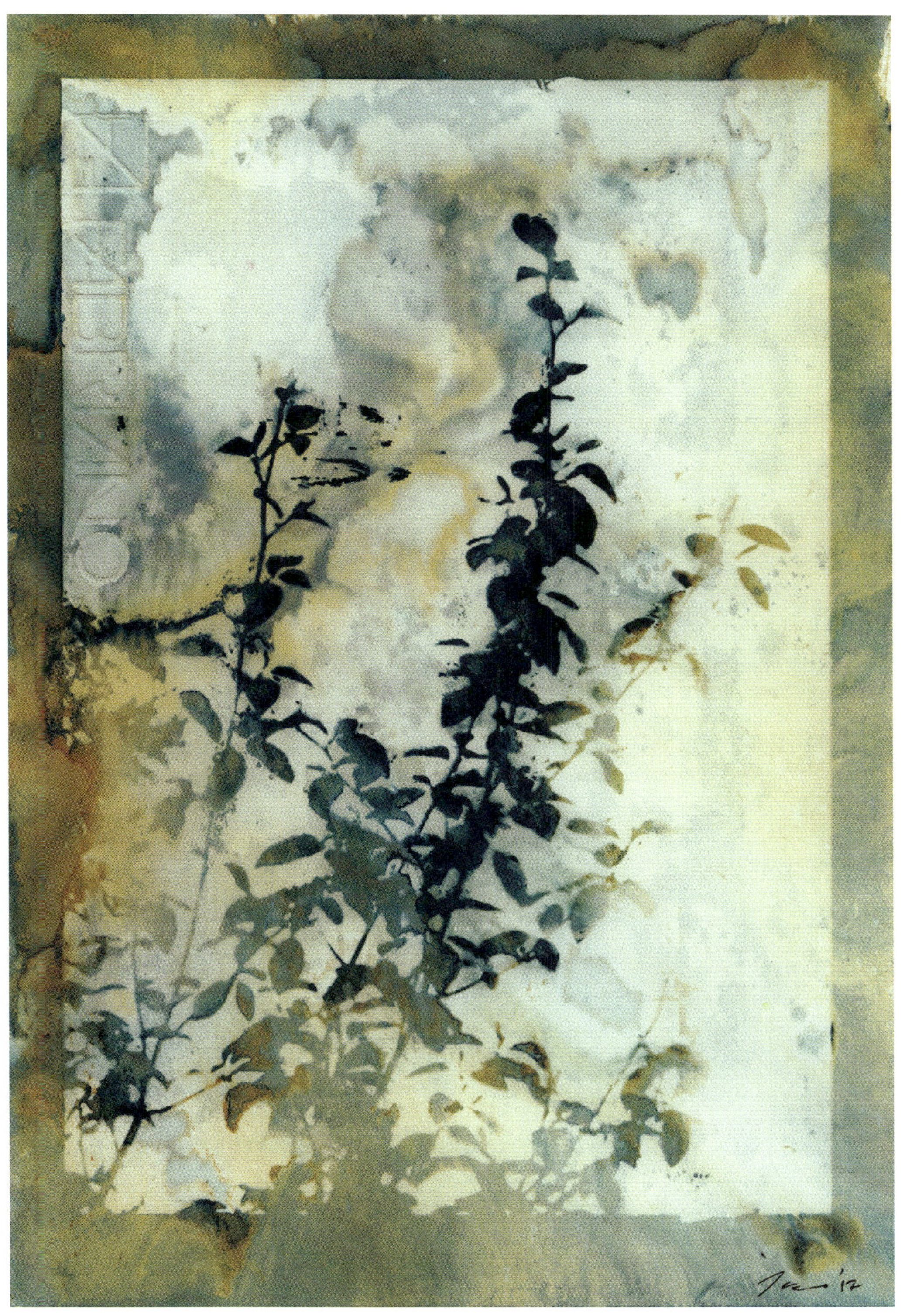

Krista McCurdy popularized the wet cyanotype process. This image showcases the beautiful unpredictability of her technique.

# Wet Cyanotypes with Vinegar, Spices, and Soap Bubbles

Wet cyanotypes are the untamed siblings of the traditional cyanotype. Playful and unpredictable, they are sometimes difficult to control. They're fascinating, but at times frustrating—they don't always behave the way you expect. When they do behave, the results can be magical.

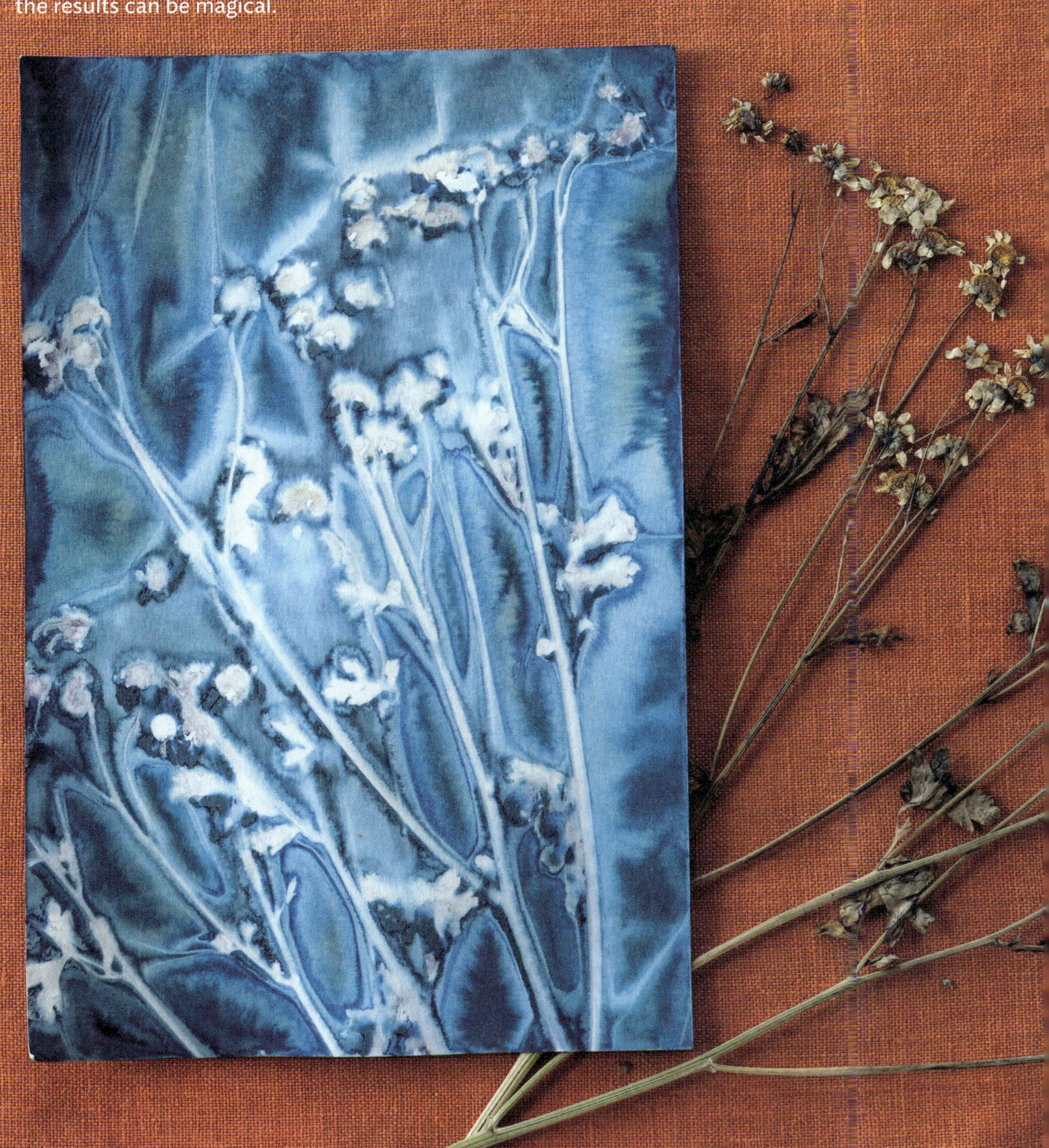

For this project, we'll explore three different types of wet cyanotypes. The washing and drying steps are the same as for "dry" cyanotypes. A wet print must be exposed to sunlight for many hours, however, so find a location where your setup won't be disturbed.

## Materials

- Sheet of prepared paper (coated with cyanotype working solution, allowed to dry, and stored in a light-safe container)
- Sheet of cardboard (or any stiff material) the same size as the glass or acrylic
- Plant material, pressed and dried or fresh, or other flat material
- White vinegar in a spray bottle
- Sheet of clear plastic film or plastic wrap larger than the paper
- Sheet of glass or acrylic larger than the paper
- Binder clips or similar fasteners
- Plastic washing tray larger than the cyanotype
- Gloves or tongs, for handling the print while rinsing (optional)
- Clothesline and clothespins or sheets of clean cardboard
- Turmeric, paprika, or other spices (optional)
- Dish soap (optional)

## WET PROCESS WITH WHITE VINEGAR

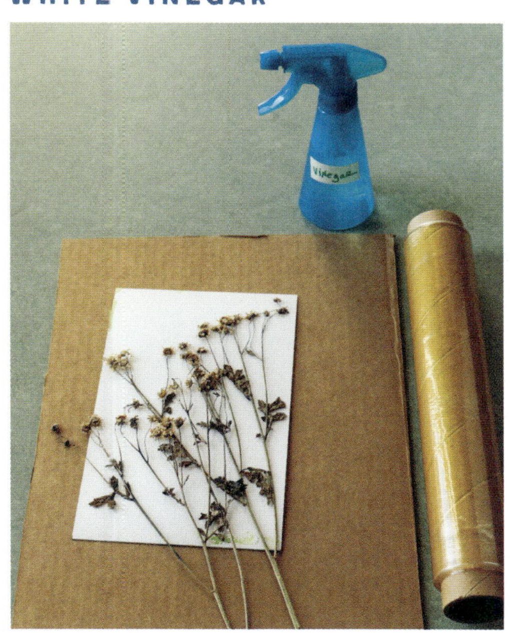

1 **SET UP.** Gather your materials in a dimly lit prep space.

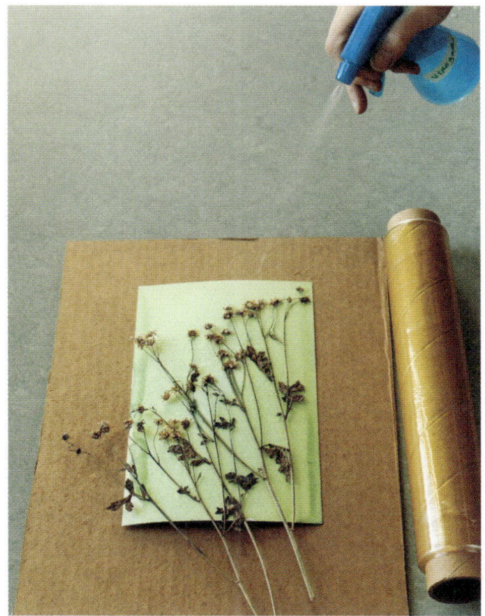

2 **ARRANGE THE COMPOSITION.** In low light, remove the sheet of paper from its light-safe container and place it on the cardboard backing with the light-green emulsion side facing up. Arrange your printing material to create a composition on the paper's emulsion side.

3 **SPRAY WITH VINEGAR.** Working in a well-ventilated area, lightly spritz the paper and printing material with vinegar until the paper is evenly wet.

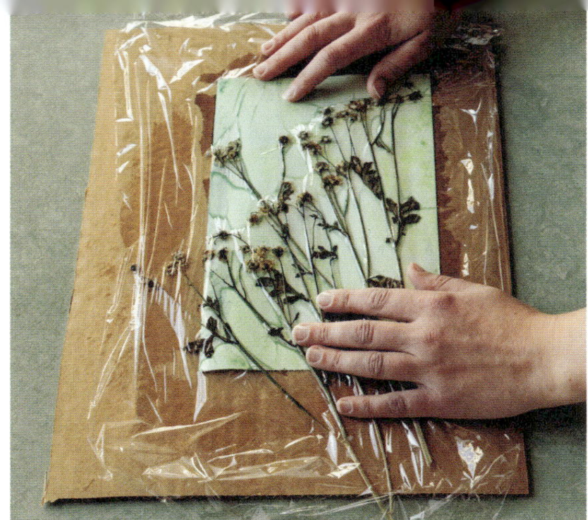

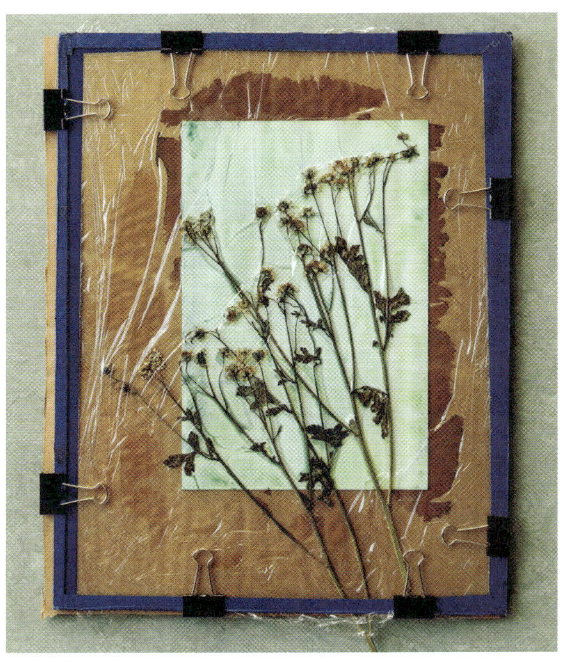

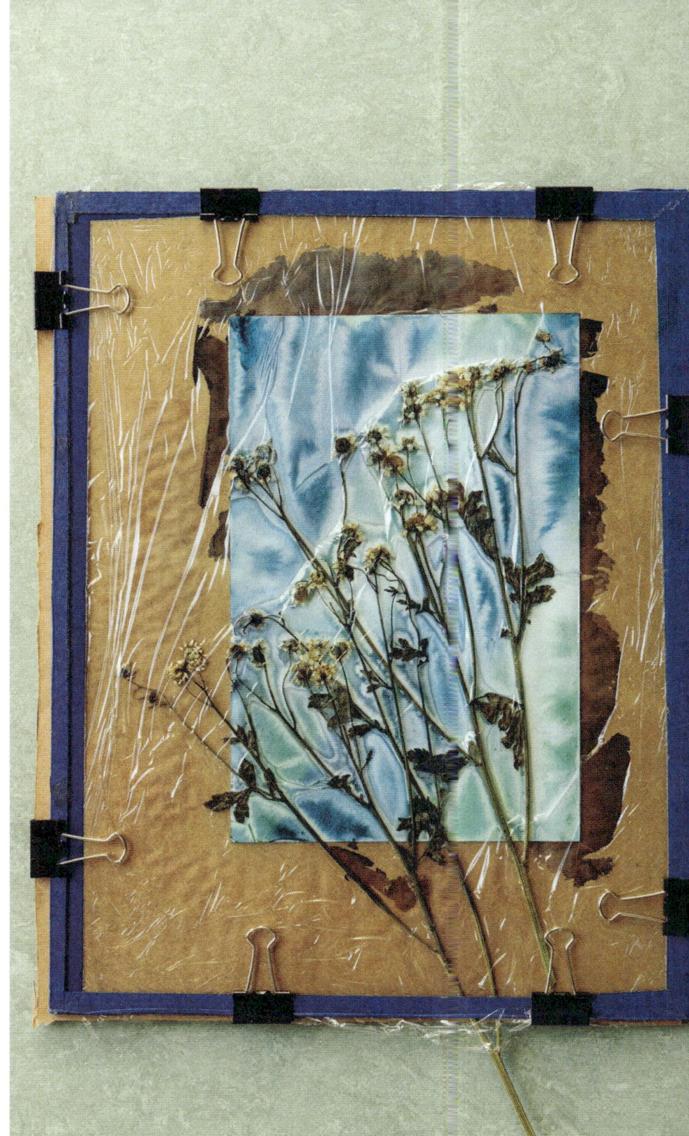

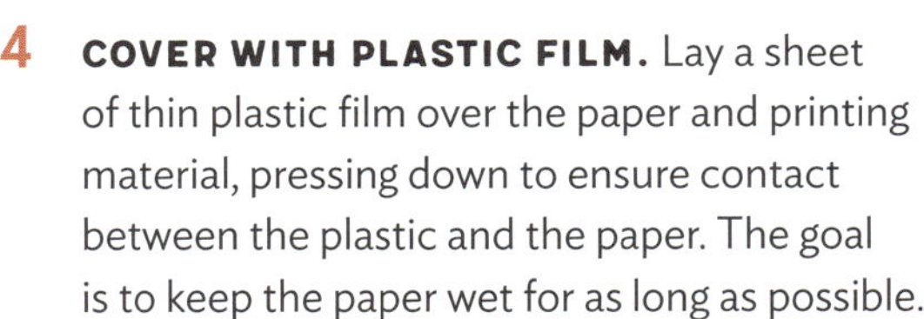

**4 COVER WITH PLASTIC FILM.** Lay a sheet of thin plastic film over the paper and printing material, pressing down to ensure contact between the plastic and the paper. The goal is to keep the paper wet for as long as possible.

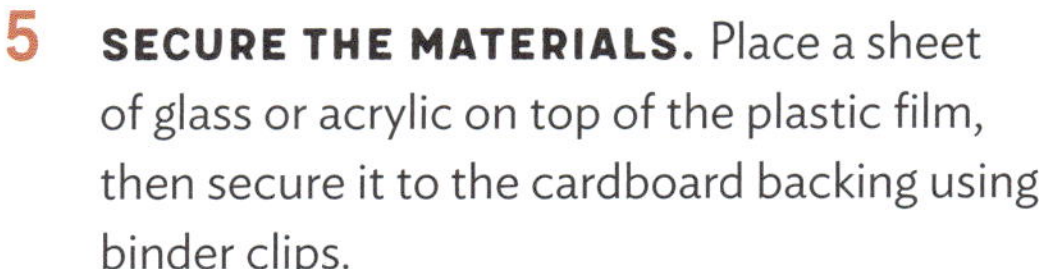

**5 SECURE THE MATERIALS.** Place a sheet of glass or acrylic on top of the plastic film, then secure it to the cardboard backing using binder clips.

**6 EXPOSE TO UV LIGHT.** Place your setup in direct UV light with the emulsion side up. Leave it exposed for at least 1 hour and up to 24 hours. You don't need to watch it closely, but notice how the coated surface changes during exposure. Areas that have fully reacted to UV light may appear darker, more vivid, or distinctly outlined. Unreacted areas may have a faint or pale quality. Trust your instincts! This process is experimental. Move to step 7 when the colors have developed to your liking.

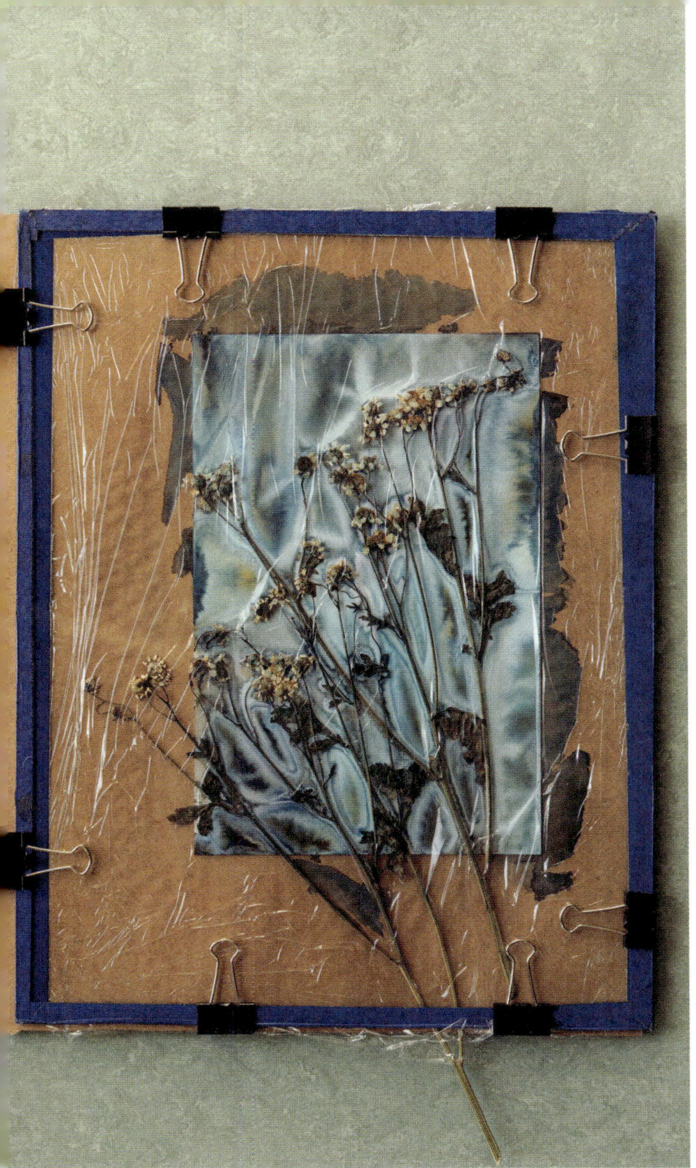

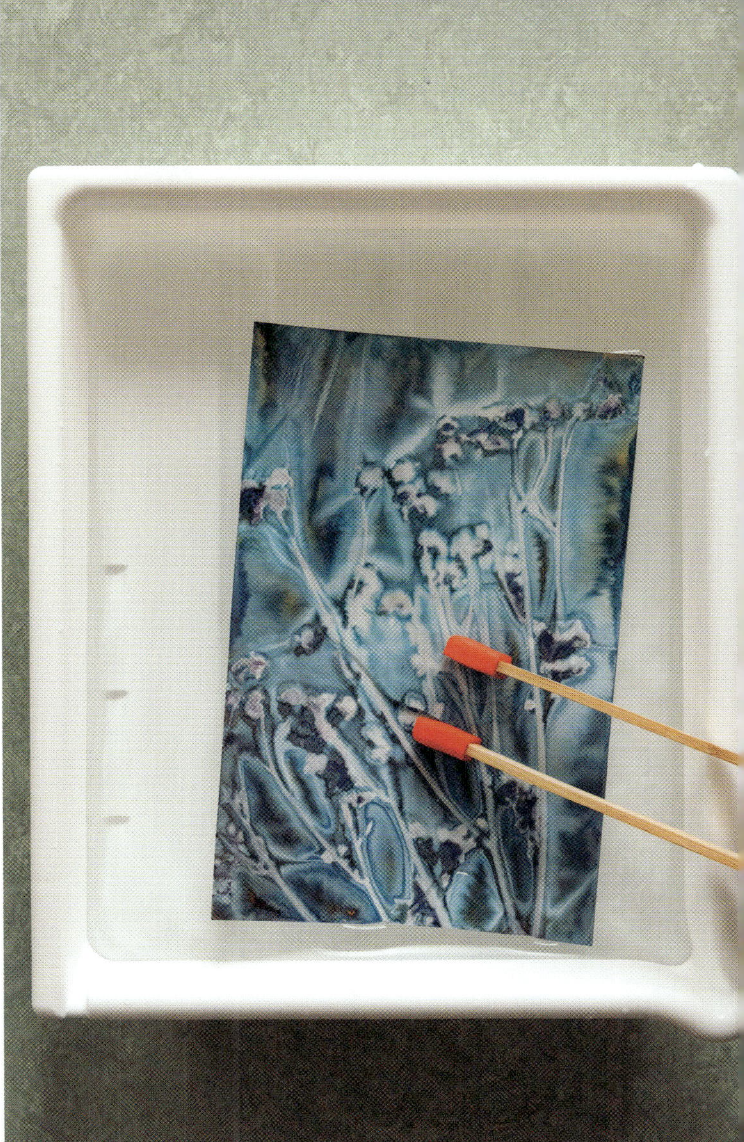

7 **DISMANTLE AND WASH.** Place the rinsing tray in your wash area and fill it with water. Remove the clips, glass or acrylic, plastic, and printing material from the paper. Place the paper in the tray; wear gloves or use tongs, if you like, to reduce skin contact with chemicals. Rinse the print in slowly running water or by filling and dumping the tray until the light-green chemicals are removed and the water is clear, 5 to 15 minutes. Keep in mind that the colors may shift during rinsing and drying.

8 **DRY THE PRINT.** Set up a clothesline or sheets of clean cardboard as a drying station, somewhere away from direct light. Hang or lay out the print and let it dry completely.

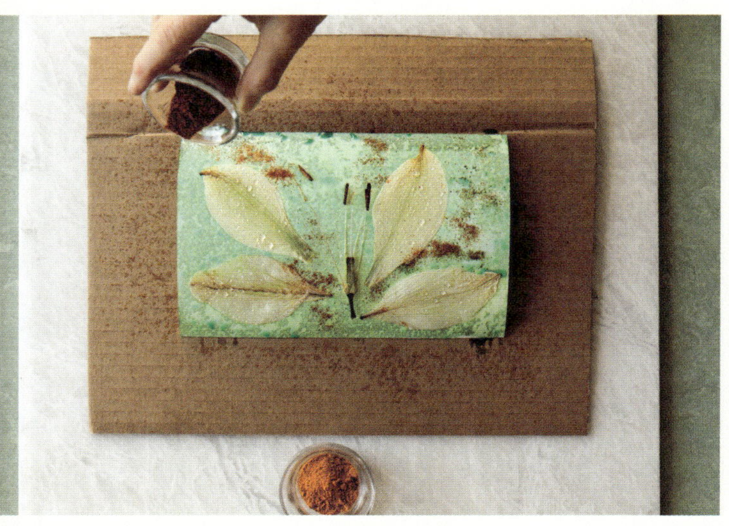

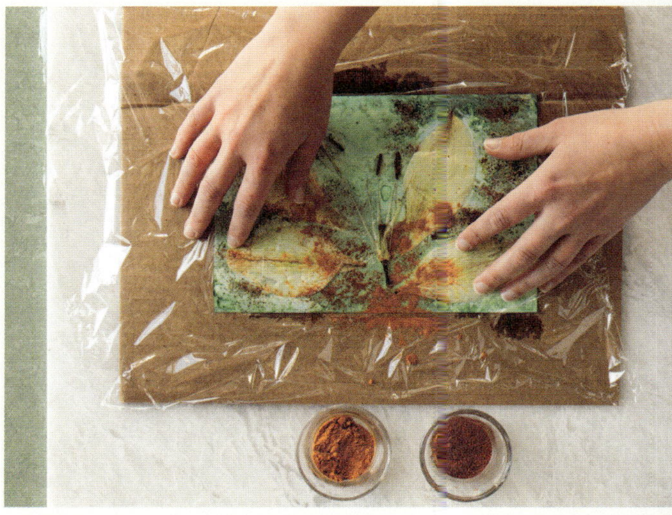

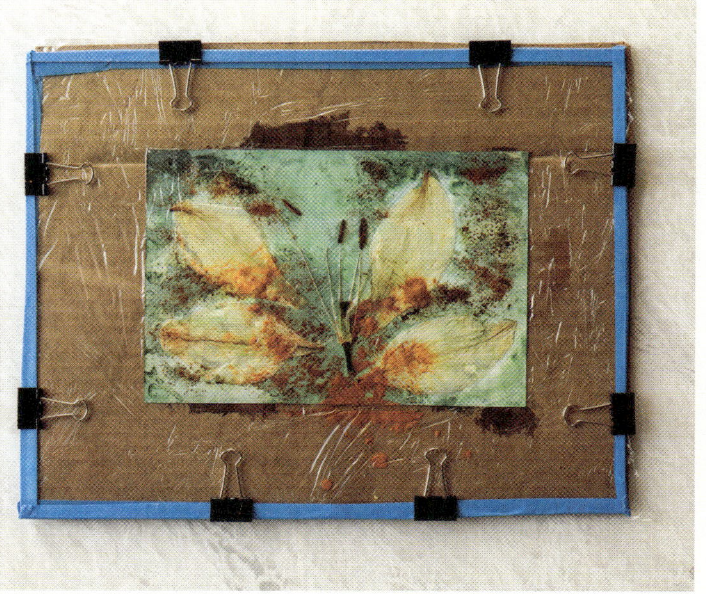

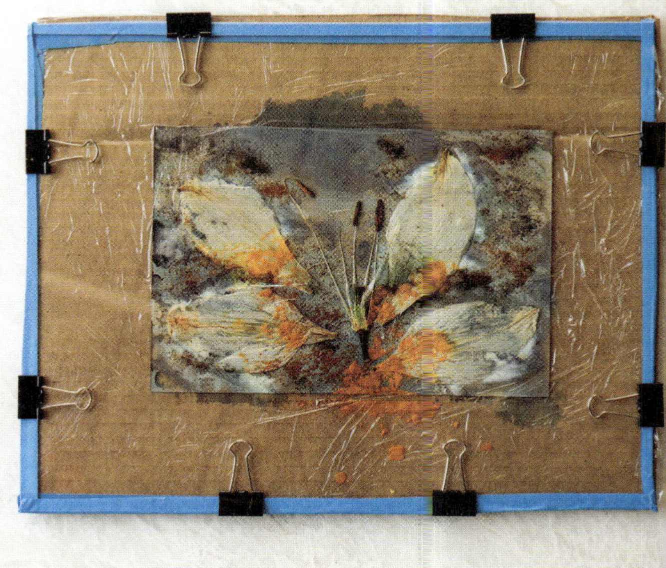

## Wet Process with Spice Dyes

Spice up a cyanotype using ground turmeric and paprika as natural dyes. Simply follow the basic steps for making a wet cyanotype, as outlined on pages 121–123.

After you wet the paper with vinegar in step 3, sprinkle turmeric (for yellow tones) and paprika (for red tones) over your composition in whatever pattern you like. You can also reverse the process and apply your spices before spraying the vinegar if you prefer.

Then cover the composition with plastic film, as described in step 4, and proceed.

You can use other spices similarly, experimenting with preparation methods, application techniques, and color tones. Consider beetroot powder, nutmeg, or other spices you may have on hand.

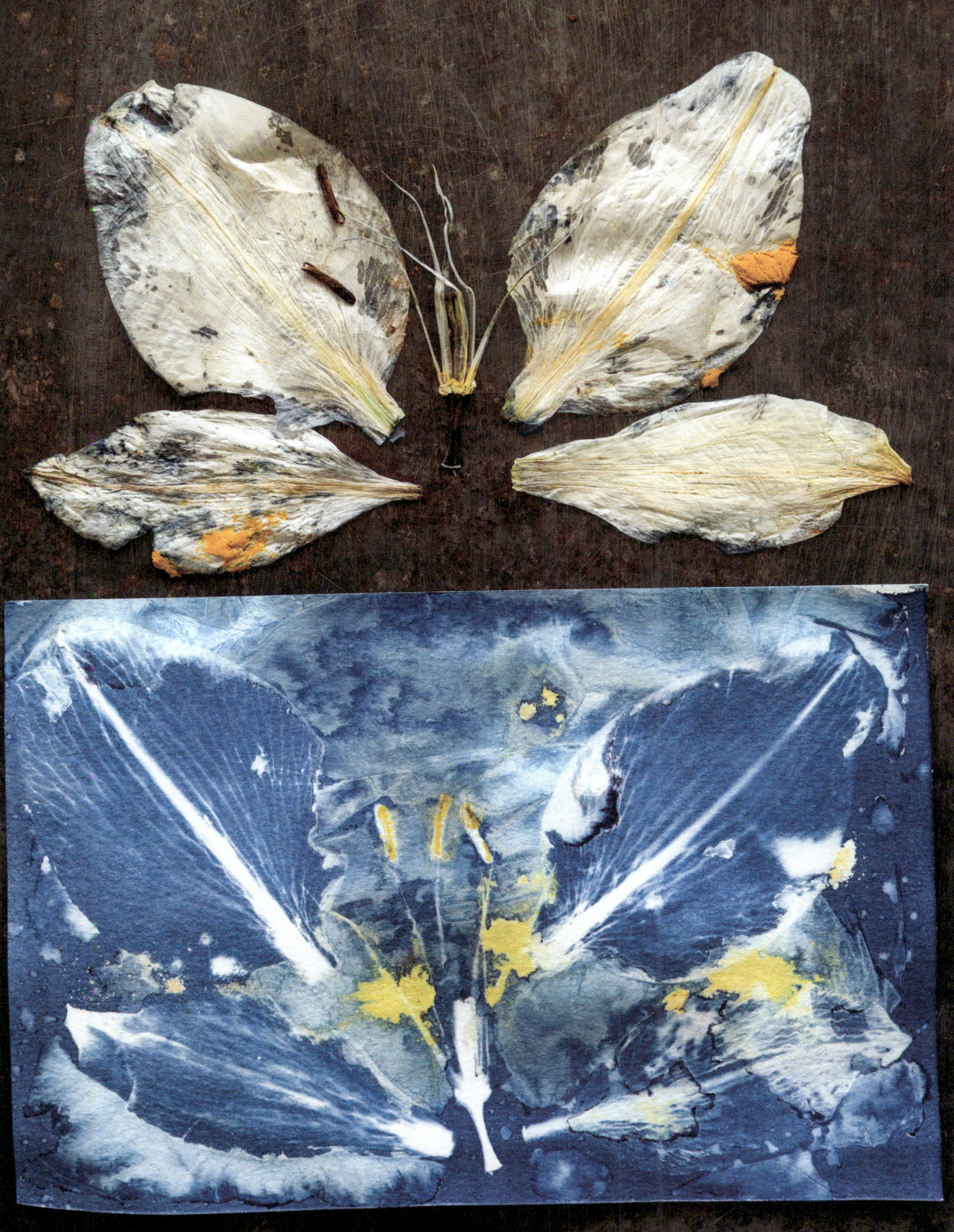

Spices can produce lovely, unexpected splashes of color.

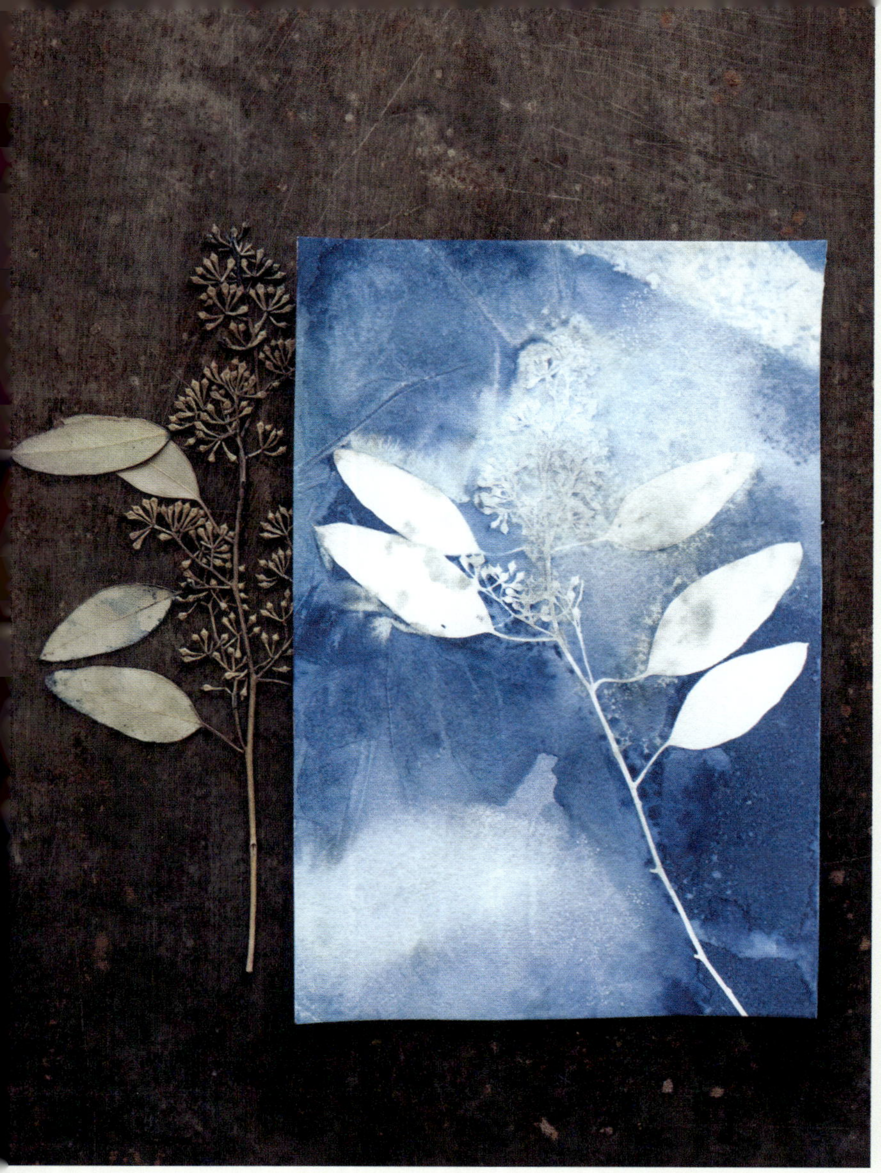

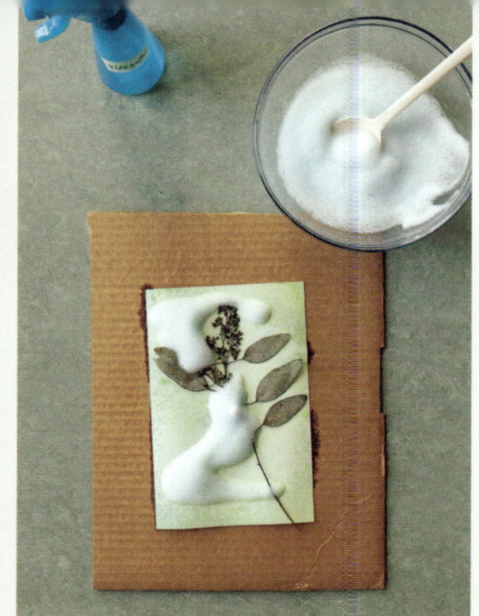

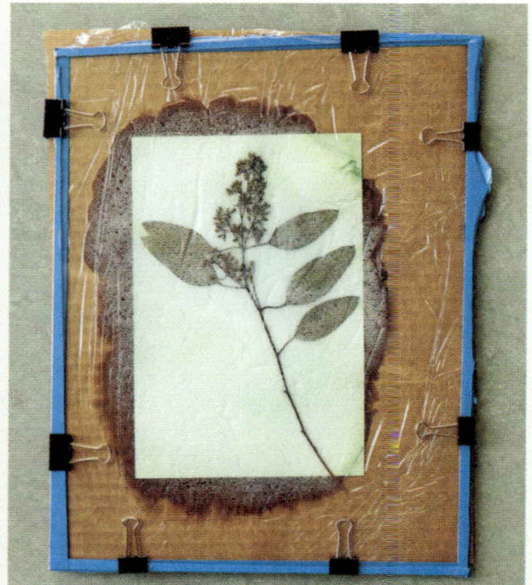

## Wet Process with Soap Bubbles

Soap bubbles are a surprising way to add texture and depth to cyanotype imagery. Again, follow the basic steps for making a wet cyanotype, as outlined on pages 121–123.

After you wet the paper with vinegar in step 3, mix up a batch of bubbles by whisking together dish soap and water in a shallow pan or bowl. Scoop up the bubbles with a spoon or your hand and gently place them on your composition.

Then cover the composition with plastic film, as described in step 4. Covering with glass or acrylic should not disturb the bubbles, but if it does, skip step 5 and proceed from there. If you choose to skip the glass, you may need to secure the paper with tape or pushpins, as it will warp once it's wet.

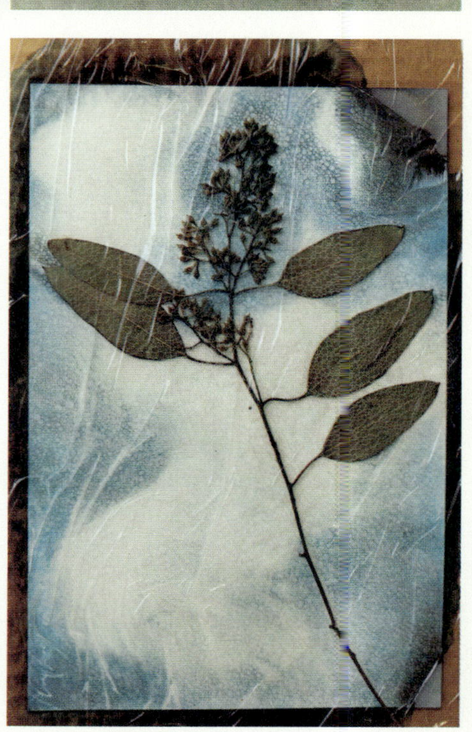

## NOTES

Be aware that printing materials used for a wet cyanotype may be altered or ruined by the vinegar, so don't use anything precious to you.

If it seems that your material might be blown out of position by the force of the spray bottle, spritz the paper with vinegar before arranging the plants (or other material) on top of it—that is, reverse steps 2 and 3.

You can skip the plastic film if you prefer, but the cyanotype chemicals will adhere to your glass or acrylic and may be difficult to clean off.

I use plastic film recycled from a variety of sources, including plastic grocery bags and the clear plastic film used to wrap up produce and various products. Plastic cling wrap used in the kitchen is another possibility.

## MORE WET CYANOTYPE EXPERIMENTS

- Combining soap bubbles and spices? Go for it!
- Try the wet process by working with freshly coated paper that has not yet dried.
- Lemon juice (citric acid) can be used in place of vinegar (acetic acid). In my experience, the results are similar, but some people report that lemon juice makes for darker blues and vinegar for softer blues.

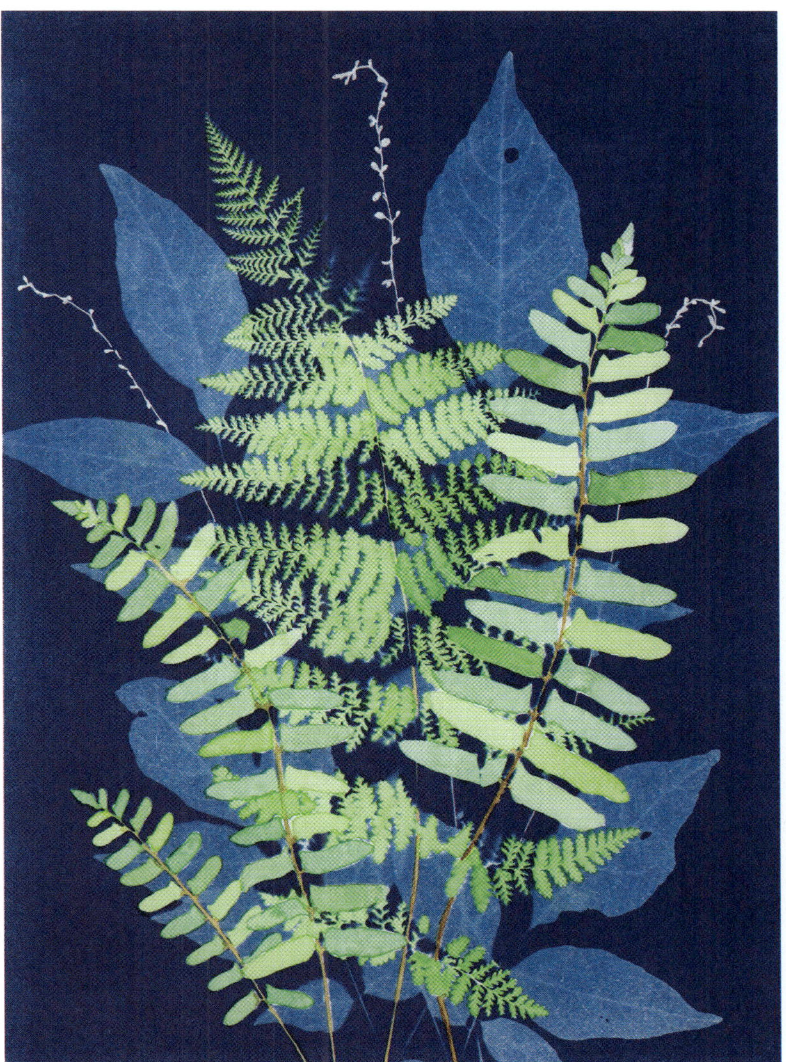

Elizabeth Booth created *Through the Woods* using the experimental wet process, extended exposure times, and watercolor paint.

# Altering Finished Cyanotypes

The creative potential of cyanotypes continues even after you've washed and fixed a print. In addition to embellishing the cyanotype with other mediums (see page 120), you can change the color of the print itself by bleaching or toning it.

Bleaching gently fades the color of a cyanotype, from a soft blue all the way to yellow depending on how long the piece is exposed to the bleaching solution.

The toning process involves soaking the print in a dye solution to add additional color. Both options allow you to move beyond the traditional blue-and-white color scheme and embrace beautiful, unexpected results.

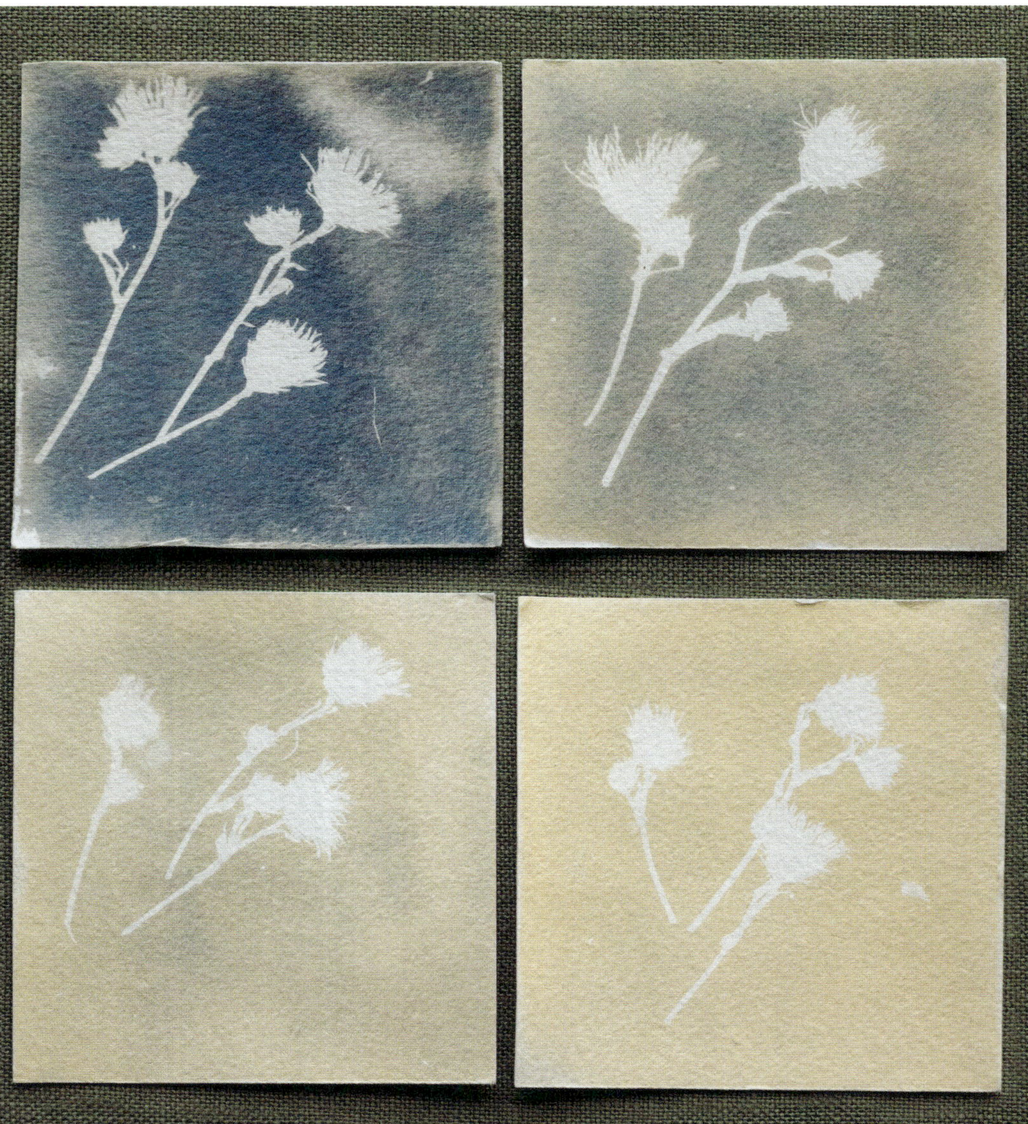

You can bleach a cyanotype as much or as little as you'd like, creating a gradient of color options.

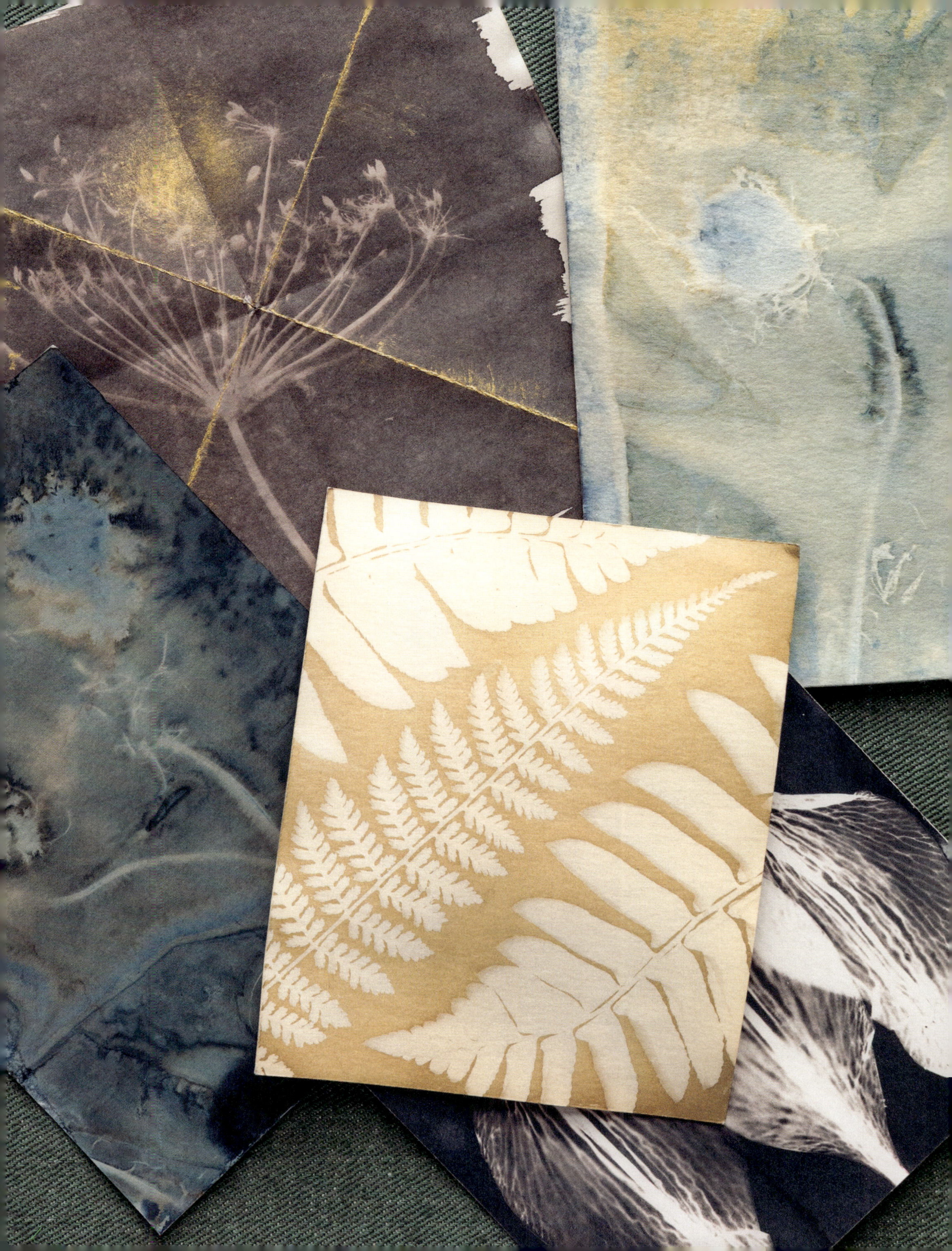

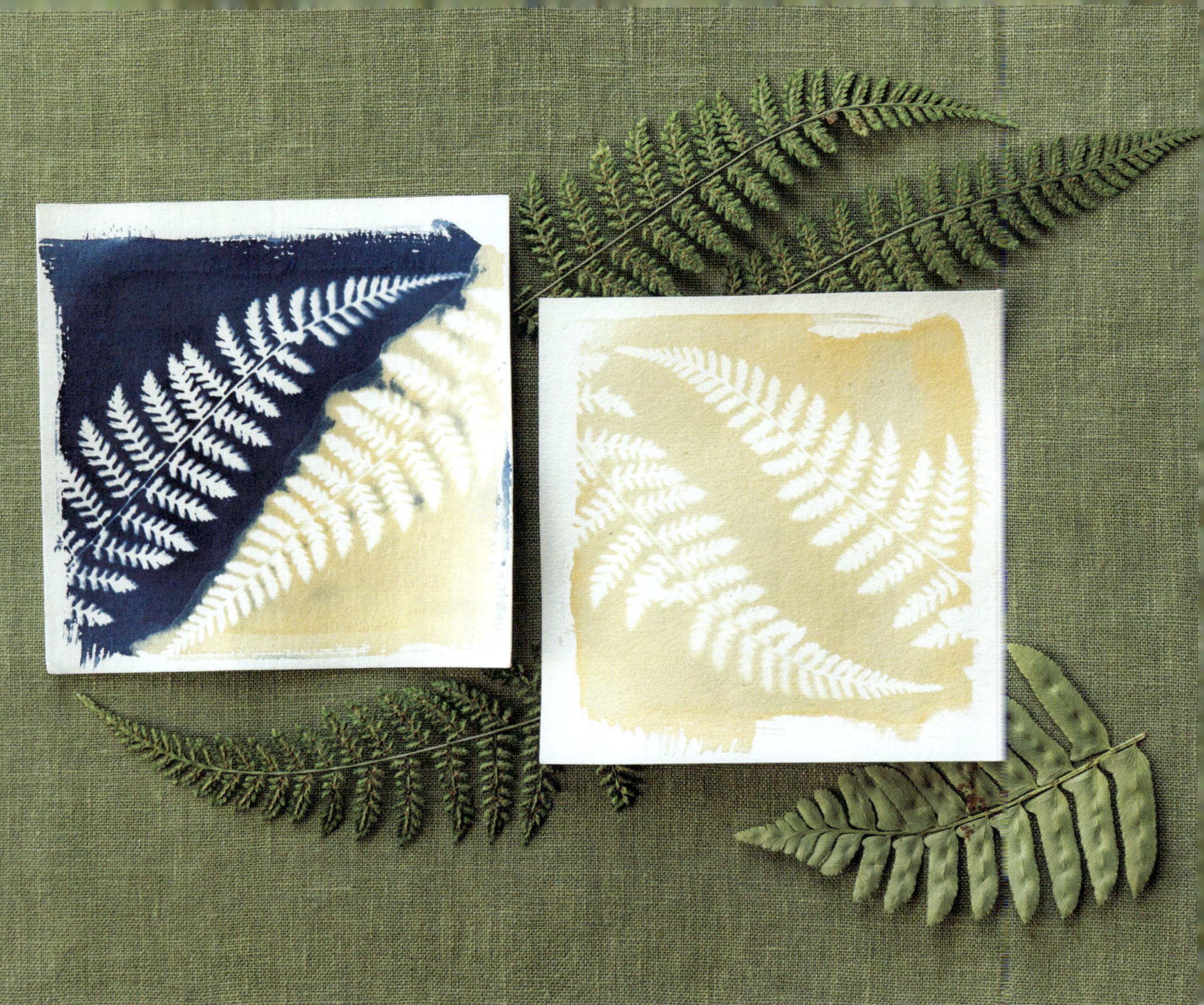

# Create a "Yellow" Cyanotype with Washing Soda

Okay, admit it—you can't stop making cyanotypes! Whether we're drawn to the classic blue and white or captivated by the unpredictability of the wet process, we all have our reasons. Sometimes, however, the results aren't exactly what we had planned. That's where this project comes in. It is perfect for making the most of our imperfect or discarded prints.

Though this project focuses on bleaching, we won't be using chlorine bleach. Instead, we'll bleach our cyanotypes with sodium carbonate (washing soda), a simple ingredient found in many laundry soaps. Washing soda raises pH and gradually shifts a cyanotype's tones from blue to purple, yellow, and eventually white.

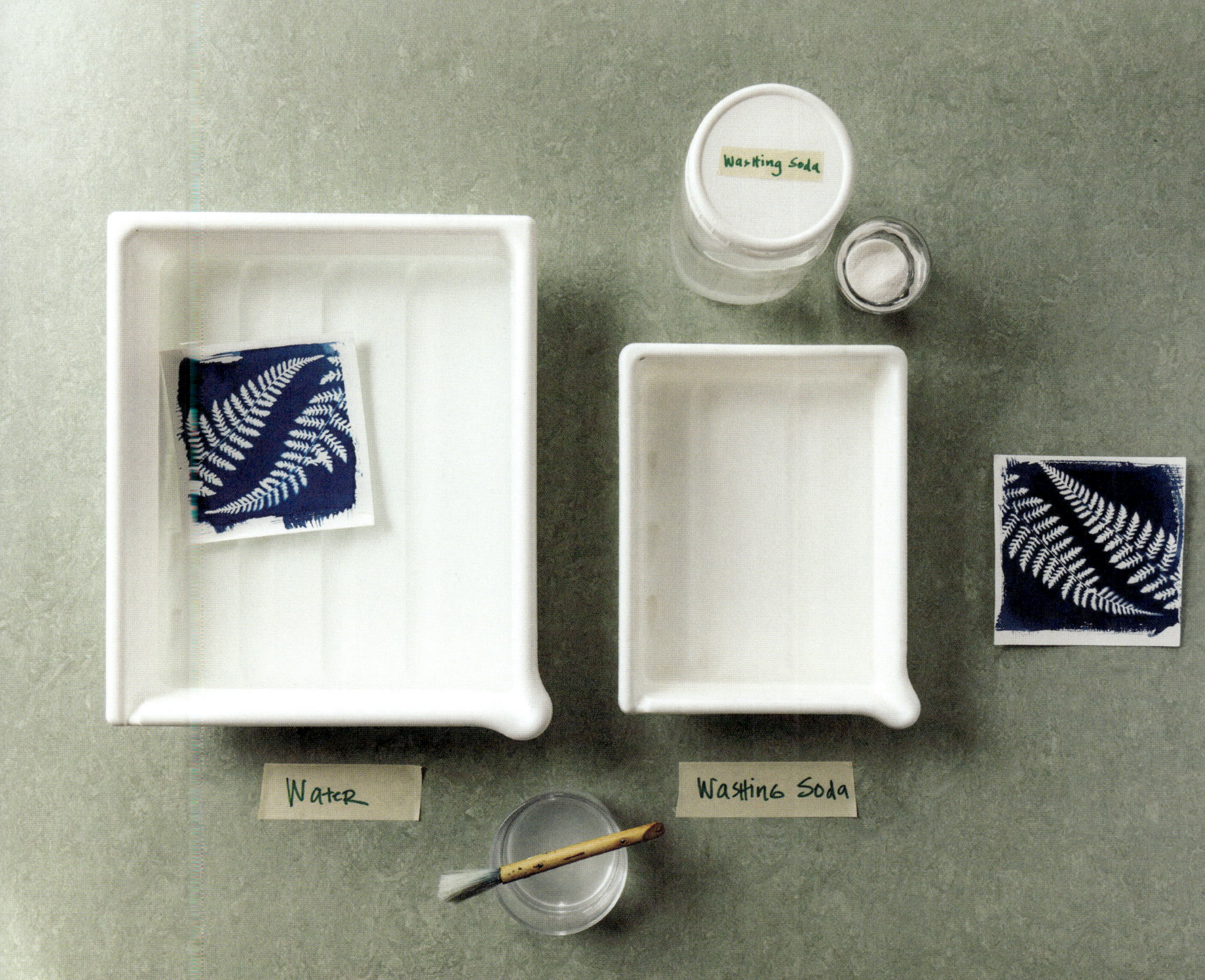


## Materials

- Washing tray (larger than the cyanotype) or paintbrush, for applying the washing soda solution
- Washing tray (larger than the cyanotype), for wetting/rinsing the cyanotype
- Finished, dried cyanotype on paper
- Washing soda (sodium carbonate) solution (½ teaspoon per 1 quart or 4 grams per 1,000 mL warm water
- Clothesline and clothespins or sheets of clean cardboard

1 **SET UP.** Arrange your materials on a work surface near a sink or other source of running water. Fill a washing tray with plain water. If you're going to bleach the entire print (option 1 below), fill the second washing tray with the washing soda solution. If you're going to spot-bleach the print (option 2 below), you can mix up the solution in any container you like. Make sure the washing soda is fully dissolved in the solution; any undissolved particles can leave white spots on your print.

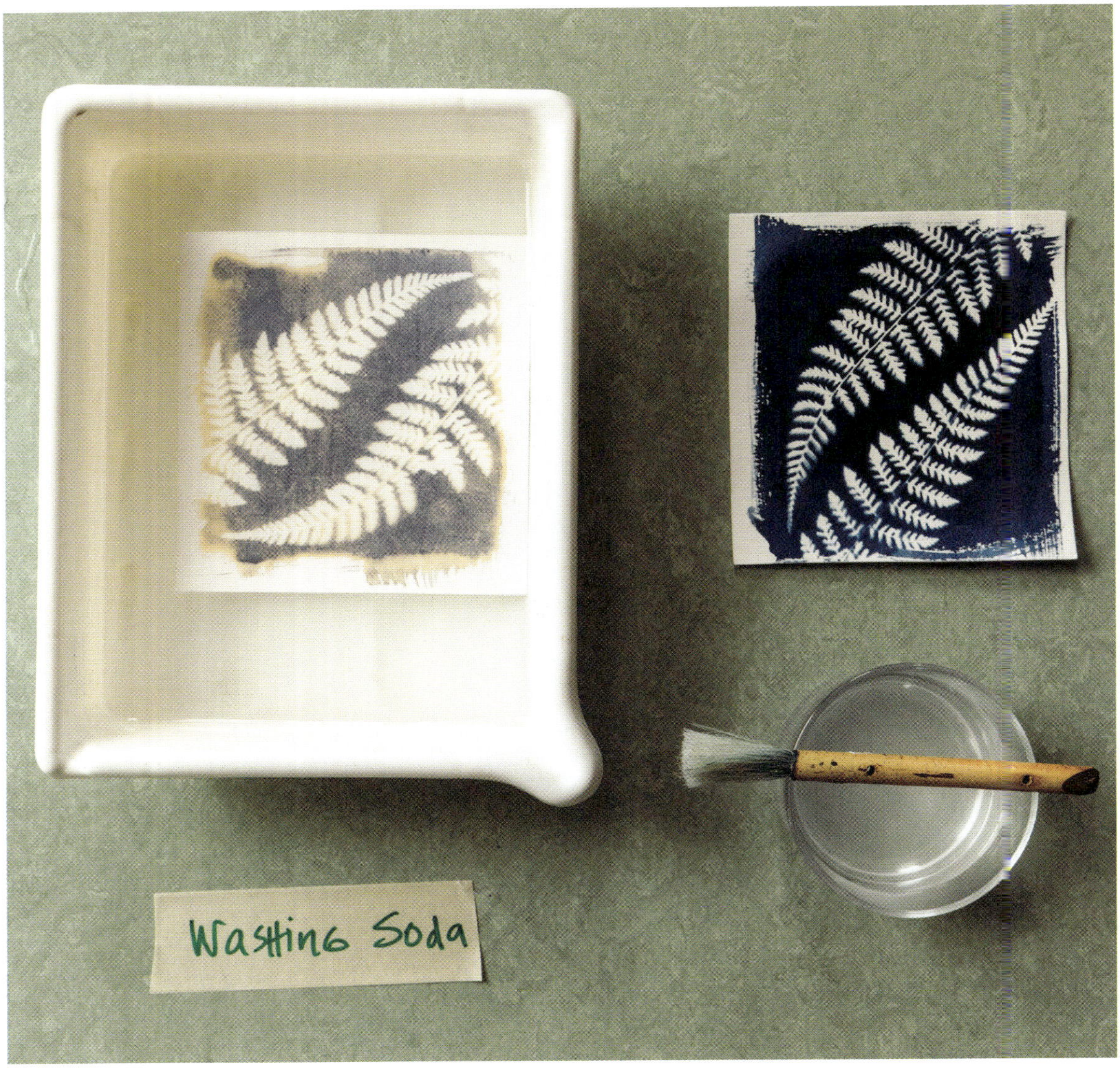

**2 APPLY THE WASHING SODA SOLUTION.** There are two options here: soaking the entire print in the washing soda solution or applying the solution to select areas of the print.

**OPTION 1:** Prewet the print by submerging it in the tray of plain water. Then submerge the print in the tray of washing soda solution.

**OPTION 2:** Do not prewet the print. Using a paintbrush, apply the washing soda solution directly to specific areas of the print. Precision bleaching of very small areas may be challenging, but using a brush allows you to control which areas are affected. (Skipping the prewetting step gives you more control over how the solution flows on the paper.)

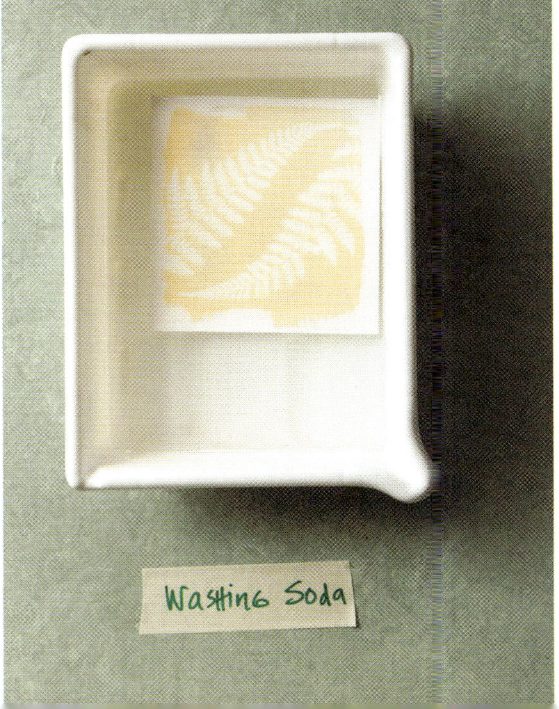

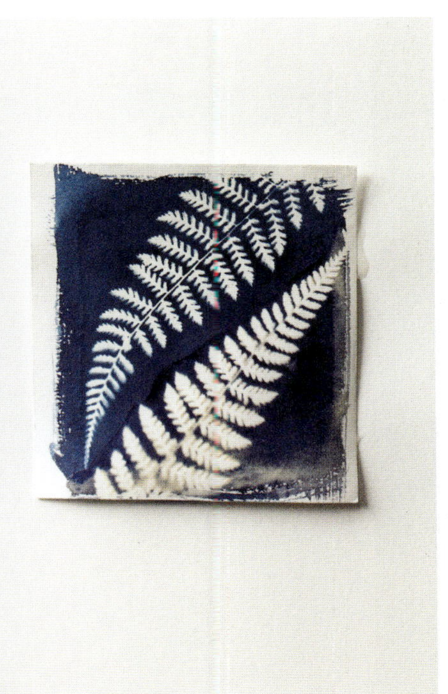

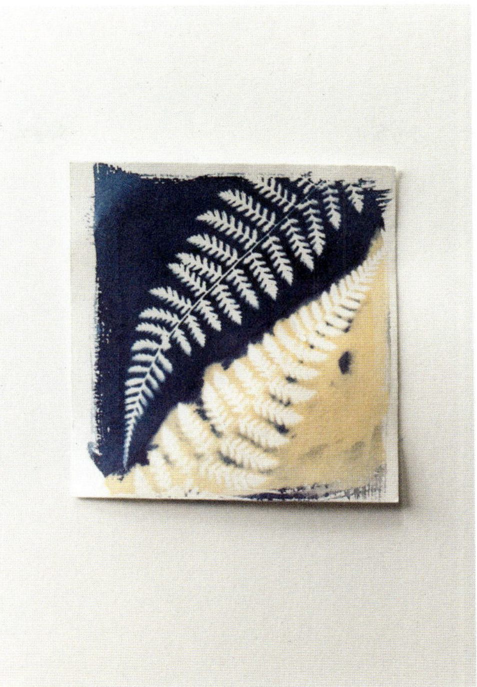

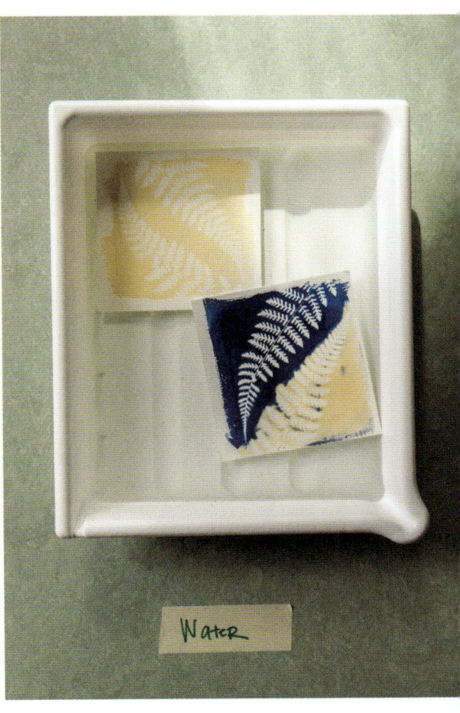


3 **OBSERVE CHANGES.** Watch the cyanotype as its color shifts from blue to purple and then yellow. Using the dilution described here, changes typically start within 15 seconds. After 20 minutes, the print may be almost fully bleached.

4 **RINSE.** Once you've achieved the desired effect, transfer the print to the tray of plain water to stop the bleaching process. Rinse in running water for 10 minutes to remove any remaining washing soda.

5 **DRY THE PRINT.** Set up a clothesline or sheets of clean cardboard as a drying station, somewhere away from direct light. Hang or lay out the print and let it dry completely.

**NOTES** The bleaching process can be preparation for the next project: toning your cyanotype with natural materials. It's also a great way to reimagine a print that is too dark.

As an alternative to sodium carbonate, you can use calcium carbonate, which can be gentler on the paper. Hard water (water with a high mineral content) or water treated with chlorine may have a similar bleaching effect if you leave a cyanotype print to soak in it for several hours.

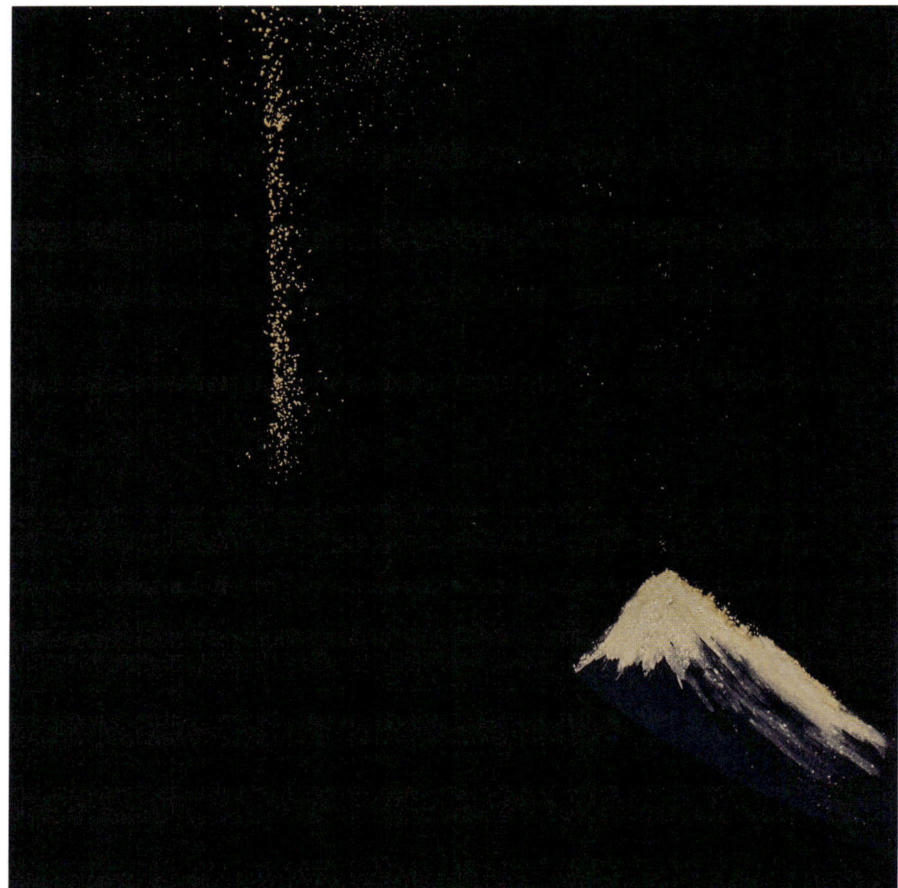

In her *Cyanoscope* series, Jeannie Hutchins bleaches selected areas of each cyanotype to create abstract images with punctuations of light.

## MAKING A LARGE CYANOTYPE

While I enjoy making smaller cyanotypes, some subjects demand larger paper. Cyanotypes by artists like Susan Weil, Robert Rauschenberg, and Meghann Riepenhoff capture the vastness of nature or human forms on large sheets, emphasizing the dramatic scale of their subjects. If you're intrigued by the idea of making a big blue cyanotype, here are some tips.

- You can purchase rolls of paper and cut them to your preferred length. I prefer 300 gsm.
- Before cutting the paper, lay out a clean drop cloth. Weight the paper and allow it to flatten for 24 hours before using.
- It can be tricky to move a large sheet of paper once you've laid out the composition. Instead, plan your composition in advance at your exposure site. Bring the sheet of paper into the light, quickly reassemble the arrangement, and then place the glass or acrylic sheets.
- Use a bathtub (if it's safe to rinse the chemicals in your area; see page 75) or a kiddie pool to rinse the print.

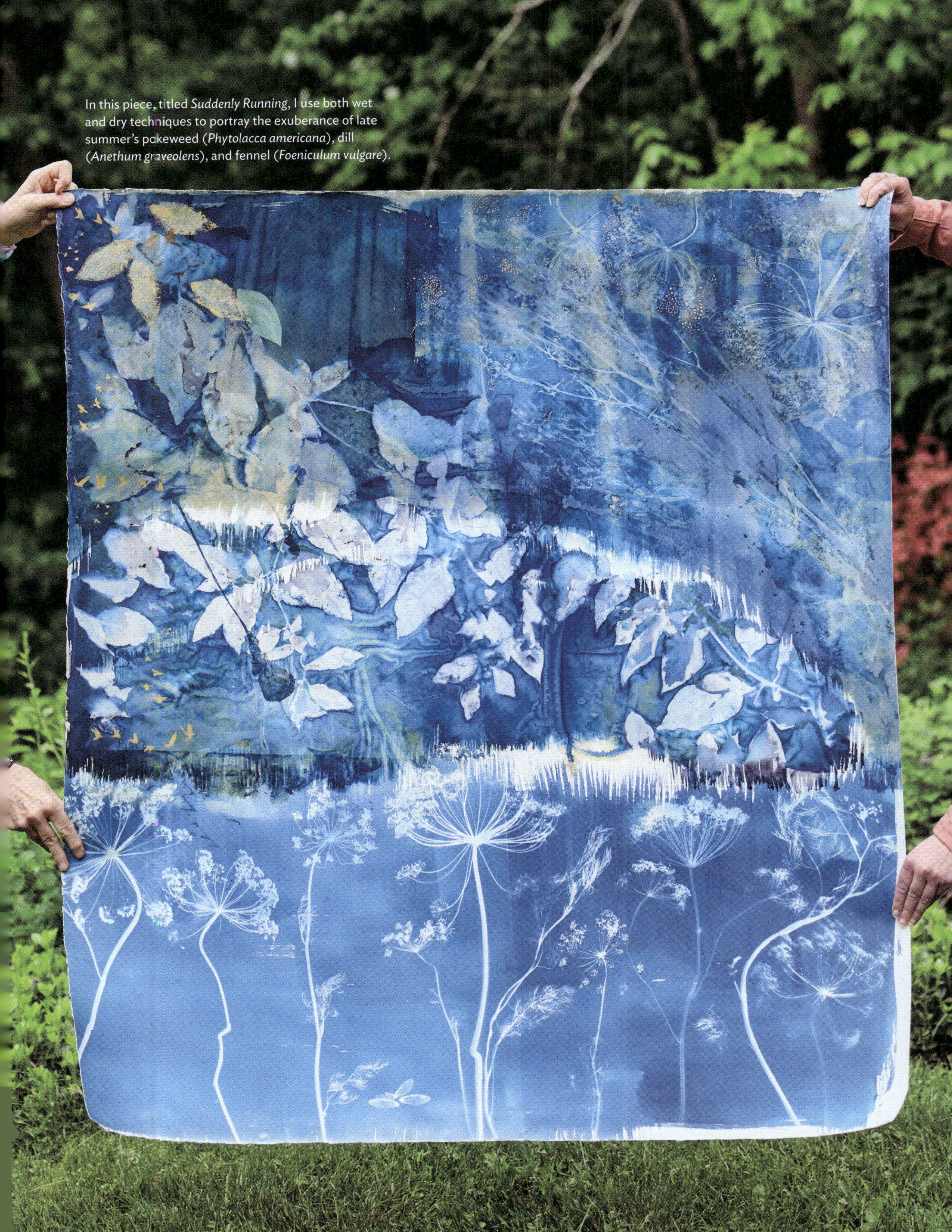

In this piece, titled *Suddenly Running*, I use both wet and dry techniques to portray the exuberance of late summer's pokeweed (*Phytolacca americana*), dill (*Anethum graveolens*), and fennel (*Foeniculum vulgare*).

# Adding Color with Toning

Toning is the process of changing the color of a cyanotype from the traditional blue to any number of other colors. You're likely familiar with sepia photographs; they are toned with a reddish-brown pigment originally derived from the common cuttlefish, whose genus name is *Sepia*.

Toning bath can be created using a variety of chemicals, but we'll focus on using plant materials. Making a toning bath is easy: You simply pour boiling water over the chopped plant material and let it infuse to extract the plant's tannins. Tannins are phenolic compounds with strong flavor and astringency, often associated with the taste of wine or tea. Some tannins are colorless and others range from brown to red. They all have unique chemical interactions that have led to their use in traditional dyeing for centuries. When a cyanotype print is submerged in a tannic toning bath, the tannins adhere to the iron salts in the emulsion, changing the hue from blue to something new.

I recommend that you approach the process of toning cyanotypes with an experimental mindset, as the results can be unpredictable. Tannins create interesting colors by reacting with the cyanotype's iron salts, but they may also stain any white or highlighted areas of the print. If your toning attempts don't turn out as you expected, keep them for future projects such as collage and card making (see page 151).

**BLEACHED VS. UNBLEACHED**

Toning is often employed on cyanotypes that have been bleached, but it can also be used with unbleached prints. Overexposed prints—those that are very dark—are often good candidates for bleaching. Lighter or underexposed prints could be toned without being bleached first. Try both to see which result you prefer.

When you are bleaching a print in preparation for toning, experiment with how much you allow the print to lighten. There is no right or wrong method here. Personally, I often remove a print from the washing soda bath when the purples start to fade and dark yellows are present, but before the print is completely bleached.

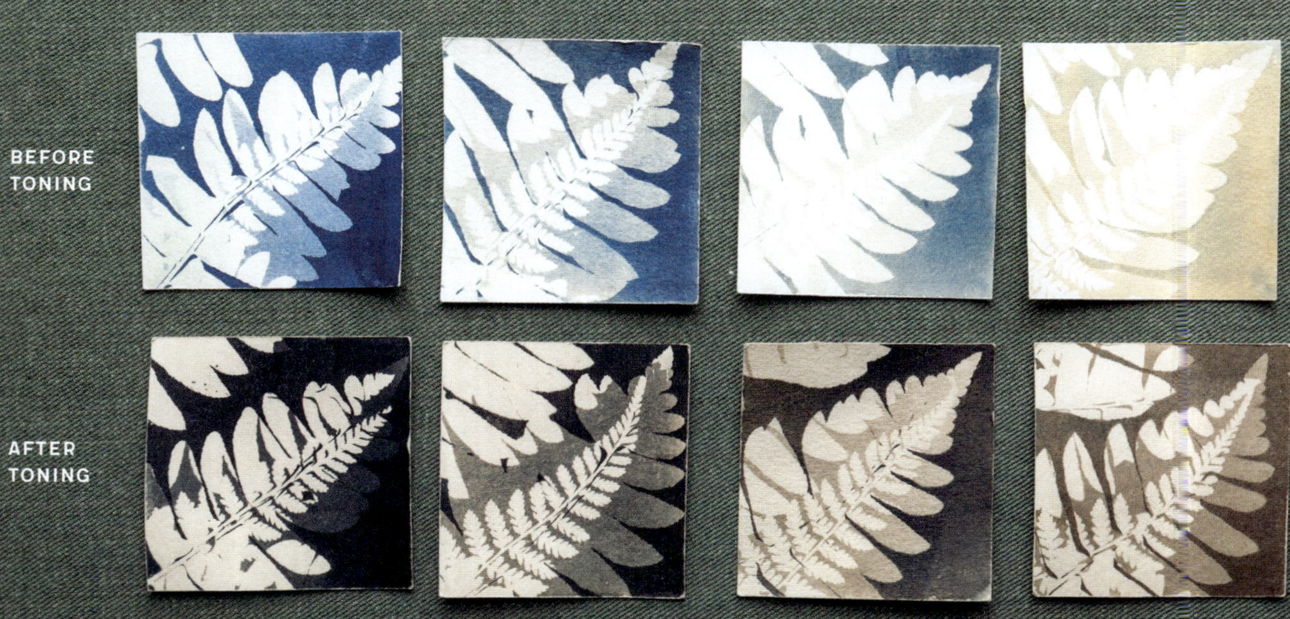


Bleaching the print before toning will impact the finished color. An unbleached print (top row, on the far left) will result in a much darker print when toned (bottom row, on the far left), whereas a bleached print (top row, on the far right) will create a lighter print (bottom row, on the far right) after being toned.

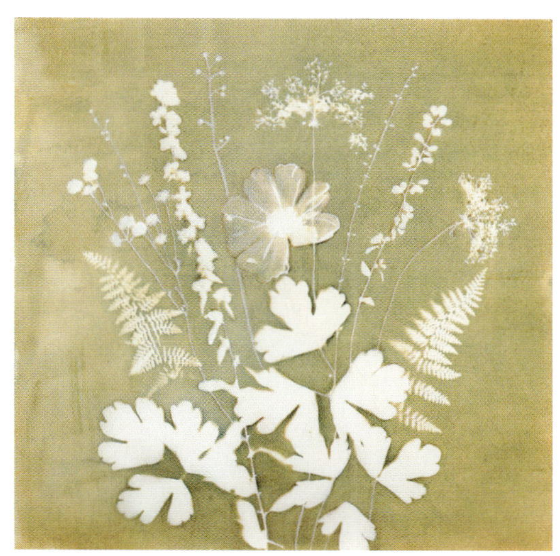

Elizabeth Booth's *Late Summer* is a cyanotype that was bleached before being toned with green tea.

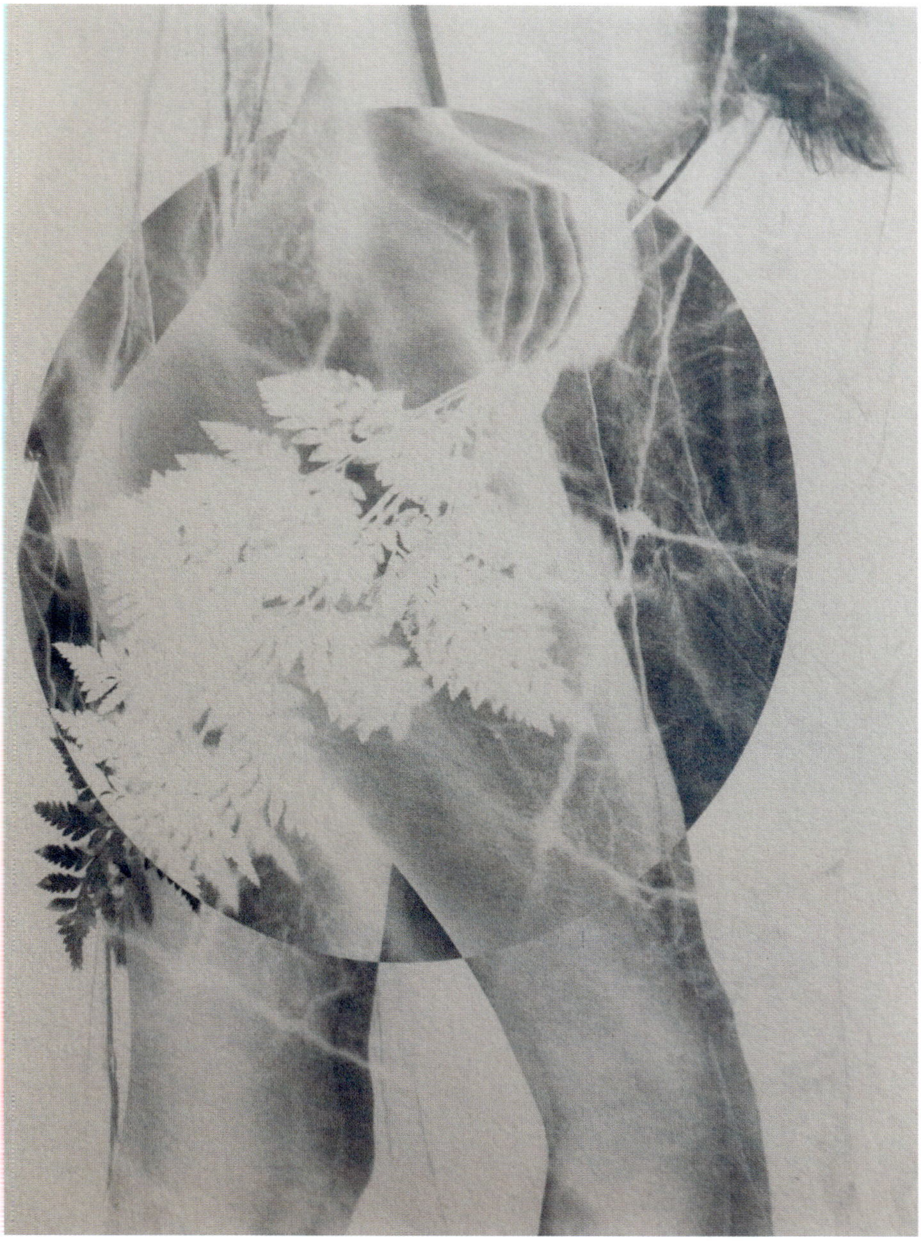

Liliana Guzmán's ethereal cyanotype *Dreaming* was created with digital negatives and botanicals, then toned with coffee and tea.

## Toning a Cyanotype with Botanicals

A wide range of plants can be used for toning, but this project will focus on three that you may already have in your cupboard: Green tea produces tones that range from greenish-black to eggplant, with warm brown highlights. Coffee yields a warm black with grayish light tones. Chopped bay leaves create dark-brown tones with yellowish highlights. Feel free to experiment with other kinds of plants. Try acorns—they are loaded with tannins!

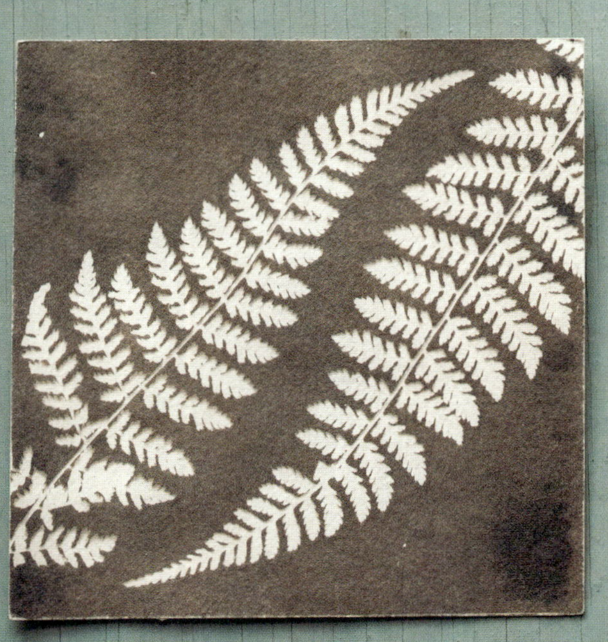

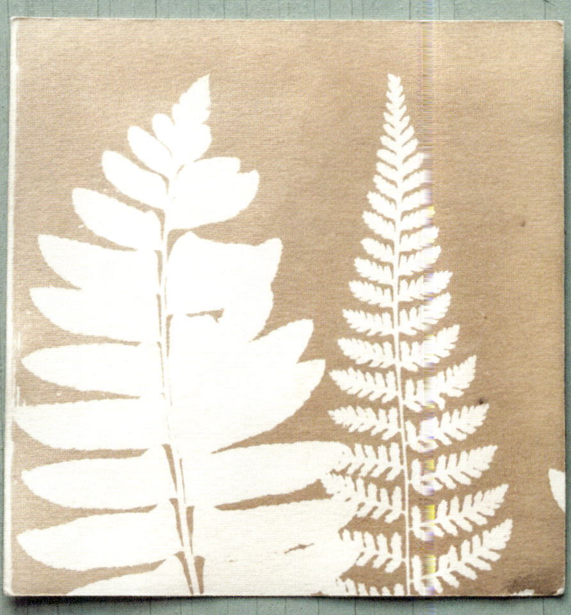

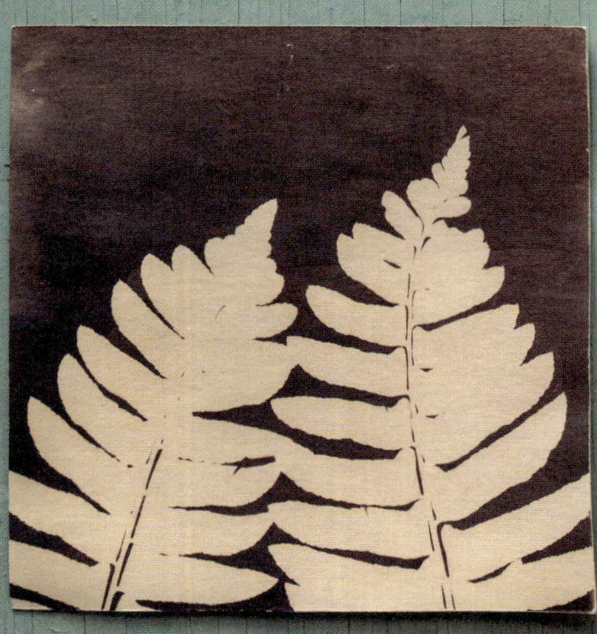

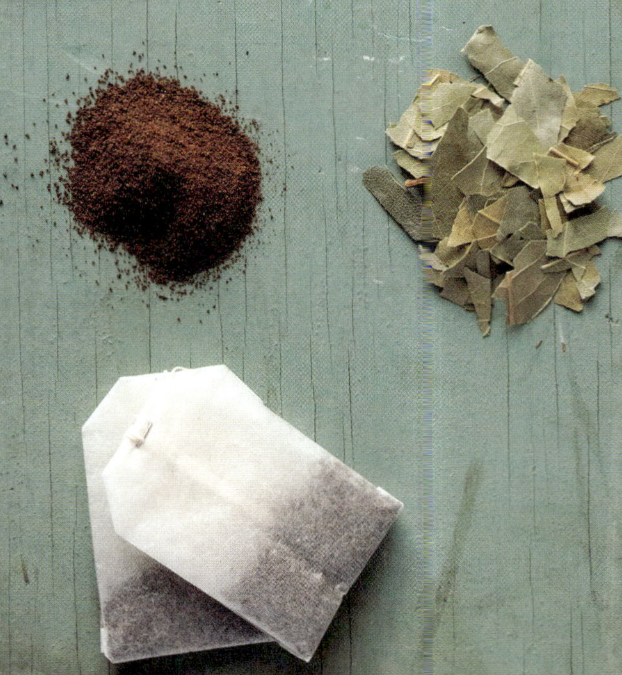

## Materials

- 4 cups or 1,000 mL boiling water
- 6 bags green tea
- ½ cup or 23 grams instant coffee granules
- ¼ cup or 12 grams dried bay leaves, chopped
- Quart-size, heat-safe container, such as a canning jar or large measuring cup
- Two washing trays larger than the cyanotype
- Finished cyanotype on paper
- Washing soda (sodium carbonate) solution (½ teaspoon per 1 quart or 4 grams per 1,000 mL warm water); optional
- Clothesline and clothespins or sheets of clean cardboard

## BLEACHING

Follow steps 1 through 4 on pages 131–133 to bleach your cyanotype if you desire. A bleached print does not need to be dried before moving to the toning step; you can slip it into the toning bath as soon as you're done rinsing it.

## TONING

If you are working with an unbleached print, allow it to dry for at least 24 hours after printing to let the emulsion harden.

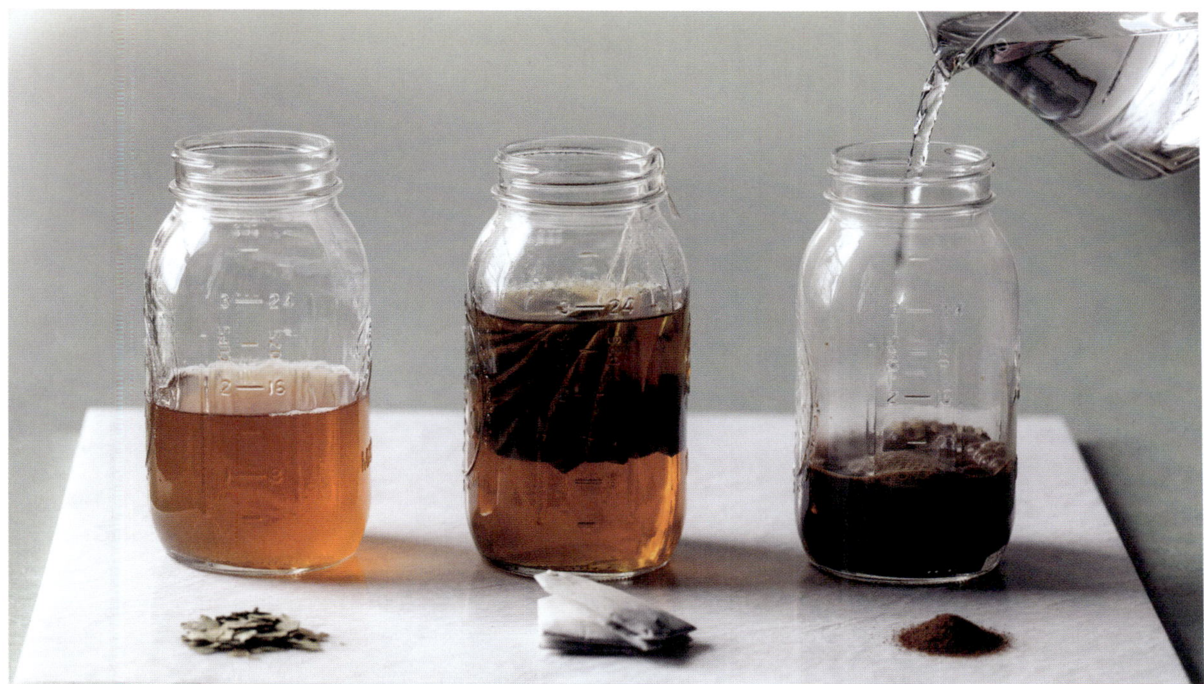

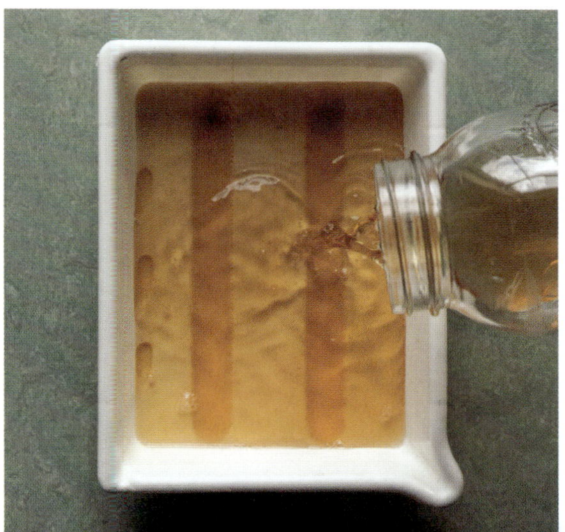

1 **BREW THE TONER.** Pour 4 cups of boiling water over the tea bags, coffee, or bay leaves in a heat-safe container. Let steep for 15 to 30 minutes, then remove the toning materials (you can compost them).

2 **PREPARE THE TONING BATH.** Pour the brewed toner into a washing tray. Agitate the solution gently to remove any air bubbles, which can leave marks on the paper.

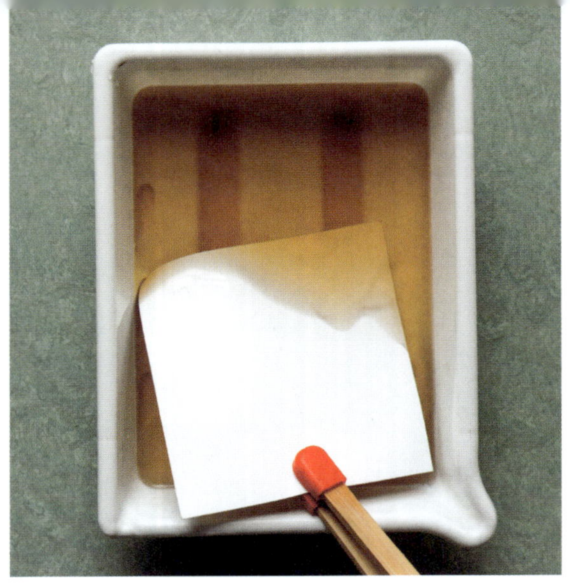

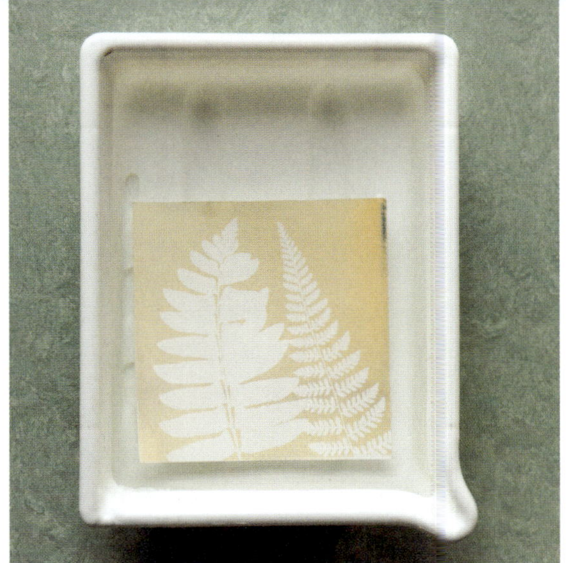

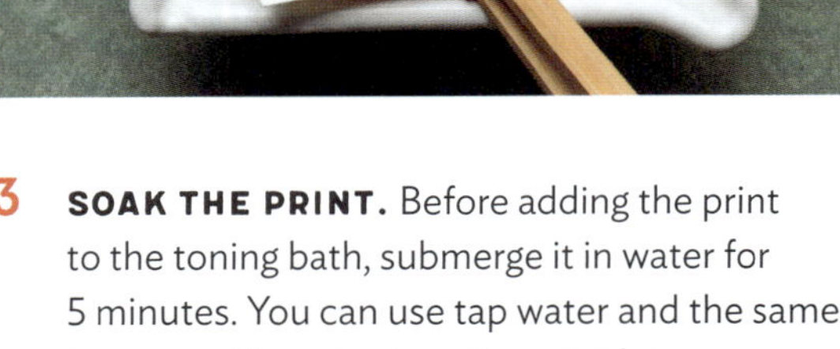

**3** **SOAK THE PRINT.** Before adding the print to the toning bath, submerge it in water for 5 minutes. You can use tap water and the same tray you will use to rinse the print later on.

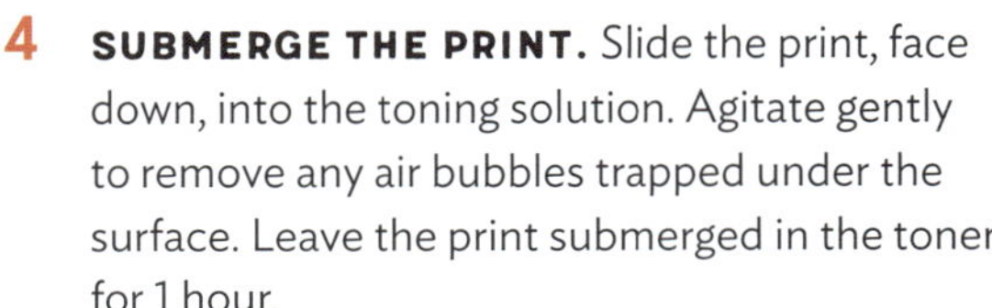

**4** **SUBMERGE THE PRINT.** Slide the print, face down, into the toning solution. Agitate gently to remove any air bubbles trapped under the surface. Leave the print submerged in the toner for 1 hour.

**5** **EVALUATE THE RESULT.** Remove the print from the toning bath to check its progress. If you are satisfied with the toning effect, move on to the next step. If you desire deeper tones, return the print to the toning bath for another 30 minutes or even longer. Prints can be toned for up to 24 hours, but longer times may increase the chance of irregular staining.

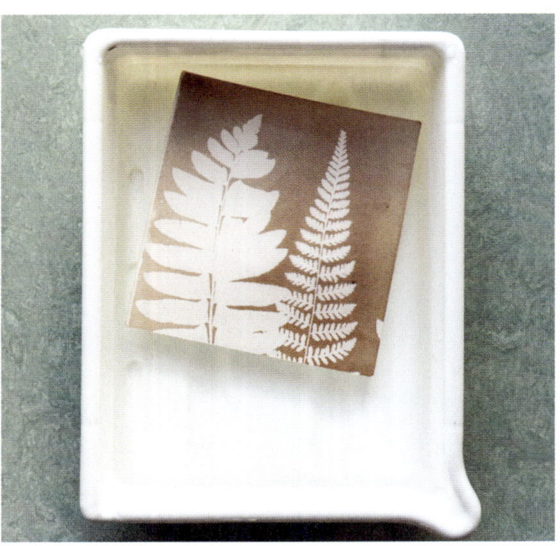

**6** **RINSE.** When you are happy with the toning effect, remove the print from the toning bath and rinse in gently running water. Then submerge the print in a tray of clean water and let sit for 10 minutes.

**7** **DRY THE PRINT.** Set up a clothesline or sheets of clean cardboard as a drying station, somewhere away from direct light. Hang or lay out the print and let it dry completely.

**NOTES** Toners quickly lose their potency, so use only freshly brewed toner.

Annette Golaz offers an in-depth description of 260 different plant toners, including the bay leaves described here, in her book *Cyanotype Toning: Using Botanicals to Tone Blueprints Naturally.*

Toner can also be made with wine tannins, which are available from wine and beer brewing suppliers.

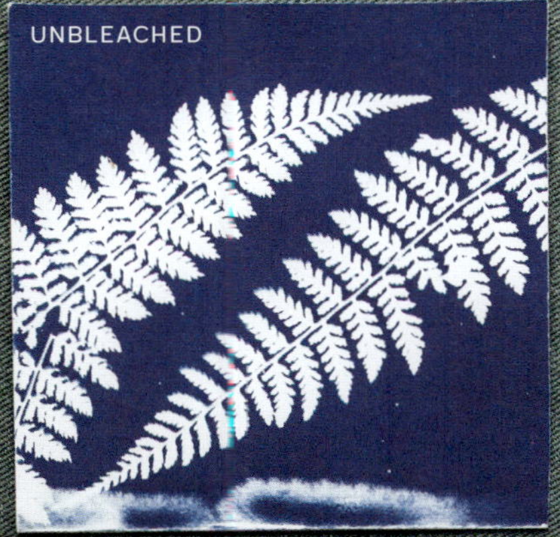
UNBLEACHED
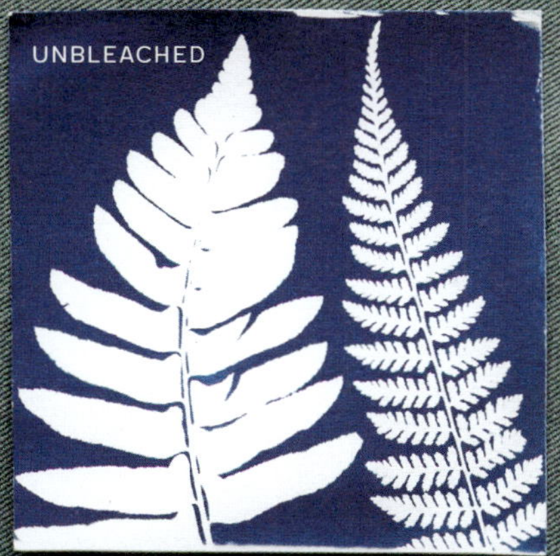
UNBLEACHED
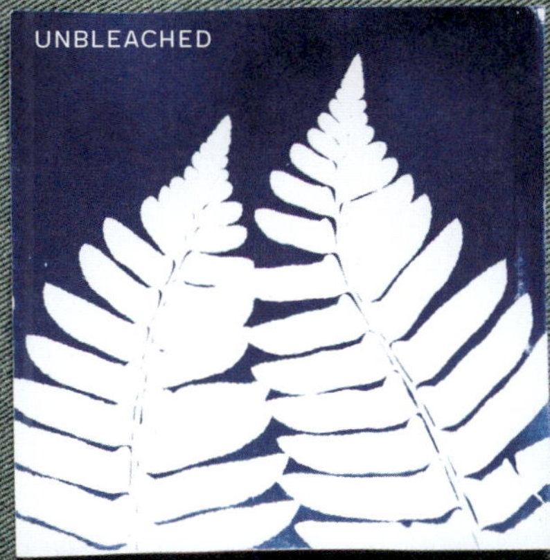
UNBLEACHED
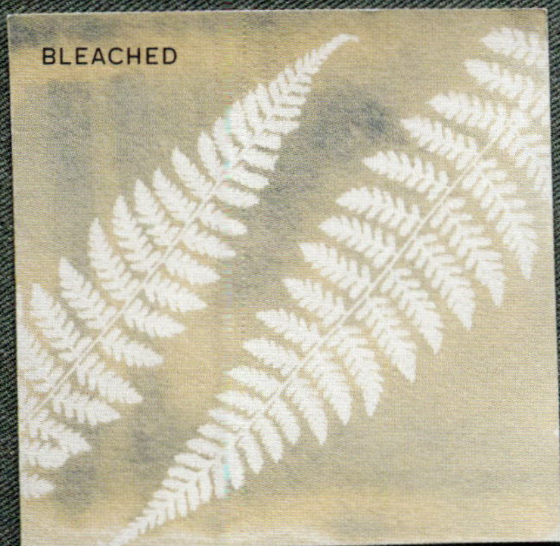
BLEACHED
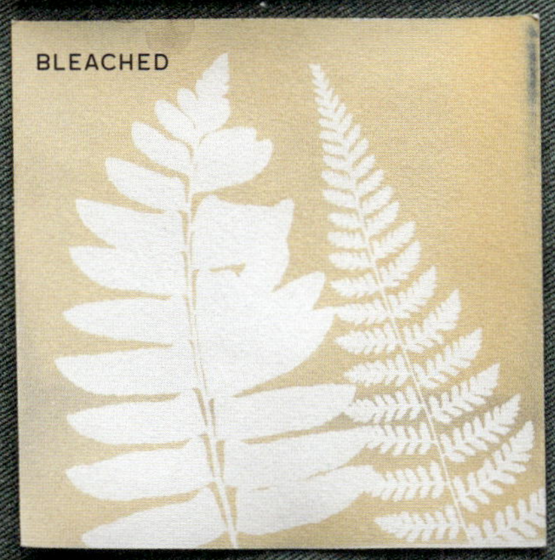
BLEACHED
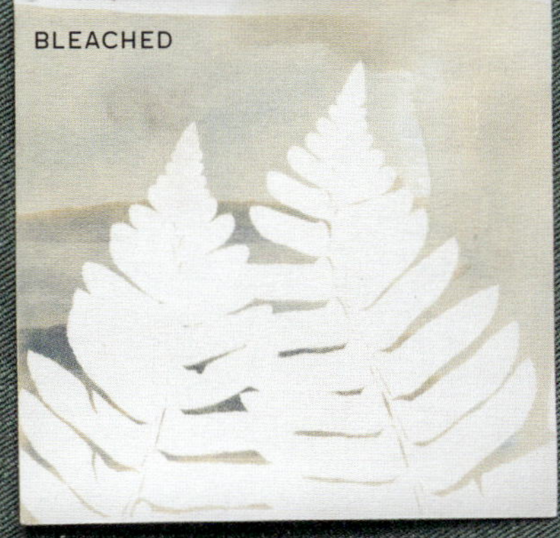
BLEACHED
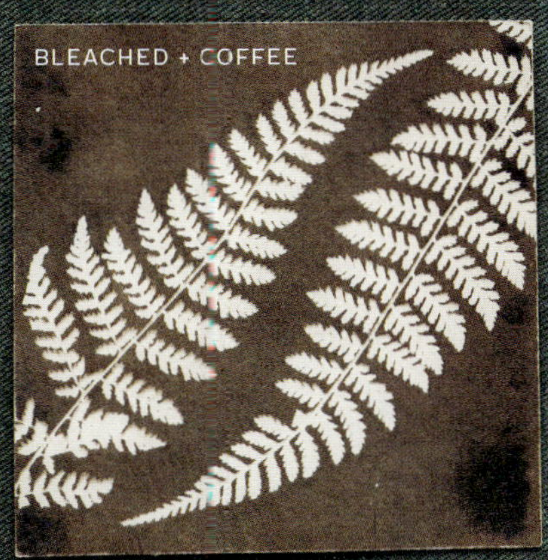
BLEACHED + COFFEE
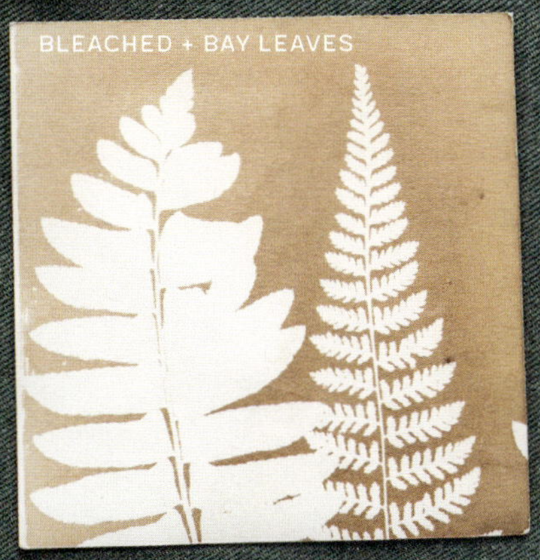
BLEACHED + BAY LEAVES
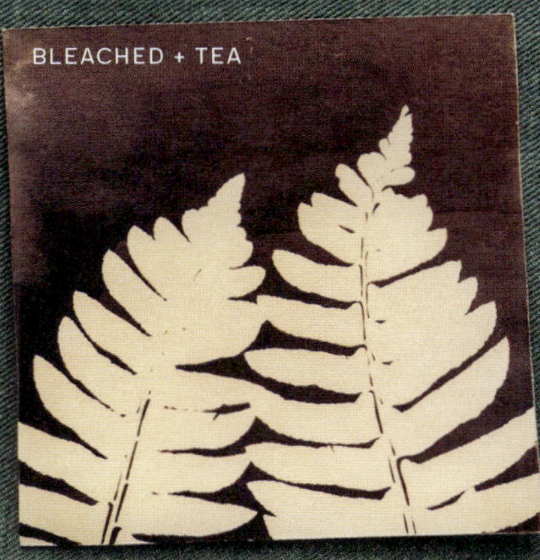
BLEACHED + TEA
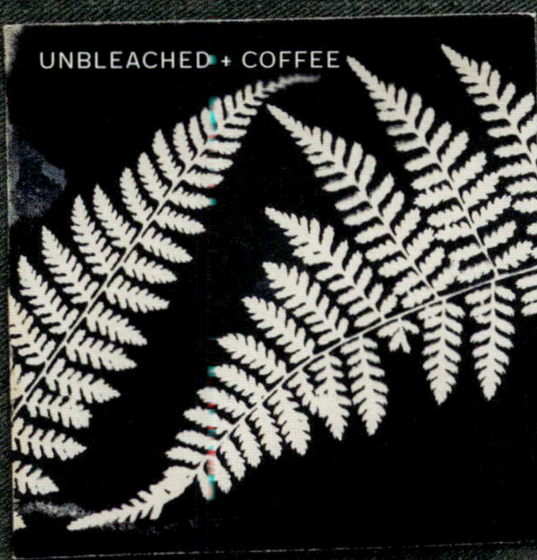
UNBLEACHED + COFFEE
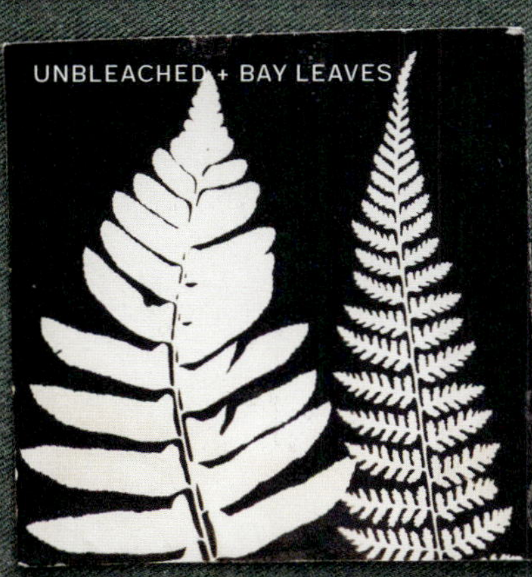
UNBLEACHED + BAY LEAVES
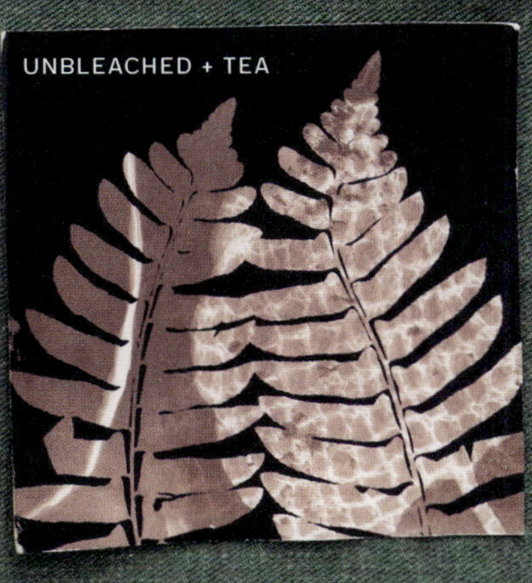
UNBLEACHED + TEA

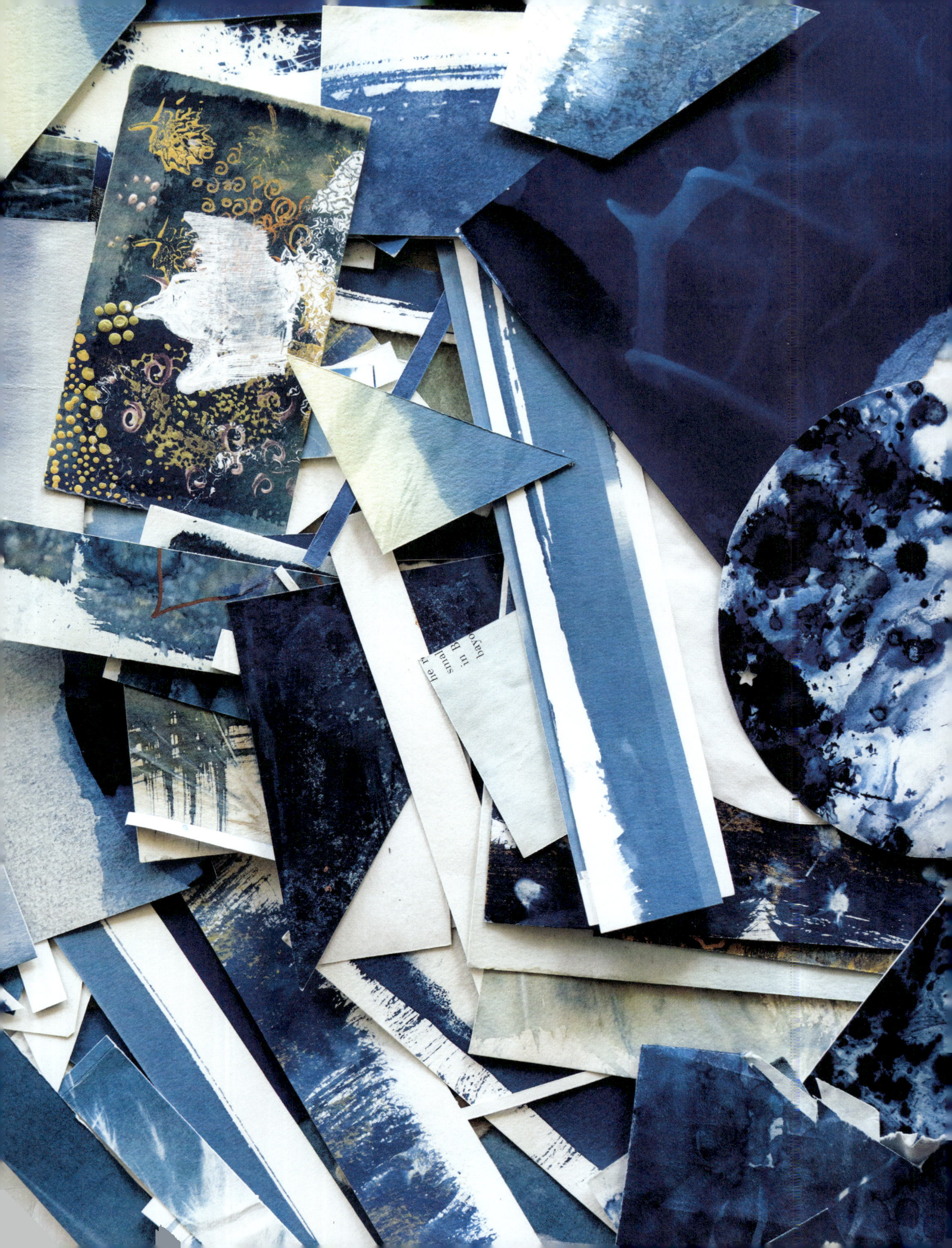

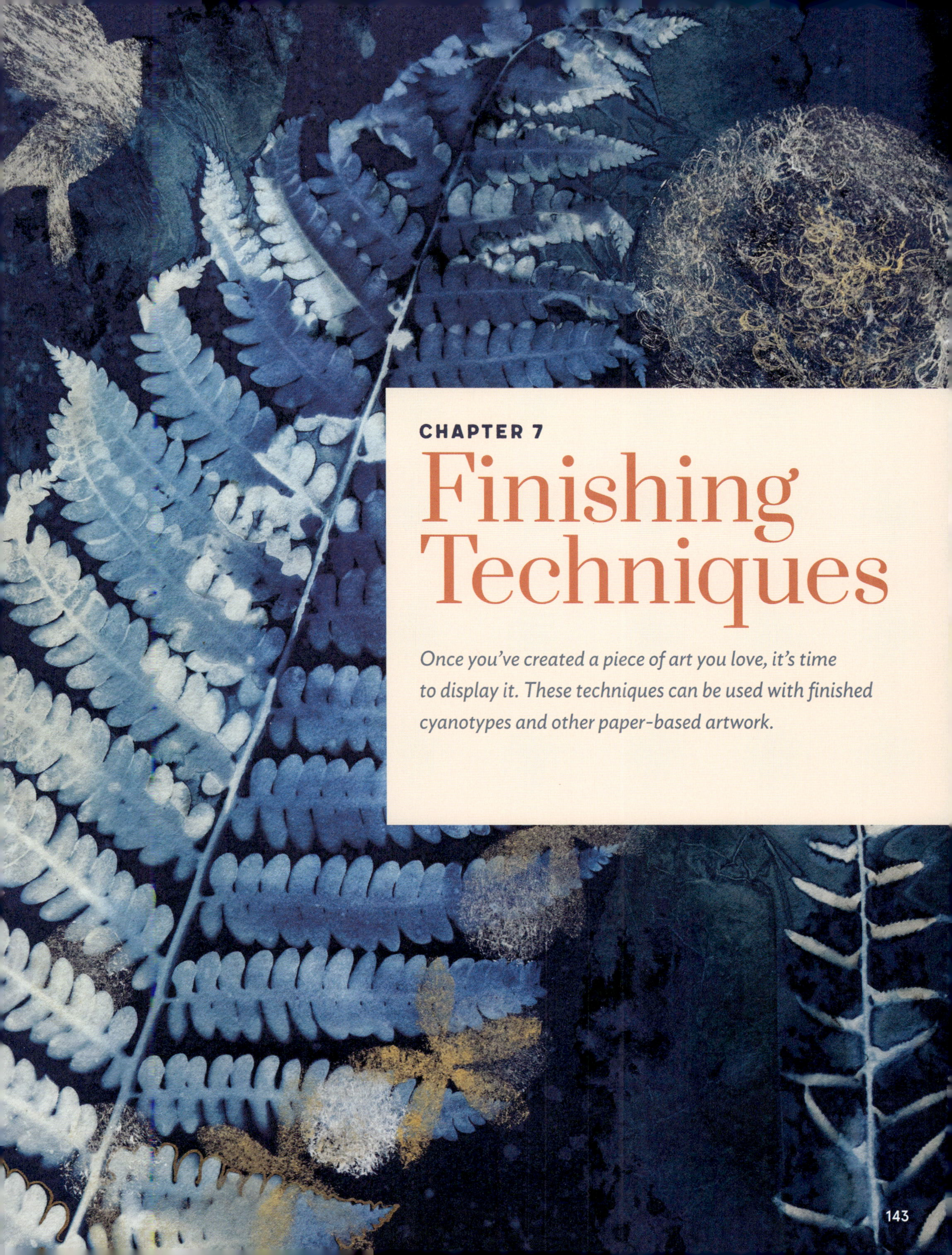

CHAPTER 7

# Finishing Techniques

*Once you've created a piece of art you love, it's time to display it. These techniques can be used with finished cyanotypes and other paper-based artwork.*

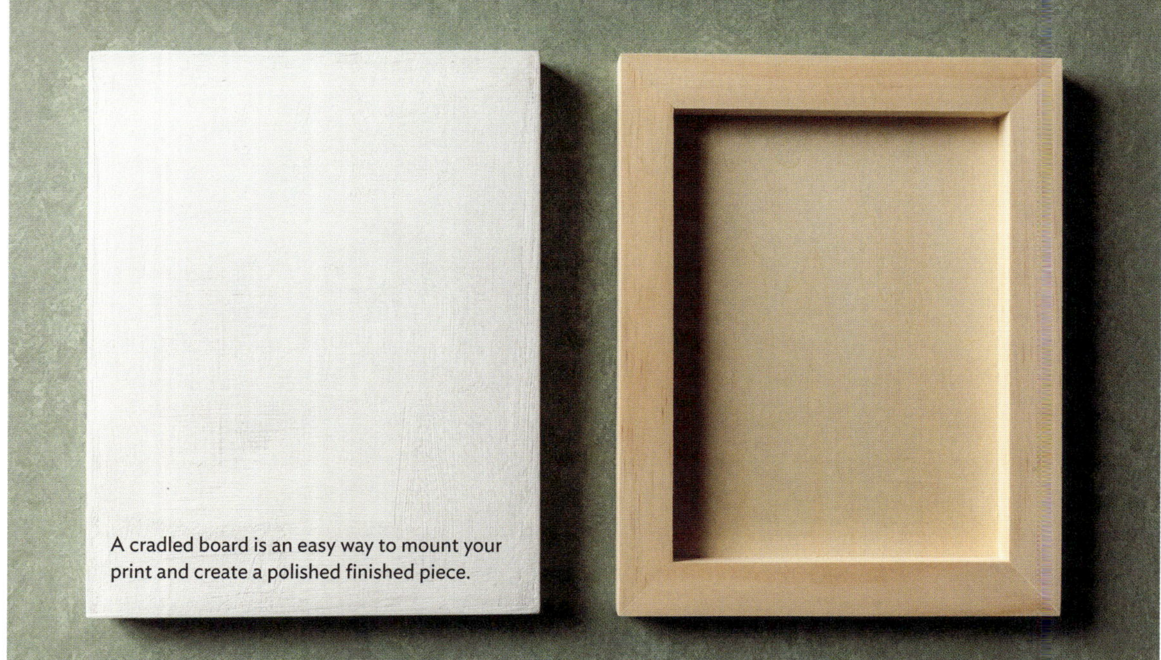

A cradled board is an easy way to mount your print and create a polished finished piece.

# Mounting and Sealing a Cyanotype

Once you've finished a piece of cyanotype art, there are still creative choices to explore. While a cyanotype can simply be displayed in a frame, there are many ways to display, preserve, and enhance a finished print.

Art made on canvas is often quite easy to display, as it is relatively sturdy and can be hung with or without a frame. Cradled boards allow you to create a similar effect for works on paper. A cradled board (sometimes just called a wood art panel) is a wooden panel with a "cradle" or frame secured on one side. Artists sometimes display a work on a cradled board to allow the viewer a more direct experience of the piece. When compared to a print set in a frame behind glass or acrylic, a cradle-mounted print is lightweight, making it easy to transport and to hang.

To mount a cyanotype on a cradled board, you'll simply apply an adhesive to the board and then press the cyanotype onto it. In one of my first attempts at this, I used PVA (polyvinyl adhesive), also known as white glue, to attach a 3 × 4-foot cyanotype onto a board. PVA dries quickly, which didn't give me enough time to smooth the paper onto the wood, resulting in bubbles and wrinkles. While PVA works for smaller cyanotypes, when working with large pieces, I recommend using an adhesive such as extra-heavy gel medium that dries more slowly.

To help a print adhere smoothly to a cradled board without any air bubbles or wrinkles, consider using a rubber brayer, a handheld roller that allows you to apply pressure to the paper, distributing the adhesive uniformly. Alternatively, you can use the edge of a credit card or similar rigid plastic tool to smooth the print onto the board, taking care not to rip or tear the paper. A heavier weight paper (300 gsm or above) will also make it easier to avoid wrinkles and bubbles.

It's best to choose a slow-drying adhesive to avoid wrinkles when mounting a cyanotype, particularly for larger pieces.

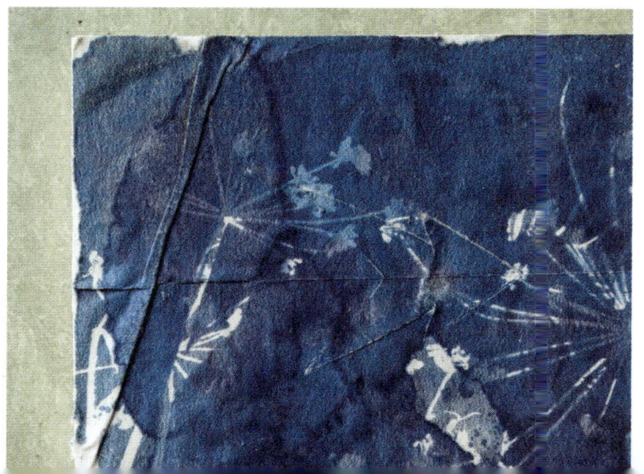

# Mounting a Cyanotype to a Cradled Board

Mounting a cyanotype creates a beautiful and professional finished piece of art that is easy to display.

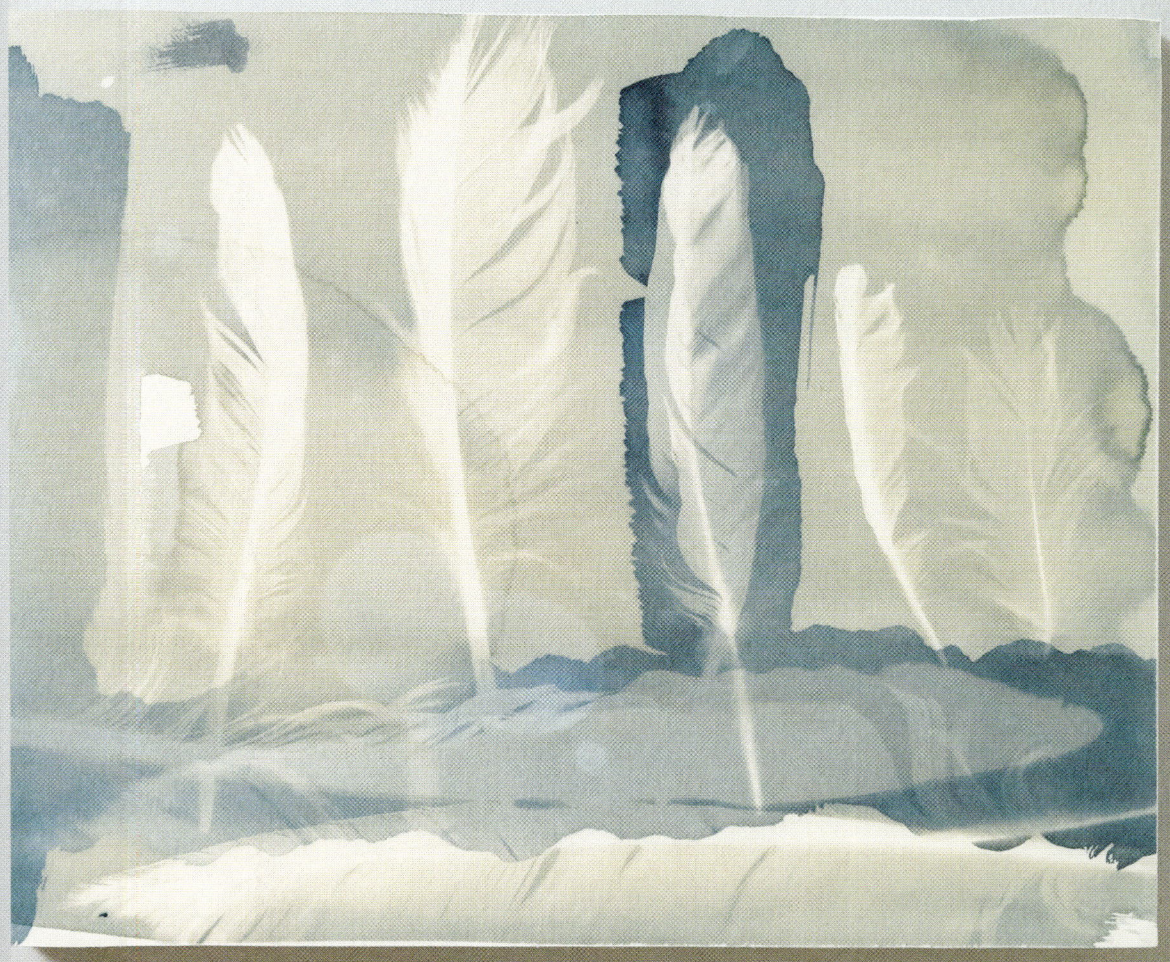

## Materials

- Gesso primer (if the cradled board is not already primed)
- Cradled board
- Kraft paper or paper towels
- Finished cyanotype, larger than the cradled board by ½ inch on all sides
- Pencil
- Adhesive (Avoid PVA and choose an extra-heavy gel medium, especially if you're mounting a large piece
- Rubber brayer
- Heavy object (to weigh down the print as it dries)
- Craft knife
- Fine (600-grit) sandpaper (optional)

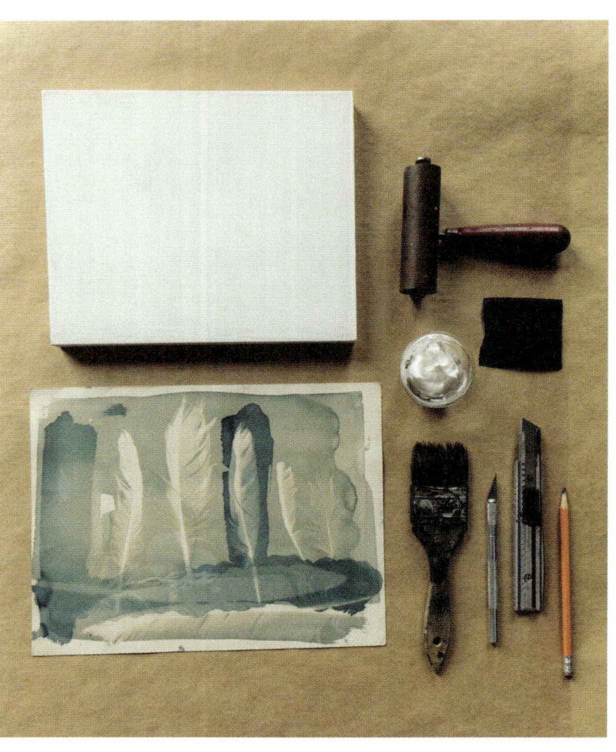

**1 PRIME THE BOARD.** Applying gesso primer to the surface of the cradled board creates a less-porous surface for the adhesive and provides a protective layer between the acid present in the wood and the paper on which the cyanotype is printed. Some cradled boards are preprimed, but if yours is not, or if you made your own, use a paintbrush to apply a layer of gesso, following the manufacturer's instructions, and let it dry completely.

**2 SET UP.** Arrange your materials and tools on your worktable and lay out some kraft paper. Place the cyanotype image side down on the kraft paper. Place the cradled board on top of it, face down. Make sure that the cyanotype is at least ½ inch larger on all sides than the board; you'll trim away the excess in step 7. Then trace around the edges with a pencil to mark the position of the board on the back of the print.

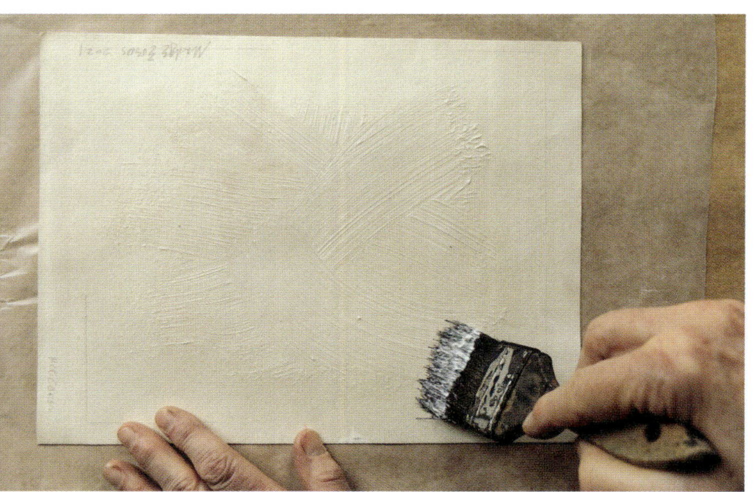

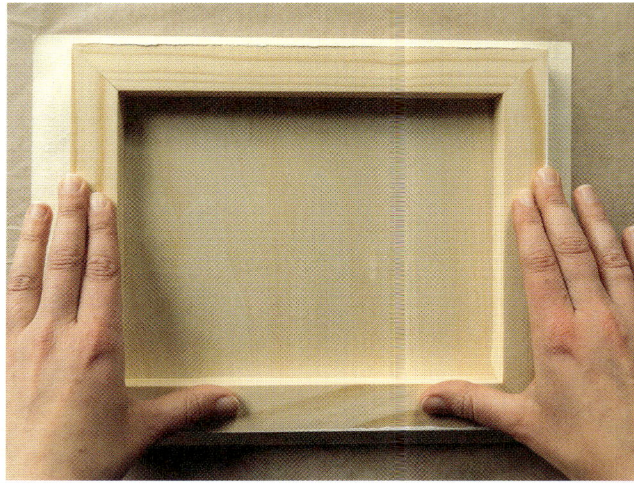

**3 APPLY THE ADHESIVE.** Flip the cradled board over, so that its front faces up, and set it aside. (Leave the cyanotype face down on the kraft paper.) Using a paintbrush, apply the adhesive to the board, starting at the center and moving toward the edges. Work quickly and apply the adhesive as evenly as possible. A thick application of gel medium is fine; any excess adhesive will dry clear.

**4 ADHERE THE CYANOTYPE TO THE SURFACE.** Pick up the board by its interior edges and place it, face down, on the wrong side of the cyanotype, aligning it with the lines you traced in step 2. Apply pressure to adhere the print to the surface of the board.

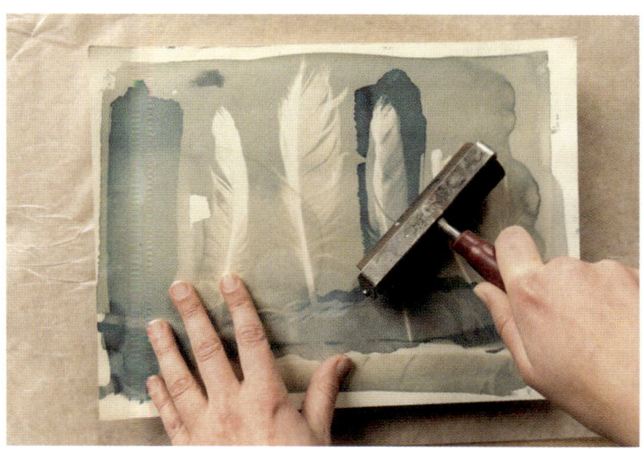

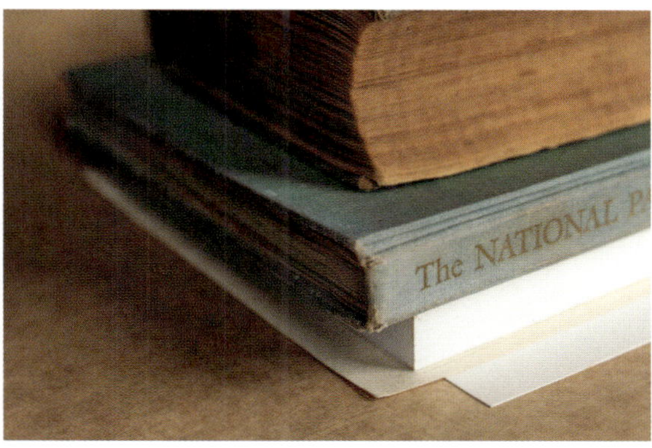


5 **SMOOTH AND REMOVE BUBBLES.** Flip the board over. Starting from the middle, roll a clean brayer across the panel to push out any bubbles.

6 **LET DRY.** Place clean paper on top of the mounted print and cover it with some kind of weight (books work well). Allow it to dry for at least 24 hours.

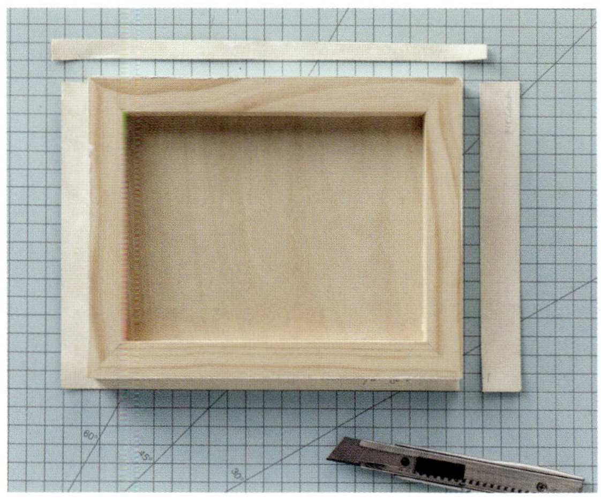

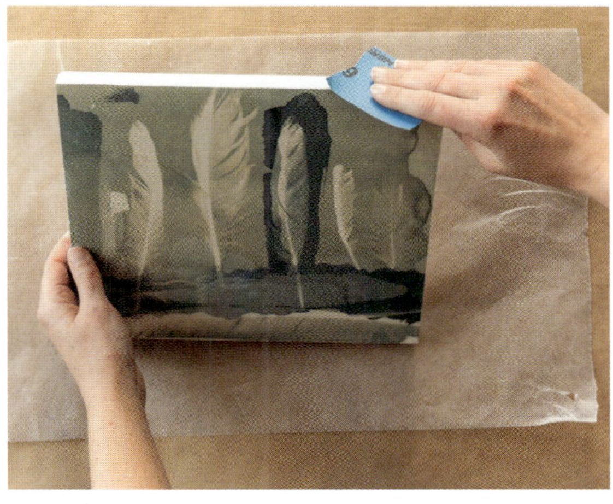

7 **TRIM PAPER EDGES.** Once the adhesive is dry, place the board with the image side down on a cutting surface. Use a sharp blade (a craft knife works well) to trim off the overhanging edges of the print.

8 **SAND THE EDGES (OPTIONAL).** If desired, use 600-grit sandpaper to lightly sand the edge where the paper meets the board. Sand downward, away from the paper, to avoid pulling the paper off the surface.

**NOTES** To hang a cradled board, use D-rings and picture wire. On each side of the frame on the back of the board, drill a pilot hole for the D-ring screws about one-third of the way down from the top. Screw in the D-rings, then attach a length of picture wire between the two rings. The board is now ready to be hung from a hook or nail.

One way to finish a cyanotype mounted on a cradled board is to apply a protective wax coating, described in the next project!

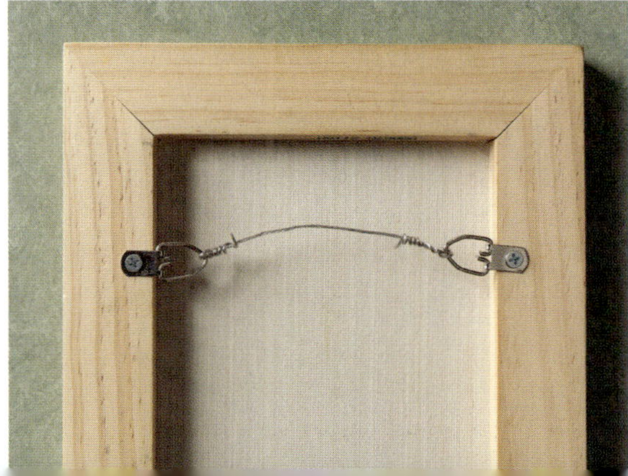

# Applying a Wax Finish

Cold wax medium (CWM) is a mixture of beeswax and odorless mineral spirits. You can find it at any art supply store or online. Artists combine CWM with oil paint and pigments; its pastelike consistency creates interesting layers and patinas. It can also be used as a finish for works on paper, to add depth, shine, and an interesting texture.

CWM offers mild protection from the elements but doesn't protect the piece from light; apply a UV spray fixative before applying the CWM to protect the finished print from UV light.

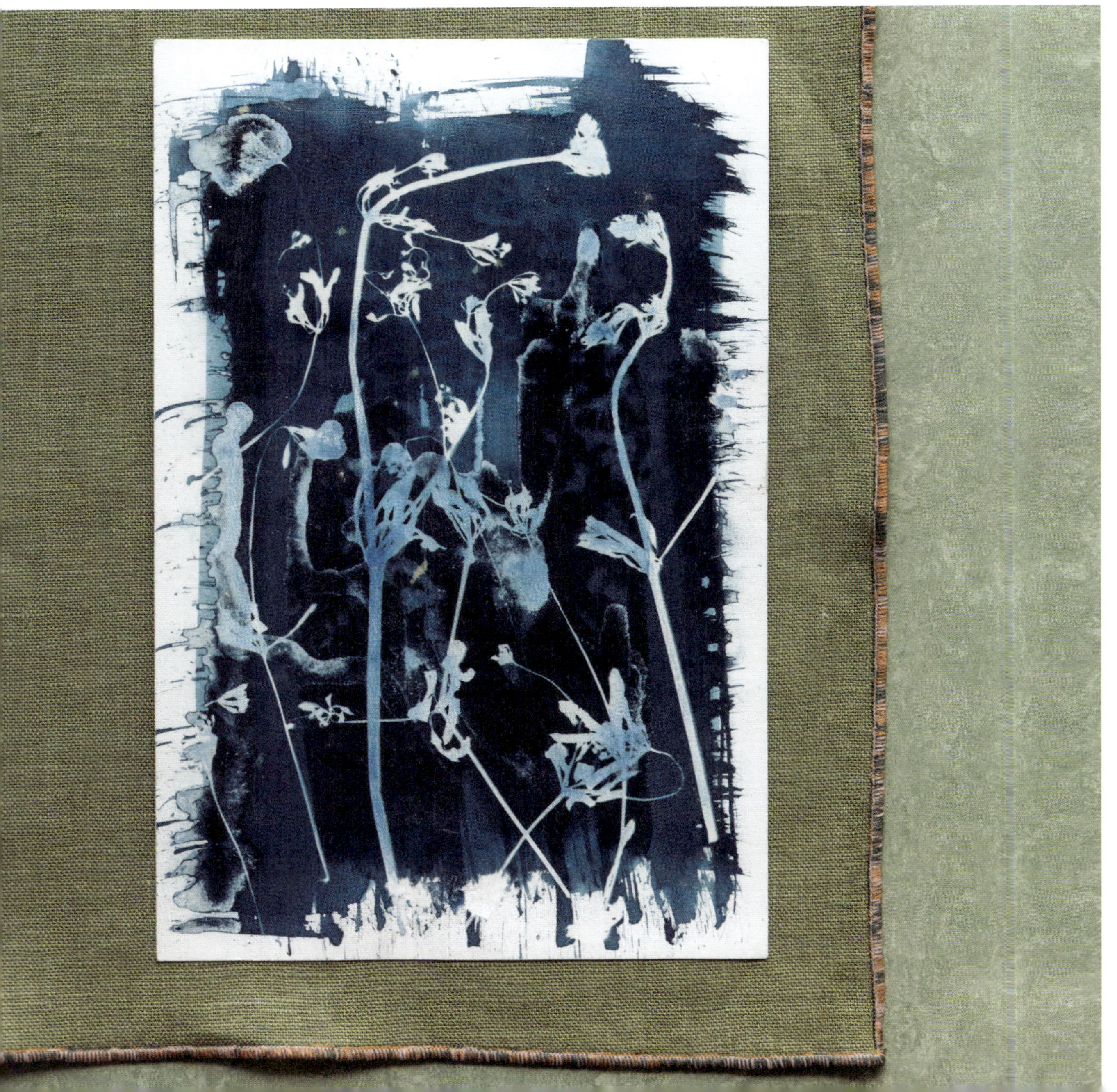

## Materials

- UV spray fixative suitable for paper
- A finished cyanotype on paper or mounted on cradled board
- Clean kraft paper or paper towels (to cover your work surface)
- Nitrile or rubber gloves
- Lint-free cloth (microfiber towels, low-lint paper towels, or linen fabric all work well)
- Cold wax medium

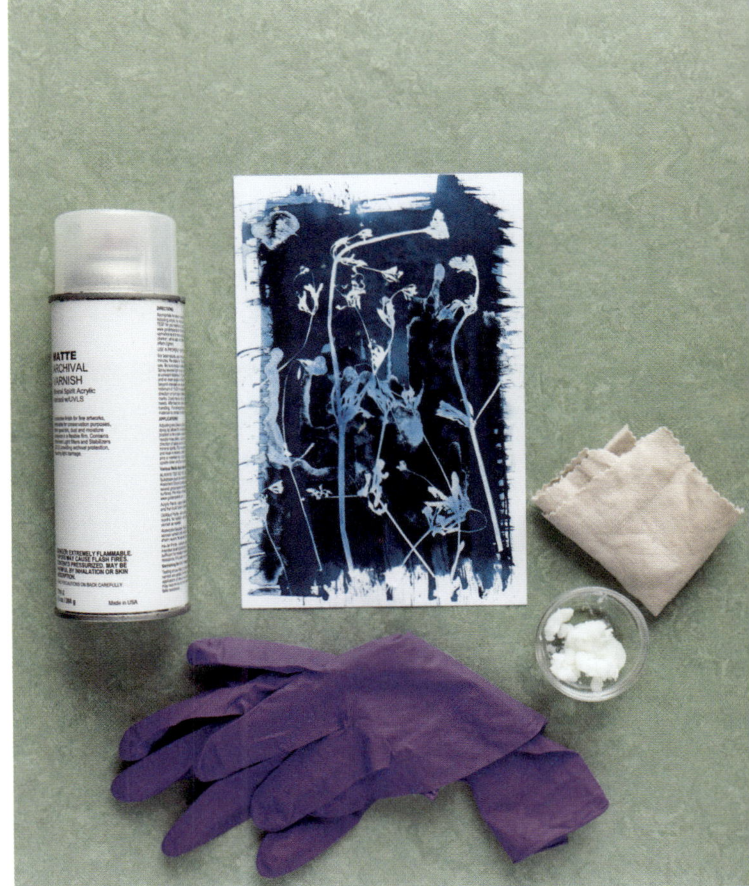

**1 APPLY SPRAY FIXATIVE.** Follow the directions on the container to apply two layers of spray fixative to your finished cyanotype. Work outside, but not in direct sunlight. Allow the first coat to dry for at least 5 hours before applying the second coat. Ensure that the fixative is completely dry before applying the CWM.

**2 SET UP.** Lay a sheet of clean paper on your work surface. Place the cyanotype print on the paper, face up. Gather the rest of your materials.

**3 APPLY WAX.** Wear nitrile or rubber gloves to protect your hands. Using a piece of lint-free cloth, scoop out a small amount of CWM. Rub the wax onto the cyanotype in a circular motion, applying a thin, even layer to completely cover the image. If your work is mounted on a cradled board and the sides of the cradle are unfinished, apply the wax to the sides as well.

Although it is not necessary, you can warm the cold wax before applying it by placing the jar in the sun. Warming the wax makes it slightly easier to apply a thin coat. However, do not heat CWM or it will liquefy.

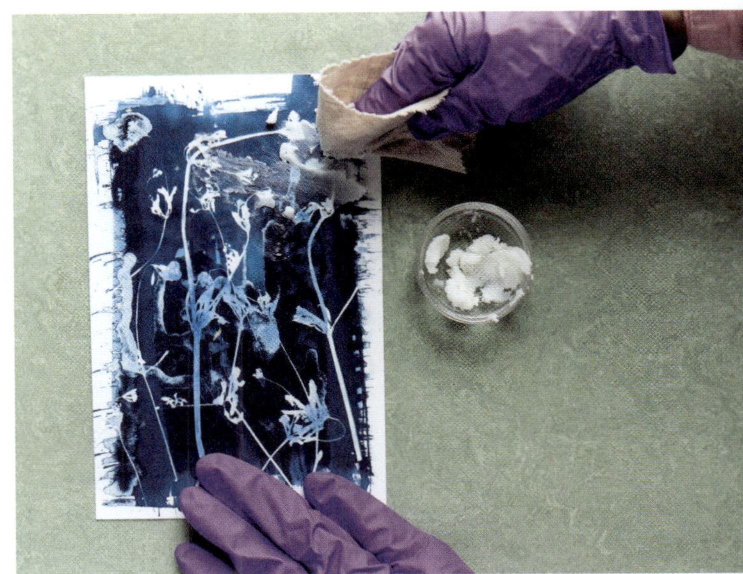

### WORKING SAFELY WITH CWM

The odorless mineral spirits present in CWM require special care. Wear protective gloves to avoid direct skin contact with CWM. Work in a well-ventilated area with doors and windows open; if necessary, use a window fan.

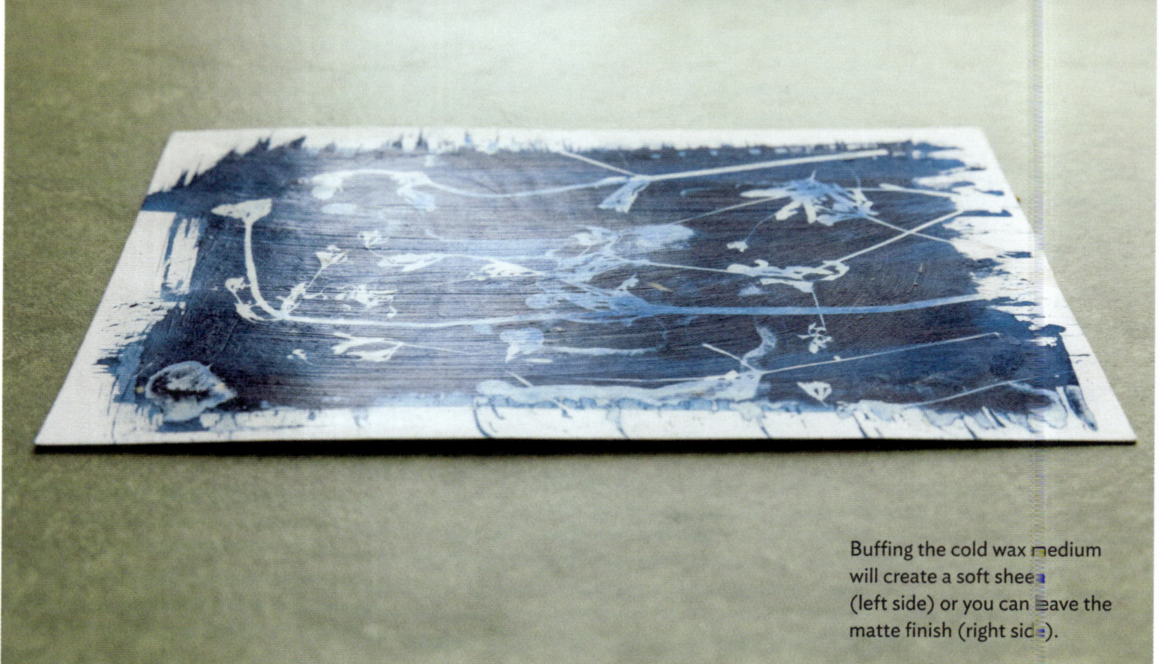

Buffing the cold wax medium will create a soft sheen (left side) or you can leave the matte finish (right side).

**4 ALLOW TO DRY.** Let your newly waxed image dry for at least 24 hours. A thick layer of wax may take longer to dry. The wax is dry when it is no longer sticky or soft.

**5 BUFF AND SHINE (OPTIONAL).** The unbuffed cyanotype print will have a matte appearance. If you like the soft matte finish, you can skip this step. Otherwise, use a fresh lint-free cloth to buff the print by rubbing in circular motions. The dull wax will begin to shine.

**6 ADD MORE LAYERS (OPTIONAL).** For more texture, repeat steps 3 through 5. Allow the wax to dry for 24 hours between each layer.

**7 CURE.** Allow another 24 hours for the wax finish to harden completely.

**NOTES** Cold wax medium will soften in extreme heat. Do not display a waxed print in direct sunlight or expose a waxed print to temperatures above 144°F/62°C (for example, in a car parked in the summer sun).

For an alternative natural finish, rub warm beeswax mixed with a few drops of lavender essential oil onto a cyanotype print with a lint-free cloth.

# Bespoke Greeting Cards and Cyanotype Collage

Writing letters and making cards by hand are becoming lost arts. Designing bespoke greeting cards using cyanotypes is one way to keep those traditions alive and share your finished art with others.

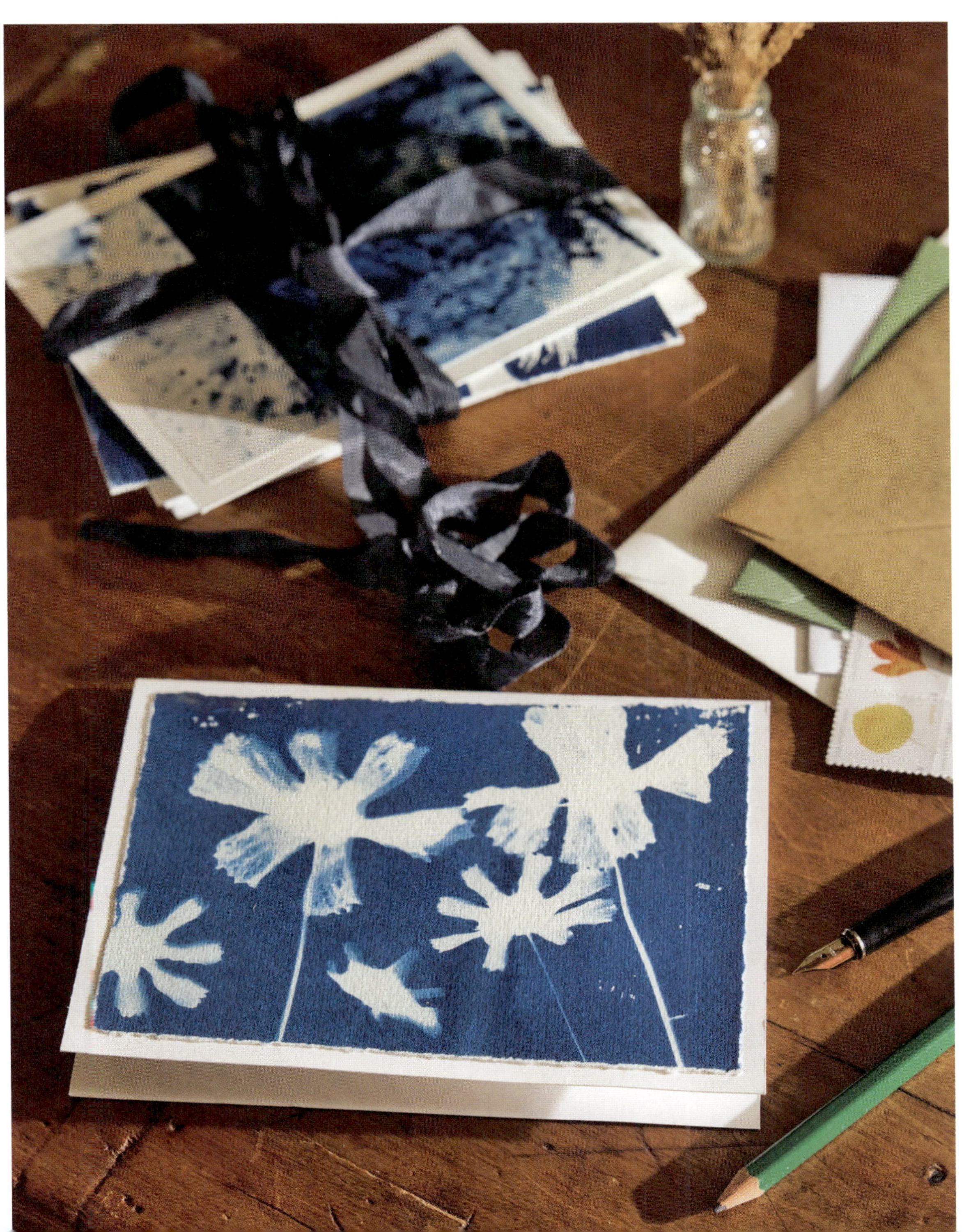

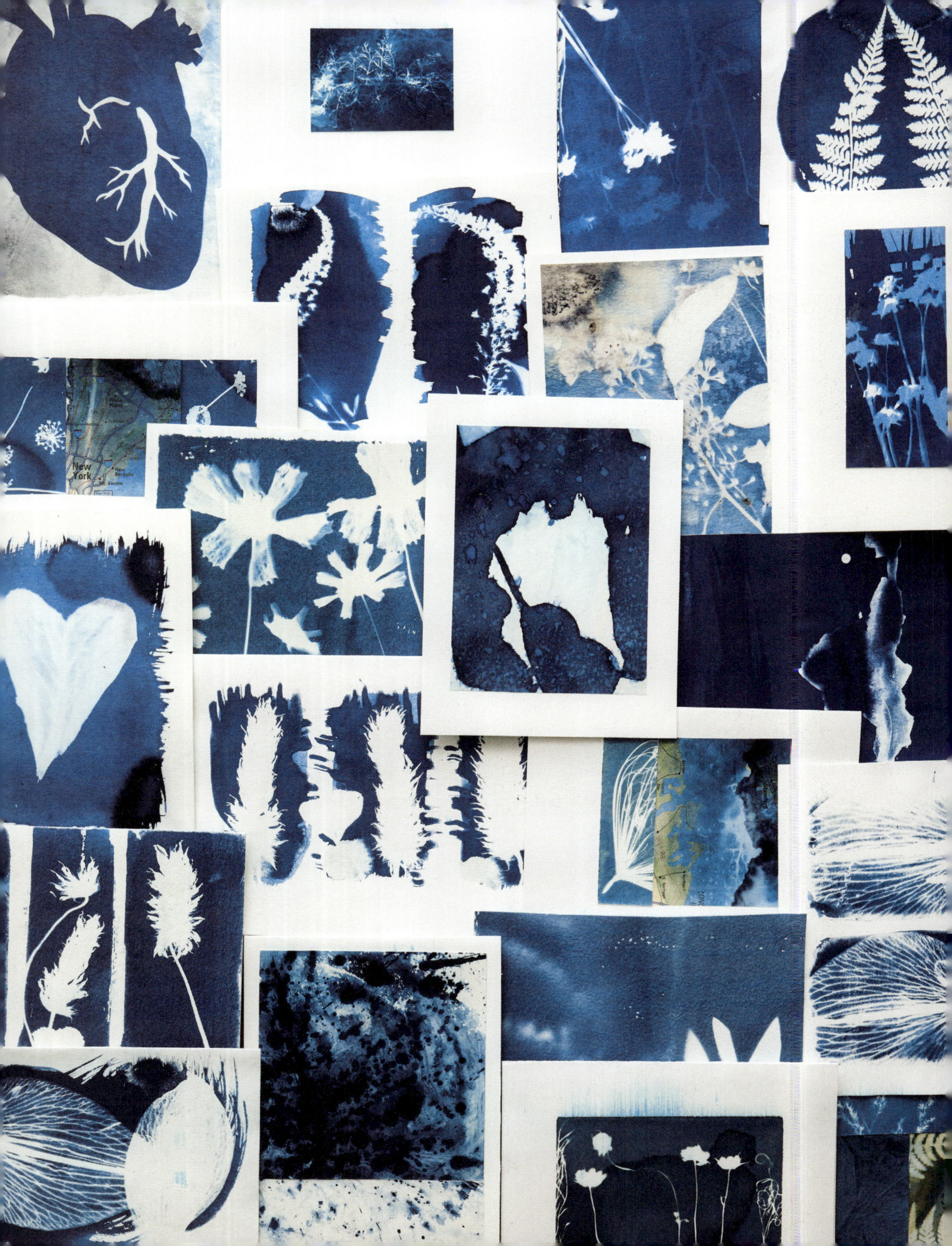
New York
New Rochelle
Mt. Vernon

The word *bespoke* is overused in marketing copy these days, but it simply means custom-made to meet the needs or tastes of the individual—like the lucky recipient of a handmade cyanotype-based card. While there are many approaches to making greeting cards, we will focus on two techniques: creating a mini cyanotype greeting card and using a collage of cyanotypes to create a card.

## CHOOSING PAPER

When designing a greeting card, consider your envelope size and use it to determine the size of paper you'll use for the card.

"A" or announcement-style envelopes come in various sizes and are typically used for invitations and greeting cards. They often feature a square flap. The following envelope sizes pair well with commonly available pads of paper.

| ENVELOPE SIZE | CORRESPONDING PAPER SIZE |
| --- | --- |
| A-6 / 4¾ inches × 6½ inches | 6 × 9-inch paper folded in half = 6 × 4½ inches (see note below) |
| A-7 / 5¼ inches × 7¼ inches | 7 × 10-inch paper folded in half = 7 × 5 inches |
| A-8 / 5½ inches × 8⅛ inches | 8 × 10-inch paper folded in half = 8 × 5 inches |

**NOTES** You can create a sheet of 6 × 9-inch paper by cutting a 9 × 12-inch sheet in half. Pads of 9 × 12-inch paper are commonly available.

Whatever size paper you choose, it should be at least 163 gsm/60# weight. Lighter-weight papers are not sturdy enough for greeting cards.

Your paper will fold more smoothly if you fold with the grain. To determine the grain of the paper, you can simply bend it gently in both directions; it will naturally bend more easily along the grain.

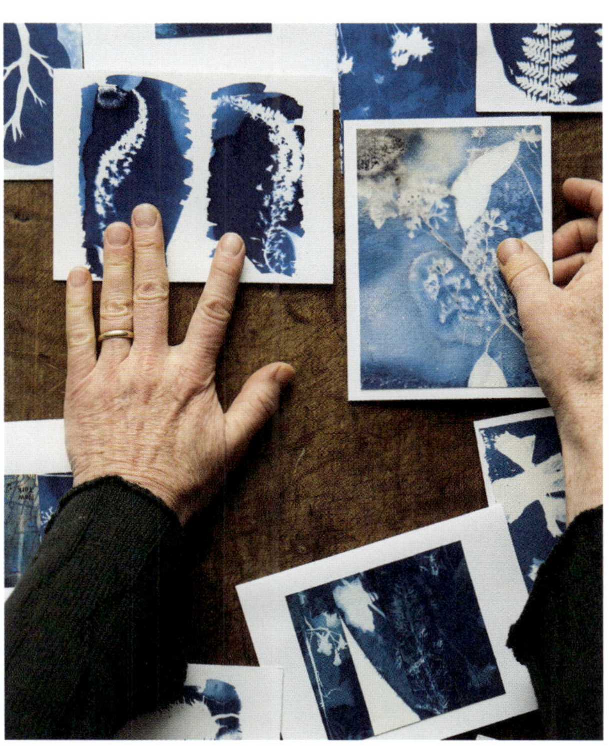

## FOLDING THE CARD

To get a crisp fold on the thick paper used for a handmade card, use a bone folder. If you don't have a bone folder, use the smooth back of a butter knife.

1 **MARK THE FOLD.** On the side of the paper you wish to use for the interior of the card, measure the spot where you intend to fold it, marking both ends of the fold. Use a pencil to make faint marks that can be erased later.

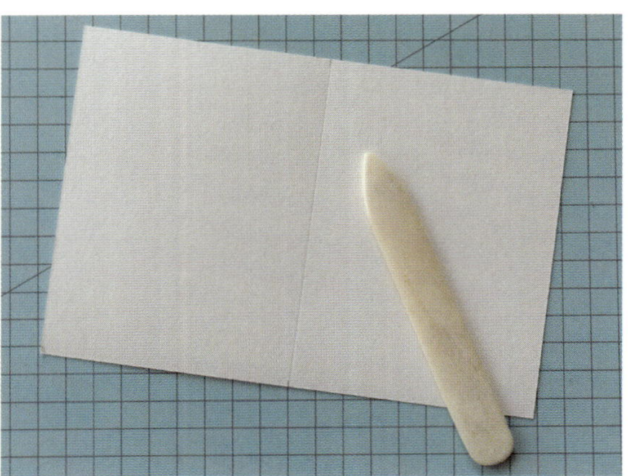

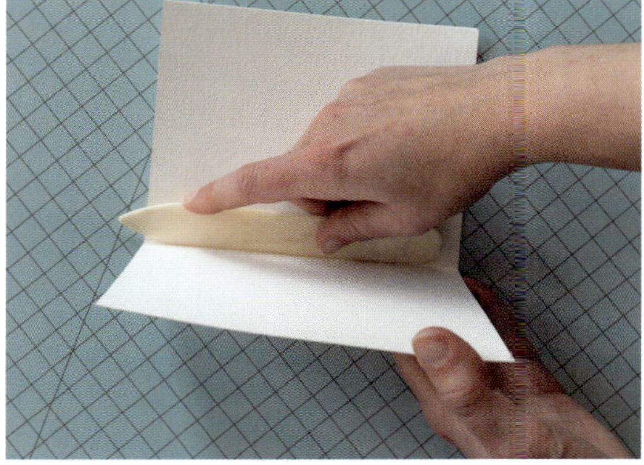

2 **SCORE THE PAPER.** Align a ruler with the marks you just made. Then place the tip of a bone folder against the ruler's edge, pressing into the paper—but not so hard that you tear the fibers. Drag the bone folder along the ruler to create a scoreline. The scoreline will be indented on the side facing up and raised on the side facing down.

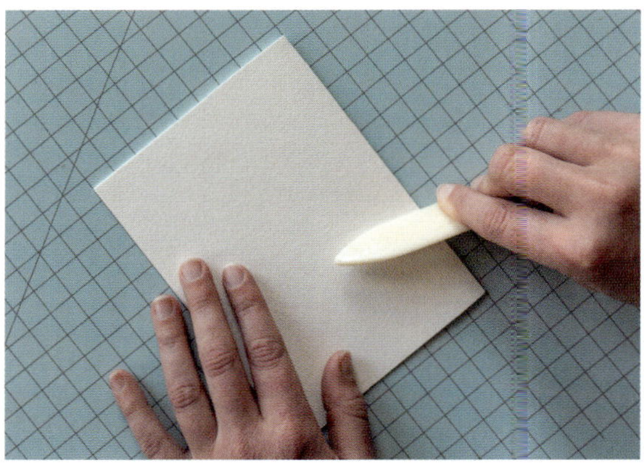

3 **CREASE THE PAPER.** Flip the paper over. Fold it along the raised side of the scoreline, using the bone folder to help create a crisp crease. (Folding toward the raised side of the scoreline gives a cleaner fold.) Gently drag the wide, flat edge of the bone folder across the folded edge, applying light pressure.

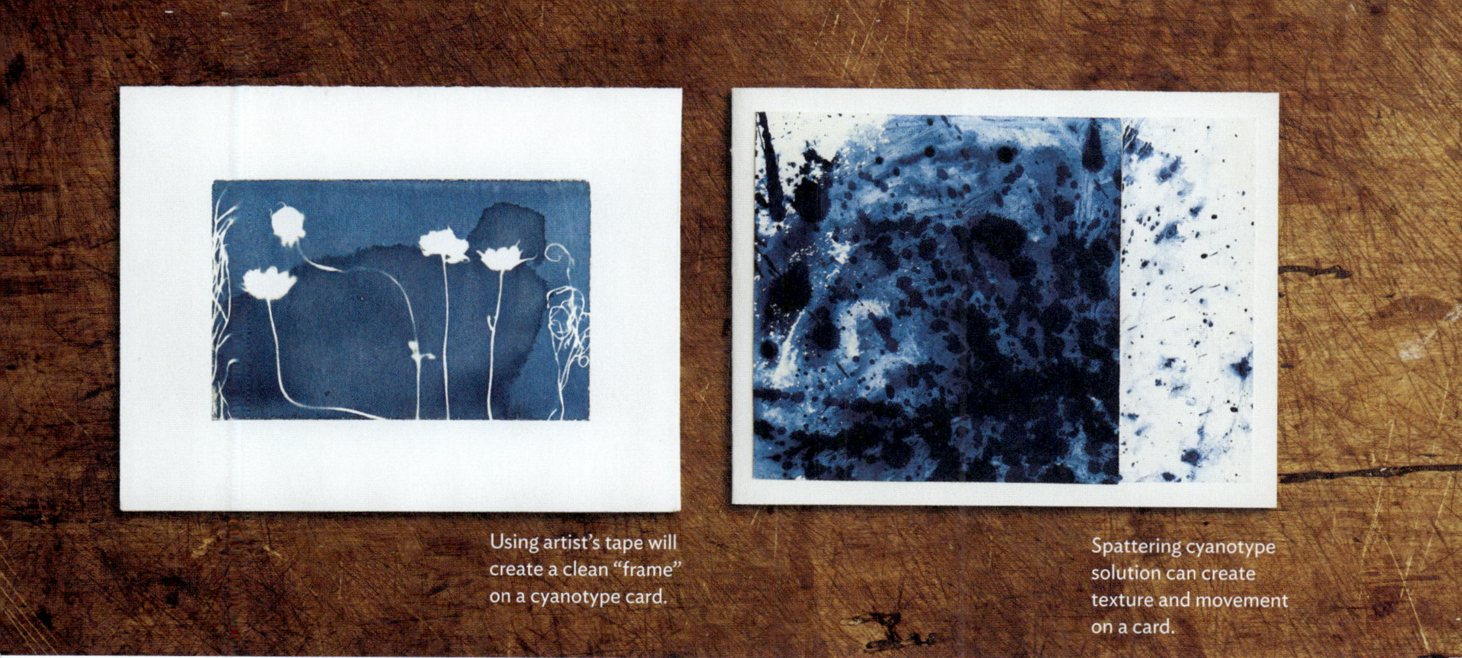

Using artist's tape will create a clean "frame" on a cyanotype card.

Spattering cyanotype solution can create texture and movement on a card.

## MAKING A MINI CYANOTYPE

Making a mini cyanotype is much the same as making a full-size one: Coat the paper, allow to dry, expose it, wash it, and dry the finished print. You can follow the instructions given for a basic botanical cyanotype on page 88. As you prepare your paper and composition, consider the following factors.

When applying cyanotype emulsion to the paper, a few drops or splatters can either detract from the composition or add a desired effect, depending on your intent.

Before applying the cyanotype emulsion, you can use artist's tape to mask the edges of the card, creating a clean border. Or you can skip the tape for a free-form look, allowing visible brushstrokes to shape your design.

If you coat the entire sheet, take care not to get the emulsion on the inside of the card. Also, consider how the card's front and back work together in your composition.

Try creating a mini diptych across the card's panels. Or experiment with a mini triptych design.

Use a stencil to make multiples for invitations, thank-you cards, or holiday-specific greetings.

## MAKING A CYANOTYPE COLLAGE

Collage offers a practical way to inventively repurpose cyanotypes that seem less than perfect but feature interesting and/or beautiful aspects. Cut these cyanotypes into various shapes, then arrange and adhere them to create a whole new art form.

- **ADHESIVE.** Use enough adhesive to secure the edges of your paper, but don't use so much that the adhesive pools. Select thin, quick-drying adhesives such as glue sticks or tacky glue.
- **BURNISHING.** Use the flat side of a bone folder or a spoon to gently burnish each collage element onto the card. Keep the card pristine by placing a clean sheet of paper over the composition before burnishing; remove the paper right after burnishing to make sure it doesn't stick.
- **DRYING.** Place a sheet of clean wax paper over the completed composition, and then add weight—a book works well. Weighting the collage helps the pieces stay adhered to the paper as the adhesive dries.

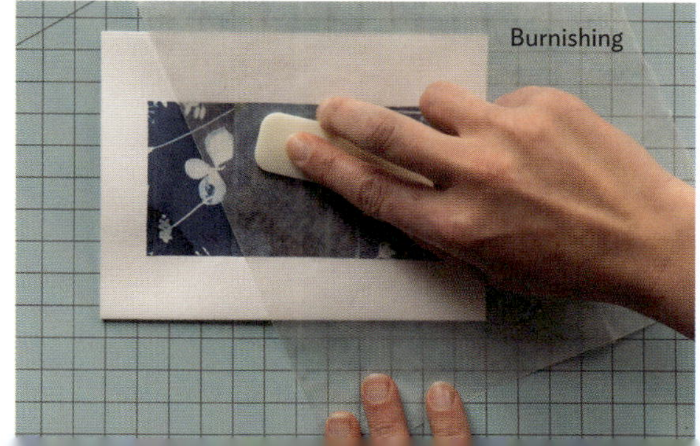

Burnishing

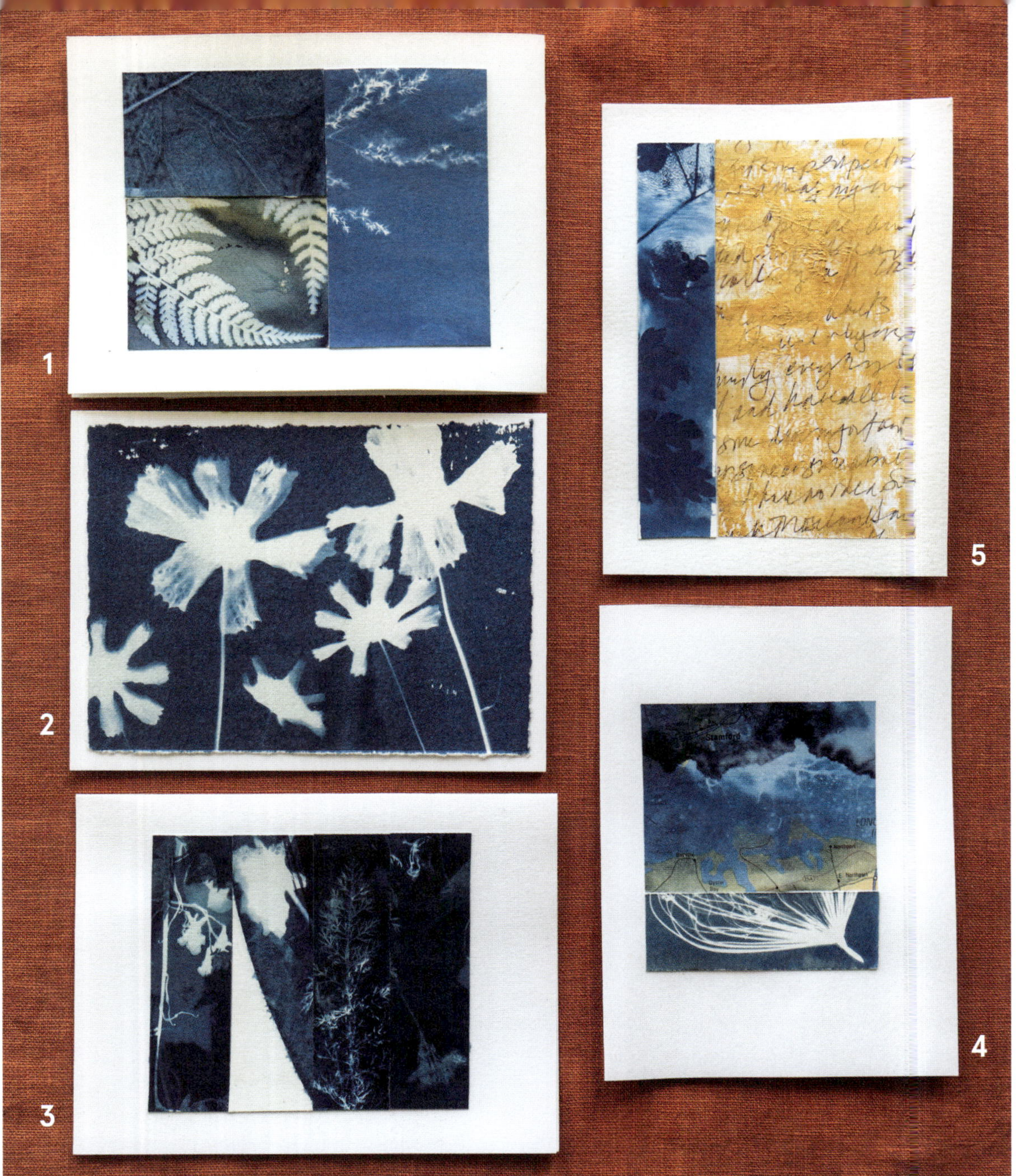


## CREATE A CARD WITH ONE (or all) OF THESE APPROACHES

1. Arrange pieces of two or more different cyanotypes for contrast.
2. Isolate one piece cut from a cyanotype and adhere it to a card—simple and effective.
3. Rearrange the pieces of a single cyanotype to make it abstract.
4. Try integrating other types of art into the collage, such as maps.
5. Incorporate new and old paper into your composition. The possibilities are endless and include old greeting cards, pages from magazines, paper from mailers, or even pages from those old journals you keep meaning to recycle (or burn). If using paper with handwritten or printed text that you want to obscure, coat with a thin layer of acrylic paint in a compatible color. Allow to dry before cutting and adhering to cards.

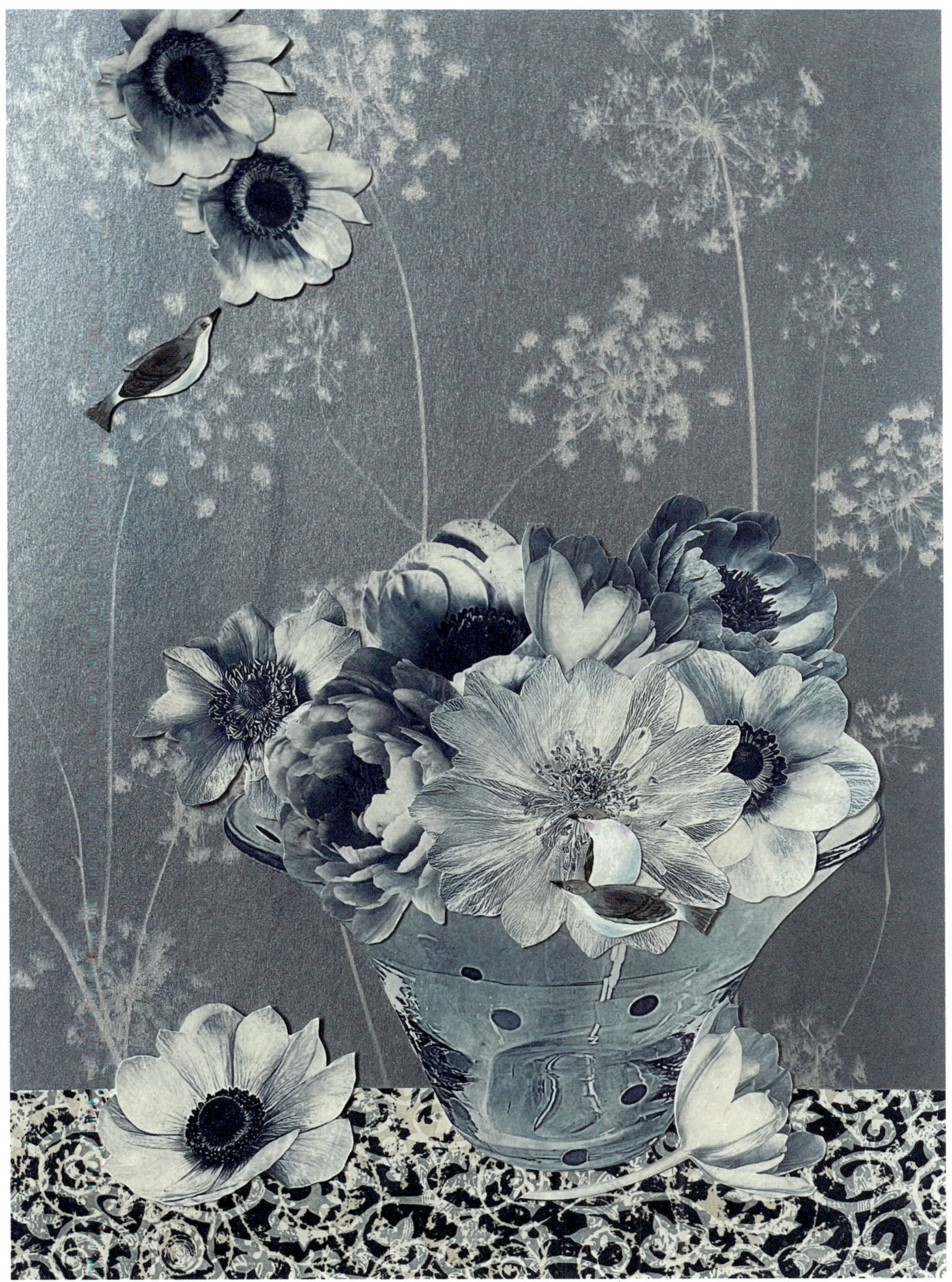

Claudia Hollister's cyanotype collage *Long Hot Summer* blends the photogram, digital negatives, and hand-designed paper to create a sense of nostalgia and wonder.

# Embellish a Cyanotype with Paint

There are many ways to alter the blue and white of a cyanotype. A simple option is to apply color directly to the print using paint, ink, or pencil.

The following are suggested materials for incorporating additional media into your cyanotype pieces. Each assumes you are starting with a completed and fully dry cyanotype on sturdy paper.

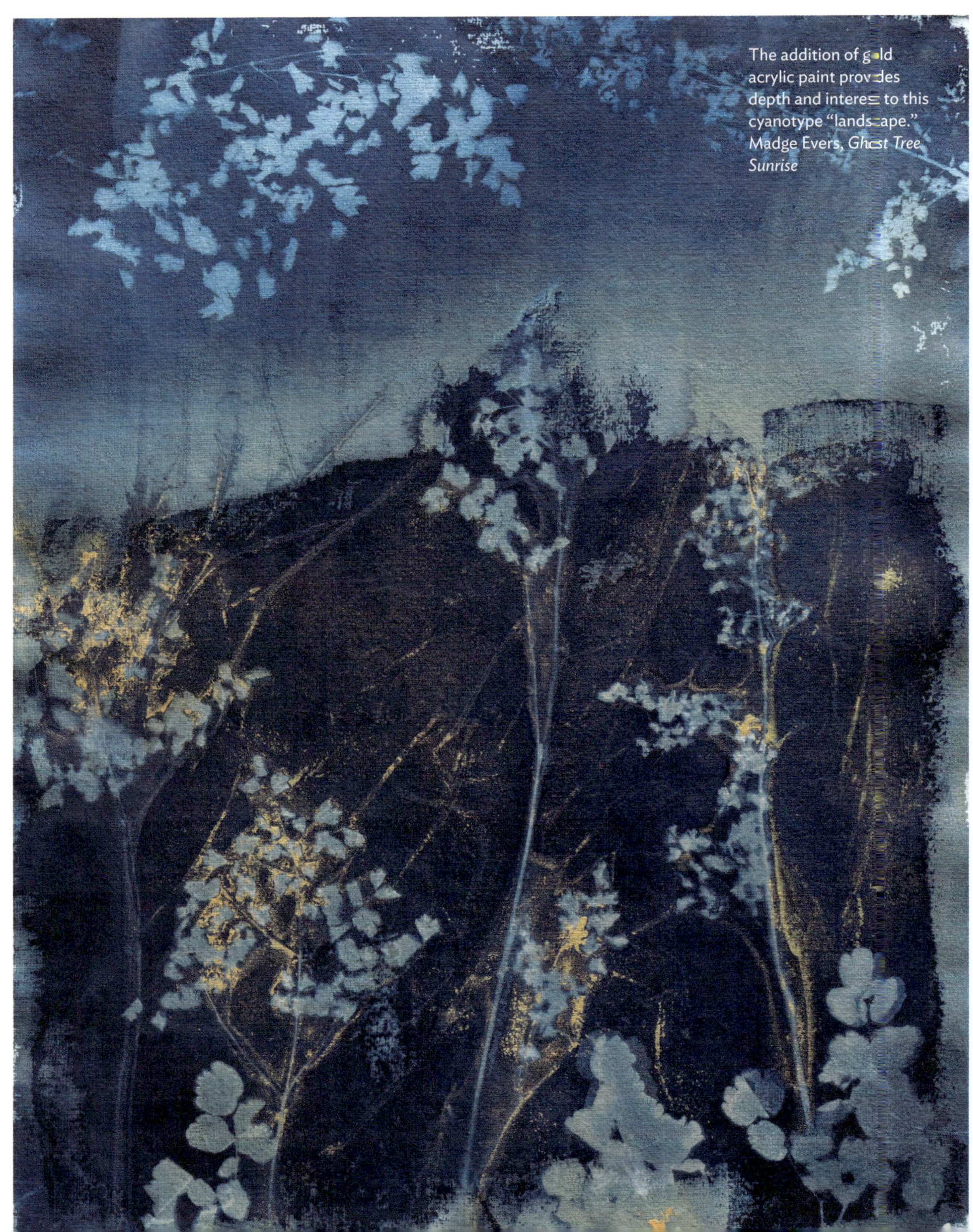

The addition of gold acrylic paint provides depth and interest to this cyanotype "landscape." Madge Evers, *Ghost Tree Sunrise*

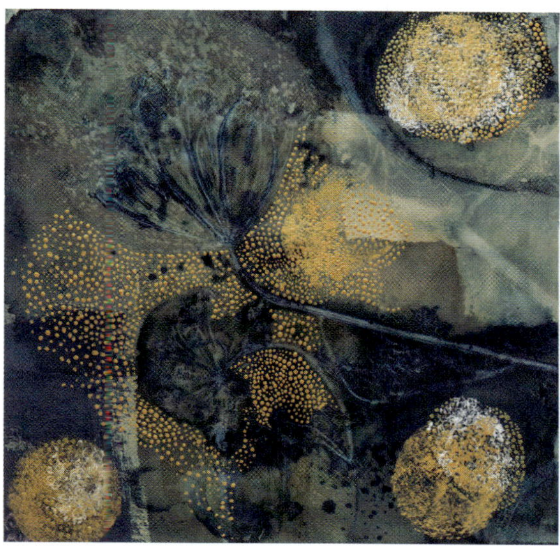

**ACRYLIC.** Madge Evers, *Sprinkle Spray*

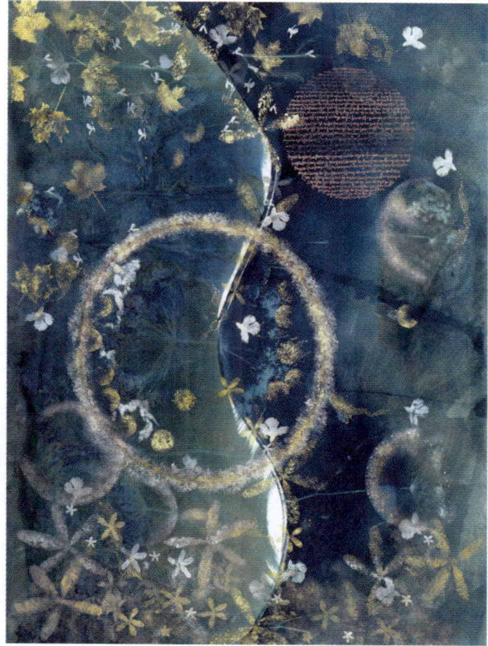

**INK.** Madge Evers, *Ring Fort, Chickadees, and Fireflies*

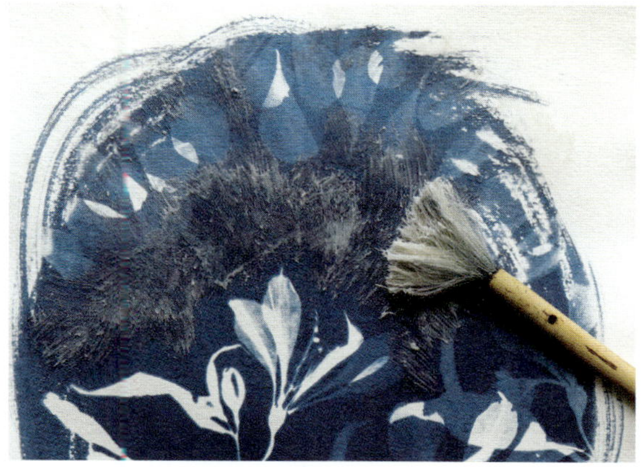

**APPLYING PUMICE GEL MEDIUM**

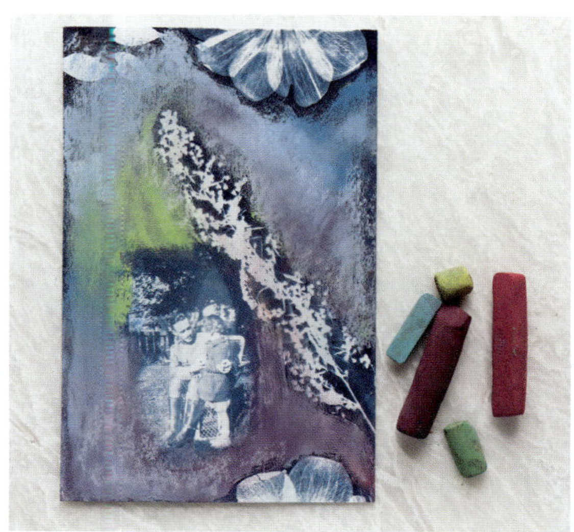

**PASTEL**

- **ACRYLIC.** Available in a wide range of colors, acrylic paint dries quickly and leaves a subtle sheen. It can also be used as an adhesive in collage work. I often use acrylics that contain mica or other reflective materials, which add a luminous quality to the piece.
- **INK.** Inks are made from a variety of materials. I typically use opaque inks to incorporate text into my cyanotype mixed-media pieces.
- **PASTEL.** Soft pastel can provide vibrant color. The paper's texture determines how well the pastel adheres: Coarse textures hold more pigment, creating bold colors, while smoother papers yield softer hues. You can add texture to a cyanotype by applying clear pastel primer or pumice gel medium, which creates a "toothy" surface for the pastel to grip.
- **GOUACHE AND WATERCOLOR.** Gouache creates flat areas of color with a matte finish. Watercolors can provide transparent color shifts over the blue and white areas of a cyanotype. (See page 160.)
- **PENCIL.** Use high-quality artist pencils. Profiled artist Linda Clark Johnson makes delicate, subtle additions to her cyanotype work with colored pencils. (See page 161.)

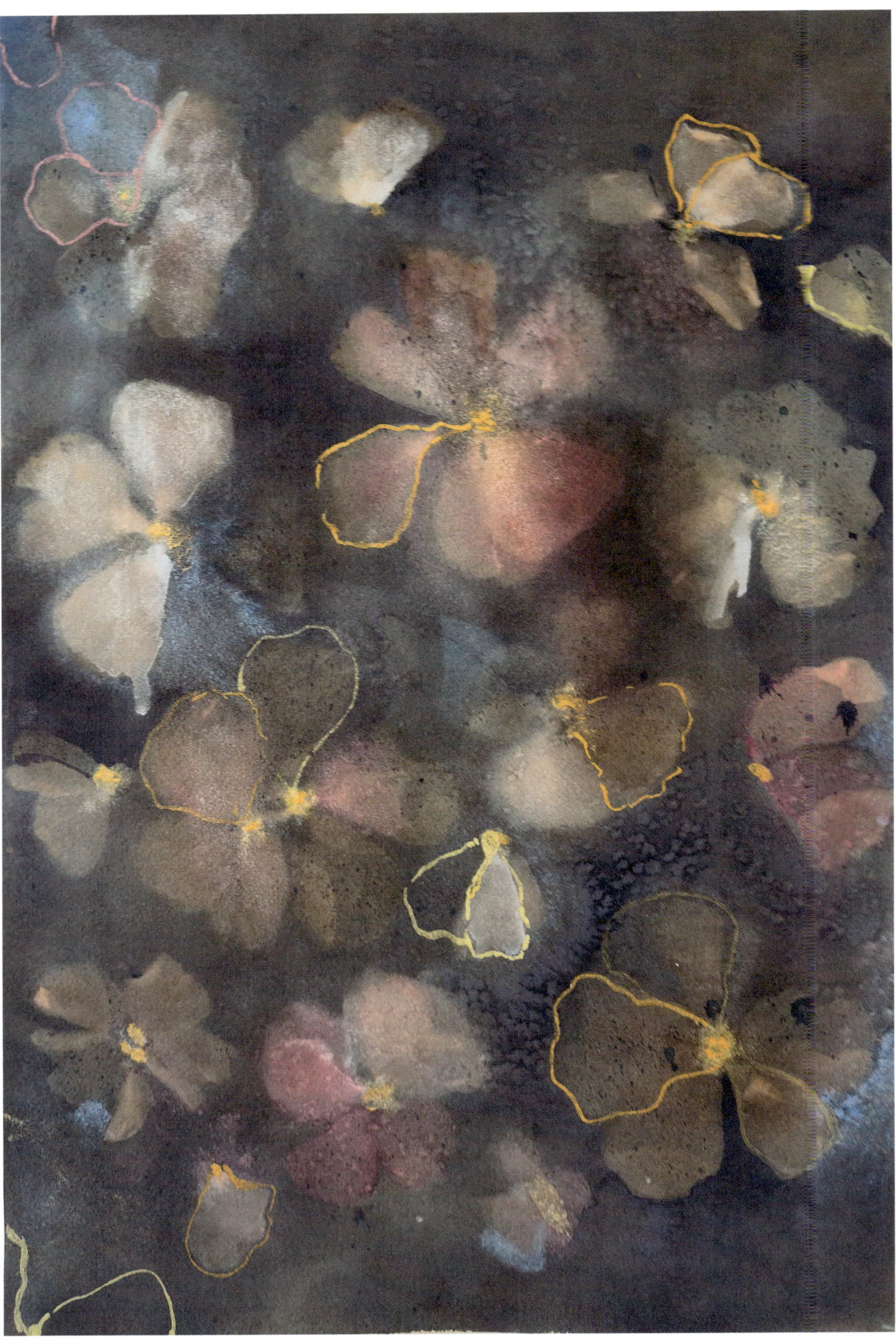

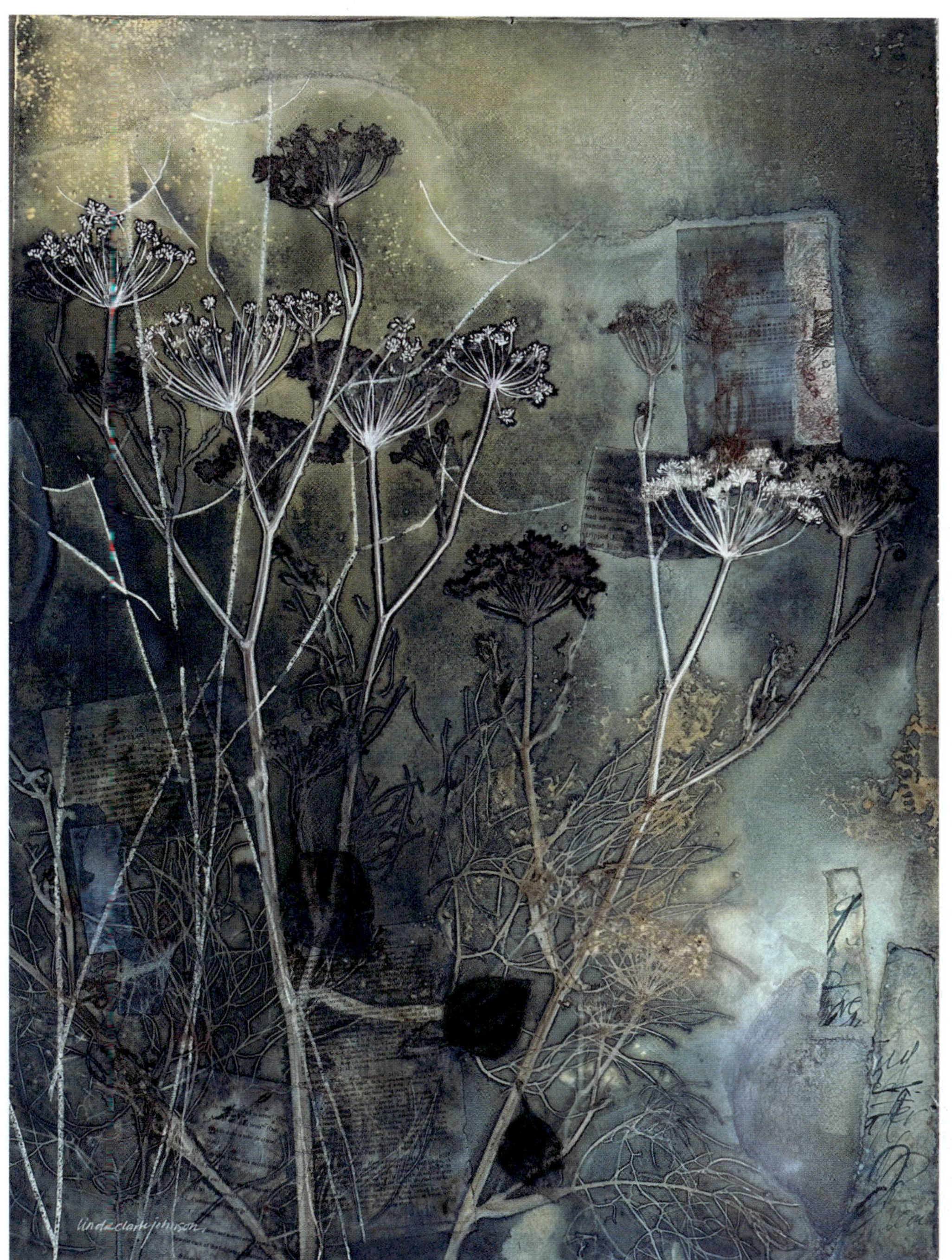


**LEFT: GOUACHE AND WATERCOLOR.**
Take inspiration from Em Crisman, who tones and adds watercolor washes to her underpaintings like in this piece titled *Becoming: Refined*.

**ABOVE: PENCIL.** Many contemporary artists use cyanotypes as a foundation for traditional media. In this piece, titled *In the Faerie Garden*, Linda Clark Johnson creates dramatic highlights with colored pencils. Johnson considers herself a painter and treats "each cyanotype print as a canvas."

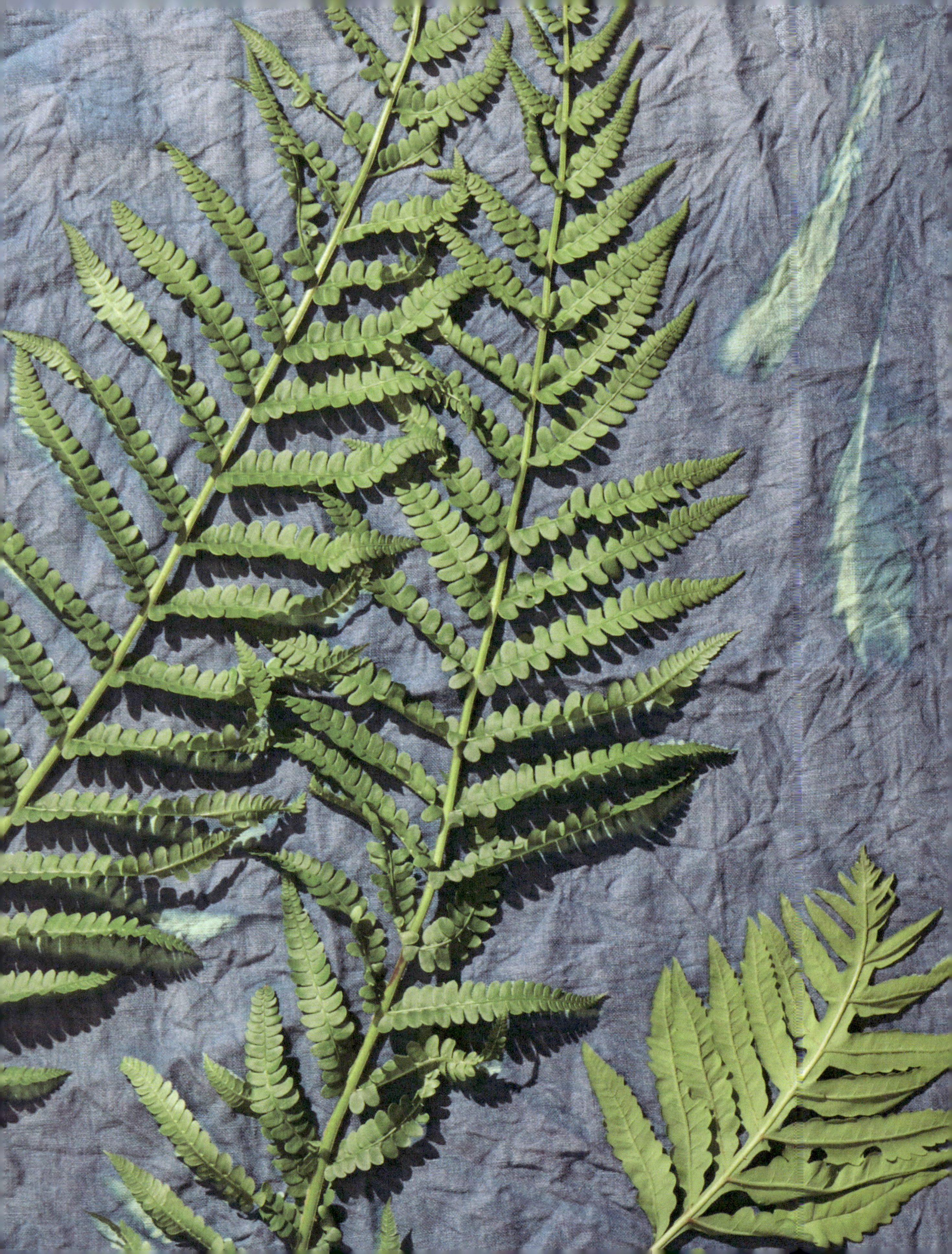

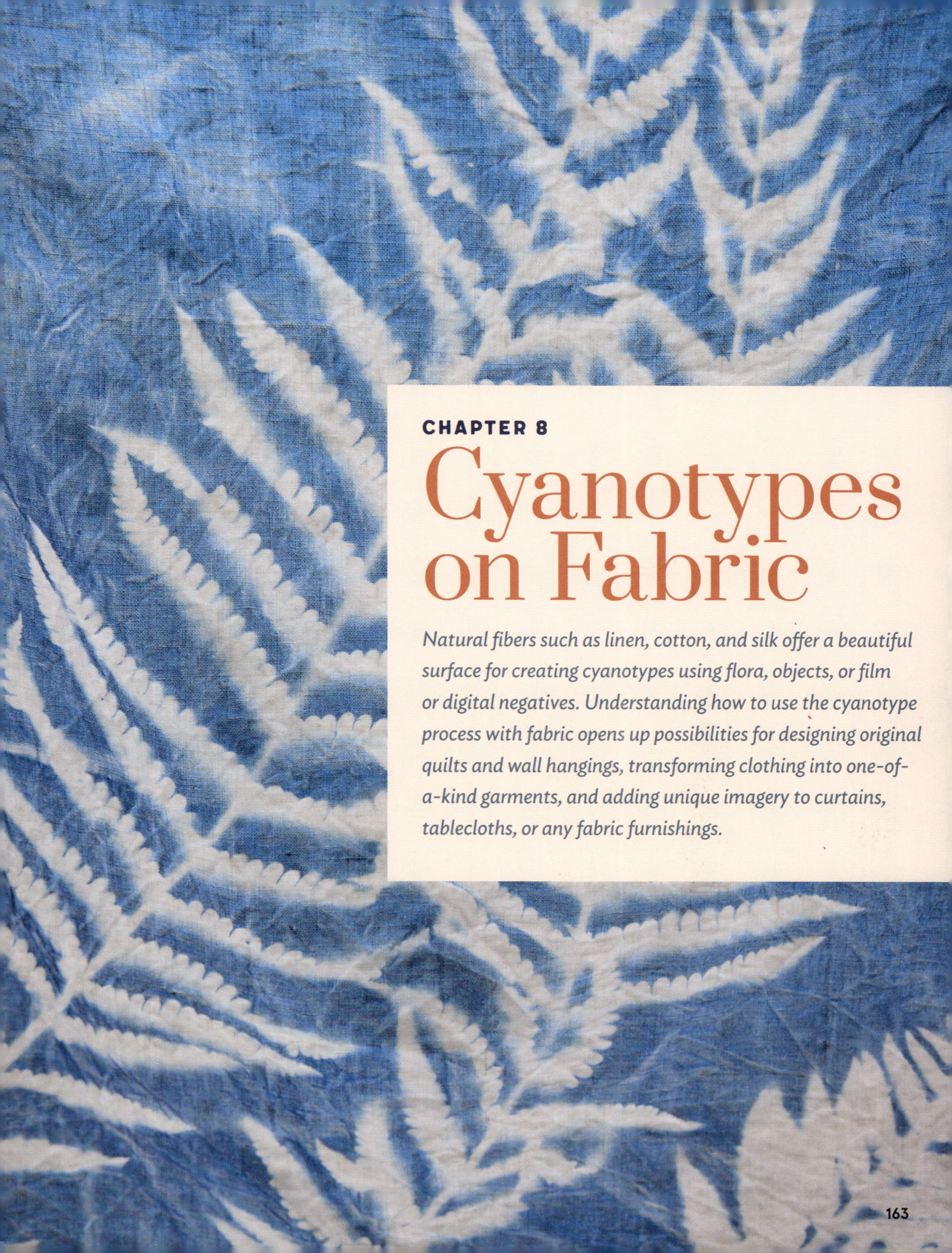

CHAPTER 8

# Cyanotypes on Fabric

*Natural fibers such as linen, cotton, and silk offer a beautiful surface for creating cyanotypes using flora, objects, or film or digital negatives. Understanding how to use the cyanotype process with fabric opens up possibilities for designing original quilts and wall hangings, transforming clothing into one-of-a-kind garments, and adding unique imagery to curtains, tablecloths, or any fabric furnishings.*

# Printing on Fabric

Working with fabric cyanotypes can be exciting but tricky. Although the chemicals used for paper and fabric are the same, fabric requires significantly more working solution than paper, and the coating process requires extra steps and considerations.

**CHOOSING A FABRIC.** The fibers of natural fabrics such as linen, cotton, and silk will absorb the cyanotype solution, but synthetic fibers resist the solution. Using synthetic fabrics or fabric blends that include both natural and synthetic fibers is not recommended; use 100 percent cotton, linen, or silk.

Many colored fabrics work beautifully with Prussian blue; you're not restricted to white or neutral-colored fabrics.

**PREPARING THE FABRIC.** If you don't want to be limited to precoated fabric, you can easily apply the cyanotype chemicals to fabric yourself, in much the same way you would with paper. However, before applying the solution there is one additional step: scouring the fabric.

Scouring involves soaking the fabric in a very hot solution of washing soda in order to remove any sizing or other chemicals in the fibers that could interfere with the absorption of the cyanotype chemicals. The same process is commonly used to prepare fabrics for dyeing with natural materials.

Precoated fabric sheets are available for purchase online if you want to skip all this fabric prep work. To get you started, I've included a project designed specifically for precoated fabric (see page 168).

**APPLYING THE SOLUTION AND PRINTING.** The amount of solution you apply can vary dramatically depending on the fabric you're using. The aim is to integrate the solution into the fabric, without applying so much that the working solution pools or drips. Adjust the amount of working solution accordingly. As always, this is an experimental process.

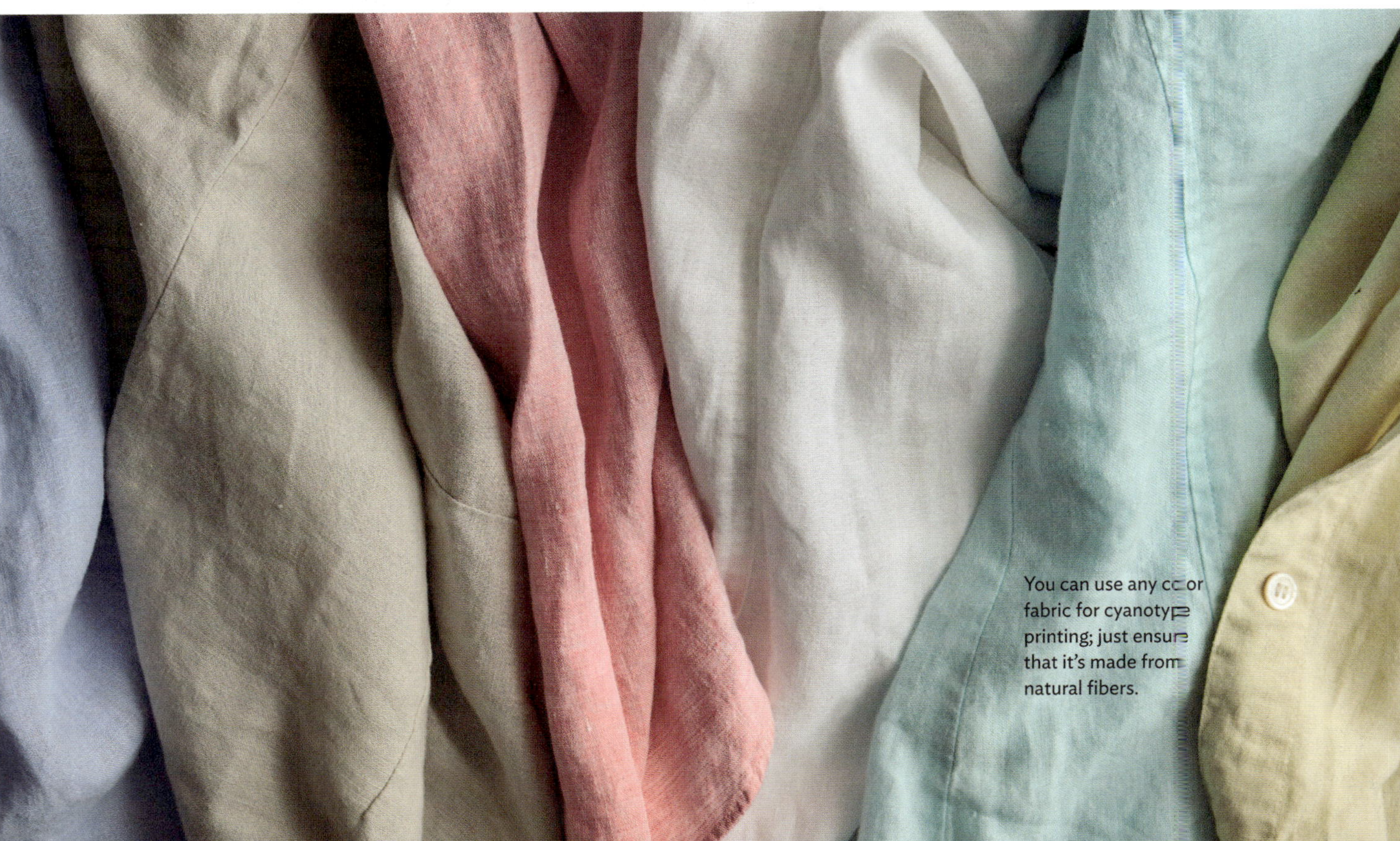

You can use any color fabric for cyanotype printing; just ensure that it's made from natural fibers.

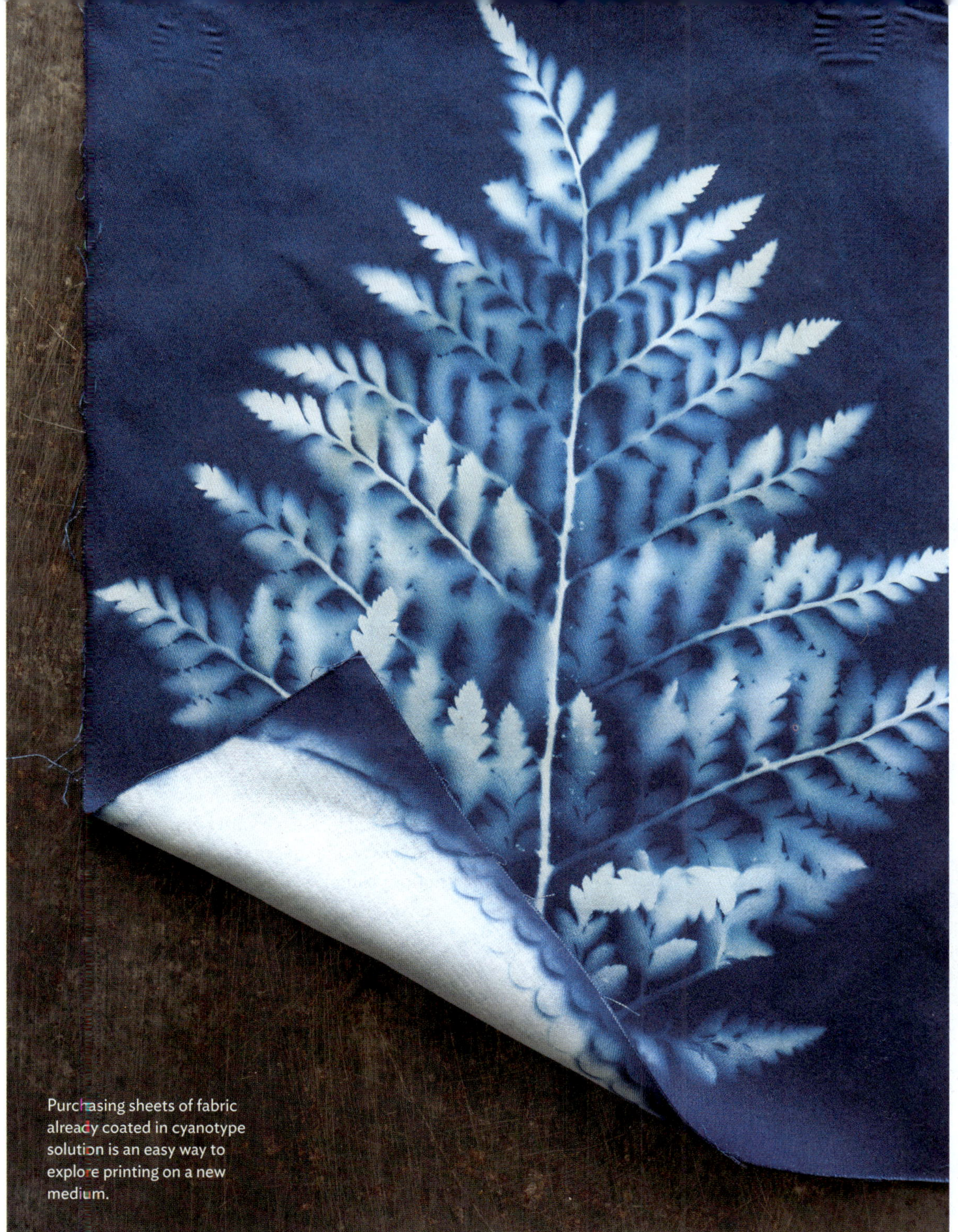

Purchasing sheets of fabric already coated in cyanotype solution is an easy way to explore printing on a new medium.

**EXPOSING AND WASHING FABRIC.** When printing on fabric, you may not observe the same distinctive silvery gray or bronze color when the exposure has run its course. I generally err on the side of overexposing rather than underexposing when working with fabric. Washing the exposed print on fabric works in much the same way as it does with paper. Since there's no need to keep the piece flat and unwrinkled as with paper, you can simply wash it in a bucket instead of a tray.

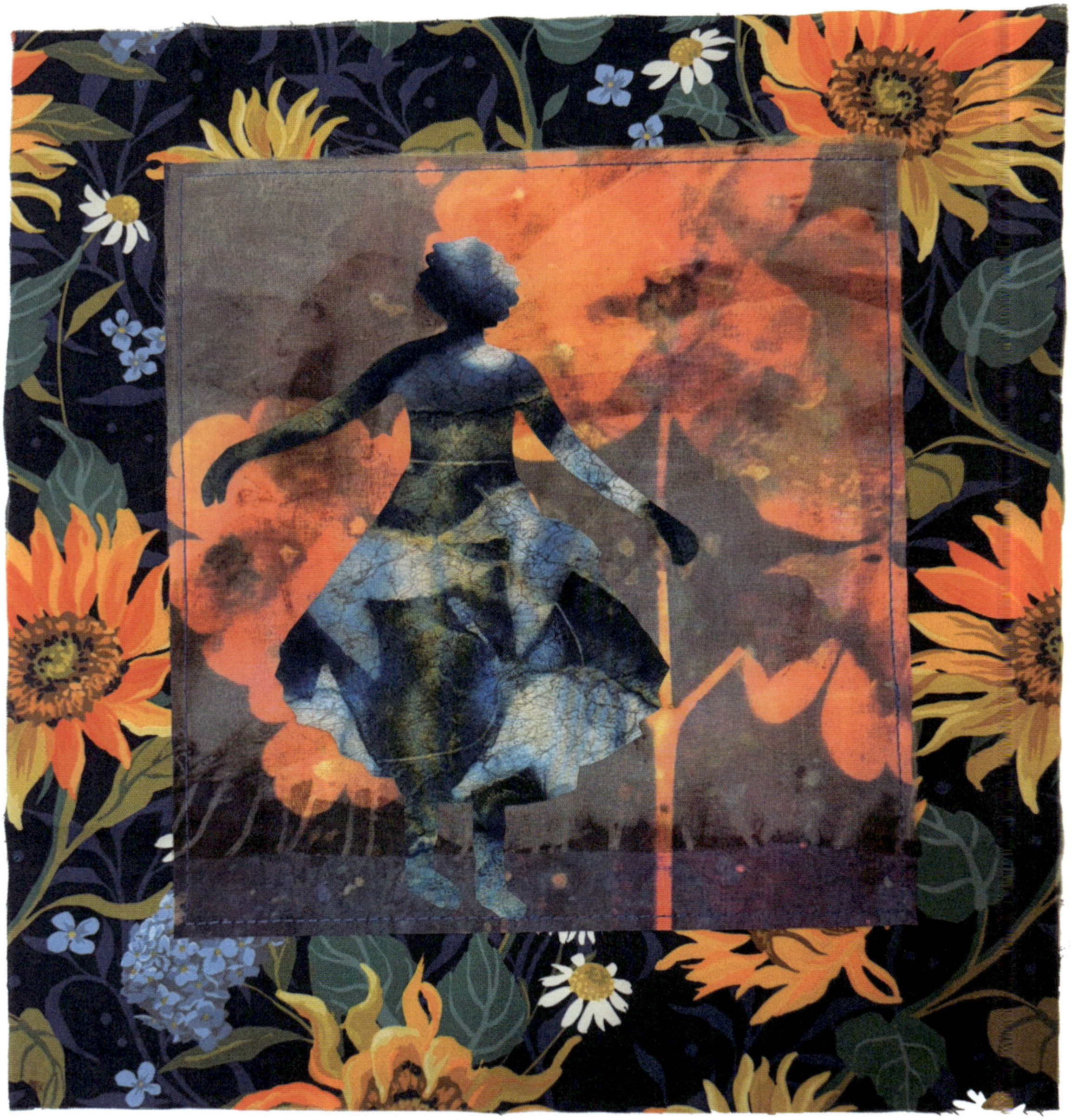

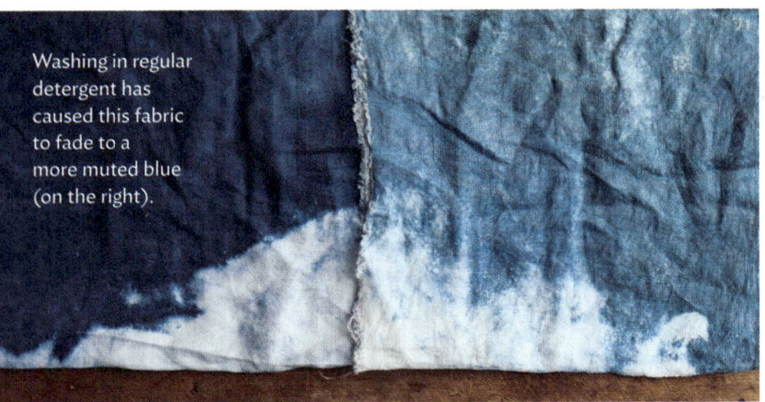
Washing in regular detergent has caused this fabric to fade to a more muted blue (on the right).

**CARING FOR CYANOTYPE-PRINTED FABRIC.** Hand-wash cyanotype-printed fabric in cool water and avoid soap or detergents with bleach, sodium, or phosphates, as these can cause fading. Fabric can be air-dried or placed in a dryer. Use products designed for delicate fabrics; see Resources on page 211 for recommendations.

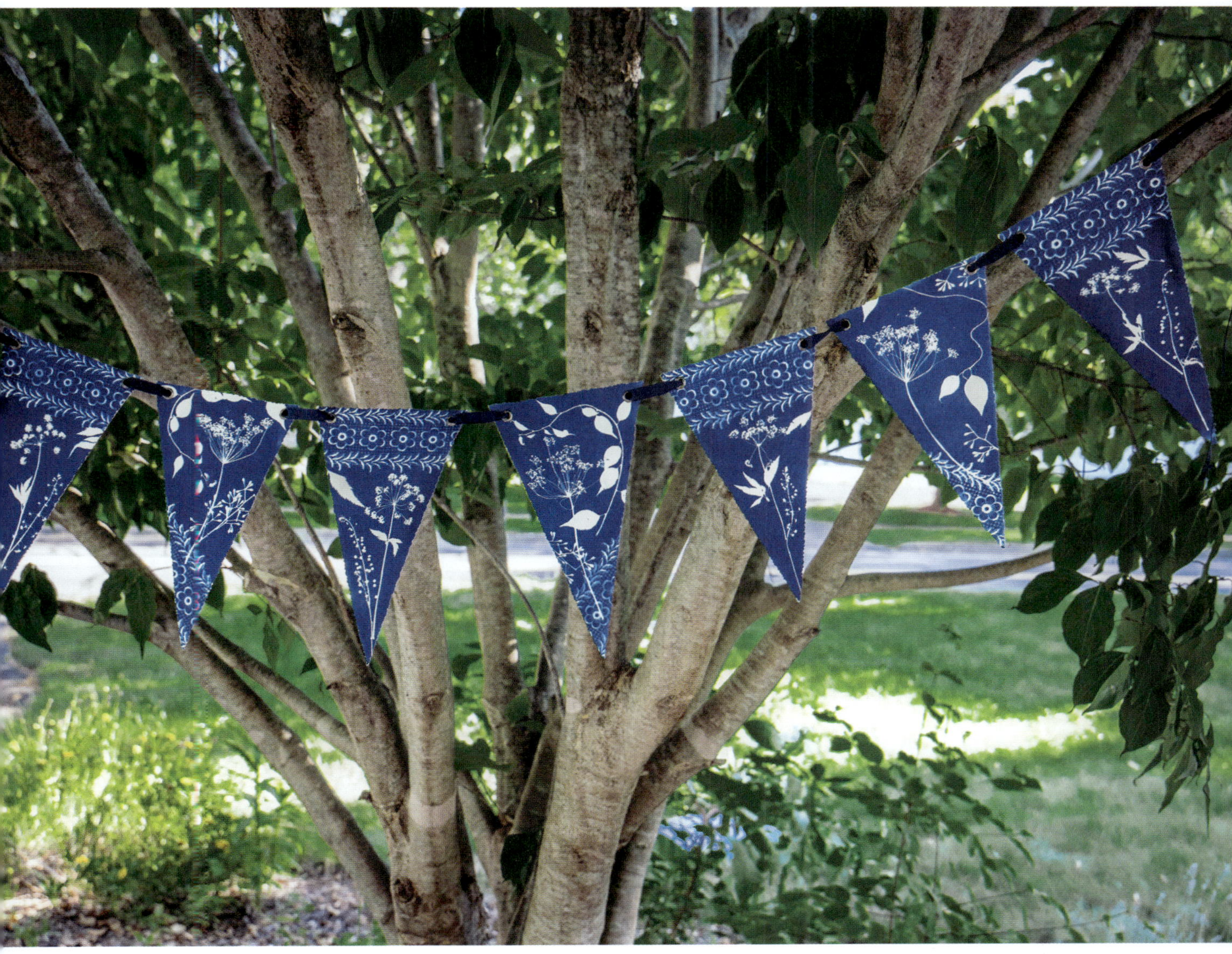

OPPOSITE: Lesley Riley's *The Thinnest Veil* employs a range of creative techniques to craft a multilayered quilt imbued with a lively narrative.

ABOVE: Erika Frank's cheerful banner features repeated patterns created with lace and botanicals.

## USING CYANOTYPE-PRINTED FABRIC

Printing on fabric opens a whole new world of creative possibilities as you consider how you'd like to use your finished piece of fabric. Of course, it can simply be a wall hanging (see page 174), but cyanotype cloth can be incorporated into quilts, sewn into bags or pouches, made into a stunning pair of curtains, or anything else you can dream up. Just remember that the fabric must be hand-washed using an appropriate soap.

# Cyanotype Stencil Prints on Fabric

If you're not ready to make a deep dive into using fabric, here's a project that allows you to dip your toe into the cyanotype sea. Pretreated fabric sheets that are coated with cyanotype chemicals and ready to expose straight out of the package are an easy way to experiment with cyanotype techniques without the need to prepare your own materials.

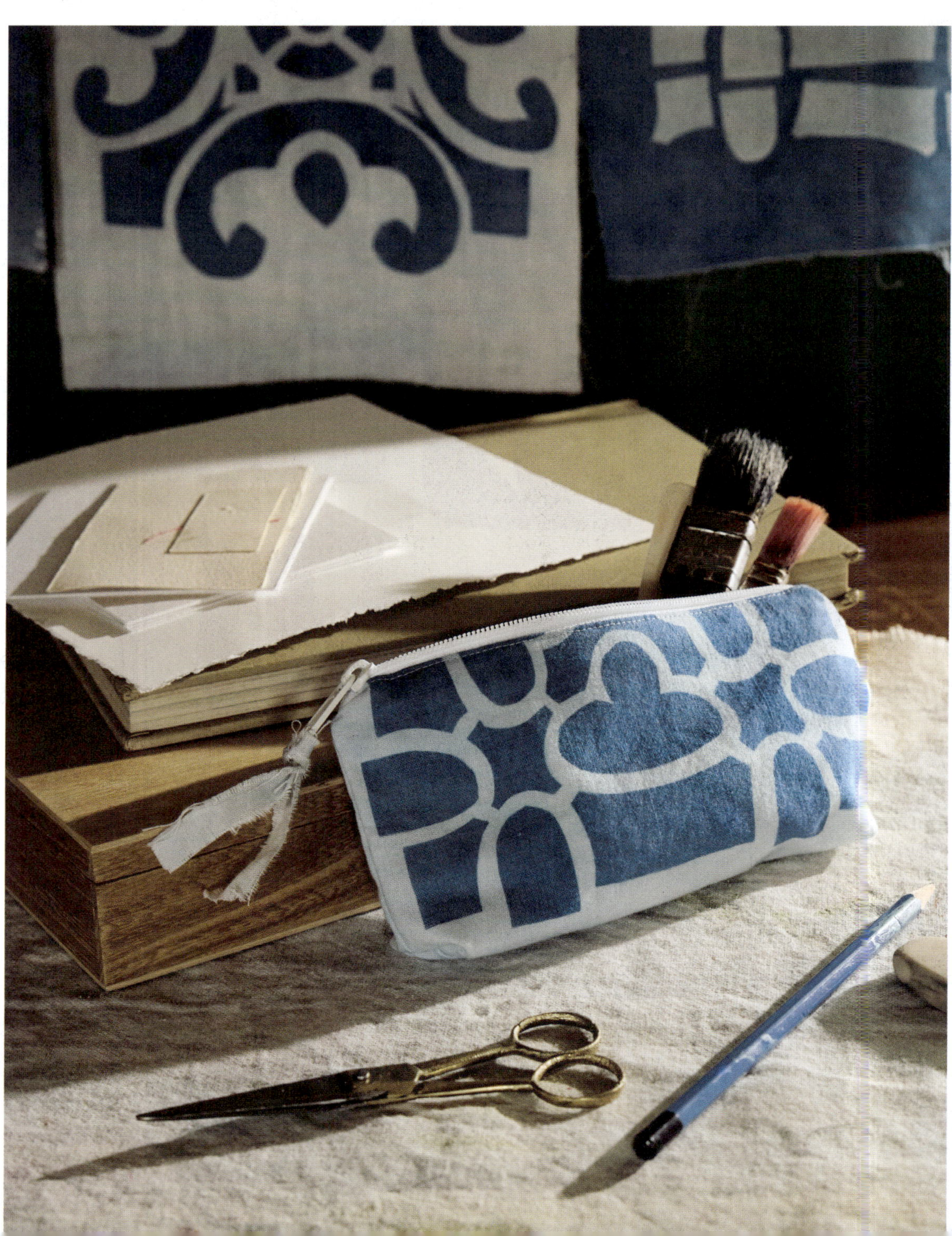

A series of 8½ × 11-inch patterned fabric sheets can be used for a sewing project, mounted on nonbuffered backing board for framing, or displayed as stand-alone pieces. The patterns can be almost identical, or varied with coordinating features to suit your project.

### Materials

- Paper with different thicknesses (see Design and Cut Your Stencil below), 8½ × 11 inches
- Pencil for drawing designs on paper
- Paper-cutting tools like scissors, craft knives, punches
- Tray or bucket for rinsing
- Pretreated fabric sheets
- Cardboard backing larger than the fabric sheet
- Plants or other printing material (optional)
- Glass or acrylic larger than the fabric sheet
- Binder clips or similar fasteners
- Clothesline and clothespins or a drying rack

## DESIGN AND CUT YOUR STENCIL

To create the patterned fabric, you'll use 8½ × 11-inch paper stencils that feature similar or coordinating designs. These stencils will block UV light and allow you to create high-contrast blue-and-white patterns. Thick paper, like card stock, will block most of the light, creating crisp patterns; thin paper, such as tissue paper, allows some UV through for lighter blue effects. You can layer multiple stencils or combine them with plants or other flat objects for more intricate designs.

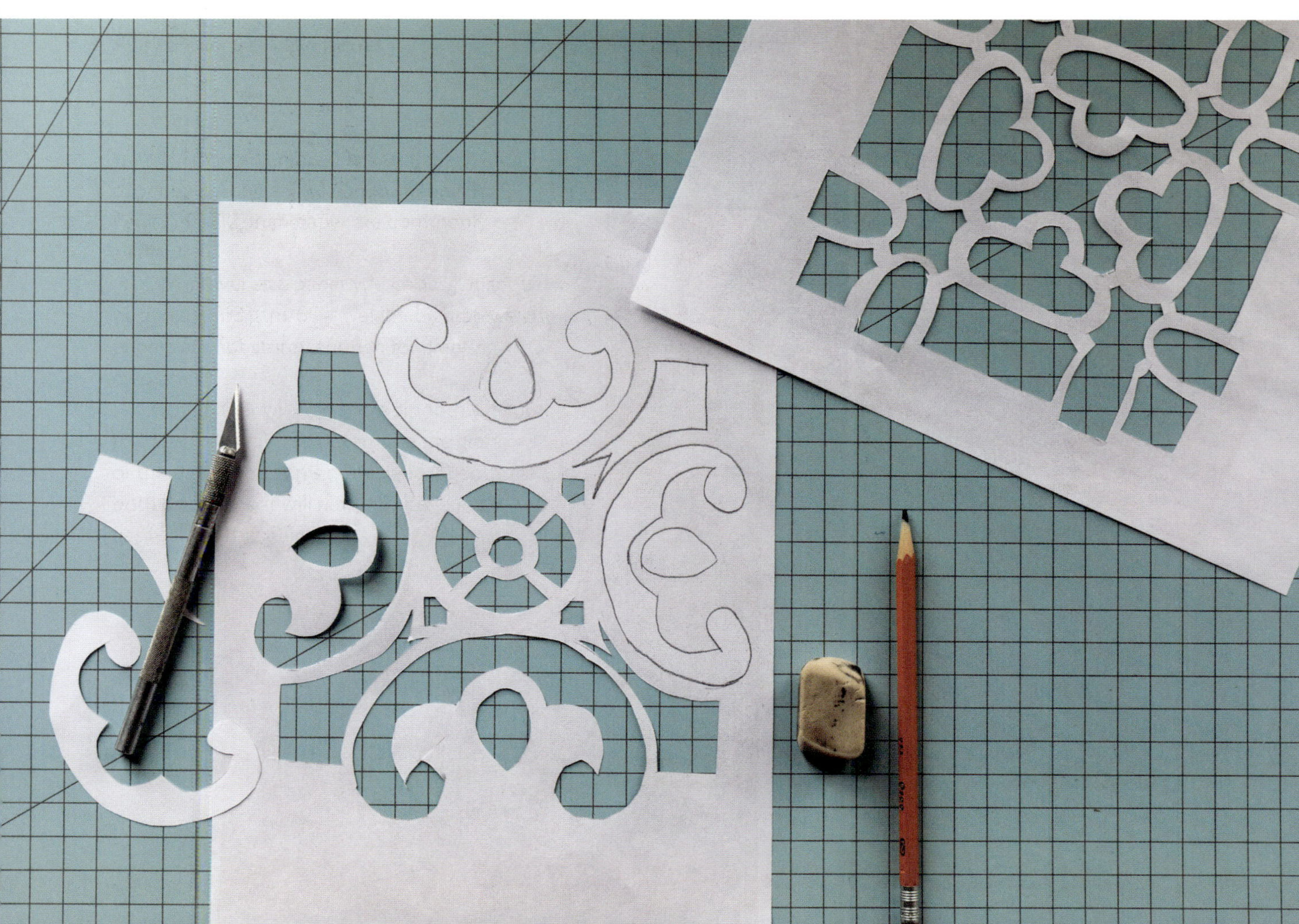

Creating a paper stencil is simple—just plan your design and sketch or trace it on paper. Then use a craft knife, scissors, or paper punches to cut out the design. Here are some tips to help you get started.

- Ensure that the paper you plan to use for stencils is the same size as, or slightly larger than, your precoated fabric.
- You can use a single stencil to make a set of fabric sheets with the same design.
- Experiment with multiple stencils to create fabric sheets featuring related but distinct patterns.
- When planning your stencil, bear in mind that the negative space (whatever parts of the stencil you cut away) will print blue.
- If you are unsure where to start, begin with simple shapes or familiar objects. Geometric designs made of lines, chevrons, grids, or even simply polka dots can all create fun results.
- Try cutting out words or phrases (or using letter punches) to create unique messages or celebrate a favorite quote.
- You can also try using purchased stencils if you'd prefer.

## PRINTING WITH A STENCIL

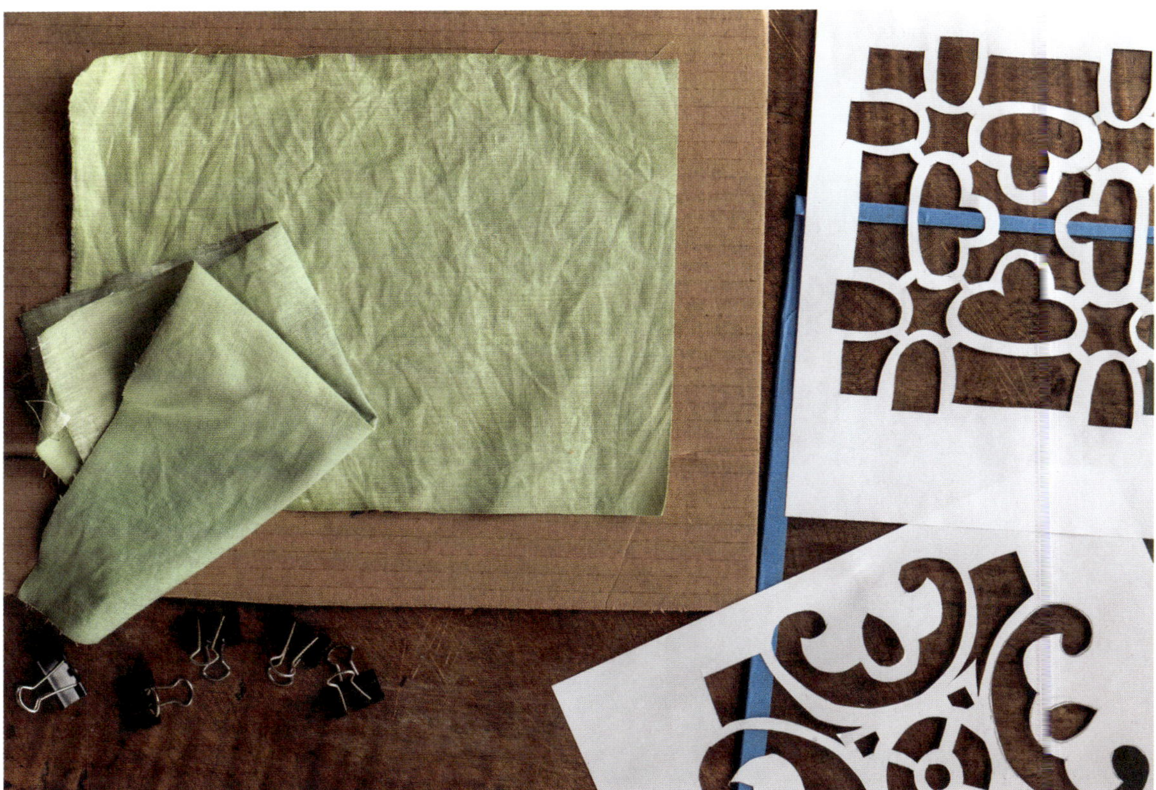

1 **SET UP.** Gather your materials in a dimly lit prep space. Set up a bucket or rinsing tray filled with water in your wash area. Set up a clothesline for drying somewhere away from direct light.

2 **ARRANGE THE COMPOSITION.** Remove the fabric sheet from its packaging and place it on the cardboard backing, smoothing out any wrinkles. Arrange your stencil(s), plant material, or other flat object on top of the fabric.

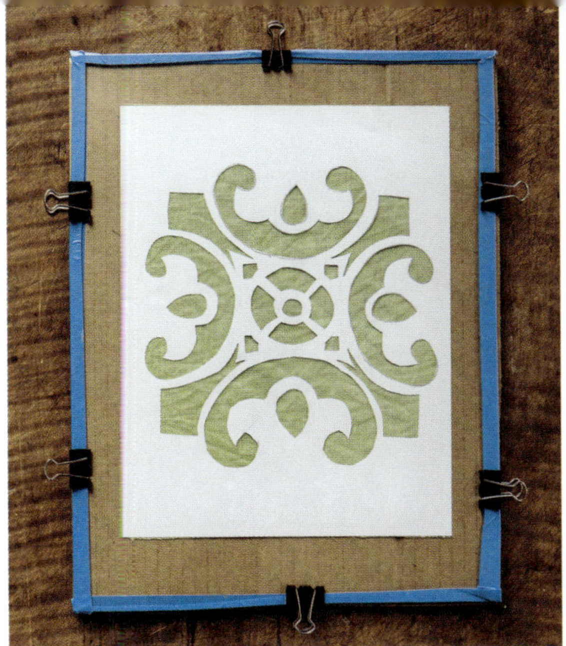

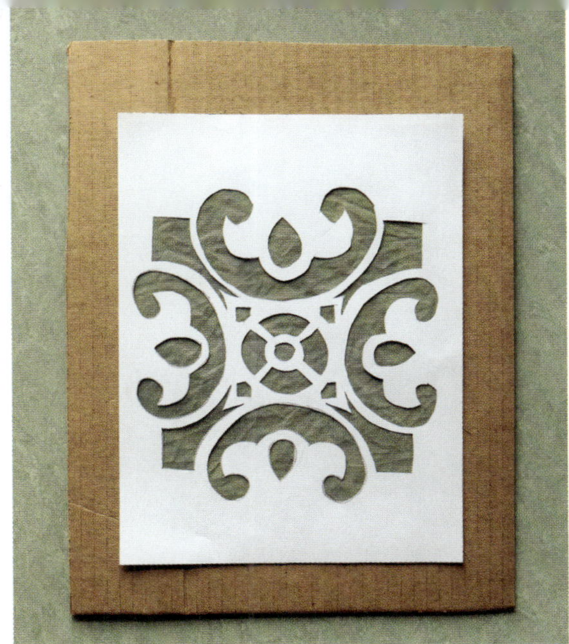

3 **SECURE THE MATERIALS.** Cover the fabric and stencils with a sheet of glass or acrylic, ensuring everything is smooth. Secure the glass or acrylic to the cardboard backing using binder clips.

4 **EXPOSE TO SUNLIGHT.** Place your setup in direct sunlight. Exposure time varies depending on sunlight strength and time of year. Overexposure is preferable to underexposure. Under a bright midday sun, you might expose the fabric for 3 to 15 minutes. The bronze color we look for to gauge the proper development of a paper print can be less apparent on fabric.

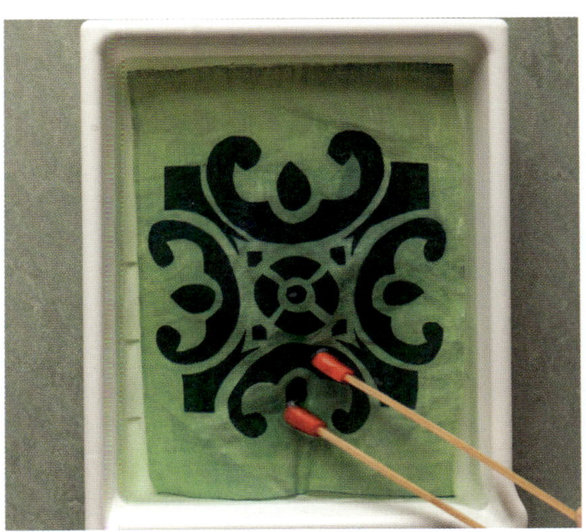

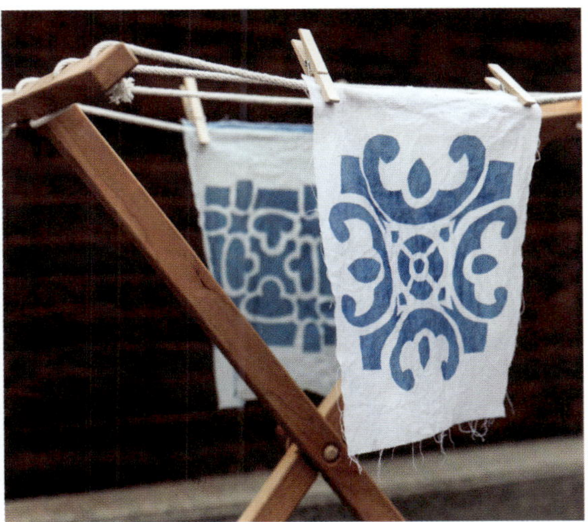

5 **DISMANTLE AND WASH.** When the fabric print is ready, move the setup out of direct sunlight. Remove the clips, glass or acrylic, and stencils. Place the fabric in water; wear gloves or use tongs, if you like. Wash in slowly running water for 5 to 15 minutes, or until the water runs clear.

6 **DRY THE PRINT.** Hang the fabric in a shaded area, away from direct light. If needed, once the fabric has dried, you can use a low-temperature iron on the back side of the fabric to smooth any wrinkles.

7 **REPEAT THE PROCESS.** Repeat steps 2–6 with the remaining fabric sheets, experimenting with patterns and compositions.

# Scouring Fabric

Scouring the fabric helps ensure that the fabric fibers absorb the cyanotype chemicals. Remember to use fabric that is composed of 100 percent natural fibers. You'll want to allow the scoured fabric to dry before using it in a cyanotype project.

## Materials

- Scale for weighing the fabric
- Fabric
- Washing soda (sodium carbonate)
- Container or bowl for mixing the washing soda solution
- Large stainless steel pot
- Kitchen thermometer, designated for craft use only
- Tongs
- Clothesline and clothespins or a drying rack

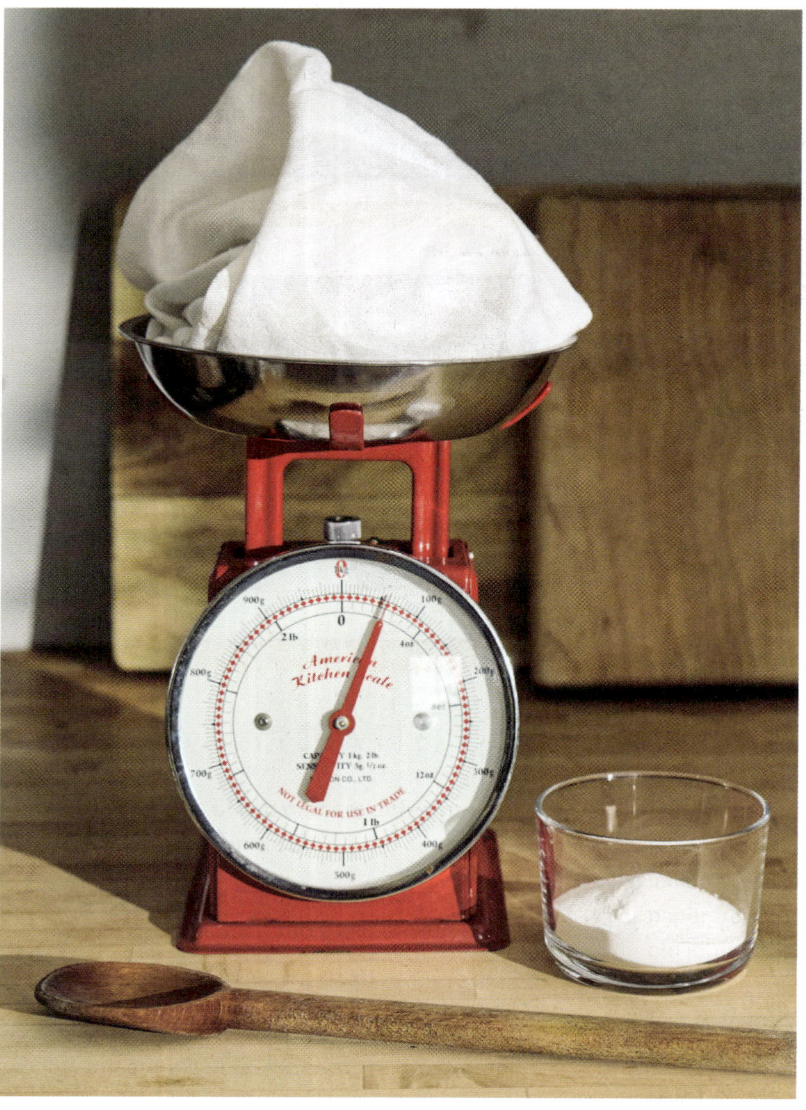


1 **PREPARE THE WASHING SODA SOLUTION.** Weigh your fabric. Then dissolve the equivalent of 2 percent of the fabric's weight in washing soda in a small amount of water. For example, for 1,000 grams of fabric, dissolve 20 grams of washing soda in ¼ cup of water.

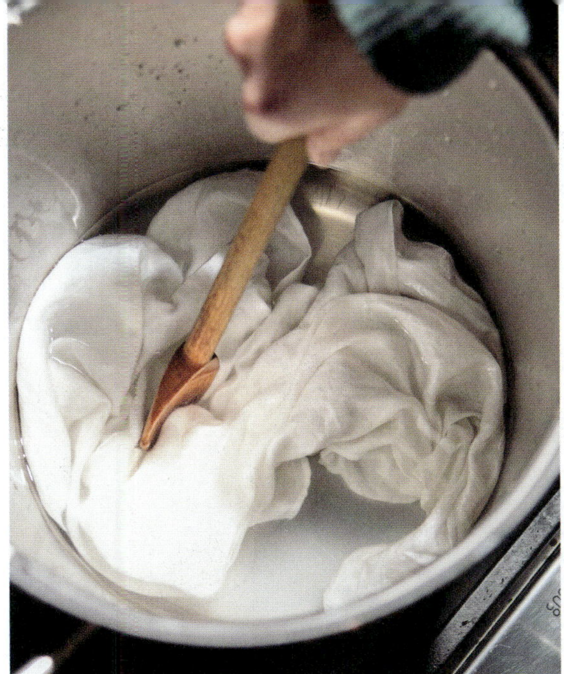

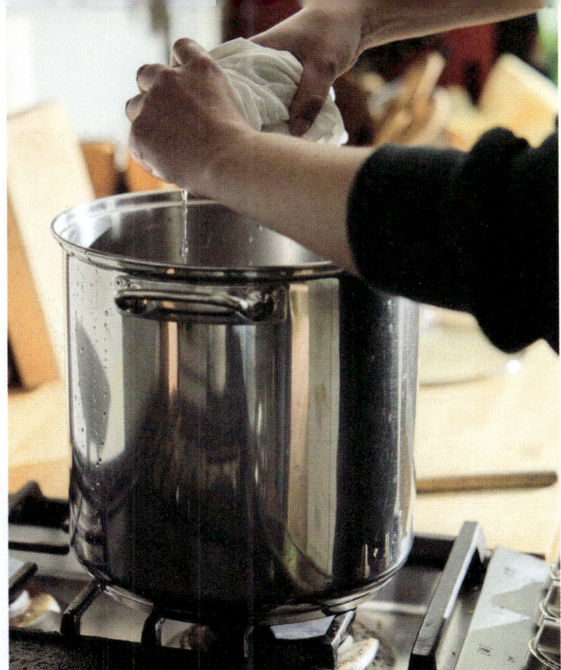

**2 WET THE FABRIC.** Place your fabric in a large stainless steel pot. Add just enough water to allow the fabric to move freely in it. Wring out the fabric and set it aside, leaving the water in the pot.

**3 HEAT.** Place the pot of water on a stovetop burner. Add the dissolved washing soda and stir well. Return the fabric to the pot and set the stove to low heat. Heat to 180°F/82°C, stirring gently; maintain this temperature for 30 minutes before removing from the heat.

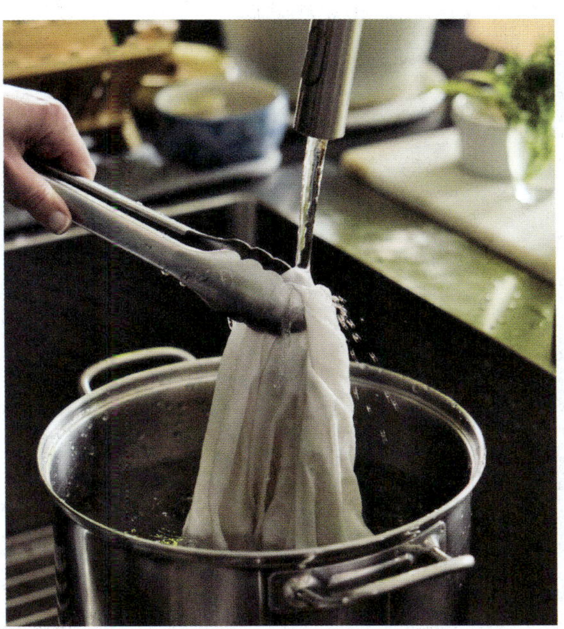

**4 RINSE.** Remove the fabric carefully using tongs (it will be hot) and rinse in cool water.

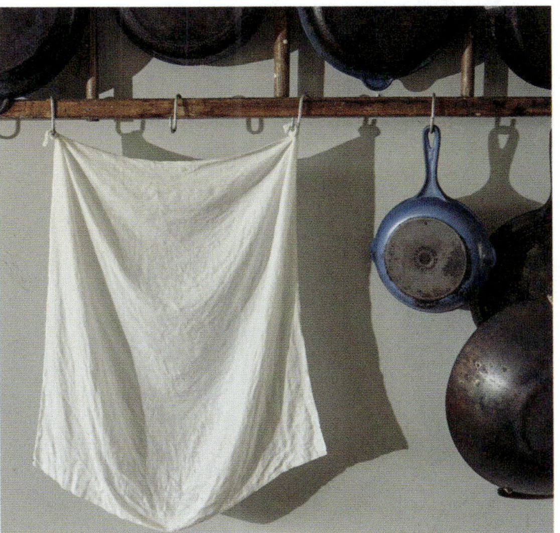

**5 DRY.** Hang the fabric on a line or over a rack to dry. Be sure it is completely dry before applying the cyanotype working solution. Wet fabric will not properly absorb the emulsion. Ironing the fabric is optional. Once your fabric has been scoured, follow the project directions to finish your piece.

# Cyanotype Wall Hanging

A wall hanging is a simple, beautiful way to display a fabric cyanotype. As with all cyanotypes, be sure to display the finished project out of direct sunlight so that it will remain vibrant. Your finished hanging can be displayed with a poster hanger, a decorative curtain rod, or quilt clips. You can leave the edges of the fabric raw for a natural look or hem the edges using a sewing machine or fusible web.

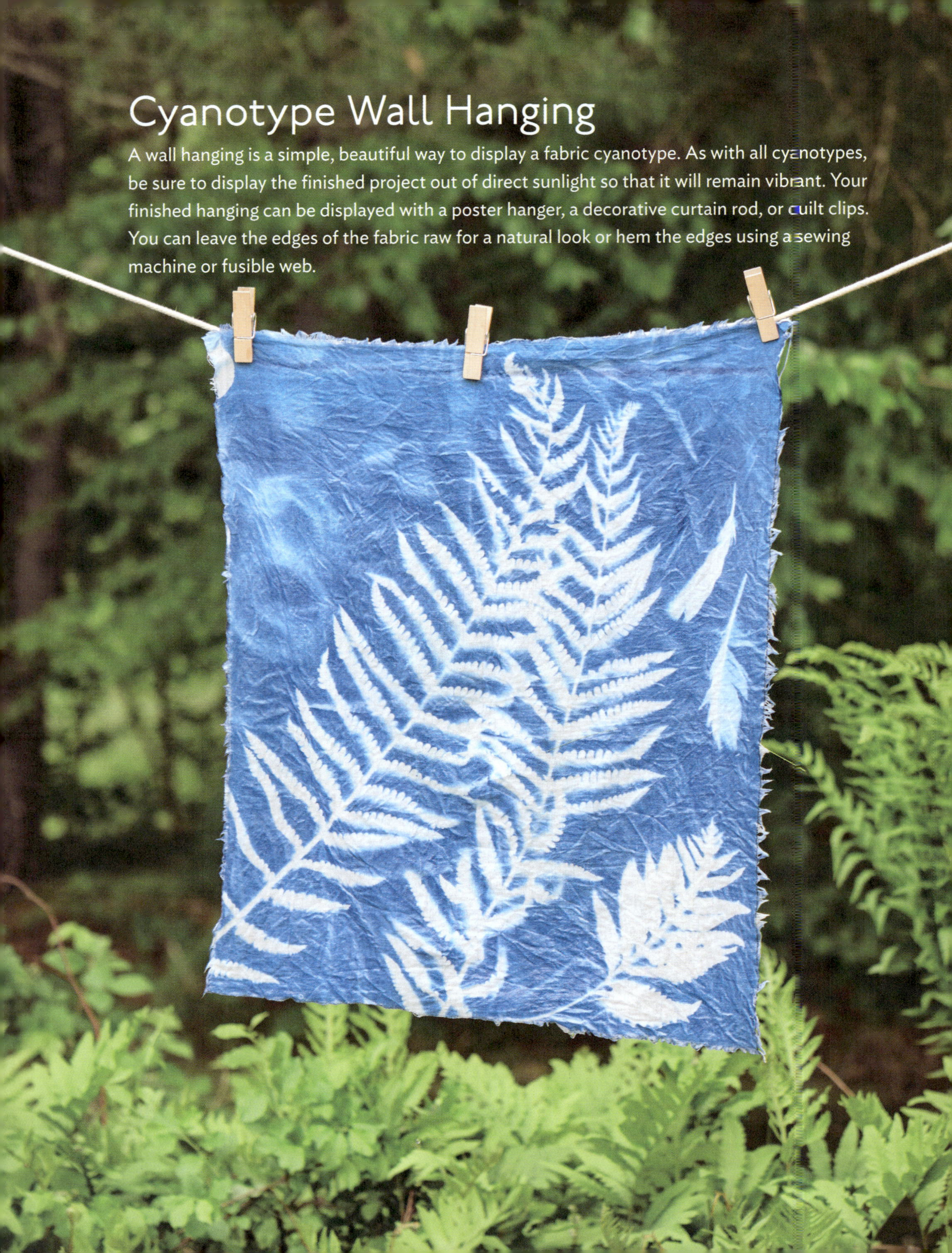

## Materials

- Stock solutions A and B
- Plastic container
- A piece of 16 × 20-inch 100 percent cotton or linen fabric that has been scoured and dried (see directions on page 172)
- Gloves (required) and tongs (optional)
- Plastic hangers, clothesline, and clothespins
- Plastic washing tray or bucket (fabric doesn't require a tray for washing)
- Plant material, pressed and dried or flat, or other printing material
- Sheet of cardboard (or any stiff material) the same size as the glass or acrylic
- Sheet of glass or acrylic larger than the fabric
- Binder clips or similar fasteners

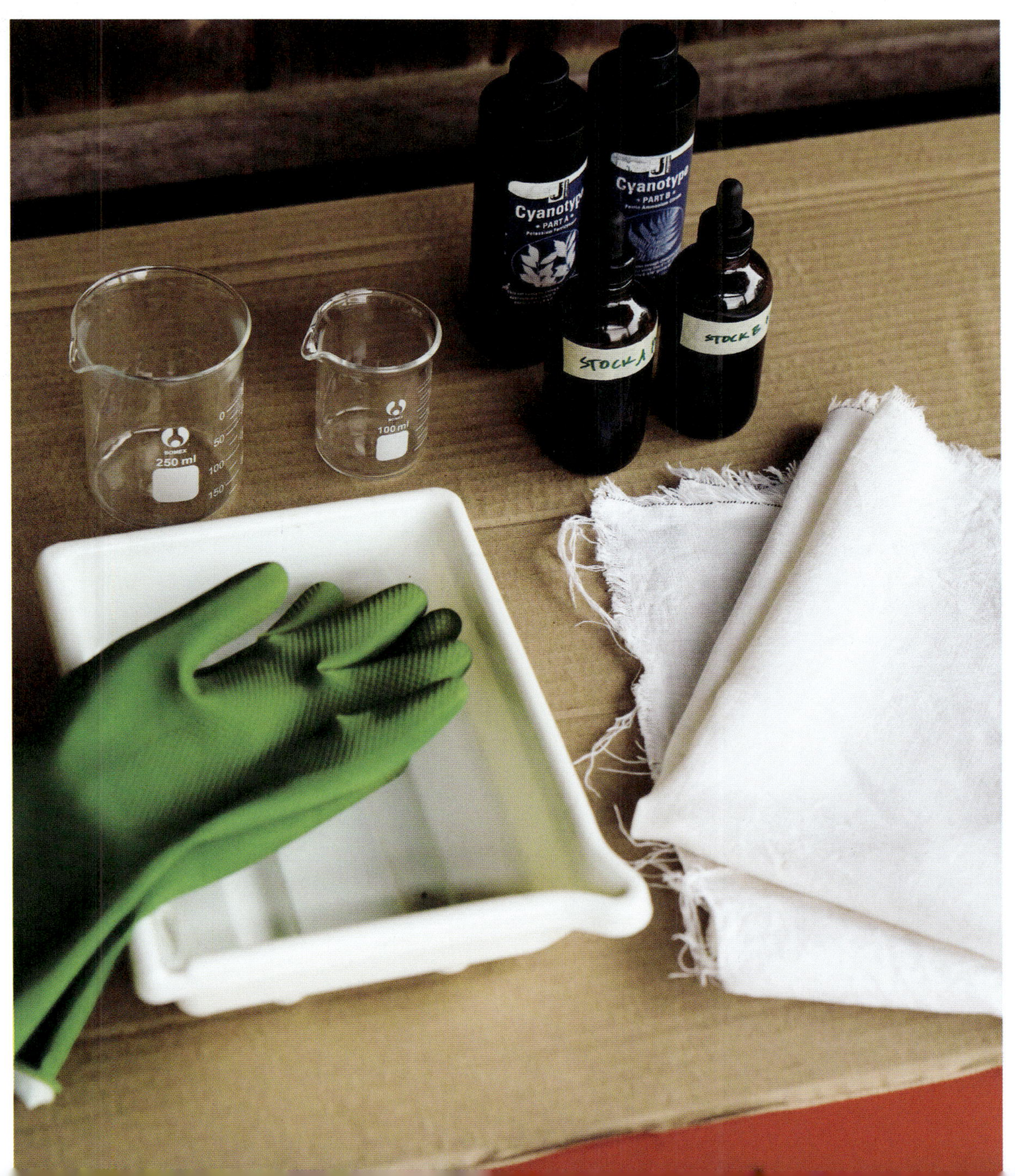

## COATING THE FABRIC

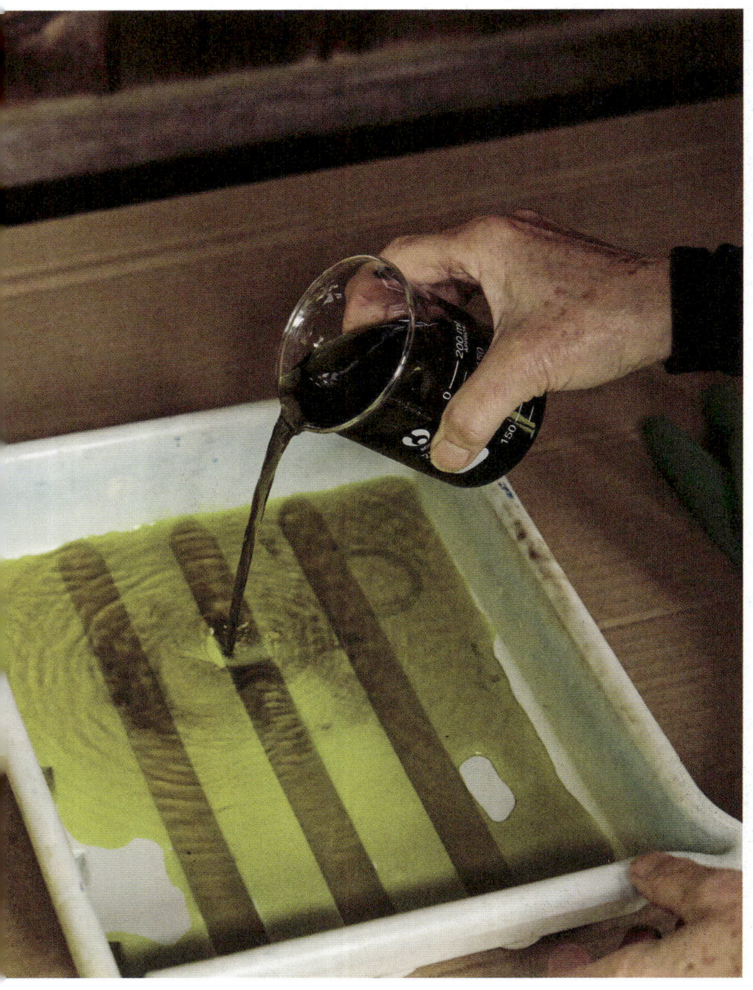


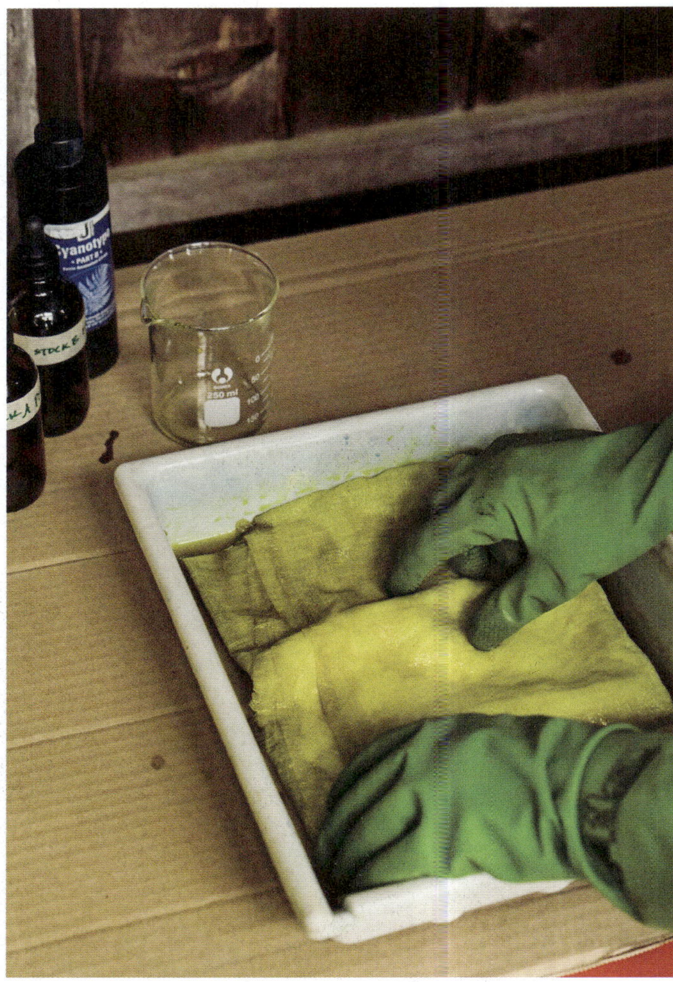




1 **MIX THE WORKING SOLUTION.** Working in a low-light setting, mix equal parts of stock solutions A and B in a plastic container large enough to hold the piece of fabric. The amount of solution you need will depend on the size of your fabric. For a 16 × 20-inch piece of cotton or linen fabric, you'll want about 150 mL or 10 tablespoons of working solution (75 mL or 5 tablespoons of each stock solution). If areas remain uncovered and your fabric has absorbed all of the solution, mix more working solution.

2 **SOAK.** Allow the fabric to sit in the solution for 5 minutes. Wearing gloves, move the fabric around from time to time to ensure even coverage. If more coverage is needed, mix up additional working solution.

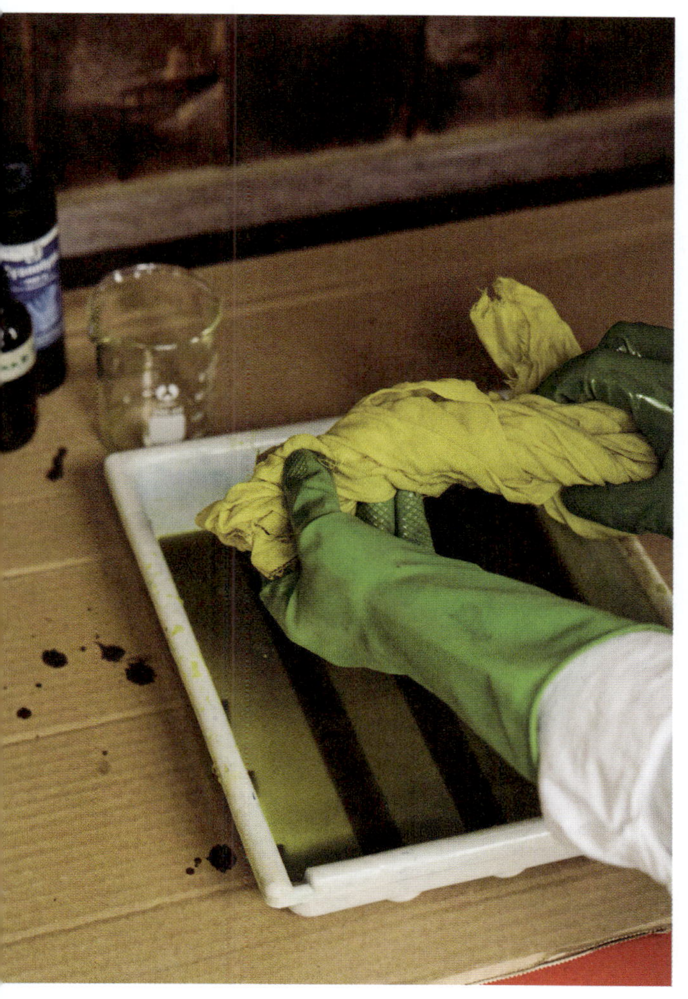

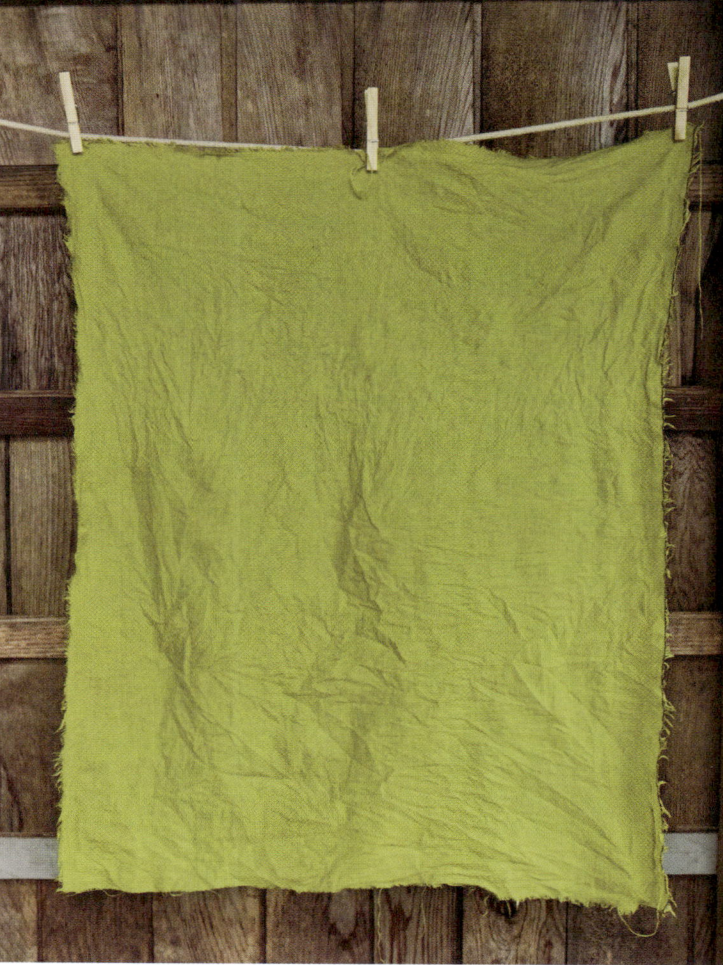

3 **WRING OUT THE FABRIC.** Wearing gloves, remove the fabric from the container, wringing out the excess solution. Pour the excess solution into a lightproof container and use within a few days. Watch out for drips, which will stain fabric and unfinished wood.

4 **DRY THE FABRIC.** Hang the fabric in a dark or low-light area. If necessary, lay a drop cloth underneath the wet fabric to catch drips. Depending on temperature and humidity, drying can take several hours. Once dry, expose and rinse or store in a lightproof container for up to 1 week.

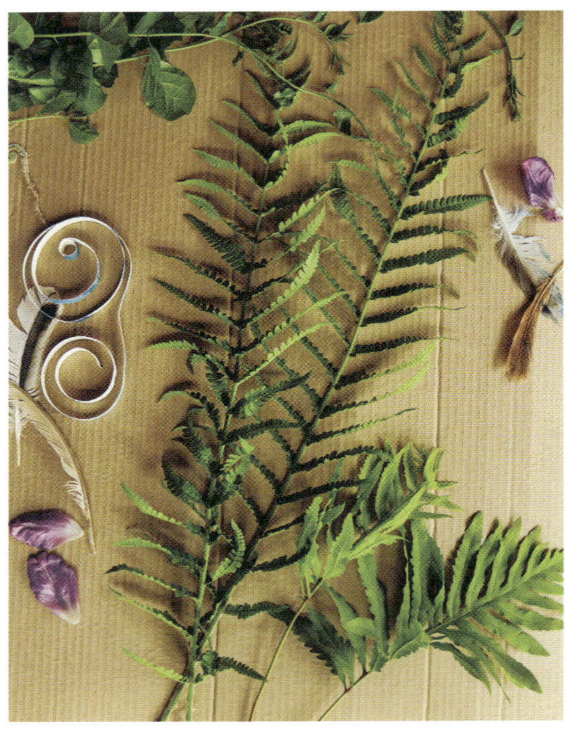

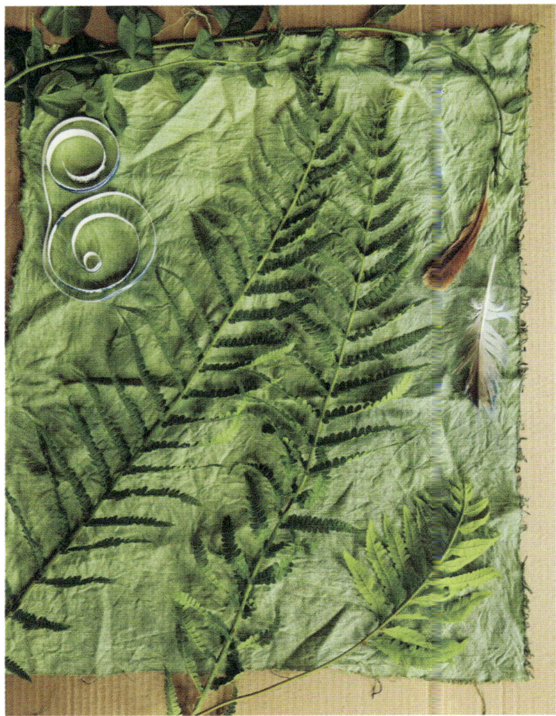

## EXPOSING AND RINSING FABRIC

1 **SET UP.** Gather your materials in a dimly lit prep space. Place a bucket or tray in your wash area and fill it with water. Set up a clothesline to dry away from direct light.

2 **ARRANGE THE COMPOSITION.** Place the fabric on the cardboard backing, smoothing out any wrinkles. Secure it with clips, if needed. Arrange your printing material on the fabric.

3 **SECURE THE MATERIALS.** Cover the fabric and printing material with a sheet of glass or acrylic. Secure the glass or acrylic to the cardboard backing with binder clips. As with securing plants to paper, the glass provides a tighter fit between the fabric and the printing material, creating a crisper rendition of the printing material.

4 **EXPOSE TO SUNLIGHT.** Place your setup in direct sunlight. Exposure time varies depending on sunlight strength and time of year. Overexposure is preferable to underexposure. Under a bright midday sun, you might expose the fabric for 3 to 15 minutes. The bronze color we look for to gauge the proper development of a paper print may be less apparent on fabric.

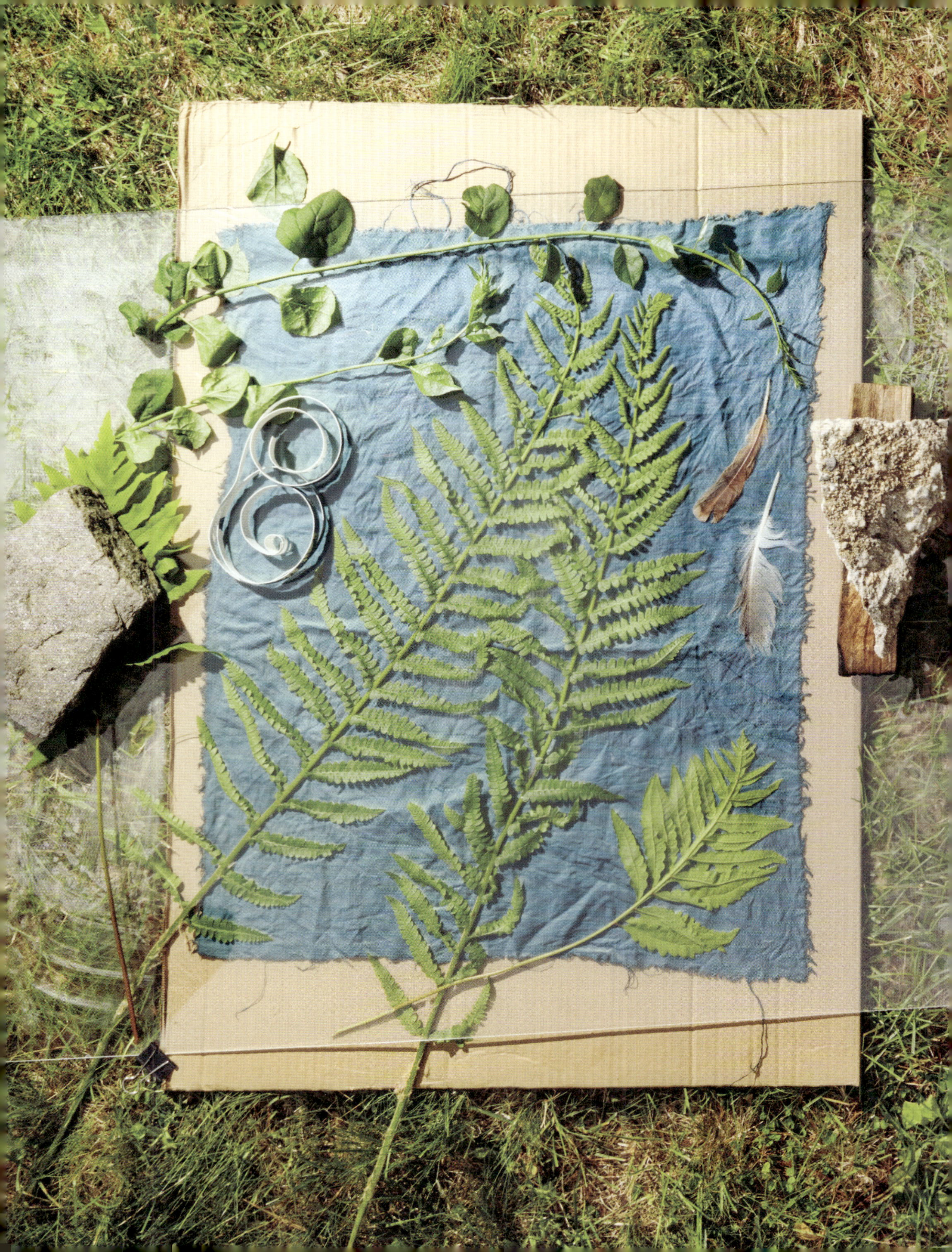

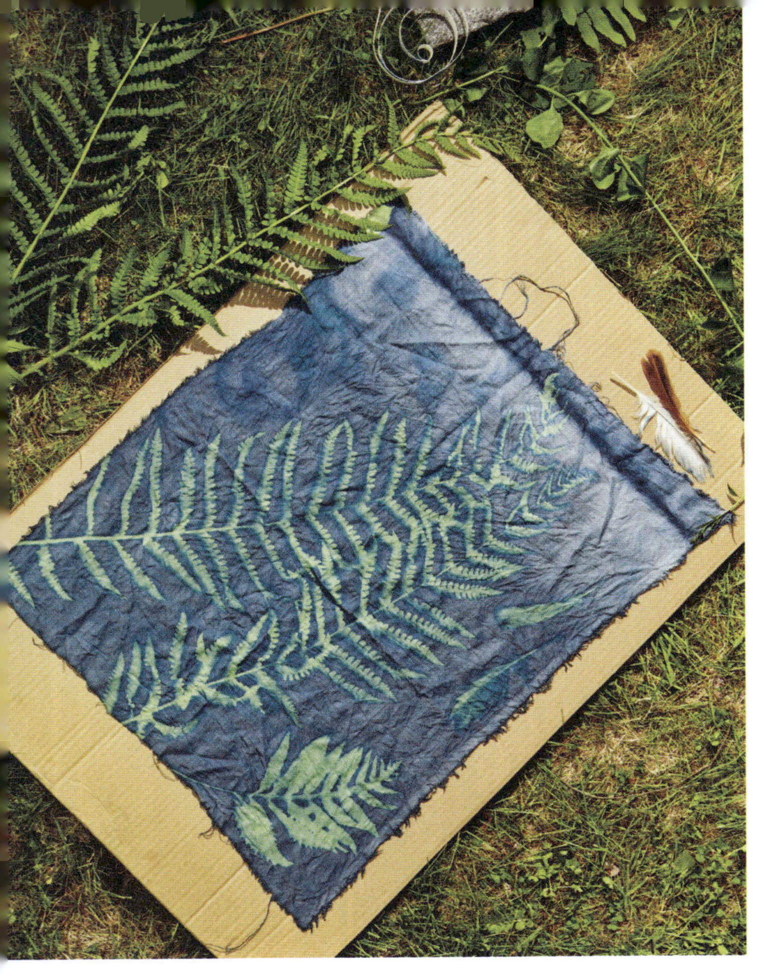

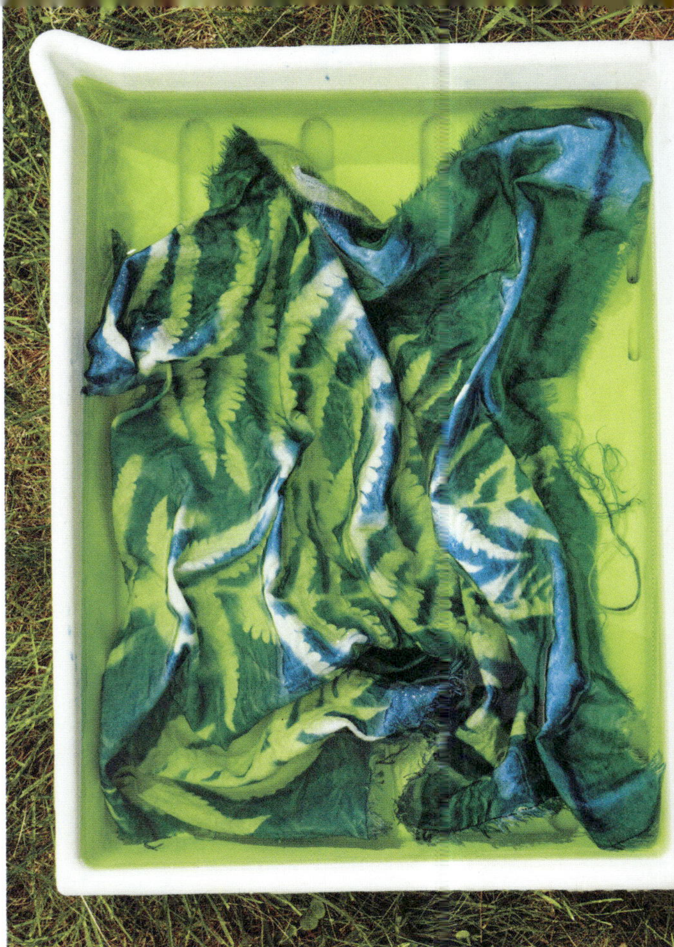

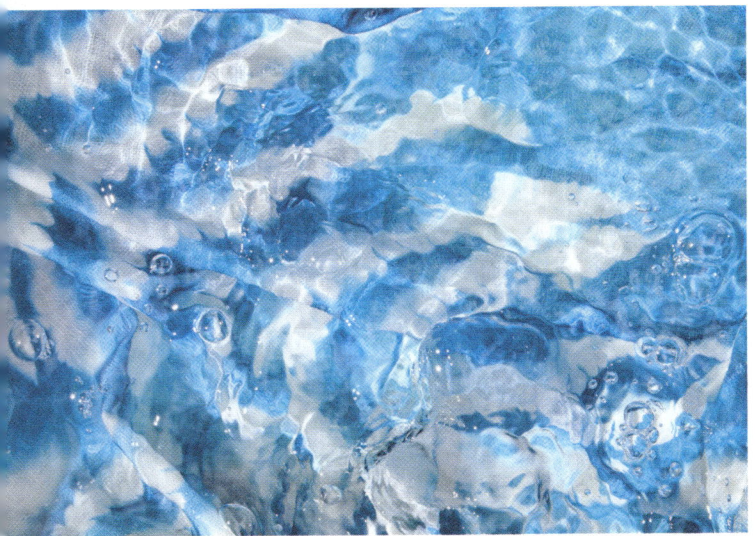

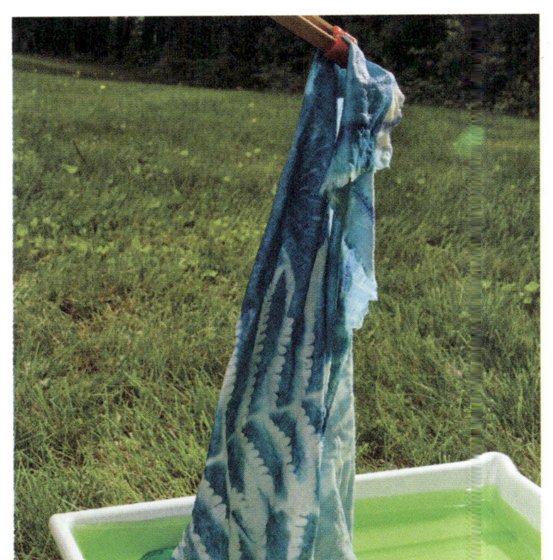

5 **DISMANTLE AND WASH.** When the fabric print is ready, move the setup out of direct sunlight. Remove the clips, glass or acrylic, and printing material. Place the fabric in water; wear gloves or use tongs, if you like. Wash in slowly running water for 5 to 15 minutes, or until the water runs clear.

6 **DRY.** Hang the fabric away from direct sun to dry. Press with a low-temperature iron on the back side of the fabric to remove wrinkles, if desired.

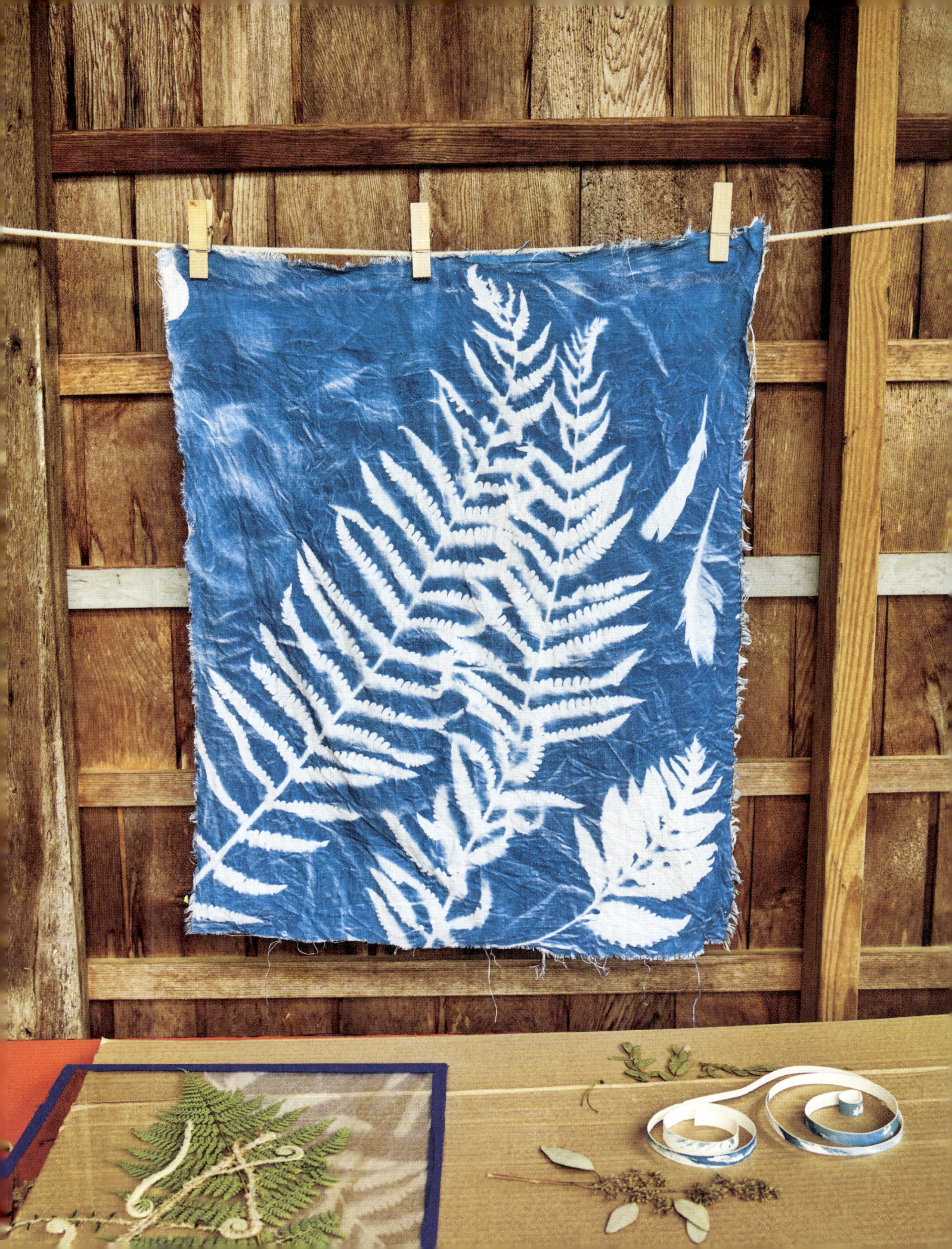

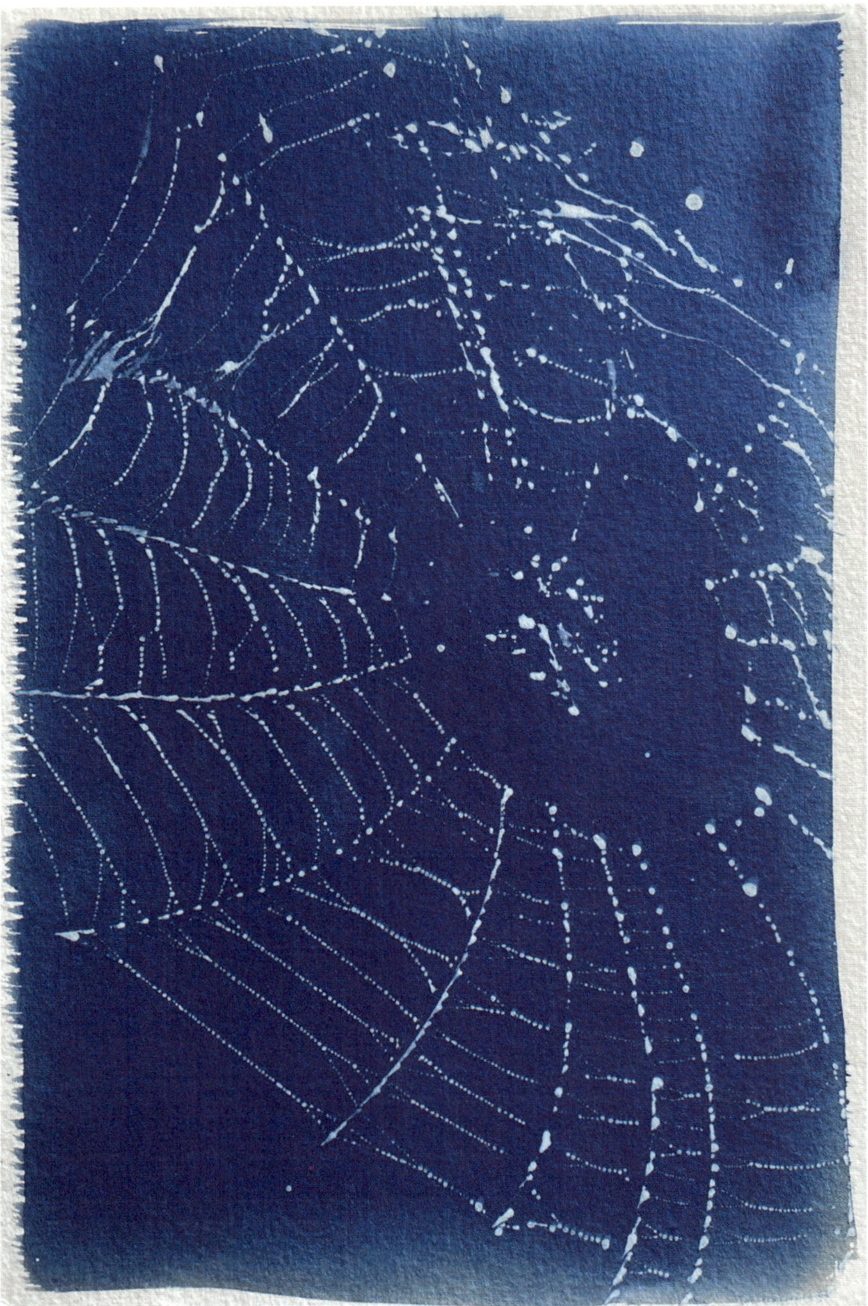

Marita Wai,
*Cobweb Study*

## BEYOND BOTANICALS

You could spend a lifetime printing with plants and never create the same composition twice. But the natural world has so much to offer. Consider unexpected objects like feathers, seashells, coral, cicada wings, seedpods, or even a spiderweb. When working with a spiderweb, artist Marita Wai recommends using a small sheet of paper and being mindful of the exposure time so that the web doesn't simply dissolve. Dew, frost, or a gentle mist of water on the web can make it easier to print with.

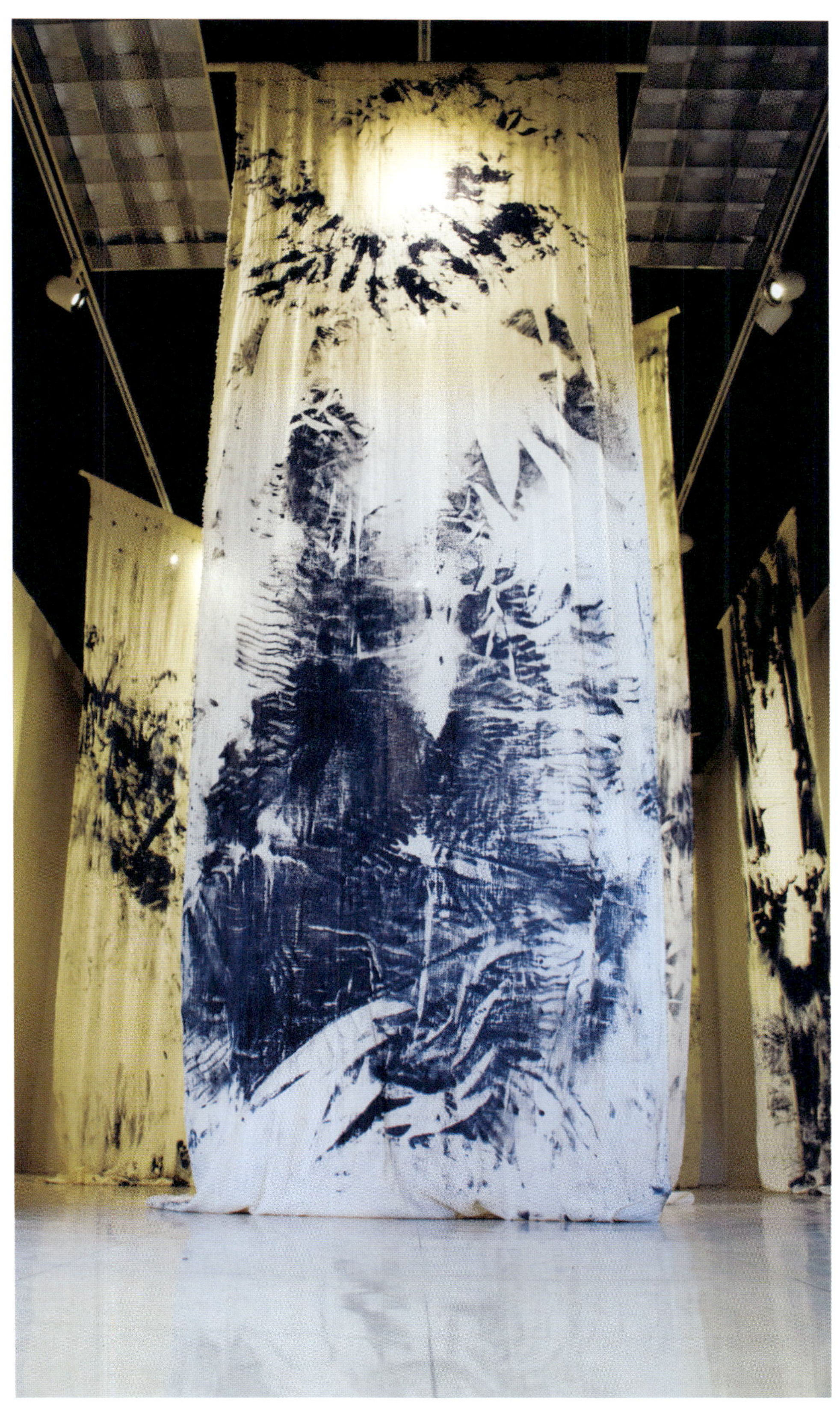

Angelea Heartsong-Redding creates self-portrait body blueprints, using cyanotype emulsion on cotton gauze, that form a map of her experiences.

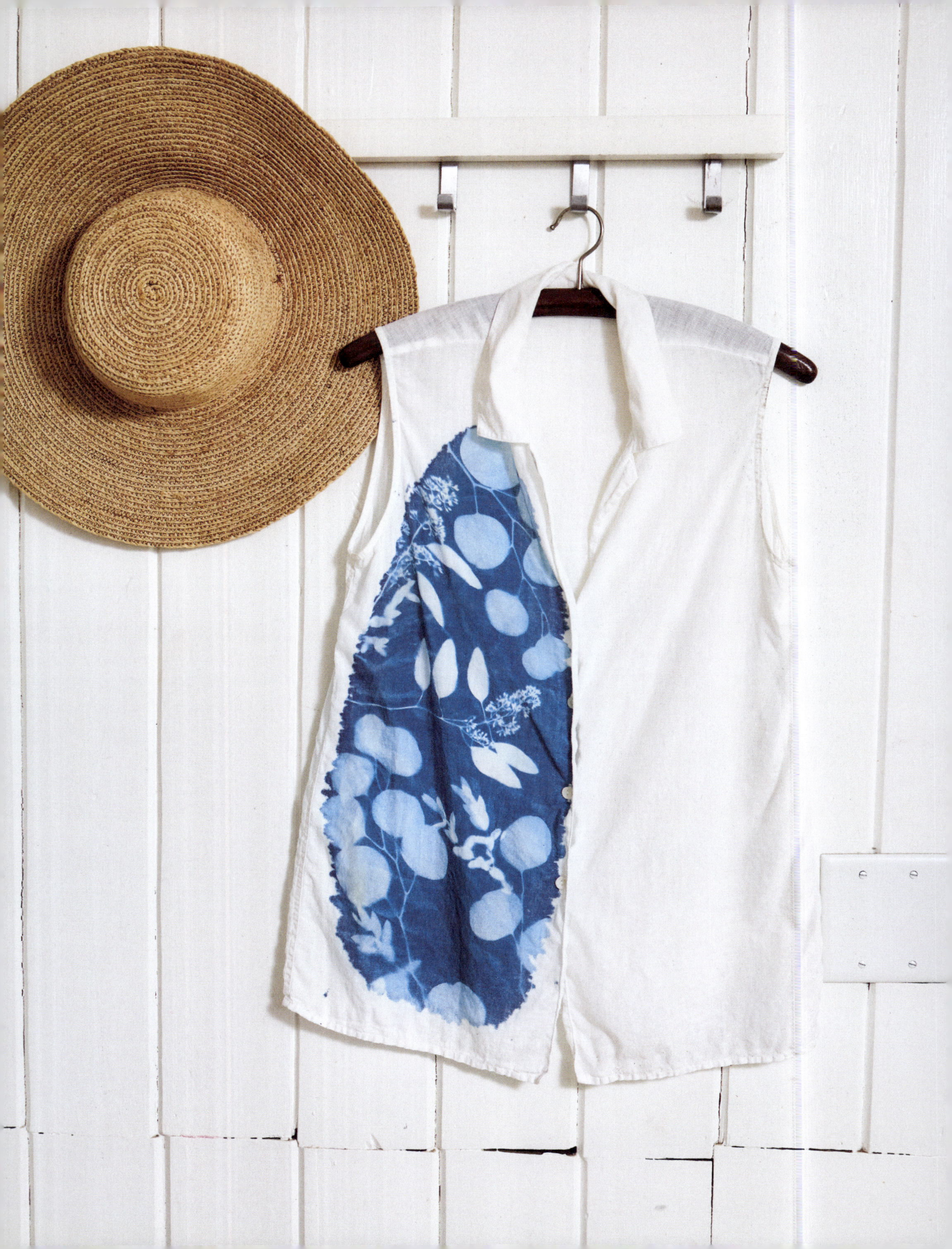

# Shirt with Botanical Embellishments

A simple shirt can become a piece of wearable art using the cyanotype process. Any style shirt works as long as it is 100 percent cotton, linen, or silk. In this project, I demonstrate on a sleeveless button-down dress shirt. I typically add cyanotype solution only to selected areas of the garment, though to create an all-blue shirt, you can immerse it in working solution as you did for the fabric wall hanging (see page 174).

### Materials

- Stock solutions A and B
- Glass or plastic container
- A cotton, silk, or linen shirt that has been scoured and dried (see directions on page 172)
- Sheet of cardboard (or any stiff material) the same size as the glass or acrylic
- Sheet of clean paper
- Hake brush or foam brush
- Plastic hangers, clothesline, and clothespins
- Plastic washing tray or bucket (fabric doesn't require a tray for washing)
- Plant material, pressed and dried or flat, or other flat material
- Sheet of glass or acrylic larger than the area of fabric you plan to coat with cyanotype solution
- Binder clips or similar fasteners
- Gloves or tongs for handling the fabric while rinsing (optional)

## COATING THE SHIRT

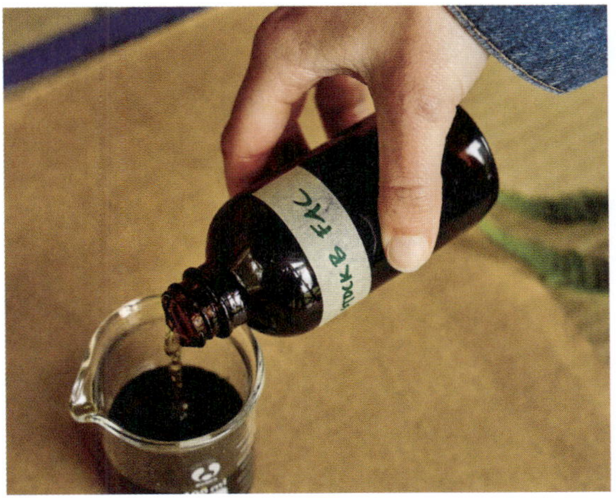


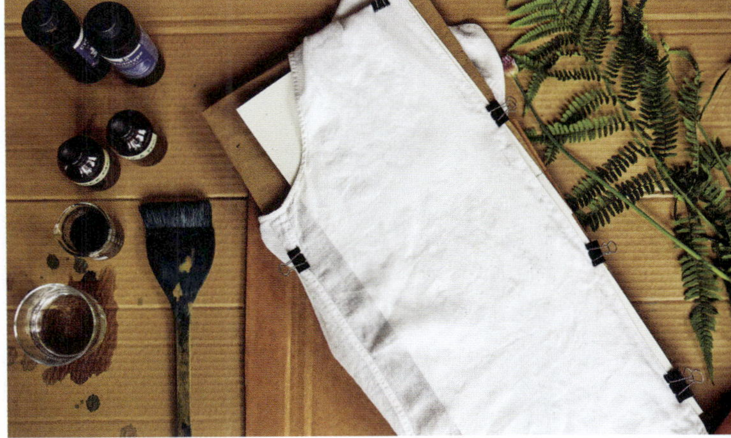

1 **MIX THE WORKING SOLUTION.** Working in a low-light setting, mix equal parts of stock solutions A and B in a glass or plastic container. The amount of solution will depend on the size of your fabric. To coat a 12 × 5-inch area of a shirt, begin with about 90 mL or 6 tablespoons of working solution (45 mL or 3 tablespoons of each stock solution). Adjust the amounts based on how much liquid is absorbed by the fabric.

2 **PREPARE THE SHIRT.** Place the area of the shirt to be printed onto a large, firm backing, like a piece of cardboard, sliding it between the front and back of the shirt, and secure with binder clips, if necessary. In order to prevent solution seeping through onto the cardboard, slide a sheet of clean paper between the cardboard backing and the shirt.

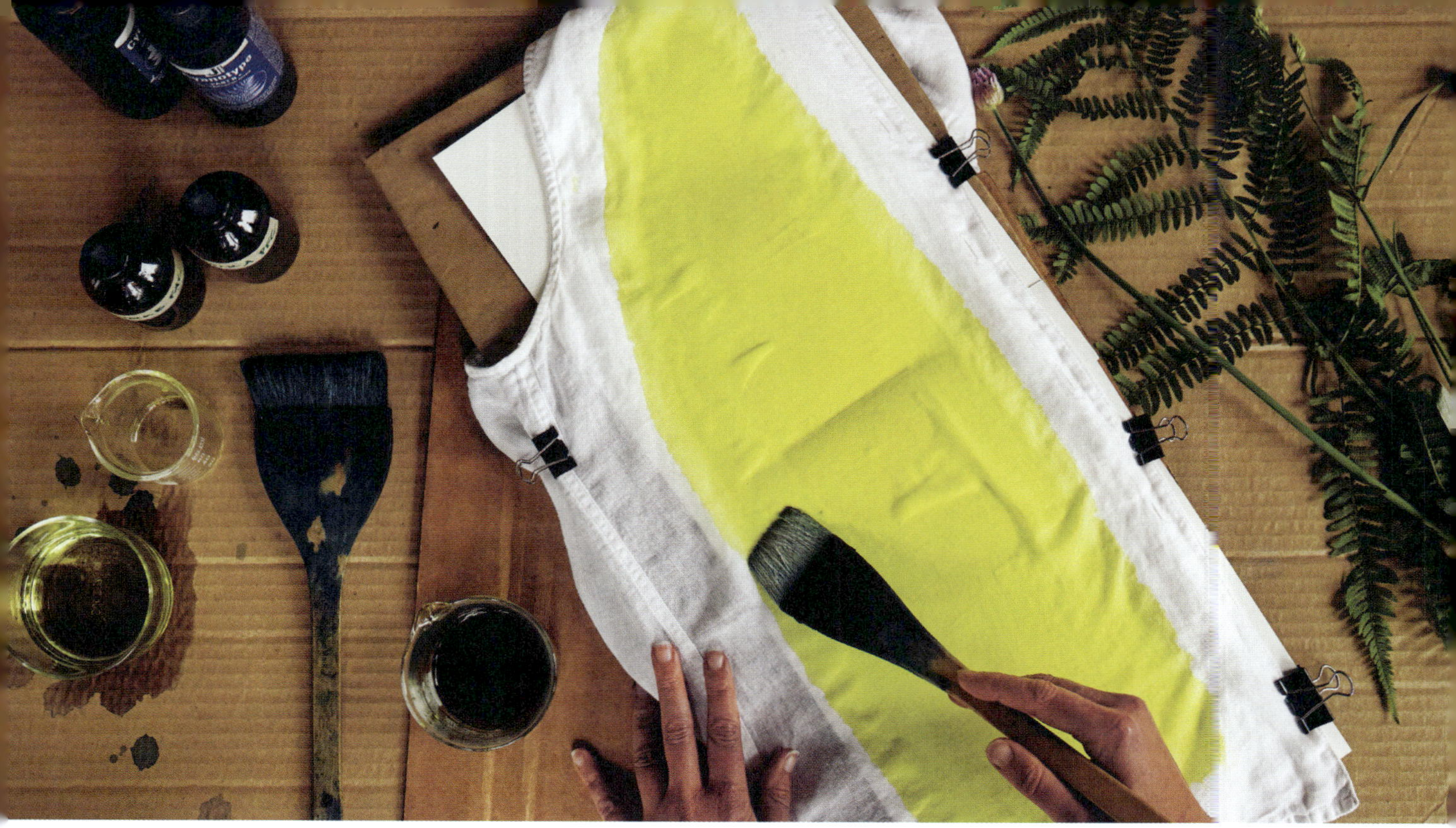

3 **APPLY THE WORKING SOLUTION.** Use a brush (I prefer a hake brush when working with fabric) to apply the working solution to the area you would like to print. It's difficult to apply working solution to fabric with precision; the liquid emulsion will tend to be absorbed by fibers all around the area of application. The imperfect lines are part of what makes the shirt interesting and beautiful.

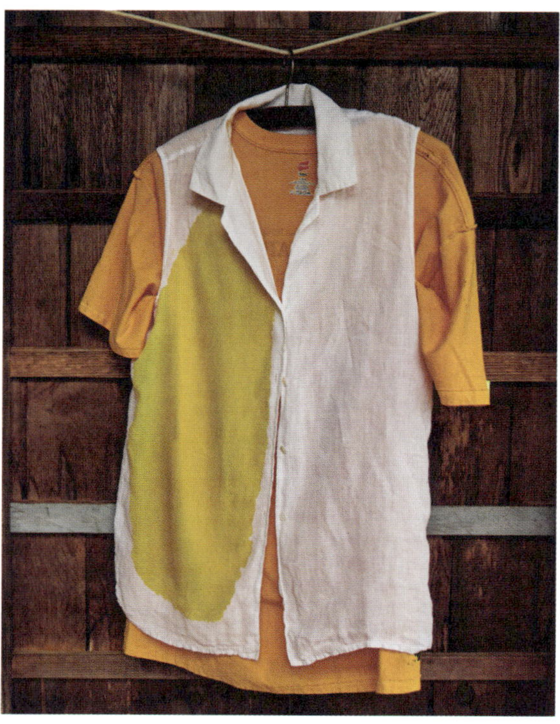

4 **DRY IN LOW LIGHT.** It's easy to accidentally transfer wet solution onto uncoated fabric. If you're printing on a button-down shirt, prevent this by placing an old T-shirt on a hanger, then hang the freshly coated shirt over the T-shirt, taking care not to allow coated areas of the shirt to touch the dry areas. It's okay for the T-shirt to get wet. If you're printing on a T-shirt, place an old T-shirt or a plastic bag over the hanger to prevent the wet coated side of the shirt from touching the dry uncoated side. Hang the shirt in a low-light location, taking care that it does not touch anything that will be stained by the cyanotype solution, like other clothing. Once dry, continue with the following steps or store in a lightproof container.

## EXPOSING AND RINSING THE SHIRT

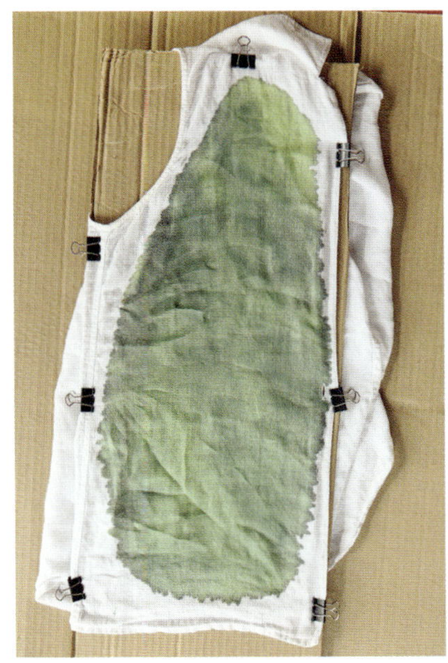

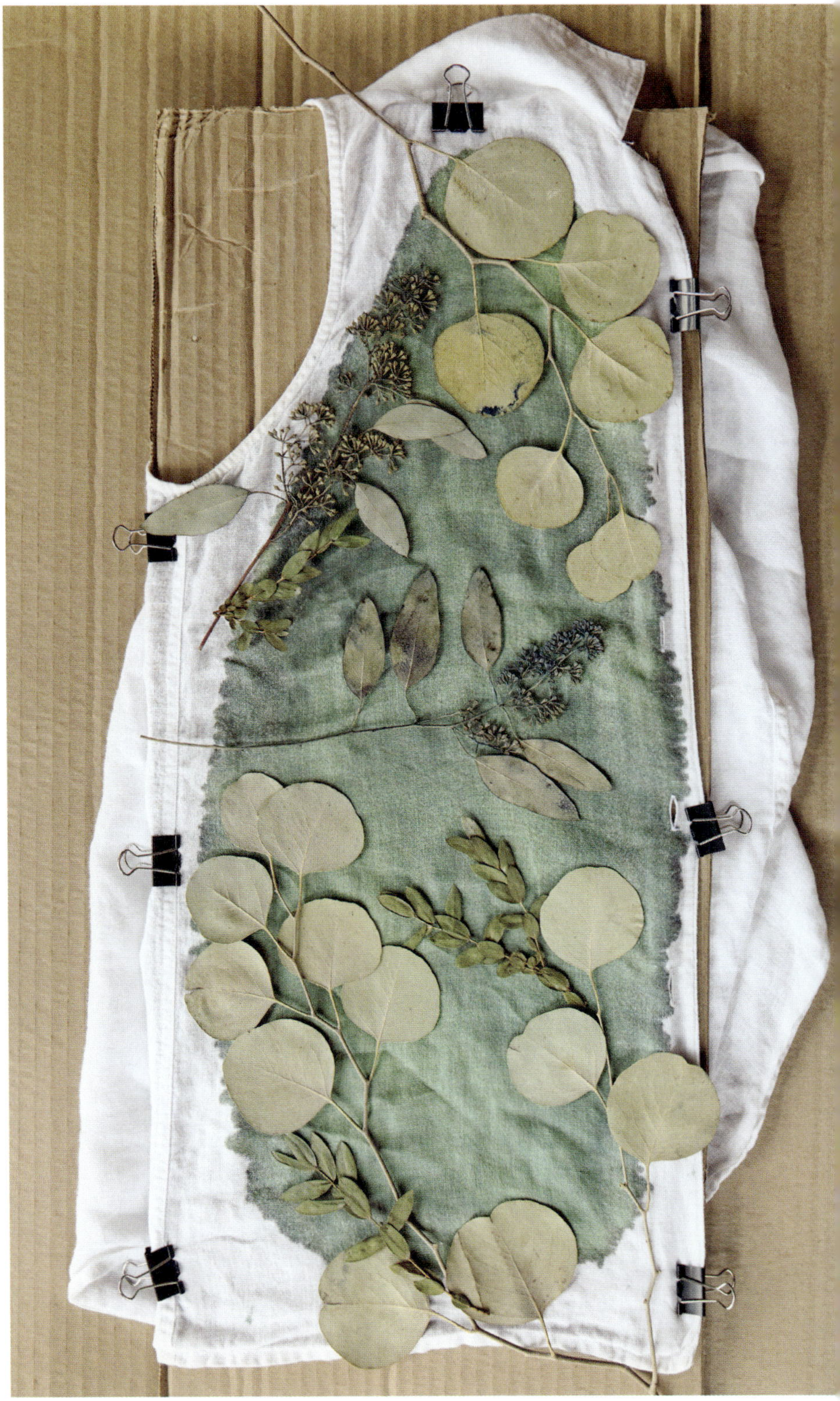

1 **SET UP.** Gather your materials in a dimly lit prep space. Place a bucket or tray in your wash area and fill it with water. Set up a clothesline where the shirt can dry away from direct light.

2 **ARRANGE THE COMPOSITION.** Place the area of the shirt with cyanotype solution onto the cardboard backing. Secure it with binder clips, if needed. Arrange your printing material onto the fabric.

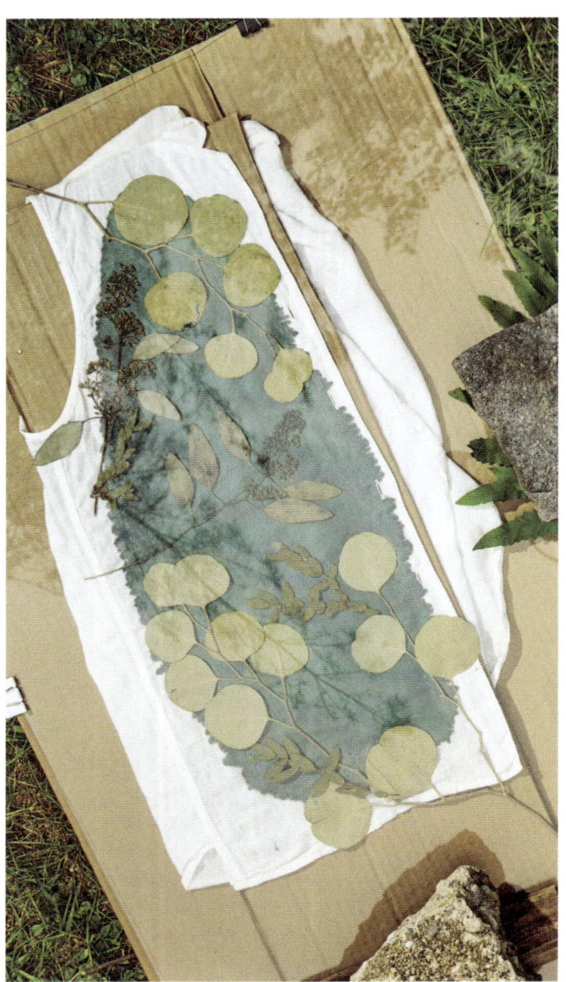

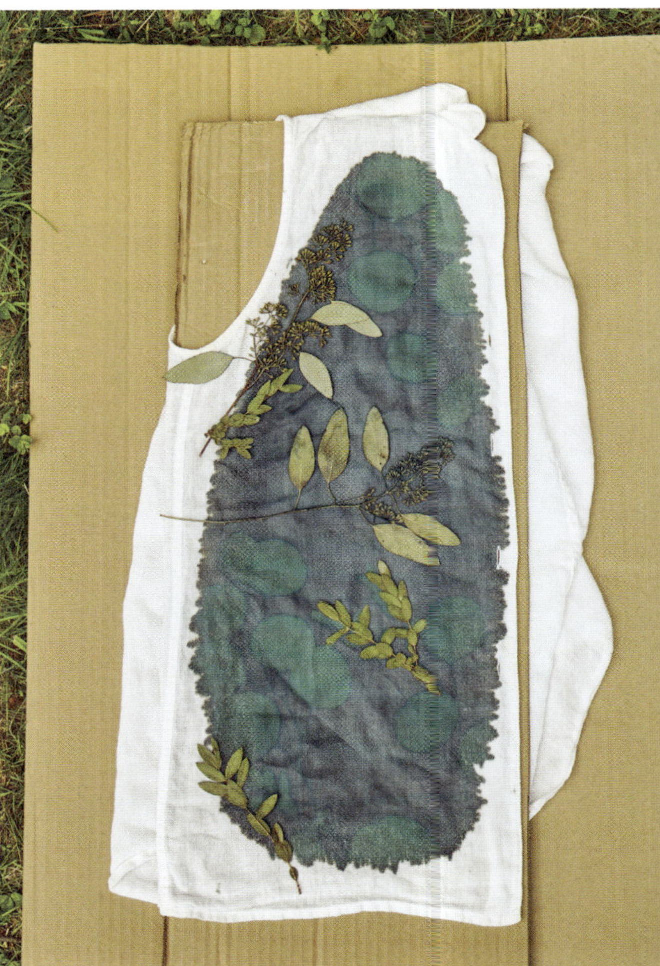

**3 SECURE THE MATERIALS.** Cover the fabric and printing material with a sheet of glass or acrylic. Secure the glass or acrylic to the cardboard backing with binder clips. As with paper, the glass provides a tighter fit between the fabric and the printing material and creates a crisper rendition of your printing object.

**4 EXPOSE TO SUNLIGHT.** Place your setup in direct sunlight. Unlike with a flat piece of cyanotype paper, a shirt can be a bit bulky. Exposure time varies depending on sunlight strength and time of year. Overexposure is preferable to underexposure. Under a bright midday sun, you might expose the fabric for 3 to 15 minutes. The bronze color we look for to gauge the proper development of a paper print may be less apparent on fabric.

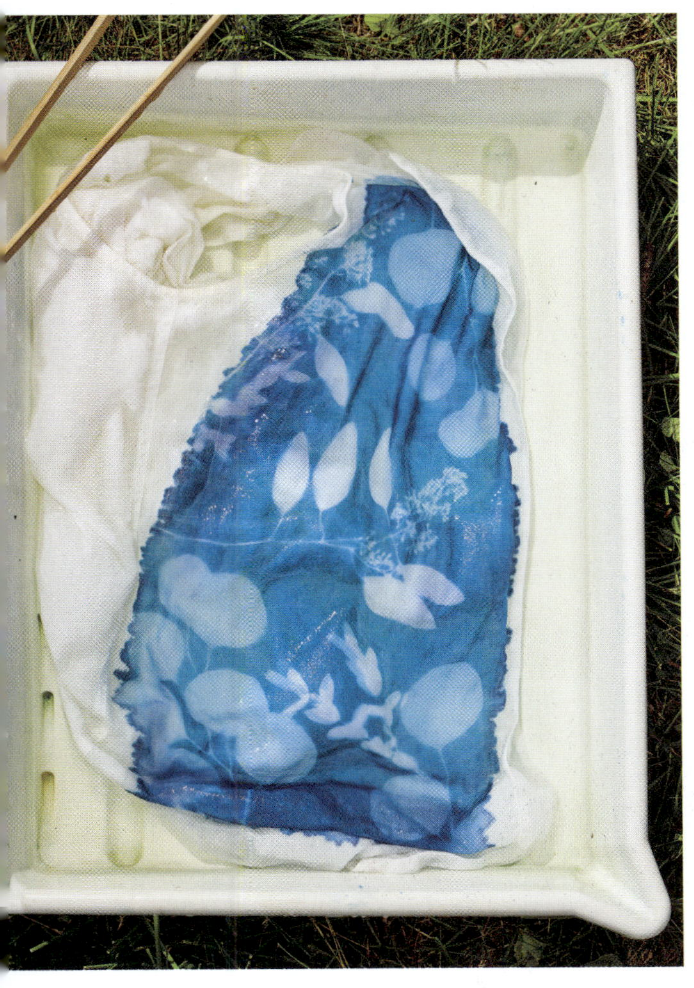

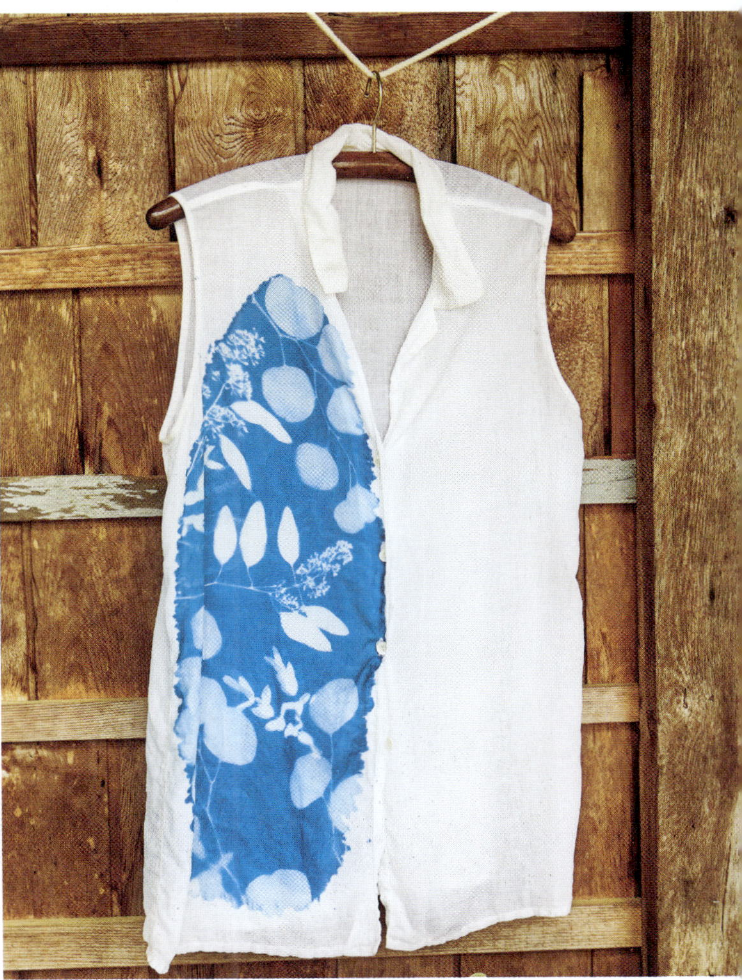

5 **DISMANTLE AND WASH.** When ready, move the setup out of direct sunlight. Remove the clips, glass or acrylic, cardboard, and printing material. Place the shirt in water; wear gloves or use tongs, if you like. Wash in slowly running water for 5 to 15 minutes, or until the water runs clear.

6 **DRY.** Hang the shirt away from direct sun to dry. Press with an iron to remove wrinkles. Follow care instructions on page 166 to keep your shirt in pristine condition.

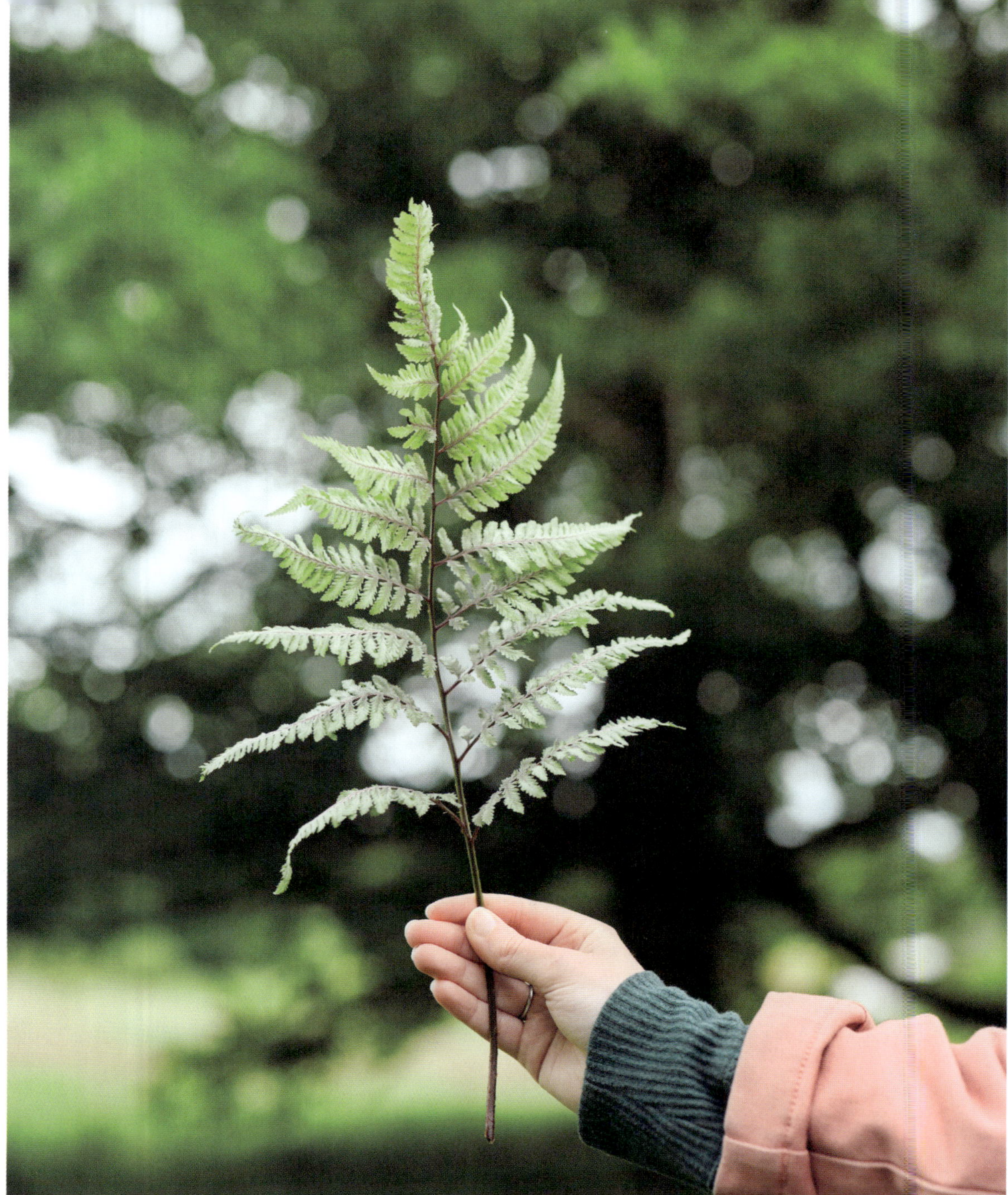

## FERNS

I love ferns! Winter walks in New England woods only deepen my admiration for them, especially when the evergreen Christmas ferns (*Polystichum acrostichoides*) push through Massachusetts snow—a sweet reminder that spring will bring plants out of dormancy to repopulate the landscape. A love for ferns is nothing new. In the nineteenth century, ferns enchanted so many people that the term *pteridomania*, or fern fever, was coined to describe the Victorian craze for all things fern-related. Pteridomania influenced arts and crafts design and extended the practice of plant cultivation from the wealthy into the homes and gardens of the middle class. The craze, however, also led to the overharvesting of wild ferns, pushing some species to the brink of extinction.

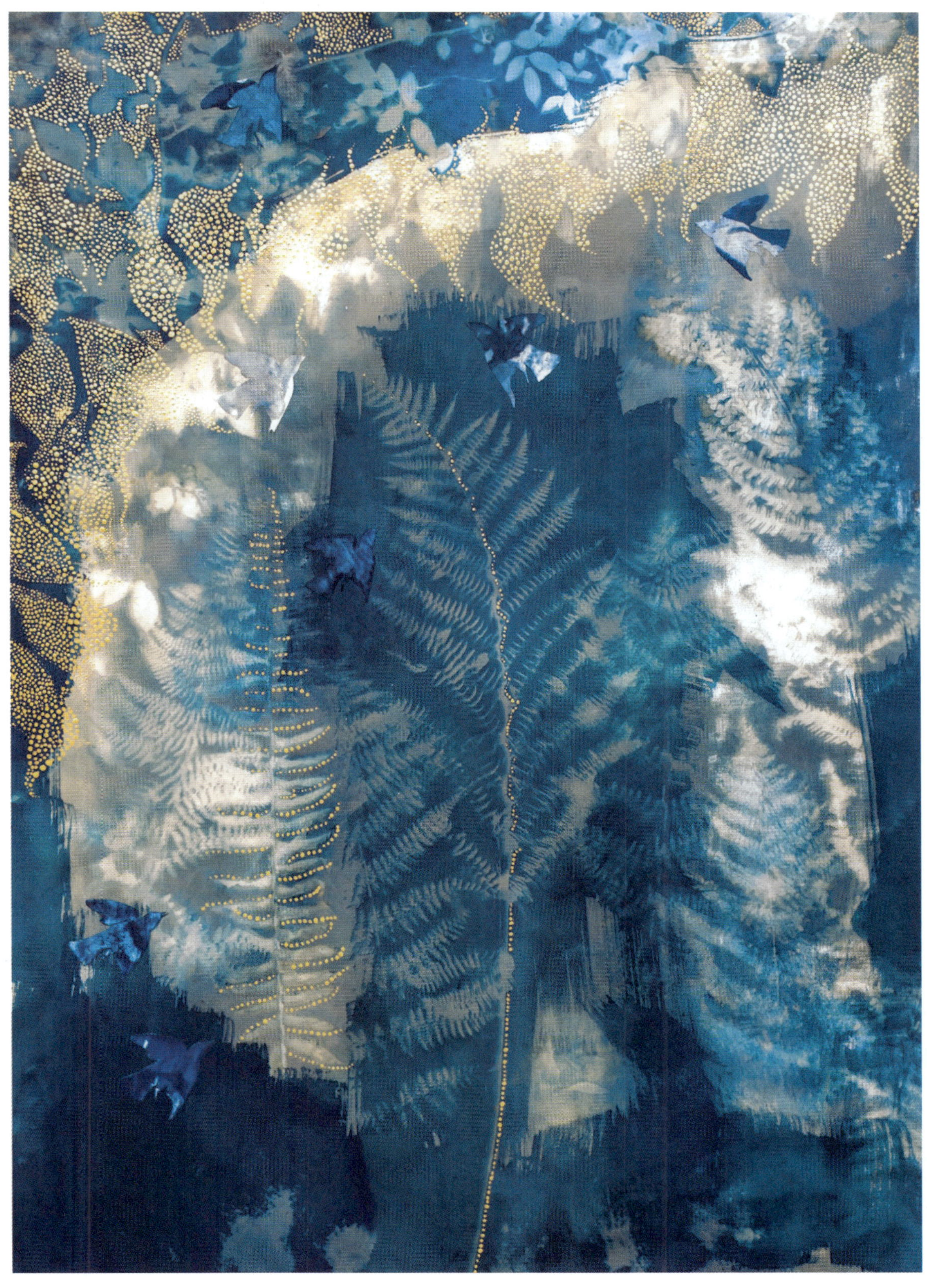

A 36 × 48-inch sheet of paper allowed me to work with very large fern fronds and make a cyanotype photogram. I then added bluebird collage elements and acrylic paint embellishments. Madge Evers, *Seven Is a Number*

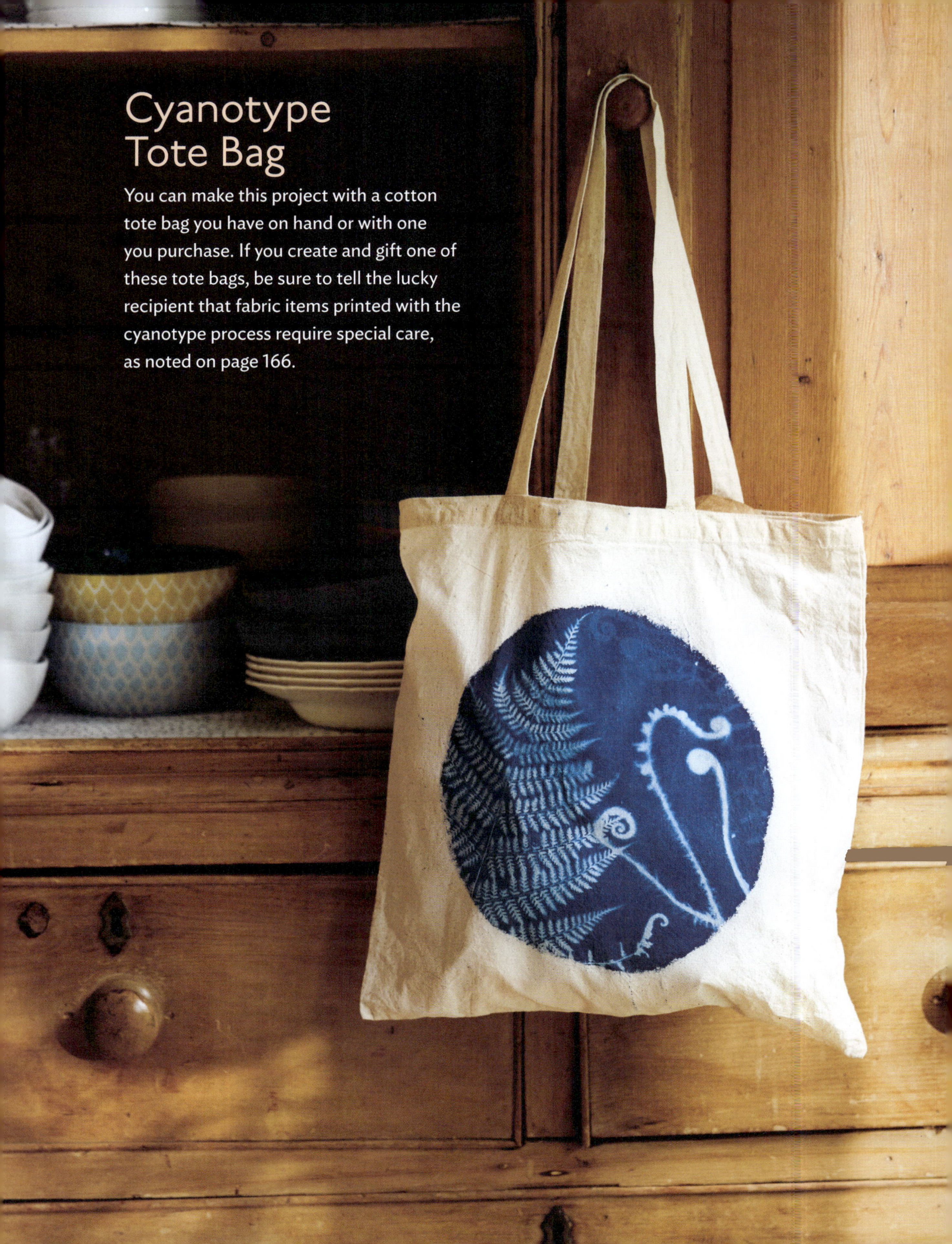

# Cyanotype Tote Bag

You can make this project with a cotton tote bag you have on hand or with one you purchase. If you create and gift one of these tote bags, be sure to tell the lucky recipient that fabric items printed with the cyanotype process require special care, as noted on page 166.

## COATING THE TOTE

### Materials

- Stock solutions A and B
- Plastic or glass container
- A 100 percent cotton tote bag, scoured and dried (see directions on page 172)
- Sheet of cardboard (or any stiff material) the same size as the glass or acrylic
- Sheet of clean paper
- Binder clips or similar fasteners
- Hake brush or foam brush
- Plastic hangers, clothes-line, and clothespins
- Plastic bucket or washing tray (fabric doesn't require a tray for washing)
- Plant material, pressed and dried or flat, or other flat material
- Sheet of glass or acrylic larger than the area of fabric you plan to coat with cyanotype solution
- Gloves or tongs for handling the fabric while rinsing (optional)

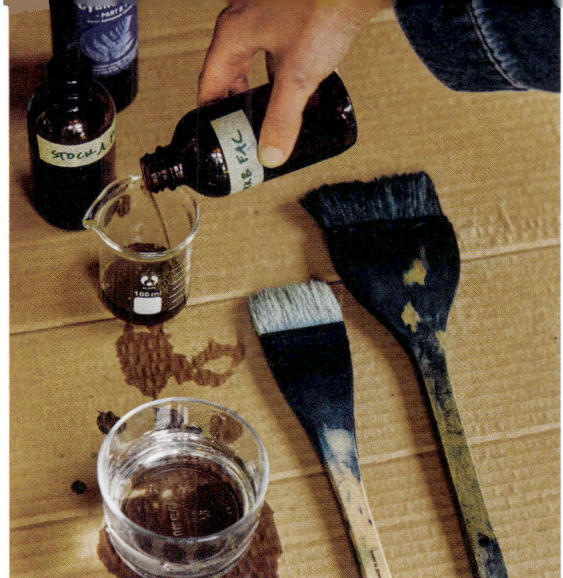

1 **MIX THE WORKING SOLUTION.** Working in a low-light setting, mix equal parts of stock solutions A and B in a plastic or glass container. To coat a 12 × 12-inch area on a tote, begin with about 90 mL or 6 tablespoons of working solution (45 mL or 3 tablespoons of each stock solution). Adjust the amounts according to how much is absorbed by the fabric.

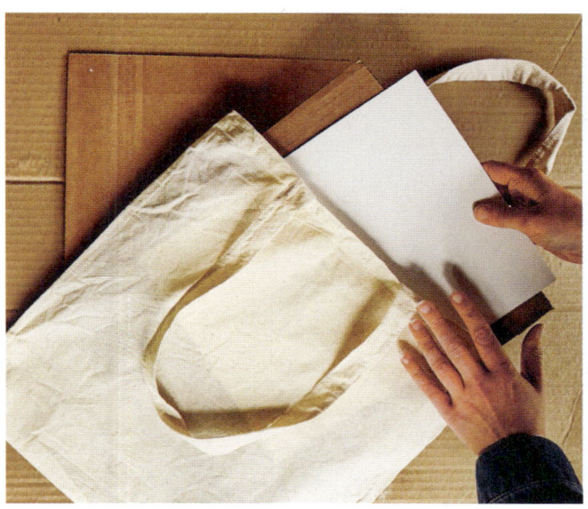

2 **PREPARE THE BAG.** Place a firm backing, like a piece of cardboard, inside the tote, sliding a sheet of clean paper between the cardboard and fabric to absorb any solution that seeps through. Secure with clips, if necessary.

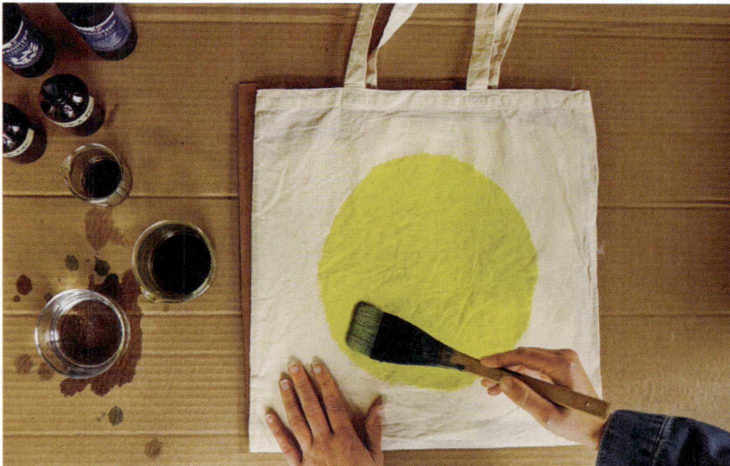

3 **APPLY THE WORKING SOLUTION.** Use a brush (I prefer a hake brush when working with fabric) to apply the working solution to the area(s) you'd like to print. It's difficult to apply working solution to fabric with precision; the liquid emulsion will tend to be absorbed by fibers all around the area of application. But that's part of the appeal! I usually apply cyanotype solution in a circular or oval shape.

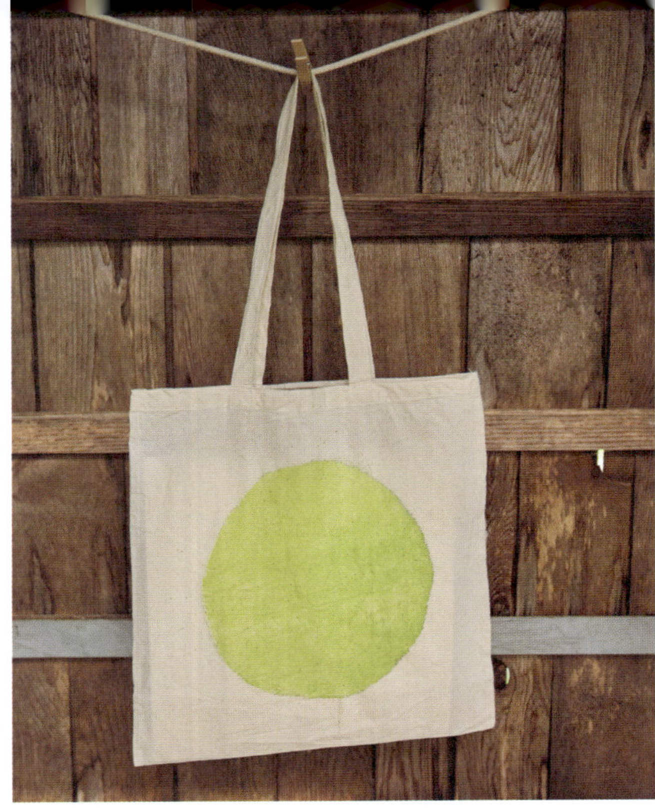

4 **DRY IN LOW LIGHT.** Allow the tote to dry in low light before exposing to UV light, taking care to hang the wet tote in a location where it will not touch anything that can be stained by cyanotype solution. Once dry, continue with the following steps or store in a lightproof container.

## EXPOSING AND RINSING THE TOTE

1 **SET UP.** Gather your materials in a dimly lit prep space. Place a bucket or tray in your wash area and fill it with water. Set up a clothesline to dry away from direct light.

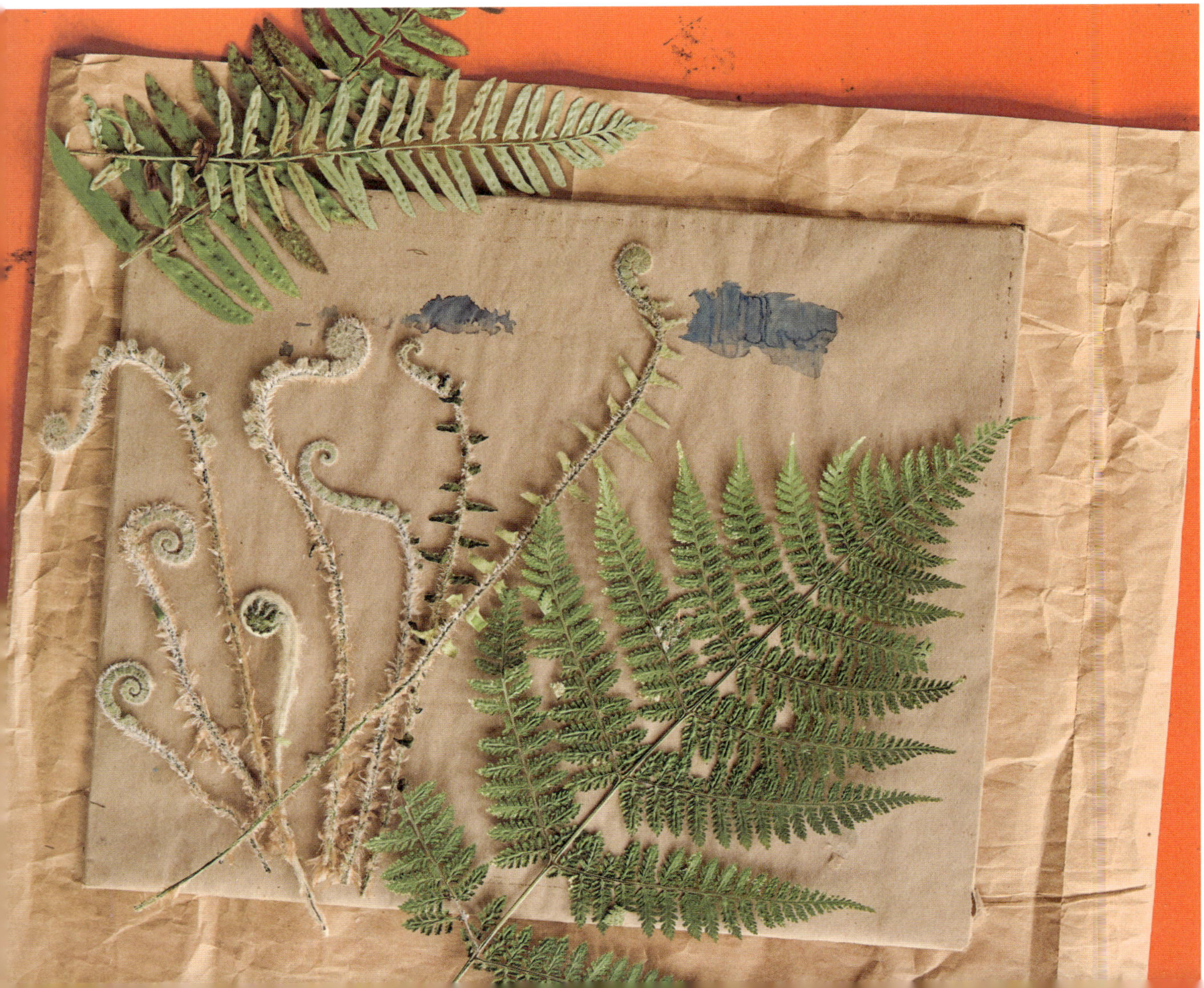

2 **ARRANGE THE COMPOSITION.** Place the area of the totebag that has been painted with cyanotype solution on a cardboard backing, securing with binder clips if needed. Arrange the printing material on the fabric.

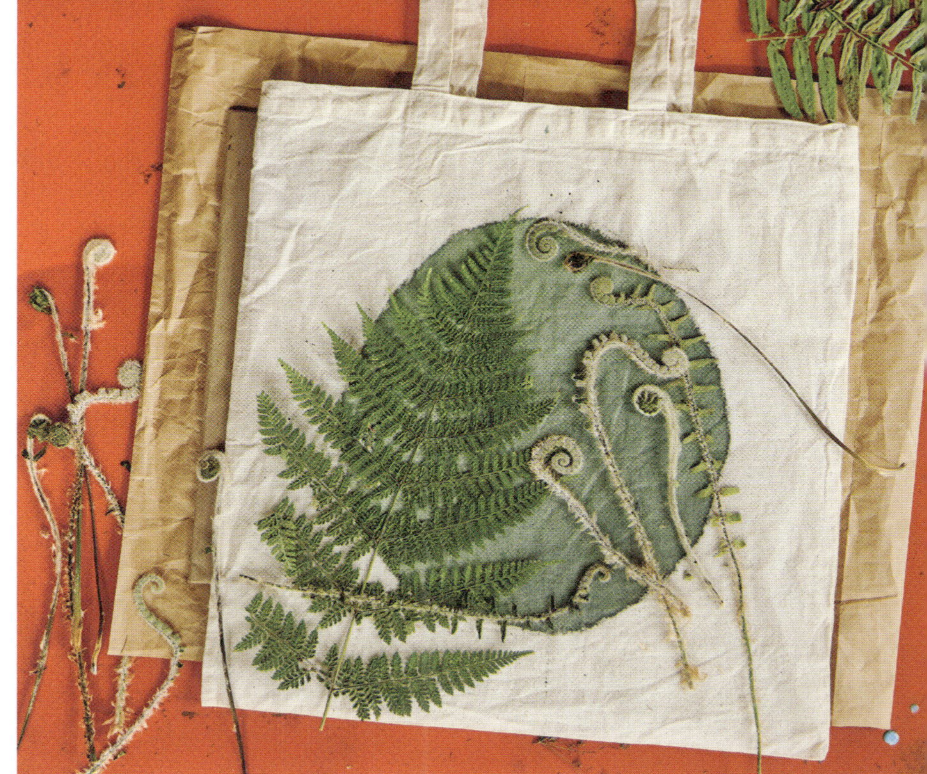

3 **SECURE THE MATERIALS.** Cover the tote and printing material with a sheet of glass or acrylic. Secure the glass or acrylic to the cardboard backing with binder clips. As when printing on paper, the glass provides a tighter fit between the fabric and printing material and creates a crisper image.

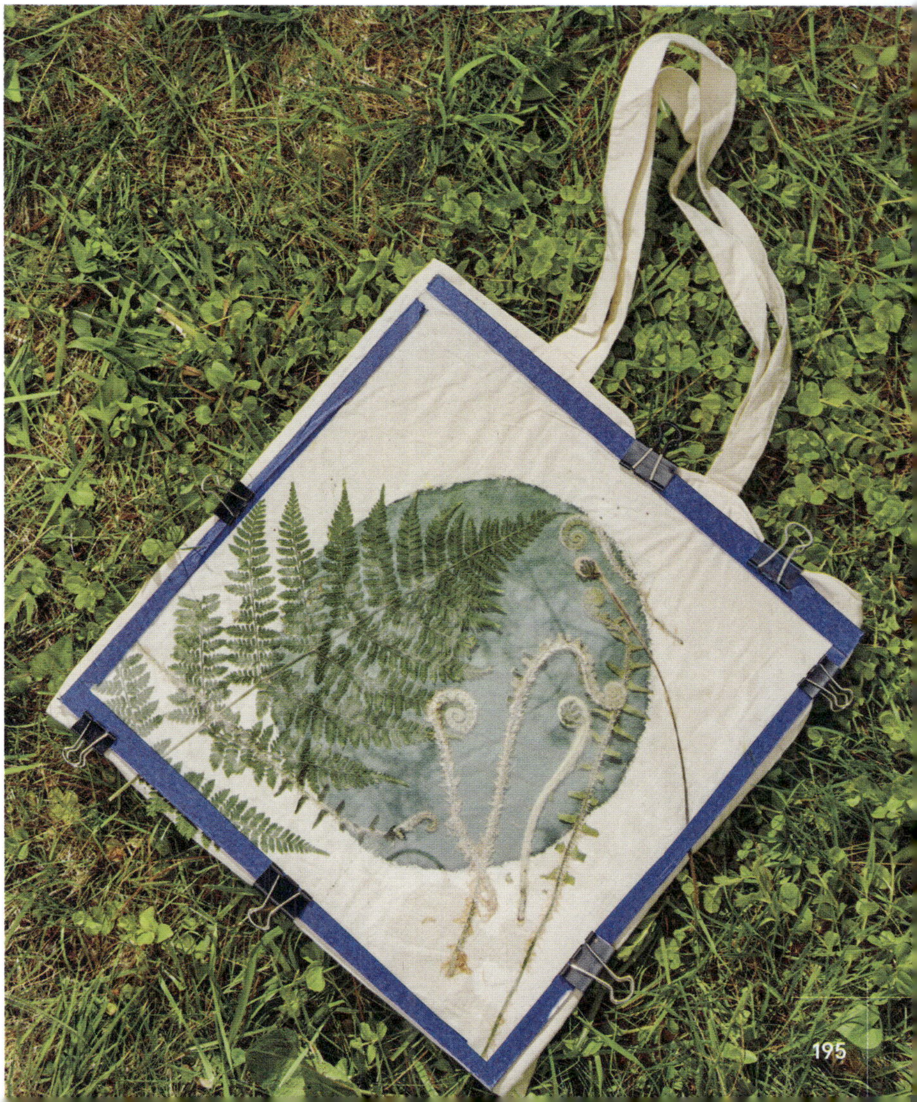

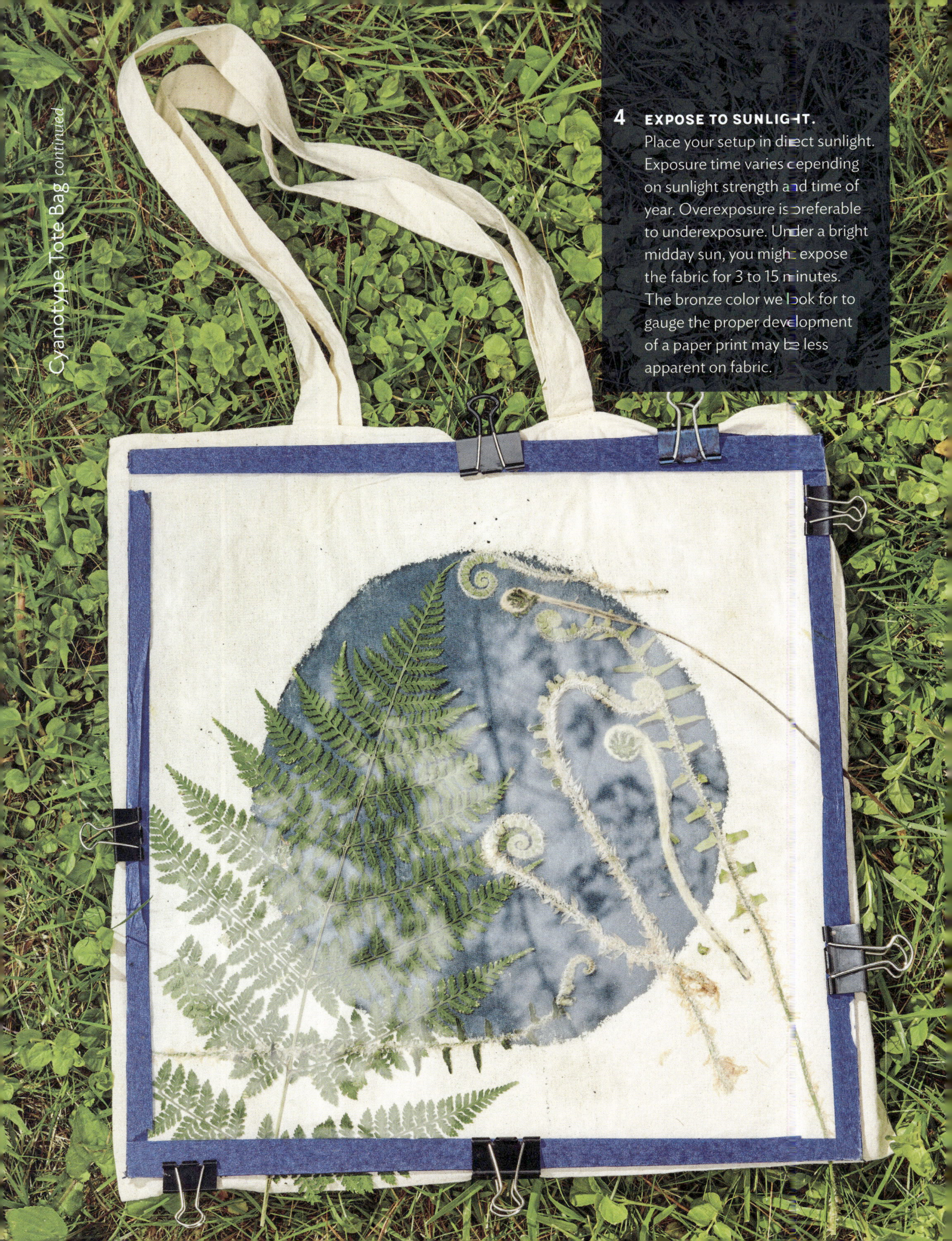

4 **EXPOSE TO SUNLIGHT.** Place your setup in direct sunlight. Exposure time varies depending on sunlight strength and time of year. Overexposure is preferable to underexposure. Under a bright midday sun, you might expose the fabric for 3 to 15 minutes. The bronze color we look for to gauge the proper development of a paper print may be less apparent on fabric.

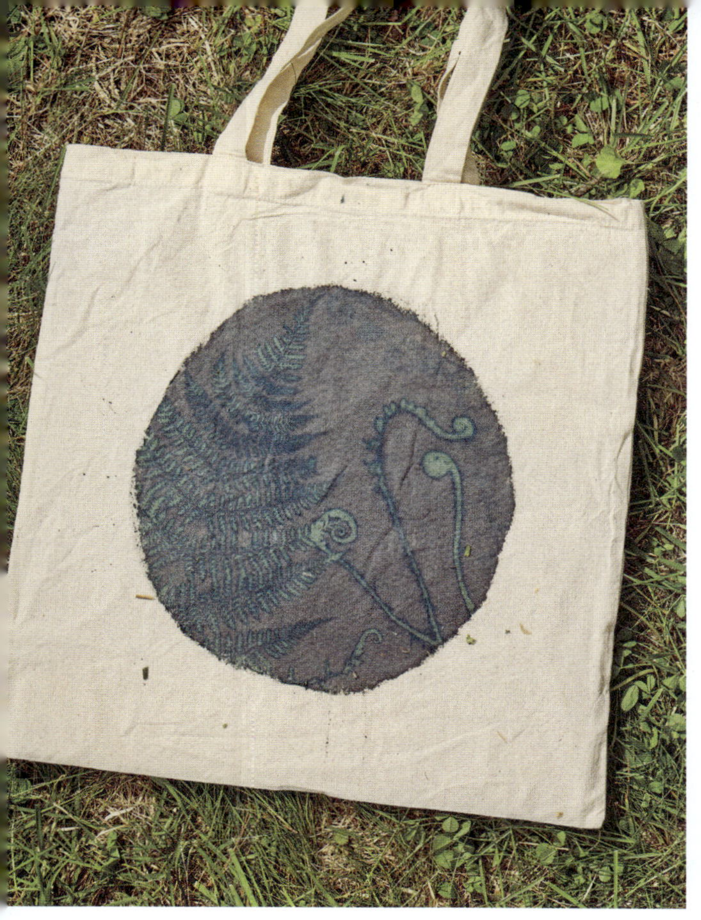

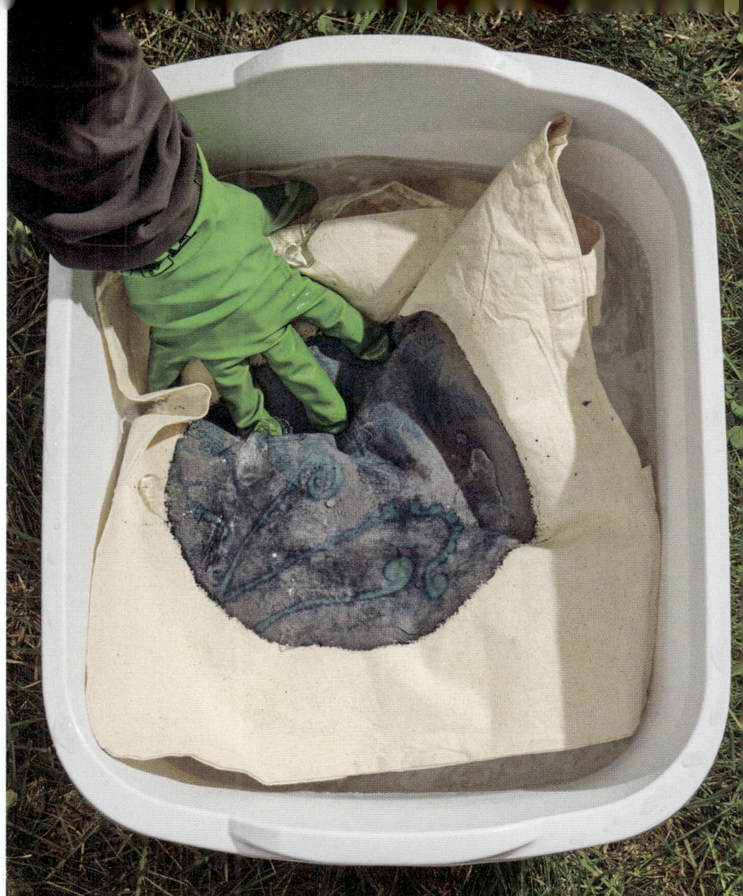

5 **DISMANTLE AND WASH.** When ready, move the setup out of direct sunlight. Remove the clips, glass or acrylic, cardboard, and printing material. Place the tote in water; wear gloves or use tongs, if you like. Wash in slowly running water for 5 to 15 minutes, or until the water runs clear.

6 **DRY.** Hang away from direct sun to dry.

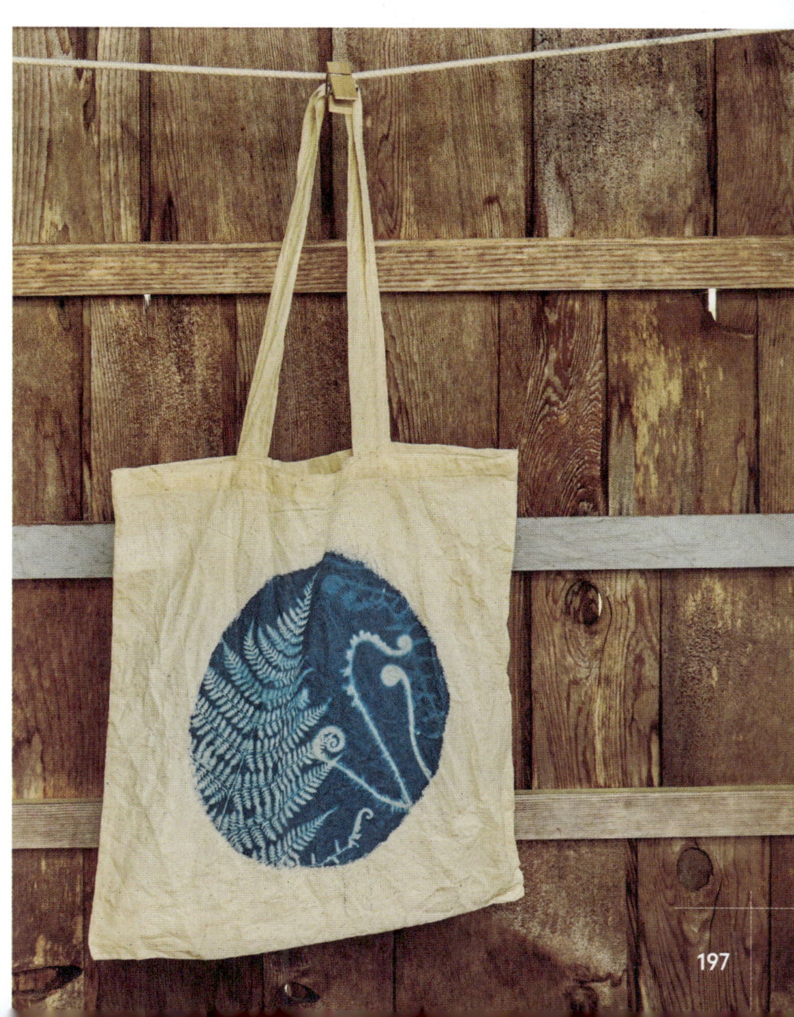

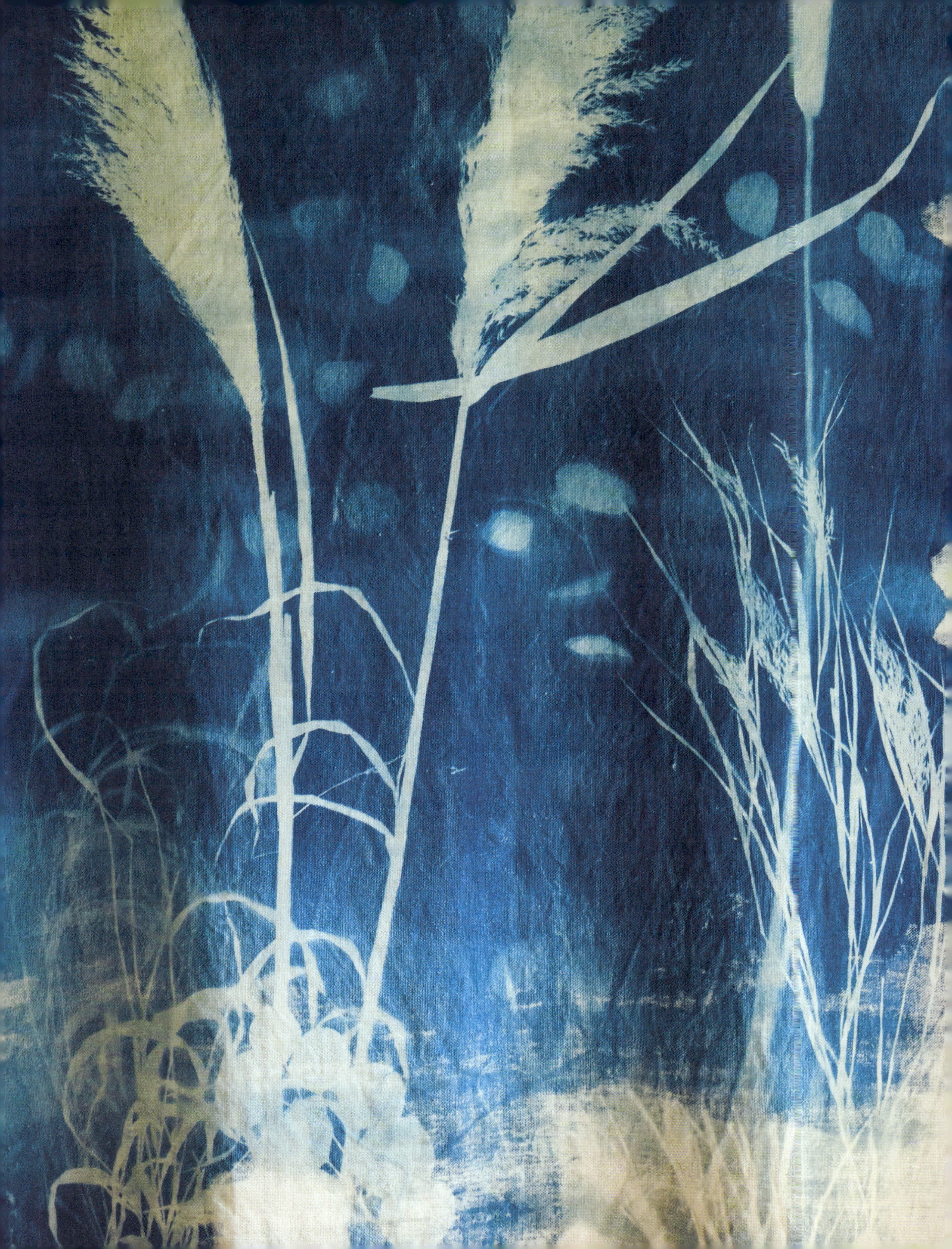

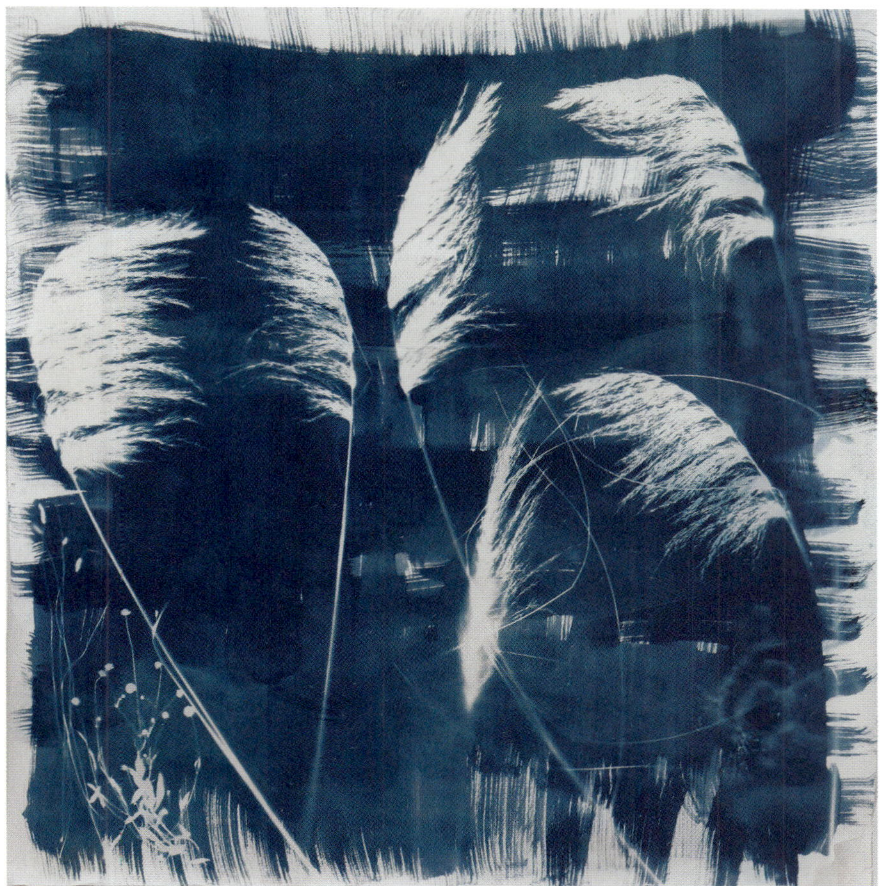

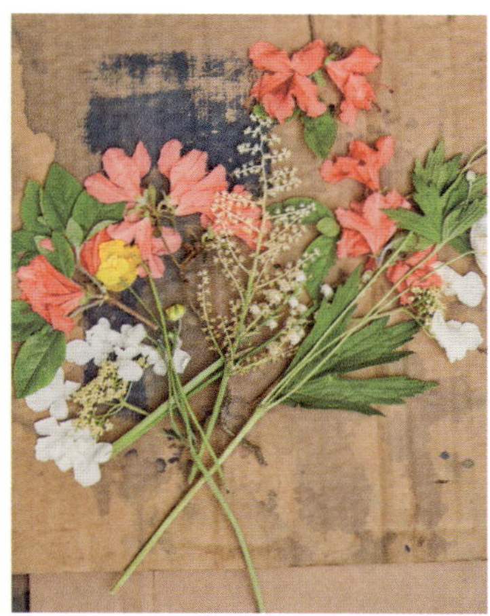

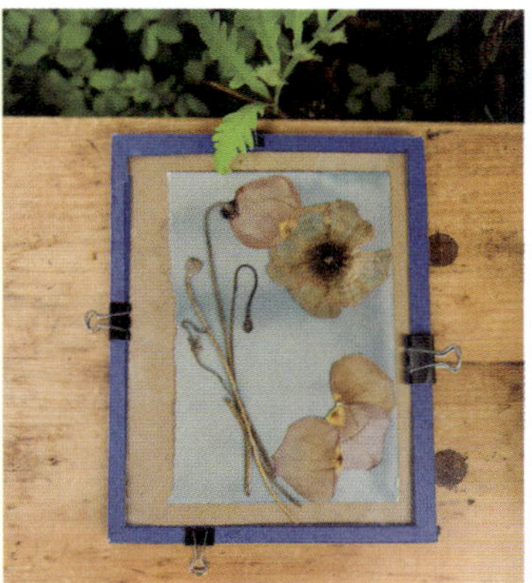

# Parting Thoughts

Thank you for taking this journey with me! Researching and writing this book has been deeply rewarding—which is not a surprise given how satisfying it is to make a cyanotype print. I've loved sharing cyanotype fundamentals and its wilder possibilities with you. Throughout, I've imagined you, the reader, learning the techniques and making them your own.

Now my curiosity is piqued, and I'd love to see what you've created. Have you made that perfect blue-and-white botanical print? Perhaps many of them? If you're inclined to share, please post your creations on Instagram and tag @_sporeplay. And if you're not active on social media but have accumulated a pile of handmade cyanotype greeting cards—or even if you'd simply like to drop me a line—I would be thrilled to hear from you! You can send correspondence to me at madgeevers.com/contact.

# More About the Artists

The work of the following artists has been featured throughout this book as a source of inspiration and to spark your own adventures in the world of cyanotypes. Below you can learn more about their process and the inspiration behind their work.

*"What keeps me engaged with cyanotype is the slow, deliberate process of creating each piece and discovering new and innovative ways of capturing and manipulating the final image. It has made me a better observer of our natural world."*

**ELIZABETH BOOTH** has been creating botanical cyanotypes with foraged and cultivated plants since 2019. She combines traditional and experimental techniques to craft multilayered cyanotypes that feature soothing compositions.

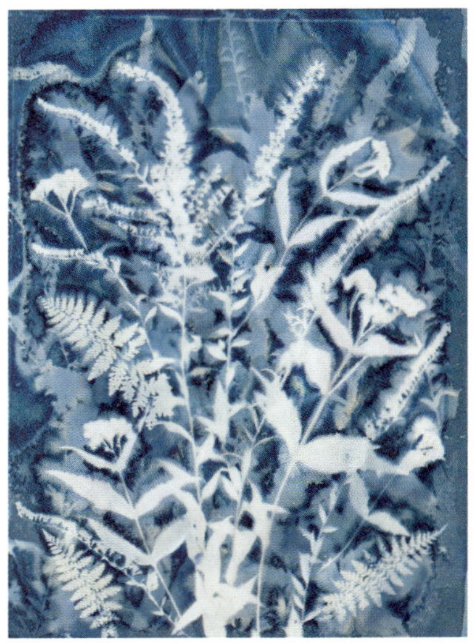

**INSTAGRAM:** @Elizabeth.Z.Booth

---

*"My use of color intentionally departs from tradition; vibrant hues emerge in both the background and foreground, illustrating how memories vary in prominence. Some aspects of our past may fade into darkness, while others remain bright and foundational, shaping who we are and who we are becoming... Ultimately, the work conveys a spiritual journey—a continuous process of becoming."*

**EM CRISMAN** blends a range of techniques and mediums into her cyanotype art, combining watercolor pigments and organic dyes. Her intuitive process involves layering these different pigments over the cyanotype, creating a piece of art that is both visually and emotionally nuanced.
**www.Emcrisman.com**

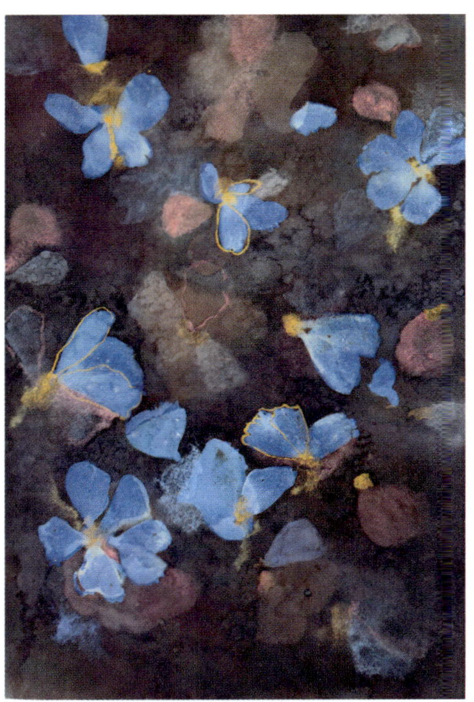

**INSTAGRAM:** @emcrismanart

**ASA CULVER** is an artist and photographer based in Arizona. She grew up in a small rural town on the East Coast and moved to Arizona in 2018 after falling in love with the southwestern landscape. She received her BFA in photography from Arizona State in 2022 and has been pursuing her artistic and photographic practice since.

**www.sunartbyasa.com**

**INSTAGRAM: @sunartbyasa**

---

*"Each print exhibits everyday objects, providing opportunities to find relatable items hidden within the blue. . . . Through my work, I invite viewers to engage with the issue of ocean pollution on a personal level. I hope to evoke a sense of responsibility and empower individuals to become advocates for change, fostering a deeper connection with our oceans."*

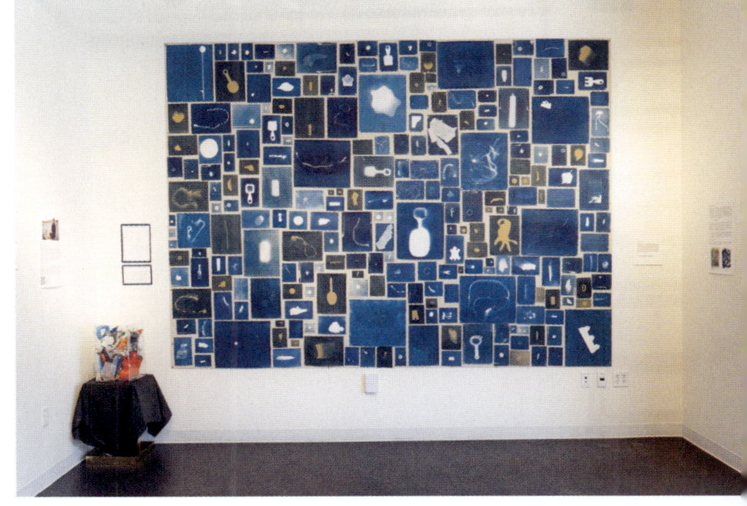

**ELIZABETH ELLENWOOD** is a photographer and Fulbright scholar whose work combines the cyanotype process with a deep reverence for the ocean to highlight issues of plastic pollution and climate change. Her surprisingly playful *Among the Tides* installation features cyanotype photograms, each representing a piece of marine debris collected during a ¾-mile walk on November 3, 2018. The work explores the complex and often fraught relationship between humanity and the oceans.

**www.elizabethellenwood.com**

*"The story of the land is in the plants that grow there, and these pieces tell that story. By carefully collecting as many specimens as possible from a single location, I try to capture a portrait of that place—a moment in time."*

**HILLARY WATERS FAYLE**'s intricate art invites you to look closely and admire each of the minute details. Her process involves creating lacelike mandalas using flower petals, leaves, and other found objects from nature, each carefully placed. Her work blends repetition and precision with the unpredictable irregularity of the organic. Each leaf and petal is slightly different, but within her compositions they combine in perfect harmony.
**www.hillarywfayle.com**

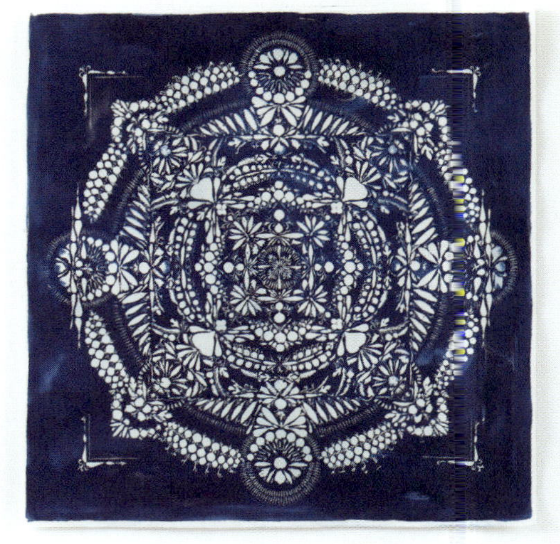

**INSTAGRAM**: @hillary.waters

---

*"Because these flowers come from one of the most meaningful places in someone's life, you can't help but want to chat with them every day. They become a part of you, your home, your moods, your ups and downs. Art with meaning is a soulful place to set yourself."*

**LINDA RUEL FLYNN** is a multidisciplinary artist who learned the art of flower preservation and botanical collage from her mother. She creates elegant compositions using meaningful flowers from clients' gardens and special-occasion bouquets, preserving their significance for a lifetime.
**www.flora-ly.com**

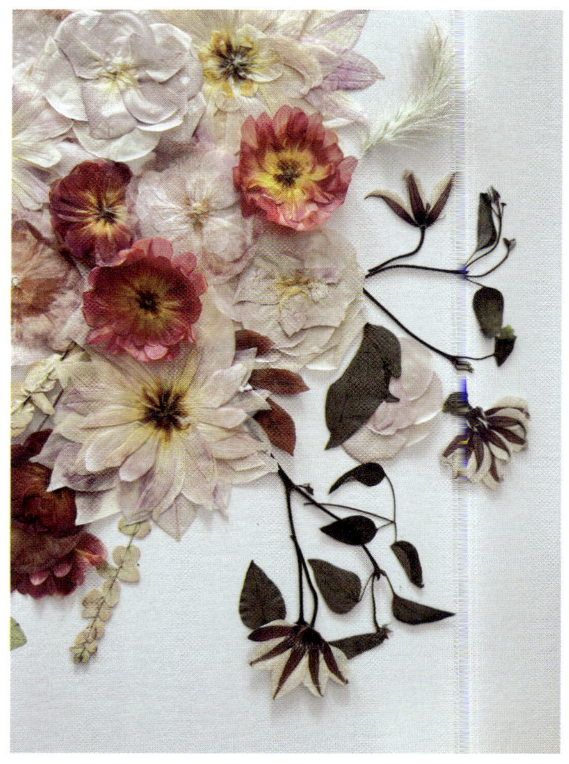

**INSTAGRAM**: @floralylinda

*"Cyanotype allows me to connect with nature in new ways. In each walk in the woods, I find inspiration in the beauty of ferns, grasses, and wildflowers, which find their way into my work. The process feels both magical and endlessly fascinating."*

**ERIKA FRANK** finds joy and fulfillment in sharing the cyanotype process with others, both as a teacher and through the creation of banners, cards, and ornaments. Working primarily with Thai mulberry paper, she incorporates found objects, lace, and botanicals to craft unique cyanotype prints, transforming everyday items into meaningful, personalized gifts.

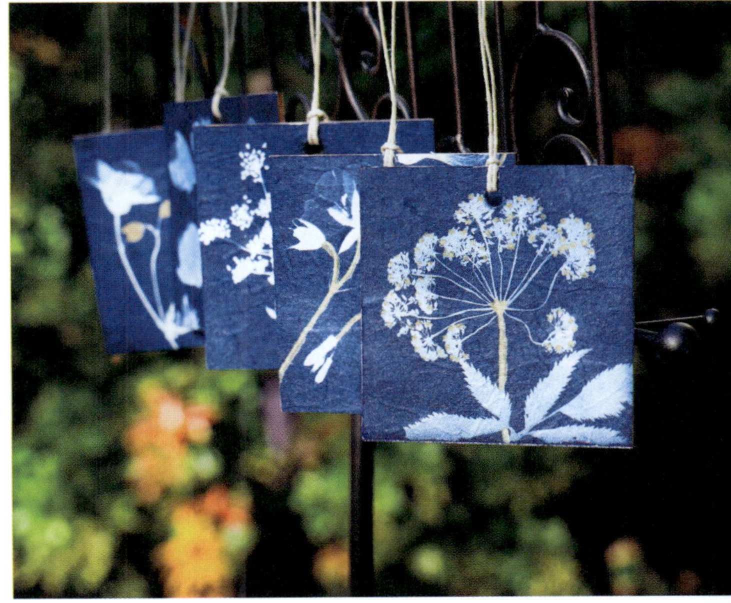

**INSTAGRAM:** @inblue_cyanotypes

---

*"Working with cyanotypes and using different botanicals, I began to see the shapes and composition of different foliage. . . . I started seeing the slight differences in the shapes of the leaves and flowers themselves. When I started working with marine mammals, I began to look at the flippers, fins, and flukes as their unique identifier, their fingerprint."*

Marine biologist **ELI ALEX GRESHAM**'s work with botanical cyanotypes taught her to pay attention to the smallest of details, attuning her to the unique shapes and composition of the plant life that surrounded her. She applies the same observational lens to her work with marine mammals, observing the distinct ridges and curves of their flippers, fins, and flukes. Each cyanotype in the *California Sea Lion Edition* depicts an animal that has had an impact on her life.

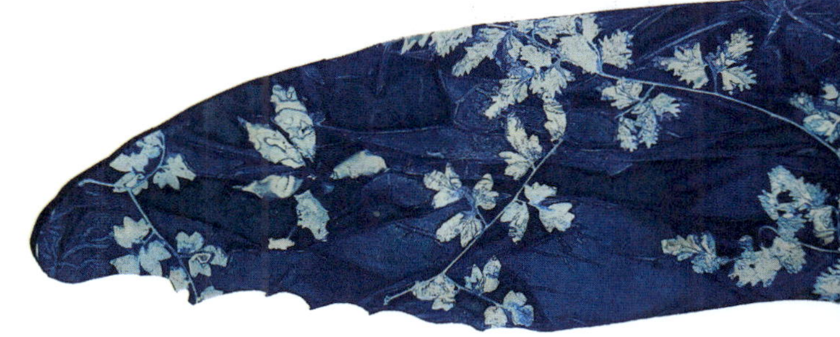

**INSTAGRAM:** @_eli.alex_

*"Incorporating cyanotype into my studio practice allows me to focus on experimentation, play, and tactility as a key part of my creative process. . . . Every step, from coating the paper to layering objects and calculating exposure, involves a certain freedom and letting go, which makes this type of alchemical photographic technique so special."*

**LILIANA GUZMÁN** is a Colombian American artist known for activating the connection between topics of the body, touch, memory, and the hidden landscapes of the self. She is the recipient of the Blue Sky Solo Show Award from Photolucida's Critical Mass 2022 and was the Rhonda Wilson Award recipient from Klompching Gallery in 2023. Raised by multiple generations of artists, she creates layered compositions with dreamlike narratives.
**www.lilianaguzman.co**

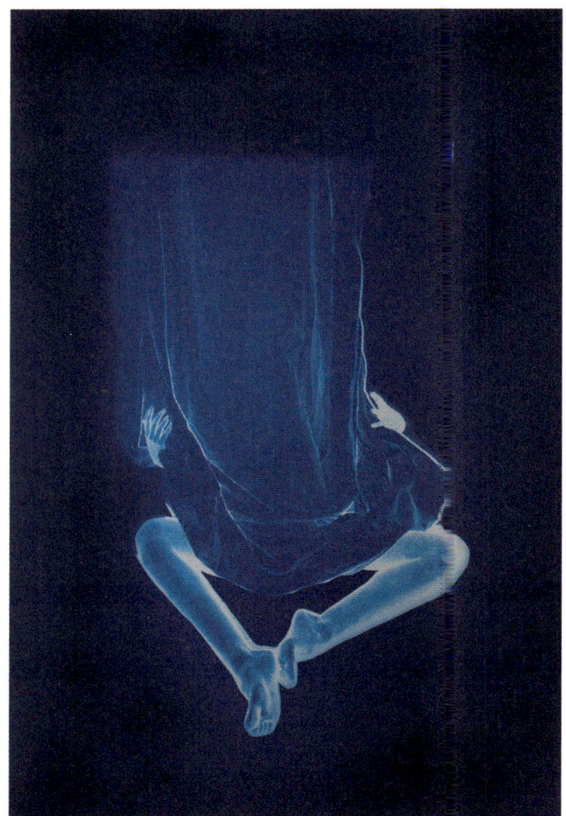

**INSTAGRAM:** @lilinessy

---

*"Through* LANDMARKS, *a series of self-portrait body blueprints, I use cyanotype emulsion on cotton gauze. . . . This historical, cameraless printing process connects me to past uses of cyanotype in scientific and architectural fields, creating blueprints and illustrations. By imprinting my body onto these fabrics, I engage with memories of trauma, transforming pain into lasting marks that deepen over time."*

**ANGELEA HEARTSONG-REDDING (H.R.)** is a photographic artist whose work delves into the contradictions within beauty, personal trauma, and the female gaze. In her *LANDMARKS* installation, H.R. coats fabric with cyanotype solution, allowing it to expose gradually over time, creating striking large-scale works that exist in a continual state of development. The series is a living archive mirroring the processes of healing and resilience the works embody.
**www.angeleahr.com**

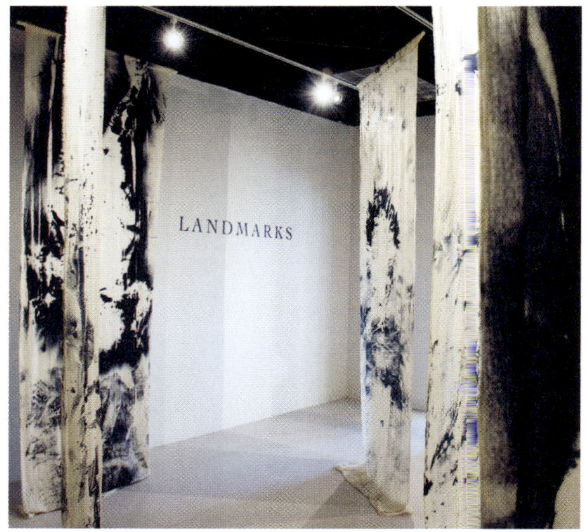


**INSTAGRAM:** @angelea-heartsong

*"My process blends chemistry, nature, artistic license, technology, and timing. My current still-life cyanotype prints and one-of-a-kind cyanotype collages showcase my garden flowers and vessels as elegant still-life floral narratives with a vintage modern twist."*

**CLAUDIA HOLLISTER** creates cyanotype-based work inspired by her deep love for the garden, focusing on intimate floral imagery. She combines traditional and experimental cyanotype techniques, utilizing unique papers, digital negatives, and the application of inks and watercolors to enhance her lush and detailed compositions.
**www.claudiahollister.com**

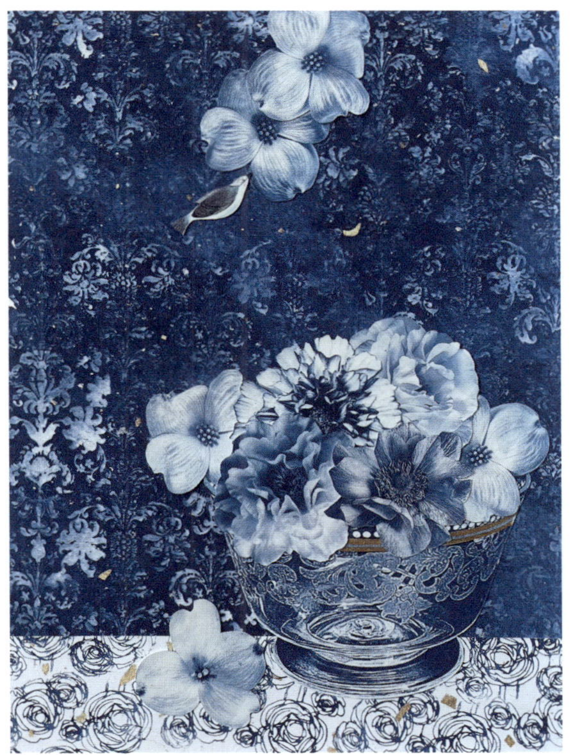

**INSTAGRAM:** @claudiahollister

---

*"Subjectivity and objectivity oscillate in interesting ways when one looks closely at the systems that make up our world. Aspects of nature that may at first appear fixed and unchanged take on fluid and fungible features when closely observed. What may seem to be highly personal can expand to something universal."*

**FRITZ HORSTMAN** brings an experimental eye to the creation of cyanotypes. Folding paper to create three-dimensional forms and intricate patterns, then treating the paper with cyanotype fluid, he exposes it to natural light. The resulting *Folded Cyanotypes* exhibit a range of elaborate textures and hues that capture a sense of depth and dimension on the page.
**www.fritzhorstman.com**

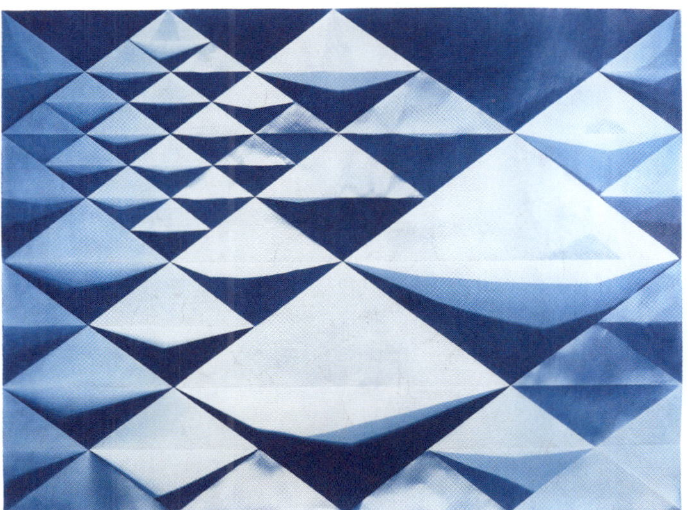

**INSTAGRAM:** @fritzhorstman

*"Photographic practice has been my outlet for exploring life's unanswerable questions. This subject matter is too esoteric and intangible to comprehend in the abstract, so I have chosen to craft physical images that best interpret where the answers may lie."*

**JEANNIE HUTCHINS** holds an MFA from Maine Media College and uses photography to explore her relationship with time, space, and universal mysteries. Her *Cyanoscapes* series begins with a midnight blue expanse, into which she introduces punctuations of light and luminosity. The resulting works evoke distant constellations, timeless geological events, and the flowing essence of matter.
**www.jeanniehutchins.com**

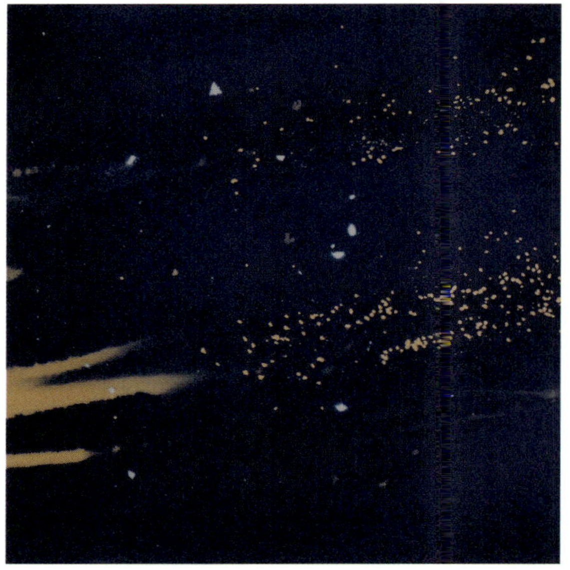

**INSTAGRAM**: **@jeanniehutchinsphotography**

---

*"Since childhood, I've been captivated by every shade of blue, the intriguing shapes of shadows, the beauty of nature, printmaking, and the artful use of negative space. Cyanotype beautifully encompasses all of these elements!"*

**LINDA CLARK JOHNSON** creates atmospheric cyanotypes with layered compositions using a combination of painting techniques, collage, and pencil work. Linda expands the possibilities of the traditional cyanotype process by incorporating wet elements, multiple exposures, selective bleaching, and natural toners. The dynamic results are full of delightful surprises.
**www.lindaclarkjohnson.com**

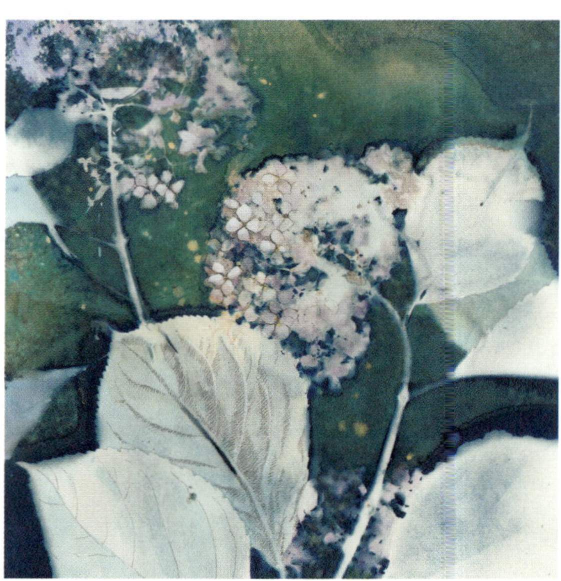

**INSTAGRAM**: **@lindaclarkjohnson**

*"At its heart, my technique is about introducing error. I discovered by introducing moisture during the exposure time, I could achieve colors beyond the traditional blue and white. I could achieve yellows, browns, greens, and varying shades of blue . . . all with just water, weather, and time."*

**KRISTA McCURDY** has a BFA in printmaking and is a self-proclaimed rule breaker, both in printmaking and with the cyanotype process. Using experimental techniques, Krista introduces wet elements into her cyanotypes before and during exposure. The results are multicolored images with a unique sense of depth and layering. Her 2017 YouTube video on creating wet cyanotypes has more than 59,000 views.

**www.kristamccurdy.com**

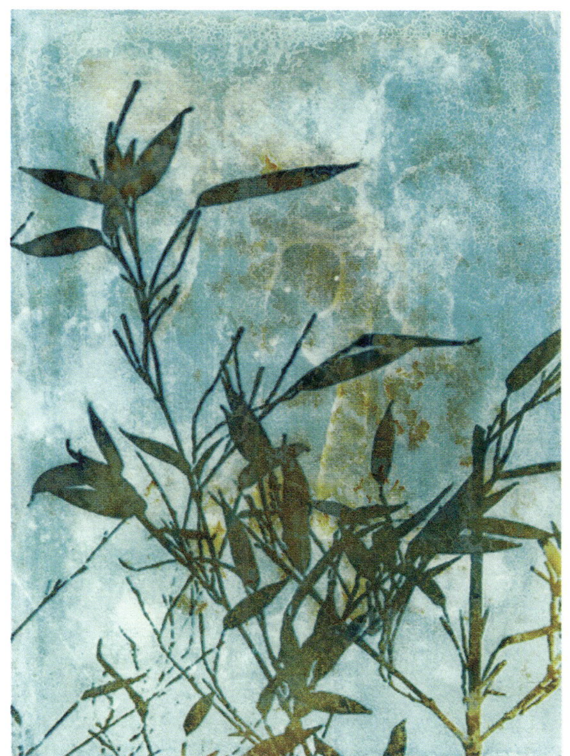

**INSTAGRAM:** **@kristamccurdy**

---

*"Cyanotypes are my spring and summer meditation—I find myself mesmerized, inspired, studying with my field guides, and foraging. Small specimens from my yard make their way onto my hand-painted cyanotype papers to expose in the sun. I typically overexpose my cyanotypes to obtain richer details, and the slowing of this process aligns with the concept of resisting convenience, part of my life's work."*

**HEATHER PALECEK** is an educator and artist who employs a range of photographic techniques, including the cyanotype process, which she creates in thoughtful collaboration with nature. Her conceptual cyanotype works originate in a deep commitment to environmental advocacy, and her delightful "gratitude flags" pay homage to the many living species with which she shares the land.

**www.heatherpalecek.com**

**INSTAGRAM:** **@heather.palecek.art**

*"It is the land that surrounds me that deeply inspires and creates a yearning to explore and express. . . . There is little more satisfying to me than a site-specific, large-scale cyanotype that helps bring nature inside."*

**SARAH BOURNE RAFFERTY**'s affinity for design is apparent in the bold graphics of her botanical cyanotypes. Inspired by the plant silhouettes she encounters during frequent walks, Sarah creates cyanotype photograms to represent specific moments in time and to act as visual poetry.

**www.atwaterdesigns.com**

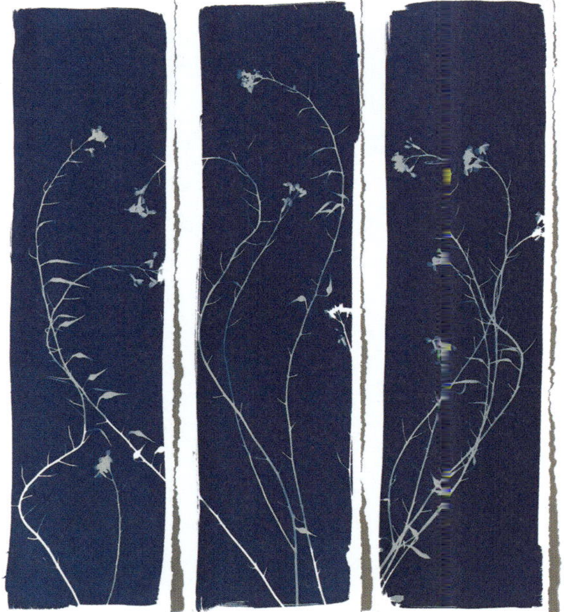

**INSTAGRAM:** @atwaterdesigns

---

*"Like many, my cyanotype journey began with leaves. I soon became smitten with wet cyanotype and began altering the process with a variety of additives that added natural color variations. Seeking even more color, I began experimenting with apps to digitally layer my blue-and-white beauties with photos of my art, textures, and other cyanotypes to create what I call Modern Botanicals."*

**LESLEY RILEY** is a mixed-media artist and quilter who creates original cyanotype prints on both paper and fabric. Blending layers of pattern and color, she combines digital tools with traditional processes to craft bold botanical imagery. Through her cyanotype work, Lesley also explores her alter ego, Lady Alchemy—the narrative embodiment of a carefree, beauty-seeking, color-loving version of herself.

**www.lesleyriley.com**

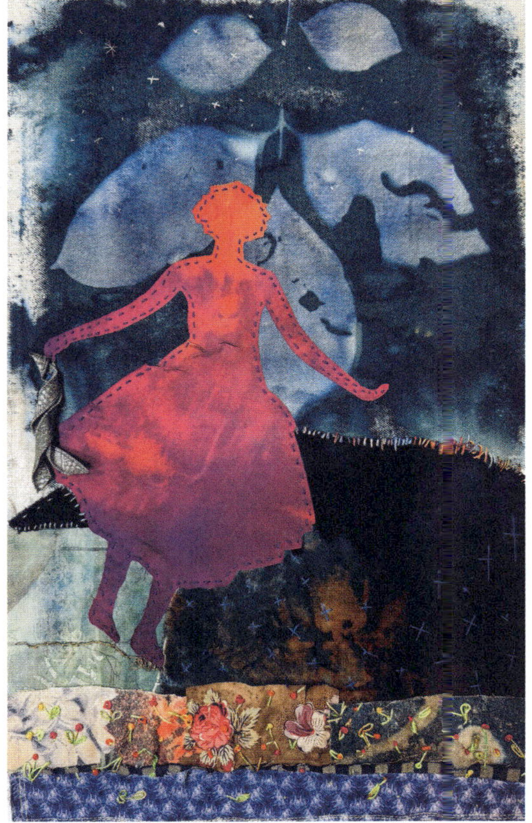

**INSTAGRAM:** @lrileyart

*"My daily life is folded into my art practice, and my inspiration comes from experiences that I hope others can easily relate to, whether it's watching a bird soar, enjoying a walk among the trees, examining the shape of a leaf, or discovering a tiny little mushroom."*

**BROOKE SAUER** combines her background in painting and photography with a profound love of nature in her cyanotype work. She creates complex, dynamic scenes, combining a variety of elements, from expressive brushwork and pressed botanicals to photographic negatives.

**www.brookesauer.com**

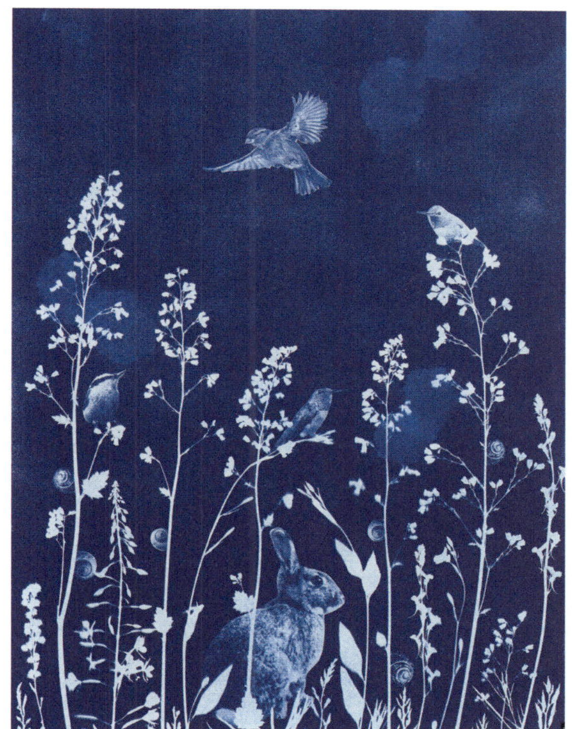

**INSTAGRAM: @biminy**

---

*"The cyanotype technique pioneered by Anna Atkins in 1843 . . . holds history, suspends time, and connects me to these women—and the viewer to their legacy. The impressionistic imagery reshapes the photographic landscape, revealing the quiet magnificence of the natural world."*

**DORA SOMOSI**, a lens-based artist and curator, creates transcendent, painterly images through a variety of photographic processes. In *By Her Side*, she uses the cyanotype process to produce a series of contact prints, some as large as 40 × 28 inches. This series offers a unique exploration of the American landscape, interwoven with the stories of 25 female artists and thinkers, inviting viewers into an immersive and layered narrative.

**www.dorasomosi.com**

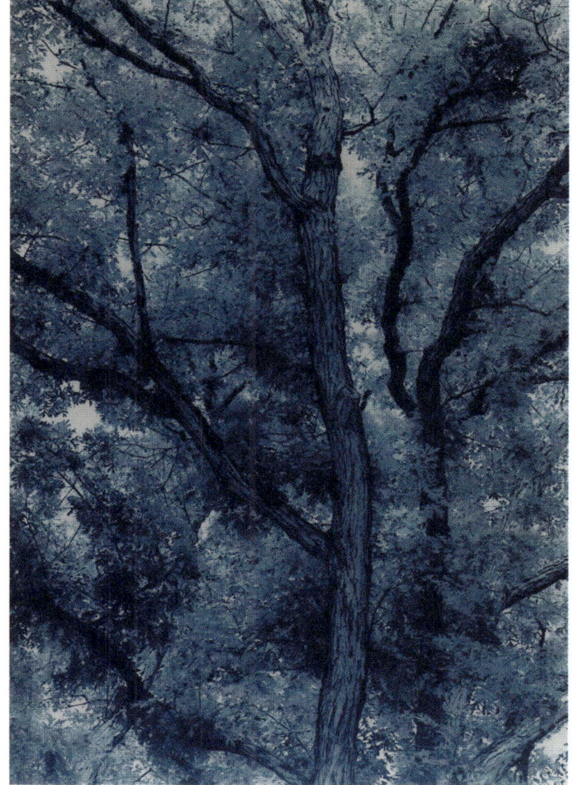

**INSTAGRAM: @dorasomosiphotography**

*"I grew up on a remote island on the West Coast of Canada, surrounded by the natural world, and spent my childhood days between the forest and the sea. Through my art and the process of cyanotype, I strive to bring the beauty and magic of nature into everyday life and inspire curiosity about plants and flowers."*

**MARITA WAI** is an artist who creates modern botanical X-rays using foraged plants and flowers from her tiny garden in London, England. In addition to a beautifully curated Instagram feed, Marita has developed a unique technique that blends art and anatomy, offering a stunning, visual exploration of the inner workings of plants.
**www.maritawai.com**

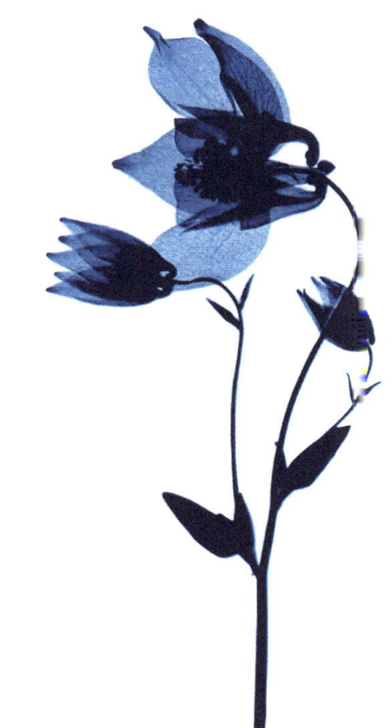

**INSTAGRAM:** @maritawaistudio

---

*"My large West Sussex countryside garden in the UK continually displays itself in new guises. The growth, death, and rebirth of plants and trees provides a never-ending palette for me as a photographic artist."*

**ELIZABETH ZESCHIN** is a professional photographer and neopictorialist whose transcendent imagery evokes a sense of the otherworldly. Drawing on the cyanotype's historical connection to the origins of photography, she uses a view camera to capture garden plants and statuary, creating contact prints from 8 × 10-inch film negatives; she also makes botanical photograms. Her work has been exhibited throughout the UK, including solo shows at the Chelsea Arts Club, the Royal Photographic Society, and "Victorian Modern" at Zimmer Stewart Gallery in 2024.
**www.elizabethzeschin.com**

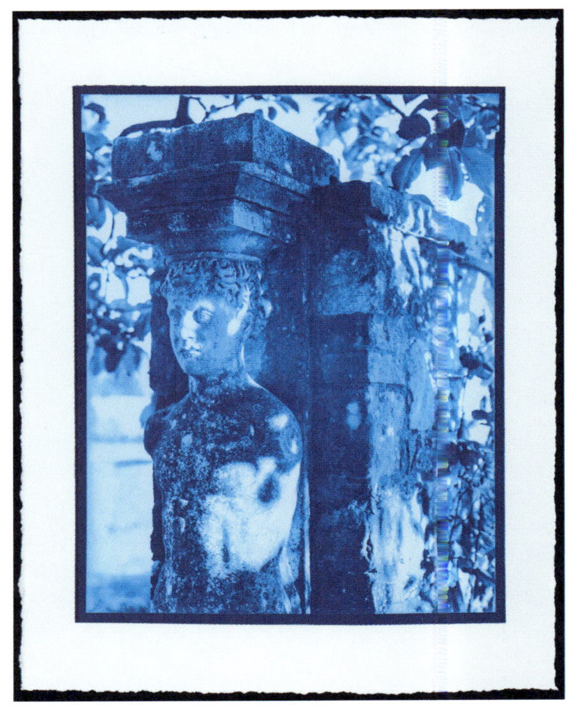

**INSTAGRAM:** @zeschin

# Resources

## EDUCATIONAL RESOURCES

### Online Learning

Christina Anderson's study of 85 papers: https://www.alternativephotography.com/massive-paper-chart/

Directions for a DIY UV LED exposure unit: https://www.alternativephotography.com/build-a-uv-led-box-for-cyanotypes/ *and* https://www.youtube.com/watch?v=6YrT6zxT_Wo

How to Make a Digital Negative: https://www.alternativeprocesses.org/post/how-to-make-a-digital-negative

Madge's DIY exposure unit on page 53 uses an Everbeam 365nm 50-watt UV LED black light.

### Books

Anderson, Christina Z. *Cyanotype: The Blueprint in Contemporary Practice*. Routledge, 2019.

Burns, Nancy Kathryn, and Kristina Wilson. *Cyanotypes: Photography's Blue Period*. Worcester Art Museum, 2016.

Chalmers, Angela. *Creative Cyanotype: Techniques and Inspiration*. Crowood Press, 2023.

Golaz, Annette. *Cyanotype Toning: Using Botanicals to Tone Blueprints Naturally*. Routledge, 2022.

Hiebert, Helen. *The Art of Papercraft: Unique One-Sheet Projects Using Origami, Weaving, Quilling, Pop-Up, and Other Inventive Techniques*. Storey Publishing, 2022.

Popova, Maria. *Figuring*. Pantheon Books, 2019.

Richardson, Melissa, and Amy Fielding. *The Modern Flower Press: Capturing the Beauty of Nature*. Abrams, 2022.

## RECOMMENDED RETAILERS

**B&H**
800-606-6969
https://www.bhphotovideo.com/
*A good source for chemicals, precoated and uncoated paper, precoated fabric, contact print frames, photo trays*

**Bostick & Sullivan**
505-474-0890
https://www.bostick-sullivan.com/
*A good source for UV exposure boxes and print frames*

**Cyanotype Store**
800-894-9410
https://cyanotypestore.com/
*A good source for precoated paper and fabric*

**Forestry Suppliers**
800-647-5368
https://www.forestry-suppliers.com/
*A good source for plant presses*

**Jacquard Products**
800-442-0455
https://www.jacquardproducts.com/
*A good source for chemicals, both bulk and dry kits; precoated fabric; and an online digital negative generator, specifically calibrated for cyanotypes. This free resource is available at https://jacquardcyanotype.com.*

**Lineco**
800-322-7775
https://www.lineco.com
*A good source for unbuffered interleaving tissue, glassine, mat board*

**Photographers' Formulary**
800-922-5255
https://stores.photoformulary.com/
*A good source for bulk chemicals and liquid and dry kits, contact print frames*

**Redimat**
877-873-1011
https://www.redimat.com
*A good source for unbuffered mat board*

# RECOMMENDED MATERIALS

The materials listed here can be found at a wide variety of retailers and art suppliers.

## Adhesive for Thin Paper

Yasutomo Nori Paste

## Archival Spray Fixative

Winsor & Newton Professional Fixative
Golden Matte Archival Varnish

## Commercial Papers

Below are some recommended papers that work well for cyanotypes. The work and extensive research of Christina Z. Anderson, author of the thorough and beautiful *Cyanotype: The Blueprint in Contemporary Practice,* was invaluable as I explored various kinds of paper. Anderson shares test results for 136 different papers in her book (and very generously online, too), offering an in-depth examination beyond this list.

**ARCHES AQUARELLE.** Currently my preferred paper for creating work, both large and small. It's made with 100 percent cotton, is acid-free and pH neutral, and is sized with gelatin to give the paper strength. This paper comes in a variety of weights and sizes. I use the hot-press (smooth) surface in natural white with a weight of 356 gsm/156#. I purchase the paper in rolls, which require some gymnastics to cut but allow for more flexibility when creating works of varying sizes. Standard sizes are available in pads and in large sheets.

**BERGGER COT 320.** A highly recommended 100 percent cotton paper made specifically for alternative photo processes, including the cyanotype process. Christina Anderson lists it among papers she considers "trouble-free" for making cyanotypes.

**CANSON XL WATERCOLOR.** This is the paper I use when conducting cyanotype workshops; it's sturdy, prints beautifully, and is an excellent value. Most of the projects in this book work well with Canson XL Watercolor. Available in a range of pad sizes or in rolls, this acid-free watercolor paper is made with 100 percent cellulose, has a cold-press (rough) surface, and is a standard watercolor weight of 300 gsm/140#. It can handle multiple coats of emulsion and washings, if necessary.

**HAHNEMÜHLE SUMI-E.** Hahnemühle's Sumi-E paper, made from 100 percent cellulose, is acid-free and has a smooth cold-pressed surface. At 80 gsm, it is thin and absorbent. Cyanotypes made with Sumi-E print a deep blue. The lightweight texture of this paper is excellent for collage work.

**LEGION STONEHENGE.** A 100 percent cotton, acid-free paper with a smooth surface, Stonehenge is made in the United States. At 250 gsm, it's more lightweight than other cotton papers, but sturdy. It's available in various forms, including 22 × 30-inch sheets with two deckled edges, pads, and rolls, and in several tones suitable for the cyanotype process, including fawn, steel gray, and kraft.

**LEGION THAI KOZO.** This lightweight, 35 gsm paper is made in Thailand from 100 percent kozo/mulberry fibers harvested from living trees. The paper is very thin but strong, and excellent for collage. Take care when washing kozo paper because it likes to wrinkle and fold.

## Cold Wax Medium

Gamblin
Dorland's

## Delicate Fabric Wash

Eucalan

## Microwave Flower Press

Microfleur

# Bibliography

## INTRODUCTION


"Bertha Jacques." Elizabeth Houston Gallery. https://www.elizabethhoustongallery.com/project/bertha-jacques/.

"Blueprints." Susan Weil, accessed March 1, 2024. https://susanweil.com/blueprints/.

"Booklet of 'Photographs of British Algae: Cyanotype Impressions' by Anna Atkins: Science Museum Group Collection." Science Museum Group, accessed February 10, 2024. https://collection.sciencemuseumgroup.org.uk/objects/co17028/booklet-of-photographs-of-british-algae-cyanotype-impressions-by-anna-atkins-booklet-cyanotype.

Burns, Nancy Kathryn, and Kristina Wilson, eds. *Cyanotypes: Photography's Blue Period.* Worcester Art Museum, 2016. Exhibition catalog.

"Burton Holmes and His Cyanotype Postcards: Postcard History." *Postcard History*, accessed February 13, 2024. https://postcardhistory.net/2020/08/burto.

"Cyanotypes of British Algae by Anna Atkins (1843)." The Public Domain Review, accessed March 31, 2024. https://publicdomainreview.org/collection/cyanotypes-of-british-algae-by-anna-atkins-1843/.

Daniel, Malcolm. "William Henry Fox Talbot (1800–1877) and the Invention of Photography." Heilbrunn Timeline of Art History, 2000. https://www.metmuseum.org/toah/hd/tlbt/hd_tlbt.htm.

Matta, Maragarita. "Exhibition Review: Ice: Meghann Riepenhoff." *Musée*, September 26, 2022. https://museemagazine.com/culture/2022/9/13/exhibition-review-ice-meghann-riepenhoff.

Muzdakis, Madeleine. "Cyanotype: The Photographic Process That 'Blue' Everyone Away 170 Years Ago." My Modern Met, accessed September 16, 2020. https://mymodernmet.com/cyanotype-photography/.

"Nancy Wilson-Pajic." A.I.R. Gallery, accessed October 14, 2024. https://www.airgallery.org/nancy-wilson-pajic.

Perri, Natalie. "The Evolution of Blueprints: Why They Are No Longer Blue." *Unraveling Archi*, accessed May 17, 2023. https://www.unravelingarchitecture.com/post/the-evolution-of-blueprints-why-they-are-no-longer-blue (site discontinued).

Popova, Maria. *Figuring.* Pantheon Books, 2019.

Santiago, Ximena. "Factory of Two: Matson Jones Blueprints for Window Display." Robert Rauschenberg Foundation, accessed March 17, 2024. https://www.rauschenbergfoundation.org/sites/default/files/2023-04/Santiago_FactoryofTwo_Oct21.pdf.

Sunday, Sarah. "An Interview with Spotlight Artist: Meghann Riepenhoff." *Musée*, March 19, 2019. https://museemagazine.com/features/2019/3/19/an-interview-with-spotlight-artist-meghann-riepenhoff.

Tate. "'Photogenic Painting, Untitled 74/13', Barbara Kasten, 1974." Tate, January 1, 1974. https://www.tate.org.uk/art/artworks/kasten-photogenic-painting-untitled-74-13-t15267.

Wikipedia, s.v. "Xerox," accessed March 18, 2024, https://en.wikipedia.org/wiki/Xerox.

Williams, Lisa Hayes, and Vincent Broqua. *Fritz Horstman: Folded Light.* New Britain Museum of American Art, Municipal Bonds, and Planthouse Gallery, 2024.


## CHAPTERS 1–4


Anderson, Christina Z. *Cyanotype: The Blueprint in Contemporary Practice.* Routledge, 2019.

Chalmers, Angela. *Creative Cyanotype: Techniques and Inspiration.* Crowood Press, 2023.

Enfield, Jill. *Jill Enfield's Guide to Photographic Alternative Processes: Popular Historical & Contemporary Techniques.* Focal Press, 2017.

Hiebert, Helen. *The Art of Papercraft: Unique One-Sheet Projects Using Origami, Weaving, Quilling, Pop-Up, and Other Inventive Techniques.* Storey Publishing, 2022.

James, Christopher. *The Book of Alternative Photographic Processes*, 3rd ed. Cengage Learning. 2015.

Ware, Mike. "Simple Cyanotype." Accessed June 7, 2024. https://www.mikeware.co.uk/downloads/SimpleCyan.pdf.

"What Is the Rule of Thirds? A Guide for Beginners." *Photography Life*, accessed August 27, 2024. https://photographylife.com/the-rule-of-thirds.


## CHAPTER 5


Celley, Courtney. "Don't Touch These Plants!" US Fish & Wildlife Service. https://www.fws.gov/story/dont-touch-these-plants.

"Cyanotypes." Fraenkel Gallery. https://fraenkelgallery.com/exhibitions/christian-marclay-cyanotypes.

Given, Craig. "How to Scan 35mm Slides." Craig Edward Given, March 14, 2018. https://www.craiggiven.com/blog/2018/3/14/how-to-scan-35mm-slides.

Mueller, Nora. "In Pursuit of Madness: 'Pteridomania' and the Historic Fascination with Ferns." *Garden Collage Magazine*, August 4, 2016. https://gardencollage.com/wander/gardens-parks/ferb-obsession/.

Richardson, Melissa, and Amy Fielding. *The Modern Flower Press: Capturing the Beauty of Nature*. Abrams, 2022.

Roach, Margaret. “Pressing Plants, with Herbarium Curator Linda Lipsen.” A Way to Garden, August 27, 2023. https://awaytogarden.com/pressing-plants-with-herbarium-curator-linda-lipsen/.

Rudnick, Les. “History, Early 1800s,” in *The Photogram—A History*, accessed September 14, 2024. https://www.photograms.org/chapter02.html.

“The Photograms Catalogue Raisonné.” Moholy-Nagy Foundation, accessed July 25, 2024. https://www.moholy-nagy.org/photograms/.

## CHAPTER 6

Golaz, Annette. *Cyanotype Toning: Using Botanicals to Tone Blueprints Naturally*. Routledge, 2022.

McCurdy, Krista. “The Original Wet Cyanotype Process.” Krista McCurdy, May 29, 2017. https://krista-mccurdy.squarespace.com/home/https/wwwkristamccurdycom/wetcyanotype.

O’Brien, Alan. “How I Make Cyanotypes.” Alan O’Brien Photography, October 11, 2023. https://obrienphotography.co.uk/how-i-make-cyanotypes/.

“Speck of Stardust: Mandy Kerr’s Wet Cyanotypes.” *Lomography*, June 7, 2020. https://www.lomography.com/magazine/344465-speck-of-stardust-mandy-kerr-s-wet-cyanotypes.

## CHAPTER 7

Webster, Carol Ann. “How to Glue Printed Paper to a Wood Panel.” https://carolannwebster.com/blog-2/how-to-mount-paper-on-board.

“What Is Cold Wax Medium?” Cold Wax Academy, May 15, 2024. https://coldwaxacademy.com/about-cwm/.

## CHAPTER 8

“How to Scour.” Botanical Colors. https://botanicalcolors.com/how-to-scour/.

Fabbri, Malin. “Preparing the Canvas: Cloth, Paper and Natural Fibre Fabrics for Cyanotypes.” Alternative Photography, June 20, 2021. https://www.alternativephotography.com/preparing-the-canvas-cloth-paper-and-natural-fibre-fabrics-for-cyanotypes/.

# Art Credits

## TITLE PAGE

Madge Evers, *Very Blue Poppies*, cyanotype on handmade paper, 8 × 10 inches, 2021

## INTRODUCTION

Dora Somosi, *Imogen Cunningham, Oakland, CA*, cyanotype contact print on paper, 26 × 18½ inches, 2022

Dora Somosi, *Toni Morrison, Nyack, NY*, cyanotype contact print on paper, 28 × 36 inches, 2023

Madge Evers, *Crowd Pleaser*, cyanotype, 18 × 24 inches, 2022

Brooke Sauer, *Travelogue*, cyanotype on paper, 15 × 21 inches, 2023

Madge Evers, *Tree Fern*, cyanotype, 81 × 54 inches, 2023

Elizabeth Zeschin, *Papaver Somniferum*, cyanotype photogram, 16 × 13 inches, 2024

Elizabeth Zeschin, *Anemone Hupensis*, cyanotype photogram, 16 × 13 inches, 2024

Madge Evers, *Luminous Blue*, cyanotype, 8 × 10 inches, 2023

Madge Evers, *Luminous Herbarium*, spore print, 12 × 18 inches, 2022

Madge Evers, *Poppy Parts*, cyanotype on handmade paper, 8 × 10 inches, 2021

Madge Evers, *Holdovers*, cyanotype on Sumi-e paper, 11 × 15 inches, 2024

Beverly Wilgus, *Homage to Sir John Herschel*, cyanotype on paper

Asa Culver, *Staying Afloat*, cyanotype on cotton, 2025

Fritz Horstman, *Folded Cyanotype 298*, cyanotype on paper, 13 × 17 inches, 2024

Fritz Horstman, *Folded Cyanotype 322*, cyanotype on paper, 27½ × 39 inches, 2024

Elizabeth Ellenwood, *Nov 3, 2018 Collection, Studio Wall*, Installation of 240 cyanotype prints, 7 × 9 feet, 2018

## CHAPTER 1

Sarah Bourne Rafferty, *Field Dance*, cyanotype, 20 × 24 inches, 2024

Image of cyanotype kit: photo by Taylor Drouhard

## CHAPTER 2

Madge Evers, *Sandhill Crane + Ferns*, cyanotype altered book page, 10 × 13 inches, 2022

Eli Alex Gresham, *Moose*, cyanotype on paper, 11¾ × 4¼ inches, 2024

Hillary Waters Fayle, *Hortus*, cyanotype on paper, 24 × 24 inches, 2020. Photo credit: David Hunter Hale

Brooke Sauer, *The Invitation*, cyanotype on paper, 44 × 30 inches, 2019

## CHAPTER 3

Heather Palecek, *This Bag Is Not a Toy*, mixed-media lumen/cyanotype prints, 4 × 4 inches (installation of multiple prints), 2021

Elizabeth Booth, *Queen Anne's Lace*, multiexposure cyanotype, 9 × 12 inches, 2024

## CHAPTER 4

Madge Evers, *Dune Shack Feathers*, cyanotype on handmade paper, 8 × 10 inches, 2021

## CHAPTER 5

Linda Ruel Flynn, *McAvoy*, pressed botanicals (protea, peonies, ranunculus, delphinium, tulip, roses, hellebore, greens) on archival board, 25 × 25 inches, 2023

Madge Evers, *Undersea World of Poppies II*, cyanotype, 15 × 22 inches, 2021

Christian Marclay, *Allover (Tori Amos, Garth Brooks, Rush, and Others)*, 2008, cyanotype on 156lb Cold Press Aquarelle Arches, 51½ × 96⅝ inches (130.8 × 245.4 cm)

Elizabeth Ellenwood, *November 3 Collection, Plastic Bag*, cyanotype, 14 × 17 inches, 2018

Heather Palecek, *Toilet Paper Art*, traditional cyanotype on paper, 10 × 10 inches, March, 2020

Liliana Guzmán, *Waiting*, cyanotype contact print on paper, 8 × 11 inches, 2021

Unidentified photographer, cyanotype, 5 × 7 inches, circa 1900

Madge Evers, *A Garden Grows*, cyanotype collage and cold wax medium, 9 × 12 inches, 2020

Dora Somosi, *Edna St. Vincent Millay, Steepletop, Austerlitz, NY*, cyanotype contact print on paper, 28 × 36 inches, 2022

Claudia Hollister, *Luscious Waves*, cyanotype contact print on paper, 10½ × 8 inches, 2022

## CHAPTER 6

Madge Evers, *Six Beauty Tips*, cyanotype, 11 × 15 inches, 2021

Krista McCurdy, *Shadows and Traces*, wet cyanotype on paper, 11 × 14 inches, 2017

Elizabeth Booth, *Through the Woods*, multiexposure cyanotype, watercolor, and pen, 9 × 12 inches, 2024

Jeannie Hutchins, *Volcano*, cyanotype chemogram on rag paper, 14 × 14 inches, 2020

Madge Evers, *Suddenly Running*, cyanotype, 54 × 46 inches, 2025

Elizabeth Booth, *Late Summer*, cyanotype toned with green tea and enhanced with white charcoal pencil, 12 × 12 inches, 2023

Liliana Guzmán, *Dreaming*, toned cyanotype contact print on paper, 9 × 12 inches, 2020

## CHAPTER 7

Claudia Hollister, *Long Hot Summer*, collage with cyanotype photogram, hand-printed paper, and cyanotype contact print, 16 × 12 inches, 2023

Madge Evers, *Ghost Tree Sunrise*, cyanotype and acrylic, 16 × 20 inches, 2021

Madge Evers, *Sprinkle Spray*, cyanotype and acrylic, 12 × 12 inches, 2023

Madge Evers, *Ring Fort, Chickadees, and Fireflies*, cyanotype, ink, and acrylic, 36 × 48 inches, 2024

Em Crisman, *Becoming: Refined*, toned cyanotype and watercolor on paper, 14 × 20 inches, 2024

Linda Clark Johnson, *In the Faerie Garden*, wet cyanotype, collage, watercolor, and colored pencil, 22½ × 30 inches, 2024

## CHAPTER 8

Lesley Riley, *The Thinnest Veil*, wet-cyanotype print machine-stitched onto vintage and tea-dyed artist-designed fabric with attached velvet leaf, 16 inches × 22 inches, 2022

Erika Frank, banner, cyanotype on paper, each 5 × 8 inches, 2023

Marita Wai, *Cobweb Study II*, cyanotype, 8 × 10 inches, 2024

Angelea Heartsong-Redding, *The Shape of Shame*, undeveloped cyanotype emulsion on cotton gauze, 144 × 44 inches, 2021

Madge Evers, *Seven Is a Number*, cyanotype, collage, acrylic, wax on cradled board, 36 × 48 inches, 2022

Madge Evers, *Ten Beauty Tips*, cyanotype, 11 × 14 inches, 2022

## MORE ABOUT THE ARTISTS

Elizabeth Booth, *Front Field*, wet process cyanotype, 14 × 20 inches, 2024

Em Crisman, *Becoming II*, toned cyanotype and watercolor on paper, 14 × 20 inches, August 2024

Asa Culver, *Staying Afloat*, cyanotype on cotton, 2025

Elizabeth Ellenwood, *Nov 3, 2018 Collection*, Studio Wall, Installation of 240 cyanotype prints, 7 × 9 feet, 2018

Hillary Waters Fayle, *Botanical Blueprint/Portrait of Place: Grace Farms, CT*, cyanotype on paper, 36 × 36 inches, July 2022, photo credit: David Hunter Hale

Linda Ruel Flynn, *Botanical Collage* (detail), pressed botanicals: dahlias, clematis, roses, grass, and greens on archival board, 12 × 20 inches, 2023

Erika Frank, *Ornaments*, cyanotype on mulberry paper and wood, 3 × 3 inches, 2023

Eli Alex Gresham, *Digit*, Cyanotype on watercolor paper, 10½ × 4½ inches, November 2022

Liliana Guzmán, *Her*, digital negative cyanotype on Arches Platine, 9 × 12 inches, 2019

Angelea Heartsong-Reddy, *LANDMARKS*, undeveloped cyanotype emulsion on cotton gauze, 144 × 44 inches, 2021

Claudia Hollister, *Enchanted Evening*, cyanotype collage on mulberry paper, 16 × 12 inches, 2024

Fritz Horstman, *Folded Cyanotype 302*, cyanotype fluid on paper, 16½ × 22½ inches, 2024

Jeannie Hutchins, *Misssing Baryon Particle*, cyanotype chemogram on rag paper, 10 × 10 inches, 2017

Linda Clark Johnson, *Cottage Garden*, wet cyanotype with watercolor, graphite, colored pencil, 20 × 20 inches, 2017

Krista McCurdy, *Leafy Bamboo*, wet cyanotype, 5 × 7 inches, 2017

Heather Palecek, *Gratitude Flags*, cyanotype on cotton, 6 × 6 inches, each, 2023–2024

Sarah Bourne Rafferty, *Speaking My Language*, cyanotype triptych, 28 × 30 inches, 2024

Lesley Riley, *Lessons in Flight*, hand-stitched and embroidered cyanotype collage with hand-dyed silk, velvet, vintage textiles, and metallic ribbon, 11½ × 18 inches, 2023

Brooke Sauer, *Dreaming in the Daylight*, cyanotype on paper, 21 × 15 inches, 2024

Dora Somosi, *Emily Dickinson, Amherst, MA*, hand-coated cyanotype contact print, 28 × 36 inches, 2022

Marita Wai, *Aqueligea Botanical X-Ray*, digital print based on original cyanotype, 8 × 10 inches, 2024

Elizabeth Zeschin, *Parham Caryatid*, cyanotype, digital negative from film negative, 20 × 16 inches, 2024

# Acknowledgments

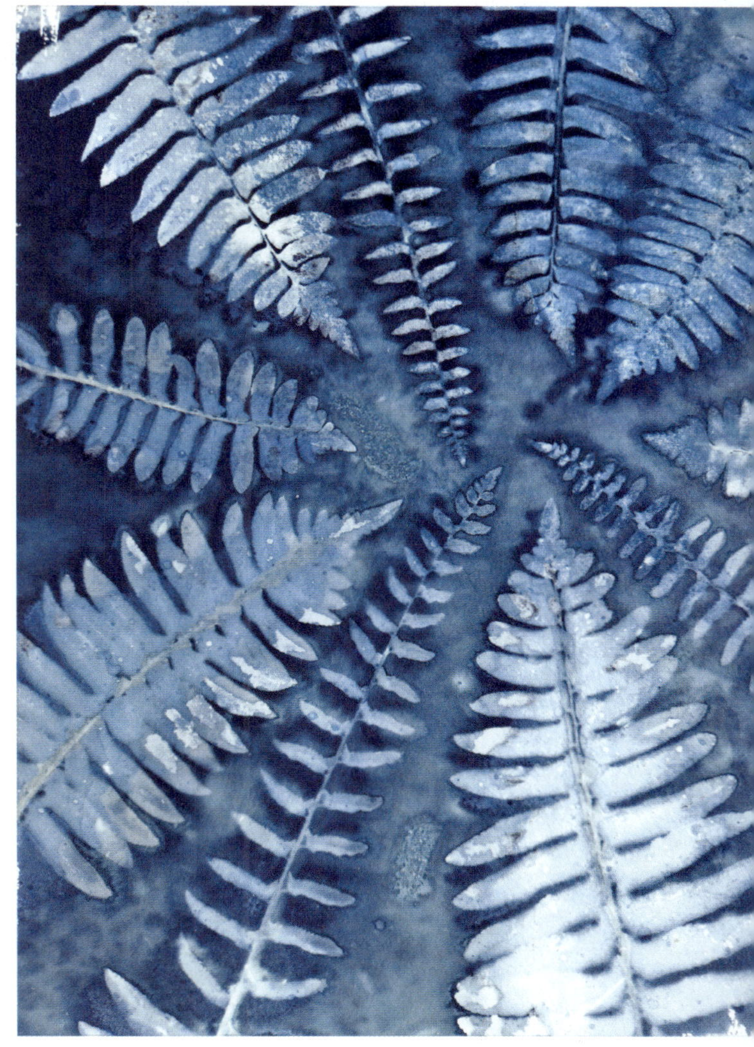

I am deeply grateful to the many people who made this book possible.

Sincere thanks to the excellent team at Storey. Thank you, Deborah Balmuth, for planting the initial seeds that grew into this project-based book on the cyanotype process. To Nancy Ringer, for thoughtful attention to my ideas and the craft of writing in the early stage—your insight was invaluable. Thank you to Carolyn Eckert for an impeccable eye and dreamy art direction. And thanks to photographers Mars Vilaubi and Kristin Teig for bringing the words and projects to life. So many thanks to my editor, Gwen Hawkes, whose enthusiasm, kindness, and steady guidance made the process a pleasure.

To the artists whose beautiful cyanotype-based work elevate these pages—thank you.

To every student who has attended a cyanotype workshop with me—thank you for sharing in the excitement and joy of the cyanotype process.

To my Friday-night writing group, your considerate feedback over the years has supported my evolving voice as a writer—thank you, dear writers.

To Cassie, your enthusiasm for the ever-changing reservoir landscape is an inspiration; thank you for showing me new ways to look at the world.

To Jesse, thank you for approaching adventure with an open and kind heart and encouraging me to do the same.

To Ellie, thank you for sharing the large and the small, the easy and the difficult, and for filling my life with possibility.

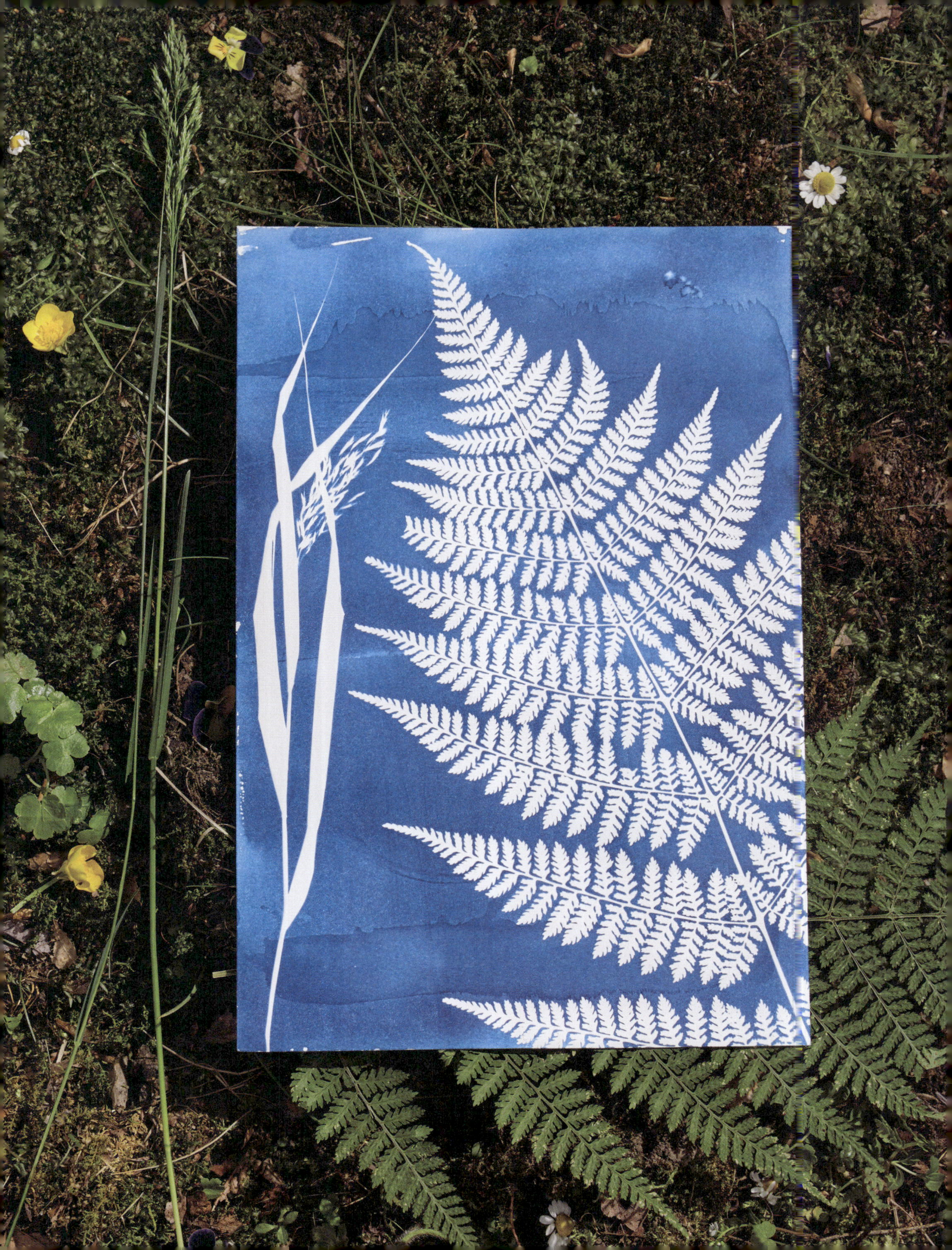

# Index

## A



## B



## C

# D



# E



# F

# G



# H



# I



# J



# K



# L



# M



# N

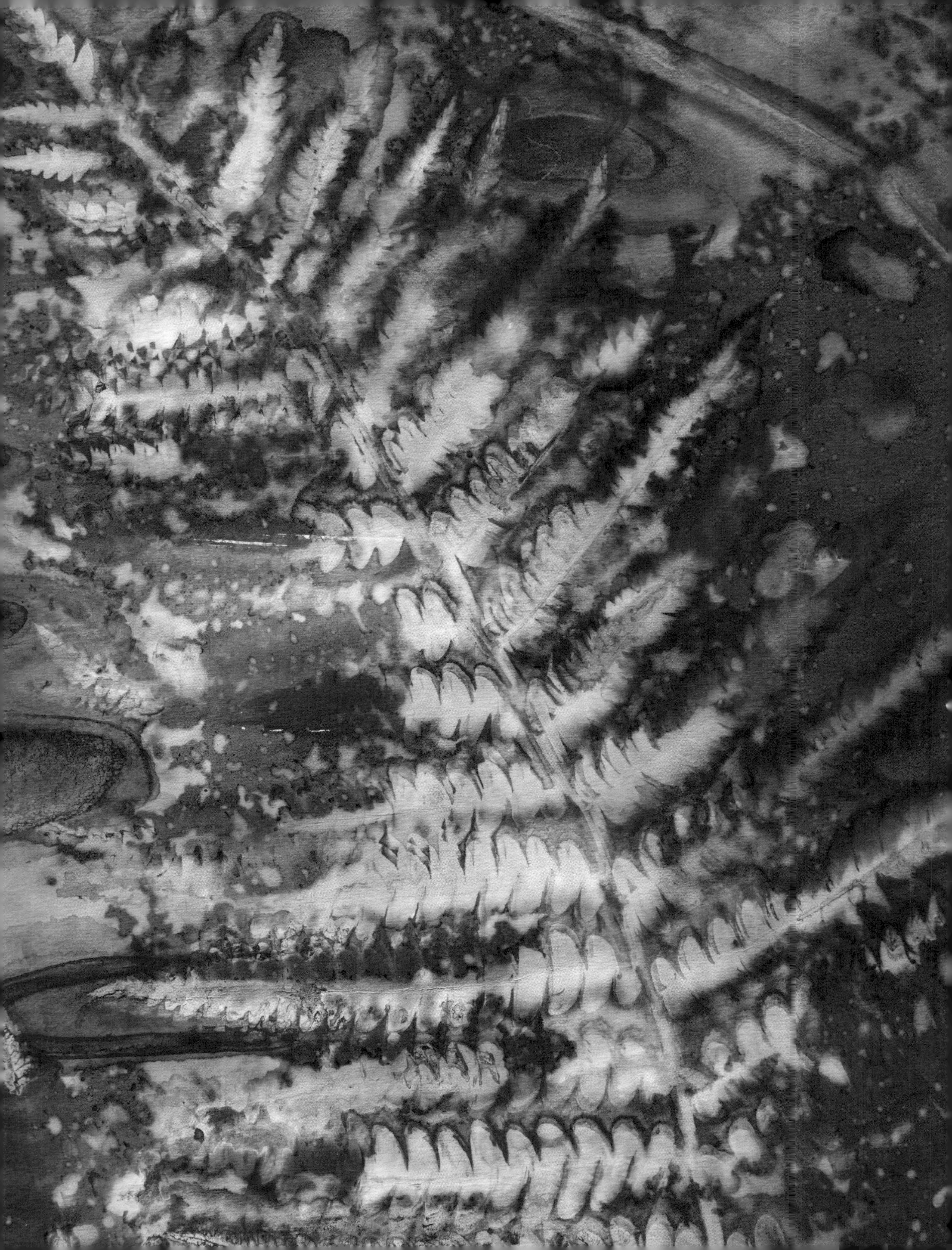

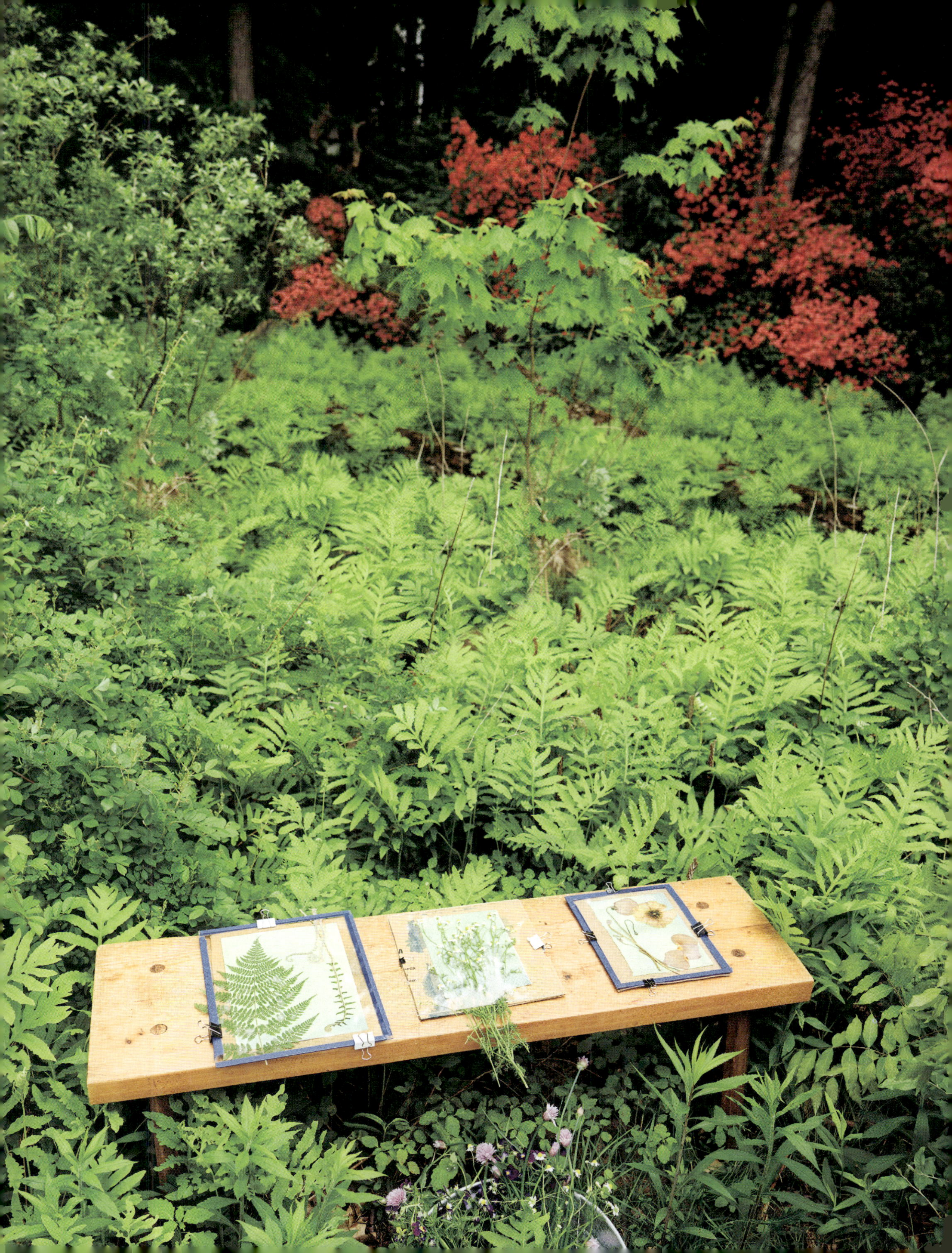

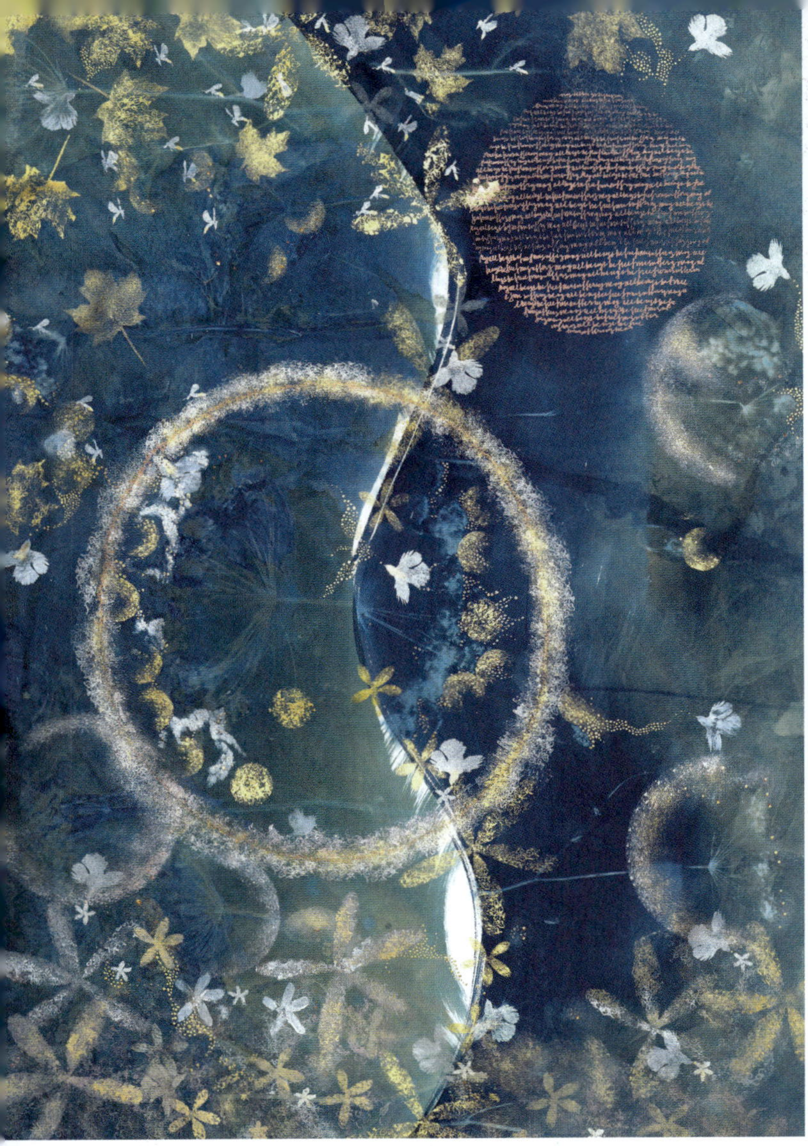

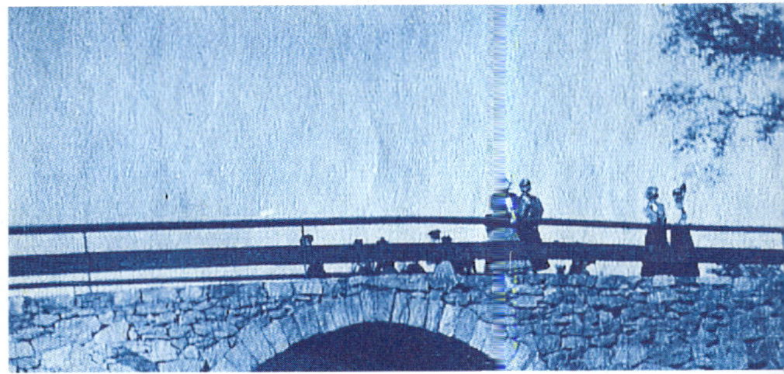

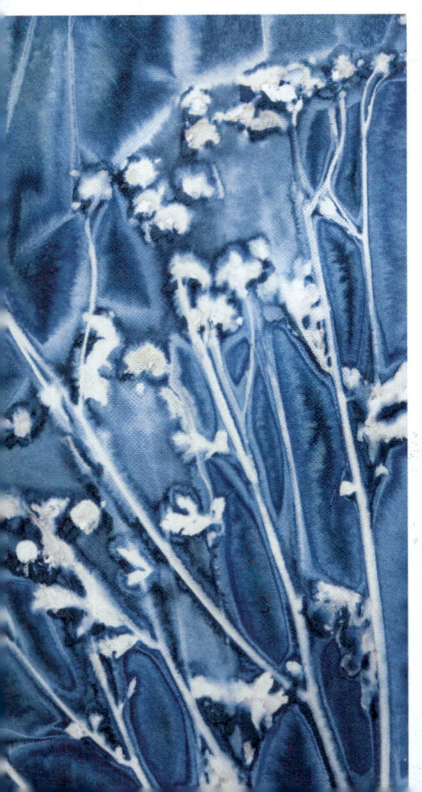

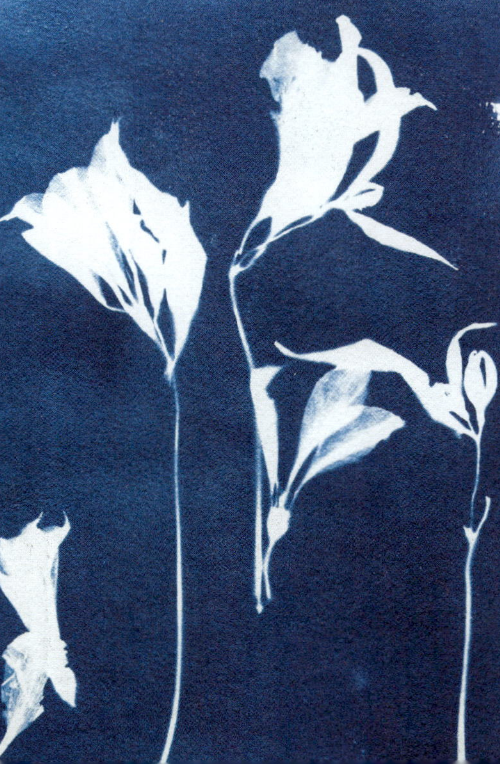

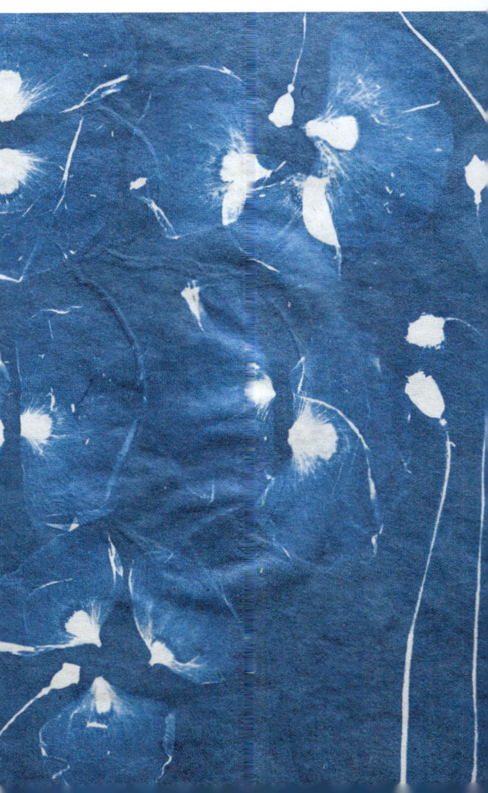